PROVIDENCE PUBLIC LIBRARY
3 1116 01047 2774

Encyclopedia of American Wrestling

Mike Chapman

Leisure Press
Champaign, Illinois

Library of Congress Cataloging-in-Publication Data

Chapman, Mike, 1943-
Encylopedia of American wrestling / by Mike Chapman
p. cm.
Bibliography: p.
ISBN 0-88011-342-1
1. Wrestling--United States--History. I. Title.
GV1198.12.C43 1990
796.8'12'0973--dc20 89-2701
CIP

ISBN: 0-88011-342-1

Developmental Editor: June I. Decker, PhD
Assistant Editors: Holly Gilly, Timothy Ryan
Copyeditor: Bruce Owens
Proofreader: Wendy Nelson
Production Director: Ernie Noa
Typesetter: Cindy Pritchard
Text Design: Keith Blomberg
Text Layout: Jayne Clampitt
Cover Design: Jack Davis
Cover Photo: The Mat Corner, Inc.
Printer: Versa Press

Printed in the United States of America

10 9 8 7 6 5 4 3 2 1

Leisure Press
A Division of Human Kinetics Publishers, Inc.
Box 5076, Champaign, IL 61825-5076
1-800-342-5457
1-800-334-3665 (in Illinois)

Contents

Forewords

It's always nice to be recognized, especially when one does something extraordinary or unique. Too often records, facts, and accomplishments disappear with time. This book will help to ensure that this does not happen in the world of amateur wrestling.

Contained within this massive volume of knowledge are many of the individual recognitions that often get forgotten. Now, with this book, those that have made their marks in our great sport can prove it!

Not only is this history for those who have achieved meaningful accomplishments, but a volume like this is fun reading for anyone who is interested in our sport. Many eyebrows will be raised by readers who know people but really had no idea of their past involvement with wrestling.

The work contains an incredible amount of information, ranging from the pinnacle to the beginnings and including records from not only the World and the Olympic Championships but also from the Junior National Tournaments, where many great careers began or ended.

Therefore, this book is a must for the overall growth of our sport. I recommend it to all fans of wrestling.

Dan Gable

World and Olympic champion
1980 and 1984 Olympic coach
Head coach, University of Iowa

Although amateur wrestling seemingly has come into prominence only within the last 4 decades, it is by no means a new sport. Wrestling has a long and rich heritage, dating back more than 5,000 years. In the ancient Olympic Games, successful wrestlers commanded great honor and respect, with the tales of their athletic accomplishments preserved through the centuries.

Now, Mike Chapman, author of many books and articles on wrestling, has dedicated himself to a very special task—renewing and preserving the rich history the sport commands in modern times. *The Encyclopedia of American Wrestling* not only records the events and dates and highlights, but it includes many of the fascinating stories behind the events, giving the reader the flavor of the time and making this truly a ''reader's'' book.

Whether you are a wrestler, coach, parent, or sports enthusiast, this book will inform and enlighten you and perhaps even change the way you have traditionally accepted and interpreted the sport. At the same time, it also honors many of our wrestling heroes of past and present. This is a book for everyone's wrestling library.

Enjoy!

Lee Kemp

Three-time NCAA champion
Three-time world champion

Preface

Baseball may be the national pastime of our magnificent country when it comes to sporting activities, but wrestling is the national heartbeat.

Wrestling in America pre-dates all other sports. It was practiced by the native Americans, the Indian tribes that flourished long before the Europeans arrived. Wrestling was popular in the Civil War camps of the North, and our greatest American hero, Abraham Lincoln, was reportedly a skilled grappler in his youth. No sport can match wrestling for its longevity on the American scene.

As a newspaper journalist and freelance writer for the past 20 years, I have devoted a considerable amount of time and energy reporting on the sport. In 1986, I began a 2-year stint as director of communications at USA Wrestling, the sport's national governing body. In that position, I was constantly fielding questions from all corners of the country. Most of them revolved around the sport's rich past.

It was obvious to me that the sport of wrestling was lacking an essential element in that there was not a single compilation of facts one could turn to for information. Many of the records concerning the development of the sport and the great men who helped create the sport's rich heritage were clouded in the mists of time and were in danger of disappearing forever.

Records are essential to the welfare of any sport, for they keep the heroes and accomplishments of the past alive. Records foster an interest in days long gone and trigger a hope in the future. The achievements of former stars in all sports are the building blocks for the aspirations of new generations. What would baseball be without its memories of Babe Ruth, boxing without Jack Dempsey, golf without Arnold Palmer, or football without Jim Thorpe, Red Grange, and Walter Payton?

I became determined to assemble a book of wrestling records, an encyclopedia of the sport. It was a task that at times seemed hopelessly immense, beyond the scope of one person. But, fortunately, I had support to draw on. Although I have attended 17 National Collegiate Athletic Association tournaments and have read voraciously on the subject for 2 decades, I felt I needed even more background than that. I sought out many of the wrestling figures of the past and tapped into their resources and memories in my attempt to make this book as authoritative and factual as possible.

Among those who have lent great assistance are Bob Dellinger, curator of the National Wrestling Hall of Fame in Stillwater, Oklahoma, and a man who truly loves the sport; Don Sayenga of Bethlehem, Pennsylvania, one of wrestling's finest historians; Ron Good, editor of *Amateur Wrestling News* in Oklahoma City; and Ed Ewoldt of Wheaton, Illinois, who has devoted years to studying the sport.

My quest for information has taken me by phone to the offices of the Amateur Athletic Union, the United States Olympic Committee, the NCAA headquarters, the National Association of Intercollegiate Athletics offices, and the National Junior College Athletic Association office. I was fortunate to have the resources of the National Wrestling Hall of Fame at my disposal during my tenure as director of communications at USA Wrestling.

The most difficult task has been the search for missing pieces of information to complete various sections. Often, as in the case of the Tbilisi Tournament, records are quite incomplete and memories a bit faulty. Therefore, I owe a huge debt to Jess Hoke, the late founder of *Amateur Wrestling News*, and to the men and women who have followed in his wake. The role *Amateur Wrestling News* has played in the record keeping of wrestling is beyond measure.

Although I make no claim that all the information presented here is 100 percent accurate, I do claim that the effort to compile it accurately was 100 percent. I left no stone unturned in my determination to provide records and the most factual account of events possible. There are many items that I believe wrestling fans will find fresh and of great interest, items uncovered through hundreds of hours of laborious research and conversations.

Through the years, I have reported on dozens of sports, from major football bowl games to world heavyweight title fights. I have met many exciting sports personalities, stars like Muhammad Ali, Dick Butkus, and Lou Ferrigno (the Incredible Hulk of television fame). And yet the athletes I admire most are the great amateur wrestlers of America. In my opinion, men like Dan Hodge, Dan Gable, Bill Koll, Robin Reed, Stanley Henson, Peter Mehringer, Lee Kemp, Mark Schultz, John Smith, and Lou Banach are among the finest athletes this country has ever produced. They are as close as I will ever come to rubbing shoulders with the heroes of ancient Greece and Sumer.

This book is a labor of love. It is dedicated to all the wrestlers in American history and to the thousands of men and women who, like me, have appreciated their efforts.

Chapter 1

The History of Wrestling in America

The sport of wrestling has a long and distinguished history in the United States, extending all the way back before the Age of Discovery. Wrestling was a favorite sporting activity and pastime of the various Indian tribes that inhabited the North American continent, and it was brought to the colonies by the hardy settlers who sailed from Europe in the 1500s and 1600s.

The sport flourished in the 1700s in upstate Vermont, where it was called "collar and elbow" due to the habit of the two wrestlers hooking up to start a match by gripping each other's collarbone and elbow. In the following century, the sport spread steadily southward and westward into the ever-expanding frontier. Abraham Lincoln, the nation's 16th president and a man some historians consider the greatest figure ever born in the western hemisphere, was proud of his wrestling skills as a backwoodsman in Kentucky and Illinois. It is reported that he assumed command of a small group of soldiers during the Black Hawk Wars by outwrestling another aspirant to the command.

During the Civil War, many of the soldiers of the Union army entertained themselves with no-holds-barred wrestling matches behind the tents. It was here, in an unrestrained atmosphere, that "catch-as-catch-can" wrestling found a home. Whereas the Europeans favored a more controlled style known as *Greco-Roman*, which allowed no holds below the waist, their American counterparts preferred a style more in step with the American character. This wide-open brand of wrestling eventually became known as *freestyle.*

When the best American catch-as-catch-can grapplers of the 1890s and early 1900s discovered they could earn money with their wrestling skills, a professional sport was born. At first, the contests were very similar to amateur matches, except there was no time limit, and submission and choke holds were allowed.

Around 1900, Tom Jenkins, a millwright from the vicinity of Cleveland, Ohio, who had lost his vision in one eye, became a national wrestling hero. His popularity was comparable to that of John L. Sullivan, then the heavyweight boxing champion of the world. Jenkins was a wrestler with a powerful, punishing style, and he asked no quarter and gave none. He ruled the American scene handily until 1905, when an Iowa farmboy named Frank Gotch stunned the sporting world by stripping Jenkins of his title. Their series of eight matches is considered among the most brutal sporting events ever, each match lasting well over an hour.

With the American title tucked away, Gotch went after the famed "Russian Lion," George Hackenschmidt, the acknowledged world champion. Born in Estonia, Hackenschmidt was a physical marvel. He set world records in weightlifting and attracted overflow crowds in Europe whenever he wrestled. He was undefeated in over 400 matches and was considered unbeatable when he came to Chicago in 1908 to face Gotch.

Gotch won the title in a classic showdown and beat the Russian Lion again in 1911 as over 30,000 fans flocked to witness the titanic match, jamming brand new Comiskey Park, the mammoth stadium named for owner Charles Comiskey. The match marked the high tide of professional wrestling in America. After Gotch died of uremic poisoning in 1917 at the age of 40, the sport was never the same. Eventually, it degenerated into acting affairs replete with embarrassing embellishments.

Amateur wrestling coexisted peacefully alongside its professional counterpart for many years. The first Amateur Athletic Union (AAU) "national" tournament was held in New York City in 1888, with just two weight classes contested. As professional wrestling grew more theatrical, the gap between the two branches of wrestling grew wider.

It is generally agreed that the first dual meet in the United States between two colleges took place on March 21, 1903, when Yale University traveled to New York City to tangle with Columbia University. The meet ended in a 2-2 tie.

However, intramural wrestling was popular at Yale (located in New Haven, Connecticut) for nearly 30 years prior to the dual meet with Columbia. Reportedly, wrestling as a sporting activity within the college atmosphere was flourishing all across the East prior to the turn of the century. Charles Morrow Willson, in his book *The Magnificent Scufflers* (1959), wrote that "a check of the scholastic records for 1900 and 1901 indicates that wrestling was then accredited or officially admitted by not fewer than 46 well-known colleges and universities, including most of the Ivy League and both West Point and Annapolis" (p. 75).

It is a matter of record that West Point had a wrestling coach as early as 1921. He was the old professional star Tom Jenkins, and he stayed at West Point for 14 years until his retirement in 1935.

According to Willson, wrestling was also prospering at that time in the high school ranks. He quotes Frederic Thompson, a reporter for The Associated Press, as saying that "as of 1901 wrestling was available in approximately one thousand high schools and preparatory schools throughout the United States" (p. 75).

The first dual meet between high school teams is lost in the mists of time, but the first structured state high school tournament is believed to have been held in Ames, Iowa, in 1921. The victorious team from Cedar Rapids Washington High School had the advantage of being coached by the legendary Farmer Burns, a man who competed in over 6,000 professional wrestling matches. He also discovered Frank Gotch and served as his trainer for many years.

Although such eastern schools as Yale, Cornell, Princeton, and Penn State are considered the unofficial collegiate team champions of the early 1900s, the first great official college power was Oklahoma A&M College. The school, located in Stillwater, Oklahoma (the site of the Great Land Rush of 1889), first fielded a team in 1915, losing to Texas, 17.5-7.5. Then, in 1916, Edward Clark Gallagher became the head coach—and the sport was never the same.

Gallagher was a standout football player and track star for the Aggies, but he fell in love with wrestling after graduating. He was particularly fascinated with leverage and with techniques that could make an average man a champion. He then set about studying the sport, traveling to Vermont to talk with the old collar-and-elbow stars and returning to Oklahoma with the knowledge and an innovative sense that would make his Aggie teams almost unbeatable.

At the same time, wrestling was blossoming in Iowa, largely due to the immense popularity of Gotch and Burns. To a state full of athletic youngsters, these men were heroes to be emulated. Gallagher in Oklahoma and Gotch and Burns in Iowa established the all-important wrestling traditions that would allow their descendants to rule the sport of collegiate wrestling for nearly 7 decades.

The first official National Collegiate Athletic Association (NCAA) Tournament was held in Ames, Iowa, in 1928. Although no official team score was kept, Gallagher's A&M men won four of the seven weight classes and has since been accorded the status of winning the first NCAA team title. In the following 57 NCAA Tournaments, a school from either Iowa or Oklahoma would win all but three of the team titles!

The AAU organization controlled the freestyle and the Greco-Roman scenes for nearly 90 years before being challenged by the United States Wrestling Federation (USWF). The USWF held its first Senior Open Tournament in 1969 in Evanston, Illinois. The organization grew steadily and took on the AAU in a long and often bitter struggle for control of the sport.

In 1982, USA Wrestling was formed from the USWF and became the national governing body for the sport. In 1986, the International Wrestling Federation (FILA), the international governing body for wrestling, made USA Wrestling a permanent member.

Amateur wrestling continued to grow steadily through the decades. By 1988 an estimated 12,500 junior high and high schools offered wrestling programs, as did 450 colleges on all levels. It is estimated that nearly 700,000 athletes participated in some form of wrestling program, including programs for kids, in all 50 states in 1988.

According to figures from the National High School Association headquarters in 1988, wrestling is the eighth-largest sport in terms of participants and the fifth largest in the NCAA list of sports.

From the wigwams of the native American Indians to the tents of the Civil War soldiers and the small towns of Vermont, Iowa, and Oklahoma, the sport has withstood the test of time. It has spread across the nation and endures as a sporting activity that stirs men's spirits.

Chronology of Important Moments in Wrestling History

1888—The first organized AAU "national" tournament is held in New York City.

1896—The first Olympic Games of the modern era are held in Athens, Greece (no wrestling competition, however).

1904—The United States first enters Olympic wrestling competition in St. Louis, Missouri (in fact, all the wrestlers entered were from the United States).

1912—The International Wrestling Federation (FILA), which deals exclusively with wrestling, is founded at the 1912 Olympic Games in Antwerp, Belgium.

1928—The first NCAA Tournament is held in Ames, with Ed Gallagher coaching Oklahoma A&M (now Oklahoma State) to the unofficial team title.

1947—Tiny Cornell College in Mount Vernon, Iowa, becomes the first school outside of Oklahoma to win the NCAA team title and the first of four Iowa colleges to win the title. Coach: Paul Scott.

1951—The first Pan-American Games are held in Buenos Aires, Argentina, and the United States wins four gold medals in eight freestyle weight classes (no Greco-Roman is held).

1953—Pennsylvania State wins the NCAA team title, the first school outside of Iowa and Oklahoma to do so. Coach: Charles Speidel.

1958—The National Association of Intercollegiate Athletics (NAIA) holds its first tournament, with the team title going to Mankato State University in Minnesota. Coach: Rummy Macias.

1960—The first Junior College National Championships are held, with the team title going to Lamar Junior College of Colorado. Coach: Dan Sniff.

1961—The first "official" World Championships participated in by the United States are held in Yokohama, Japan. The U.S. freestyle team, coached by Raymond Swartz, finishes sixth, as does the Greco-Roman team, coached by Dr. Dale Thomas.

1963—The first Midlands Wrestling Tournament is held in LaGrange, Illinois, with the University of Michigan winning. Coach: Cliff Keen.

—The first NCAA Division II Tournament is held, with the team title going to Western State Colorado. Coach: Tracy Borah.

1965—Iowa State University wins the first of its six NCAA team titles under Coach Dr. Harold Nichols.

1967—Michigan State becomes only the second team outside Oklahoma and Iowa and the first Big Ten team to win the NCAA team title. Coach: Grady Peninger.

1969—The first USWF (now USA Wrestling) National Tournaments for senior athletes are held. The Mayor Daley Youth Foundation club of Chicago wins both the freestyle and the Greco-Roman team titles. Coach: Terry McCann.

—Richard Sanders (114.5 pounds) and Fred Fozzard (180.5) become the first Americans to win gold medals at the Freestyle World Championships.

—The first Junior World Championships are held in Boulder, Colorado. The United States crowns five freestyle champions but none in Greco-Roman.

1971—The Junior National Tournament, sponsored by USA Wrestling, is born in Iowa City, Iowa, and evolves into the largest wrestling tournament in the world. The first year it is only freestyle, but Greco-Roman starts in 1972.

1972—Dan Gable (149.5) and Wayne Wells (163) become the first U.S. wrestlers to win titles at both the World Championships and the Olympic Games.

1974—The first NCAA Division III Tournament is held, with the team title going to Wilkes College in Pennsylvania. Coach: John Reese.

1975—Greco-Roman competition is included in the Pan-American Games for the first time, and the United States wins seven gold medals in the 10 weight classes.

—The University of Iowa wins its first NCAA team title, becoming the fourth school from Iowa to do so. Coach: Gary Kurdelmeier.

1976—The National Wrestling Hall of Fame in Stillwater, Oklahoma, is dedicated on September 11, 1976, with 14 legendary figures inducted.

1978—The University of Iowa wins the first of nine straight NCAA team titles under coach Dan Gable.

1982—The USWF replaces the AAU as wrestling's national governing body, the result of a decision made by the American Arbitration Association, ending a long battle.

1984—The United States claims its first medals in Greco-Roman competition at the Olympics, with Steve Fraser (198) and Jeff Blatnick (286) winning golds.

1985—Mike Houck becomes the first American to win a gold medal in the Greco-Roman World Championships, capturing the 198-pound title in Kolbotn, Norway.

1986—USA Wrestling is recongized by FILA as its permanent representative.

1987—The University of Iowa is thwarted in its bid to become the only team in any sport to win 10 straight NCAA team titles when cross-state rival Iowa State University wins the title. Coach: Jim Gibbons.

1988—Arizona State University becomes the first school west of the Rocky Mountains to win the NCAA team title and represents only the fifth state ever to have won. Coach: Bobby Douglas.

Chapter 2

The Olympic Games

No sporting event in the history of the world has stirred the souls of men and women as profoundly as the Olympic Games. From the birth of the Games in ancient Olympia, Greece, in 776 B.C., to its rebirth in Athens in 1896, to the Games of Seoul, South Korea, in 1988, the Olympic flame burns deep in the collective consciousness of all humanity.

America harbors a special feeling for its Olympic stars. In a poll taken in 1987 by the Epcot Center in Disney World on behalf of the United States Olympic Committee (USOC) and published in the November 1987 issue of *The Olympian Magazine,* Americans overwhelmingly listed Olympians as their most honored and respected sports heroes. The Olympic spirit is as much a part of the American dream as is becoming a business tycoon or a Hollywood film star.

Despite the huge success the Olympics have experienced recently, the modern era of the Olympic Games had a modest beginning in 1896. Only 13 nations and a total of 311 athletes participated. The United States "team" consisted of just 13 athletes, a loose grouping of men who had competed in various sports clubs on the East Coast and who were curious enough to test themselves against Europeans.

All the competition was held at one site, and little advance publicity of the event was given. Only nine sports were on the agenda: cycling, fencing, gymnastics, lawn tennis, shooting, swimming, track and field, weightlifting, and wrestling. Just how far the Olympic Games have come since then is evidenced by the swimming event of 1896. The swimmers were taken into a nearby bay by boat and dumped into icy water. The first swimmer to reach shore, regardless of the stroke used, was the winner—a far cry from today's format with lanes colorfully marked in beautiful pools, electronic timing clocks, and the like.

The Olympic concept fired the world's imagination and caught on quickly. The Paris Games of 1900 attracted 1,330 athletes from 22 countries, including the first women, but wrestling was left off the list of scheduled events.

The third Olympic Games, in 1904, were hosted by the United States in St. Louis, Missouri. However, only 12 countries were on hand, with a total of 625 athletes. The trip to America was considered too costly for most European countries.

Still, many athletes were not taking the Olympics all too seriously. A small mailman from Cuba entered the torturous marathon and finished fourth, but not without pausing along the way to chat with spectators and even taking a detour into an apple orchard to wolf down some green apples, which gave him an upset stomach and forced him to sit and rest for a while.

The wrestling competition in 1904 was completely one-sided, as only Americans showed up. All seven gold medal winners were from the United States as were all other place winners. The final medal count for all sports had the United States with 209 medals, only 13 for runner-up Germany, and 10 for third-place Cuba.

The 1908 Olympics were held in London, and the host country of Great Britain was the runaway winner in medals by a 141-46 margin over the United States. A total of 20 countries participated, and the U.S. team brought 121 athletes. Great Britain even dominated wrestling, where it won 11 of 15 medals.

However, it was here that diminutive George Mehnert set a standard for U.S. matmen that stood for 80 years. He had won the 115-pound weight class in 1904 and took top honors at 119 pounds in 1908, making him America's only two-time Olympic champion. A native of Newark, New Jersey, who earned his living as a paper cutter, Mehnert won six national titles and lost just one match in a 7-year span. He was considered the best wrestler at the 1908 Games.

"Mehnert showed form quite above any other man in the whole contest," stated the official report of the British Olympic Association for the 1908 Games, as quoted by Bob Dellinger when writing Mehnert's biography in the official National Wrestling Hall of Fame induction program. Mehnert "undoubtedly was the most scientific, both in attack and defense, of any wrestler taking part in the Games."

Of the six-man American team, only George Dole joined Mehnert as a place winner. Dole, a former two-time AAU national champion from Yale, captured the 132.5-pound gold medal. Ironically, he was the man who inflicted Mehnert's sole defeat during the latter's 7-year stretch.

The 1912 Olympic Games in Stockholm, Sweden, were a grand spectacle, attracting 2,547 athletes from 28 nations. Daily attendance averaged between 20,000 and 30,000, and much of the action was spectacular. The unquestioned star of the Games was a Sac and Fox Indian from the plains of Oklahoma. Jim Thorpe turned in one of the most stunning performances in athletic history by winning both the pentathlon (5 track-and-field events) and the decathlon (10 events)!

Perhaps Thorpe should have tried for a spot on the American wrestling team, as he was reputed to be a good "backyard-style" grappler as a young man. As it was, only two Americans participated in wrestling (which was limited to Greco-Roman this time), and neither man placed.

World War I canceled the 1916 Olympic Games, which were scheduled for Berlin, Germany, and the 1920 games were held in Antwerp, Belgium. The United States, relatively unaffected by the war in comparison to war-ravaged Europe, was entering into the Era of Good Feelings of the Roaring Twenties and sent a full team. A total of 26 U.S. wrestlers went to Antwerp, but they came back with just one gold medal.

Charles Ackerley, although never a national champion, won the gold medal in the 119-pound freestyle class, defeating teammate Samuel Gerson in the finals. But by all accounts, the United States should have won a gold medal in the heavyweight class. There, Nat Pendleton, a former mat star from Columbia University, earned a silver medal.

The powerful Pendleton, winning AAU national titles in 1916 and 1920, looked like a solid bet to win the gold medal in Antwerp. His training partner at the New York Athletic Club, Paul Berlenbach, made the team at 175 pounds but could not compete after suffering an injury prior to the start of the Olympics.

Pendleton, fluent in several languages, eventually wound up in Hollywood and appeared in nearly 100 films as a well-known character actor. Berlenbach became the professional light-heavyweight boxing champion of the world and in 1974 was inducted into the National Boxing Hall of Fame. Their remarkable sagas are highlighted in "Wrestling's Greatest Story" in chapter 5.

Bitter feelings lingered after World War I, and Germany was not invited to participate in the Paris Olympics of 1924. Still, 44 nations were on hand, along with 3,092 athletes. A crowd estimated at 625,000 braved a heat wave that sent temperatures soaring to the 113-degree mark, and the huge turnout proved that the Olympic movement was on solid footing.

The 1924 Olympic Games were very successful from a wrestling standpoint, as the United States went home with four gold medals, one silver, and one bronze. Two champions of those Games, Robin Reed (134) and Russell Vis (145), have long been considered two of the greatest wrestlers in American history.

Reed took up the sport in Portland, Oregon, and won AAU national titles in 1921, 1922, and 1924. It is a matter of record that he never lost a match at any time, at any place, to anybody. He is generally regarded as the most feared and punishing wrestler of all time, a man who would break an opponent's arm if the mood struck him to do so.

"Had the rules permitted, he might well have won a handful of gold medals," mentions Reed's biographical sketch at the National Wrestling Hall of Fame." In the Pacific Northwest tryouts for the Olympic team he entered four weight classes, from 145 pounds to 191, and won all four. It is well established that he could pin almost every member of the U.S. Olympic team, including the gold medalists at 191 pounds and heavyweight."

No less an authority than Don Sayenga, one of the nation's most recognized wrestling historians, feels that Reed is the roughest wrestler the United

States ever produced. Dr. Dale Thomas, coach at Oregon State University for 3 decades and a former Olympian and national champion, supports that opinion.

Vis had lost just one match during his long amateur career when he moved up several weights just to see if he could defeat a much larger wrestler. Like Reed, Vis grew up in Oregon, but he moved to Los Angeles in 1919. He captured four straight AAU national titles and breezed to the Olympic gold medal with little difficulty.

Although it is unknown whether Vis and Reed ever worked out against each other, they did not meet in a head-to-head bout at any time during their great careers. Vis once wrote that Reed was the second-best wrestler he ever saw, behind only the legendary professional from Nebraska, John Pesek, another wrestler who was feared far and wide.

Reed once wrote, "My greatest discussions were with John Pesek and Farmer Burns. Ah! Those were the masters!" Burns was the legendary professional from Iowa who trained Frank Gotch and played an instrumental role in the emergence of Iowa as a wrestling powerhouse. Both Reed and Vis competed in the professional ranks for several years but grew to despise the required theatrics.

Olympic champions Robin Reed and Russel Vis, 1924. (Courtesy of National Wrestling Hall of Fame)

The other wrestling gold medalists at the Paris Games were John Spellman (191.5) and Harry Steele (heavyweight). Two athletes who won gold medals in other events at the 1924 Olympics became world renowned in later years. Johnny Weissmuller took home three golds in swimming and then went on to become the most famous movie-screen Tarzan of all time. Benjamin Spock was a member of the winning crew team and became the famous baby doctor.

Forty-six nations and 3,014 athletes competed in the 1928 Olympics in Amsterdam, The Netherlands. The U.S. team, under the supervision of General Douglas MacArthur, sailed to the competition aboard the SS *President Roosevelt* and lived aboard it during the Games. For the third straight Olympics, the United States led the medal count. But only one American wrestler, Allie Morrison, came home with a gold.

Morrison was born and raised in Marshalltown, Iowa, but wrestled at the University of Illinois. Morrison, undefeated in his entire collegiate career, won three AAU national titles before gaining the 134-pound Olympic crown that Reed had claimed 4 years earlier.

When the Olympics returned to the United States in 1932, the country was in the depths of the Great Depression. Despite that sobering fact, Los Angeles put on the finest show ever witnessed in athletic circles. Nine years of preparation resulted in magnificent settings for the sports, and 550 cottages were built specifically for housing the athletes.

An 18-year-old girl from Beaumont, Texas, stole the show. Mildred "Babe" Didrickson won gold medals in the javelin throw and the 80-meter hurdles and placed second in the high jump, losing the gold medal on a technicality. She went on to earn acclaim as the greatest woman athlete of all time, the female counterpart of the great Jim Thorpe.

Three wrestlers won gold medals on the home turf. Bobby Pearce (123) and Jack Van Bebber (158.5) were Oklahoma A&M products, and Pete Mehringer (191.5) was an all-American football player at the University of Kansas.

Pearce was NCAA champion in 1931 and runner-up in 1932. He won AAU national titles in 1930 and 1931, starring on the same Oklahoma A&M team with Van Bebber, who never lost in college, winning three NCAA and four AAU national titles. The only loss of his entire career came in an early round of the 1932 Olympic trials, but he bounced back to make the team with little difficulty.

At the Los Angeles Olympics, Van Bebber almost missed out on a chance to compete for the gold medal. He discovered at the last minute that the competition times had been changed, and he took off on a 6-mile walk-run from his cottage to the arena. A passing motorist recognized him and gave him a ride. He showed up just in time to defeat Finland's Eino Leino, a four-time Olympian.

Van Bebber's status as an all-time great was cemented in a 1950 poll in which national sports authorities voted him one of the country's top-10 amateur athletes in any sport in the first half century.

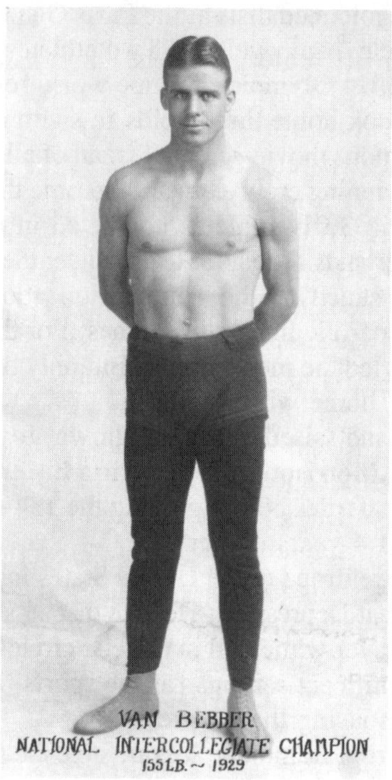

Jack Van Bebber, the first wrestler to win three NCAA titles and an Olympic gold medal. (Courtesy of National Wrestling Hall of Fame)

Mehringer's career began when he and his brothers, living on a Kansas farm, bought a mail-order instruction book written by Farmer Burns and Frank Gotch. He hitchhiked to the state wrestling tournament as a senior and won. At the University of Kansas, he became a football all-American and NCAA runner-up in the heavyweight class.

For the Olympic trials, Mehringer cut to 191.5 pounds and made the team. He also tried out at heavyweight and defeated Northwestern University's Jack Riley, the man who had edged him in the NCAA tournament. Selecting the lower weight, Mehringer won the Olympic gold medal with little difficulty, and Riley finished second at heavyweight.

Mehringer remained in the Los Angeles area for decades. He taught himself to be an electrical engineer and went to work for the city. He also moonlighted in the movies, appearing as a stuntman in nearly 50 films. His first assignment sent him to the jungles of Guatemala, where he became Tarzan (doubling for star Herman Brix, the 1928 Olympic shot-put silver medalist) in *New Adventures of Tarzan*. Later, he doubled for Bob Hope, wrestling a man in a gorilla suit. Mehringer played in the *Chicago Tribune* All-Star

Football Game and played 5 years of professional football. He also wrestled professionally for a short time.

The Berlin Games of 1936 are the most talked-about Olympics ever held. They were made famous by the growing Nazi dread, by the huge amounts of money spent on the preparation for the Games, by Adolf Hitler, and especially by Jesse Owens. The indomitable Owens strode away from the packed track stadium (crowds of 100,000 were common) with four gold medals and a reputation as the greatest track star of all time.

From a wrestling standpoint, the Berlin Olympics were mediocre. The United States crowned just one champion, Frank Lewis (158.5), a rangy graduate of Oklahoma A&M. Lewis scored four pins, then lost to Sweden's Ture Andersson but wound up with the gold medal on the points system. Overall, Germany grabbed 101 medals and the United States 57.

World War II ruined just about everything in the 1940s, and the Olympics were no exception. The Games were scheduled for Tokyo, Japan, in 1940 and for London, England, in 1944 but were canceled by the largest conflict ever seen on the face of the earth.

London was, however, the site of the 1948 Olympics. Despite the fact that devastation from the Great War was still evident, the 14th Olympic Games were a smashing success. A total of 59 nations entered 4,099 athletes, and huge crowds were on hand for nearly every event.

The most outstanding athlete to emerge from the Games was a 17-year-old California high school student named Bob Mathias. Defying all odds, Mathias became the youngest Olympic champion in American history, winning the decathlon in just his third try ever at the grueling event.

Glen Brand (174) and Henry Wittenberg (191.5) brought home gold medals in wrestling, and Germ Leeman (125.5) earned a silver and Leland Merrill (160.5) a bronze. Brand, an NCAA champion at Iowa State, earned his spot on the team in a series of ferocious tryouts with Joe Scarpello of Iowa. In London, he scored four relatively easy victories for the crown.

Wittenberg used the Olympics to enhance his already solid reputation as one of America's greatest mat stars of all time. With seven AAU national titles behind him, Wittenberg defeated the University of Minnesota's Verne Gagne for his berth on the team. He then scored three pins and three decisions to grab his Olympic crown. The final standings found the United States back on top with a total of 84 medals to runner-up Sweden's 46.

Helsinki, Finland, was the site of the 1952 Olympic Games, which are memorable for several reasons. Little was known in the United States about Finland, and Helsinki was the smallest city ever to host the Games. Any doubts about the Finns' ability to stage the Games were quickly dispelled. "What the visitors found were superb facilities, hosts who were models of efficiency and courtesy, and exciting contests memorable for their dramatic moments," wrote The Associated Press and Grolier in *Pursuit of Excellence: The Olympic Story* (1979, p. 192).

However, not all was blissful. The 1952 Olympics saw the return of the Soviet Union to the Games and also marked the infusion of heavy politics into the Olympics. The Soviets had not participated since 1912. They had been invited to the 1948 Olympics and sent a large squad of coaches and trainers to study and take notes. Arriving in Helsinki, athletes from the Soviet Union and other Eastern Bloc countries demanded to be headquartered in housing that was separate from the rest of the world's athletes.

The *Pursuit of Excellence* reports, "For whatever reasons the Soviets insisted on segregated quarters and the IOC [International Olympic Committee] permitted them; [but] when the athletes of the two camps came together in training before the Games opened and in the contests themselves, they mingled without incident. In fact, the 1952 Helsinki Games are remembered as the best of all Olympics" (p. 191).

Mathias repeated as decathlon champion, becoming the only two-time winner of that event. The other great star of the 1952 Games was Finland's Emil Zatopek, who won gold medals in both the 5,000- and the 10,000-meter races as well as the marathon. Zatopek is considered one of the two or three greatest long-distance runners ever. His wife, Dana, also won a gold medal in the javelin throw.

Bill Smith (160.5), a two-time NCAA champion at Iowa State Teachers College, became America's only wrestling winner. And even Smith was not certain about his gold medal for a while. The long and lanky master of the "whizzer" (an arm bar used in a defensive posture to keep the foe at bay) scored five victories but lost a close decision to Sweden's Per Berlin. Taking the awards stand, Smith was surprised to be directed to the top spot. He thought he had placed third, but he had actually won under the complicated scoring system.

Two other Americans earned silver medals and came within a whisker of golds. Tommy Evans (147.5) won four matches easily and appeared to be far superior to defending world champion Olle Anderberg, taking the Swedish star down seven times and giving up no takedowns. However, under international freestyle rules at the time, no points were awarded for takedowns but only for exposing a foe's back to the mat. Despite his 7-0 takedown edge, Evans wound up losing a controversial decision as Anderberg won the gold.

New York's Henry Wittenberg (191.5), attempting to become the United States' first two-time gold medal winner since George Mehnert in 1908, came out of retirement. He won four matches and lost one close decision, winding up with a silver. Josiah Henson (136.5) earned a bronze. The United States maintained its overall athletic supremacy at the 1952 Olympics, outscoring the Soviet Union in the total medal count by a 76-71 margin.

Following on the heels of the Soviet invasion of Hungary, the 1956 Olympics in Melbourne, Australia, were viewed by many around the world as an East-West rivalry between the Soviet Union and the United States. If that was the case, the United States came out on the short end, taking home 32 gold medals and 74 medals overall to the Soviet Union's 37 golds and 98 overall.

In wrestling, the United States was denied a gold medal for the first time since 1912. But it took a very controversial call by a Soviet mat judge against America's brightest hope, Dan Hodge, to make it happen. Hodge, a member of the 1952 team as a 19-year-old, was considered almost unbeatable by the time the 1956 Olympics arrived. He had won two NCAA titles at the University of Oklahoma without a close match, and his tremendous strength was legendary in American mat circles. In Melbourne, he scored four pins and found himself pitted against the defending world champion from Bulgaria, Nikola Stanchev. Hodge held an 8-1 lead late in the bout when the two men hit the mat, fell apart, and stood back up.

In a stunning development, the Bulgarian's hand was raised in triumph. A Soviet mat judge had called Hodge on a touch fall as he rolled through on his back, even though the two wrestlers were not touching at the time. Hodge came back to battle a Soviet (174) for the silver medal and punished him with a painful three-quarter nelson before pinning him.

Thirty years later, an Australian official who was touring the United States labeled the call that cost Hodge a gold medal the worst he had seen in 3 decades of international wrestling. More disturbing, it marked the beginning of years of disputes between wrestling groups at international meets, as such questionable calls became the norm rather than the exception.

The Melbourne Games were the first time that the United States competed in Greco-Roman since 1912. Although no American won a medal, James Holt (160.5) and Dale Thomas (191.5) finished fifth.

American athletes, most notably a boxer named Cassius Clay, stole the show at the 1960 Olympics in Rome, Italy. The 18-year-old from Louisville, Kentucky, as well known for his loquaciousness as for his punching, carried a 162-8 lifetime record into the Games and emerged with a gold medal. He turned professional 2 months later and, as Muhammad Ali, became the best-known person in the world, winning the world heavyweight title three times.

Other great American champions at Rome were runner Wilma Rudolph, decathlete Rafer Johnson, and the basketball team, which featured such stars as Oscar Robertson, Jerry West, and Jerry Lucas. And the American wrestling team turned in one of its finest performances as well.

Three wrestlers—Terry McCann (125.5), Shelby Wilson (147.5), and Doug Blubaugh (160.5)—won gold medals. McCann, a two-time NCAA champion at Iowa and a native of Chicago, lost one match but roared back with a vengeance. He pinned a Soviet in just 30 seconds and gained round-robin victories over Poland and Bulgaria to earn his championship.

Wilson was undefeated in his four matches, including a win over the Soviet Union's defending world champion, Vladimir Sinjavskij. Blubaugh, who had been a teammate of Wilson's at Ponca City High School in Oklahoma as well as at Oklahoma State University, traveled the roughest path. Wrestling seven matches, he scored six falls and was named Outstanding Wrestler. One of his victims was Iran's fabled Emamali Habibi, a five-time world champion. Behind in the scoring, Blubaugh threw Habibi to his back and pinned him before a stunned crowd of nearly 8,000.

"One of the most satisfying features of our Olympic competition this year was the manner in which the United States wrestlers trounced the haughty Russians," reported *Amateur Wrestling News*. "In five matches that brought the two countries together on the mat, the United States won four, including victories over three world champions, by Elliott Simons, Shelby Wilson and Ed DeWitt."

Turkey won the wrestling team title with 52 points, and the United States was second with 37. The Soviets were third with 27 points. Although the Soviet Union failed to win a single gold medal in wrestling in Rome, it still outdistanced the United States in total medals, 103-71. A total of 83 countries brought 5,348 athletes to Rome, and more countries won medals than ever before.

Tokyo moved into the Olympic spotlight in 1964. Although the Japanese showed that they had taken a huge step forward in rebounding from the shocking loss of World War II, the United States took a large step backward in wrestling. Japan went all out to support the Olympics, rebuilding major portions of Tokyo and spending $3 billion. Ninety-four nations brought 5,500 athletes, and world and Olympic records tumbled right and left.

Don Schollander became the first swimmer to win four gold medals in one Olympics, Joe Frazier emerged from a Philadelphia slaughterhouse to capture the heavyweight gold medal in boxing, Billy Mills raised the pride of native Americans with his stirring 10,000-meter triumph, and Peter Snell put New Zealand on the athletic map with great victories in the 800- and the 1,500-meter runs.

But the closest the United States came to a wrestling title was the third-place finish by Dan Brand (191.5) in freestyle. In Greco-Roman, Ron Finley (138.5) and Dick Wilson (114.5) just missed medals, placing fourth. Overall, the United States actually edged the Soviet Union in gold medals, 36-30, but finished second in total medals by a 96-90 count.

Unfortunately, the 1968 and 1972 Olympics will probably be remembered as much for the circumstances that surrounded them as for the performances of the athletes. Mexico City, Mexico, hosted the 1968 Olympics at a time when the United States was trying to cope with civil unrest, stemming in large part from the Vietnam War and the assassinations of Martin Luther King Jr. and Robert Kennedy.

Sprinters Tommie Smith and John Carlos offered a black power salute on the victory stand and were expelled from the Olympic Village and suspended by the USOC. George Foreman waved a tiny American flag in the ring after knocking out a Soviet boxer to win the heavyweight boxing title, and Bob Beamon staggered the world track community with the most incredible leap in track history. In the rarefied air of Mexico City, Beamon shattered the world record in the long jump by nearly 2 feet, sailing 29 feet, 2-1/2 inches.

Rick Sanders (114.5) and Don Behm (125.5) each won silver medals in freestyle wrestling, but that was as close as the wrestlers could come to taking home the gold. Once again, the United States had the greatest medal haul, topping the Soviets in gold, 45-29, and overall, 107-91.

As troubled as the Mexico City Olympics Games were, they hardly scratched the surface of the tragedy that struck Munich, West Germany, in 1972. Early in the morning of September 5, eight terrorists wearing athletic garb stormed into the Israeli team's quarters and fired weapons. When it was over, a stunned world heard that 11 Israeli athletes and officials had been killed by a group calling itself the Black Septemberists.

The rest of the Games belonged mostly to Mark Spitz, who left Germany with indelible memories. Spitz, an American Jew from California, won seven gold medals to become a national hero. But a bitter moment arose at the basketball arena when the Soviet Union was apparently given several extra seconds on the scoreboard clock and then responded with a very controversial 51-50 win over the U.S. team. It was America's first loss in Olympic basketball, and the team refused to accept the silver medal.

It was a very different story in the wrestling arena, where the United States was excelling like never before. Coach Bill Farrell saw his team earn three gold medals, two silvers, and one bronze. Iowan Dan Gable (149.5), who once won 181 straight matches in high school and college competition, sailed through six bouts without surrendering a single point. Although he was hampered by a severe knee injury and was suffering a cut above his left eye that required seven stitches, Gable scored three pins and routed West Germany's 1964 silver medalist, 20-0, on his way to winning the gold medal.

Wayne Wells (163), fourth in the 1968 Olympics and the 1970 world champion, also turned in an amazing performance. The former University of Oklahoma star made the U.S. team while studying for his law exams and won the gold medal despite suffering cracked ribs.

The most surprising wrestler was Ben Peterson, a native of Wisconsin. Just months after graduating from Iowa State, where he won two NCAA titles, Peterson was entering his first international meet. He tied his Soviet foe, Genndai Strakhov, in the opening bout, 4-4, then rattled off four straight wins to earn the gold medal.

Ben's brother, John (180.5), earned a silver medal, and the two became the talk of the wrestling world. Rick Sanders (125.5), finishing second in 1968, had to settle for the silver medal again, losing a 4-2 match to Japan's Hideaki Yanagida. Sanders was killed a short time later when the automobile that picked him up while he was hitchhiking in Yugoslavia went off a cliff.

The most frustrating match concerning a U.S. wrestler since the Dan Hodge affair in 1956 centered around 450-pound heavyweight Chris Taylor. In a tough draw, he was paired with many-time world champion Alexander Medved of the Soviet Union in the opening round. Medved was awarded a very controversial point for Taylor's stalling, which turned out to be the difference in a 3-2 victory for the Soviet. Taylor wound up with four straight wins and the bronze medal. The call was so controversial that the official who made the call was banned from the rest of the tourney. Jimmy Carr (114.5) of Pennsylvania failed to place but did have the honor of being the youngest athlete, at age 17, to make a U.S. Olympic wrestling team.

When the Games were over, the Soviets could boast of the brightest star at the 1972 Olympics in tiny gymnast Olga Korbut and of the most medals, with a 99-93 edge over the United States. The Soviets also had more gold medals, 50-33. The Munich Olympics set a record for the most countries (122) and for the most participants (7,147) but also for the worst tragedy.

The Games needed to rebound from the disaster of Munich in an impressive fashion, but Montreal, Canada, provided an Olympics marred by political wrangling and huge financial overruns. Security, which was absolutely essential after the terrorism of Munich, cost $100 million. A walkout by much of black Africa in protest over a racial situation involving New Zealand took many of the world's top runners from the competition. The dispute with New Zealand and Taiwan reduced the number of teams from 122 in 1972 to just 88. Despite that loss, there were 7,356 entrants, a record number.

The stars of the Olympics were many, ranging from boxers Sugar Ray Leonard and brothers Leon and Michael Spinks to decathlete Bruce Jenner. But no athlete came away with a greater fan and press following than did Rumania's Nadia Comaneci, who attained perfection several times on her way to winning three gold medals in gymnastics.

The Soviets dominated wrestling thoroughly, leaving Montreal with 12 gold medals, including 5 in freestyle. The only American champion was John Peterson (180.5), who improved one notch from his silver medal performance of 4 years earlier. Peterson, wrestling masterfully, never really had a close match. He defeated 1975 world champion Adolf Seger of West Germany, 14-4, and then routed 1974 world champion Viktor Novajilov of the Soviet Union, 20-4.

John's brother, Ben (198), a gold medalist in 1972, was forced to settle for the silver this time around. The Soviet Union's Levan Tediashvili, one of the most respected matmen of all time, defeated John in 1972 to win the gold and moved up a weight in 1976 to stop Ben from repeating. Joining Ben as silver medalists were Lloyd Keaser (149.5) and Russ Hellickson (220), and Gene Davis (136.5) and Stan Dziedzic (163) finished third. The closest the Greco-Roman team came to a medal was at 220, where Brad Rheingans placed fourth.

Perhaps the most surprising development of the 1976 Olympics was the third-place finish of the United States in the gold medal count. The Soviets went home with 47 gold medals (115 medals overall), whereas East Germany left with 40 (90 overall) and the United States with 34 (94 overall). With just 17 million people, East Germany is only one twelfth the size of the United States.

The 1980 and 1984 Olympics were among the most disappointing in the history of the Games. Wracked by considerable political disagreements, the Games were exploited by the United States and the Soviet Union as a means of expressing political viewpoints. President Jimmy Carter announced that the United States would boycott the 1980 Games in Moscow in protest of the Soviet invasion of Afghanistan, and the Soviets responded by boycotting the 1984 Games in Los Angeles.

The 1980 boycott cost the United States an excellent chance of winning the freestyle title in wrestling. The team was loaded with great stars, including world champions Lee Kemp (163) and Chris Campbell (180.5). Chances were also excellent that the United States would gain its first medal in Greco-Roman, with wrestlers like Dan Chandler (180.5), Mark Johnson (198), and Brad Rheingans (220) in the lineup. It was not to be, however. Russ Hellickson, the 1980 freestyle captain and another prime candidate for a gold medal, articulated how most of the 1980 wrestling Olympians felt in later years: "I guess the thing that gets the most discouraging or disheartening about [the boycott] is that very few people relate to what happened in 1980," Hellickson told Dave Kelch of Ohio State University's *Scarlet and Gray* magazine (March 1988, p. 19). "I've been asked on a number of occasions, 'I see here by your record in 1976 you won a silver medal and in 1980 you were the captain and you didn't win anything. What happened, a letdown?' See, that kind of thing just aggravates the thought of what the Olympics all represented."

The wrestling team that competed in Los Angeles 4 years later was equally strong. The United States captured seven gold medals in freestyle and its first medals in Greco-Roman. Bobby Weaver (105.5), Randy Lewis (136.5), Dave Schultz (163), Mark Schultz (180.5), Ed Banach, (198), Lou Banach (220), and Bruce Baumgartner (286) were far too powerful and too skilled for the wrestlers who showed up, and all seven won gold medals with relative ease. How well they would have done against the Eastern Bloc teams will never be known, but they are Olympic champions for all time.

Freestyle coach Dan Gable said the Americans would have been quite successful regardless of the Soviet presence: "The way these guys were wrestling, any of them would have had a shot with anyone in the world. We would still have done very, very well."

Michigan's Steve Fraser (198) and New York's Jeff Blatnick (286) made history in Los Angeles, each winning gold medals in Greco-Roman. Fraser racked up five wins, including a 4-1 victory over three-time world champion Frank Andersson of Sweden. Blatnick was just 2-1 in his bouts but captured the gold with a dramatic 2-0 victory over Thomas Johansson of Sweden.

After winning his final bout, Blatnick sank to the mat in a prayerful pose, thankful for overcoming cancer to compete. His story became one of the most publicized to come out of the 1984 Olympics, and Blatnick was selected to carry the U.S. flag in the closing ceremonies.

Two other Greco-Roman athletes won medals, bringing the U.S. total in that sport to four. Greg Gibson (220) gained a silver and James Martinez (149.5) a bronze. Other freestyle medal winners were Barry Davis (125.5) and Andy Rein (149), who both earned silvers.

The 1988 Olympics were the first "full" Games since Montreal in 1976. A total of 162 nations sent teams to Seoul, South Korea. The United States earned seven wrestling medals, including the first ever Greco-Roman medal in a full Olympics when Dennis Koslowski finished third at 220 pounds.

The freestyle team fared well, but not as well as American fans had expected. Bruce Baumgartner missed in his bid to become the first two-time gold medal winner since George Mehnert in 1908, losing in the finals at 286 pounds to old rival David Gobedjichvili of the Soviet Union, 3-1. Mark Schultz, also bidding for his second gold medal, injured a knee and finished sixth at 180.5 pounds.

But John Smith and Ken Monday, a pair of former Oklahoma State University stars, came home with gold medals. Smith reeled off seven straight wins at 136.5 pounds, while Monday scored eight consecutive wins at 163 pounds. Other medal winners on the freestyle team were Nate Carr, third at 149.5, and Bill Scherr, third at 220 pounds.

At the conclusion of the 1988 Olympics, 244 wrestlers had represented the United States in 16 Olympic Games (not including the 1980 team). Forty-seven Americans had earned gold medals, 31 of them had earned silver medals, and 22 had earned bronze medals.

Six men—Bill Kerslake, Dick Wilson, Wayne Baughman, Ben Peterson, Dan Chandler, and Mark Fuller—gained positions on three Olympic teams each. Only six men—Mehnert, Wittenberg, Sanders, Ben Peterson, John Peterson, and Baumgartner—have won medals in two different Olympics. Wittenberg was the oldest gold medalist at 33 years, 309 days of age (1948), while Mehringer was the youngest at 22 years, 17 days (1932).

For more complete records of U.S. wrestling champions and teams, see Tables 2.1 and 2.2.

Table 2.1
United States Olympic Wrestling Champions

1904 Freestyle (St. Louis, MO)	
Benjamin H. Bradshaw	135
Robert Curry	105
Charles Erickson	158
Bernhulf Hansen	+158
George N. Mehnert	115

Isidor G. Niflot	125
Otto F. Roehm	145

1908 Freestyle (London)

George S. Dole	132
George N. Mehnert	119

1920 Freestyle (Antwerp, Belgium)

Charles E. Ackerly	119

1924 Freestyle (Paris)

Robin Reed	134
John T. Spellman	191.5
Harry Steel	+191.5
Russell J. Vis	145

1928 Freestyle (Amsterdam)

Allie R. Morrison	134

1932 Freestyle (Los Angeles, CA)

Peter J. Mehringer	191.5
Robert E. Pearce	123
Jack F. Van Bebber	158.5

1936 Freestyle (Berlin)

Frank W. Lewis	158.5

1948 Freestyle (London)

Glen Brand	174
Henry Wittenberg	191.5

1952 Freestyle (Helsinki, Finland)

William T. Smith	160.5

1960 Freestyle (Rome)

Douglas M. Blubaugh	160.5
Terrence J. McCann	125.5
Shelby A. Wilson	147.5

1972 Freestyle (Montreal)

Dan M. Gable	149.5
Benjamin L. Peterson	198
Wayne A. Wells	163

1976 Freestyle (Montreal)

John A. Peterson	180.5

1984 Freestyle (Los Angeles, CA)

Edward J. Banach	198
Louis D. Banach	220
Randy S. Lewis	136.5
David Schultz	163
Mark Schultz	180.5
Robert Weaver	105.5
Bruce R. Baumgartner	+220

1984 Greco-Roman (Los Angeles, CA)

Jeffrey C. Blatnick	+220
Steven H. Fraser	198

1988 Freestyle (Seoul)

Kenneth Monday	163
John Smith	136.5

Table 2.2
United States Olympic Team Results

Name	Class	Place
1904 Freestyle (St. Louis, MO)[a]		
Gustav Bauers	115	2
William Beckmann	158	2
Benjamin H. Bradshaw	135	1
Charles E. Clapper	135	3
Robert Curry	105	1
Charles Erickson	158	1
Bernhulf Hansen	+158	1
John Hein	105	2
Frank Kungler	+158	2
Theodore McLeer	135	2
George N. Mehnert	115	1
William L. Nelson	115	3
Isidor G. Niflot	125	1
Otto F. Roehm	145	1
Z.B. Strebler	125	3
Rudolph Tesing	145	2
Gus Thiefenthaler	105	3
F.C. Warmbold	+158	3
August Wester	125	2

Name	Class	Place
Jerry E. Winholtz	158	3
Albert Zirkel	145	3
1908 Freestyle (London)		
John Craige	160.5	Eliminated, second round
George S. Dole	132.5	1
John H. Krug	146.5	Eliminated, second round
George N. Mehnert	119	1
Frank Narganes	160.5	Eliminated, second round
Lee J. Talbot	+160.5	
1912 Greco-Roman (Stockholm, Sweden)		
William J. Lyshon	132	Eliminated, second round
George W. Retzer Jr.	132	Eliminated, second round
1920 Freestyle (Antwerp, Belgium)		
Charles E. Ackerly	119	1
Paul Berlenbach	. . .	Alternate
Angus M. Frantz	152	4
Samuel N. Gerson	119	2
Charles F. Johnson	152	3
Ferdinand H. Kirchman	. . .	Alternate
Walter Maurer	176	3
George Metropoulos	134	Eliminated, first round
Fred J. Meyer	+176	3
B. Olson	. . .	Alternate
Nathanael Pendleton	+176	2
John R. Redman	176	4
Joseph M. Shimmon	134	Eliminated, second round
John Vorhes	. . .	Alternate
Philip Weems	. . .	Alternate
George M. Pinneo, coach		
1920 Greco-Roman (Antwerp, Belgium)		
Adrian R. Brian	132	Eliminated, third round
Daniel V. Gallery	132	Eliminated, third round
Frank M. Maichle	181.5	Eliminated, third round
George Metropoulos	148.5	Eliminated, third round
Nathanael Pendleton	181.5	Eliminated, second round
Oral R. Swigart	148.5	Eliminated, second round
Henry I. Szymanski	165	Eliminated, fifth round
Alexander M. Weyand	+181.5	4
Edward E. Wilkie	+181.5	5

Name	Class	Place
Paul D. Zanoline	165	Eliminated, second round
George M. Pinneo, coach		
	1924 Freestyle (Paris)	
Simon H. Brown	134	Alternate
Roger L. Flanders	+191.5	Eliminated, second round
Bryan Hines	123	3
William B. Johnson	158.5	4
Guy H. Lookabaugh	158.5	Eliminated, sixth round
C. Milton MacWilliam	123	Eliminated, first round
Perry Martter	145	Eliminated, first round
Chester Newton	134	2
William B. Quinn	191.5	Alternate
Robin Reed	134	1
E.B. Rogers	145	Alternate
Herschel A. Smith	174	Eliminated, second round
John T. Spellman	191.5	1
Harry Steel	+191.5	1
Charles W. Strack	191.5	Eliminated, first round
Orion Stuteville	174	Alternate
Kenneth Truckenmiller	158.5	Alternate
Russell J. Vis	145	1
Walter D. Wright Jr.	174	Eliminated, first round
Wilfrid E. Cann, coach		
Charles W. Streit Jr., manager		
Wilbur Hutsell, trainer		
	1928 Freestyle (Amsterdam)	
Lloyd Otto Appleton	158.5	2
Leslie Beers	158.5	Alternate
Clarence Berryman	145	6
Heywood L. Edwards	191.5	4
Ed George	+191.5	4
Ralph W. Hammonds	174	4
Robert Hewitt	123	5
Arthur L. Holding	123	Alternate
Allie R. Morrison	134	1
Ralph A. Prunty	145	Alternate
James Reed	123	Alternate
George D. Rule	174	Alternate
Auree B. Scott	174	Alternate
Charles W. Strack	191.5	Alternate

Name	Class	Place
George M. Pinneo, coach		
Charles W. Streit Jr., manager		
Wilfrid E. Cann, trainer		
1932 Freestyle (Los Angeles, CA)		
Lloyd Otto Appleton	174	Alternate
George W. Ashford	123	Alternate
Conrad C. Caldwell	191.5	Alternate
Melvin C. Clodfelter	145	4
Carl J. Dougovito	158.5	Alternate
Maynard F. Harman	145	Alternate
Robert William Hess	174	4
Peter J. Mehringer	191.5	1
Lyle Morford	134	Alternate
Edgar Nemir	134	2
Robert E. Pearce	123	1
John Horn Riley	+191.5	2
Ralph Teague	+191.5	Alternate
Jack F. Van Bebber	158.5	1
Hugo Otopalik, coach		
Charles W. Streit Jr., manager		
1936 Freestyle (Berlin)		
Ben L. Bishop	145	Alternate
Dale E. Brand	123	Alternate
Ray Clemons	191.5	5
Roy Harvey Dunn	+191.5	Eliminated, second round
Orville W. England	174	Alternate
A. Ross Flood	123	2
C. Edward Knight	158.5	Alternate
Frank W. Lewis	158.5	1
Charles McDaniel	191.5	Alternate
Francis E. Millard	134	2
Fred Parkey	123	Alternate
Howell A. Scobey Jr.	+191.5	Alternate
Harley DeWitt Strong Jr.	145	Eliminated, third round
Richard L. Voliva	174	2
William H. Thom, coach		
Edward C. Gallagher, honorary coach		

Name	Class	Place
Charles W. Streit Jr., manager		
Clarence A. Gallagher, trainer		
1948 Freestyle (London)		
Glen Brand	174	1
Leland Christensen	114.5	Alternate
John A. Fletcher	147.5	Alternate
Verne C. Gagne	191.5	Alternate
Richard Hutton	+191.5	Eliminated, third round
William Jernigan	114.5	Eliminated, third round
William Koll	147.5	5
Gerald G. Leeman	125.5	2
Malcolm MacDonald	125.5	Alternate
Robert R. Maldegan	+191.5	Alternate
Leland Merrill	160.5	3
Hal L. Moore	136.5	6
William J. Nelson	160.5	Alternate
Joseph Scarpello	174	Alternate
Leo A. Thomsen	136.5	Alternate
Henry Wittenberg	191.5	1
Art Griffith, coach		
Clifford P. Keen, manager		
1952 Freestyle (Helsinki, Finland)		
Jack Lee Blubaugh	125.5	Alternate
Bill D. Borders	125.5	Eliminated, third round
Samuel J. Coursen	114.5	Alternate
Leonard J. DeAugustino	136.5	Alternate
Jay Thomas Evans	147.5	2
John A. Fletcher	147.5	Alternate
Herbert L. Haberlach	+191.5	Alternate
Josiah Henson	136.5	3
Dan Allen Hodge	174	Eliminated, third round
William R. Kerslake	+191.5	5
Joseph J. Krufka	174	Alternate
James C. LaRock	160.5	Alternate
R. Hugh Peery	114.5	Eliminated, third round
William T. Smith	160.5	1
Dale O. Thomas	191.5	Alternate
Henry Wittenberg	191.5	2
Raymond H. Swartz, coach		
Buel R. Patterson, manager		

Name	Class	Place
1956 Freestyle (Melbourne, Australia)		
Lee Dale Allen	125.5	Eliminated, second round
Richard Beattie	160.5	Surgery[b]
Frank A. Bettucci	147.5	Injured[c]
Peter Steele Blair	191.5	3
Richard A. Delgado	114.5	5
Jay Thomas Evans	147.5	5
William E. Fischer	160.5	Eliminated, third round
Dan Allen Hodge	174	2
William R. Kerslake	+191.5	Eliminated, third round
Myron W. Roderick	136.5	4
David H. McCuskey, coach		
Commander C. Shuford Swift, manager		
1956 Greco-Roman (Melbourne, Australia)		
Jay Thomas Evans	147.5	Eliminated, second round
James Jay Holt	160.5	5
Dale Folsom Lewis	+191.5	Eliminated, second round
James C. Peckham	174	Eliminated, third round
Alan H. Rice	136.5	Eliminated, second round
Dale O. Thomas	191.5	5
Kent Harold Townley	125.5	Eliminated, third round
J. Richard Wilson	114.5	Eliminated, third round
Joseph R. Scalzo, coach		
Commander C. Shuford Swift, manager		
1960 Freestyle (Rome)		
Douglas M. Blubaugh	160.5	1
Daniel O. Brand	191.5	5
Edward DeWitt	174	4
Louis D. Giani	136.5	Injured, withdrew fourth round
William R. Kerslake	+191.5	Eliminated, fourth round
Terrence J. McCann	125.5	1
E. Gray Simons	114.5	5
Shelby A. Wilson	147.5	1
Port G. Robertson, coach		
John Mandel, manager		
1960 Greco-Roman (Rome)		
Lee Dale Allen	136.5	Eliminated, fourth round
Russell A. Camilleri	174	Eliminated, fourth round

Name	Class	Place
Fritz Fivian	160.5	Eliminated, second round
Howard George	191.5	Eliminated, second round
Larry Lauchle	125.5	Eliminated, second round
Dale Folsom Lewis	+191.5	Eliminated, second round
Ben A. Northrup	147.5	Eliminated, second round
J. Richard Wilson	114.5	Eliminated, fourth round
M. Briggs Hunt, coach		
John Mandel, manager		
	1964 Freestyle (Tokyo)	
David C. Auble	125.5	4
Daniel O.Brand	191.5	3
Gerald G. Conine	213.5	6
Bobby E. Douglas	138.5	4
Larry D. Kristoff	+213.5	Eliminated, third round
Gregory K. Ruth	154	6
E. Gray Simons	114.5	Eliminated, fourth round
Charles E. Tribble	171.5	Failed to weigh in for second round
Rex A. Peery, coach		
Fendley A. Collins, manager		
	1964 Greco-Roman (Tokyo)	
R. Wayne Baughman	191.5	Eliminated, fourth round
James E. Burke	154	Eliminated, third round
Russell A. Camilleri	171.5	Eliminated, fourth round
Ronald L. Finley	138.5	4
Andrew Fitch	125.5	Eliminated, third round
W. Patrick Lovell	213.5	Eliminated, second round
Robert J. Pickens	+213.5	6
J. Richard Wilson	114.5	4
Dean L. Rockwell, coach		
Fendley A. Collins, manager		
	1968 Freestyle (Mexico City)	
Donald Behm	125.5	2
Steven L. Combs	171.5	Eliminated, fifth round
Bobby E. Douglas	138.5	Injured, withdrew second round
Larry D. Kristoff	+213.5	5
Jesse Lewis	213.5	6
Thomas Peckham	191.5	4
Richard Sanders	114.5	2
Wayne A. Wells	154	4

Name	Class	Place
Jay Thomas Evans, coach		
Manuel Gorriaran, manager		
1968 Greco-Roman (Mexico City)		
R. Wayne Baughman	191.5	5
David G. Hazewinkel	125.5	Eliminated, fourth round
James A. Hazewinkel	138.5	Eliminated, fourth round
Werner Holzer	154	6
Larry Lyden	171.5	Eliminated, second round
Robert Roop	+213.5	Eliminated, third round
Henk Schenk	213.5	Eliminated, second round
Richard Tamble	114.5	Eliminated, second round
Henry Wittenberg, coach		
Dominick Torio, manager		
1972 Freestyle (Munich)		
Jimmy Carr	114.5	Eliminated, third round
Gene Davis	136.5	Eliminated, third round
Dan M. Gable	149.5	1
Sergio Gonzalez	105.5	Eliminated, third round
Benjamin L. Peterson	198	1
John A. Peterson	180.5	2
Richard Sanders	125.5	2
Henk Schenk	220	Eliminated, second round
Chris Taylor	+220	3
Wayne A. Wells	163	1
Bill Farrell, coach		
Russell Houk, manager		
1972 Greco-Roman (Munich)		
R. Wayne Baughman	198	Eliminated, third round
Robert Buzzard	149.5	Eliminated, second round
Buck Deadrich	220	Eliminated, second round
David G. Hazewinkel	125.5	Eliminated, second round
James A. Hazewinkel	136.5	Eliminated, second round
Wayne A. Holmes	105.5	Eliminated, second round
Gary Neist	163	Eliminated, second round
J. Robinson	180.5	Eliminated, third round
James C. Steiger	114.5	Injured, withdrew second round
Chris Taylor	+220	Eliminated, second round
Alan H. Rice, coach		
Captain Stephen M. Archer, manager		

Name	Class	Place
	1976 Freestyle (Montreal)	
Joe M. Corso	125.5	Eliminated, third round
Gene Davis	136.5	3
Stanley J. Dziedzic	163	3
James A. Haines	114.5	Eliminated, third round
Russell Hellickson	220	2
Jimmy Jackson	+220	Eliminated, third round
Lloyd W. Keaser	149.5	2
Benjamin L. Peterson	198	2
John A. Peterson	180.5	1
William Rosado	105.5	Eliminated, second round
Major R. Wayne Baughman, coach		
Russell Houk, manager		
	1976 Greco-Roman (Montreal)	
Gary Alexander	136.5	Eliminated, second round
Daniel C. Chandler	180.5	Eliminated, third round
Michael Farina	105.5	Eliminated, third round
Evan Johnson	198	Eliminated, third round
William "Pete" Lee	+220	5
Patrick J. Marcy	149.5	Eliminated, third round
John Matthews	163	Eliminated, second round
Brad Rheingans	220	4
Joseph Sade	125.5	Eliminated, fourth round
Bruce Thompson	114.5	Eliminated, third round
James C. Peckham, coach		
Vaughan Hitchcock, manager		
	1980 Freestyle (Moscow)[d]	
John Azevedo	125.5	
Chris Campbell	180.5	
Russell Hellickson	220	
Lee Kemp	163	
Randy S. Lewis	136.5	
Gene Mills	114.5	
Benjamin L. Peterson	198	
Robert Weaver	105.5	
Greg Wojciechowski	+220	
Charles Yagla	163	
Dan M. Gable, coach		
Stanley J. Dziedzic, manager		

Name	Class	Place
1980 Greco-Roman (Moscow)[d]		
Jeffrey C. Blatnick	+220	
Daniel C. Chandler	180.5	
Mark A. Fuller	105.5	
Brian Gust	125.5	
Mark Johnson	198	
John Matthews	163	
Thomas Minkel	149.5	
Daniel Mello	136.5	
Brad Rheingans	220	
Bruce Thompson	114.5	
Lee Dale Allen, coach		
Major R. Wayne Baughman, manager		
1984 Freestyle (Los Angeles, CA)		
Edward J. Banach	198	1
Louis D. Banach	220	1
Bruce R. Baumgartner	+220	1
Barry A. Davis	125.5	2
Joe A. Gonzales	114.5	Eliminated, third round
Randy S. Lewis	136.5	1
Andrew R. Rein	149.5	2
David Schultz	163	1
Mark Schultz	180.5	1
Robert Weaver	105.5	1
Dan M. Gable, coach		
Stanley J. Dziedzic, assistant coach		
1984 Greco-Roman (Los Angeles, CA)		
Jeffrey C. Blatnick	+220	1
Christopher L. Catalfo	163	Eliminated, fourth round
Daniel C. Chandler	180.5	Eliminated, second round
Frank S. Famiano	125.5	5
Steven H. Fraser	198	1
Mark A. Fuller	105.5	Eliminated, second round
Gregory P. Gibson	220	2
Bert A. Govig	114.5	Failed to weigh in
Abdurrahim Kuzu	136.5	4
James M. Martinez	149.5	3

Name	Class	Place
Ronald L. Finley, coach		
Pavel Katsen, assistant coach		
	1988 Greco-Roman (Seoul)	
Anthony Amado	125.5	Eliminated, second round
Issac Anderson	136.5	6
David Butler	163	Eliminated, fourth round
Michial Foy	198	Eliminated, third round
Mark A. Fuller	105.5	Eliminated, third round
Dennis Koslowski	220	3
Duane Koslowski	286	8
John Morgan	180.5	7
Andy Seras	149.5	Eliminated, fourth round
Shawn Sheldon	114.5	Eliminated, second round
Pavel Katsen, coach		
Thomas Minkel, assistant coach		
	1988 Freestyle (Seoul)	
Bruce Baumgartner	286	2
Nate Carr	149.5	3
Kenneth Chertow	114.5	Eliminated, third round
Barry Davis	125.5	Eliminated, third round
Kenneth Monday	163	1
Bill Scherr	220	3
Jim Scherr	198	5
Mark Schultz	180.5	6
John Smith	136.5	1
Tim Vanni	105.5	4
James Humphrey, coach		
Dan M. Gable, assistant coach		

[a]The competition consisted of the National AAU Championships and attracted 41 entries, all from the United States. Only the medalists are listed.

[b]Beattie was replaced by Fischer after an appendectomy.

[c]Bettucci was replaced by Evans after an injury at the site of the Games.

[d]The 1980 Games were boycotted by the United States.

Chapter 3

The World Championships

Freestyle and Greco-Roman

The history of the world wrestling tournament is confusing and somewhat difficult to trace. According to FILA (the international wrestling body), the first recognized world championships took place in 1896 in Athens at the first Olympic Games of the modern era. It was not a very large tournament, however, as only two countries participated in just one weight class.

From that shaky start, it was a long road to a truly competitive world championship. Except on Olympic years, tournaments were held almost yearly in Europe for decades, often with just two or three weight classes contested. They were mostly in the Greco-Roman style, which was the favored European form at the time. Nonetheless, FILA lists those meets as world championships in its official handbook.

Perhaps the best early attempt at holding a world wrestling meet came in September 1938, when the top four freestyle teams from the 1936 Olympics assembled in Stockholm for a "wrestle-off." The United States was represented by champions of the 1938 AAU National Tournament and finished second. The American team defeated Hungary, 5-2, and Germany, 4-3, but lost to host Sweden, 4-3. Hungary edged Germany, 4-3, to finish third behind Sweden and the United States.

Members of the American squad included Joe McDaniel (123) of Oklahoma A&M, Francis Millard (134) of Massachusetts, and John Harrell (191) of Oklahoma A&M. The trio won all three of their bouts and could therefore be considered "world champions" by some. Harrell, in fact, pinned all three of his foes, including the Swedish star Azel Cadier, who was European champion at the time and was nicknamed "the perfect wrestler" by European mat enthusiasts.

The United States might have won the team title had not one of its finest wrestlers, Stanley Henson of Oklahoma A&M, suffered a dislocated shoulder that forced him to the sidelines. He was favored in the match against Sweden at 145 pounds but was not able to compete, and the United States forfeited the weight class.

According to FILA, eight world tournaments were held between 1938 and 1961. In 1951 the AAU decided to send a team consisting of the winners at the national meet held in San Diego, California. The world tourney was held in Tokyo, and the U.S. team was quite unfamiliar with the rules. The best effort was turned in by Wenzel Hubel (174), who placed fourth. Others placing were Alan Rice, Newt Copple, and Jim Rose, all fifth, and Dale Thomas, who placed sixth.

The next effort by the United States was in 1961, when it sent a full team of freestyle and Greco-Roman wrestlers to the world tournament in Yokohama, Japan. That event, held in June 1961, is generally considered by U.S. authorities to be the first official world championships.

The freestyle team, coached by Raymond Swartz of the U.S. Naval Academy, scored 11.5 points and finished sixth. Iran won the title with 41 points, followed by the Soviet Union (33), Turkey (26), Japan (15), and Hungary (13). The best American effort was turned in by lanky Dan Brand (198), a former University of Nebraska standout who was fourth. Dick Wilson (114.5) and Mike Rodriguez (147.5) finished fifth. Carmen Molino (125.5), Lee Allen (136.5), Earl "Skip" Perillo (160.5), and Russ Camilleri (174) were sixth, and Dale Lewis (heavyweight) did not place.

The Greco-Roman team, coached by Dale Thomas of Oregon State, also finished sixth. It was led by Ben Northrup (147.5), who was fourth. Wilson and Brand both doubled in Greco-Roman and took fifth, and Joe Gomes (125.5) and Pat Lovell (heavyweight) were sixth. Other members of the Greco-Roman team were Ron Finley (136.5) and Bill Weick (160.5), who did not place.

In 1962, the World Championships came to the United States, with Toledo, Ohio, hosting. Both teams placed sixth again. Bill Smith coached the freestylers, while Hallow Wilson coached the Greco-Roman team. The tournament marked the emergence of the Soviet Union as the top wrestling country in the world, replacing Iran as the freestyle champion and winning the Greco-Roman title for the second straight year.

The United States earned its first medals in the World Championships in 1962, when Jim Ferguson (171.5) and Dan Brand (191.5) won bronze medals in freestyle and Jim Burke (154) did the same in Greco-Roman. All three were members of the San Francisco Olympic Club.

The 1962 tournament in Toledo proved a success on several fronts. A record number 27 countries participated, and the 12 sessions attracted a total attendance of 29,800. It also marked the first time that foam-rubber mats were used in an international meet, and there was a sizeable media turnout. According to *Amateur Wrestling News*, nearly 150 members of the nation's television, radio, and newspaper professions were on hand.

In 1965 in Manchester, England, Bobby Douglas (138.5) and Larry Kristoff (heavyweight) became the first U.S. wrestlers to place as high as second in freestyle. Their performances set the stage for a pair of Oregon products to make history in the 1969 World Championships. Competing in Mar del Plata, Spain, Rick Sanders (114.5) and Fred Fozzard (180.5) won the first gold medals for the United States. Sanders pinned his first four foes and scored a 7-4 victory over Mohammad Ghrbani of Iran in the finals.

Fozzard posted pins over Mongolia, the Soviet Union, and Finland and decisions over Germany and Iran. In the round-robin, he dropped a close decision to Bulgaria but was awarded the gold medal when the Soviet and Bulgarian wrestlers were disqualified for attempting to fix their final bout. Both were thrown out of the tournament, and no second- or third-place medals were awarded.

"Bill Farrell, U.S. freestyle coach, had sensed a possible collusion and alerted friendly officials," reported *Amateur Wrestling News*. "The move when it came was so obvious that the match was stopped immediately and disqualification resulted."

In 1970, Oklahoma's Wayne Wells (163) became the nation's third world champion. Wells did not have a close match as he posted five straight wins in Edmonton, Canada. He was leading his Soviet foe, Nodarr Khorkashvili, 5-0, in the finals when the Soviet withdrew, citing an injury to his shoulder. In the opening round, Wells defeated France's 1967 world champion, Daniel Robin, 4-1. The gold medal climaxed a steady climb by the determined Wells. He had placed fourth in the Olympics in 1968 and second in the 1969 World Championships.

In 1971, Iowa's Dan Gable became the fourth American to earn a world title. The 1971 World Championships in Sofia, Bulgaria, was the largest world mat meet ever held, drawing 280 freestyle participants from 41 countries. Gable posted four pins and scored decisive victories over his Soviet and Bulgarian foes to become world champion at the age of 22 years, 11 months. One year later, Wells and Gable made U.S. history by becoming the first two matmen to win world and Olympic titles.

Maryland's Lloyd Keaser, a graduate of the U.S. Naval Academy, was the fifth wrestler to win a world title, taking the 149.5-pound gold medal in 1973. Keaser scored six victories and battled to a tie with the Soviet Union's Nasrulla Nasrullajev on his way to earning the crown.

America's sixth world champion was Pennsylvania's Stan Dziedzic, who wrestled at Slippery Rock State College. Dziedzic moved up from a bronze medal effort at the 1976 Olympics to capture the 163-pound title in 1977. He lost a 7-6 match to Bulgaria's Alexander Nanev but scored seven wins, including a pin of Iran silver medalist Mansuor Barzegar, who beat Nanev, 10-2.

On August 27, 1978, Ohio's Lee Kemp became the seventh and youngest American to win a world title when he scored a 7-4 triumph over Alexander Nanev to clinch the 163-pound gold medal. Kemp's effort was all the more impressive considering it was his first major international meet and considering that two of his victims, West Germany's Martin Knosp and Nanev, both became world champions in the years to follow.

Kemp was only 21 years, 8 months old when he captured his first world title. He came back to win the world championship at the same weight in

Stan Dziedzic (left) and Lee Kemp in a battle of world champions. (Courtesy of USA Wrestling)

1979 and again in 1982. He was third in 1981, losing to Knosp on a very controversial call. By 1988, he was America's most successful competitor in the World Championships, having won three gold medals. He also won three NCAA titles for the University of Wisconsin and narrowly missed becoming the first four-time NCAA champion when he lost a split decision to Iowa's Chuck Yagla in the finals as a freshman.

Chris Campbell, the former University of Iowa star by way of New Jersey, breezed to the 1981 world title at 180.5 pounds to become the eighth world champion from the United States. He defeated Hungary's 1979 world champion, Istan Kovacs, 7-1, in one round and Bulgaria's Efraim Kamerov, 4-1, in the finals. Campbell was voted the meet's Most Technically Prepared Wrestler.

Two years later, Dave Schultz, a native of California who wrestled at the University of Oklahoma, took over where Kemp left off and won the world title at 163 pounds. Schultz had placed third at 180.5 the year before and traveled a tough road to the gold medal in 1983. He battled defending world champion Knosp to a 2-2 tie, then rattled off five straight wins. In the finals, he trailed the Soviet Union's Taram Magomadov, 4-0, before rallying for an 11-6 triumph.

Although Kemp stood in 1988 as America's only three-time champion at the World Championships, he was joined as a three-time world champion (including the Olympics) by Mark Schultz. Like Kemp, a former three-time NCAA champion (at the University of Oklahoma), Schultz won the Olympics in 1984 and the World Championships in both 1985 and 1987.

In 1985, Schultz breezed to the title without a close call in his six matches, defeating Bulgaria's Nanev in the finals, 10-5. He slipped to seventh in the 1986 meet but roared back to take the title again in 1987, defeating defending world champion Nanev again in the finals, 3-1.

Bill Scherr joined Schultz as world champion in 1985, taking the 198-pound title. Scherr, a native of tiny Mobridge, South Dakota, won an NCAA title at the University of Nebraska and seven straight matches at the world meet, including a victory over Iran's Hasan Mohebbi in the finals, 7-4.

Bruce Baumgartner, a native of New Jersey who competed for Indiana State University, was world champion at 286 pounds in 1986. Baumgartner cracked the Soviet Union's 25-year stranglehold on the heavyweight world title with four straight wins, including a 6-2 triumph over 1985 world champion David Godedjichvili. Baumgartner had also beaten the Soviet champion two other times in 1986—at the Goodwill Games and at the World Cup.

Joining Mark Schultz as a gold medalist in 1987 was young John Smith. The Oklahoma native won the gold medal at 136.5 pounds, becoming the second-youngest world champion ever (behind Kemp). Smith pinned one foe and outscored the other six by a combined 61-14 margin, including a 5-4 win over defending world champion Khaser Isaev of the Soviet Union. He followed up the world victory by winning his second straight NCAA title and compiling a winning streak of 90 matches, the second-longest streak in NCAA history behind Gable's 100.

Dave and Mark Schultz hold the distinction of being the only brothers to win world and Olympic titles for the United States. However, the Petersons, Ben and John, each earned Olympic gold medals.

Although 12 U.S. wrestlers have won a total of 15 world freestyle gold medals, Mike Houck stands alone in Greco-Roman. In 1985, in Kolbotn, Norway, he finished first at 198 pounds and became the first American to win the world championship in Greco-Roman. He defeated three-time world champion Frank Andersson of Sweden along the way, 6-5, and in the finals defeated three-time world champion Igor Kanygin of the Soviet Union by passivity disqualification. Houck had won the U.S. national title in both 1984 and 1985 but was defeated by Steve Fraser for the 1984 Olympic team spot by a single point. Fraser went on to capture the gold medal in Los Angeles.

The first American to earn a medal in Greco-Roman at the World Championships was Jim Burke (154), who finished third in 1962 in Toledo, Ohio. James Raschke (heavyweight) matched that effort the following year, but it was not until Dave Hazewinkel (125.5) in 1970 that America could boast of a silver medal.

Mark and Dave Schultz, the only brothers in American history to each win a world and an Olympic title. (Courtesy of USA Wrestling)

Perhaps the most versatile wrestler the United States has ever produced at the international level is Greg Gibson, a former University of Oregon star who excelled for many years with the U.S. Marine Corps. After establishing a Marine Corps record in the obstacle course, the powerful 220-pounder went on to capture medals in all three major forms of wrestling competition at the international level. He won a gold medal in the 1981 World Sombo Tournament (Sombo is Soviet judo, allowing submission holds), a silver medal in the 1983 World Freestyle Tournament, and a silver medal in Greco-Roman in the 1984 Olympics.

The Soviet Union has dominated the world wrestling scene for most of the past 3 decades. The reasons are several, according to top American authorities. Of utmost importance are (a) the government's total support and sponsorship, (b) year-long training programs that allow athletes to train as hard and as long as Americans work at jobs, and (c) team depth. It has been estimated that 10 times as many athletes participate in wrestling in the Soviet Union as in any other country.

The most successful international-style wrestler in history was Alexander Medved of the Soviet Union. Medved won a total of 10 world championships in weight classes ranging from 97 kilograms to 100-plus (heavyweight). He captured Olympic titles in 1964, 1968, and 1972 and world titles in 1962, 1963, 1966, 1967, 1969, 1970, and 1971. He lost just 2 of 73 international matches.

Medved was born September 16, 1937, in the small Ukrainian town of Belaya Tserkov. His father was a forest ranger. Medved entered the army at the age of 17 and became a national hero for his wrestling exploits. When he retired after the 1972 Olympics, a full house of 6,000 attended his farewell party at the Sports Palace in Minsk.

Another Soviet wrestler, Valeriy Rezantsev, turned in a remarkable string of performances by winning seven straight world titles in Greco-Roman, all in the same weight class (198). Rezantsev won two Olympic titles in that string (in 1972 and 1976).

Osamu Watanabe of Japan compiled an incredible record while winning three world freestyle titles at 138 pounds. He never lost once in over 300 matches. He breezed to world titles in 1962 and 1963 and captured an Olympic gold medal in 1964. He competed in 186 international bouts without surrendering a single point and scored 120 pins.

For U.S. results in the World Championships, see Table 3.1.

Table 3.1
World Championships, United States Results (Since 1961)

Name	Class	Place
	1961 Freestyle (Yokohama, Japan)	
Richard Wilson	114.5	5
Carmen Molino	125.5	5
Lee Allen	136.5	6
Michael Rodriguez	147.5	5
Earl Perillo	160.5	6
Russell Camilleri	174	6
Daniel Brand	191.5	4
Dale Lewis	Heavyweight	
Raymond Swartz, coach (Team placed 6th)		
	1961 Greco-Roman (Yokohama, Japan)	
Richard Wilson	114.5	5
Joseph Gomes	125.5	6
Ronald Finley	136.5	
Ben Northrup	147.5	
William Weick	160.5	
Russell Camilleri	174	
Daniel Brand	191.5	
Patrick Lovell	Heavyweight	
Dale Thomas, coach (Team placed 6th)		

Name	Class	Place
1962 Freestyle (Toledo, OH)		
Richard Wilson	114.5	
David Auble	125.5	4
Ronald Finley	138.5	4
Gregory Ruth	154	5
James Ferguson	171.5	3
William Farrell	191.5	
Daniel Brand	213.5	3
Merrell Solowin	Heavyweight	
William Smith, coach (Team placed 6th)		
1962 Greco-Roman (Toledo, OH)		
Richard Wilson	114.5	
Carmen Molino	125.5	
Lee Grubbs	138.5	
James Burke	154	3
Rudy Williams	171.5	5
Russell Camilleri	191.5	
Patrick Lovell	213.5	6
Hallow Wilson	Heavyweight	5
Dean Rockwell, coach (Team placed 6th)		
1963 Freestyle (Sofia, Bulgaria)		
Andrew Fitch	114.5	6
David Auble	125.5	
Ronald Finley	138.5	4
Gregory Ruth	154	3
Dean Lahr	171.5	4
Russell Camilleri	191.5	6
Russell Winer	213.5	
Merrell Solowin	Heavyweight	
Myron Roderick, coach (Team placed 6th)		
1963 Greco-Roman (Halsingborg, Sweden)		
Andrew Fitch	114.5	
Carmen Molino	125.5	
Bobby Douglas	138.5	
Ben Northrup	154	
Dennis Fitzgerald	171.5	

Name	Class	Place
Wayne Baughman	191.5	
James Ferguson	213.5	
James Raschke	Heavyweight	3
Dominick Torio, coach (Team placed 14th)		

1964 (an Olympic year)

1965 Freestyle (Manchester, England)

Name	Class	Place
Richard Sanders	114.5	
Bobby Douglas	138.5	
James Burke	154	
Russell Camilleri	171.5	
Wayne Baughman	191.5	5
Gerald Conine	213.5	
Larry Kristoff	Heavyweight	3
William Smith, coach (Team placed 6th)		

1965 Greco-Roman (Tampere, Finland)

Name	Class	Place
Richard Sanders	114.5	
Bobby Douglas	138.5	
James Burke	154	
Russell Camilleri	171.5	
Wayne Baughman	191.5	
Gerald Conine	213.5	
Larry Kristoff	Heavyweight	
William Smith, coach (Team did not place)		

1966 Freestyle (Toledo, OH)

Name	Class	Place
Richard Sanders	114.5	3
Fred Powell	125.5	5
Bobby Douglas	138.5	2
Werner Holzer	154	4
Len Kauffman	171.5	4
Dean Lahr	191.5	5
Jess Lewis	213.5	
Larry Kristoff	Heavyweight	2
William Smith, coach (Team placed 3rd)		

Name	Class	Place
1966 Greco-Roman (Toledo, OH)		
James Hazewinkel	114.5	6
Charles Coffee	125.5	
Ronald Finley	138.5	6
Ben Northrup	154	
Russell Camilleri	171.5	
Wayne Baughman	191.5	
Gerald Conine	213.5	
James Raschke	Heavyweight	
Dale Thomas, coach (Team did not placc)		
1967 Freestyle (New Delhi, India)		
Richard Sanders	114.5	2
Richard Sofman	125.5	
Michael Young	138.5	
Werner Holzer	154	
Patrick Kelly	171.5	
Wayne Baughman	191.5	6
Harry Houska	213.5	
Larry Kristoff	Heavyweight	3
William Smith, coach (Team placed 4th)		
1967 Greco-Roman (Bucharest, Hungary)		
David Hazewinkel	114.5	
James Hazewinkel	125.5	
Charles Coffee	138.5	
Rudy Williams	171.5	
Gary Stenslund	213.5	
Thomas Evans, coach (Team did not place)		
1968 (an Olympic year)		
1969 Freestyle (Mar del Plata, Spain)		
Dale Kestel	114.5	5
Richard Sanders	114.5	1
Donald Behm	125.5	2
Michael Young	136.5	5
Bobby Douglas	149.5	4
Wayne Wells	163	2
Fred Fozzard	180.5	1
Henk Schenk	198	3

Name	Class	Place
Larry Kristoff	220	2
Rocky Rasley	Heavyweight	5
William Farrell, coach (Team placed 2nd)		
1969 Greco-Roman (Mar del Plata, Spain)		
Art Chavez	114.5	
David Hazewinkel	125.5	3
James Hazewinkel	136.5	4
Robert Buzzard	149.5	
Larry Lyden	163	5
Phil Wells	180.5	
Buck Deadrich	198	6
Alan Rice, coach (Team placed 9th)		
1970 Freestyle (Edmonton, Canada)		
Joe Orta	105.5	
John Morley	114.5	5
Donald Behm	125.5	5
Michael Young	136.5	3
Bobby Douglas	149.5	3
Wayne Wells	163	1
Fred Fozzard	180.5	5
Bill Harlow	198	2
Larry Kristoff	220	2
Greg Wojciechowski	Heavyweight	4
William Farrell, coach (Team placed 2nd)		
1970 Greco-Roman (Edmonton, Canada)		
Dale Kestel	105.5	
William Davids		
David Hazewinkel	125.5	2
James Hazewinkel	136.5	
Abdul Raheem Ali	149.5	
Richard Mihal	163	
J Robinson	180.5	4
Wayne Baughman	198	
Willie Williams	220	6
Chris Taylor	Heavyweight	4
Alan Rice, coach (Team placed 8th)		

Name	Class	Place
1971 Freestyle (Sofia, Bulgaria)		
Sergio Gonzalez	105.5	6
Jimmy Carr	114.5	
Donald Behm	125.5	2
Gene Davis	136.5	
Dan Gable	149.5	1
Mike Gallego	163	
John Peterson	180.5	
Russell Hellickson	198	3
Larry Kristoff	220	
Buck Deadrich	Heavyweight	
Douglas Blubaugh, coach (Team placed 5th)		
1971 Greco-Roman (Sofia, Bulgaria)		
Wayne Holmes	105.5	
Dale Kestel	114.5	
David Hazewinkel	125.5	
James Hazewinkel	136.5	
Gary Alexander	149.5	
Gary Neist	163	
J Robinson	180.5	5
Wayne Baughman	198	
Willie Williams	220	
Ronald Finley, coach (Team placed 15th)		
1972 (an Olympic year)		
1973 Freestyle (Teheran, Iran)		
David Range	105.5	
Henry Geller	114.5	
Donald Behm	125.5	4
Larry Morgan	136.5	4
Lloyd Keaser	149.5	1
Stan Dziedzic	163	
John Peterson	180.5	3
Ben Peterson	198	
James Duschen	220	
Mike McCready	Heavyweight	
Wayne Baughman, coach (Team placed 5th)		

Name	Class	Place
1973 Greco-Roman (Teheran, Iran)		
Karoly Kancsar	105.5	
Bruce Thompson	114.5	
Joseph Sade	125.5	
Gary Alexander	136.5	
Phil Frey	149.5	
Abdul Raheem Ali	163	
Mike Gallego	180.5	
Willie Williams	198	
James Duschen	220	
Mack McCready	Heavyweight	
Lee Allen, coach (Team did not place)		
1974 Freestyle (Istanbul, Turkey)		
William Rosado	105.5	
Gary Breece	114.5	
Jan Gitcho	125.5	
James Humphrey	136.5	
Gene Davis	149.5	6
Stan Dziedzic	163	5
Gregory Hicks	180.5	
Vincent Paolano	198	
John Bowlsby	220	
Mike McCready	Heavyweight	
Wayne Baughman, coach (Team placed 13th)		
1974 Greco-Roman (Katowice, Poland)		
Karoly Kancsar	104.5	6
Bruce Thompson	114.5	
Brian Gust	125.5	
Reid Lamphere	136.5	
Patrick Marcy	149.5	
Abdul Raheem Ali	163	
Joseph Nigos	180.5	
Willie Williams	198	6
William Galler	220	
James Peckham, coach (Team placed 12th)		

Name	Class	Place
1975 Freestyle (Minsk, USSR)		
Larry Baltezore	105.5	
James Haines	114.5	
Mark Massery	125.5	4
James Humphrey	136.5	4
Gene Davis	149.5	6
Carl Adams	163	5
Gregory Hicks	180.5	5
Russell Hellickson	198	4
Ben Peterson	220	4
Michael McCready	Heavyweight	5
Wayne Baughman, coach (Team placed 5th)		
1975 Greco-Roman (Minsk, USSR)		
Karoly Kancsar	105.5	5
Bruce Thompson	114.5	
Daniel Mello	125.5	
Gary Alexander	136.5	
Patrick Marcy	149.5	
Abdul Raheem Ali	163	
Daniel Chandler	180.5	
Willie Williams	198	
Bradley Rheingans	220	
William Van Worth	Heavyweight	6
James Peckham, coach (Team placed 14th)		
1976 (an Olympic year)		
1977 Freestyle (Lausanne, Switzerland)		
Randal Miller	114.5	
Jack Reinwand	125.5	3
James Humphrey	136.5	2
Chuck Yagla	149.5	
Stan Dziedzic	163	1
Chris Campbell	180.5	5
Laurent Soucie	198	
Mike McCready	220	
John Bowlsby	Heavyweight	
Dan Gable, coach (Team placed 4th)		

Name	Class	Place
1977 Greco-Roman (Goteborg, Sweden)		
James Howard	105.5	
Michael Fleming	114.5	
Brian Gust	125.5	
Reid Lamphere	136.5	
Patrick Marcy	149.5	
John Matthews	163	
Daniel Chandler	180.5	6
Mitch Hull	198	
Jeff Simons	220	4
William "Pete" Lee	Heavyweight	6
Lee Allen, coach (Team placed 13th)		
1978 Freestyle (Mexico City)		
William Rosado	105.5	
James Haines	114.5	3
Randy Lewis	125.5	
Tim Cysewski	136.5	
James Humphrey	149.5	
Lee Kemp	163	1
John Peterson	180.5	3
Ben Peterson	198	5
Larry Bielenberg	220	6
Greg Wojciechowski	Heavyweight	5
Dan Gable, coach (Team placed 5th)		
1978 Greco-Roman (Mexico City)		
Wilfredo Leiva	105.5	
Michael Fleming	114.5	
Daniel Mello	125.5	
Abdurrahim Kuzu	136.5	
Tom Minkel	149.5	
John Matthews	163	4
Dan Chandler	180.5	6
Jeff Simons	198	
Bradley Rheingans	220	4
Craig Schoene	Heavyweight	
Lee Allen, coach (Team placed 9th)		

Name	Class	Place
1979 Freestyle (San Diego, CA)		
Bob Weaver	105.5	2
James Haines	114.5	2
Joe Corso	125.5	3
Andre Metzger	136.5	3
Chuck Yagla	149.5	
Lee Kemp	163	1
John Peterson	180.5	2
Laurent Soucie	198	6
Russ Hellickson	220	2
David Klemm	Heavyweight	
Dan Gable, coach (Team placed 2nd)		
1979 Greco-Roman (San Diego, CA)		
Greg Williams	105.5	
Bruce Thompson	114.5	
Daniel Mello	125.5	
Abdurrahim Kuzu	136.5	2
Gary Pelci	149.5	
John Matthews	163	
Daniel Chandler	180.5	5
Steve Fraser	198	
Bradley Rheingans	220	3
Bob Walker	Heavyweight	3
Lee Allen, coach (Team placed 4th)		
1980 (an Olympic year)		
1981 Freestyle (Skoplje, Yugoslavia)		
Bill Rosado	105.5	3
Joe Gonzales	114.5	5
Joe Corso	125.5	
Mike Land	136.5	5
Andy Rein	149.5	4
Lee Kemp	163	3
Chris Campbell	180.5	1
Dan Lewis	190	
Greg Gibson	220	2
Harold Smith	Heavyweight	5
Gene Davis, coach (Team placed 3rd)		

Name	Class	Place
1981 Greco-Roman (Oslo, Norway)		
Mark Fuller	105.5	
Wilfredo Leiva	114.5	
Dan Mello	125.5	
Abdurrahim Kuzu	136.5	6
Scott Bliss	149.5	
James Andre	163	
Dan Chandler	180.5	
Mike Houck	198	
Greg Gibson	220	4
Ron Carlisle	Heavyweight	
Wayne Baughman, coach (Team did not place)		
1982 Freestyle (Edmonton, Canada)		
Tim Vanni	105.5	6
Joe Gonzales	114.5	3
John Azevedo	125.5	4
Randy Lewis	136.5	4
Andre Metzger	149.5	4
Lee Kemp	163	1
Dave Schultz	180.5	3
Mitch Hull	198	
Greg Gibson	220	3
Bruce Baumgartner	Heavyweight	
James Peckham, coach (Team placed 2nd)		
1982 Greco-Roman (Katowice, Poland)		
T.J. Jones	105.5	
Lewis Dorrance	114.5	
Rob Hermann	125.5	
Abdurrahim Kuzu	136.5	
John Selmon	149.5	
John Matthews	163	
Tom Press	180.5	
Steve Fraser	198	
Greg Gibson	220	
Pete Lee	Heavyweight	6
Wayne Baughman, coach (Team did not place)		

Name	Class	Place
1983 Freestyle (Kiev, USSR)		
Bobby Weaver	105.5	5
Joe Gonzales	114.5	
Barry Davis	125.5	
Lee Roy Smith	136.5	2
Nate Carr	149.5	
Dave Schultz	163	1
Mark Schultz	180.5	
Ed Banach	198	
Greg Gibson	220	2
Bruce Baumgartner	Heavyweight	
Dan Gable, coach (Team placed 3rd)		
1983 Greco-Roman (Kiev, USSR)		
Mark Fuller	105.5	
Jeff Clark	114.5	
Robert Hermann	125.5	
Abdurrahim Kuzu	136.5	
Jim Martinez	149.5	
Jim Andre	163	
Dan Chandler	180.5	
Mike Houck	198	
Dennis Koslowski	220	6
Pete Lee	Heavyweight	
Ron Finley, coach (Team did not place)		
1984 (an Olympic year)		
1985 Freestyle (Budapest, Hungary)		
Tim Vanni	105.5	10
Joe Gonzales	114.5	4
Kevin Darkus	125.5	2
Gene Mills	136.5	
Andre Metzger	149.5	
Dave Schultz	163	3
Mark Schultz	180.5	1
Bill Scherr	198	1
Dan Severn	220	6
Bruce Baumgartner	286	3
Joe Seay, coach (Team placed 3rd)		

Name	Class	Place
1985 Greco-Roman (Kobaltn, Norway)		
T.J. Jones	105.5	5
Mark Fuller	114.5	
Rob Hermann	125.5	
Dalen Wasmund	136.5	10
Jim Martinez	149.5	3
Dale Oliver	163	
Chris Catalfo	180.5	6
Mike Houck	198	1
Greg Gibson	220	
Dennis Koslowski	Heavyweight	6
Pavel Katsen, coach (Team placed 6th)		
1986 Freestyle (Budapest, Hungary)		
Tim Vanni	105.5	6
Mike Erb	114.5	9
Barry Davis	125.5	2
Joe McFarland	136.5	2
Andre Metzger	149.5	2
Dave Schultz	163	3
Mark Schultz	180.5	7
Jim Scherr	198	3
Bill Scherr	220	
Bruce Baumgartner	286	1
Jim Humphrey, coach (Team placed 2nd)		
1986 Greco-Roman (Budapest, Hungary)		
Eric Wetzel	105.5	6
Shawn Sheldon	114.5	
Anthony Amado	125.5	9
Frank Famiano	136.5	
Jim Martinez	149.5	
David Butler	163	
Darryl Gholar	180.5	6
Derrick Waldroup	198	
Dennis Koslowski	220	7
Duane Koslowski	286	4
Pavel Katsen, coach (Team placed 6th)		

Name	Class	Place
1987 Freestyle (Claremont-Ferrand, France)		
Tim Vanni	105.5	5
Greg Robbins	114.5	
Barry Davis	125.5	2
John Smith	136.5	1
Andre Metzger	149.5	3
Dave Schultz	163	2
Mark Schultz	180.5	1
Jim Scherr	198	2
Bill Scherr	220	3
Bruce Baumgartner	286	3
Jim Humphrey, coach (Team placed 2nd)		
1987 Greco-Roman (Claremont-Ferrand, France)		
Lew Dorance	105.5	10
Shawn Sheldon	114.4	
Anthony Amado	125.5	4
Dalen Wasmund	136.5	8
Jim Martinez	149.5	10
David Butler	163	
Chris Catalfo	180.5	9
Derrick Waldroup	198	
Dennis Koslowski	220	2
Duane Koslowski	286	5
Pavel Kasten, coach (Team placed 7th)		
1988 (an Olympic year)		

Chapter 4

Other Major World Meets

Although the Olympic Games and the World Championships are certainly the most important international tournaments, American wrestlers also compete in other major meets around the globe. Ranking behind the Olympics and the World Championships are the Pan-American Games, the World Cup, and the Tbilisi Tournament in the Soviet Union.

The Pan-American Games

The first Pan-American Games were held in Buenos Aires, Argentina, in 1951. However, the concept had been conceived of almost 20 years earlier. The Mexican delegation at the 1932 Summer Olympics in Los Angeles proposed the idea of holding a Western Hemisphere sports competition as a means of fostering good relationships among countries.

A group called the Pan-American Sports Congress gathered in Buenos Aires in 1940 to plan the format and decided to hold the inaugural Pan-American Games 2 years later. However, World War II, which halted the Olympic Games, caused a postponement of the initial Pan-American Games until 1951.

When the teams finally congregated in Argentina, 21 nations were represented by 2,500 athletes. Among the 19 sports on the agenda was freestyle wrestling. The United States totally dominated, capturing medals in all eight weight classes. No Greco-Roman was held. The U.S. team was coached by legendary Lehigh University coach Bill Sheridan. Gold medal winners were Hugh Peery (114.5), Richard LeMyre (125.5), Newton Copple (136.5), and Melvin Northrup (160.5).

The 1955 Games were held in Mexico City, and the Americans took home another four gold medals. The champs from "up north" were Jack Blubaugh (125.5), Tommy Evans (147.5), Alfred Paulekas (191.5), and Bill Kerslake (heavyweight).

In 1959, the United States hosted the Pan-American Games, but not without some difficulties. Cleveland, Ohio, was originally selected as the site, but funding problems forced a shift to Chicago. The United States won 120 of the 163 gold medals handed out, including a clean sweep in wrestling. The mat champions were Dick Wilson (114.5), Dave Auble (125.5), Louis Giani (136.5), Jim Burke (147.5), Doug Blubaugh (160.5), Jim Ferguson (174), Frank Rosenmayr (191.5), and Dale Lewis (heavyweight).

Sao Paulo, Brazil, hosted the 1963 Pan-American Games, and the Americans repeated their performance of 4 years earlier, taking all the gold medals. Winning titles were Andy Fitch (114.5), William Riddle (125.5), Ron Finley (138.5), Greg Ruth (154), Dennis Fitzgerald (171.5), Jim Ferguson (191.5), Jack Barden (213.5), and Joe James (heavyweight).

It was more of the same at the 1967 competition in Winnipeg, Canada. Americans swept it all for the third straight tournament, leaving with eight more gold medals. Richard Sofman (105.5), Rick Sanders (125.5), Mike Young (138.5), Gerald Bell (154), Pat Kelly (171.5), Wayne Baughman (191.5), Harry Houska (213.5), and Larry Kristoff (heavyweight) were the new mat kings of the hemisphere.

The United States was cleaning up in Pan-American Games competition, and it was no misrepresentation to say it was more difficult to win the U.S. national title than it was to win a Pan-American Games title.

However, the situation began to shift in 1971 in the sixth Pan-American Games. There, in Cali, Columbia, the Cubans began to show marked progress. The weight classes increased from 8 to 10, and the United States won just 7 of them. One indication that the field was getting tougher was the performance by Wayne Wells (163), who won the world title in 1970 but slipped to second in Cali. American winners were Sergio Gonzales (105.5), Don Behm (125.5), Dave Pruzansky (136.5), Dan Gable (149.5), Russ Hellickson (198), Jeff Smith (213.5), and Dominic Carollo (heavyweight).

When the Games returned to Mexico City in 1975, Greco-Roman competition was added for the first time. The United States captured seven gold medals as Bruce Thompson (114.5), Dan Mello (125.5), Pat Marcy (149.5), Dan Chandler (180.5), Willie Williams (198), Brad Rheingans (220), and Bill Van Worth (heavyweight) all won titles. In freestyle, five Americans won: Lloyd Keaser (149.5), Greg Hicks (180.5), Ben Peterson (198), Russ Hellickson (220), and Mike McCready (heavyweight).

The 1979 competition in Puerto Rico was made notorious by the actions of U.S. basketball coach Bobby Knight, who was charged with striking a police officer during an argument with another man. Knight was tried in absentia and was the subject of controversy for years as the case dragged on.

Meanwhile, on the wrestling mats, the United States reverted to old form, winning all 10 freestyle weights and 5 of the Greco-Roman weights. The freestyle champions were Bill Rosado (105.5), Gene Mills (114.5), Joe Corso (125.5), Andre Metzger (136.5), Andy Rein (149.5), Lee Kemp (163), Dan Lewis (180.5), Roy Baker (198), Russ Hellickson (220), and Jimmy Jackson (heavyweight). Greco-Roman champions were Bruce Thompson (114.5), John Matthews (163), Dan Chandler (180.5), Brad Rheingans (220), and Pete Lee (heavyweight).

The ninth Pan-American Games, held in Caracas, Venezuela, were soured by hard feelings over poor housing and a drug scandal. Fifteen athletes from 10 nations were stripped of medals, and 11 U.S. athletes decided to withdraw rather than undergo drug tests. The Cubans shocked the United States on the mat, winning the team titles in both styles. The United States managed just four freestyle gold medals and one in Greco-Roman.

Freestyle champions were Barry Davis (125.5), Randy Lewis (136.5), Lee Kemp (163), and Greg Gibson (220). The only U.S. gold medalist in Greco-Roman was Steve Fraser (198). The quality of the competition was such that Mark Schultz (180.5), destined to win the Olympics in 1984 and the World Championships in 1985, placed only fifth.

The Pan-American Games returned to the United States in 1987 amid considerable fanfare. Benefitting from the excitement generated by the 1984 Olympics in Los Angeles, the 1987 Pan-American Games were a big hit in the United States, drawing close to 1.5 million spectators to Indianapolis, Indiana. In addition, a record 6,000 athletes, representing 38 countries, participated.

The U.S. wrestling team, however, again had to take a back seat to the Cubans. The Cubans, well supported financially by the government and buoyed by extensive training with the Soviets, stepped forward as a world wrestling power by nipping the United States in freestyle, 88-86, and in Greco-Roman, 96-88. American freestyle champions were John Smith (136.5), Andre Metzger (149.5), Dave Schultz (163), Mark Schultz (180.5), Bill Scherr (220), and Bruce Baumgartner (heavyweight). David Butler (163), Chris Catalfo (180.5), and Duane Koslowski (286) were the Greco-Roman winners.

When the 1987 Games drew to a close, the United States had won 64 gold medals in 10 competitions in freestyle. In Greco-Roman, the count was 15 gold medals in 4 competitions (see Table 4.1).

Table 4.1
Pan-American Games: United States Results

Name	Class	Place
	1951 Freestyle (Buenos Aires, Argentina)	
Hugh Peery	114.5	1
Richard LeMyre	125.5	1
Newton Copple	136.5	1
Gerald Maurey	147.5	2
Melvin Northrup	160.5	1
Louis Holland	174	2
Donald McCann	191.5	3

Name	Class	Place
Ralph Schmidt	Heavyweight	2
Billy Sheridan, coach (Team placed 1st)		

1955 Freestyle (Mexico City)

Name	Class	Place
Michael Krishart	114.5	3
Jack Blubaugh	125.5	1
Alan Rice	136.5	2
Tommy Evans	147.5	1
Melvin Northrup	160.5	2
Wenzel Hubel	174	2
Alfred Paulekas	191.5	1
Williams Kerslake	Heavyweight	1
Fendley Collins, coach (Team placed 1st)		

1959 Freestyle (Chicago, IL)

Name	Class	Place
Dick Wilson	114.5	1
Dave Auble	125.5	1
Louis Giani	136.5	1
James Burke	147.5	1
Doug Blubaugh	160.5	1
James Ferguson	174	1
Frank Rosenmayr	191.5	1
Dale Lewis	Heavyweight	1
Claude Reeck, coach (Team placed 1st)		

1963 Freestyle (Sao Paulo, Brazil)

Name	Class	Place
Andrew Fitch	114.5	1
William Riddle	125.5	1
Ronald Finley	138.5	1
Gregory Ruth	154	1
Dennis Fitzgerald	171.5	1
James Ferguson	191.5	1
Jack Barden	213	1
Joe James	Heavyweight	1
Charles Parker, coach (Team placed 1st)		

1967 Freestyle (Winnipeg, Canada)

Name	Class	Place
Richard Sofman	114.5	1
Richard Sanders	125.5	1
Michael Young	138.5	1
Gerald Bell	154	1

Name	Class	Place
Patrick Kelly	171.5	1
Wayne Baughman	191.5	1
Harry Houska	213.5	1
Larry Kristoff	Heavyweight	1
James Miller Jr., coach (Team placed 1st)		

1971 Freestyle (Cali, Columbia)

Name	Class	Place
Sergio Gonzales	105.5	1
Randal Miller	114.5	
Donald Behm	125.5	1
David Pruzansky	136.5	1
Dan Gable	149.5	1
Wayne Wells	163	2
Bob Anderson	180.5	2
Russ Hellickson	198	1
Dominic Carollo	220	1
Jeff Smith	Heavyweight	1
Doug Blubaugh, coach (Team placed 1st)		

1975 Freestyle (Mexico City)

Name	Class	Place
David Range	105.5	2
Jim Haines	114.5	2
Jim Humphrey	125.5	3
Lloyd Keaser	149.5	1
Carl Adams	163	2
Greg Hicks	180.5	1
Ben Peterson	198	1
Russ Hellickson	220	1
Mike McCready	Heavyweight	1
Bill Weick, coach (Team placed 1st)		

1975 Greco-Roman (Mexico City)

Name	Class	Place
Karoly Kancsar	105.5	2
Bruce Thompson	114.5	1
Dan Mello	125.5	1
Gary Alexander	136.5	2
Pat Marcy	149.5	1
Mike R. Jones	163	2
Dan Chandler	180.5	1
Willie Williams	198	1
Brad Rheingans	220	1

Name	Class	Place
Bill Van Worth	Heavyweight	1
Ron Finley, coach (Team placed 1st)		
1979 Freestyle (Puerto Rico)		
Bill Rosado	105.5	1
Gene Mills	114.5	1
Joe Corso	125.5	1
Andre Metzger	136.5	1
Andrew Rein	149.5	1
Lee Kemp	163	1
Dan Lewis	180.5	1
Roy Baker	198	1
Russ Hellickson	220	1
Jimmy Jackson	Heavyweight	1
Gene Davis, coach (Team placed 1st)		
1979 Greco-Roman (Puerto Rico)		
Gregg Williams	105.5	3
Bruce Thompson	114.5	1
Brian Gust	125.5	2
John Hughes	136.5	3
Gary Pelcl	149.5	2
John Matthews	163	1
Dan Chandler	180.5	1
Jerome Schmitz	198	2
Brad Rheingans	220	1
Pete Lee	Heavyweight	2
James Peckham, coach (Team placed 1st)		
1983 Freestyle (Caracas, Venezuela)		
Richard Salamone	105.5	2
Charles Heard	114.5	2
Barry Davis	125.5	1
Randy Lewis	136.5	1
Lennie Zalesky	149.5	2
Lee Kemp	163	1
Mark Schultz	180.5	5
Peter Bush	198	3
Greg Gibson	220	1
Bruce Baumgartner	Heavyweight	2
J Robinson, coach (Team placed 2nd)		

Name	Class	Place
1983 Greco-Roman (Caracas, Venezuela)		
T.J. Jones	105.5	2
Mark Fuller	114.5	2
Rob Hermann	125.5	3
Dan Mello	136.5	3
James Martinez	149.5	2
James Andre	163	2
Dan Chandler	180.5	3
Steve Fraser	198	1
Dennis Koslowski	220	2
Ronald Carlisle	Heavyweight	3
Ron Finley, coach (Team placed 2nd)		
1987 Freestyle (Indianapolis, IN)		
Tim Vanni	105.5	2
Greg Robbins	114.5	2
Ken Chertow	125.5	
John Smith	136.5	1
Andre Metzger	149.5	1
Dave Schultz	163	1
Mark Schultz	180.5	1
Jim Scherr	198	3
Bill Scherr	220	1
Bruce Baumgartner	286	1
Jim Humphrey, coach (Team placed 2nd)		
1987 Greco-Roman (Indianapolis, IN)		
Eric Wetzel	105.5	3
Shawn Sheldon	114.5	3
Anthony Amado	125.5	3
Dalen Wasmund	136.5	3
James Martinez	149.5	3
David Butler	163	1
Chris Catalfo	180.5	1
Derrick Waldroup	198	2
Dennis Koslowski	220	2
Duane Koslowski	286	1
Pavel Katsen, coach (Team placed 2nd)		

The World Cup

The first freestyle World Cup was held May 19-20, 1973, in Toledo, Ohio. The competition was conceived as a vehicle for bringing together champions from the five continents that offer wrestling (North America, South America, Europe, Asia, and Africa) and owes its existence primarily to the drive and dedication of Joseph Scalzo of Toledo.

Scalzo, a man of unusual versatility and vision, pushed for the World Cup format for years before it was adopted by FILA. His hometown of Toledo (where he worked as a lawyer, engineer, civic official, and wrestling coach) served as host of the event 13 times in the first 14 years it was held.

The Soviets have dominated the competition from the outset, winning 11 team titles. The United States has won 2 titles outright, and the two countries tied in 1986. The first American victory came in 1980. "The USA/AAU National Team gained the world's No. 1 ranking for the first time March 30 by scoring an emotional 7-3 triumph over the Soviet Union to win the eighth World Cup of Freestyle Wrestling," reported Don Krone in the April 15, 1980, edition of *Amateur Wrestling News*. "In the 21-year history of head-to-head competition between the national clubs of the U.S. and the USSR, the Americans had never emerged victorious. A crowd of 6,000 at the University of Toledo's Centennial Hall overworked their vocal chords for the two-hour encounter in a stirring display of patriotism."

The team, coached by Dan Gable, received a letter of congratulations from U.S. Senator John Glenn of Ohio, the first American astronaut to orbit the earth. "I think Glenn was in orbit once," said Gable after the historic victory. "That's where I am right now."

Scoring key wins for the United States were Bobby Weaver (105.5) and Dave Schultz (149.5). Weaver rallied from a 5-0 deficit to pin 1972 Olympic champion Roman Dmitriev in 4 minutes, 57 seconds, and Schultz scored a last-second tilt to edge Nikolai Petrenko, 6-5. Other American winners were Gene Mills (114.5), Lee Kemp (163), John Peterson (180.5), Ben Peterson (198), and Jimmy Jackson (heavyweight).

The second U.S. triumph, a 6-4 victory, came in Toledo in 1982 and was witnessed by nearly 6,000 flag-waving fans. Winning for the American team were Adam Cuestas (105.5), Joe Gonzales (114.5), Lee Kemp (163), Mark Schultz (180.5), Howard Harris (198), and Greg Gibson (220). Harris was trailing Vladimir Batnya, 7-2, when he pinned him with just 23 seconds remaining in the match.

The United States would not boast of another title until 1986, and this they had to share with the Soviets. Propelling the United States to its 5-5 tie were Gene Mills (136.5), Nate Carr (163), Jim Scherr (198), Dan Severn (220), and Bruce Baumgartner (heavyweight). The crucial win came in the final match, when Baumgartner pinned the Soviets' defending world champion, David Gobedjichvili, in just 1 minute, 23 seconds.

The quality of the World Cup competition was most evident in 1986. There were seven world champions in the field, but only two were victorious at the Cup.

Trelleborg, Sweden, was the site of the first Greco-Roman World Cup competition, held December 1-2, 1980. Competing countries were the United States, the Soviet Union, Japan, Africa, and Sweden. The United States finished third behind the Soviet Union and Sweden and crowned two champs, Abdurrahim Kuzu (136) and Greg Gibson (220).

Because Greco-Roman wrestling is not nearly as popular as freestyle in countries like the United States and Japan, the World Cup has experienced difficulties in maintaining consistency. The tournament was not held in 1981 and 1983. After the first six competitions (through 1987), Kuzu and Gibson remained the only American champions. Gibson also won titles in 1984 and 1985 (See Table 4.2).

Table 4.2
World Cup: United States Results

Name	Class	Place
	1973 Freestyle (Toledo, OH)	
David Range	105.5	3
Jimmy Carr	114.5	3
Don Behm	125.5	2
Doug Moses	136.5	3
Lloyd Keaser	149.5	1
Stan Dziedzic	163	3
John Peterson	180.5	1
Ben Peterson	198	2
Russ Hellickson	220	2
Mike McCready	Heavyweight	2
Bill Farrell, coach (Team placed 2nd)		
	1974 Freestyle (Las Palmas, Canary Islands)	
David Range	105.5	4
Jim Haines	114.5	4
Richard Sofman	125.5	4
David Pruzansky	136.5	4
Gene Davis	149.5	2
Stan Dziedzic	163	3
Greg Hicks	180.5	2
Peter Leiskau	198	4
Greg Wojciechowski	220	3
Mack McCrady	Heavyweight	4
Bill Weick, coach (Team placed 4th)		

Name	Class	Place
1975 Freestyle (Toledo, OH)		
David Range	105.5	3
Chris Sones	114.5	3
Mark Massery	125.5	1
Doug Moses	136.5	4
Joe Tice	149.5	4
Stan Dziedzic	163	1
John Peterson	180.5	1
Kenn Linn	198	3
Greg Wojciechowski	220	4
Mike McCready	Heavyweight	2
Larry Kristoff, coach (Team placed 3rd)		
1976 Freestyle (Toledo, OH)		
Bill Rosado	105.5	3
Terry Hall	114.5	4
Jan Gitcho	125.5	2
Lloyd Ford	136.5	3
Gene Davis	149.5	2
Carl Adams	163	3
Greg Hicks	180.5	2
Brad Rheingans	198	1
Greg Wojciechowski	220	3
Mike McCready	Heavyweight	2
Larry Kristoff, coach (Team placed 3rd)		
1977 Freestyle (Toledo, OH)		
Bobby Weaver	105.5	2
Jim Haines	114.5	3
Jack Reinwand	125.5	2
Jim Humphrey	136.5	4
Chuck Yagla	149.5	2
Stan Dziedzic	163	1
Wade Schalles	180.5	2
Bud Palmer	198	2
Harold Smith	220	2
Jimmy Jackson	Heavyweight	1
Dan Gable, coach (Team placed 2nd)		

Name	Class	Place
	1978 Freestyle (Toledo, OH)	
Rich Salamone	105.5	2
Jim Haines	114.5	1
Jack Reinwand	125.5	3
Tim Cysewski	136.5	2
Dave Schultz	149.5	2
Wade Schalles	163	2
Mark Leiberman	180.5	1
Laurent Soucie	198	2
Russ Hellickson	220	1
Jimmy Jackson	Heavyweight	1
Dan Gable, coach (Team placed 2nd)		
	1979 Freestyle (Toledo, OH)	
Billy Rosado	105.5	2
Mike McArthur	114.5	4
Jack Reinwand	125.5	2
Tim Cysewski	136.5	1
Chuck Yagla	149.5	1
Lee Kemp	163	1
Mark Lieberman	180.5	2
Ben Peterson	198	2
Fred Bohna	220	2
Jimmy Jackson	Heavyweight	1
Dan Gable, coach (Team placed 2nd)		
	1980 Freestyle (Toledo, OH)	
Bobby Weaver	105.5	1
Gene Mills	114.5	1
Nick Gallo	125.5	2
Andre Metzger	136.5	2
Dave Schultz	149.5	1
Lee Kemp	163	1
John Peterson	180.5	1
Ben Peterson	198	1
Larry Bielenberg	220	2
Jimmy Jackson	Heavyweight	1
Dan Gable, coach (Team placed 1st)		

Name	Class	Place
1980 Greco-Roman (Trelleborg, Sweden)		
Mark Fuller	105.5	3
Todd Rosenthal	114.5	
Rob Hermann	125.5	
Abdurrahim Kuzu	136.5	1
Dave Butler	149.5	
John Matthews	163	3
Phil Lanzatella	180.5	3
Mark Johnson	198	3
Greg Gibson	220	1
Jeff Blatnick	Heavyweight	2
Wayne Baughman, coach (Team placed 3rd)		
1981 Freestyle (Toledo, OH)		
Bobby Weaver	105.5	2
Gene Mills	114.5	1
Ricky Dellagatta	125.5	3
Andre Metzger	136.5	3
Dave Schultz	149.5	2
Lee Kemp	163	1
Chris Campbell	180.5	1
Howard Harris	198	2
Greg Gibson	220	2
Jimmy Jackson	Heavyweight	2
Dan Gable, coach (Team placed 2nd)		
1981 Greco-Roman (not held)		
1982 Freestyle (Toledo, OH)		
Adam Cuestas	105.5	1
Joe Gonzales	114.5	1
Gene Mills	125.5	2
Randy Lewis	136.5	2
Andy Rein	149.5	2
Lee Kemp	163	1
Mark Schultz	180.5	1
Howard Harris	198	2
Greg Gibson	220	2
Bruce Baumgartner	Heavyweight	2
Dan Gable, coach (Team placed 1st)		

Name	Class	Place
1982 Greco-Roman (Budapest, Hungary)		
T.J. Jones	105.5	
Lewis Dorrance	114.5	
Rob Hermann	125.5	
Dave Nelson	136.5	3
Jim Martinez	149.5	
James Andre	163	
Tom Press	180.5	
Mike Houck	198	
Greg Gibson	220	3
Pete Lee	Heavyweight	3
Dan Chandler and Karoly Kancsar, coaches (Team placed 5th)		
1983 Freestyle (Toledo, OH)		
Adam Cuestas	105.5	1
Joe Gonzales	114.5	2
Gene Mills	125.5	2
LeeRoy Smith	136.5	2
Nate Carr	149.5	2
Dave Schultz	163	2
Chris Campbell	180.5	1
Mitch Hull	198	3
Harold Smith	220	2
Bruce Baumgartner	Heavyweight	2
Dan Gable, coach (Team placed 2nd)		
1983 Greco-Roman (not held)		
1984 Freestyle (Toledo, OH)		
Bobby Weaver	105.5	1
Joe Gonzales	114.5	1
Mike Land	125.5	2
LeeRoy Smith	136.5	2
Lennie Zalesky	149.5	2
Lee Kemp	163	
Chris Campbell	180.5	1
Ed Banach	198	2
Greg Gibson	220	2
Bruce Baumgartner	Heavyweight	1
Dan Gable, coach (Team placed 2nd)		

Name	Class	Place
1984 Greco-Roman (Seinajoki, Finland)		
T.J. Jones	105.5	2
Shawn Sheldon	114.5	3
Rob Hermann	125.5	2
Dalen Wasmund	136.5	2
Andy Seras	149.5	5
Chris Catalfo	163	2
Tom Press	180.5	6
Steve Fraser	198	4
Greg Gibson	220	1
Ron Carlisle	286	3
Pavel Katsen and Joe DeMeo, coaches (Team placed 3rd)		
1985 Freestyle (Toledo, OH)		
Rich Salamone	105.5	2
Randy Willingham	114.5	2
Barry Davis	125.5	2
Pete Schuyler	136.5	4
Bill Nugent	149.5	2
Dave Schultz	163	1
Mark Schultz	180.5	2
Bill Scherr	198	2
Dan Severn	220	2
Bruce Baumgartner	286	2
Al Bevilacqua, coach (Team placed 2nd)		
1985 Greco-Roman (Lund, Sweden)		
T.J. Jones	105.5	
Shawn Sheldon	114.5	4
Rob Hermann	125.5	4
Dalen Wasmund	136.5	
James Martinez	149.5	2
David Butler	163	4
Chris Catalfo	180.5	2
Steve Goss	198	
Greg Gibson	220	1
Dennis Koslowski	Heavyweight	2
Floyd Winter and Pavel Katsen, coaches (Team placed 3rd)		

Name	Class	Place
1986 Freestyle (Toledo, OH)		
Tim Vanni	105.5	3
Eddie Woodburn	114.5	3
Barry Davis	125.5	3
Gene Mills	136.5	2
Andre Metzger	149.5	2
Nate Carr	163	1
Jim Scherr	180.5	1
Bill Scherr	198	2
Dan Severn	220	1
Bruce Baumgartner	286	1
Joe Seay, coach (Team tied with USSR for 1st place)		
1986 Greco-Roman (Oak Lawn, IL)		
Eric Wetzel	105.5	3
Lew Dorrance	114.5	5
Anthony Amado	125.5	3
Frank Famiano	136.5	3
Andy Seras	149.5	2
David Butler	163	3
Darrell Gholar	180.5	4
Michael Carolan	198	4
Dennis Koslowski	220	2
Duane Koslowski	286	3
Pavel Katsen, coach (Team placed 3rd)		
1987 Freestyle (Ulaan Bator, Mongolia)		
Eddie Woodburn	105.5	
Mark Schwabb	114.5	3
Kevin Darkus	125.5	
Joe McFarland	136.5	3
John Giura	149.5	
Ken Monday	163	1
Rico Chiapparelli	180.5	
Duane Goldman	198	
Kirk Trost	220	1
Tom Erickson	286	2
Bobby Douglas, coach (Team placed 3rd)		

Name	Class	Place
1987 Greco-Roman (Albany, NY)		
Lew Dorrance	105.5	3
Shawn Sheldon	114.5	
Eric Seward	125.5	4
Buddy Lee	136.5	2
Andy Seras	149.5	2
David Butler	163	2
John Morgan	180.5	
Derrick Waldroup	198	
Dennis Koslowski	220	2
Jeff Blatnick	286	3
Pavel Katsen, coach (Team placed 3rd)		
1988 Freestyle (Toledo, OH)		
Tim Vanni	105.5	3
Joe Gonzales	114.5	1
Kevin Darkus	125.5	4
Joe McFarland	136.5	1
Andre Metzger	149.5	2
Ken Monday	163	2
Mike Sheets	180.5	2
Jim Scherr	198	2
Bill Scherr	220	2
Bruce Baumgartner	286	2
Jim Humphrey, coach (Team placed 2nd)		
1988 Greco-Roman (Athens, Greece)		
Lew Dorrance	105.5	2
Shawn Sheldon	114.5	2
Anthony Amado	125.5	4
Isaac Anderson	136.5	3
Andy Seras	149.5	3
David Butler	163	3
John Morgan	180.5	3
Mike Houck	198	3
Phil Lanzatella	220	4
Craig Pittman	286	2
Pavel Katsen, coach (Team placed 3rd)		

The Tbilisi Tournament

In the viewpoint of many, the annual mat meet held in the city of Tbilisi in the Soviet Union is the most competitive wrestling tournament in the world. The Tbilisi Tournament, known officially as the International Wrestling Championships, was created in 1961. However, it was not until 1971 that the United States and seven other nations accepted invitations to participate.

"This is the toughest tournament in the world. The Olympics are nowhere near as hard," Dan Gable, coach of the American team, told the author in 1988. Gable ought to know, as he owns gold medals from the World Championships, the Olympics, and the Tbilisi Tournament. Tbilisi is so tough, he explained, because the Soviets often enter as many as 10 wrestlers in each weight class.

In 1985, for instance, the Soviet Union had 100 entries in the total field of 156 and swept victories in all 10 weight classes. Twelve Soviets entered 1 weight class (114.5) and won the first 7 places. However, according to tournament rules, each country can win only 1 medal per weight class, so the Soviet athletes who placed 2nd through 7th were not medal winners, and the wrestler from Germany, who was actually 8th, went home with the silver medal.

Tbilisi, a city of about 700,000 people, is located in the province of Georgia. It is a major transportation and economic center of the Soviet Union and has a long, rich heritage that dates back to the fourth century A.D., when it was founded by Persia. Tbilisi has been ruled by Moslems, Turks, Arabs, Khazars, Iranians, and Mongols in its long and checkered past.

The first American winner at Tbilisi was former Michigan State star Don Behm (125.5), whose performance led the United States to a second-place finish in the 1971 team race. Winning silver medals for the American squad were Dan Gable (149.5), Wayne Wells (163), Larry Kristoff (220), and Chris Taylor (heavyweight). Mike Young (136.5) and Bill Harlow (198) won bronze medals, and Steve Combs (180.5) failed to place.

Gable lost, 3-2, to Soviet Vasily Kozakhov on a very controversial note. He scored what seemed to be the winning takedown with plenty of time remaining on the score clock, but the Soviets said time had expired and denied the takedown. Gable soundly defeated Kozakhov in a dual meet several days later.

The following year, Gable (149.5) breezed to the title and was presented a bear cloak as the outstanding wrestler. At a banquet following the meet, the Soviet coach announced that his primary goal was to find a Soviet wrestler who could defeat Gable in the 1972 Olympics. He was, however, unsuccessful in his search.

Other U.S. winners through 1988 were Ben Peterson (198) in 1973, Russ Hellickson (198) in 1974, Wade Schalles (163) in 1976, Gene Mills (114.5) in 1980, Joe Gonzales (114.5) in 1982, Andy Rein (149.5) in 1983, Dave Schultz (163) in 1984 and 1987, Bruce Baumgartner (heavyweight) in 1986, Jim Scherr (198) in 1987, and Ken Monday (163) in 1988.

Schalles' effort in 1976 was remarkable; he pinned all six of his opponents, including two world champions. A year later, Dave Schultz made the team as a senior in high school and earned a bronze medal at 149.5. He pinned a Romanian and a German, decisioned a Soviet, and lost to a German and a Soviet.

Gene Mills' performance in 1980 was memorable in that he won the tourney without a bad mark. He scored five pins and an 18-0 win by passivity on his way to the 114-pound title.

The trip to Tbilisi is extremely demanding, and American wrestlers are often treated in a manner less than first class in terms of travel and accommodations. The fashion of awarding placcs has led to considerable confusion over the years, and records are not all they ideally could be. Table 4.3 presents a list of American wrestlers who have competed at Tbilisi since 1971. Their medal place finishes are listed first, and, where known, their actual place winnings are listed second in parentheses.

Table 4.3
Tbilisi Tournament: United States Results

Name	Class	Place
	1971	
No entry	105.5	
John Morley	114.5	3
Don Behm	125.5	1
Mike Young	136.5	3
Dan Gable	149	2
Wayne Wells	163	2
Steve Combs	180.5	
Bill Harlow	198	3
Larry Kristoff	220	2
Chris Taylor	Heavyweight	2
Werner Holzer, coach		
	1972	
No entry	105.5	
John Morley	114.5	10
Dwayne Keller	125.5	5
Gene Davis	136.5	
Mike Young	136.5	

Name	Class	Place
Dan Gable	149.5	1
Mike Gallego	163	9
John Peterson	180.5	9
Russ Hellickson	198	4
Buck Deadrich	220	5
Doug Blubaugh and Myron Roderick, coaches		
	1973	
Bob Orta	105.5	
Greg Johnson	114.5	
Don Fay	125.5	
Dave Pruzansky	136.5	
Lloyd Keaser	149.5	3
Stan Dziedzic	163	
John Peterson	180.5	
Ben Peterson	198	1
Vince Paolano	220	
Greg Wojciechowski	Heavyweight	
Jim Peckham, coach		
	1974	
Wayne Holmes	105.5	3
Sergio Gonzales	114.5	5
Jan Gitcho	125.5	8
Larry Morgan	136.5	
Lloyd Keaser	149.5	2
Joe Wells	163	2
John Peterson	180.5	3
Russ Hellickson	198	1
Buck Deadrich	220	2
Mike McCready	Heavyweight	2
Jim Peckham and Bill Weick, coaches		
	1975	
Miguel Salin	105.5	4
Jim Breece	114.5	6
Dan Sherman	125.5	5
Jim Humphrey	136.5	3
Tom Milkovich	149.5	(Injury)
Wade Schalles	163	3

Name	Class	Place
Bill Bragg	180.5	2
Larry Amundson	198	3
Barry Walsh	220	5
Jim Woods	Heavyweight	4
Bill Weick, coach		
	1976	
Stan Opp	105.5	
Myron Shapiro	114.5	
Nabil Gutelov	125.5	
Doug Moses	136.5	3
Dwayne Keller	136.5	
No entry	149.5	
Wade Schalles	163	1
Stan Dziedzic	163	
John Peterson	180.5	
Mark Lieberman	180.5	
Ben Peterson	198	2
Jerry Washington	220	
Mike McCready	Heavyweight	2
J Robinson, coach		
	1977	
Mike Frick	136.5	3
Tim Cysewski	136.5	
Dave Schultz	149.5	3
Brady Hall	180.5	
Laurent Soucie	198	
Tom Hazell	220	2
Bob Walker	Heavyweight	
Wade Schalles, coach		
	1978	
Rich Salamone	105.5	
Jim Haines	114.5	
Chuck Davis	114.5	
Joe Corso	125.5	
Mark Mangianti	125.5	
Steve Barrett	136.5	5
Craig Horswill	136.5	
Chuck Yagla	149.5	
Floyd Hitchcock	180.5	
Laurent Soucie	198	
Tom Burns	220	

Name	Class	Place
Larry Avery	Heavyweight	2
Shelby Wilson, coach		
	1979	
Bill Rosado	105.5	
Jim Haines	114.5	
Joe Corso	125.5	
Pat Milkovich	136.5	
Tim Cysewski	136.5	
Dave Schultz	149.5	
Chuck Yagla	163	2
Mark Churella	163	
Chris Campbell	180.5	
Charles Gadsen	180.5	
Laurent Soucie	198	3
Harold Smith	220	
Stan Dziedzic, coach		
	1980	
Bill Rosado	105.5	7
Gene Mills	114.5	1
Joe Corso	125.5	6
Randy Lewis	136.5	3
Jim Humphrey	149.5	3
Dave Schultz	163	2
Bruce Kinseth	163	
Chris Campbell	180.5	4
Don Shuler	180.5	9
Roy Baker	198	
Larry Bilenberg	220	2
Fred Bohna	220	
Stan Dziedzic, coach		
	1981	
Rich Salamone	105.5	
Bill DePaoli	114.5	
John Azevedo	125.5	
LeeRoy Smith	136.5	4
Andy Rein	149.5	
Dave Schultz	163	
Chris Campbell	180.5	4
Steve Fraser	198	
Eric Wais	198	

Name	Class	Place
Greg Gibson	220	3
Jeff Blatnick	286	
Stan Dziedzic, coach		
	1982	
Tim Vanni	105.5	6
Joe Gonzales	114.5	1
Gene Mills	125.5	
Mike Land	136.5	5
Scott Trizino	149.5	
Roye Oliver	163	4
Mark Schultz	180.5	4
Willie Gadsen	198	4
Greg Gibson	220	
Mike Evans	Heavyweight	
Jim Peckham, coach		
	1983	
Tim Vanni	105.5	
Tom Dursee	114.5	
John Azevedo	125.5	3 (7)
LeeRoy Smith	136.5	
Randy Lewis	136.5	
Andre Metzger	149.5	
Andy Rein	149.5	1
Dave Schultz	163	2 (7)
Roye Oliver	163	
Mitch Hull	198	3 (5)
Chris Campbell	198	6
Greg Gibson	220	2
Bruce Baumgartner	Heavyweight	2 (3)
J Robinson, coach		
	1984	
Bobby Weaver	105.5	2
Randy Willingham	114.5	2 (7)
Barry Davis	125.5	2 (7)
LeeRoy Smith	136.5	(Ill)
Randy Lewis	136.5	(Ill)
Lennie Zalesky	149.5	2 (6)
Dave Schultz	163	3
Lee Kemp	163	(Injury)
Chris Campbell	180.5	(Injury)
Bruce Baumgartner	Heavyweight	1
Dan Gable, coach		

Name	Class	Place
	1985	
Cory Baze	105.5	
Randy Willingham	114.5	3 (9)
Kevin Darkus	125.5	4 (7)
Charlie Heard	125.5	
Darryl Burley	136.5	2 (3)
Bill Nugent	149.5	
Jesse Reyes	149.5	
Nate Carr	163	3 (12)
Jim Scherr	180.5	2 (4)
Don Shuler	180.5	
Bill Scherr	198	2 (4)
Dan Severn	220	2 (5)
Bruce Baumgartner	Heavyweight	2
Mike Holcomb	Heavyweight	
Gene Davis, coach		
	1986	
Tim Vanni	105.5	
Michael Pilione	114.5	
Barry Davis	125.5	
John Smith	136.5	
John Giura	149.5	
Eddie Urbano	163	
Murray Crews	163	
Jon Lundberg	180.5	
Jim Hall	198	
Wayne Cole	220	
Craig Pittman	Heavyweight	
Al Bevilacqua and Dave Schultz, coaches		
	1987	
Mark Schwab	114.5	3
Barry Davis	125.5	4
Joe McFarland	136.5	4
Eddie Urbano	149.5	3
Dave Schultz	163	1
Ken Monday	163	3
Wayne Catan	180.5	3
Jim Scherr	198	1
Duane Goldman	198	6
Bill Scherr	220	4
Morris Johnson	286	4
Al Bevilacqua and Joe Wells, coaches		

Name	Class	Place
	1988	
Larry Nicholson	105.5	
Eddie Woodburn	114.5	
Karl Glover	125.5	
John Orr	136.5	
John Giura	149.5	
Ken Monday	163	1
Eddie Urbano	163	
Rico Chiapparelli	180.5	5
Mike Sheets	180.5	8
Jim Scherr	198	3
Bill Scherr	220	3
Kirk Trost	220	4
Tom Erickson	286	
Craig Pittman	286	
Greg Strobel, coach		

*Records are often incomplete.

Chapter 5

The AAU National Freestyle Championships

The oldest and longest-running wrestling tournament in the United States is the AAU National Tournament. It began in 1888 in New York City and endured for a full century. It was dealt a crippling blow in 1982, when USA Wrestling emerged as the national governing body of wrestling after a long and often-bitter battle between the AAU and the USWF. The nation's oldest wrestling tournament survived, but its numbers and reputation were substantially reduced.

Professional sports were popular all across America at the dawn of the 20th century, and amateur athletes grew interested in competing among themselves. They were mostly part-time athletes who wanted to compete for fun rather than for money. Although the professional athletes were much admired, particularly in boxing and wrestling, those men who formed the first national amateur athletic groups were not about to tangle with the professionals.

An interest in holding national competitions for rowing and tennis led to the development of the National Association of Amateur Athletes (NAAA) in 1879. In 1887, the NAAA held a "national" wrestling tournament in New York City. The tournament was limited to wrestlers who weighed less than 135 pounds (professionals were usually much larger men) in an effort to keep the professionals from competing. The winner of that meet is now known only as L. Chenoweth of the Pastime Athletic Club. He became the first recorded "national" wrestling champion.

But many of the participating clubs were not happy with the NAAA and in 1888 met at the New York Athletic Club to discuss options. According to Don Sayenga in *Amateur Wrestling News*, these clubs "formed the Amateur Athletic Union for the expressed purpose of displacing the NAAA as the governing body for amateur athletics in the USA and setting up stringent new standards to protect the concept of amateurism."

The AAU held its first "national" meet the following year on April 6, 1888, at the Metropolitan Opera House in New York City. A crowd estimated at 3,000 was on hand to watch athletes compete in boxing, wrestling, and fencing in a roped ring erected on a stage. The wrestling competition was divided into weight classes of under 120 pounds and under 158 pounds. So many wrestlers entered the meet that preliminary wrestle-offs were held during the week preceding the finals. The winners of the tournament were the first AAU national champions. John Steil took the under-120 title, and Dr. Shell won in the heavier division.

Four weight classes were offered the next year, and the tournament continued to expand periodically in the coming decades. The first team champion was recognized in 1913: the Bronx Church House Team of New York City.

Several wrestlers won more than just a single weight division in the early years. Because the competition began with the lowest weight classes, wrestlers were able to compete in one division and then continue up the ladder. Max Wiley captured two titles in 1900 and claimed three the following year at 135, 145, and 158. Wiley, a rugged member of the Rochester YMCA, would sit in the stands in his long-underwear outfit and smoke cigars between sessions. He ended his career with a total of nine titles, the last coming in 1908.

Another very successful wrestler in the early years was George Mehnert, a rugged little scrapper who won six titles at 115 and 125. Mehnert, a paper cutter by trade who was a vegetarian, also won Olympic gold medals in 1904 and 1908.

One of the greatest of the early AAU champions was Earl Caddock, a lanky grappler who learned his craft at the YMCA in Atlantic, Iowa. Competing for the Hebrew Institute of Chicago, Caddock won titles at 175 pounds in 1914 and 1915, also capturing the heavyweight crown the latter year. Shortly afterward, he turned professional and followed in the footsteps of another Iowan, Frank Gotch, considered by many experts to be the greatest professional wrestler of all time.

Caddock was a protégé of Gotch, and in 1916, just a year before his death, Gotch labeled Caddock the finest mat technician he had ever seen. It was a viewpoint held by many of the amateur stars of the era. According to Don Sayenga, Fred Meyer, a winner of several AAU titles, "verifies [Caddock] was the genuine article, a man who knew a thousand holds."

In 1917, Caddock tangled with the then world professional champion Joe Stetcher of Nebraska and won the title in what many regard as the last legitimate professional title bout. Caddock remained a fan of the amateur sport and was invited to speak to high school wrestling teams throughout his lifetime.

Two other early-day stars were Nat Pendleton and Paul Berlenbach. Pendleton won AAU national titles in 1916 and 1920 and was silver medalist in the 1920 Olympics at heavyweight. He then moved to Hollywood and became a top character actor for decades.

Pendleton's primary training partner at the New York Athletic Club was Paul Berlenbach, who was national champion in 1922 and 1923. In fact,

Paul Berlenbach, AAU national wrestling champion and professional world light-heavyweight boxing champion. (Courtesy of *The Ring* magazine)

Berlenbach captured AAU national titles in both wrestling and boxing in one weekend in 1923 and then went on to become the light-heavyweight boxing champion of the world. The amazing stories of Pendleton and Berlenbach are highlighted on pages 82-84.

Although the AAU national tournament was the domain of the club stars in the first 2 decades of the 20th century, the collegiate athletes began to make their presence felt in the middle 1920s. The rugged grapplers from the Midwest and Southwest colleges were developing at an early age and were anxious to compete on any amateur level available to them.

But the man who many consider the greatest AAU star of all time had a limited scholastic wrestling background. Henry Wittenberg never wrestled at Dickinson High School in Jersey City, New Jersey, as he excelled in football. But he took to wrestling quickly after enrolling at the City College of New York. There, working with coach Joe Sapora, a two-time NCAA champion while at Illinois, Wittenberg progressed quickly. He placed third and second in the NCAA tournaments in 1938 and 1939, respectively.

In 1940, Wittenberg traveled to Ames, Iowa, and won the 174-pound title at the AAU nationals. It was the first of eight such triumphs for Wittenberg and was also the start of an incredible record of consistency.

"One thing that's not certain is the exact number of matches won by Henry," wrote Dan Sayenga in *Amateur Wrestling News*. "Whatever the number is, it is doubtless the American record for consecutive victories, because Henry didn't lose another bout [after the NCAA meet in 1939] for 13 years! The best guess is somewhere around 350 wins in a row."

After earning a master's degree at Columbia, Wittenberg joined the New York City police force and entered as many meets as his work schedule would allow. In 1948 he became the only noncollegiate to make the Olympic team and won a gold medal at 198 pounds at the London Games. He retired, then came back to earn a silver medal in the 1952 Olympics at the age of 33 years, 10 months.

Other great stars emerged in the 1950s as the AAU Freestyle Championships took on a status almost equal to the NCAA Tournament. Bill Kerslake, a huge man who did not compete in wrestling in college, won eight straight AAU national heavyweight titles, beginning in 1953 and extending through 1960. He also won seven Greco-Roman titles for a total of 15 AAU national championships.

In 1956, Dan Hodge turned in a remarkable performance in a 10-day period that was climaxed at the AAU nationals in Tulsa, Oklahoma. As a junior at

Dan Hodge, winner of AAU freestyle and Greco-Roman titles in 1956. (From the Chapman collection)

the University of Oklahoma, he won the Big Eight Conference title with two falls, the NCAA title with four falls, the AAU freestyle title with six falls, and then the AAU Greco-Roman title with four falls—three national titles with 16 straight pins!

In the 1960s, M.A. "Doc" Northrup earned himself a bevy of admirers by competing in AAU meets in his late 50s. He wrestled collegiately in the 1930s for Washington State University and captured AAU national titles in 1943, 1944,and 1945. He came back in 1955 to win a fourth AAU national title at 160.5 and continued wrestling until he was almost 60 years old.

At 57, Northrup entered the tough Phoenix Open and won three matches before bowing out. The veterinarian said he wrestled to offset a severe case of arthritis. "If I wasn't wrestling and keeping in shape I wouldn't be able to move," Northrup said at the Phoenix Open. Northrup's son, Ben, was also an AAU national champion, and both men competed in the Olympics.

The final major AAU national tournament was held in Lincoln, Nebraska, in 1982. Fittingly, the New York Athletic Club took the team title, its 12th in 14 years. The field was so talented that there were six former NCAA champions in one class alone (136.5). The winner, LeeRoy Smith of the Sunkist Kids, was named Outstanding Wrestler.

Other champions at the 1982 tournament were Bill Rosado (105.5) of the Sunkist Kids, Bobby Weaver (114.5) and Gene Mills (125.5) of the New York Athletic Club, Andy Rein (149.5) and Lee Kemp (163) of the Wisconsin

Two great champions of the 1970s, Russ Hellickson (front) and Ben Peterson, in one of several classic battles. (Courtesy of National Wrestling Hall of Fame)

Wrestling Club, Bruce Kinseth (180.5) of the Hawkeye Wrestling Club, Bill Scherr (198) of the Nebraska Wrestling Club, Greg Gibson (220) of the U.S. Marine Corps, and Bruce Baumgartner (heavyweight) of the New York Athletic Club (see Tables 5.1 and 5.2).

The AAU continued to hold a senior open tournament after 1982, but it was only a shadow of the event it once was. In fact, results from those tournaments were not turned in to *Amateur Wrestling News* and in 1988 were not available through the national AAU headquarters.

Wrestling's Greatest Story

In 1888, the first AAU "national" wrestling tournament was held in New York City. Several hundred thousand athletes have competed in wrestling since that first gathering a century ago. Innumerable great stories, both on and off the mat, have sprouted from the efforts of those athletes.

What follows here may be the single most fascinating story in wrestling history. It is a tale that involves unbelievable obstacles and staggering achievements, all tied together with a wonderful friendship that developed between two wrestlers of unique courage and skill.

One of them went on to appear in over 100 movies, the other became light-heavyweight champion of the world—but in boxing! This is the story of Nat Pendleton and Paul Berlenbach.

Pendleton was born August 9, 1895, in Davenport, Iowa, but grew up in New York City. In 1916, he won the first of two AAU national titles at 175 pounds, competing for the New York Athletic Club. He also captured an AAU national title in 1920, the same year he made the U.S. Olympic team.

At the 1920 Olympics in Antwerp, Belgium, Pendleton won the silver medal at heavyweight. But, by at least two accounts, he should have won the gold medal.

"This was the worst decision ever," wrote Fred Meyer to wrestling historian Don Sayenga nearly 6 decades after the event took place. "Pendleton was the winner of the contest, no ifs or buts." Meyer was writing from a perspective of considerable merit, as he finished third in the same Olympics in the same weight class (then, countries could enter two men per class) and saw the match firsthand.

George M. Pinneo, the U.S. coach in 1920, agreed with Meyer. In a report filed shortly after the Games concluded, Pinneo wrote, "The decision which took the final match from Mr. Pendleton was probably the most unpopular of many unsatisfactory decisions."

Prior to the Olympics, Pendleton won three Eastern Conference titles while attending Columbia University. After the Games of 1920, he worked overseas for a year and then wound up in Hollywood. There, in the film capital of the world, Pendleton found a career, appearing in well over 100 films in the 1930s and 1940s, including several of the top hits of the era.

"Producers, ignoring that he held an economics degree from Columbia, saw Pendleton as big, good-natured—and dumb," wrote David Ragan in the book *Who's Who in Hollywood: 1900-1976* (1976, p. 747). "He had the opportunity to show off his muscles as Sandor the Great in *The Great Zigfield*. Not so dumb, he starred in 1933's *Deception* in a role as wrestler that he wrote for himself" (p. 748).

The rugged-looking Pendleton also had key roles in the popular *Thin Man* series, starring debonair William Powell and Myrna Loy. But he was at his humorous best in *Buck Privates*, a movie starring the very popular comedy team of Bud Abbott and Lou Costello. He played a tough sergeant who was always harassing Costello, and he wound up refereeing a fight that the roly-poly Costello was duped into.

Well read and well traveled, Pendleton was far more than the buffoon he often was cast to be by Hollywood. In fact, he was fluent in five languages! He also maintained his interest in wrestling throughout his Hollywood days. "He used to come down to San Diego and watch the big tournament there at the naval base," said Wes Brown Jr., a longtime AAU official, in a 1988 telephone interview with the author. "He was a real great guy, and loved wrestling."

But Pendleton is only half of this story. The other half is even more incredible! Sometime during his stay with the New York Athletic Club, Pendleton befriended a semi-illiterate taxi driver named Paul Berlenbach. Though the facts are obscure, lost in the mists of time, it is known that the two athletes became fast buddies. Pendleton was able to arrange a membership for Berlenbach at the New York Athletic Club, and they began to train together. What an odd couple they were: the college-educated Pendleton was able to read and write in several languages, and the rugged cab driver could barely converse in English.

Berlenbach was born in the rough Astoria section of New York City on February 18, 1901. He suffered an attack of scarlet fever as a youth, leaving him with a serious disability, unable to speak or hear. Miraculously, at the age of 15, Berlenbach came in contact with a live electrical wire and received a tremendous shock. It jolted his system in such a way that he began to speak and hear once again.

"Berlenbach apparently developed rapidly from that point on," Don Sayenga told the author in 1988. "He and Pendleton worked out together daily at the NYAC. They were equal in ability at the time of the Olympic trials in 1920."

They both made the team, but Berlenbach was injured on the trip to Antwerp and did not compete in the 175-pound class. Instead, he watched his friend, Pendleton, battle to the finals before dropping the controversial decision.

Back in New York City, Berlenbach began dreaming of the 1924 Olympic Games. He won AAU national wrestling titles at 175 pounds in 1922 and 1923. But, while he was training at the New York Athletic Club, the boxing coach was keeping a close eye on him. He finally approached Berlenbach and told the tough-looking wrestler that he had a tremendous future ahead of him—in boxing!

Berlenbach, interested in the financial potential of boxing, tried his hand at the amateur level and won 16 of 17 bouts, including 13 by knockout. In 1923, he won the AAU national wrestling and boxing titles in a single weekend, a stunning feat of skill and endurance.

Reluctantly, Berlenbach decided to pass up the 1924 Olympics in wrestling and turn professional in boxing. He won his first 11 bouts by knockout and sported a record of 23-1-2 when he was given his golden opportunity. On May 30, 1925, he climbed into the ring in New York City to face Mike McTigue, the light-heavyweight champion of the world. Berlenbach, deaf and dumb for years until miraculously revived by a run-in with a live electrical wire, earned a 15-round decision to become a king of pugilism.

The rugged Berlenbach fought until 1933, recording an overall record of 37 wins, 8 losses, and 2 draws. He scored 30 knockouts. A magazine article in 1979 rated him the sixth-best body puncher of all time, behind Rocky Marciano (fifth) and just ahead of Jack Dempsey (seventh), pretty good company to be sure. In 1971, Berlenbach was elected to the National Boxing Hall of Fame.

"He was the original Rocky," Don Sayenga told the author in 1988. Indeed, Paul Berlenbach's story was one that even Sylvester Stallone would have found hard to believe.

Pendleton and Berlenbach lived a country apart after their days training together at the New York Athletic Club, with Pendleton at home in the hills of Hollywood and Berlenbach remaining in New York City. But their lives are forever intertwined in their amazing accomplishments.

Pendleton died in 1967 and rated a long obituary in the *New York Times*. Berlenbach survived his old friend for nearly 2 decades, finally closing his eyes for the last time in 1985.

The two are the stuff of which legends are made. Together, they represent one of the most fascinating stories in the history of amateur wrestling.

Table 5.1
AAU National Freestyle Championships

Freestyle Champions, 1889-1961

This list of national AAU champions includes every man who ever won that title in any weight class since the organization of amateur wrestling in 1888 to date.

It will be noted that the weight classes have changed at various times, usually corresponding with Olympic years, when the weight classes are made to correspond with the metric weights used in the Olympics.

The list is divided into two sections, catch-as-catch-can champions (1888-1921) and freestyle champions (1922 to date). *Don Sayenga, historian*

Catch-as-catch-can champions, 1888-1921

105-lb class

1889 J.B. Reilly (ACSN)
1890 J.B. Reilly (ACSN)
1891 F. Bertsch (AAC)
1893 C. Monnypenny (PASC)
1894 R. Bonnett (Newark NTV)
1895 J. Hiliah (Allegheny AC)
1896 H. Cotter (Bay Ridge AC)
1897 G.W. Owens (Pittsburgh AC)
1899 W. Nelson (St. George's Club, New York)
1900 W. Nelson (St. George's Club, New York)
1901 W. Karl (Metropolitan AC)
1902 W. Karl (Metropolitan AC)
1903 R. Curry (New York)
1904 R. Curry (New York)
1905 J. Hein (Ave. A. Boys' Club, New York)
1906 W. Lott (Mohawk AC)
1907 G. Taylor (Newark NTV)
1908 R. Schwartz (New York Boys' Club)
1909 G. Taylor (Newark NTV)
1910 G. Taylor (Newark NTV)
1911 H. Donaldson (Spokane AC)
1912 G. Taylor (Newark NTV)

108-lb class

1913 G. Taylor (Newark NTV)
1914 R. Goudie (Ohio Lima YMCA)
1915 R. Goudie (Ohio Lima YMCA)
1916 G. Taylor (Newark NTV)
1917 C. Benson (Swedish American AC, New York)
1918 J. Meagher (Indiana Gary YMCA)
1919 J. Meagher (Indiana Gary YMCA)
1920 C. Benson (Swedish American AC, New York)
1921 C. Benson (Swedish American AC, New York)

115-lb class

1888 J. Steil (NTV)
1889 F. Mueller (NTV)
1890 F. Mueller (NTV)
1891 E. Beck (STV)
1893 J. Holt (PASC)
1894 F. Bertsch (NTV)
1895 M. Kerwin (Kinglsey AC)
1896 R. Bonnett (Newark NTV)
1897 R. Bonnett (Newark NTV)
1899 R. Bonnett (Newark NTV)
1900 J. Renzland (St. George's Club, New York)
1901 G. Owens (Verner AC)
1902 G. Mehnert (Newark NTV)
1903 G. Mehnert (Newark NTV)
1904 G. Mehnert (Newark NTV)
1905 G. Bauer (Newark NTV)
1906 G. Bauer (Newark NTV)
1907 G. Bauer (Newark NTV)
1908 G. Mehnert (Newark NTV)
1909 G. Bauer (Newark NTV)

1910 J. Hein (New York Boys' Club)
1911 N. Chapman (San Francisco Olympic Club)
1912 W. Strohback (unat)
1913 J. Hein (New York Boys' Club)
1914 J. Vorhes (Hull House Chicago)
1915 F. Glahe (Spokane AC)
1916 K. Borsits (Indiana Gary YMCA)
1917 L. Servais (Pennsylvania U)
1918 V. Vosen (unat)
1919 M. Gans (Morris AC)
1920 S. Pammow (Chicago HI)
1921 J. Troyer (Redlands U)

125-lb class
1893 W. Troelsch (PASC)
1894 W. Reilly (MAA)
1895 W. Reilly (MAA)
1896 E. Harris (New York)
1897 A. Meanwell (New York)
1899 M. Wiley (RAC)
1900 A. Kurtzman (New York)
1901 I. Niflot (Pastime NY)
1902 I. Niflot (Pastime NY)
1903 I. Niflot (Pastime NY)
1904 I. Niflot (Pastime NY)
1905 G. Mehnert (Newark NTV)
1906 G. Mehnert (Newark NTV)
1907 G. Dole (Yale)
1908 L. Dole (Yale)
1909 L. Ruggiero (Grace AC)
1910 M. Himmelhoch (Michigan)
1911 G. Bauer (Newark NTV)
1912 G. Bauer (Newark NTV)
1913 V. Vosen (Bronx, NY)
1914 S. Vorhes (Hull House)
1915 S. Vorhes (Chicago)
1916 C. Liljehult (New York)
1917 C. Liljehult (New York)
1918 J. Felios (Chicago)
1919 M. Gans (Morris AC)
1920 A. Callas (Chicago)
1921 R. Reed (Oregon Agricultural C)

135-lb class
1889 M. Luttbeg (NYTV)
1891 A. Ullman (WAA)
1893 C. Clark (PASC)
1894 A. Lippman (St. George's Club, New York)
1895 J. McGrew (Pittsburgh)
1896 A. Ullman (Brooklyn)
1897 H. Wolff (Quaker AC)
1899 M. Wiley (Rochester)
1900 M. Wiley (Rochester)
1901 M. Wiley (Rochester)
1902 F. Cook (Newark NTV)
1903 B. Bradshaw (New York Boys' Club)
1904 B. Bradshaw (New York Boys' Club)
1905 I. Niflot (St George's AC)
1906 A. Rubin (Grace AC)
1907 B. Bradshaw (New York Boys' Club)
1908 G. Dole (Yale)
1909 S. Fleischer (EA)
1910 S. Kennedy (Chicago Lincoln TV)
1911 O. Franzke (Oregon Multnomah AAC)
1912 E. Helikman (EA)
1913 A. Anderson (Norwegian American AC)
1914 H. Jenkins (Pittsburgh AC)
1915 A. Runchey (Seattle)
1916 W. Hallas (Chicago)
1917 P. Metropoulos (Indiana Gary YMCA)
1918 S. Vorhes (Chicago)
1919 B. Johnson (Birmingham AC)
1920 G. Metropoulos (Indiana Gary YMCA)
1921 J. Hummerich (Los Angeles AC)

145-lb class
1897 W. Riggs (Philadelphia)
1899 M. Wiley (Rochester)
1900 M. Wiley (Rochester)
1901 M. Wiley (Rochester)

1902 N. Nelson (Pastime)
1903 M. Yokel (Pastime)
1904 O. Roehm (Buffalo YMCA)
1905 R. Tesing (New York)
1906 C. Clapper (New York)
1907 Richard Jaeckel (New York)
1908 M. Wiley (GAAC)
1909 C. Johnson (Swedish American AC)
1910 C. Johnson (Swedish American AC)
1911 W. Milchewski (Chicago David Park)
1912 Gus Peterson (Harlem YMCA)
1913 C. Johnson (NYAC)
1914 H. Jenkins (Pittsburgh AC)
1915 D. Burns (Spokane AC)
1916 L.Nelson (Norwegian American AC)
1917 H. Jenkins (Pittsburgh AC)
1918 A. Forst (GINS)
1919 G. Smith (Indiana Gary YMCA)
1920 W. Tikka (Finnish American AC)
1921 R. Vis (Los Angeles AC)

158-lb class

1888 Dr. Shell (ACSN)
1889 M. Lau (VBC)
1890 G. Hoskins (ACSN)
1891 P. Von Boeckman (St. George's AC)
1893 W. Osgood (PASC)
1894 F. Ellis (PASC)
1895 C. Reinicke (CTV)
1896 A. Ullman (New York)
1897 D. Chesterman (Quaker AC)
1899 A. Mellinger (New York)
1900 M. Wiley (Rochester)
1901 J. Schmucker (Vernor AC)
1902 J. Schmucker (Vernor AC)
1903 W. Beckman (WSY, NY)
1904 C. Erikson (Norwegian TS)
1905 W. Schaefer (NTV)
1906 J. McAfee (Chicago Central YMCA)
1907 F. Narganes (NYAC)
1908 C. Anderson (Boston)
1909 F. Narganes (NYAC)
1910 F. Narganes (NYAC)
1911 C. Gesek (Spokane AC)
1912 J. Smith (NYAC)
1913 J. Smith (NYAC)
1914 B. Reubin (HI Chicago)
1915 B. Reubin (HI Chicago)
1916 W. Americus (Greek American AC)
1917 C. Johnson (Boston)
1918 Stephensen (Great Lakes NS)
1919 G. Tragos (Indiana Gary YMCA)
1920 E. Leino (NYAC)
1921 C. Johnson (Boston)

175-lb class

1913 J. Varga (Lenox Hill NY)
1914 E. Caddock (Chicago)
1915 E. Caddock (Chicago)
1916 N. Pendleton (NYAC)
1917 D. Very (Pittsburgh)
1918 K. Kunert (Indiana Gary YMCA)
1919 K. Kunert (Indiana Gary YMCA)
1920 K. Kunert (Indiana Gary YMCA)
1921 F. Meyer (Chicago)

Heavyweight class

1893 Taylor Sharp (PASC)
1895 W.D. Osgood (Pennsylvania)
1904 B. Hansen (Norwegian Turn.)
1905 B. Hansen (Norwegian Turn.)
1906 J. McAfee (Chicago)
1907 J. Gundersen (Dovre SP)
1908 J. Gundersen (Dovre SP)
1909 E. Payne (New Westside AC)
1910 F. Motis (Cornell Square AC, Chicago)
1911 H. Grimm (Seattle)
1912 A. Kaino (Finnish American AC)
1913 J. Gunderson (Norwegian American AC)

1914 A. Minkley (Bankers)
1915 E. Caddock (Chicago)
1916 S. Swartz (New Haven)
1917 D. Very (Pittsburgh AC)
1918 K. Kunert (Indiana Gary YMCA)
1919 S. Czarnecke (Indiana Gary YMCA)
1920 N. Pendleton (NYAC)
1921 F. Meyer (Chicago)

Freestyle champions, 1922 to 1961

1922
118 V. Vosen (Chicago)
125.5 Achilles Callas (Chicago)
135 Robin Reed (Oregon)
147.5 Russell Vis (Los Angeles)
160 E. Wolf (New Hampshire)
174 Paul Berlenbach (NYAC)
191.5 Fred Meyer (Chicago)
UNL Fred Meyer (Chicago)

1923
112 R. Rowsey (Indiana)
118 I. Servais (NYAC)
125.5 A. Callas (Chicago)
135 J. Vorhes (Chicago)
147 R. Vis (Los Angeles)
160 E. Leino (NYAC)
174 P. Berlenbach (NYAC)
UNL K. Lappanen (Finish American AC)

1924
112 R. Rowsey (Indiana)
123 B. Hines (Northwestern)
135 R. Reed (Oregon)
147 R. Vis (Los Angeles)
160 P. Martter (Los Angeles)
174 W. Wright (New York)
191.5 Ch. Strack (Colgate)
UNL R. Flanders (unat)

1925
112 H. DeMarsh (Oklahoma)
118 G. Campbell (Oklahoma)
125.5 B. Patterson (Oklahoma)
135 L. Brigham (Oklahoma)
147.5 K. Truckenmiller (Cornell C)
160 R. Hammonds (Texas)
174 O. Stuteville (Oklahoma)
UNL R. Kruse (Multnomah)

1926
112 L. Lupton (Cornell C)
118 C. Mitchell (Multnomah)
125.5 H. Boyvey (Iowa State)
135 A. Morrison (Illinois)
147.5 R. Myers (Multnomah)
160 R. Hammonds (Texas)
174 F. Bryan (Oregon)
UNL C. Strack (Oklahoma)

1927
112 L. Pfeffer (Iowa)
118 L. Lake (Oklahoma)
125.5 A. Holding (Iowa State)
135 A. Morrison (Illinois)
147.5 R. Prunty (Ames, IA)
160 F. Collins (Oklahoma A&M)
174 G. Rule (Oklahoma A&M)
UNL R. Flanders (Oklahoma A&M)

1928
112 G. Rosenberg (Iowa Falls HS)
123 R. Hewitt (Michigan)
135 A. Morrison (Illinois)
147.5 C. Berryman (Oklahoma A&M)
160 L. Appleton (Cornell C)
174 R. Hammonds (Texas U)
191.5 E. Edwards (Navy)
UNL E. George (Michigan)

1929
112 G. Shoemaker (Lehigh)
118 T. McCrary (Cornell C)
125.5 G. Campbell (Oklahoma)
135 J. Earickson (Baltimore)
147.5 A. Tomlinson (Oklahoma)
160 B. Sherman (Multnomah)
174 K. Krough (Chicago)
UNL E. George (Michigan)

1930
112 H. Phillips (NYAC)
118 B. Pearce (Oklahoma)
125.5 J. Reed (NYAC)
135 Z. Letowt (NYAC)
147.5 O. Kapp (NYAC)
160 J. Van Bebber (Oklahoma)

174 G. Stafford (NYAC)
UNL E. McCreaddy (Oklahoma)

1931
114.5 J. Sapora (NYAC)
125.5 R. Pearce (Oklahoma)
135 L. Morford (Cornell C)
147.5 A. Tomlinson (Oklahoma)
155 O. Kapp (NYAC)
160.5 J. Van Bebber (Oklahoma)
174 C. Caldwell (Oklahoma)
UNL R. Jones (Indiana)

1932
118 L. Conti (Lenox Hill NY)
123 J. Sapora (NYAC)
135 J. Fickel (Kansas State)
147.5 B. Bishop (Pennsylvania)
158 J. Van Bebber (Los Angeles)
174 J. Schutte (NYAC)
191.5 L. Putrin (NYAC)
UNL L. Hammack (Army)

1933
125.5 M. Andes (Baltimore)
135 E. Stout (Southwest State C)
147.5 G. Sappington (Missouri)
155 G. Belshaw (Indiana)
160.5 B. Hess (Iowa State)
174 A. Sweet (Southwest State C)
UNL G. Ellison (Cornell C)

1934
112 R. Johnson (Iowa)
118 E. Thomas (Iowa)
125.5 Jack Gott (Southwest State C)
135 E. Stout (Southwest State C)
147.5 F. Stout (Southwest State C)
155 E. Kielhorn (Iowa)
160.5 O. England (Southwest State C)
174 G. Martin (Iowa State)
UNL R. Teague (Southwest State C)

1935
112 R. Myers (Indiana)
118 Rex Perry (Oklahoma)
125.5 R. Flood (Oklahoma)
135 R. Rasor (Oklahoma)
147.5 L. Tomlinson (Central State)
155 Frank Lewis (Oklahoma)
160.5 O. England (Southwest State C)
174 L. Ricks (Oklahoma)
UNL R. Teague (Southwest State C)

1936
112 C.E. Ritchie (California)
118 J. McDaniels (Oklahoma)
123 R. Flood (Oklahoma)
135 F. Parkey (Oklahoma)
147.5 L. Fegg (Oklahoma)
158 G. Belshaw (Indiana)
174 R. Voliva (Chicago)
191 L. Ricks (Oklahoma)
UNL R. Dunn (Oklahoma)

1937
112 Charles Peterson (New York)
118 M. Croft (Brigham Young)
123 W. Duffy (Indiana)
135 G. Hanks (Southwest State C)
147.5 E. Bruno (California)
158 W. Jacobs (Baltimore YMCA)
174 A. Crawford (Wilmington YMCA)
191.5 W. Norton (Southwest State C)
UNL R. Vaughan (New Jersey)

1938
112 Charles Peterson (New York)
118 J. Speicher (Michigan)
123 J. McDaniels (Oklahoma)
135 F. Millard (North Adams YMCA)
147.5 S. Henson (Oklahoma A&M)
158 W. Jacobs (Baltimore YMCA)
174 A. Crawford (Wilmington YMCA)
191.5 J. Harrell (Oklahoma)
UNL C. Gustafson (Minnesota)

1939
112 H. Farrell (New Jersey)
118 T. Imoto (Fullerton JC)
123 E. Collins (NYAC)
135 B. Renfo (Southwest State C)
147.5 D. Taylor (NYAC)
158 W. Jacobs (Baltimore YMCA)
174 A. Crawford (NYAC)

191.5	V. Cavagnaro (Oregon)
UNL	M. Sims (Oklahoma)
1940	
112	Gerald Leeman (Osage HS, Osage, IA)
118	C. Fredericks (Purdue)
123	Dale E. Hanson (unat, Minneapolis)
134	R. Chaney (unat, Iowa Falls, IA)
145	E. Viskocil (unat, Osage, IA)
158	Edward Blake (Baltimore YMCA)
174	Henry Wittenberg (YMCA West, New York)
191	Edward H. Valorz (U of Chicago alumni)
1941	
112	H. Farrell (unat, Indiana)
118	J. McDaniels (unat, Oklahoma)
123	H. Byrd (U of Oklahoma)
134	D. Lee (Baltimore Y)
145	C. Soukas (Greek American AC)
158	H. Faucett (unat, Indiana)
174	H. Wittenberg (YMCA West, New York)
191	G. Frei (NYAC)
UNL	L. Mashi (YMCA, New York)
1942	
115	Bill Curtis (Crescent Club, Tulsa)
121	Bob Barber (Minnesota)
128	Sid Marks (Crescent Club, Tulsa)
135	Douglas Lee (Baltimore YMCA)
145	Dave Arndt (Crescent Club, Tulsa)
155	Vernon Logan (Crescent Club, Tulsa)
165	Joe Scarpello (Vental HS, Omaha, NE)
175	Garnett Inman (Bowman Field, KY)
191	Sam Santo (Camp Polk, LA)
UNL	Leonard Levy (U of Minnesota)
1943	
114.5	F. Preston (Cornell C)
121	P. McDaniel (Oklahoma A&M)
128	C. Ridenour (Penn State)
135	M. Jennings (Michigan State)
147.5	B. Maxwell (Michigan State)
155	R. Roberts (McBurney Y, New York)
160.5	Dr. M.A. Northrup (SF Olympic)
174	D. Thomas (Cornell C)
191.5	H. Wittenberg (New York)
UNL	R. Metzgar (Yew York)
1944	
114.5	C. Parks (Baltimore YMCA)
121	M. McDonald (Navy)
125.5	F. Barkovich (Penn)
135	V. Cronhardt (Baltimore YMCA)
147.5	L. Cowell (Westside YMCA)
155	E. Tomick (Baltimore YMCA)
160.5	E. Blake (Baltimore YMCA)
174	Dr. M.A. Northrup (SF Olympic)
191.5	H. Wittenberg (Westside YMCA)
UNL	R. Vaughan (Lancaster, PA)
1945	
114.5	Grady Peninger (Tulsa)
121	Bill Klein (Oklahoma State)
125.5	Richard Dickerson (Oklahoma City)
135	Clifford McFarland (Oklahoma City)
147.5	Gale Miklos (Michigan State)
155	Doug Lee (Baltimore YMCA)
160.5	M.A. Northrup (SF Olympic)
174	James Dernehl (Navy)
191.5	Robert Wilson (Navy)
UNL	Richard Vaughan (Lancaster, PA)

1946

114.5	Arlie Curry (Tulsa)
121	Dick Hauser (Waterloo, IA)
125.5	Ed Collins (NYAC)
135	Lowell Lange (Waterloo, IA)
147.5	James Miller (Ithaca YMCA)
155	Robert Roemer (California)
160.5	Doug Lee (Baltimore YMCA)
174	Frank Bissell (NYAC)
191	Henry Wittenberg (Westside YMCA, New York)
UNL	Mike DeBiase (California)

1947

114.5	Grady Peninger (Oklahoma)
121	Charles Ridenour (NYAC)
125.5	Louis Kachiroubas (Illinois)
135	Lowell Lange (Cornell C)
147.5	James Miller (Ithaca)
155	Orville Long (Southwestern Tech)
160.5	Doug Lee (Baltimore YMCA)
174	Dale Thomas (Cornell C)
191	Henry Wittenberg (New York)
UNL	Ray Gunkel (Purdue)

1948

114.5	Malcolm McDonald (Navy)
125.5	Robert Kitt (Navy)
135	Lee Thomson (Cornell C)
147.5	Newt Copple (Nebraska)
155	Bill Nelson (ISTC)
160.5	Leland Merrill (NYAC)
174	Dale Thomas (Marion, IA)
191	Henry Wittenberg (New York)
UNL	Ray Gunkle (Purdue)

1949

114.5	Arnold Plaza (Purdue)
121	John Harrison (ISTC)
125.5	Russ Bush (ISTC)
135	Lowell Lange (Cornell C)
147.5	Keith Young (ISTC)
155	Bill Nelson (ISTC)
160.5	Bill Smith (ISTC)
174	Shuford Swift (Navy)
191	Verne Gagne (Minnesota)
UNL	Robert Maldegan (Michigan)

1950

114.5	John Harrison (ISTC)
121	Arnold Plaza (Purdue)
125.5	Dick Hauser (Cornell C)
135	Lowell Lange (Carnell C)
147.5	Keith Young (ISTC)
155	Bill Nelson (ISTC)
160.5	Bill Smith (ISTC)
174	Shuford Swift (Baltimore)
191	David Whinfrey (Rutgers)
UNL	Fred Stocker (ISTC)

1951

114.5	George Creason (Long Island)
121	John Lee (Harvard)
125.5	Gene Lybbert (ISTC)
135	Bill Armstrong (Oklahoma A&M)
147.5	Bob Hoke (Michigan)
155	Keith Young (ISTC)
160.5	Bill Smith (ISTC)
174	Louis Holland (Wyoming)
191.5	Harry Lanzi (Toledo)
UNL	Carl Abell (Cleveland)

1952

114.5	Sidney Nodland (Long Island)
125	Jack Blubaugh (Armed Forces)
135	Josiah Henson (Armed Forces)
147.5	Newt Copple (Illinois)
160.5	James LaRock (New York)
174	Shuford Swift (Armed Forces)
191.5	Henry Wittenberg (New York)
UNL	Richard Clark (New York)

1953

114.5	Richard Delgado (Navy)
125.5	Richard Hauser (Washington)
135	Jim Sinadinos (Michigan State)
147.5	Newt Copple (Illinois)
160.5	James LaRock (New York)
174	Dan Hodge (Illinois)
191.5	Dale Thomas (Michigan State)
UNL	Bill Kerslake (Cleveland)

1954

114.5	Richard Delgado (Navy)
125.5	Jack Blubaugh (Tulsa)
135	Tommy Evans (Tulsa)
147.5	Shozo Sasahara (Tokyo)
160.5	Jay Holt (San Francisco)
174	Dan Hodge (Tulsa)
191.5	Dale Thomas (Michigan State)
UNL	Bill Kerslake (Cleveland)

1955

114.5	Katsuhoshi Yakayama (Japan)
125.5	Shuhei Iwano (Japan)
135	Motoichi Matohashi (Japan)
147.5	Joe Scandura (New York)
160.5	Dr. Melvin Northrup (San Francisco)
174	Wenzel Hubel (Kentucky)
191.5	Tim Woodin (Ithaca)
UNL	Bill Kerslake (Cleveland)

1956

114.5	Richard Delgado (Navy)
125.5	Bill Carter (Tulsa)
135	Allan Rice (NYAC)
147.5	Tommy Evans (Tulsa)
160.5	Bill Fisher (Sooner AC)
174	Dan Hodge (Sooner AC)
191.5	Pete Blair (Navy)
UNL	Bill Kerslake (Cleveland)

1957

114.5	Takashi Hirata (Japan)
125.5	Terry McCann (Tulsa)
135	Masashi Kokubo (Japan)
147.5	Tommy Evans (Tulsa)
160.5	Doug Blubaugh (Tulsa YMCA)
174	Meb Turner (NYAC)
191.5	Tim Woodin (Michigan)
UNL	Bill Kerslake (Cleveland)

1958

114.5	Tsuruhisa Torikura (Japan)
125.5	Terry McCann (Tulsa)
135	Mitsuo Ikeda (Japan)
147.5	Newt Copple (Nebraska)
160.5	Larry TenPas (Army)
174	Wenzel Hubel (Los Angeles)
191.5	Frank Rosenmayr (San Francisco)
UNL	Bill Kerslake (Cleveland)

1959

114.5	Dick Wilson (Toledo)
125.5	Terry McCann (Tulsa)
135	S. Nichiwaki (Japan)
147.5	Newt Copple (Nebraska)
160.5	Fritz Fivan (Oregon State)
174	Jim Ferguson (Michigan State)
191.5	Frank Rosenmayr (San Francisco)
UNL	Bill Kerslake (Cleveland)

1960

114.5	Gil Sanchez (Colorado)
125.5	Carmen Molino (NYAC)
135	Linn Long (Colorado)
147.5	Frank Betucci (NYAC)
160.5	Doug Blubaugh (NYAC)
174	Jim Ferguson (unat)
191.5	Frank Rosenmayr (San Francisco)
UNL	Bill Kerslake (Cleveland)

1961

114.5	Dick Wilson (Toledo)
125.5	U. Imaizumi (Japan)
135	Lee Allen (Multnomah AC)
147.5	Mike Rodriguez (Michigan)
160.5	Steve Friedman (NYAC)
174	Russ Camilleri (San Francisco)
191.5	Dan Brand (San Francisco)
UNL	Dale Lewis (Oklahoma)

Table 5.2
AAU National Freestyle Championships
Place Winners, 1962-1982

1962

Team	Points
1. San Francisco Olympic Club	40
2. New York AC	37
3. Tokyo Club, Self Defense Club—Japan	20
5. Hazel Park (MI)	18
6. Chuo University (Japan)	10
7. Oklahoma AC	8
8. Oregon State University	7
9. Ithaca Grapplers, Navy, Simi HS (CA) Hosei University (Japan)	4
13. University of Nebraska, Waseda U (Japan)	2

Place winners

114.5-lb class
1. Horyuka Harada (Japan)
2. Takashi Hirata (NYAC)
3. Andy Fitch (NYAC)
4. Jyo Umezana (Oklahoma AC)

125.5-lb class
1. Dave Auble (NYAC)
2. Bill Riddle (Hazel Park AC)
3. Masaki Hatta (Oklahoma AC)
4. Mitsmori Toshi (Japan)

138.5-lb class
1. Osamu Watanabe (Japan)
2. Lee Allen (Multnomah AC)
3. Ron Finley (Oregon State)
4. Nobuyuki Motokawa (Simi HS)

154-lb class
1. Kazuo Abe (Japan)
2. Mike Rodriguez (Hazel Park AC)
3. Jim Burke (SFOC)
4. Greg Ruth (NYAC)

171.5-lb class
1. Jim Ferguson (SFOC)
2. Russ Camilleri (SFOC)
3. Dennis Fitzgerald (Hazel Park AC)
4. Roy Conrad (unat)

191.5-lb class
1. Shunichi Kawano (Japan)
2. Bill Farrell (NYAC)
3. Jack Stanbro (Ithaca Grapplers)
4. Sven Holm (SFOC)

213.5-lb class
1. Dan Brand (SFOC)
2. Bob McDermott (NYAC)
3. Isamu Otsuka (Japan)
4. Joe James (Oklahoma AC)

UNL class
1. Jiro Seki (Japan)
2. Pat Lovell (SFOC)
3. Hallow Wilson (Navy)
4. Jim Raschke (U of Nebraska)

1963

Team	Points
1. San Francisco Olympic Club	47
2. New York AC	37
3. Multnomah AC	12
4. University of Colorado, Southern Illinois University	10
6. Oklahoma AC	7
7. Phoenix Wristlock, University of Toledo	5
9. San Bernardino, Navy	2

Place winners

114.5-lb class
1. Takashi Hirata (NYAC)
2. Kenzo Kawajiri (Japan)

3. Hiroaki Aoki (NYAC)
4. Faber Jenkins (Navy)

125.5-lb class
1. Norio Tominaga (Japan)
2. Masaki Koisumi (Japan)
3. Dave Auble (NYAC)
4. Joe Gomes (SFOC)

138.5-lb class
1. Haruo Abe (Japan)
2. Masaru Hashimoto (Japan)
3. Linn Long (unat)
4. Tomio Saishu (SFOC)

154-lb class
1. Greg Ruth (NYAC)
2. Bill Weick (SFOC)
3. Werner Holzer (SFOC)
4. Mike Rodriguez (unat)

171.5-lb class
1. Dean Lahr (U of Colorado)
2. Dennis Fitzgerald (unat)
3. Ed DeWitt (Multnomah)
4. Jim Ferguson (SFOC)

191.5-lb class
1. Russ Camilleri (SFOC)
2. Wayne Buaghman (Oklahoma AC)
3. Jack Stanbro (NYAC)
4. Charles Tribble (San Bernardino)

213.5-lb class
1. Dan Brand (SFOC)
2. Pat Lowell (SFOC)
3. Russ Winer (Phoenix Wristlock)
4. Jim McGowan (SFOC)

UNL class
1. Larry Kirstoff (Southern Illinois U)
2. Garry Stensland (Multnomah)
3. Merrell Solowin (U of Toledo)
4. Bill Farrell (NYAC)

1964

Team	Points
1. New York AC	50
2. San Francisco Olympic Club	38
3. Illinois	15
4. Oregon State University	14
5. Cowboy AC	11
6. Japan	10
7. Hazel Park (MI)	9
8. San Bernardino YMCA, Air Force	7
10. Tokyo University	4
11. Multnomah AC	2

Place winners

114.5-lb class
1. Hiroaki Aoki (NYAC)
2. Tadaki Hatta (Cowboy AC)
3. Terry Finn (Illinois)
4. Okla Johnson (Hazel Park, MI)

125.5-lb class
1. Gray Simons (NYAC)
2. Dave Auble (NYAC)
3. Masaaki Hatta (Cowboy AC)
4. Andy Fitch (NYAC)

138.5-lb class
1. Mitsuo Hara (Japan)
2. Ron Finley (SFOC)
3. Chikara Murano (NYAC)
4. Richard Leonardo (NYAC)

154-lb class
1. Greg Ruth (NYAC)
2. Jim Burke (SFOC)
3. Mamoru Shimizu (Tokyo U)
4. Gerry Grenier (NYAC)

171.5-lb class
1. Len Kauffman (Oregon State U)
2. Charles Tribble (San Bernardino YMCA)
3. Steve Combs (Illinois)
4. Bruce Glenn (unat)

191.5-lb class
1. Russ Camilleri (SFOC)
2. Wayne Baughman (Air Force)
3. Morgan Peters (NYAC)
4. Mike Wittenberg (Cornell U)

213.5-lb class
1. Dan Brand (SFOC)
2. Jack Barden (Hazel Park, MI)

3. Art Makinster (Oregon State U)
4. Bob McDermott (NYAC)

UNL class
1. Jim Raschke (NYAC)
2. Bob Pickens (Illinois)
3. Pat Lovell (SF Olympic)
4. Garry Stensland (Multnomah AC)

1965

Team	*Points*
1. Multnomah AC	27
2. New York AC	25
3. San Francisco Olympic Club	20
4. Chicagoland WC	16

Place winners

114.5-lb class
1. Ray Sanchez (Cheyenne, WY)
2. Dwayne Keller (Kennewick, WA)
3. Bill Bush (Binghamton, NY)
4. Dale Kestel (Garden City, MI)

125.5-lb class
1. Rick Sanders (Multnomah AC)
2. K. Ikeda (Japan)
3. David Pruzansky (Passaic, NJ)
4. John Hahn (Chula Vista, CA)

138.5-lb class
1. Chikara Murano (NYAC)
2. Linn Long (Boulder, CO)
3. Mac Motokawa (Brigham Young)
4. Bob Evans (Chicagoland WC)

154-lb class
1. Jim Burke (SFOC)
2. Bob Douglas (Oklahoma State)
3. Orlando Iacovelli (NYAC)
4. Jerry Pamp (SFOC)

171.5-lb class
1. Russ Camilleri (SFOC)
2. Len Kauffman (Oregon State U)
3. Pat Kelly (Chicagoland WC)
4. Frank Hankin (Phoenix Wristlock)

191.5-lb class
1. Wayne Baughman (Air Force)
2. Pat Clock (Portland OR)
3. Morgan Peters (NYAC)
4. Mike Wittenberg (NY City)

213.5-lb class
1. Jerry Conine (Multnomah AC)
2. Jack Stanbro (NYAC)
3. Bob McDermott (NYAC)
4. Art Makinster (Oregon State U)

UNL class
1. Larry Kristoff (Chicagoland WC)
2. Garry Stensland (Multnomah AC)
3. Mike McGann (Fort Ord)
4. Jim Skelton (12th Naval District)

1966

Team	*Points*
1. Mayor Daley Youth Foundation	

Other team statistics are unavailable.

Place winners

114.5-lb class
1. Ray Sanchez (unat, Cheyenne, WY)
2. Dwayne Keller (Kenewick, WA)
3. Kenichi Kanno (unat, Eugene, OR)
4. Peter Wallach (Reed C)

125.5-lb class
1. Richard Sofman (Penatiquit AC)
2. Rick Sanders (Multnomah AC)
3. Fred Powell (NYAC)
4. Jim Hazewinkel (St. Cloud State)

138.5-lb class
1. Mac Motokawa (Brigham Young)
2. Linn Long (Colorado)
3. Ron Finley (SF Olympic)
4. Gerald Bell (NYAC)

154-lb class
1. Werner Holzer (MDYF)
2. Orlando Iacovelli (NYAC)

3. Mohammed Sadrzadeh (Phoenix Wristlock)
4. Bob Douglas (MDYF)

171.5-lb class
1. Steve Combs (MDYF)
2. Len Kauffman (unat, Corvallis, OR)
3. Jeff Stephen (NYAC)
4. Russ Camilleri (SFOC)

191.5-lb class
1. Dean Lahr (Boulder, CO)
2. Pat Clock (Multnomah AC)
3. Lt. Wayne Baughman (Air Force)
4. Fran Ferraro (NYAC)

213.5-lb class
1. Ken Johnston (Boulder, CO)
2. Jess Lewis (unat, Corvallis, OR)
3. Dom Carollo (El Camino C)
4. Jerry Conine (Multnomah AC)

UNL class
1. Larry Kristoff (MDYF)
2. Jim Raschke (Lincoln, NE)
3. Garry Stensland (Multnomah AC)
4. Bruce Wilhelm (unat, Stillwater, OK)

1967

Team	*Points*
1. Mayor Daley Youth Foundation	40
2. Michigan WC	19
3. Multnomah AC	18
4. New York AC	17

Place winners

114.5-lb class
1. Noriyuki Sizuki (Japan)
2. Tadaaki Hatta (MDYF)
3. John Miller (Multnomah AC)
4. Greg Johnson (Michigan WC)

125.5-lb class
1. Rich Sanders (Multnomah AC)
2. Masaaki Hatta (Michigan WC)
3. Dan Gable (Iowa State U)
4. Rich Sofman (Army)

138.5-lb class
1. Bob Buzzard (Michigan WC)
2. Mike Young (unat)
3. Gerald Bell (NYAC)
4. Bill Stuart (NYAC)

154-lb class
1. Bobby Douglas (Michigan WC)
2. Werner Holzer (MDYF)
3. Dan Direnzo (NYAC)
4. Lee Ehrler (UCLA)

171.5-lb class
1. Pat Kelly (MDYF)
2. Greg Ruth (NYAC)
3. Ed DeWitt (Multnomah AC)
4. Steve Combs (MDYF)

191.5-lb class
1. Bill Harlow (Michigan WC)
2. Wayne Baughman (Air Force)
3. Larry Lyden (Minnesota)
4. Tom Peckham (unat)

213.5-lb class
1. Henk Schenk (Army)
2. Charles Tribble (Phoenix Wristlock)
3. Joe James (MDYF)
4. Gene Libal (Nebraska)

UNL class
1. Larry Kristoff (MDYF)
2. Curley Culp (Arizona State U)
3. Wayne Corser (Bay Area)
4. Bob Roop (unat)

1968

Team	*Points*
1. San Francisco Olympic Club	36
2. New York AC	30

Place winners

114.5-lb class
1. Arthur Chavez (SFOC)
2. Tustomu Hoshino (Japan)
3. Ray Stapp (Oklahoma State U)
4. John S. Miller (Multnomah AC)

125.5-lb class
1. Richard Sofman (NYAC)
2. Masaaki Hatta (Michigan WC)
3. James P. Hanson (Air Force)
4. Don Behm (MDYF)

138.5-lb class
1. Masamitsu Ichiguchi (NYAC)
2. Mike Young (Brigham Young)
3. Sam Al-Karaghouli (Michigan WC)
4. Funiaki Nakamura (NYAC)

154-lb class
1. Bobby Douglas (Michigan WC)
2. Jerry Bell (NYAC)
3. Orlando Iacovelli (NYAC)
4. Lee Ehrler (SFOC)

171.5-lb class
1. Mike Gallego (SFOC)
2. Jeff Stephens (NYAC)
3. Don Morrison (unat)
4. Mike Carroll (Oklahoma State U)

191.5-lb class
1. Russ Camilleri (SFOC)
2. Tom Peckham (unat, Ames, IA)
3. Wayne Baughman (Air Force)
4. Ben Cooper (Southern Illinois U)

213.5-lb class
1. Henk Schenk (Army)
2. Gerald Conine (San Bernardino U)
3. Buck Deadrich (SFOC)
4. Jess Lewis (Oregon State U)

UNL class
1. Larry Kristoff (MDYF)
2. Curley Culp (Phoenix Thunderbirds)
3. Dale Stearns (unat, Iowa)
4. Ron Wright (unat, Laramie, WY)

1969

Team	*Points*
1. Michigan WC	35
2. New York AC	33
3. Iowa State	25
4. Army	24

Place winners

105.5-lb class
1. Dale Kestel (Michigan WC)
2. Bill Davids (Michigan WC)
3. Richard Vaughn (SFOC)
4. Joe Orta (Nebraska)

114.5-lb class
1. Yasuo Katsumura (Nebraska AC)
2. John Miller (Oregon)
3. John Morley (NYAC)
4. Steve Lampe (Iowa State U)

125.5-lb class
1. Toshio Nakano (Japan)
2. Michio Tomino (Nebraska)
3. Masaaki Hatta (Michigan WC)
4. Richard Sofman (NYAC)

136.5-lb class
1. Dan Gable (Iowa State U)
2. David Pruzansky (Passaic, NJ)
3. Ted Parker (MDYF)
4. Noriaki Kiguchi (MDYF)

149.5-lb class
1. Fumiaki Nakamura (NYAC)
2. Len Borchers (SFOC)
3. Bob Tomasovic (Oregon State U)
4. Mark Miller (NYAC)

163-lb class
1. Lee Dietrick (Michigan WC)
2. Joe Bavaro (NYAC)
3. Orlando Iacovelli (NYAC)
4. Kim Snider (Oregon State U)

180.5-lb class
1. Len Kauffman (Army)
2. Chuck Jean (Iowa State U)
3. Mickey Carroll (Northern Arizona U)
4. Jason Smith (Iowa State U)

198-lb class
1. Buck Deadrich (MDYF)
2. Henk Schenk (Army)
3. Don Buzzard (Michigan WC)
4. Jim Duschen (Iowa State U)

220-lb class
1. Jess Lewis (Oregon State U)
2. Gene Libal (Nebraska AC)

3. Steve Shippos (NYAC)
4. Mike Wilson (Iowa State U)

UNL class
1. Dale Stearns (Iowa)
2. Jim Homan (Army)
3. Greg Wojciechowski (Toledo U)
4. George Chaplin (Air Force)

1970

Team	*Points*
1. New York AC	59
2. Multnomah AC	21
3. Mayor Daley Youth Foundation	17
4. Iowa Grapplers	16
5. Air Force	14
6. Michigan WC	11
7. Toledo University	10

Place winners

105.5-lb class
1. Bob Orta (unat)
2. Stan Opp (unat)
3. David Herrera (unat)
4. Brad Thompson (Minnesota)

114.5-lb class
1. John Morley (NYAC)
2. Yasua Katsumura (NYAC)
3. Robert Pina (NYAC)
4. Gil Garcia (Colorado U)

125.5-lb class
1. Richard Sanders (Multnomah AC)
2. Masaaki Hatta (Michigan WC)
3. John Miller (Multnomah AC)
4. Sigeki Mitera (Japan)

136.5-lb class
1. Mike Young (unat)
2. Kelichi Nakayama (NYAC)
3. Tom Huff (Air Force)
4. David Pruzansky (Temple U)

149.5-lb class
1. Dan Gable (Iowa Grapplers)
2. Joe Seay (unat)
3. Mark Miller (NYAC)
4. Fumiaki Nakamura (NYAC)

163-lb class
1. Wayne Wells (unat)
2. Jerry Bell (NYAC)
3. Lonny Gallagher (NYAC)
4. Bobby Douglas (Iowa Grapplers)

180.5-lb class
1. J Robinson (NYAC)
2. Ed DeWitt (Army)
3. Mike Bradley (Michigan WC)
4. Steve DeVries (unat)

198-lb class
1. Wayne Baughman (Air Force)
2. Bill Harlow (MDYF)
3. Tom Peckham (Iowa Grapplers)
4. Henk Schenk (Oregon State U)

220-lb class
1. Larry Kristoff (MDYF)
2. Bernie Hospodka (U of Nebraska at Omaha)
3. Roy Frantz (NYAC)
4. Len Pettigrew (Ashland C)

UNL class
1. Greg Wojciechowski (Toledo U)
2. Chris Taylor (unat)
3. Tim Kopitar (Bay Area Salto Club)
4. Dale Stearns (Iowa City WC)

1971

Team	*Points*
1. New York AC	93
2. Athletes in Action	44
3. Army	34.5
4. San Francisco Olympic Club	27.5
5. Multnomah AC	25.5
6. Mexico	24
7. Penn Grapplers	18
8. Air Force	13
9. Michigan WC	12
10. West Chester	10.5
11. Mayor Daley Youth Foundation	9

Team	*Points*
12. University of Tampa	8
13. Venezuela, John Long Club	7
15. Minnesota WC	5
16. Kentucky	4
17. Cleveland WC, University of Iowa	3
19. Steinborn's Gym	1

Place winners

105.5-lb class
1. Wayne Holmes (unat)
2. Fidel Torres (Army)
3. Lee Klepper (NYAC)
4. Brad Thompson (Minnesota WC)
5. Alfredo Olvera (Mexico)
6. Oscar Luna (Venezuela)

114.5-lb class
1. John Morley (NYAC)
2. Enrique Jemenez (Mexico)
3. Stan Opp (unat)
4. Dan Blakinger (unat)
5. Jose Bravo (Venezuela)
6. Eric Waterd (Penn Grapplers)

125.5-lb class
1. Michi Tanaka (NYAC)
2. Moises Lopez (Mexico)
3. Ted Levine (Penn Grapplers)
4. Terry Magoon (Army)
5. Steve Nativ (U of Iowa)
6. Carlos Conzalez (Venezuela)

136.5-lb class
1. Rick Sanders (MAC)
2. David Pruzansky (Penn Grapplers)
3. Doug Smith (AIA)
4. Ron Rosso (NYAC)
5. Massao Hattori (NYAC)
6. (tie) William Camp (Army) and William Komloske (Army)

149.5-lb class
1. Gene Davis (AIA)
2. James Tanniehill (Army)
3. Fumi Nakamura (NYAC)
4. Mike Murray (Kentucky)
5. Tom Milkovich (Michigan State U)
6. Doug Parsen (SFOC)

163-lb class
1. Jerry Bell (NYAC)
2. Lonny Gallagher (NYAC)
3. Mke Gallego (SFOC)
4. (tie) Gary Neist (Army) and Gary Rushing (AIA)
6. Joe Bavaro (NYAC)

180.5-lb class
1. Russ Camilleri (SF Olympic)
2. Mike Bradley (Michigan WC)
3. James Lee (West Chester)
4. Bob Anderson (AIA)
5. Jack Zindel (Michigan WC)
6. Steve DeVries (U of Iowa)

198-lb class
1. Wayne Baughman (Air Force)
2. Fletcher Carr (U of Tampa)
3. Vince Paolano (NYAC)
4. (tie) Buck Deadrich (SFOC) and Randall Forrest (West Chester)
6. Greg Zindel (Michigan WC)

220-lb class
1. (tie) Dominic Carrollo (AIA) and Henk Schenk (Multnomah AC)
3. Jeff Smith (John Long Club)
4. Julian McPhillips (NYAC)
5. John Clabaugh (Kentucky)
6. Art Rutzen (NYAC)

UNL class
1. Greg Wojciechowski (Toledo U)
2. Mike Kelley (MCYF)
3. Norm Mosch (unat)
4. Steve Shippos (NYAC)
5. Michael Clark (unat)
6. Ronald Cooper (Cleveland AC)

1972

Team	*Points*
1. New York AC	87
2. Army	56
3. Multnomah AC	30
4. Air Force	29

Team	*Points*
5. San Francisco Olympic Club	27
6. Michigan WC	26
7. Ohio WC	21
8. Oklahoma City AC, Minnesota WC, U.S. Marine Corps	10

Place winners

105.5-lb class
1. Dale Kestel (Michigan WC)
2. Wayne Holmes (Ohio WC)
3. Katsuyoshi Takamura (Japan)
4. Bruce Thompson (Minnesota WC)
5. Brad Thompson (Minnesota WC)
6. Richard Vaughn (SF Peninsula)

114.5-lb class
1. John Morley (NYAC)
2. Sergio Gonzales (Southland WC)
3. Frank Von Stralen (San Diego State U)
4. Ed Knecht (Westlake, OH)
5. Ted Alexander (Florida WC)
6. Albert Tschirhart (Canada)

125.5-lb class
1. John Miller (Multnomah AC)
2. Ken Melchoir (Army)
3. Stewart Pruzansky (NYAC)
4. Ray Stapp (Oklahoma City AC)
5. Gary Franke (Army)
6. Don Fay (NYAC)

136.5-lb class
1. Ikeno (NYAC)
2. Rich Sanders (Multnomah AC)
3. Osamu Sakamoto (Japan)
4. Dave Auble (SFOC)
5. Jim Hanson (Air Force)
6. John Geyer (Army)

149.5-lb class
1. Mike Young (Boise, ID)
2. Kaoru Enomato (Japan)
3. Fumi Nakamura (NYAC)
4. Roger Young (Ohio WC)
5. Pat Marcy (Minnesota WC)
6. Jim Tanniehill (Army)

163-lb class
1. Wayne Wells (Oklahoma City AC)
2. Lonny Gallagher (NYAC)
3. Stan Dziedzic (NYAC)
4. Jeff Callard (Oklahoma City AC)
5. Charles Shepherd (USMC)
6. Mike Gallego (SFOC)

180.5-lb class
1. J Robinson (Army)
2. Floyd Hitchcock (NYAC)
3. William Halsey (USMC)
4. Jesse Rawls (Indiana)
5. Russ Camilleri (SFOC)
6. Jack Zindel (Michigan WC)

198-lb class
1. Wayne Baughman (Air Force)
2. Ken Levels (Ohio WC)
3. Floyd Winter (Army)
4. Samuel Muldrow (Army)
5. Shemas Owen (SFOC)
6. Dave Boren (Eastern Kentucky)

220-lb class
1. Buck Deadrich (SFOC)
2. Henk Schenk (Multnomah)
3. Vince Paolano (NYAC)
4. Michael Kelly (Florida)
5. J. McPhillips (NYAC)
6. Bill Galler (MDYF)

UNL class
1. Greg Wojciechowski (Torio)
2. Harry Geris (Canada)
3. Paul Goble (Air Force)
4. Barry Walsh (Minnesota WC)
5. Ed Floyd (JCAC)
6. Joe Bertolone (Ohio WC)

1973

Team	*Points*
1. New York AC	79
2. Ohio WC	40
3. Wisconsin WC	38
4. Athletes in Action	36

Team	*Points*
5. Michigan WC	21
6. Army	20

Place winners

105.5-lb class
1. David Range (Ohio WC)
2. Wayne Holmes (Ohio WC)
3. Mike Perusky (Waukegan, IL)
4. Mike McArthur (Minnesota, WC)
5. Tom Jeffrey (NYAC)
6. Vita Vee (unat)

114.5-lb class
1. Dale Kestel (Michigan WC)
2. Stan Opp (Freeman SD)
3. Norman Knight (Army)
4. Henry Geller (DYF)
5. Robin Netzley (Ohio WC)
6. James Haimes (unat)

125.5-lb class
1. Don Behm (East Lansing, MI)
2. James Carr (Erie YM)
3. John Morley (NYAC)
4. Jitsushi Furutani (NYAC)
5. Jan Gitcho (unat)
6. Stewart Pruzansky (NYAC)

136.5-lb class
1. Dave Pruzansky (NYAC)
2. Tetsu Ikeno (NYAC)
3. Darrell Keller (Stillwater, OK)
4. Doug Moses (unat)
5. Garry Barton (Army)
6. Curtis Scott (Air Force)

149.5-lb class
1. Lloyd Keaser (USMC)
2. Larry Morgan (California Poly)
3. Art Holden (AIA)
4. Fumiaki Nakamura (NYAC)
5. Brad Smith (unat)
6. Brian Schmidt (NYAC)

163-lb class
1. Carl Adams (Ames, IA)
2. Stan Dziedzic (NYAC)
3. Jim Tanniehill (Army)
4. Jerry Bell (NYAC)
5. Joseph Carr (Eric YM)
6. Joseph Wells (unat)

180.5-lb class
1. John Peterson (Wisconsin WC)
2. Greg Hicks (AIA)
3. Mike Bradley (Michigan WC)
4. Bob Anderson (AIA)
5. Bill Reinbolt (Ohio WC)
6. Floyd Hitchcock (NYAC)

198-lb class
1. Ben Peterson (Wisconsin WC)
2. Vince Paolano (NYAC)
3. Willie Williams (Chicago)
4. Roland Boose (Ohio WC)
5. John Logan (Boston Union)
6. Bill McDaniel (unat)

220-lb class
1. Russ Helickson (Wisconsin WC)
2. Henk Schenk (Multnomah AC)
3. Greg Wojciechowski (Torio AC)
4. Kenneth Levels (Ohio WC)
5. James Metzler (Indianapolis)
6. Mike Kelly (unat)

UNL class
1. Chris Taylor (Ames, IA)
2. Michael McCready (AIA)
3. Robert Johnson (Minnesota WC)
4. James Woods (unat)
5. Robert Fouts (unat)
6. Bruce Conger (Las Vegas YM)

1974

Team	*Points*
1. New York AC	80
2. Athletes in Action	56
3. Ohio WC	55
4. Wisconsin WC	36
5. Mayor Daley Youth Foundation, Mexico	17
7. San Francisco Peninsula Grapplers	14

Team	Points
8. Toledo	12
9. Bay Area WA, Central Coast	10

Place winners

105.5-lb class
1. David Range (Garfield Heights, OH)
2. Chuck Davis (Grove City, OH)
3. Alfredo Olvera (Mexico)

114.5-lb class
1. Sergio Gonzalez (Venice, CA)
2. James Haines (Arcadia, WA)
3. Heikichi Adegawa (NYAC)

125.5-lb class
1. Richard Sofman (NYAC)
2. Norman Hatchett (Cincinnati)
3. Dan Sherman (AIA)

136.5-lb class
1. Don Behm (East Lansing, MI)
2. David Pruzansky (NYAC)
3. Tetsu Ikeno (NYAC)

149.5-lb class
1. Gene Davis (AIA)
2. Larry Morgan (Bakersfield, CA)
3. Neil Duncan (NYAC)

163-lb class
1. Stan Dziedzic (NYAC)
2. Wade Schalles (Hollidaysburg, PA)
3. Lon Gallagher (NYAC)

180.5-lb class
1. Greg Hicks (AIA)
2. Edward Vatch (Madison, WI)
3. John Peterson (AIA)

198-lb class
1. Peter Lieskau (Wisconsin WC)
2. David Curby (Ann Arbor, MI)
3. Vincent Paolano (NYAC)

220-lb class
1. Greg Wojciechowski (Toledo U)
2. Russ Winer (Phoenix, AZ)
3. Gary Sommer (Racine, WI)

UNL class
1. Mack McCrady (Watsonville, CA)
2. Mike McCready (AIA)
3. Jeff Epperson (Middletown, OH)

1975

Team	Points
1. Athletes in Action	71
2. New York AC	62
3. Ohio WC	44
4. Mayor Daley Youth Foundation	43
5. Hawkeye WC	36
6. Armed Forces	26

Place winners

105.5-lb class
1. Dave Range (Ohio WC)
2. Wayne Holmes (Ohio WC)
3. Bill Rosado (Tucson Conquistadores)
4. Lawrence Baltezore (Armed Forces)
5. Joe Cliffe (MDYF)
6. Jim Reizer (unat)

114.5-lb class
1. John Morley (NYAC)
2. Jim Haines (Wisconsin, WC)
3. Randy Miller (unat)
4. Terry Hall (Armed Forces)
5. Chris Sones (Armed Forces)
6. Heikichi Adegawa (NYAC)

125.5-lb class
1. Mark Massery (MDYF)
2. Dan Sherman (AIA)
3. Richie Sofman (NYAC)
4. Dennis Goldberg (NYAC)
5. Andy Daniels (Ohio WC)
6. Tom Schuler (Armed Forces)

136.5-lb class
1. Doug Moses (Hawkeye WC)
2. Mu Chang (AIA)
3. Kiyoshi Abe (NYAC)
4. Jim Humphrey (Ohio WC)
5. Don Behm (MDYF)
6. Tim Cysewski (unat)

149.5-lb class
1. Gene Davis (AIA)
2. Lloyd Keaser (Armed Forces)
3. Larry Morgan (Hawkeye WC)
4. Joe Tice (unat)

5. Larry Johnson (MDYF)
6. Reid Lamphere (AIA)

163-lb class
1. Carl Adams (Iowa State WC)
2. Wade Schalles (unat)
3. Stan Dziedzic (NYAC)
4. Jeff Callard (Rhino WC)
5. Joe Wells (Hawkeye WC)
6. Allyn Cooke (AIA)

180.5-lb class
1. John Peterson (AIA)
2. Greg Hicks (AIA)
3. Greg Strobel (unat)
4. Bob Anderson (AIA)
5. Brady Hall (UCLA WC)
6. Mike Gallego (SF Olympic)

198-lb class
1. Russ Hellickson (Wisconsin WC)
2. Ben Peterson (Iowa State WC)
3. Tom Hazell (Cowboy WC)
4. Larry Amundson (AIA)
5. Rick Arnold (San Diego WF)
6. Verlyn Strellner (MDYF)

220-lb class
1. Greg Wojciechowski (Toledo U)
2. John Bowlsby (unat)
3. Vince Paolano (NYAC)
4. Walter Grote (NYAC)
5. Henk Schenk (Multnomah AC)
6. Ken Levels (Ohio WC)

UNL class
1. Mike McCready (Hawkeye WC)
2. Larry Avery (unat)
3. Tony Policare (NYAC)
4. Jeffrey Epperson (Ohio WC)
5. John Major (Rhino WC)
6. Forrest Waugh (Ohio WC)

1976

Team	Points
1. New York AC	101
2. Hawkeye WC	54
3. Ohio WC	46
4. Arizona AC	25
5. Michigan WC, Mayor Daley Youth Foundation	23
7. U.S. Marine Corps	21
8. Wisconsin WC	15
9. Multnomah AC	10
10. Minnesota WC	2

Place winners

105.5-lb class
1. Bill Rosado (Arizona AC)
2. Phil Drenik (Ohio WC)
3. David Range (Ohio WC)
4. Billy Ree (unat, Oklahoma)
5. Larry Baltezore (Army)
6. Randy Wallen (unat, Washington)

114.5-lb class
1. Jim Haines (Wisconsin WC)
2. John Morley (NYAC)
3. Ed Knecht (Arizona WC)
4. Bill DiPaoli (California State, Palo Alto)
5. (tie) Ray Takahashi (Thunder Bay WC) and Bob Orta (NYAC)

125.5-lb class
1. Jan Gitcho (Hawkeye)
2. Mark Mangianti (Michigan, WC)
3. Dennis Goldberg (NYAC)
4. James Brown (Ohio WC)
5. Joe Corso (Purdue U)
6. Tom Schuler (NYAC-USMC)

136.5-lb class
1. Kiyoshi Abe (NYAC)
2. Jim Humphrey (Ohio AC)
3. Phil Parker (unat)
4. Mark Massery (MDYF)
5. Don Behm (MDYF)
6. Mark Hawald (John Carroll U)

149.5-lb class
1. Lloyd Keaser (USMC)
2. Larry Morgan (Hawkeye WC)
3. Brian Schmidt (NYAC)
4. Dave Foxen (NYAC)
5. Joe Tice (San Francisco AC)
6. Sam Jones (Multnomah AC)

163-lb class
1. Stan Dziedzic (NYAC)
2. Jeff Callard (unat, Oklahoma)
3. Ron Ray (MDYF)
4. Leo Kocher (MDYF)
5. Dan Muthler (USMC)
6. Larry Johnson (MDYF)

180.5-lb class
1. Brad Hall (unat, California)
2. Wade Schalles (Hawkeye)
3. Mark Lieberman (NYAC)
4. Mel Renfro (unat, Louisiana)
5. Tom Muir (Michigan, WC)
6. Mike Lieberman (NYAC)

198-lb class
1. Ben Peterson (Ames, IA)
2. Vince Paolano (NYAC)
3. Tery Paice (Canada)
4. Jeff Simons (USMC)
5. Tom Hazell (Cowboy WC)
6. John Johnson (MDYF)

220-lb class
1. Russ Hellickson (Wisconsin, WC)
2. Larry Bielenberg (Oregon State U)
3. Henk Schenk (Multnomah AC)
4. Walter Grote (NYAC)
5. Greg Wojciechowski (Toledo Area WA)
6. (tie) Buck Deadrich (unat, California) and Tom Herr (Temple AC)

UNL class
1. Mike McCready (Hawkeye WC)
2. Larry Avery (Michigan, WC)
3. Harry Geris (Canada)
4. Carl Dambman (AIA)
5. Jeff Epperson (NYAC)
6. Jim Witzleb (unat, Iowa)

1977

Team	*Points*
1. New York AC	81
2. Ohio WC	31
3. Michigan WC	25
4. Hawkeye WC	24
5. Wisconsin WC	15
6. U.S. Marine Corps	9
7. Air Force, Navy	2

Place winners

105.5-lb class
1. Bill Rosado (Bakersfield Express)
2. Robert Weaver (NYAC)
3. Richard Salamone (NYAC)
4. Jorge Frias (Mexico)
5. Greg Durand (Minneapolis, MN)
6. Mark Ohriner (Las Vegas YMCA)

114.5-lb class
1. Kiyoto Shimizu (Japan)
2. Heikichi Adegawa (Japan)
3. Mike Farina (Cyclone WC)
4. Ed Knecht (Bakersfield Express)
5. Randy Miller (Michigan WC)
6. Mark Mysynk (Iowa City, IA)

125.5-lb class
1. Akira Yamagi (Japan)
2. Jack Reinwand (Wisconsin WC)
3. Joe Corso (Hawkeye WC)
4. Bryan Evans (Sooner AC)
6. Scott Pacino (NYAC)

136.5-lb class
1. Jim Humprhey (Bakersfield Express)
2. Tim Cysewski (Hawkeye WC)
3. Don Behm (MDYF)
4. Kenichi Horii (Japan)
5. Nick Gallo (NYAC)
6. Mike Frick (NYAC)

149.5-lb class
1. Chuck Yagla (Hawkeye WC)
2. Larry Morgan (Bakersfield Express)
3. Brian Schmidt (NYAC)
4. Pete Galea (Cyclone WC)
5. David Foxen (NYAC)
6. Reid Lamphere (AIA)

163-lb class
1. Stan Dziedzic (NYAC)
2. Mark Churella (Michigan WC)
3. Dan Zilverberg (Minnetonka, MN)
4. Dave Schultz (SF Peninsula Grapplers)
5. (tie) Bruce Kinseth (Iowa City, IA) and Ethan Reeve (Ohio WC)
6. John Janaiak (NYAC)

180.5-lb class
1. Mark Lieberman (NYAC)
2. Larry Zilverberg (Minnetonka, MN)
3. Wade Schalles (Bakersfield Express)
4. Dan Schuler (Bakersfield Express)
5. Brady Hall (Bakersfield Express)
6. Chris Campbell (Hawkeye WC)

198-lb class
1. Ben Peterson (Marantha WC)
2. Tom Hazell (Bakersfield Express)
3. Laurent Soucie (Wisconsin WC)
4. William Halsey (USMC)
5. Mitch Hull (Wisconsin WC)
6. Aurel Balainu (NYAC)

220-lb class
1. Harold Smith (NYAC)
2. Yatsu Yoshiaki (Japan)
3. Fred Bohna (Bakersfield Express)
4. Mike McCready (Hawkeye WC)
5. Scott Jerabek (Madison, WI)
6. Walter Grote (NYAC)

UNL class
1. Greg Wojciechowski (Ohio WC)
2. Larry Avery (Michigan WC)
3. John Bowlsby (Waterloo, IA)
4. Jeff Epperson (NYAC)
5. Don Malm (MDYF)
6. Churck Pinta (Navy)

1978

Team	*Points*
1. New York AC	77
2. Hawkeye WC	76
3. Sunkist Kids	65

Place winners

105.5-lb class
1. Bob Weaver (NYAC)
2. Bill Rosado (Sunkist Kids)
3. Richard Salamone (NYAC)
4. Wilfredo Leiva (USMC)
5. Jim Jones (Navy)
6. Darryl Cone (Las Vegas YM)
7. Ishikawa Toshimitsu (Japan)
8. Tim Schultz (Hawkeye WC)

114.5-lb class
1. Jim Haines (Wisconsin WC)
2. Mike McArthur (AIA)
3. Peter Morelli (NYAC)
4. Isamitsu Kariba (Japan)
5. Ed Knecht (Sunkist Kids)
6. Joe Gonzales (USMC)
7. Dwain Burkholder (Hawkeye WC)
8. Oscar Luna (Venezuela)

125.5-lb class
1. Tomiyama Hideaki (Japan)
2. Joe Corso (Hawkeye WC)
3. Mark Mangianti (Sunkist Kids)
4. Jack Reinwand (Wisconsin WC)
5. Dan Mello (Bakersfield Express)
6. Keith Whelan (St. Louis CC)
7. Tom Husted (Wisconsin WC)
8. (tie) Bruce Brotzman (Wisconsin WC) and Dennis Goldberg (NYAC)

136.5-lb class
1. Tim Cysewski (Hawkeye WC)
2. Taga Tsuneo (Japan)
3. Randy Lewis (Hawkeye WC)
4. TiHamer Toth-Fejel (NYAC)
5. Nick Gallo (NYAC)
6. Frank DeAngelis (Oklahoma Underdogs)
7. Jim Carr (Ohio WC)
8. T.D. Hawkins (Titan WC)

149.5-lb class
1. Jim Humphrey (Oklahoma Underdogs)
2. Mike Taylor (Bakerfield Express)
3. Dave Foxen (NYCA)
4. Dick Knorr (Sunkist Kids)
5. Nakamura Shinubo (Japan)
6. Steve Barrett (Cowboy WC)
7. Reid Lamphere (AIA)
8. LeeRoy Smith (Cowboy WC)

163-lb class
1. Chuck Yagla (Hawkeye WC)
2. Mark Churella (Sunkist Kids)
3. Jan Sanderson (unat)
4. Roye Oliver (Sunkist Kids)
5. Dan Muthler (USMC)
6. Joe Sloan (AIA)
7. Joe Zuspann (Cyclone WC)
8. Wade Schalles (NYAC)

180.5-lb class
1. John Peterson (AIA)
2. Mark Lieberman (NYAC)
3. Don Shuler (Sunkist Kids)
4. Chris Campbell (Hawkeye WC)
5. Larry Zilverberg (Sunkist Kids)
6. Charlie Gadson (Cyclone WC)
7. Dave Schultz (Cowboy WC)
8. Tom Muir (Michigan WC)

198-lb class
1. Ben Peterson (Wisconsin WC)
2. Bud Palmer (Hawkeye WC)
3. Laurent Soucie (Hawkeye WC)
4. Roy Baker (NYAC)
5. Eric Wais (Cowboy WC)
6. Mitch Hull (Wisconsin WC)
7. Mike Mann (Marshalltown, IA)
8. Bill Bragg (Colorado Springs WC)

220-lb class
1. Larry Bielenberg (Sunkist Kids)
2. Jeff Simons (USMC)
3. Harold Smith (Ohio WC)
4. Jeff Blatnick (Adirondack Three-Style WC)
5. John Sefter (NYAC)
6. Walter Grote (NYAC)
7. Ed Herman (Hawkeye WC)
8. Barry Walsh (Michigan WC)

UNL class
1. Greg Wojciechowski (Ohio WC)
2. Mike McCready (Hawkeye WC)
3. Greg Gibson (Bakersfield Express)
4. Tom Burns (Hawkeye WC)
5. Jim Murray (Navy)
6. Jeff Epperson (NYAC)
7. Carl Dambman (AIA)
8. Jerry Anderson (Cyclone WC)

1979

Team	*Points*
1. New York AC	87
2. Hawkeye WC	69
3. Wisconsin WC	68
4. Athletes In Action	26
5. Minnesota WC	24
6. Sunkist Kids	18
7. Navy	11
8. Cyclone WC	9

Place winners

105.5-lb class
1. Bob Weaver (NYAC)
2. Sun Jab Do (South Korea)
3. Richard Salamone (NYAC)
4. Tim Schultz (Cyclone WC)
5. Steve Porter (Sun Prairie, WI)
6. Craig Hallock (Hawkeye WC)

114.5-lb class
1. Tom Dursee (NYAC)
2. Kyn Kim Jong (South Korea)
3. Pat Finlan (Winconsin WC)
4. Tae Ogil (South Korea)
5. Paul Widerman (Massachusetts)
6. Jody Perry (Colorado)

125.5-lb class
1. Joe Corso (Hawkeye WC)
2. John Azevedo (Sunkist Kids)
3. Jim Haines (Wisconsin WC)
4. Bruce Brotzman (Wisconsin WC)
5. Koi Zumi Junichi (Japan)
6. Gene Mills (Syracuse U)

136.5-lb class
1. Andre Metzger (Oklahoma Underdogs)
2. Keith Mourlam (Hawkeye WC)
3. Taga Tsuneo (Japan)
4. Nick Gallo (NYAC)
5. Mike Frick (Navy)
6. Tim Cysewski (Hawkeye WC)

149.5-lb class
1. Chuck Yagla (Hawkeye WC)
2. Roger Frizzel (Oklahoma Underdogs)
3. Hiramatzu Yoshitaka (Japan)
4. Scott Bliss (Oregon)
5. Steve Barrett (AIA)
6. Dave Foxen (NYAC)

163-lb class
1. LeRoy Kemp (Wisconsin WC)
2. Dave Schultz (AIA)
3. Bruce Kinseth (Hawkeye WC)
4. Mike DeAnna (Hawkeye WC)

5. Dan Zilverberg (Minnesota WC)
6. Jon Jackson (California)

180.5-lb class
1. Dan Lewis (Fullerton WC)
2. Larry Zilverberg (Minnesota WC)
3. Mark Lieberman (NYAC)
4. Ed Banach (Hawkeye WC)
5. Jerry Schmitz (Minnesota WC)
6. Perry Hummell (Cyclone WC)

198-lb class
1. Laurent Soucie (Wisconsin WC)
2. Brady Hall (Santa Monica WC)
3. Roy Baker (NYAC)
4. Greg Gibson (USMC)
5. Mitch Hull (Wisconsin WC)
6. George Bowman (Minnesota WC)

220-lb class
1. Russ Hellickson (Wisconsin WC)
2. Steve Day (Illinois)
3. John Sefter (NYAC)
4. Wyatt Wishart (Canada)
5. Jeff Simons (USMC)
6. Harold Smith (Kentucky)

UNL class
1. Greg Wojciechowski (Ohio WC)
2. Bob Walker (AIA)
3. Tom Burns (Hawkeye WC)
4. Dave Osenbaugh (Cyclone WC)
5. Erland Van Lidth de Jeude (NYAC)
6. Dennis Mills (New Jersey)

1980

Team	*Points*
1. New York AC	113.50
2. Sunkist Kids	72
3. Hawkeye WC	60
4. Wisconsin WC	38
5. Oklahoma Underdogs	27
6. Cyclone WC	20
7. Light Tower WC (Edison, NJ)	14
8. U.S. Marine Corps	9
9. Army	1.33
10. Navy	1.33

Place winners

105.5-lb. class
1. Bob Weaver (NYAC)
2. Adam Cuesta (Sunkist Kids)
3. Richard Salamone (NYAC)
4. Bill Rosado (Sunkist Kids)
5. Lew Dorrance (USMC)
6. (tie) T.J. Jones (Navy) and Shinichi Ishikawa (Japan)

114.5-lb class
1. Joe Gonzales (Sunkist Kids)
2. Tom Dursee (NYAC)
3. Bill DePaoli (NYAC)
4. Randy Miller (Lexington, KY)
5. Kanno Koichi (Japan)
6. Ronald Jones (Light Tower WC)

125.5-lb class
1. Joe Corso (Hawkeye WC)
2. Gene Mills (NYAC)
3. Jim Haines (Wisconsin WC)
4. Mark Mangianti (Sunkist Kids)
5. (tie) John Azevedo (Sunkist Kids) and Rod Buttery (NYAC)

136.5-lb class
1. Ricky Dellagatta (NYAC)
2. Randy Lewis (Hawkeye WC)
3. Nick Gallo (NYAC)
4. Tihamer Toth-Fejel (Sunkist Kids)
5. Kenneth Mallory (NYAC)
6. Eric Fobert (Canada)

149.5-lb class
1. Jim Humphrey (Oklahoma Underdogs)
2. Andre Metzger (Oklahoma Underdogs)
3. Scott Trizzino (Hawkeye WC)
4. Doug Parise (NYAC)
5. Andy Rein (Wisconsin WC)
6. Chuck Yagla (Hawkeye WC)

163-lb class
1. Bruce Kinseth (Hawkeye WC)
2. Dave Schultz (Oklahoma Underdogs)
3. Marc Mongeon (Team Canada)
4. Scott Heaton (Sunkist Kids)
5. Roye Oliver (Sunkist Kids)
6. Gary Kessel (NYAC)

180.5-lb class
1. Chris Campbell (Cyclone WC)
2. Mark Lieberman (NYAC)
3. John Janiak (NYAC)
4. Clark Davis (Team Canada)
5. Jeffrey Parker (Light Tower WC)
6. Thomas Martucci (Light Tower WC)

198-lb class
1. Ben Peterson (Wisconsin WC)
2. Dan Lewis (Sunkist Kids)
3. Laurent Soucie (Wisconsin WC)
4. Charlie Gadson (Cyclone WC)
5. Roy Baker (NYAC)
6. Howard Harris (Sunkist Kids)

220-lb class
1. Russ Hellickson (Wisconsin WC)
2. Larry Bielenberg (Sunkist Kids)
3. Greg Gibson (USMC)
4. Dan Severn (Sunkist Kids)
5. Michael Koppel (Team Canada)
6. (tie) Mike Rotunda (NYAC), Alan Hyncia (Army), and Hiroski Obayashi (Japan)

UNL class
1. Bruce Baumgartner (NYAC)
2. Tom Burns (Hawkeye WC)
3. Dean Phinney (Hawkeye WC)
4. Paul Curka (Light Tower WC)
5. Mike Haschak (Sunkist Kids)
6. Michael Steffens (Lancaster, WI)

1981

Team	*Points*
1. Sunkist Kids	132
2. New York AC	63
3. Oklahoma Underdogs	40
4. U.S. Marine Corps	33
5. Athletes in Action	25

Place winners

105.5-lb class
1. Bill Rosado (Sunkist Kids)
2. Tim Vanni (Sunkist Kids)
3. Paul Widerman (NYAC)
4. Rich Salamone (NYAC)
5. Lewis Dorrance (USMC)
6. Luis Sanchez (Mexico)

114.5-lb class
1. Joe Gonzales (Sunkist Kids)
2. Dan Glenn (Hawkeye WC)
3. Lewis Dorrance (USMC)
4. Luis Sanchez (Mexico)
5. Tom Dursee (NYAC)
6. Pat Finlan (Wisconsin WC)

125.5-lb class
1. John Azevedo (Sunkist Kids)
2. Dan Cuestas (Sunkist Kids)
3. Adam Cuestas (Sunkist Kids)
4. Ed Knecht (Sunkist Kids)
5. Bill DePaoli (NYAC)
6. Mark Zimmer (Oklahoma Underdogs)

136.5-lb class
1. LeeRoy Smith (Cowboy WC)
2. Mike Land (Cyclone WC)
3. Mike McArthur (AIA)
4. Chuck Ludeman (Wisconsin WC)
5. Keith Mourlam (Hawkeye WC)
6. Bill Marino (NYAC)

149.5-lb class
1. Andy Rein (Wisconsin WC)
2. Lewis Sondgeroth (USMC)
3. Tihamer Toth-Fejel (Sunkist Kids)
4. Davis Fozzen (NYAC)
5. Doug Parise (NYAC)
6. Jim Martinez (Minnesota WC)

163-lb class
1. David Schultz (Oklahoma Underdogs)
2. Roye Oliver (Sunkist Kids)
3. Roger Frizzell (Oklahoma Underdogs)
4. Mike Taylor (Sunkist Kids)
5. Steve Suder (AIA)
6. Bill Dykeman (NYAC)

180.5-lb class
1. Dan Zilverberg (Sunkist Kids)
2. John Janiak (NYAC)
3. Jim Hall (Oklahoma Underdogs)
4. Rey Martinez (Cowboy WC)
5. Andy Tsarnas (Spartan WC)
6. Don Shuler (AIA)

198-lb class
1. Eric Wais (Oklahoma Underdogs)
2. Willie Gadson (Cyclone WC)
3. Dan Lewis (Sunkist Kids)
4. Charlie Gadson (Cyclone WC)
5. Drew Whitfield (AIA)
6. Tom Hazel (Sunkist Kids)

220-lb class
1. Greg Gibson (USMC)
2. Mike Evans (AIA)
3. Jeff Blatnick (Adirondack Three-Style WC)
4. Russ Hellickson (Wisconsin WC)
5. Dave Severn (Sunkist Kids)

UNL class
1. Jimmy Jackson (Sunkist Kids)
2. Ron Carlisle (USMC)
3. James Mitchell (Sunkist Kids)
4. Mike Euker (Wisconsin WC)
5. Dan Cook (Sunkist Kids)
6. Mike Rotunda (NYAC)

1982

Team	*Points*
1. New York AC	85
2. Sunkist Kids	61
3. U.S. Marine Corps	29
4. Wisconsin WC	28
5. Nebraska Olympic Club	25
6. Oklahoma Underdogs	22
7. Athletes in Action	15
8. Michigan WC	7

Place winners

105.5-lb class
1. Bill Rosado (Sunkist Kids)
2. Rich Salamone (NYAC)
3. Bernardo Olivera (Mexico)
4. Tim Vanni (Sunkist Kids)
5. Randy Ohta (Sunkist Kids)
6. Eric Wetzel (USMC)

114.5-lb class
1. Bob Weaver (NYAC)
2. Joseph Spinazzola (NYAC)
3. Anthony Amado (USA Oregon)
4. Alfred Gutierrez (Sunkist Kids)
5. Michael Erb (Sunkist Kids)
6. Emiro Marquez (Venezuela)

125.5-lb class
1. Gene Mills (NYAC)
2. Barry Davis (Hawkeye WC)
3. Randy Willingham (Cowboy WC)
4. John Azevedo (Sunkist Kids)
5. Karl Glover (Sunkist Kids)
6. William DePaoli (NYAC)

136.5-lb class
1. LeeRoy Smith (Cowboy WC)
2. Randy Lewis (Hawkeye WC)
3. Ricky Dellagatta (NYAC)
4. Mike Land (Cyclone WC)
5. Darryl Burley (unat)
6. Kenneth Mallory (NYAC)

149.5-lb class
1. Andy Rein (Wisconsin WC)
2. Andre Metzger (Oklahoma Underdogs)
3. Bill Nugent (Sunkist Kids)
4. Lewis Sonderoth (USMC)
5. Al Freeman (Nebraska OC)
6. Jessie Reyes (Sunkist Kids)

163-lb class
1. Lee Kemp (Wisconsin WC)
2. Roye Oliver (Sunkist Kids)
3. Mike DeAnna (Hawkeye WC)
4. John Dwyer (Team Canada)
5. Ken Sheets (Indiana WC)
6. Steven Suder (AIA)

180.5-lb class
1. Bruce Kinseth (Hawkeye WC)
2. David Schultz (Oklahoma Underdogs)
3. Dan Chaid (Oklahoma Underdogs)
4. Peter Capone (NYAC)
5. Jim Scherr (Nebraska OC)
6. Scott Mansur (USA Oregon)

198-lb class
1. Bill Scherr (Nebraska OC)
2. Charlie Gadson (Cyclone WC)
3. Steve Fraser (Michigan WC)
4. Clark Davis (Team Canada)

5. Dan Lewis (Sunkist Kids)
6. Howard Harris (Sunkist Kids)

220-lb class
1. Greg Gibson (USMC)
2. Mike Evans (AIA)
3. Richard Deschatelets (Team Canada)
4. Dan Severn (Sunkist Kids)
5. Louis DiSerafino (NYAC)
6. Josh Washington (Sunkist Kids)

UNL class
1. Bruce Baumgartner (NYAC)
2. Ron Carlisle (USMC)
3. Gary Albright (Nebraska OC)
4. Erland Van Lidth de Jeude (NYAC)
5. Dan Cook (Sunkist Kids)
6. Michael Euker (Wisconsin WC)

Chapter 6

The United States Freestyle Senior Open

USA Wrestling

It can be argued that the U.S. Freestyle Senior Open is the roughest wrestling tournament in the country. It certainly did not start out that way when the first meet was held in Evanston, Illinois, in 1969. Less than 100 wrestlers, all over 17 years of age, were on hand for that rather inauspicious debut held under the direction of the USWF.

Yet the tournament, originally in competition with the AAU National Freestyle Championships, continued to evolve through the 1970s. When the USWF was officially seated as the sport's national governing body in 1982 (after being renamed USA Wrestling and ending a lengthy struggle with the AAU for bragging rights in the nation), the tournament developed an even stronger reputation. The AAU nationals fell by the wayside, and the USA Wrestling Freestyle Senior Open Championships became the major freestyle meet in the country. By 1987, a total of 392 wrestlers were in the field, including 38 former NCAA all-Americans and 11 former Olympians.

In 1969 the Mayor Daley Youth Foundation club of Chicago became the first team champion and went on to claim a total of five team titles in the first 6 years the tournament was held. The first individual champions were Mike Kaye (105.5) and Chuck Rosetti (114.5) of Illinois, Larry Owings (149.5) of Washington, Len Pettigrew (198) of Ohio, and Ted Parker (125.5), Don Behm (136.5), Vic Marcucci (163), Les Armes (180.5), Mike Kelly (220), and Larry Kristoff (heavyweight), all of Mayor Daley. Behm was voted Outstanding Wrestler.

The quality of competition was high that first year. Behm and Kristoff were former Olympic silver medal winners, and Owings and Marcucci were former NCAA champions at the University of Washington and Iowa State, respectively.

The tournament began in Illinois, then crisscrossed the country. By 1988 it had been held in such diverse settings as Fort Collins, Colorado; Stillwater, Oklahoma; Chapel Hill, North Carolina; Madison, Wisconsin; Hempstead, New York; Eugene, Oregon; and Reno and Las Vegas, Nevada.

Annually, the tournament draws the best freestyle wrestlers in the country, all anxious to earn the right to call themselves national champion. In 1988, Bruce Baumgartner won his seventh title at heavyweight to tie Richard Salamone (105.5) for the most championships. Lee Kemp won five crowns at 163 pounds.

In 1986, the tournament split into two divisions to recognize the various sizes of the clubs across the country. Teams with more than 10 athletes competed in Division I, whereas teams with 10 wrestlers or less competed in Division II.

In 1987, Dave Schultz turned in one of the finest performances in the history of the tournament. Schultz pinned all nine of his opponents at 163 pounds, including three-time NCAA champions Jim Zalesky and Nate Carr. In 1988, he moved up to 180.5 and won again, tying brother Mark Schultz as a four-time champion.

The Sunkist Kids of Tempe, Arizona, was the most consistent team champion during the 1980s. Sponsored by Art Martori and coached by Bobby Douglas, the Sunkist Kids racked up six straight championships from 1983 through 1988.

For an overall view of the history of the U.S. national freestyle champions, see Table 6.1.

Table 6.1
USA Wrestling National Freestyle Senior Open Championships

1969
(at Northwestern University, Evanston, IL)

Team	Points
1. Mayor Daley Youth Foundation	67
2. Ashland College	12
3. Northwestern University, University of Washington, Illinois WC	10

Place winners

105.5-lb class
1. Mike Kaye (unat)
2. H. Geller (unat)
3. K. Fender (unat)
4. (tie) R. Woodward and Bruce Beam (both unat)

114.5-b class
1. Chuck Rossetti (Illinois WC)
2. S. Verner (unat)
3. J. Bissell (unat, Michigan State U)
4. G. Snodgrass (unat)

125.5-lb class
1. Ted Parker (MDYF)
2. T. Hatta (MDYF)
3. J. Anderson (Northern Michigan U)
4. C. Angello (Ashland C)

136.5-lb class
1. Don Behm (MDYF)
2. M. Hattori (Japan)
3. N. Kiguchi (Japan)
4. M. Fox (unat)

149.5-lb class
1. Larry Owings (U of Washington)
2. R. Ouellet (unat, Michigan State U)
3. K. Lowrance (unat, Michigan State U)
4. J. Hansen (unat)

163-lb class
1. Vic Marcucci (MDYF)
2. Joe Wells (Iowa)
3. J. Lee (unat)
4. E. Bates (MDYF)

180.5-lb class
1. Les Armes (MDYF)
2. J. Klein (unat)
3. B. Pauss (Northwestern U)
4. D. Smith (MDYF)

198-lb class
1. Len Pettigrew (Ashland)
2. C. Arnold (Northwestern U)
3. G. Ponatelli (MDYF)
4. D. Patitz (unat)

220-lb class
1. Mike Kelley (MDYF)
2. D. Demski (unat, Colorado State U)

Heavyweight
1. Larry Kristoff (MDYF)
2. J. Smith (unat, Michigan State U)
3. B. Billberg (MDYF)
4. D. Kraft (Northwestern U)

1970
(at Oklahoma State University, Stillwater, OK)

Team	*Points*
1 Mayor Daley Youth Foundation	74
2. Athletes in Action	20
3. Oklahoma City AC	12
4. Mexico Poly	6

Place winners

105.5-lb class
1. Stan Opp (South Dakota State U)
2. Scott Verner (MDYF)
3. Richard Vaughn (California)
4. Alfred Olvera (Mexico)

114.5-lb class
1. Ron Oglesby (MDYF)
2. Terry Henry (Perry, OK)
3. Enrique Jimenez (Mexico)
4. Gilbert Garcia (Colorado)

125.5-lb class
1. Rick Sanders (Portland)
2. Yoshiro Fujita (Stillwater)
3. Dwayne Keller (Stillwater)
4. Ron Thrasher (Stillwater)

136.5-lb class
1. Darrell Keller (Stillwater)
2. Dave Pruzansky (New Jersey)
3. Roger Weigel (Oregon)
4. Wayne Monts (Colorado)

149.5-lb class
1. Bob Douglas (Iowa)
2. Larry Owings (Washington)
3. Bob Buzzard (MDYF)
4. Gene Davis (AIA)

183-lb class
1. Wayne Wells (OCAC)
2. Greg Hicks (AIA)
3. John Williams (Stillwater)
4. Phil Fitgerald (Stillwater)

180.5-lb class
1. Fred Fozzard (Stillwater)
2. Bob Anderson (AIA)
3. Steve Combs (MDYF)
4. Willie Williams (MDYF)

198-lb class
1. Bill Harlow (MDYF)
2. Jim Duschen (MDYF)
3. Larry Amundsen (AIA)
4. Daryl Williamson (OCAC)

220-lb class
1. Larry Kristoff (MDYF)
2. Ken Oswell (Washington)
3. Gerald Winnard (Stillwater)

Heavyweight
1. Mike Kelley (MDYF)
2. Bill Galler (MDYF)
3. Gene Libal (Nebraska)
4. Harry Geris (Stillwater)

1971
(at Oklahoma State University, Stillwater, OK)

Team	*Points*
1 Athletes in Action	41.33
2. Mayor Daley Youth Foundation	33
3. West Germany	24
4. Oklahoma City AC, Air Force	10
6. Multnomah AC, Lansing WC	7

Place winners

105.5-lb class
1. Scott Verner (MDYF)
2. Sergio Gonzalez (UCLA)
3. Joe Cliff (MDYF)

114.5-lb class
1. Everett Gomez (Oklahoma State U)
2. Mario Sabatini (West Germany)
3. Tom Phillips (Oregon State U)

125.5-lb class
1. Dwayne Keller (Oklahoma State U)
2. Ron Thrasher (Oklahoma State U)
3. Billy Martin (Norfolk,VA)

136.5-lb class
1. Gene Davis (AIA)
2. Yoshiro Fujita (Oklahoma State U)
3. Bernd Fleig (West Germany)

149.5-lb class
1. Dan Gable (Ames, IA)
2. Jeff Callard (Lansing, MI)
3. David Dominick (Oklahoma State U)

163-lb class
1. Wayne Wells (Oklahoma City AC)
2. Fred Hicks (AIA)
3. Adolf Seeger (West Germany)

180.5-lb class
1. Jack Zindel (Lansing, MI)
2. Peter Neumaier (West Germany)
3. Larry Amundson (AIA)

198-lb class
1. Wayne Baughman (Air Force)
2. Russ Hellickson (MDYF)
3. Greg Strobel (Oregon State U)

220-lb class
1. Larry Kristoff (MDYF)
2. Henk Schenk (Multnomah AC)
3. John Lightner (AIA)

Heavyweight
1. Nick Carollo (AIA)
2. Harry Geris (Oklahoma State U)

1972
(at Oklahoma State University, Stillwater, OK)

Team	*Points*
1 Mayor Daley Youth Foundation	74
2. Oklahoma City AC	33
3. Athletes in Action	25
4. Ohio WC, San Francisco Olympic Club	20
6. Southland WC (CA)	13
7. Hawkeye Club	8
8. Air Force	3
9. Winona Mat Club (MN), Phoenix Wristlock Club	2
(Japanese Team 56, Mexico 1; these teams cannot compete for team title)	

Place winners

105.5-lb class
1. Wayne Holmes (Ohio WC)
2. Hiromasa Niijima (Japan)
3. Joe Cliffe (MDYF)
4. Henry Geller (MDYF)
5. Dennis Switzky (Kansas State U)

6. Gilbert Medrano (unat, Dodge City, KS)

114.5-lb class

1. Toshinori Atsumi (Japan)
2. Robert Dieli (Ohio WC)
3. Steve Breece (unat, Tulsa, OK)
4. Bob Orta (unat, Nebraska)
5. Scott Miller (Winona Mat Club)
6. Enrique Jimenez (Mexico)

125.5-lb class

1. Hideaki Yanagida (Japan)
2. Don Behm (MDYF)
3. Ted Parker (MDYF)
4. Ray Stapp (OCAC)
5. Dale Brumit (unat, Arizona)
6. Mike Johnson (unat, Colorado)

136.5-lb class

1. Kiyoshi Abe (Japan)
2. Rick Sanders (Portland, OR)
3. Gene Davis (AIA)
4. James Hanson (Air Force)
5. Doug Smith (AIA)
6. Keith Lowrance (Norfolk)

149.5-lb class

1. Kikuo Wada (Japan)
2. Dave Maple (MDYF)
3. Larry Owings (U of Washington)
4. Hajime Shinjo (U of Washington)
5. Stephen Randall (unat, Oklahoma State U)
6. Bob Buzzard (MDYF)

163-lb class

1. Wayne Wells (OCAC)
2. Mike Gallego (SFOC)
3. Joe Wells (MDYF)
4. Greg Hicks (AIA)
5. Wade Schalles (Clarion State)
6. Mike R. Jones (Oregon State U)

180.5-lb class

1. Fred Fozzard (OCAC)
2. Steve Combs (MDYF)
3. John Lightner (AIA)
4. John Peterson (Stout State U)
5. Les Armes (Oklahoma State U)
6. Ralph Orr (Southland WC)

198-lb class

1. Russ Hellickson (MDYF)
2. Bill Harlow (MDYF)
3. Geoff Baum (OCAC)
4. Ben Peterson (Iowa State U)
5. Pat Clock (Oswego, OR)
6. Willie Williams (MDYF)

220-lb class

1. Buck Deadrich (SFOC)
2. Nick Carollo (AIA)
3. Henk Schenk (Portland, OR)
4. Jim Hagen (Oregon State U)
5. Russ Winer (Phoenix Wristlock)
6. Bill Galler (MDYF)

Heavyweight

1. Jeff Smith (Southland WC)
2. Dale Stearns (Hawkeye Club)
3. Mike Kelly (MDYF)
4. Rick Kepler (Kansas City)
5. Mike Day (Northern Illinois U)
6. Mike Henry (Cypress, CA)

1973
(at Colorado State University, Fort Collins, CO)

Team	*Points*
1 Mayor Daley Youth Foundation	57
2. Athletes in Action	56
3. International WC (Stillwater, OK)	30
4. Ohio WC, San Francisco Olympic Club, New York AC	20
7. Treasure Valley WC	15
8. Michigan WC	12
9. Utah WF	5.5
10. CDOM Mexico	5
11. Oregon WC, Sterling WC (CO)	3

Place winners

105.5-lb class
1. Wayne Holmes (Ohio WC)
2. Joe Cliffe (MDYF)
3. Fumio Tomino (unat, McCook, NE)
4. Ron Snyder (Treasure Valley WC)

114.5-lb class
1. Dale Kestel (Michigan WC)
2. Chris Sones (unat, Iowa City)
3. Tatsuro Yamazaki (International WC)
4. Steve Hart (Oregon WC)

125.5-lb class
1. Yoshiro Fujita (International WC)
2. Terry Henry (unat, Oklahoma State U)
3. Jan Gitcho (MDYF)
4. Jeff Lamphere (unat, U of Minnesota)

136.5-lb class
1. Darrell Keller (International WC)
2. Jim Humphrey (Ohio WC)
3. Don Behm (MDYF)
4. Kyung Mu Chang (AIA)

149.5-lb class
1. Mike Young (Treasure Valley WC)
2. Bob Bergen (unat, Portland State U)
3. Gene Davis (AIA)
4. Rondo Fehlberg (Utah WF)

163-lb class
1. Stan Dziedzic (NYAC)
2. Marlin Grahn (unat, Portland State)
3. Ron Ray (MDYF)
4. Rich Lawinger (unat, U of Wisconsin)

180.5-lb class
1. Greg Hicks (AIA)
2. J Robinson (NYAC)
3. Ed Vatch (unat, U of Wisconsin)
4. Bob Anderson (AIA)

198-lb class
1. Willie Williams (MDYF)
2. Ralph Vandro (SFOC)
3. Larry Amundson (AIA)
4. Raul Garcia (CDOM Mexico)

220-lb class
1. Buck Deadrich (SFOC)
2. Nick Carollo (AIA)
3. Jim Duschen (MDYF)
4. Ken Levels (unat, Hiram, OH)

Heavyweight
1. Mike McCready (AIA)
2. Vic Mittleberg (MDYF)
3. Robert Fouts (unat, Waterloo, IA)
4. Doug Malay (Sterling WC)

1974
(at Colorado State University, Fort Collins, CO)

Team	*Points*
1 Mayor Daley Youth Foundation	74
2. Athletes in Action	44
3. Stronghold Youth	14
4. Wisconsin WC	13
5. Ohio WC	3

Place winners

105.5-lb class
1. Dan Cliffe (MDYF)
2. William Damiter (MDYF)
3. Bill Van Cleve (unat, Washington U)
4. John Siscon (U.S. International WC)

114.5-lb class
1. Jim Haines (unat, Wisconsin U)
2. Tom Scott (unat, Portland State U)
3. Bob Dieli (unat, Colorado State U)
4. Mike McArthur (Minnesota WC)
5. Rick Coward (U.S. International WC)
6. Steve Hart (Oregon WC)

125.5-lb class
1. Dan Sherman (AIA)
2. Mark Massery (MDYF)
3. Ted Parker (MDYF)
4. Gary Wallman (unat, Nebraska)
5. Scott Conkwright (unat, U of North Carolina)
6. Alan Karstetter (Utah WF)

136.5-lb class
1. Dwayne Keller (unat, Oklahoma State U)
2. Doug Moses (Stronghold)
3. Shuichi Shoji (Oregon WC)
4. Reid Lamphere (AIA)

5. Mark Sanderson (Utah WF)
6. Edward Jackson (MDYF)

149.5-lb class
1. Joe Tice (U.S. International WC)
2. David Scherer (North Dakota WC)
3. Hajime Shinjo (unat, U of Washington)
4. Bob Bergen (Portland State WC)
5. Mike Winberry (Greeley WC)
6. Kit Shaw (unat, Central Washington)

163-lb class
1. Mike R. Jones (Oregon State U)
2. Leo Kocher (MDYF)
3. Jan Sanderson (unat, U of Iowa)
4. Bob Kuhn (AIA)
5. Terry Rusher (unat, U of Colorado)
6. Dave Maple (unat, Oklahoma State U)

180.5-lb class
1. Bob Anderson (AIA)
2. Verlyn Strellner (MDYF)
3. Ed Vatch (unat, U of Wisconsin)
4. Dan Wagemann (unat, U of Iowa)
5. Tom Muir (unat, Michigan State U)
6. Steve DeVries (Wisconsin WC)

198-lb class
1. Bill Harlow (MDYF)
2. Greg Strobel (Oregon State U)
3. Bob Bragg (Stronghold)
4. Willie Williams (MDYF)
5. Nick Carollo (AIA)
6. Rich Calderon (unat, U of Washington)

220-lb class
1. Russ Hellickson (Wisconsin WC)
2. James Duschen (MDYF)
3. Tom Hazell (unat, Oklahoma State U)
4. Ken Levels (Ohio WC)
5. Larry Bielenberg (unat, Oregon State U)
6. Jim Waschek (unat, U of Iowa)

Heavyweight
1. Mike McCready (AIA)
2. Larry Avery (unat, Michigan State U)
3. Greg Williams (unat, Columbia Basin JC)
4. Doug Malay (unat, Colorado)
5. Lou Roberts (Treasure Valley WC)
6. P.J. Braun (U.S. International WC)

1975
(at University of North Carolina, Chapel Hill, NC)

Team	*Points*
1 New York AC	75
2. Athletes in Action	34
3. Wisconsin WC	26
4. Mayor Daley Youth Foundation	23
5. Lock Haven	15
6. Florida International WC, Minnesota WC	14
8. Louisiana State	12
9. Tampa Bay WC	9
10. Hawkeye WC	8
11. Middle Tennessee WC	4
12. U.S. Marine Corps	3
13. San Francisco Olympic Club, Air Force	2
15. Florida WC, Western NYWC, East Carolina	1

Place winners

105.5-lb class
1. Gary Uram (Lock Haven)
2. Larry Horton (unat, North Carolina)

114.5-lb class
1. John Morley (NYAC)
2. Lee Klepper (NYAC)
3. Gary Moore (unat, New Jersey)
4. Tom Busman (Florida International)
5. Peter Horton (unat, North Carolina)
6. Rick Canaday (unat, Indiana)

125.5-lb class
1. Jack Reinwand (unat, Wisconsin)
2. Gary Breece (unat, North Carolina)
3. Dan Sherman (AIA)
4. Dennis Goldberg (NYAC)
5. Mohamad Ghorbani (Middle Tennessee State U)
6. Eddie Rew (AIA)

136.5-lb class
1. Dwayne Keller (unat, Oklahoma State U)

2. Kiyoshi Abe (NYAC)
3. Kyung Mu Chang (AIA)
4. Jeff Rippey (Lock Haven)
5. Jeff Lamphere (Minnesota WC)
6. Craig Horswill (unat, Wisconsin)

149.5-lb class
1. Paul Gillespie (NYAC)
2. Larry Morgan (Hawkeye WC)
3. Reid Lamphere (AIA)
4. Neil Duncan (NYAC)
5. Gordon Connell (Middle Tennessee State U)
6. Albert Pedrinan (NYAC)

163-lb class
1. Dave Maple (MDYF)
2. Chuck Yagla (unat, Iowa)
3. David Kinchen (Florida International)
4. Rickey Schade (Florida International)
5. James Callard (Air Force)
6. Al Strangl (Western NYWC)

180.5-lb class
1. Greg Hicks (AIA)
2. Peter Leiskau (Wisconsin WC)
3. Laurent Soucie (Wisconsin WC)
4. Jim Jackson (USMC)
5. Len Gallagher (NYAC)
6. Phil Mueller (East Carolina)

198-lb class
1. Mel Renfro (Louisiana State U)
2. Willie Williams (MDYF)
3. Steve Strellner (NYAC)
4. Henry Shaffer (AIA)
5. Billy King (Florida International)
6. Lawrence Parker (unat, North Carolina)

220-lb class
1. Russ Hellickson (Wisconsin WC)
2. Vince Paolano (NYAC)
3. Walter Grote (NYAC)
4. Bill Galler (MDYF)
5. Glen Vissers (unat, Wisconsin)
6. Larry Bergman (Tampa WC)

Heavyweight
1. Larry Avery (Michigan WC)
2. Dan Kraft (Tampa Bay WC)
3. Gene Santoli (NYAC)
4. Tom Herr (unat, Pennsylvania)
5. Buck Deadrich (SFOC)
6. Mark Totten (Florida WC)

1976
(at Madison, WI)

Team	*Points*
1 Hawkeye WC	66
2. Mayor Daley Youth Foundation	36
3. Wisconsin WC	26
4. Ohio WC	20
5. U.S. Marine Corps	11

Place winners

105.5-lb class
1. Bill Ree (Cowboy WC)
2. Randy Wollen (unat, Washington)
3. Dennis Reed (unat, Wisconsin)

114.5-lb class
1. Jim Haines (unat, Wisconsin)
2. Chris Sones (Hawkeye WC)
3. Everett Gomez (unat, Oklahoma)
4. Brad Thompson (unat, Wisconsin)
5. Mark Mysnyk (unat, New York)
6. Jim Reizer (unat, Illinois)

125.5-lb class
1. Don Behm (MDYF)
2. Mark Massery (MDYF)
3. Joe Corso (Hawkeye WC)
4. Jack Reinwand (Wisconsin WC)
5. Mike Land (Iowa State WC)
6. Billy Martin (unat, Oklahoma)

136.5-lb class
1. Jim Humphrey (Ohio WC)
2. Jim Miller (Hawkeye WC)
3. Craig Horswill (Wisconsin WC)
4. Doug Moses (Hawkeye WC)
5. Brad Jacot (Club Northwest)
6. Alray Johnson (unat, Pennsylvania)

149.5-lb class
1. Larry Morgan (Hawkeye WC)
2. Lloyd Keaser (USMC)
3. Bruce Kinseth (unat, Iowa)
4. Dale Spies (Wisconsin WC)

5. Tom Adams (Wisconsin WC)
6. Ken Snyder (Hawkeye WC)

163-lb class
1. Joe Wells (Hawkeye WC)
2. Ron Ray (MDYF)
3. Terry Kramer (unat, Wisconsin)
4. Jeff Callard (Rhino WC)
5. Leo Kocher (MDYF)
6. Terry Limmex (unat, Wisconsin)

180.5-lb class
1. Wade Schalles (unat, Pennsylvania)
2. Mel Renfro (unat, Louisiana)
3. Don Stumpf (unat, Illinois)
4. Steve Lawinger (unat, Wisconsin)
5. Randy Hill (unat, Wisconsin)
6. Brady Hall (California IWA)

198-lb class
1. Ben Peterson (Iowa State WC)
2. Tom Hazell (Cowboy WC)
3. Verlyn Strellner (MDYF)
4. Jeff Simons (USMC)
5. Ron Jeidy (unat, Wisconsin)
6. Dennis Stearns (Hawkeye WC)

220-lb class
1. Russ Hellickson (Wisconsin WC)
2. Ken Levels (Ohio WC)
3. Scott Jerabek (unat, Wisconsin)
4. Steve Duerst (unat, Wisconsin)
5. Duane Fritchie (unat, Missouri)
6. Michael Glasman (unat, Wisconsin)

Heavyweight
1. Mike McCready (Hawkeye WC)
2. David Porter (unat, Michigan)
3. Carl Dambman (AIA)
4. Rob Whisman (Iowa State WC)
5. Harry Geris (AMWC Canada)
6. Phillip Thingvold (unat, Wisconsin)

1977
(at University of Oregon, Eugene, OR)

Team	Points
1 Bakersfield Express	70
2. Oregon WC	45
3. U.S. Marine Corps, Wisconsin	12
5. Mayor Daley Youth Foundation, Michigan WC	8

Place winners

105.5-lb class
1. Hiromi Nara (Bellingham, WA)
2. Doug Higley (Clearfield, UT)
3. Bill Van Cleve (Bellingham, WA)
4. Randy Ohta (Oregon WC)

114.5-lb class
1. Bill Anderson (Umpqua MC)
2. Dave Bentley (USMC)
3. Tim Teasley (Fortuna, CA)

125.5-lb class
1. John Azevedo (Bakersfield Express)
2. Bernie Kleiman (MDYF)
3. Steve Hart (Oregon WC)
4. Thomas Goodwin (Palouse Hills WC)

136.5-lb class
1. Jim Humphrey (Bakersfield Express)
2. Larry Marshall (Oregon WC)
3. Carlos Rodriquez (U of California)
4. Larry Nugent (SOSC Mat Club)
5. Dan Mello (Bakersfield Express)
6. Jerald Nikodym (USMC)

149.5-lb class
1. Larry Morgan (Bakersfield Express)
2. Scott Bliss (Oregon WC)
3. Steve Morris (Viking Club)
4. Mikel Salazar (U of California)
5. Ken Williams (Tanstaafl)
6. Tony Byrne (Eagle WC)

163-lb class
1. Wade Schalles (Bakersfield, CA)
2. Mark Churella (Michigan WC)
3. Michael Taylor (Bakersfield Express)
4. Joe Tice (Bakersfield, CA)
5. Robert McDowell (Spartan WC)
6. Joe Seay (Bakersfield Express)

180.5-lb class
1. Don Shuler (Virtuous Knight WC)
2. Brady Hall (Bakersfield Express)
3. Dan Lewis (Southern California WC)
4. Marty Ryan (Oregon State U)

5. Michael Anderson (Bakersfield Express)
6. Dennis Graham (Viking WC)

198-lb class
1. Laurent Soucie (Wisconsin WC)
2. Bill Bragg (Oregon WC)
3. Greg Strobel (Corvallis, OR)
4. Mike Johnson (Bakersfield Express)
5. Gary Casey (Southern California WC)
6. Rich Calderon (Spartan WC)

220-lb class
1. Fred Bohna (Bakersfield Express)
2. Howard Harris (Oregon State U)

Heavyweight
1. Greg Gibson (Oregon WC)
2. Mike Wagner (Viking WC)
3. Chuck Pinta (Ackley, IA)
4. Chris Wright (USMC)
5. Earl Goshorn (Lake Stevens, WA)

1978
(at Hofstra University, Hempstead, NY)

Team	Points
1 New York AC	114
2. Hawkeye WC	62
3. Athletes in Action	30
4. Hofstra WC	15
5. York County AC (Maine)	6.5
6. Florida WC	2
7. East Los Angeles WC	1

Place winners

105.5-lb class
1. Rich Salamone (NYAC)
2. David Epstein (Columbia U)
3. no place
4. Kevin Honness (unat, New York)

114.5-lb class
1. Ed Knecht (Sunkist Kids)
2. Peter Morelli (NYAC)
3. Heikichi Adegawa (NYAC)
4. Michael Whitfield (AIA)

125.5-lb class
1. Joe Corso (Hawkeye WC)
2. Richard Hone (Syracuse)
3. Wayne Smith (AIA)
4. Richard Numa (unat, New Jersey)

136.5-lb class
1. Tim Cysewski (Hawkeye WC)
2. Nick Gallo (NYAC)
3. Keith Mourlam (Hawkeye WC)
4. William Racich (NYAC)

149.5-lb class
1. Brian Schmidt (NYAC)
2. Tihamer Toth-Fejel (NYAC)
3. David Foxen (NYAC)
4. Joseph Miller (NYAC)

163-lb class
1. Chuck Yagla (Hawkeye WC)
2. Jody Sloan (AIA)
3. William Keck (Hofstra U)
4. Randy Bates (NYAC)

180.5-lb class
1. Mark Lieberman (NYAC)
2. John Peterson (AIA)
3. John Raver (Ohio WC)
4. Joe Carr (unat, Kentucky)

198-lb class
1. Roy Baker (NYAC)
2. Don McCorkel (NYAC)
3. Earl Boyes (York County AC)
4. Ben Smith (unat, New York)

220-lb class
1. Walter Grote (NYAC)
2. John Sullivan (Hofstra U)
3. Steven Strellner (NYAC)
4. Vincent Paolano (unat, New York)

Heavyweight
1. John Bowlsby (Hawkeye WC)
2. Mike McCready (Hawkeye WC)
3. Ken Levels (Erie)
4. Carl Dambman (AIA)

1979
(at University of Wisconsin, Madison, WI)

Team	Points
1 Hawkeye WC	80.5
2. New York AC	75
3. Sunkist Kids	44
4. Wisconsin WC	39

Place winners

105.5-lb class
1. Bob Weaver (NYAC)
2. Bill Rosado (Sunkist Kids)
3. Rich Salamone (NYAC)
4. Tim Schultz (Northern Michigan)
5. Todd Rosenthal (MDYF)
6. Craig Hallock (Hawkeye WC)

114.5-lb class
1. Ed Knecht (Sunkist Kids)
2. Randy Willingham (unat, Oklahoma State U)
3. Tom Dursee (NYAC)
4. Pat Finlan (Wisconsin WC)
5. Jeff Hannum (Hawkeye WC)
6. Dean Quam (unat)

125.5-lb class
1. Jack Reinwand (Wisconsin WC)
2. Joe Corso (Hawkeye WC)
3. Mark Mangianti (Sunkist Kids)
4. Gene Mills (NYAC)
5. Bill DePaoli (NYAC)
6. Mark Mysnyk (Hawkeye WC)

136.5-lb class
1. Tim Cysewski (Hawkeye WC)
2. Randy Lewis (Hawkeye WC)
3. Keith Mourlam (Hawkeye WC)
4. Nick Gallo (NYAC)
5. Bob Antonacci (Cyclone WC)
6. Craig Horswill (Wisconsin WC)

149.5-lb class
1. Scott Trizzino (Hawkeye WC)
2. Andre Metzger (Oklahoma Underdogs)
3. LeeRoy Smith (Oklahoma State U)
4. Yoshi Hiranuma (NYAC)
5. Jim Farina (unat, Illinois)
6. David Foxen (NYAC)

163-lb class
1. Lee Kemp (Wisconsin WC)
2. Bruce Kinseth (Hawkeye WC)
3. Jan Sanderson (Hawkeye WC)
4. Gary Kessel (NYAC)
5. Al Pedrinan (NYAC)
6. Grant Smith (Wisconsin WC)

180.5-lb class
1. Mark Lieberman (NYAC)
2. Perry Hummel (Cyclone WC)
3. Jim Hall (Oklahoma Underdogs)
4. Lanny Davidson (Hawkeye WC)
5. Jeff Dillman (unat)
6. Ed Banach (Hawkeye WC)

198-lb class
1. Ben Peterson (Maranatha WC)
2. Mitch Hull (Wisconsin WC)
3. Dan Severn (Sunkist Kids)
4. Eric Wais (Oklahoma State U)
5. Roy Baker (NYAC)
6. Charlie Heller (NYAC)

220-lb class
1. Larry Bielenberg (Sunkist Kids)
2. Walter Grote (NYAC)
3. Mike Early (unat)
4. Doug Stein (Maranatha WC)
5. Terry St. Louis (Kazoo WC)
6. Rich Hay (AIA)

Heavyweight
1. Mike McCready (Hawkeye WC)
2. Erland van Lidth de Jeude (NYAC)
3. John Bowlsby (Hawkeye WC)
4. Jack Campbell (NYAC)
5. Dennis Kipnis (Wisconsin WC)
6. Bob Veitch (Kazoo WC)

1980
(at Hofstra University, Hempstead, NY)

Team	Points
1 New York AC	91
2. Wisconsin WC	56
3. Hawkeye WC	45

Team	Points
4. Cowboy WC	14
5. Cyclone WC	10
6. Baton Rouge WC, Sunkist Kids	8

Place winners

105.5-lb class
1. Richard Salamone (NYAC)
2. Daniel Smith (Connecticut)

114.5-lb class
1. Bob Weaver (NYAC)
2. Bill DePaoli (Pennsylvania)
3. Tom Dursee (NYAC)
4. Ronald Jones (New Jersey)
5. Pat Finlan (Wisconsin WC)
6. Paul Weideman (NYAC)

125.5-lb class
1. Jack Reinwand (Wisconsin WC)
2. Jim Haines (Wisconsin WC)
3. Mike Picozzi (Cyclone WC)
4. Tom Husted (New Jersey)
5. Mark Zimmer (Wisconsin WC)
6. Bruce Brotzman (Wisconsin WC)

136.5-lb class
1. Tim Cysewski (Hawkeye WC)
2. Ken Mallory (NYAC)
3. Keith Mourlam (Hawkeye WC)
4. Aaron Thomas (Liberty)

149.5-lb class
1. LeeRoy Smith (Cowboy WC)
2. Doug Parise (New Jersey)
3. Chuck Yagla (Hawkeye WC)
4. Dave Foxen (NYAC)
5. Gene Nighman (Cornell U)
6. Jim Lord (Cyclone WC)

163-lb class
1. Lee Kemp (Wisconsin WC)
2. Gary Kessel (NYAC)
3. Greg Sargis (Michigan)
4. Roy Lobdell (NYAC)
5. Brian Surage (New Jersey)
6. Chris Bovanovic (New Jersey)

180.5-lb class
1. Mark Lieberman (NYAC)
2. Mark Churella (Sunkist Kids)
3. Jeff Parker (Baton Rouge WC)
4. Lanny Davidson (Hawkeye WC)
5. Terry Jones (Cowboy WC)
6. John Hanrahan (NYAC)

198-lb class
1. Roy Baker (NYAC)
2. Peter Zamzow (Wisconsin WC)
3. Charlie Gadson (Cyclone WC)
4. Willie Gadson (Cyclone WC)
5. Kent Rawhouser (Wisconsin WC)
6. Eric Moll (Baton Rouge WC)

220-lb class
1. Russ Hellickson (Wisconsin WC)
2. Michael Kappel (Quebec)
3. Steve Strellner (NYAC)
4. Peter Pauline (NYAC)
5. Emad Faddoul (NYAC)
6. Terry St. Louis (Kalamazoo)

Heavyweight
1. Mike McCready (Hawkeye WC)
2. Bruce Baumgartner (NYAC)
3. Tom Burns (Hawkeye WC)
4. Kevin Lank (York County AC)

1981
(at University of Northern Iowa, Cedar Falls, IA)

Team	Points
1 Wisconsin WC	66
2. New York AC	65
3. Hawkeye WC	52
4. Cowboy WC	30

Place winners

105.5-lb class
1. Rich Salamone (NYAC), unopposed

114.5-lb class
1. Tom Dursee (NYAC)
2. Pat Finlan (Wisconsin WC)
3. Robin Morris (Wisconsin WC)
4. Ron Gutiurrez (unat)

125.5-lb class
1. Joe Corso (Hawkeye WC)
2. John Thorn (Cyclone WC)
3. Randy Willingham (Cowboy WC)

4. Barry Davis (Hawkeye WC)
5. Mark Zimmer (Oklahoma Underdogs)
6. Mark Perry (Cowboy WC)

136.5-lb class
1. Keith Mourlam (Hawkeye WC)
2. Mike Land (Cyclone WC)
3. Kenneth Mallory (NYAC)
4. Ricky Dellagatta (NYAC)
5. Ryan Kaufman (Maverick WC)
6. Paul Glynn (unat)

149.5-lb class
1. Andy Rein (Wisconsin WC)
2. Doug Parise (NYAC)
3. Kenny Monday (Cowboy WC)
4. Jim Lord (Cyclone WC)
5. Jim Martinez (Minnesota WC)
6. Mark Schmitz (Wisconsin WC)

163-lb class
1. Lee Kemp (Wisconsin WC)
2. Chuck Yagla (Hawkeye WC)
3. Roye Oliver (Maverick WC)
4. Ernie Vatch (Huskie WC)
5. Craig Wiklund (Minnesota WC)
6. John Sauerland (NYAC)

180.5-lb class
1. Rey Martinez (Cowboy WC)
2. Tom Press (Hawkeye WC)
3. Jay Llewellyn (U of Northern Iowa)
4. Terry Jones (Cowboy WC)
5. Bruce Arvold (U of Northern Iowa)
6. James Bruck (unat)

198-lb class
1. Mitch Hull (Wisconsin WC)
2. Charlie Gadson (Cyclone WC)
3. Steve Fraser (Michigan WC)
4. Colin Kilrain (NYAC)
5. Kirk Myers (U of Northern Iowa)
6. Joe Gormally (U of Northern Iowa)

220-lb class
1. Laurent Soucie (Wisconsin WC)
2. Roy Baker (NYAC)
3. Jim Latanski (Huskie WC)

Heavyweight
1. Bruce Baumgartner (NYAC)
2. Mike McCready (Hawkeye WC)
3. Jeff Grier (unat)
4. Mike Euker (Wisconsin WC)
5. Perry Kaufman (Cowboy WC)
6. Steve Wilbur (Hawkeye WC)

1982
(at University of Northern Iowa, Cedar Falls, IA)

Team	Points
1 Wisconsin WC	53
2. Hawkeye WC	42
3. New York AC	32
4. Cowboy WC	30

Place winners

105.5-lb class
1. Rich Salamone (NYAC)
2. Eric Wetzel (USMC)
3. Matt Wilkinson (Purdue WC)
4. Alan Rivera (Wildcat WC)

114.5-lb class
1. Tom Dursee (NYAC)
2. Joe Spinnazola (NYAC)
3. Mike Farina (Minnesota WC)
4. Mike Froeschle (Iowa)

125.5-lb class
1. Randy Willingham (Cowboy WC)
2. Davie Martin (Cowboy WC)
3. Pat Pickford (U of Northern Iowa)
4. Ed Giese (Minnesota)

136.5-lb class
1. Keith Mourlam (Hawkeye WC)
2. John Grassinger (Oklahoma Underdogs)
3. Dale Johnson (Cowboy WC)
4. Bob Pronk (Ontario)

149.5-lb class
1. Andy Rein (Wisconsin WC)
2. Lewis Sondgeroth (USMC)
3. Jim Lord (Cyclone WC)
4. Al Freeman (Nebraska)

163-lb class
1. Lee Kemp (Wisconsin WC)
2. Mike DeAnna (Hawkeye WC)

3. Kenny Monday (Cowboy WC)
4. Pete Galea (Wildcat WC)

180.5-lb class
1. Bruce Kinseth (Hawkeye WC)
2. Tom Press (Minnesota WC)
3. Jim Scherr (Nebraska)
4. Dennis Limmex (Wisconsin WC)

198-lb class
1. Mitch Hull (Wisconsin WC)
2. Bill Scherr (Nebraska)
3. Perry Hummell (Cyclone WC)
4. Rey Martinez (Cowboy WC)

220-lb class
1. Randy Taylor (Illinois)
2. Randy McFadden (U of Northern Iowa)
3. Gary Grundahl (Wisconsin WC)
4. Scott Donlea (South Dakota)

286-lb class
1. Gary Albright (Nebraska)
2. Dean Phinney (Hawkeye WC)
3. Jeff Grier (Wildcat WC)
4. Fred McGaver (Wisconsin WC)

1983
(at University of Wisconsin, Madison, WI)

Team	*Points*
1 Sunkist Kids	80
2. New York AC	69
3. Hawkeye WC	40
4. Wisconsin WC	21
5. Cyclone WC	18
6. U.S. Marine Corps, Team Canada	16
8. Bison WC	12
9. Wildcat WC	11
10. Cowboy WC	10

Place winners

105.5-lb class
1. Rich Salamone (NYAC)
2. Tim Vanni (Sunkist Kids)
3. Paul Wiederman (NYAC)
4. Richard Bailey (USMC)
5. James Blake (Michigan WC)
6. Brett Cook (NYAC)

114.5-lb class
1. Joe Gonzales (Sunkist Kids)
2. Charlie Heard (Sunkist Kids)
3. Tom Dursee (NYAC)
4. Michael Pilione (NYAC)
5. Ed Woodburn (Sunkist Kids)
6. Joe Spinazzola (NYAC)

125.5-lb class
1. Joe Corso (Bison WC)
2. Barry Davis (Hawkeye WC)
3. John Azevedo (Sunkist Kids)
4. Gene Mills (NYAC)
5. Randy Willingham (Cowboy WC)
6. Steve Maurey (AIA)

136.5-lb class
1. Rick Dellagatta (NYAC)
2. LeeRoy Smith (Cowboy WC)
3. Mike Land (Cyclone WC)
4. Davie Goodspeed (Wisconsin WC)
5. Ken Mallory (NYAC)
6. Larry Nugent (Sunkist Kids)

149.5-lb class
1. Bill Nugent (Sunkist Kids)
2. Doug Parise (NYAC)
3. Lennie Zalesky (Hawkeye WC)
4. Harlan Kistler (Hawkeye WC)
5. Bob Bury (NYAC)
6. Steve Babyak (UA Ohio)

163-lb class
1. Lee Kemp (Wisconsin WC)
2. Dave Schultz (Sunkist Kids)
3. Jim Zalesky (Hawkeye WC)
4. Mark Schmitz (Wisconsin WC)
5. Lindley Kistler (Hawkeye WC)
6. Dan Hartvikson (Canada)

180.5-lb class
1. Chris Campbell (Cyclone WC)
2. Jim Scherr (Sunkist Kids)
3. Jon Lundberg (AIA)
4. Dave Fitzgerald (Hawkeye WC)
5. Peter Capone (NYAC)
6. Doug Cox (Canada)

198-lb class
1. Pete Bush (Hawkeye WC)
2. Steve Fraser (Michigan WC)
3. Clark Davis (Team Canada)
4. Mitch Hull (Wisconsin WC)
5. Drew Whitfield (AIA)
6. Craig Pittman (USMC)

220-lb class
1. Greg Gibson (USMC)
2. Harold Smith (Wildcat WC)
3. Richard Deschatelets (Team Canada)
4. Dan Lewis (Sunkist Kids)
5. Wayne Brightwell (Team Canada)
6. John Daugherty (NYAC)

Heavyweight
1. Bruce Baumgartner (NYAC)
2. Jimmy Jackson (Sunkist Kids)
3. Tab Thacker (Sunkist Kids)
4. Rod Chamberlin (Wildcat WC)
5. Dave Klemm (Oklahoma Underdogs)
6. Kahlan O'Hara (Sunkist Kids)

1984
(at University of Oklahoma, Norman, OK)

Team	*Points*
1 Sunkist Kids	101
2. New York AC	73
3. Hawkeye WC	22
4. Athletes in Action	21
5. Michigan AC	18
6. Wisconsin WC	13
7. Wildcat WC	12
8. Cowboy WC	9
9. U.S. Marine Corps	4

Place winners

105.5-lb class
1. Rich Salamone (NYAC)
2. Paul Widerman (Hawkeye WC)
3. Bill Rosado (Sunkist Kids)
4. Tim Vanni (Sunkist Kids)
5. Jim Martin (unat)
6. Leroy Witherspoon (NYAC)

114.5-lb class
1. Charlie Heard (Sunkist Kids)
2. Adam Cuestas (Sunkist Kids)
3. Randy Willingham (Cowboy WC)
4. Tom Dursee (NYAC)
5. Ed Knecht (Sunkist Kids)
6. Mike Pilione (NYAC)

125.5-lb class
1. Joe Corso (NYAC)
2. John Azevedo (Sunkist Kids)
3. Joe McFarland (Michigan WC)
4. Orlando Caceres (NYAC)
5. Randy Majors (Hawkeye WC)
6. Marvin Gasner (unat)

136.5-lb class
1. Rick Dellagatta (NYAC)
2. Darryl Burley (unat)
3. Ryan Kaufman (Hawkeye WC)
4. Barry Davis (Hawkeye WC)
5. Dave Goodspeed (Wisconsin WC)
6. Dan Cuestas (AIA)

149.5-lb class
1. Andre Metzger (unat)
2. Steve Barrett (AIA)
3. Andy Rein (Wisconsin WC)
4. Harlan Kistler (Hawkeye WC)
5. Doug Parise (NYAC)
6. Al Freeman (Sunkist Kids)

163-lb class
1. Dave Schultz (Sunkist Kids)
2. Roye Oliver (Sunkist Kids)
3. Mike DeAnna (Hawkeye WC)
4. Nate Carr (Cyclone WC)
5. Rick O'Shea (Sunkist Kids)
6. Ken Sheets (NYAC)

180.5-lb class
1. Mark Schultz (Sunkist Kids)
2. Don Shuler (AIA)
3. Wayne Catan (NYAC)
4. Jim Scherr (Sunkist Kids)
5. Kevin Benson (USA Oregon)
6. Brad Anderson (Army)

198-lb class
1. Steve Fraser (Michigan WC)
2. Bill Scherr (Sunkist Kids)

3. Charlie Gadson (Cyclone WC)
4. Mitch Hull (Wisconsin WC)
5. Lou DiSerafino (Wisconsin WC)
6. Colin Kilrain (NYAC)

220-lb class
1. Harold Smith (Wildcat WC)
2. Dan Severn (Sunkist Kids)
3. John Dougherty (NYAC)
4. Craig Pittman (Cowboy WC)
5. James Phills (Hawkeye WC)
6. George Fears (USMC)

Heavyweight
1. Bruce Baumgartner (NYAC)
2. Tab Thacker (Sunkist Kids)
3. Gary Albright (Sunkist Kids)
4. Ron Carlisle (USMC)
5. Kahlan O'Hara (Sunkist Kids)
6. Matt Ghaffari (NYAC)

1985
(at Lock Haven University, Lock Haven, PA)

Team	*Points*
1 Sunkist Kids	139
2. New York AC	72
3. U.S. Marine Corps	24
4. Athletes in Action	16
5. Hawkeye WC	11
6. Edinboro WC	8
7. Wildcat WC	4
8. Adirondack Three-Style WA	2
9. Army, Air Force	1

Place winners

105.5-lb class
1. Tim Vanni (Sunkist Kids)
2. Rich Salamone (NYAC)
3. Eric Wetzel (USMC)
4. Jess Norton (Miami)
5. Dan Smith (Southington)
6. Michael Fingman (Golden Bears)

114.5-lb class
1. Jim Martin (NYAC)
2. Joe Spinazzola (NYAC)
3. Dan Buzza (Penn State WC)
4. Ed Woodburn (Sunkist Kids)
5. Stephen Bierdrycki (USMC)
6. Scott Kitchen (Air Force)

125.5-lb class
1. Charlie Heard (Sunkist Kids)
2. Kevin Darkus (Cyclone WC)
3. Anthony Amado (Sunkist Kids)
4. John Loomis (Sunkist Kids)
5. Ed Giese (AIA)
6. Darren Stevens (Sunkist Kids)

136.5-lb class
1. Darryl Burley (Lehigh WC)
2. Gary Bohay (Sunkist Kids)
3. Gene Mills (NYAC)
4. Buddy Lee (USMC)
5. Steve DePetro (Wildcat WC)
6. Larry Nugent (Sunkist Kids)

149.5-lb class
1. Bill Nugent (Sunkist Kids)
2. Lenny Zalesky (Hawkeye WC)
3. Andre Metzger (NYAC)
4. Jim Martinez (Minnesota WC)
5. Al Freeman (Wildcat WC)
6. Jesse Reyes (Sunkist Kids)

163-lb class
1. Kenny Monday (Sunkist Kids)
2. Mike DeAnna (Edinboro)
3. Murray Lee Crews (AIA)
4. Eddie Urbano (Sunkist Kids)
5. Isreal Sheppard (Sunkist Kids)
6. Jeff Cardwell (Sunkist Kids)

180.5-lb class
1. Mike Sheets (Sunkist Kids)
2. Jim Scherr (Sunkist Kids)
3. Booker Benford (Sunkist Kids)
4. Mark VanTine (Louisiana State)
5. Jon Lundberg (AIA)
6. Eric Burgel (NYAC)

198-lb class
1. Mark Schultz (Sunkist Kids)
2. Bill Scherr (Sunkist Kids)
3. Don Shuler (AIA)
4. Pete Bush (Hawkeye WC)
5. Jim Hall (NYAC)
6. Todd Paterson (Army)

220-lb class
1. Greg Gibson (USMC)
2. Dan Severn (Sunkist Kids)
3. John Dougherty (NYAC)
4. Kahlan O'Hara (Sunkist Kids)
5. Phil Lanzatella (ATWC)
6. James Johnson (Sunkist Kids)

Heavyweight
1. Bruce Baumgartner (NYAC)
2. Andy Schwab (NYAC)
3. Tom Erickson (Sunkist Kids)
4. Rick Peterson (NYAC)
5. Matt Ghaffari (Sunkist Kids)
6. Ron Carlisle (USMC)

1986
(at Las Vegas, NV)

Team	*Points*
Division I	
1. Sunkist Kids	148
2. New York AC	52
Division II	
1. Hawkeye WC	17
2. Wildcat WC, Athletes in Action	14

Place winners

105.5-lb class
1. Rich Salamone (NYAC)
2. Tim Vanni (Sunkist Kids)
3. Phil Ogan (Navy)
4. Jay Olinger (AIA)
5. Anthony Rizzo (NYAC)
6. Mitch Kimbrell (South Carolina WC)

114.5-lb class
1. Joe Gonzales (Sunkist Kids)
2. Adam Cuestas (Sunkist Kids)
3. Mike Erb (AIA)
4. Joe Spinzzola (NYAC)
5. Ed Giese (Wildcat WC)
6. Cory Baze (Sunkist Kids)

125.5-lb class
1. Kevin Darkus (Cyclone WC)
2. Barry Davis (Hawkeye WC)
3. Charlie Heard (Sunkist Kids)
4. Steve Knight (Hawkeye WC)
5. Bill Starke (NYAC)
6. Rob Calabrese (NYAC)

136.5-lb class
1. John Smith (Sunkist Kids)
2. Joe McFarland (Cliff Keen)
3. Gary Bohay (Sunkist Kids)
4. Gene Mills (NYAC)
5. John Loomis (Sunkist Kids)
6. Pete Schuyler (NYAC)

149.5-lb class
1. Andre Metzger (NYAC)
2. Andy Rein (unat, Wisconson)
3. Eddie Urbano (Sunkist Kids)
4. John Giura (unat, Wisconsin)
5. Jim Martinez (Minnesota WC)
6. Dave McKay (Team Canada)

163-lb class
1. Dave Schultz (Sunkist Kids)
2. Ken Monday (Sunkist Kids)
3. Jim Zalesky (Hawkeye WC)
4. Murray Crews (AIA)
5. Johnny Johnson (Sunkist Kids)
6. Ardeshir Asgari (Sunkist Kids)

180.5-lb class
1. Mark Schultz (Sunkist Kids)
2. Mike Sheets (Sunkist Kids)
3. Booker Benford (Sunkist Kids)
4. Chris Rinke (Team Canada)
5. Jon Lundberg (AIA)
6. Melvin Douglas (Sunkist Kids)

198-lb class
1. Jim Scherr (Wildcat WC)
2. Serge Marcil (Team Canada)
3. Dan Chaid (Sunkist Kids)
4. Douglas Perkins (Sunkist Kids)
5. Jeff Weatherman (Panther WC)
6. Mike Porcelli (NYAC)

220-lb class
1. Dan Severn (Sunkist Kids)
2. Greg Gibson (USMC)
3. Bill Scherr (Sunkist Kids)
4. James Johnson (Sunkist Kids)
5. John Dougherty (NYAC)
6. Mike Blaske (USMC)

286-lb class
1. Bruce Baumgartner (NYAC)
2. Tom Erikson (Sunkist Kids)
3. Morris Johnson (Sunkist Kids)
4. Matt Ghaffair (Sunkist Kids)
5. Bill Hyman (NYAC)
6. Mike Connors (ATWC)

1987
(at Las Vegas, NV)

Team	*Points*
Division I	
1. Sunkist Kids	84
2. New York AC	35
3. Gopher WC	11
Division II	
1. Foxcatcher	47
2. Hawkeye WC	25
3. Wildcat WC	18
4. U.S. Marine Corps	13

Place winners

105.5-lb class
1. Takashi Irie (Japan)
2. Tim Vanni (Sunkist Kids)
3. Larry Nicholson (Southern California)
4. David Range (Buckeye WC)
5. Masaru Higashino (Japan)
6. Leroy Witherspoon (unat)

114.5-lb class
1. Mitsuru Sato (Japan)
2. Joe Gonzales (Sunkist Kids)
3. Greg Robbins (Hawkeye WC)
4. Jeff Henderson (Michigan WC)
5. Jim Sanchez (unat)
6. Ed Woodburn (Sunkist Kids)

125.5-lb class
1. Barry Davis (Hawkeye WC)
2. Charlie Heard (Sunkist Kids)
3. Ken Chertow (NYAC)
4. Steve Knight (unat)
5. Karl Glover (Southern California)
6. Toshio Asakura (Japan)

136.5-lb class
1. Takum Adach (Japan)
2. Joe McFarland (Foxcatcher)
3. Steve DePetro (Wildcat WC)
4. Satoru Goitbuka (Japan)
5. Glenn Goodman (Foxcatcher)
6. John Orr (NYAC)

149.5-lb class
1. Andre Metzger (Foxcatcher)
2. John Giura (NYAC)
3. Eddie Urbano (Sunkist Kids)
4. David McKay (Burnaby)
5. Mark Manning (unat)
6. Al Freeman (Foxcatcher)

163-lb class
1. Dave Schultz (Foxcatcher)
2. Nate Carr (Sunkist Kids)
3. Kenny Monday (Sunkist Kids)
4. Jim Zalesky (Gopher WC)
5. Greg Elinsky (NYAC)
6. Murray Crews (Sunkist Kids)

180.5-lb class
1. Mark Schultz (Foxcatcher)
2. Melvin Douglas (Gopher WC)
3. Jon Lundberg (AIA)
4. Greg Okoorian (Southern California)
5. Fred Little (Sunkist Kids)
6. Lindley Kistler (Hawkeye WC)

198-lb class
1. Jim Scherr (Wildcat WC)
2. Dan Chaid (Sunkist Kids)
3. Duane Goldman (Hawkeye WC)
4. Wayne Catan (NYAC)
5. Doug Cox (Team Canada)
6. Michael Porcelli (NYAC)

220-lb class
1. Bill Scherr (Sunkist Kids)
2. Greg Gibson (USMC)
3. Wayne Cole (Sunkist Kids)
4. Bill Hyman (Foxcatcher)
5. Larock Benford (USMC)
6. Bob Kopecky (unat)

286-lb class
1. Bruce Baumgartner (NYAC)
2. Tom Erikson (Sunkist Kids)

3. Dean Hall (Edinboro)
4. Craig Pittman (USMC)
5. Andy Schwab (NYAC)
6. Javier Armengan (unat)

1988
(at Reno, NV)

Team	*Points*
Division I	
1. Sunkist Kids	138
2. New York AC	54
Division II	
1. Foxcatcher	39
2. Gopher WC	30
3. Hawkeye WC	25
4. Cyclone WC	17

Place winners

105.5-lb class
1. Tim Vanni (Sunkist Kids)
2. Rich Salamone (NYAC)
3. David Range (Buckeye WC)
4. Larry Nicholson (Foxcatcher)
5. Paul Widerman (Foxcatcher)
6. Bernard Au (Hawaii)

114.5-lb class
1. Joe Gonzales (Sunkist Kids)
2. Jack Cuvo (East Stroudsburg)
3. Paul Kriemeyer (Hawkeye WC)
4. Michael Erb (Foxcatcher)
5. Ed Woodburn (Sunkist Kids)
6. Pablo Saenz (Sunkist Kids)

125.5-lb class
1. Kevin Darkus (Cyclone WC)
2. Charlie Heard (Sunkist Kids)
3. Mitch Ostburg (Team Canada)
4. Orlando Caceres (NYAC)
5. Brad Gustafson (Sunkist Kids)
6. Ken Chertow (NYAC)

136.5-lb class
1. John Smith (Sunkist Kids)
2. Randy Lewis (Hawkeye WC)
3. Jim Jordan (Buckeye WC)
4. Paul Hughes (Team Canada)
5. Larry Nugent (Sunkist Kids)
6. Pete Schuyler (NYAC)

149.5-lb class
1. Nate Carr (Sunkist Kids)
2. John Giura (NYAC)
3. Dave McKay (Burnaby)
4. Karl Monaco (NYAC)
5. Mike Schmidlin (unat)
6. Junior Saunders (Sunkist Kids)

163-lb class
1. Kenny Monday (Sunkist Kids)
2. Jim Zalesky (Gopher WC)
3. Marty Kistler (Hawkeye WC)
4. Eddie Urbano (Sunkist Kids)
4. Murray Crews (Sunkist Kids)
6. Stewart Carter (Cyclone WC)

180.5-lb class
1. Dave Schultz (Foxcatcher)
2. Steve Klock (Navy)
3. Chris Barnes (Sunkist Kids)
4. Greg Okoorian (Foxcatcher)
5. Roye Oliver (Sunkist Kids)
6. Kevin Jackson (Cyclone WC)

198-lb class
1. Melvin Douglas (Gopher WC)
2. Mike Foy (Gopher WC)
3. Dan Chaid (Foxcatcher)
4. Jim Scherr (Wildcat WC)
5. Booker Benford (Sunkist Kids)
6. Doug Cox (Burnaby)

220-lb class
1. Bill Scherr (Sunkist Kids)
2. Dan Severn (Sunkist Kids)
3. Kirk Trost (Cliff Keen)
4. John Dougherty (NYAC)
5. Wayne Cole (Sunkist Kids)
6. Larock Benford (USMC)

286-lb class
1. Bruce Baumgartner (NYAC)
2. Tom Erikson (Sunkist Kids)
3. Jim Nielsen (unat)
4. Matt Ghaffari (Sunkist Kids)
5. Joel Greenlee (unat)
6. James Weber (NYAC)

Chapter 7

The Greco-Roman Nationals

AAU and USA Wrestling

Although Greco-Roman wrestling has its roots in ancient Greece, it was very popular in Switzerland and other Alpine countries in the 1200s. It resurfaced again in France in the mid 1800s and quickly spread to the rest of the European nations.

Greco-Roman was far more popular than freestyle in Europe, due in part to its status as a classical sport. Wrestlers from the continent felt that it was a more suitable form of wrestling than was the wide-open, catch-as-catch-can style favored by the less sophisticated Americans. They believed the ancient Greeks had disdained wrestling on the ground and were interested only in "on-the-feet" maneuvers. Because no holds below the waist are allowed in Greco-Roman, a premium is placed on upper-body strength, pummeling, and position.

In 1896 the modern Olympic era began, and Greco-Roman was the preferred style in the early Games. In fact, in 1912 it was the only style offered in the Olympics held in Sweden. Although Sweden and Finland were the dominant countries in the early part of the century, by 1950 the Soviet Union, Hungary, Turkey, and Bulgaria had moved to the forefront.

The style took a long time to gain a foothold in the United States. "After the 1920 Olympics, Bill Streit of the AAU tried to stimulate some interest in Greco-Roman and held national tournaments in 1929 and 1934 without attracting much attention," wrote Don Sayenga in *Amateur Wrestling News* in 1973. "No further participation in the Olympics was considered . . . until Greco-Roman was revived in the 1950s."

Although the AAU held its first freestyle meet in 1887, it was not until 1953 that it sanctioned a national tournament in Greco-Roman. Eight champions were crowned: Jerry Davis (114.5) of Nebraska at Omaha, Vern Whitney (125.5) of Purdue, Jerry Wilson (136.5) of Camp LeJeune, Walt Romanowski

(147.5) of Purdue, Jack Grubbs (160.5) of Missouri, Ahmet Senol (174) of Purdue, Dale Thomas (191) of Michigan State, and Bill Kerslake (heavyweight) of Cleveland.

Kerslake, who eventually became an aerospace research engineer at the National Aeronautics and Space Administration (NASA), captured seven straight titles at heavyweight. Wayne Baughman of the Air Force surpassed that number eventually, winning eight AAU Greco-Roman national titles.

The USA Wrestling National Tournament, earlier known as the USWF tournament, began in 1969. Its first winners were Mike Kaye (105.5), Chuck Rossetti (114.5), and Bob Birnberg (125.5), all of Illinois; Noriaki Kiguchi (136.5) of Japan; Larry Owings (149.5) of Washington; John Klein (180.5) of California; and Sam Parker (163), Johnny Johnson (198), Roy Worthington (220), and Bob Billberg (heavyweight), all of the Mayor Daley Youth Foundation club of Chicago.

Wayne Baughman added a USA Wrestling national title in 1972 to his eight AAU titles for a total of nine. But the man with the most Greco-Roman national titles by 1988 was Willie Williams. The former Illinois State University star grabbed 4 AAU and 7 USA Wrestling championships for a total of 11 Greco-Roman national championships, all at 198 pounds.

Another great Greco-Roman specialist was Dan Chandler. The former University of Minnesota star won five AAU titles and five USA Wrestling titles (mostly at 180.5). He also represented the United States in three Olympics and won the gold medal at the 1975 and the 1979 Pan-American Games.

Men like Dean Rockwell in Michigan and Joseph Scalzo in Ohio were pioneers in the development of Greco-Roman, and college stars like Baughman (Oklahoma) lent great prestige to the sport when they began winning national Greco-Roman titles. But Greco-Roman received its largest boost from former collegiate stars Steve Fraser (Michigan) and Jeff Blatnick (Springfield) when both won gold medals in the 1984 Olympics in Los Angeles. In 1985, Mike Houck became the first American to win a world title in Greco-Roman.

It was estimated that by 1988 there were only 200 serious practitioners of Greco-Roman wrestling in the United States, compared to 400,000 in the Soviet Union. The U.S. pockets of strength were basically in three areas: Albany, New York; Minneapolis, Minnesota; and the armed services.

The roots of Greco-Roman are buried deep in the Minnesota soil. "In recent years there has been a trend toward specialization in Greco-Roman wrestling, and those interested in the promotion of this style have seen much improvement in our national quality that they [hope] will result in improving our representation in international competition," wrote Jess Hoke in the May 21, 1977, edition of *Amateur Wrestling News*. "The Minnesota Wrestling Club has been the dominant force in this upgrading of Greco-Roman wrestling. Under Alan Rice, a former collegiate star at the University of Minnesota and a member of the first G-R Olympic team in 1956, the club has produced more international Greco-Roman wrestlers than the rest of the na-

Mike Houck, the only world Greco-Roman champion in U.S. history. (Courtesy of National Wrestling Hall of Fame)

tion combined. They have just won the national AAU Greco-Roman championship for the 9th time in 11 years."

In the late 1960s and early 1970s, the Hazewinkel twins, Dave and James, brought recognition to the sport with their accomplishments. The Minnesota Wrestling Club continued to flourish into the 1980s, giving rise to stars like Dan Chandler, Brad Rheingans, James Martinez, and the Koslowski brothers, Dennis and Duane.

The sport received a considerable boost in the 1980s with the arrival of Pavel Katsen to the United States. Katsen was born and raised in the Soviet Union and competed in Greco-Roman for many years in the Soviet system. He emigrated to the United States in 1979 and began coaching American teams. His influence on the American Greco-Roman scene was immense. He was an assistant coach for the 1984 Olympics and head coach for the 1988 Games in Seoul. "I owe a lot of my success to Pavel," Fraser told the author 4 years after winning his gold medal in 1984. "He made me a believer. Working with him, I began to see the way to success. Hc is a great motivator and a great organizer."

In a 4-year span between 1981 and 1985, the United States climbed from 18th to 6th in the world tournament. Clearly, Greco-Roman was making progress on all fronts, ranging from performance to publicity. Credit was due to the impact of clubs like the Minnesota Wrestling Club, to coaches like Katsen, and to wrestlers like Fraser.

For an overview of the history of U.S. Greco-Roman national champions, see Tables 7.1 and 7.2.

Table 7.1
AAU Greco-Roman National Championships (1953-1982)

Name	Class
1953	
Jerry Davis (Omaha YMCA)	114.5
Vern Whitney (Purdue U)	125.5
Jerry Wilson (Camp LeJeune)	136.5
Walter Romanowski (Purdue U)	147.5
Jack Grubbs (Ritenour YMCA, MO)	160.5
Ahmet Senol (Purdue U)	174
Dale Thomas (Michigan State College)	191
Bill Kerslake (Case Tech, Cleveland)	Heavyweight
1954	
Richard Delgado (11th Naval District)	114.5
Lee Allen (Multnomah AC)	125.5
Safi Taha (Ford Recreation Club, Dearborn, MI)	136.5
Normal Gill (Michigan State C)	147.5
Jay Holt (SF Rowing Club)	160.5
James Connor (SF Olympic Club)	174
Dale Thomas (unat, Michigan)	191
William Kerslake (Chase AC, Cleveland)	Heavyweight
1955	
Katsuhoshi Akayama (Japan Wrestling Federation)	114.5
Epsuma Imada (Japan)	125.5
Tadashi Mumajiu (Japan)	136.5
Newton Copple (NYAC)	147.5
Henrick Hansen (McBurney YMCA)	160.5
Jim Peckham (Boston, YMCA)	174
Bob Steckle (Canada)	191
William Kerslake (unat, Cleveland)	Heavyweight
1956	
Ray Osborne (SF Olympic Club)	114.5
Jack Blubaugh (Tulsa YMCA)	125.5
Allan Rice (NYAC)	136.5
Jerry Maurey (Sooner AC)	147.5
Khalil Taha (Ford WC)	160.5
Dan Hodge (Sooner AC)	174
Ken Maidlow (Michigan State U)	191
Bill Kerslake (Case AC, Cleveland)	Heavyweight

Name	Class
1957	
Richard Wilson (Toledo U)	114.5
Lee Allen (Multnomah AC)	125.5
Tom Hall (3rd Army)	136.5
Frank Szecsi (Ford Wrestling Center)	147.5
Khalil Taha (Ford Wrestling Center)	160.5
Barry Billington (UCLA)	174
Robert Steckle (Kitchener YMCA)	191
Bill Kerslake (unat, Cleveland)	Heavyweight
1958	
Richard Wilson (unat, Ohio Association)	114.5
Jerry Wager (unat, Ohio Association)	125.5
Nabora Ikedo (Chuo Japan)	136.5
Bud Betz (USMC)	147.5
Frank Fejes (SF Olympic Club)	160.5
Zselt Csiba (unat, Portland OR)	174
Frank Rosenmayr (SF Olympic Club)	191
Bill Kerslake (unat, Cleveland)	Heavyweight
1959	
Dick Wilson (unat, Ohio Association)	114.5
Masaaki Hatta (Cowboy AC)	125.5
Eisuke Kitamura (Kansai U, Japan)	136.5
Ben Northrup (SF Olympic Club)	147.5
Fred Boger (Irving Park, Chicago)	160.5
Julius Beno (SF Olympic Club)	174
Adnan Kaisy (SF Olympic Club)	191
Bill Kerslake (unat, Cleveland)	Heavyweight
1960	
Gilbert Sanchez (Takedown Club, Lamar, CO)	114.5
Lynn Griffith (unat, Lamar, CO)	125.5
Lee Allen (Multnomah AC)	136.5
Larry Wright (unat, Oregon Association)	147.5
Joe Vastag (SF Olympic Club)	160.5
Russ Camilleri (U.S. Air Force)	174
Frank Rosenmayr (SF Olympic Club)	191
Hallow Wilson (Navy, HI)	Heavyweight
1961	
Dick Wilson (Toledo U)	114.5
Joe Gomes (SF Olympic Club)	125.5
Lee Allen (Multnomah (AC)	136.5
Fred Boger (Chicago Y)	147.5

Name	Class
Julius Beno (SF Olympic Club)	160.5
Russ Camilleri (SF Olympic Club)	174
Zoltan Pentek (NYAC)	191
Pat Lovell (SF Olympic Club)	Heavyweight
1962	
Sakurama Koji (Tokyo Club, Japan)	114.5
Masamitsu Ichiguichi (Tokyo Club, Japan)	125.5
Nobuyuki Motokawa (Simi HS, CA)	138.5
Toshivoki Sawauchi (Tokyo Club, Japan)	154
Rudy Williams (Taha Grapplers)	171.5
Ron Lewis (Navy, HI)	191.5
Dan Brand (SF Olympic Club)	213.5
Hallow Wilson (Navy, HI)	Heavyweight
1963	
Hiroka Aoki (NYAC)	114.5
Masaki Kiosomi (Japan)	125.5
Ron Finley (unat)	138.5
Yasuo Horikawa (Japan)	154
Bruce Glenn (unat)	171.5
Wayne Baughman (Oklahoma AC)	191.5
Dan Brand (SF Olympic Club)	213.5
Gary Stensland (Multnomah AC)	Heavyweight
1964	
Horoaki Aoki (NYAC)	114.5
Takao Ikeucai (Japan)	125.5
Sam Boone (Long Island Grapplers)	138.5
Ben Northrup (SF Olympic Club)	154
Rudy Williams (Taha AC)	171.5
Russ Camilleri (SF Olympic Club)	191.5
Dan Brand (SF Olympic Club)	213.5
Jim Raschke (NYAC)	Heavyweight
1965	
Rich Henjyoji (Multanomah AC)	114.5
Clem Crow (NYAC)	125.5
Chikara Murano (NYAC)	138.5
Bob Douglas (Oklahoma State U)	154
Russ Camilleri (SF Olympic Club)	171.5
Wayne Baughman (Air Force)	191.5
Art Makinster (Oregon State U)	213.5
Gary Stensland (Multnomah AC)	Heavyweight

Name	Class
1966	
Masashi Ryoba (Japan)	114.5
Jim Hazewinkel (St. Cloud State U)	125.5
Mac Motokawa (Brigham Young U)	138.5
Bob Douglas (Mayor Daley YF)	154
Russ Camilleri (SF Olympic Club)	171.5
Rudy Williams (Michigan WC)	191.5
Jerry Conine (Multnomah AC)	213.5
Larry Kristoff (Mayor Daley YF)	Heavyweight
1967	
Dave Hazewinkel (Minnesota)	114.5
Tomino Michio (NYAC)	125.5
Charles Coffee (Minnesota)	138.5
Ben Northrup (SF Olympic Club)	154
Rudy Williams (Michigan WC)	171.5
Wayne Baughman (U.S. Air Force)	191.5
Gary Stensland (Multnomah AC)	213.5
Larry Kristoff (Mayor Daley YF)	Heavyweight
1968	
Arthur Chavez (SF Olympic Club)	114.5
I. Yamamoto (Japan)	125.5
James Hazewinkel (Minnesota)	138.5
Fred Lett (Minnesota)	154
Larry Lyden (Minnesota)	171.5
Wayne Baughman (U.S. Air Force)	191.5
Jess Lewis (Oregon State U)	213.5
Bob Johnson (Minnesota)	Heavyweight
1969	
Billy Davids (Michigan WC)	105
Yasuo Katsumura (NAC)	114.5
Dave Hazewinkel (Army)	125.5
Jim Hazewinkel (Army)	136.5
Kenshiro Natsunami (NYAC)	149.5
James Tanniehill (Minnesota WC)	163.0
Rudy Williams (Michigan WC)	180.5
Wayne Baughman (Air Force)	198.0
Robert Roop (Mayor Daley YF)	220.0
Larry Kristoff (Mayor Daley YF)	Heavyweight

Name	Class
1970	
Stanley Opp (South Dakota)	105
Dale Kestel (Michigan WC)	114.5
Dave Hazewinkel (Minnesota)	125.5
Yasuo Ishii (Japan)	
Masao Hatlori (NYAC)	136.5
Phil Frey (Army)	149.5
Larry Lyden (MAWA)	163.0
Rudy Williams (Cleveland)	180.5
Wayne Baughman (U.S. Air Force)	198.0
Jim Duschen (Mayor Daley YF)	220.0
Chris Taylor (Muskegon WC)	Heavyweight
1971	
Karoly Kancsar (Nebraska)	105
Enrique Jimenez (Mexico)	114.5
Dave Hazewinkel (Minnesota WC)	125.5
Jim Hazewinkel (Minnesota WC)	136.5
Phil Frey (Army)	149.5
Larry Lyden (Minnesota WC)	163.0
Khosrow Vazin (Minnesota WC)	180.5
Wayne Baughman (U.S. Air Force)	198.0
Hank Schenk (Multnomah AC)	220.0
Jeff Smith (Michigan)	Heavyweight
1972	
Karoly Kancsar (Nebraska)	105
Mike Thomson (USMC)	114.5
Dave Hazewinkel (Army)	125.5
Gary Alexander (Minnesota)	136.5
Phil Frey (Oregon)	149.5
Larry Lyden (Minnesota)	163.0
Jay Robinson (Army)	180.5
Wayne Baughman (U.S. Air Force)	198.0
Henk Schenk (Multnomah AC)	220
Greg Wojciechowski (Ohio)	Heavyweight
1973	
Karoly Kancsar (Nebraska)	105
Bruce Thompson (Minnesota)	114.5
Joe Sade (Oregon)	125.5
Gary Alexander (Minnesota)	136.5

Name	Class
Phil Frey (Oregon)	149.5
Mike Jones (Oregon)	163.0
James Tanniehill (Army)	180.5
Willie Williams (Mayor Daley YF)	198.0
Greg Wojciechowski (Ohio)	220.0
Mack McCrady (California)	Heavyweight
1974	
Karoly Kancsar (Minnesota)	105.5
Bruce Thompson (unat)	114.5
Susumo Hagihare (Oregon)	125.5
Gary Alexander (Minnesota WC)	136.5
Pat Marcy (Minnesota WC)	149.5
Abdul Tanniehill (Army)	163.0
Larry Lyden (Minnesota)	180.5
Willie Williams (Mayor Daley YF)	198
Greg Wojciechowski (Ohio)	220
Mike McCready (AIA)	Heavyweight
1975	
Karoly Kancsar (California)	105.5
Bruce Thompson (Minnesota WC)	114.5
Brian Gust (Minnesota WC)	125.5
Gary Alexander (Minnesota WC)	136.5
Lloyd Keaser (USMC)	149.5
Abdul Raheem Ali (U.S.Army)	163.0
Dan Chandler (Minnesota WC)	180.5
Willie Williams (Mayor Daley YF)	198
Henk Schenk (Multnomah AC)	220
Mike McCready (Hawkeye WC)	Heavyweight
1976	
Karoly Kancsar (California)	105
Chris Sones (Hawkeye WC)	114.5
Bruce Thompson (Minnesota WC)	125.5
Hachiro Oishi (NYAC)	136.5
Larry Morgan (Hawkeye WC)	149.5
John Matthews (Michigan)	163.0
Dan Chandler (Minnesota WC)	180.5
Willie Williams (Mayor Daley YF)	198.0
Brad Rheingans (Minnesota WC)	220.0
Mike McCready (Hawkeye WC)	Heavyweight

Name	Class
1977	
James Howard (USMC)	105.5
Enrique Jiminez (Mexico)	114.5
Brian Gust (Minnesota)	125.5
Hashiro Oishi (unat)	136.5
Dave Schultz (San Francisco)	149.5
Abdul Raheem Ali (Minnesota WC)	163
Dan Chandler (Minnesota WC)	180.5
Bill Bragg (Oregon WC)	198
Brad Rheingans (Minnesota WC)	220
Bob Walker (AIA)	Heavyweight
1978	
Wilfredo Leiva (USMC)	105.5
James Howard (USMC)	114.5
Bruce Thompson (Minnesota WC)	125.5
Abdurrahim Kuzu (Nebraska)	136.5
Abdul Raheem Ali (Minnesota WC)	149.5
John Matthews (Michigan WC)	163
Dan Chandler (Minneapolis)	180.5
Frank Anderson (Sweden)	198
Brad Rheingans (Minnesota WC)	220
Greg Wojciechowski (Toledo Area WC)	Heavyweight
1979	
Greg Williams (San Francisco)	105.5
Ray Pavia (U.S. Air Force)	114.5
Bruce Thompson (Minnesota)	125.5
Hachiro Oishi (NYAC)	136.5
Abdul Raheem Ali (Minnesota WC)	149.5
John Matthews (Michigan WC)	163
Dan Chandler (Minneapolis)	180.5
Frank Anderson (Sweden)	198
Brad Rheingans (Minnesota WC)	220
Greg Wojciechowski (Toledo Area WC)	Heavyweight
1980	
Mark Fuller (SF Peninsula Grapplers)	105.5
John Hartupee (Michigan WC)	114.5
Bruce Thompson (Land of Lakes, MN)	125.5
Abdurrahim Kuzu (NAC, Nebraska)	136.5
Doug Yeats (Canada)	149.5
John Matthews (Michigan WC)	163

Name	Class
Louis Santerre (Canada)	180.5
Laurent Soucie (Wisconsin WC)	198
Brad Rheingans (Minnesota WC)	220
Jeff Blatnick (Adirondack Three-Style WA)	Heavyweight
1981	
T.J. Jones (Navy)	105.5
Mark Fuller (Little C AC)	114.5
Dan Mello (USMC)	125.5
Frank Famiano (ATWA)	136.5
Doug Yeats (Canada)	149.5
John Matthews (Michigan WC)	163
Tom Press (Minnesota WC)	180.5
Steve Fraser (Michigan WC)	198
Greg Gibson (USMC)	220
Pete Lee (Grand Rapids)	Heavyweight
1982	
T.J. Jones (U.S. Navy)	105.5
Wilfredo Leivia (USMC)	114.5
Dan Mello (USMC)	125.5
Abdurrahim Kuzu (Nebraska OC)	136.5
Doug Yeats (Canada)	149.5
David Schultz (Oklahoma Underdogs)	163
Dan Chandler (Twin City)	180.5
Mike Houck (Minnesota WC)	198
Jeff Blatnick (ATWA)	220
Ron Carlisle (USMC)	Heavyweight

Table 7.2

Greco-Roman National Championships
USA Wrestling (1969-1988)

1969
(at Evanston, IL)

Team	Points
1. Mayor Daley Youth Foundation	47
2. Illinois WC	17
3. University of Washington	10
4. University of Iowa, Illinois State University	7
6. Northwestern University	4

Champions

105.5-lb class
Mike Kaye (unat)

114.5-lb class
Chuck Rosetti (Illinois WC)

125.5-lb class
Bob Birnberg (unat)

136.5-lb class
Noriaki Kiguchi (Japan)

149.5-lb class
Larry Owings (U of Washington)

163-lb class
Sam Parker (MDYF)

180.5-lb class
John Klein (unat)

198-lb class
Johnny Johnson (MDYF)

220-lb class
Roy Worthington (MDYF)

Heavyweight
Bob Billberg (MDYF)

1970
(at Fullerton, CA)

Team	*Points*
1. Southland WC	65
2. Cerritos WC	24
3. Bakersfield WC	21
4. Riverside WC	14

Place winners

105.5-lb class
1. Kancsar (Southland WC)
2. Pivac (Southland WC)
3. Bright (Cerritos WC)

114.5-lb class
1. Montellano (Mexico City Polytech)
2. Gonzales (Tri Lg. WC)
3. Zorich (LACC)

125.5-lb class
1. Eli (SFPG)
2. Howard (Riverside WC)
3. Raikes (Sugarfoot WC)

136.5-lb class
1. Nerio (Southland WC)
2. Rodriguez (Riverside WC)
3. Watanabe (Southland WC)
4. Cortez (Mexico City)

149.5-lb class
1. Seay (Bakersfield WC)
2. Frazier (SF Peninsula Grapplers)
3. Manley (Southland WC)
4. Ruz (Southland WC)

163-lb class
1. West (U of Oregon)
2. Sherman (SF State)
3. Cunningham (Southland WC)
4. Likens (SF Peninsula Grapplers)

180.5-lb class
1. Sipe (Newport)
2. Anderson (AIA)
3. West (Cerritos WC)
4. Miller (Cerritos WC)

198-lb class
1. Wright (Southland WC)
2. Hargrave (Southland WC)
3. Ohai (Cerritos WC)
4. Newcomb (SF Peninsula Grapplers)

220-lb class
1. Winer (SFOC)
2. Mills (Southland WC)
3. Johnson (Fullerton JC)
4. Schramm (California Tech)

Heavyweight
1. Smith (Cerritos WC)
2. Wright (Treasure Valley WC)
3. Moyer (Phoenix Wristlock)
4. Johnson (California Tech)

1971
(at Eugene, OR)

Team

1. Mayor Daley Youth Foundation
2. Minnesota WC

(Team scores not available)

Place winners

105.5-lb class
1. Maas (West Germany)
2. Karoly (unat)
3. Geller (MDYF)

114.5-lb class
1. Huber (West Germany)
2. Nagao (Japan)
3. Takahashi (Japan)

125.5-lb class
1. Hazewinkel (Minnesota WC)
2. Iokumi (Japan)
3. Kida (U.S. International)

136.5-lb class
1. Hazewinkel (Minnesota WC)
2. Fox (MDYF)
3. Little (Bakersfield WC)

149.5-lb class
1. Schoendorfer (West Germany)
2. Pond (Oregon State U)
3. Frey (U.S. Army)

163-lb class
1. Schroeter (West Germany)
2. Seay (Bakersfield WC)
3. Likens (Penn Grapplers)

180.5-lb class
1. Sipe (unat)
2. West (unat)
3. Crumley (Oregon State U)

198-lb class
1. Williams (MDYF)
2. Yoshida (Japan)
3. Haghi (Iran)

220-lb class
1. Hellickson (MDYF)
2. Stioham (unat)
3. Stapleton (Oregon)

Heavyweight
1. Kopitar (California Poly)
2. Schwarz (West Germany)
3. Dulaney (Southern Oregon State U)

1972
(at Eugene, OR)

Team	*Points*
1. Mayor Daley Youth Foundation	82
2. Armed Forces	53
3. University of Oregon	34
4. Minnesota WC	25
5. San Francisco Olympic Club	21
6. Oregon State University	15
7. International WC, Mexico	13
9. Multnomah AC	12
10. Bakersfield WC	9

Place winners

105.5-lb class
1. Cliffe (MDYF), unopposed

114.5 class
1. Jiminez (Mexico)
2. Thompson (Air Force)
3. Gellar (MDYF)
4. Goward (International WC)
5. Cliffe (MDYF)
6. Olvero (Mexico)

125.5-lb class
1. Parker (MDYF)
2. Scott (Air Force)
3. Melchior (Air Force)
4. Keady (unat)

5. Dickson (Oregon State U)
6. Steiger (International WC)

136.5-lb class
1. Hazewinkel (Minnesota WC)
2. Shoji (U of Oregon)
3. Mello (Portland WC)
4. Williams (U of Oregon)
5. Oilar (U of Oregon)
6. Moore (Capital City Mat)

149.5-lb class
1. Hazewinkel (Minnesota WC)
2. Buzzard (MDYF)
3. Asuma (International WC)
4. Smith (Oregon City)
5. Tanniehill (Air Force)
6. Alexander (Minnesota WC)

163-lb class
1. Jones (Oregon State U)
2. Seay (Bakersfield WC)
3. Owings (Washington WC)
4. Grahn (Portland WC)
5. Hatch (Air Force)
6. Bugajski (MDYF)

180.5-lb class
1. Camilleri (SFOC)
2. Halsey (Air Force)
3. Strellner (MDYF)
4. Combs (MDYF)
5. Bugajski (Air Force)
6. Sipe (Washington WC)

198-lb class
1. Baughman (Air Force)
2. Harlow (MDYF)
3. Williams (MDYF)
4. Hines (U of Oregon)
5. Bledsoe (Portland WC)
6. Strobel (Oregon State U)

220-lb class
1. Schenk (Multnomah)
2. Deadrich (SFOC)
3. Winter (Air Force)
4. Duschen (MDYF)
5. Dove (International WC)

Heavyweight
1. Strobel (U of Oregon)
2. Galler (MDYF)
3. Jones (unat)

1973
(at Lansing, MI)

Team	Points
1. Mayor Daley Youth Foundation	63
2. Athletes in Action	40
3. Michigan WC	33.5
4. CDOM Mexico	24
5. Rhino WC	17.5
6. Wolfpack WC	14
7. Army, New York AC	13
8. U.S. Marine Corps	11

Place winners

105.5-lb class
1. Olvera (CDOM Mexico)
2. Cliffe (MDYF)
3. Wolf (Michigan WC)

114.5-lb class
1. Jimenez (CDOM Mexico)
2. Zorick (unat)
3. Weir (unat)

125.5-lb class
1. Sones (unat)
2. Gust (Wolfpack WC)
3. Turner (MDYF)
4. Schuler (USMC)

136.5-lb class
1. Lamphere (AIA)
2. Fox (MDYF)
3. Davids (unat)
4. Alexander (Wolfpack WC)

149.5-lb class
1. Minkel (Michigan WC)
2. Willer (Rhino WC)
3. Keaser (USMC)
4. Palcl (Wolfpack WC)

163-lb class
1. Tanniehill (Army)
2. Martin (MDYF)
3. Kocher (MDYF)
4. Hulburt (Michigan WC)

180.5-lb class
1. Robinson (NYAC)
2. Anderson (AIA)
3. Bradley (Michigan WC)
4. Strellner (MDYF)

198-lb class
1. Williams (MDYF)
2. Chastain (unat)
3. Stapleton (unat)
4. Quinn (Michigan WC)

220-lb class
1. Duschen (MDYF)
2. Carollo (AIA)
3. Carlson (unat)
4. Souheaver (unat)

Heavyweight
1. McCready (AIA)
2. Major (Rhino WC)
3. Rivera (unat)

1974
(at Ypsilanti, MI)

Team	Points
1. Twin Cities WC	74
2. Mayor Daley Youth Foundation	61.5
3. Rhino WC	44
4. Army	37
5. Michigan WC, Athletes in Action	22

Place winners

1. Cliffe (MDYF), unopposed

114.5-lb class
1. Singleton (Rhino WC)
2. Cliffe (MDYF)
3. Thompson (Twin Cities WC)

125.5-lb class
1. Gust (Twin Cities WC)
2. Clardy (Twin Cities WC)
3. Szymula (unat)

136.5-lb class
1. Alexander (Twin Cities WC)
2. Oishi (Tampa WC)
3. Lamphere (AIA)

149.5-lb class
1. Marcy (Twin Cities WC)
2. Pelcl (Twin Cities WC)
3. Willer (Rhino WC)

163-lb class
1. Tanniehill (Army)
2. Chandler (Twin Cities WC)
3. Mathews (Michigan WC)

180.5-lb class
1. Bradley (Rhino WC)
2. Zindel (Michigan WC)
3. Grunseth (Army)

198-lb class
1. Williams (MDYF)
2. Strellner (MDYF)
3. Curby (Rhino WC)

220-lb class
1. Levels (Hiram College)
2. Winter (Army)
3. Halbert (Twin Cities WC)

Heavyweight
1. McCready (AIA)
2. Major (Rhino WC)
3. Baker (Southwestern Michigan)

1975
(at Iowa City, IA)

Team	Points
1. Minnesota WC	57.33
2. Hawkeye WC	35
3. Mayor Daley Youth Foundation, Michigan WC	30
4. Michigan WC	30
5. Armed Forces	20
6. Tampa Bay WC	12
7. Wisconsin WC, New York AC	6

Place winners

105.5-lb class
1. Goldsmith (Illinois)
2. N.Z. Bryant Jr. (Michigan WC)
3. Sams (U of Washington)
4. DePaoli (Pennsylvania WC)

114.5-lb class
1. Learned (Colorado)
2. Velez (Colorado)
3. J. Bryant (Michigan WC)
4. Zorick (Los Angeles)

125.5-lb class
1. Gust (Minnesota WC)
2. Yamagata (San Juan WC)
3. Frakes (unat)
4. Shaw (unat)

136.5-lb class
1. Oishi (Tampa Bay WC)
2. Alexander (Minnesota WC)
3. Cyscwski (Hawkeye WC)
4. Davids (Rhino WC)
5. Sherman (unat)
6. Brooks (unat)

149.5-lb class
1. Marcy (Minnesota WC)
2. Willer (Rhino WC)
3. Smith (Hawkeye WC)
4. Morris (MDYF)
5. Stuebing (Oregon WC)
6. Patterson (unat)

163-lb class
1. Ali (Armed Forces)
2. Matthews (Michigan WC)
3. Pelcl (Minnesota WC)
4. Yagla (Hawkeye WC)
5. Dalton (Colorado Olympic WA)
6. Breedlove (Hawkeye WC)

180.5-lb class
1. Chandler (Minnesota WC)
2. Bradley (Michigan WC)
3. Soucie (Wisconsin WC)
4. Holm (Hawkeye WC)
5. Wells (Hawkeye WC)
6. Miller (Minnesota WC)

198-lb class
1. Williams (MDYF)
2. Bohna (unat)
3. Strellner (NYAC)
4. Kearns (unat)
5. Coon (unat)

220-lb class
1. Galler (MDYF)
2. Linn (Armed Forces)
3. Miller (Minnesota WC)
4. Palm (unat)
5. Young (unat)

Heavyweight
1. McCready (Hawkeye WC)
2. Jackson (Michigan WC)
3. Van Lidth De Jeude (MIT)
4. Stewart (MDYF)
5. Witzleb (Hawkeye WC)
6. (tie) Davidson (unat), Sowers (Minnesota WC), Potts (unat)

1976
(at St. Louis, MO)

Team	*Points*
1. Mayor Daley Youth Foundation	63.50
2. Hawkeye WC	30
3. Minnesota WC	24.33
4. Michigan WC	23
5. Army	22.33
6. San Francisco Peninsula Grapplers	16
7. U.S. Marine Corps	14
8. New York AC	12
9. Ohio WC	8
10. Tampa Bay WC	3
11. Air Force	2
12. Blue Springs WC	1

Place winners

114.5-lb class
1. Kelly (unat)
2. Whelan (unat)
3. Whelan (unat)
4. Bryant Jr. (Michigan WC)

125.5-lb class
1. Sones (Hawkeye WC)
2. Clardy (Minnesota WC)
3. Schuler (USMC)
4. Ancona (MDYF)

136.5-lb class
1. Oishi (NYAC)
2. Turner (MDYF)

3. Miller (MDYF)
4. McArdle (Army)

149.5-lb class
1. Morgan (Hawkeye WC)
2. Keaser (USMC)
3. Horpel (SFPG)
4. Kenworthy (unat)

163-lb class
1. Matthews (Michigan WC)
2. Pelcl (Minnesota WC)
3. Andre (Minnesota WC)
4. Johnson (MDYF)

180.5-lb class
1. Ali (Army)
2. Bradley (Michigan WC)
3. Stumpf (MDYF)
4. Hines (MDYF)

198-lb class
1. Williams (MDYF)
2. Calderon (SFPG)
3. Silver (unat)
4. Alday (Tampa Bay WC)

220-lb class
1. Galler (MDYF)
2. Levels (Ohio WC)
3. Winter (Army)
4. Gangware (unat)

Heavyweight
1. Jackson (unat)
2. Lee (MDYF)
3. McCready (Hawkeye WC)
4. Geris (unat)

1977
(at Iowa City, IA)

Team	*Points*
1. Minnesota WC	92
2. Michigan WC	51.5
3. Mayor Daley Youth Foundation	39
4. Hawkeye WC	20
5. Wisconsin WC, Bakersfield Express	8

Place winners

105.5-lb class
1. Cliffe (MDYF)
2. Bryant (Michigan WC)
3. Horton (North Carolina)

114.5-lb class
1. Whelan (Gateway WC)
2. Lockwood (California)
3. Smith (Illinois)

125.5-lb class
1. Clardy (Minnesota WC)
2. Shaw (Minnesota WC)
3. Causey (MDYF)

136.5-lb class
1. Gust (Minnesota WC)
2. Meilo (Bakersfield Express)
3. Kuzy (Nebraska)

149.5-lb class
1. Marcy (Minnesota WC)
2. Wells (Michigan WC)
3. Hughes (Minnesota WC)

163-lb class
1. Matthews (Minnesota WC)
2. Pelcl (Minnesota WC)
3. Yagla (Hawkeye WC)

180.5-lb class
1. Chandler (Minnesota WC)
2. Noon (Army)
3. Plautz (Erie CC)

198-lb class
1. Williams (MDYF)
2. Soucie (Wisconsin WC)
3. Chastain (Michigan WC)

220-lb class
1. Rheingans (Minnesota WC)
2. McCready (Hawkeye WC)
3. Galler (MDYF)

Heavyweight
1. Lee (Michigan WC)
2. Levels (Pennsylvania)
3. Bowlsby (Hawkeye WC)

1978
(at Iowa City, IA)

Team	*Points*
1. Mayor Daley Youth Foundation	89
2. Hawkeye WC	36
3. Michigan WC	35
4. Minnesota WC	17
5. Atlanta Takedown Club, York County (ME)	12

Place winners

105.5-lb class
1. Rosenthal (MDYF)
2. Fair (unat)
3. Powers (unat)

114.5-lb class
1. Blackman (MDYF)
2. Cliffe (MDYF)
3. Zorick (unat)
4. Jones (MDYF)

125.5-lb class
1. Thompson (Minnesota WC)
2. McNelis (unat)
3. Owens (Michigan WC)
4. Hatchett (unat)

136.5-lb class
1. Gust (Minnesota WC)
2. Turner (MDYF)
3. Souris (Atlanta TC)
4. Miller (MDYF)

149.5-lb class
1. Eon (York County AC)
2. Mallory (unat)
3. Bland (MDYF)
4. Jordan (Minnesota WC)

163-lb class
1. Yagla (Hawkeye WC)
2. Sherman (unat)
3. Stensgard (unat)
4. Omer (Michigan WC)

198-lb class
1. Williams (MDYF)
2. Longmire (MDYF)
3. Harlan (Michigan WC)
4. Kirkwood (Patriot AC)

220-lb class
1. Stevens (Hawkeye WC)
2. Daniels (MDYF)
3. Simpson (unat)
4. Nelson (Minnesota AAU)

Heavyweight
1. Bowlsby (Hawkeye WC)
2. Lee (Michigan WC)
3. Jeffries (Atlanta TC)

1979
(at Blaine, MN)

Team	*Points*
1. Haddad WC	78
2. Michigan WC	63
3. Mayor Daley Youth Foundation	37
4. Terre Haute WC	27
5. Hawkeye WC	25
6. U.S. Marine Corps	12

Place winners

105.5-lb class
1. Boden (Michigan WC)
2. Rosenthal (MDYF)

114.5-lb class
1. Steiner (MDYF)
2. Wimberley (Florida)
3. Gutierrez (Twin Cities WC)

125.5-lb class
1. Thompson (Haddad WC)
2. Clardy (Terre Haute WC)
3. Hartupee (Michigan WC)

136.5-lb class
1. Gust (Haddad WC)
2. Turner (MDYF)
3. Angerillo (Minnesota WC)

149.5-lb class
1. Minkel (Michigan WC)
2. Ali (Terre Haute WC)
3. Jordan (Haddad WC)

163-lb class
1. Andre (Haddad WC)
2. Matthews (Michigan WC)
3. Vavrosky (USMC)

180.5-lb class
1. Johnson (Hawkeye WC)
2. Bradley (Michigan WC)
3. Jackson (USMC)

198-lb class
1. Chandler (Haddad WC)
2. Williams (Terre Haute WC)
3. Lovrien (Haddad WC)

220-lb class
1. Rheingans (Haddad WC)
2. Galler (MDYF)
3. Walker (Redbird WC)

Heavyweight
1. McCready (Hawkeye WC)
2. Slizewski (Michigan WC)
3. Swenson (unat)

1980
(at Franklin Park, IL)

Team	*Points*
1. Haddad WC	98
2. Michigan WC	26
3. Mayor Daley Youth Foundation	18
4. Wisconsin WC	8
5. Hawkeye WC	6
6. Huskie WC	3

Place winners

105.5-lb class
1. Rosenthal (Illinois)
2. Pierre (unat)

114.5-lb class
1. Johnson (MDYF)
2. Zorick (California)

125.5-lb class
1. Thompson (Haddad WC)
2. Owens (Michigan WC)
3. Powers (Illinois WC)

136.5-lb class
1. Hughes (Haddad WC)
2. Burke (Oklahoma Underdogs)
3. Turner (MDYF)
4. Parent (Michigan WC)
5. Lamphere (Haddad WC)
6. Whitish (Michigan WC)

149.5-lb class
1. Metzger (Oklahoma Underdogs)
2. Trainer (Michigan WC)
3. Nighman (unat)
4. Stone (USMC)

163-lb class
1. Andre (Haddad WC)
2. Dermendjian (Haddad WC)
3. Vavrosky (USMC)
4. Stensgard (Haddad WC)
5. Delaney (Haddad WC)
6. Pheanis (Huskie WC)

180.5-lb class
1. Chandler (Haddad WC)
2. Press (Haddad WC)
3. Schultz (Oklahoma Underdogs)
4. Hall (Oklahoma Underdogs)
5. Kasprowicz (Michigan WC)
6. Eisley (Michigan WC)

198-lb class
1. Houck (Haddad WC)
2. Hull (Wisconsin WC)
3. Bragg (Colorado Springs WC)
4. Soucie (Wisconsin WC)
5. Craig (Huskie WC)
6. Hurley (Michigan WC)

220-lb class
1. Hays (unat)
2. Vavrosky (Haddad WC)

Heavyweight
1. Blatnick (Haddad WC)
2. Carlisle (USMC)
3. McCready (Hawkeye WC)
4. Zupancic (Michigan WC)

1981
(at Arlington Heights, IL)

Team	*Points*
1. Twin Cities WC	74
2. Michigan WC	62
3. Navy	51
4. Redbird WC	22
5. Wisconsin WC	3

Place winners

105.5-lb class
1. Jones (USMC)
2. Rivera (unat)

114.5-lb class
1. Rosenthal (Redbird WC)
2. Stewart (Navy)
3. Wager (Navy)
4. Zorick (unat)
5. Wilkinson (unat)

125.5-lb class
1. Herman (Navy)
2. Hartupee (Michigan WC)
3. Covers (unat)

136.5-lb class
1. Kuzi (Nebraska OC)
2. Hughes (Twin Cities WC)
3. Nelson (SFPL)
4. Schatz (Redbird WC)
5. Parent (Michigan WC)
6. Nobles (Navy)

149.5-lb class
1. Johnson (Michigan WC)
2. Minkel (Michigan WC)
3. Benintende (U.S. Navy)
4. Trainor (Michigan WC)
5. Lord (Cyclone WC)
6. Bellis (Redbird WC)

163-lb class
1. Andre (Twin Cities WC)
2. Pelcl (Twin Cities WC)
3. Jolly (unat)
4. Jahad (unat)
5. Hernandez (Navy)
6. Miller (Michigan WC)

180.5-lb class
1. Chandler (Twin Cities WC)
2. Gross (Michigan WC)
3. Delany (Twin Cities WC)
4. Fisher (Wisconsin WC)
5. Dergo (unat)
6. Dergo (unat)

198-lb class
1. Ali (Twin Cities WC)
2. Llewellyn (Illinois WC)
3. Houck (Twin Cities WC)
4. Harlan (Michigan WC)
5. Krogstad (unat)

Wilcox (Maverick WC) did not wrestle

220-lb class
1. Simons (Michigan WC)
2. Press (Twin Cities WC)
3. Walker (Redbird WC)
4. Tidwell (Navy)
5. Brown (unat)

Heavyweight
1. Grier (unat)
2. Zupancic (Michigan WC)
3. Chamberlin (Hoosier WC)
4. Paloucek (Illinois WC)
5. Nelson (Twin Cities WC)
6. Gear (Navy)

1982
(at Arlington Heights, IL)

Team	*Points*
1. Minnesota WC	83
2. U.S. Marine Corps	71
3. Armed Forces WC	58
4. Michigan WC	27
5. Hawkeye WC	5
6. Wildcat WC, Wisconsin WC	3
8. Cowboy WC	2

Place winners

105.5-lb class
1. Dorrance (USMC)
2. Serrato (AFWC)

3. Jones (AFWC)
4. Wetzel (USMC)
5. Bailey (USMC)
6. Rivera (Wildcat WC)

114.5-lb class
1. Leiva (USMC)
2. Rosenthal (unat)
3. Farina (Minnesota WC)
4. Burke (AFWC)
5. Singleton (Michigan WC)
6. Richards (unat)

125.5-lb class
1. Hermann (AFWC)
2. Pavia (Michigan WC)
3. Powers (unat)
4. Johnson (unat)
5. Willingham (Cowboy WC)
6. Giese (Minnesota WC)

136.5-lb class
1. Mello (USMC)
2. Wasmund (Minnesota WC)
3. Nelson (unat)
4. Ray (Hawkeye WC)
5. Parent (Michigan WC)
6. Byrd (AFWC)

149.5-lb class
1. Hughes (Minnesota WC)
2. Martinez (Minnesota WC)
3. Minkel (Michigan WC)
4. Lord (Cyclone WC)
5. Brown (AFWC)
6. Giura (Wisconsin WC)

163-lb class
1. Andre (Minnesota WC)
2. Butler (AFWC)
3. Miller (Michigan WC)
4. Pelletier (AFWC)
5. Yagla (Hawkeye WC)
6. Richman (Wisconsin WC)

180.5-lb class
1. Press (Minnesota WC)
2. Ali (Minnesota WC)
3. Campbell (AFWC)
4. Clemens (AFWC)
5. Schmitz (Minnesota WC)
6. Scherr (U of Nebraska)

198-lb class
1. Scherr (U of Nebraska)
2. Pittman (USMC)
3. Houck (Minnesota WC)
4. Fraser (Michigan WC)
5. Bernstein (Minnesota WC)
6. Shultz (Wisconsin WC)

220-lb class
1. Gibson (USMC)
2. Koslowski (Minnesota WC)
3. Williams (AFWC)
4. Johnson (unat)
5. Galler (Wildcat WC)
6. Walker (unat)

Heavyweight
1. Carlisle (USMC)
2. Hurlock (unat)
3. Lee (Michigan WC)
4. Olson (unat)
5. Albright (Nebraska)
6. Chamberlain (unat)

1983
(at Arlington Heights, IL)

Team	*Points*
1. Minnesota WC	68
2. U.S. Marine Corps	44
3. Michigan WC	40
4. Adirondack Three-Style WC	36
5. Navy	32
6. Army	15
7. San Francisco Peninsula Grapplers, Little C WC	14
9. Nebraska Olympic Club	11
10. USA Oregon	8
11. Team Canada	4

Place winners

105.5-lb class
1. Jones (Navy)
2. Sheldon (ATWA)

3. Wetzel (USMC)
4. Bailey (USMC)
5. Sterriker (Minnesota WC)
6. Serrato (Army)

114.5-lb class
1. Fuller (Little C WC)
2. Clark (ATWA)
3. Rosenthal (unat)
4. Manlicic (SFPG)
5. Yale (Navy)
6. Dorrance (USMC)

125.5-lb class
1. Hermann (Navy)
2. Amado (USA Oregon)
3. Francis (Army)
4. Genova (ATWA)
5. Hartupee (Michigan)
6. Clardy (Minnesota WC)

136.5-lb class
1. Mello (USMC)
2. Hughes (Minnesota WC)
3. Famiano (ATWA)
4. Ray (U of Iowa)
5. Nelson (Little C WC)
6. Pollard (USMC)

149.5-lb class
1. Martinez (Minnesota WC)
2. Kuzu (Nebraska OC)
3. Pelcl (Minnesota WC)
4. Giura (unat)
5. Placek (ATWA)
6. Johnson (unat)

163-lb class
1. Andre (Minnesota WC)
2. Pelletier (Army)
3. Butler (Navy)
4. Johnson (Michigan WC)
5. Ali (Minnesota WC)
6. Darnandzhyan (Armenian WC)

180.5-lb class
1. Goss (Michigan WC)
2. Hall (Oklahoma Underdogs)
3. Press (Minnesota WC)
4. Scherr (Nebraska OC)
5. Santerre (Team Canada)
6. Goldman (U of Iowa)

198-lb class
1. Fraser (Michigan WC)
2. Houck (Minnesota WC)
3. Pittman (USMC)
4. Nazari (SFPG)
5. Brown (SFPG)
6. Schultz (unat)

220-lb class
1. Koslowski (Minnesota WC)
2. Gibson (USMC)
3. Blatnick (ATWA)
4. Simons (Michigan WC)
5. Kallos (Team Canada)
6. Williams (Wildcat WC)

Heavyweight
1. No champion (double disqualification)
2. Carlisle (USMC) and Lee (Michigan WC)
3. Johnson (SFPG)
4. Jackson (unat)
5. Koplowitz (ATWA)
6. Smith (Wildcat WC)

1984
(at Albany, NY)

Team	*Points*
1. Adirondack Three-Style WC	69
2. Minnesota WC	66
3. U.S. Marine Corps	46
4. Michigan WC	35
5. Navy, Sunkist Kids	30
7. Army	13
8. Little C WC	12
9. New York AC	5
10. Hawkeye WC	4

Place winners

105.5-b class
1. Jones (Navy)
2. Shelton (ATWA)
3. Wetzel (USMC)
4. Ogan (Sunkist Kids)

5. Biedrycki (USMC)
6. Kenfield (ATWA)

114.5-lb class
1. Fuller (Little C AC)
2. Farina (Minnesota WC)
3. Govig (Sunkist Kids)
4. Dorrance (USMC)
5. Ohta (Sunkist Kids)
6. Yale (Navy)

125.5-lb class
1. Famiano (ATWA)
2. Hermann (Navy)
3. Amado (Sunkist Kids)
4. Seward (USMC)
5. Milonas (NYAC)
6. Clard (ATWA)

136.5-lb class
1. Mello (USMC)
2. Wasmund (Minnesota WC)
3. DeMeo (ATWA)
4. Thoefilatos (NYAC)
5. Anderson (ATWA)
6. Whelan (Navy)

149.5-lb class
1. Martinez (Minnesota WC)
2. Seras (ATWA)
3. Minkel (Michigan WC)
4. Franco (ATWA)
5. Kuzu (Sunkist Kids)
6. Bailey (Cowboy WC)

163-lb class
1. Matthews (Michigan WC)
2. Butler (Navy)
3. Oliver (ATWA)
4. Pelletier (Army)
5. Catalfo (ATWA)
6. Montano (Sunkist Kids)

180.5-lb class
1. Press (Minnesota WC)
2. Sabo (ATWA)
3. Collier (Army)
4. Anderson (Army)
5. Paquette (ATWC)
6. Harter (unat)

198-lb class
1. Houck (Minnesota WC)
2. Fraser (Michigan WC)
3. Bernstein (Minnesota WC)
4. Johnson (Hawkeye WC)
5. Lanzatella (ATWA)
6. Benford (USMC)

220-lb class
No champion (double disqualification)
2. Gibson (USMC) and Koslowski (Minnesota WC)
3. Blatnick (ATWA)
4. Fears (USMC)
5. Johnson (Sunkist Kids)
6. Jack (unat)

286-lb class
No champion (double disqualification)
2. Albright (Sunkist Kids) and Carlisle (USMC)
3. Lee (Michigan WC)
4. Watkins (Michigan WC)
5. Ware (ATWA)
6. Barber (Army)

1985
(at Ann Arbor, MI)

Team	*Points*
1. U.S. Marine Corps	61
2. Adirondack Three-Style WC	59
3. Sunkist Kids	57
4. Minnesota WC	51
5. Navy	34
6. Army	18
7. New York AC	16
8. Michigan WC	11
9. Wisconsin WC	6
10. San Francisco Peninsula Grapplers	1

Place winners

105.5-lb class
1. Jones (Navy)
2. Wetzel (USMC)
3. Connly (USMC)
4. Ramaswamy (ATWA)

114.5-lb class
1. Fuller (Sunkist Kids)
2. Sheldon (ATWA)
3. Ohta (Sunkist Kids)
4. Sanchez (unat)
5. Blake (Michigan WC)
6. Biedrycki (USMC)

125.5-lb class
1. Seward (USMC)
2. Hermann (Navy)
3. Canali (Sunkist Kids)
4. Amado (Sunkist Kids)
5. Caceres (NYAC)
6. Dawkins (Sunkist Kids)

136.5-lb class
1. Lee (USMC)
2. Wasmund (Minnesota WC)
3. Anderson (ATWA)
4. Theofilatos (NYAC)
5. Genova (ATWA)
6. Gillen (ATWA)

149.5-lb class
1. Martinez (Minnesota WC)
2. Metzger (NYAC)
3. Giura (Wisconsin WC)
4. Russell (Sunkist Kids)
5. Placek (ATWA)
6. Mann (USMC)

163-lb class
1. Butler (Navy)
2. Seras (ATWA)
3. Oliver (ATWA)
4. Black (Michigan WC)
5. Moe (Minnesota WC)
6. O'Shea (Sunkist Kids)

180.5-lb class
1. Catalfo (ATWA)
2. Scherr (Sunkist Kids)
3. Colling (Army)
4. Stuebing (Sunkist Kids)
5. Gholar (Minnesota WC)
6. Tebidor (USMC)

198-lb class
1. Houck (Minnesota WC)
2. Anderson (Army)
3. Goss (Michigan WC)
4. Hall (NYAC)
5. Carolan (Navy)
6. Osterholt (SFPG)

220-lb class
1. Gibson (USMC)
2. J. Johnson (Sunkist Kids)
3. M. Johnson (Sunkist Kids)
4. Koslowski (Minnesota WC)
5. Lanzatella (ATWA)
6. Tironi (ATWA)

286-lb class
1. Koslowski (Minnesota WC)
2. Carlisle (USMC)
3. Ware (ATWA)
4. Barber (Army)
5. Connors (ATWA)
6. Hrncir (Army)

1986
(at LaCrosse, WI)

Team	Points
Division I	
1. U.S. Marine Corps	65
2. Minnesota WC	58
3. Sunkist Kids	56
4. Adirondack Three-Style WA	47
Division II	
1. Navy	33
2. Army	24
3. Michigan WC	17

Place winners

105.5-lb class
1. Wetzel (USMC)
2. Vanni (Sunkist Kids)
3. Phil Ogan (Navy)
4. Peter Ogan (unat)

5. McNeal (Minnesota WC)
6. Ramaswamy (ATWA)

114.5-lb class
1. Sheldon (ATWA)
2. Fuller (Sunkist Kids)
3. Dorrance (USMC)
4. Biedrycki (USMC)
5. Ohta (Sunkist Kids)
6. Sterriker (Navy

125.5-lb class
1. Amado (Sunkist Kids)
2. Hermann (Navy)
3. Genova (NYAC)
4. Frank (USMC)
5. Canali (Sunkist Kids)
6. Yale (Navy)

136.5-lb class
1. Famiano (ATWA)
2. Anderson (ATWA)
3. Massey (USMC)
4. Critelli (USA Oregon)
5. Wainwright (unat)
6. Popelka (Army)

149.5-lb class
1. Martinez (Minnesota WC)
2. Seras (ATWA)
3. Giura (Wisconson WC)
4. Pollard (USMC)
5. Mann (USMC)
6. Craig (Michigan WC)

163-lb class
1. Butler (Navy)
2. Miller (Michigan WC)
3. Monday (Sunkist Kids)
4. Thomas (Army)
5. Schoonmaker (USMC)
6. McManaman (Wildcat WC)

180-lb class
1. Gholar (Minnesota WC)
2. Anderson (Army)
3. Morgan (Minnesota WC)
4. Mooney (USMC)
5. Short (Minnesota WC)
6. Cantrell (USMC)

198-lb class
1. Waldroup (Army)
2. Goss (Michigan WC)
3. Chaid (Sunkist Kids)
4. Carolan (Navy)
5. Johnson (USMC)
6. Stephens (USMC)

220-lb class
1. Koslowski (Minnesota WC)
2. Gibson (USMC)
3. J. Johnson (Sunkist Kids)
4. Tironi (ATWA)
5. Blaske (USMC)
6. Galler (Mercer Island)

286-lb class
1. Koslowski (Minnesota WC)
2. Carlisle (USMC)
3. M. Johnson (Sunkist Kids)
4. Pittman (USMC)
5. Lanzatella (ATWA)
6. Connors (ATWA)

1987
(at Schenectady, NY)

Team	*Points*
Division I	
1. U.S. Marine Corps	76
2. Adirondack Three-Style WA	66
3. Minnesota WC	52
4. Navy	40
5. Sunkist Kids	31
Division II	
1. Army	22
2. New York AC	19
3. Michigan WC	9
4. Air Force	2

Place winners

105.5-lb class
1. Wetzel (USMC)
2. Jones (Navy)
3. Dorrance (USMC)
4. Vanni (Sunkist Kids)
5. Gomez III (Colorado)
6. Ramaswamy (ATWA)

114.5-lb class
1. Sheldon (ATWA)
2. Biedrycki (USMC)
3. Caracci (NYAC)
4. Mays (Navy)
5. Ohta (USA Oregon)
6. Owens (Army)

125.5-lb class
1. Seward (USMC)
2. Amado (Sunkist Kids)
3. Hermann (Navy)
4. Genova (NYAC)
5. Ohta (USA Oregon)
6. Owens (Army)

136.5-lb class
1. Famiano (ATWA)
2. Wasmund (Minnesota WC)
3. Lee (USMC)
4. Barsegian (Sunkist Kids)
5. Massey (USMC)
6. Theofilatos (NYAC)

149.5-lb class
1. Martinez (Minnesota WC)
2. Seras (ATWA)
3. Giura (NYAC)
4. Pollard (USMC)
5. Mann (USMC)
6. Trainor (Michigan WC)

163-lb class
1. Butler (Navy)
2. Miller (Michigan WC)
3. Thomas (Army)
4. Oliver (ATWA)
5. Air (U.S. Air Force)
6. Patay (Sunkist Kids)

180.5-lb class
1. Catalfo (ATWA)
2. Stuebin (Sunkist Kids)
3. Morgan (Minnesota WC)
4. Anderson (NYAC)
5. Gholar (Minnesota WC)
6. Ryan (ATWA)

198-lb class
1. Waldroup (Army)
2. Carolan (Navy)
3. Catalfo (ATWA)
4. Stephens (USMC)
5. Chaid (Sunkist Kids)
6. Lanzatella (Army)

220-lb class
1. Koslowski (Minnesota WC)
2. Gibson (USMC)
3. Johnson (Sunkist Kids)
4. Tironi (ATWA)
5. Benford (USMC)
6. Thomas (Navy)

286-lb class
1. Koslowski (Minnesota WC)
2. Pittman (USMC)
3. Blatnick (ATWA)
4. Carlisle (USMC)
5. Barber (Army)
6. Katz (ATWA)

1988
(at Cedar Rapids, IA)

Team	*Points*
Division I	
1. U.S. Marine Corps	76
2. Gopher WC	59
Division II	
1. Sunkist Kids	37
2. Army	36

Place winners

105.5-lb class
1. Jones (Navy)
2. Wetzel (USMC)
3. Rabinovitz (Army)
4. Henson (Missouri)
5. Ogan (Navy)
6. Tocci (Gold Medal)

114.5-lb class
1. Sheldon (ATWA)
2. Fuller (Sunkist Kids)
3. Biedrycki (USMC)
4. Ilg (Army)
5. Blake (Michigan WC)
6. Ussery (USMC)

125.5-lb class
1. Barseghian (Sunkist Kids)
2. Frank (USMC)
3. Hermann (Navy)
4. Mahan (USMC)
5. Stanley (Navy)
6. Dodge (ATWA)

136.5-lb class
1. Wasmund (Minnesota WC)
2. Anderson (ATWA)
3. Seward (USMC)
4. Popelka (Army)
5. Melchiore (Hawkeye WC)
6. Lee (USMC)

149.5-lb class
1. Pollard (USMC)
2. Brown (Air Force)
3. Mann (USMC)
4. Trainor (Michigan WC)
5. Marino (NYAC)
6. Healy (Fighting Illini WC)

163-lb class
1. Thomas (Army)
2. Seras (ATWA)
3. Butler (Navy)
4. Jones (Air Force)
5. Brown (Army)
6. Oliver (ATWA)

180.5-lb class
1. Gholar (Minnesota WC)
2. Morgan (Minnesota WC)
3. Osterholt (Sunkist Kids)
4. Couture (Army)
5. Elben (USMC)
6. Court (Minnesota WC)

198-lb class
1. Carolan (Sunkist Kids)
2. Giles (USMC)
3. Anderson (ATWA)
4. Johnson (USMC)
5. Foy (Minnesota WC)
6. Stephens (USMC)

220-lb class
1. Koslowski (Minnesota WC)
2. Tironi (ATWA)
3. Lanzatella (Army)
4. Johnson (Sunkist Kids)
5. Benford (USMC)
6. Bullins (USMC)

286-lb class
1. Koslowski (Minnesota WC)
2. Pittman (USMC)
3. Koplovitz (ATWA)
4. Koontz (Panther WC)
5. Johnson (Sunkist Kids)
6. Katz (ATWA)

Chapter 8

The Collegiate Nationals

Since the beginning of the twentieth century, college wrestling has crowned thousands of champions. The NCAA, NAIA, and junior college organizations each hold their own yearly championship meets.

NCAA Tournament: Division I

At the start of the 1900s, the top college wrestling teams were located in the East. Although no national collegiate tournament was held until 1928, *Amateur Wrestling News*, the nation's foremost wrestling publication, selected unofficial national champion teams for the time period from 1905 to 1928. The designated champions for each of the first 18 years are eastern schools.

According to *Amateur Wrestling News*, Yale had the nation's best wrestling team in the years 1905 through 1910. From 1911 through 1921, eastern schools such as Cornell, Princeton, Penn State, and Navy joined Yale as unofficial national champions.

In 1922, a midwestern school made its first appearance on the *Amateur Wrestling News* list when Iowa State College in Ames tied Navy for the top spot. In 1923, it was Cornell (Ithaca, New York) and Iowa State leading the pack. But the power shift was complete by 1924: from that point on, with just one notable exception, states of the Midwest and Southwest ruled the world of collegiate wrestling.

In particular, Oklahoma and Iowa became the wrestling capitals of the country. It did not happen overnight, however. Both states were catapulted into their triumphant roles by the toil and leadership of men who were destined to become legends. In Oklahoma, that man was Edward Clark Gallagher. The emergence of Iowa in the 1920s can be traced to the hero status attained a decade earlier by two men: professional stars Frank Gotch and Farmer Burns.

"I don't think there's any doubt that men like Gotch and Burns really gave wrestling its impetus in this state," said Cornell College's Paul Scott, the first coach to lead an Iowa college to an NCAA team title (Chapman, 1981, p. 20). It was a sentiment echoed by many other coaches on both the high school and the college level across the state.

But Iowa also received a substantial boost when Charlie Mayser brought his Yale background to Ames. Mayser borrowed from the rich eastern wrestling tradition and sowed those seeds on the path plowed by Gotch and Burns to create a wrestling kingdom in Iowa.

Mayser entered Yale in 1900 and was largely responsible for the staging of the first collegiate dual meet in 1903 between Yale and Columbia. In 1915, Mayser became athletic director at Iowa State College, bringing with him to Ames his great affection for wrestling. While coaching football at Iowa State, he began a wrestling program, and five of his eight mat squads went unbeaten.

In 1918, Mayser became the first chairman of the collegiate wrestling rules committee, and he served in that capacity for 4 years. In 1921, Mayser played the key role as Iowa became the first state to hold a state high school wrestling tournament.

"He was one of the first coaches to insist that his wrestlers go for the fall at all times, regardless of the score, adding greatly to the sport's appeal," Bob Dellinger, curator of the National Wrestling Hall of Fame, reported in the official program when Mayser was inducted as a charter member.

Mayser's efforts were very instrumental in building a scholastic wrestling base in Iowa, and they paved the way for the young coach who replaced him at Iowa State. Hugo Otopalik was a star football player and wrestler at Nebraska and was offered the Iowa State job in 1924 when Mayser resigned to become athletic director at Franklin and Marshall College in Pennsylvania. Otopalik accepted and stayed for 29 years.

The Yale influence had first touched Iowa State through Mayser and struck again through Otopalik, though once removed. At Nebraska, Otopalik had been coached by Dr. Raymond Clapp, who had been a pole-vault star at Yale in 1896. Clapp earned a medical degree at Keokuk College in Iowa, then moved on to Lincoln, Nebraska, where he formed a wrestling team in 1915. Otapolik was his brightest star.

Clapp's role in the history of amateur wrestling was considerable. Four years prior to helping Otopalik host the first NCAA meet, he had organized the Missouri Valley Tournament, which evolved into the Big Eight Conference Tournament. He also served for 17 years, from 1928 until 1945, as chairman of the NCAA Wrestling Rules Committee.

In 1928, Clapp and Otopalik worked ceaselessly to stage the first official NCAA wrestling tournament. "This idea [of an NCAA tournament] was not received with enthusiasm in all parts of the nation," wrote Don Sayenga in *Amateur Wrestling News*. "But with immense support from his former pupil, Hugo Otopalik at Iowa State, Dr. Clapp succeeded in scheduling the first NCAA meet for the end of March in Ames."

The meet was not popular among the nation's wrestlers, as it took a back seat to the Olympic trials. An estimated 2,500 wrestlers competed in the 1928 Olympic trials in sites around the country, but only 40 wrestlers entered the first NCAA Tournament in Ames. No team scores were kept, but the squad from Oklahoma A&M (which became Oklahoma State University in 1957) won four titles in the seven weight divisions. Aggie winners were Harold DeMarsh (115), Melvin Clodfelter (145), George Rule (175), and Earl McCready (heavyweight). The other three schools with champions were Northwestern (Ralph Lupton at 125), Iowa State (Arthur Holding at 135), and Iowa (Leslie Beers at 158).

While Mayser, Clapp, and Otopalik were paving the way for Iowa State's wrestling juggernaut, Gallagher was doing just as much by himself down in Stillwater, Oklahoma. The former Aggie football and track star fell in love with wrestling after graduating from Oklahoma A&M, and he focused his attention on wrestling with a fervor seldom seen before or since in any sport.

Gallagher graduated from Oklahoma A&M in 1909 with a degree in electrical engineering but could not stay away from athletics. He coached for a brief spell at Baker University in Kansas, then returned to his alma mater as athletic director in 1916. Oklahoma A&M fielded its first team a year earlier (on April 2, 1915), losing to a more experienced University of Texas team. One of Gallagher's highest priorities as athletic director was to improve the wrestling fortunes at Oklahoma A&M. And improve them he did!

A summer's trip to Vermont to learn from the old elbow-and-collar grapplers paid huge dividends back in Oklahoma. In the often-windy plains town of Stillwater, Gallagher supplemented the knowledge he gained in Vermont with his own brand of genius, wrapped up in raw instincts and ingenuity.

"He applied his engineering knowledge of leverage and stress to the development of more than 300 wrestling holds," wrote Bob Dellinger in the official National Wrestling Hall of Fame program at the induction of Gallagher. "He was the first to organize systematic practice situations, and devoted close attention to diet and training methods."

Gallagher's efforts were richly rewarded. His teams became the scourge of the nation. In Gallagher's 23 years as coach, the Aggies posted a remarkable record of 138-4-5. They racked up 19 undefeated seasons and at one point won 68 dual meets in a row. In 13 NCAA tournaments, the Aggies (later to become the Cowboys) earned 10 team titles and shared an 11th title. Individually, Gallagher products collected 37 NCAA titles and three Olympic gold medals.

Oklahoma A&M was listed by *Amateur Wrestling News* as unofficial team champion from 1925 to 1928 and captured official NCAA team titles in 1929, 1930, 1934, and 1935. Factions were still bickering about whether a team score should be a part of the tournament, and team scores were dismissed in 1931, 1932, and 1933.

The Oklahoma A&M success fired a competitive urge in Norman, just 60 miles south of Stillwater, and the University of Oklahoma decided to start a program. It hired Aggie graduate Paul Keen as its coach. Keen, a basketball and football star at Oklahoma A&M, never wrestled in college. But he had studied the sport under Gallagher, and his brother, Cliff, had been an Aggie mat star.

Keen took over the Sooner program in 1928 and just 5 years later led his underdog squad to a tremendous upset of the Aggies. The 13.5-12.5 victory before a packed arena in Stillwater snapped a 68-match, 10-year winning streak compiled by Gallagher's men.

In 1936, Keen led the Sooners to the NCAA crown. It was the first national title in any sport for the Sooners, who were paced by three-time champion Wayne Martin (134) and Harry Broadbent (174).

The Aggies returned to rule the roost the next 7 years in a row, from 1937 through 1946 (with the NCAA taking time out for World War II from 1943 to 1945). Along the way, however, there was a changing of the guard. The legendary Gallagher's health had been deteriorating for several years, and on August 28, 1940, he died of pneumonia and complications at the age of 53.

Art Griffith, a highly successful coach at Tulsa Central High School, was selected as Gallagher's successor. In 1941 he became the first rookie coach to lead his team to the national championship. Competing at Lehigh, Pennsylvania, Oklahoma A&M scored 37 points to outdistance runner-up Michigan State by 11. Going all the way for their new coach were Alfred Whitehurst (136), David "Buddy" Arndt (145), Earl Van Bebber (155), and Virgil Smith (165)—four Aggie champs in eight divisions!

In 1947, the first of the four Iowa colleges to win the NCAA team title halted the long victory run by the state of Oklahoma. Coached by the dynamic Paul Scott, tiny Cornell College, a school of just 600 students in picturesque Mount Vernon, tore a path through the amateur wrestling world in 1947. The Purple posted a 12-0-1 record in dual meets, whipping Eastern Intercollegiate Wrestling Association (EIWA) champion Lehigh, 36-0, and upending Big Seven champion Iowa State and Big Ten champion Illinois.

At the NCAA Tournament in Champaign, Illinois, Scott's crew racked up 32 points for a runaway victory. Iowa State Teachers College (now the University of Northern Iowa) was second with 19 points, whereas the mighty Aggies slipped to third with 15. Paving the way for the Purple were a pair of freshman champs from West Waterloo High School, the same high school that would produce Dan Gable 2 decades later.

Richard Hauser claimed the 121-pound title for Cornell, and teammate Lowell Lange won the first of his three NCAA titles at 136 pounds. Three different Iowa colleges won six of the eight NCAA individual titles that year. Iowa State Teachers College had three champions in Russell Bush (128), Bill Koll (145), and Bill Nelson (165), and the University of Iowa had one champion in Joe Scarpello (175).

Oklahoma State returned to the top spot in 1948 and 1949, but in 1950 a second Iowa school claimed a title. Iowa State Teachers College, coached by Dave McCuskey, outscored Purdue by a 30-16 margin to win the crown in its own gymnasium. Champions were Keith Young (145), destined to be-

Bill Koll lifting an opponent during the 1948 season. (Courtesy of National Wrestling Hall of Fame)

come a three-timer; Nelson (155), winning his third; and Bill Smith (165), destined to become an Olympic champion 2 years later, winning his second.

The following season (1951) was the "Year of the Sooner." The University of Oklahoma, under coach Port Robertson, became the talk of the wrestling community when it halted Oklahoma A&M's winning streak at 76, 19-8. The Sooners crushed defending champion Iowa State Teachers College twice, then beat the Aggies in a second dual by the same score.

At the NCAA Tournament, Phil Smith (157) was the only champion from Oklahoma, but it was just enough to slip past Lehigh, 24-23. The Sooners repeated in 1952 in Fort Collins, Colorado, edging Iowa State Teachers College by a 22-21 margin.

But in 1953, a team from the East rose up once again. Penn State reminded fans of the glory days of Yale when it hosted the NCAA Tournament in State College, Pennsylvania, and outscored runner-up Oklahoma by a 21-15 margin. Penn State, coached by Charlie Speidel, had just one champion in Hudson Samson (191) and used team balance for the win. Former champion Cornell of Iowa was third, while former champions Oklahoma A&M and Iowa State Teachers College tied for fourth.

For the next 11 years, it was an Oklahoma show. The Aggies rolled off six straight team titles, surrendered the title in 1960 to Oklahoma, then rattled off two more. Oklahoma won again in 1963, and the Aggies took it back to Stillwater in 1964.

Even a change of coaches could hardly slow down the Oklahoma State (formerly A&M) express. Griffith stepped down after the 1956 season, leaving behind a legacy of eight NCAA championships in 13 years and a dual meet record of 78-7-4. Taking his place was young, intense Myron Roderick, who, although just 23 years old at the time he began coaching, hardly skipped a beat in continuing the great Cowboy tradition. His first squad was just fourth in the NCAA Tournament in 1957, but the following year the Cowboys were back on the top.

Between Oklahoma in Norman and Oklahoma State in Stillwater, it seemed to many mat fans that the Oklahoma dynasty would never end. Then came 1965 and a new kid on the block. During the late 1940s and early 1950s, Iowa State had slipped from its heady success of earlier years. When Otopalik fell ill and died unexpectedly following the 1953 season, the Cyclones went searching for a new coach. They found Harold Nichols at Arkansas State College.

Nichols grew up on a farm outside Cresco, Iowa, and wrestled for Cliff Keen at the University of Michigan. Keen was an undefeated wrestler for Gallagher in the middle 1920s, and it was Keen's brother, Paul, who led Oklahoma to its first title. Nichols and his brother, Don, were both NCAA champions at Michigan, and Harold started the wrestling program at Arkansas State, where he developed a reputation as a coach who would face any team at any time.

Nichols was offered the Iowa State job and moved to Ames with a mission: He wanted to knock Oklahoma off its perch as king of the mat world.

The Cyclones finished in a tie for 26th at the 1956 NCAA Tournament and leaped all the way to third the following season. They were second in 1958, 1959, and 1960 and placed second again in 1963 and third in 1964. But in 1965, the Cyclones became the third Iowa college to win the NCAA title, nipping Oklahoma State, 87-86, in a dramatic battle that extended all the way to the final match of the tournament.

Iowa State had just one champion in Tom Peckham (177) but racked up a bundle of points in the consolations, many in head-to-head showdowns with the Cowboys. It was the beginning of a new era in wrestling, as Nichols placed considerable emphasis on going for the pin, just as Mayser had done 5 decades earlier.

But Oklahoma State was not about to concede anything to its Big Eight rival. Roderick is generally acknowledged as one of the slickest takedown artists in amateur history, and his style of "take-'em-down-and-let-'em-up" ran directly contrary to Nichols' style of "turn-'em-over-and-pin-'em." The contrast made for some of the most exciting showdowns in wrestling history.

The Cowboys regained the title in 1966 by a 79-70 margin over Iowa State, and Oklahoma was just a point behind the Cyclones. But in 1967, a former Oklahoma State star led an outsider to the NCAA title. Grady Peninger was an NCAA runner-up for Griffith in 1949 and took over for former Aggie great Fendley Collins as coach of Michigan State in 1963.

Under Peninger, the Spartans became the terror of the Big Ten, rolling to seven consecutive conference titles. Champions Dale Anderson (137) and George Radman (167) led the Spartan charge at the national tourney at Kent State in Ohio in 1967, and for only the second time since 1928 the NCAA champion was a college from outside Oklahoma and Iowa.

It was back to normal in 1968, however, as Oklahoma State recaptured its championship. For the next 7 years, the three Big Eight powers kept the title among themselves, but in 1969 Roderick retired following a sixth-place finish at the NCAA Tournament. In 13 years at the helm, Roderick had lassoed seven NCAA championships and compiled a dual meet record of 140-10-7, including an all-time record of 84 in a row.

As in replacing Gallagher with Griffith, Oklahoma State turned to the high school coaching ranks to replace Roderick. The man they selected was former Oklahoma State matman Tommy Chesbro. In 1971, his second year at the helm, Chesbro led the Cowboys to their 27th team crown behind champions Yoshiro Fujita (126), Darrell Keller (142), and Geoff Baum (177).

Iowa State recaptured the team title in 1972 with a 103-72.5 spread over Michigan State. Winning titles for coach Nichols were Carl Adams (158), Ben Peterson (190), and 440-pound Chris Taylor (heavyweight). The Cyclones repeated in 1973, but in 1974 Stan Abel coached the Sooners of Oklahoma into the top spot. In one of the tightest finishes ever, Oklahoma scored 69.5 points to 67 for Michigan, 64 for Oklahoma State, and 63 for Iowa State. Sooner champions were Gary Breece (118) and Rod Kilgore (158).

The Oklahoma schools were about to enter a long drought, however. In 1975, a new dynasty was dawning in Iowa City, and through 1988 neither Oklahoma team had been able to capture another NCAA title.

Like Harold Nichols, Gary Kurdelmeier was a product of Cresco, Iowa. He competed for coach Dave McCuskey at the University of Iowa, winning the 177-pound NCAA title in 1958. He replaced the retiring McCuskey as Hawkeye coach in 1973 and startled the wrestling world by hiring Dan Gable, who was Nichols' greatest star at arch-rival Iowa State, as assistant coach.

Gable won 181 straight high school and college matches over a 7-year period, earning worldwide acclaim for his obsessive training routine at Iowa State. In 1972, he captured the 149.5-pound Olympic gold medal without surrendering a single point in six matches.

The Kurdelmeier-Gable combination took the Hawkeyes to unprecedented heights. In just their third year, they gave the University of Iowa its first NCAA team title, scoring 102 points in Princeton, New Jersey. The Hawkeyes rolled up a 25-point margin over second-place Oklahoma with champions Chuck Yagla (150) and Dan Holm (158) leading the way.

The Hawkeyes repeated in convincing fashion the following year in Tucson, Arizona, outscoring runner-up Iowa State, 123.25-85.75. Oklahoma State was third with just 64.5 points.

Three-time NCAA champion Jimmy Jackson (left) against Greg Gibson in the 1976 NCAA finals in Tucson, Arizona. (Courtesy of USA Wrestling)

It was like old times at the NCAA Tournament in Oklahoma City in 1977, with Big Eight powers Iowa State and Oklahoma State finishing first and second, respectively, knocking Iowa to third. It was Gable's first year as coach following Kurdelmeier's retirement. But the handwriting was on the wall. Iowa, coached by Gable, would closely resemble the Oklahoma State dynasty that was coached by Gallagher.

The Hawkeyes edged Iowa State by a mere half point to reclaim the title in 1978 at College Park, Maryland. The performance was all the more ironic because not a single Iowa wrestler won a title.

It was the start of something big in Iowa City. The Hawkeyes, under Gable, captured nine NCAA titles in a row, tying the all-time record in any sport. Only the Yale golf teams of the early 1900s and the Southern California track teams of the 1940s had performed so well.

Going for the all-time record of 10 in a row at College Park in 1987, the Hawkeyes were upset by an old nemesis. Young Jim Gibbons replaced Nichols in 1986 and in just his second season coached his Cyclones to their seventh team title, shattering the Iowa drive for the record. Four Iowa Staters won titles: Billy Kelly (126), Tim Krieger (150), Stewart Carter (167), and Eric Voelker (190).

In 1988 the Arizona State Sun Devils, coached by Bobby Douglas, made history by becoming the first team west of the Rocky Mountains to win the team championship. Like Iowa in 1978, the Sun Devils did not win a title, but they placed all seven of their qualifiers and scored 93 points to 85.5 for runner-up Iowa and 83.75 for third-place Iowa State.

The Arizona State triumph came in Ames at the 60th anniversary of the first official NCAA Tournament. It was a fitting testimonial to the growth of the sport, which began in the East and has continued to spread westward.

By 1988, only nine schools had claimed the NCAA team championship under official conditions. Oklahoma State leads the way with 27 titles, with the University of Iowa second at 11. Iowa State and the University of Oklahoma each has won 7 titles. Five schools—Cornell College of Iowa, Iowa State Teachers College, Penn State, Michigan State, and Arizona State—have corralled 1 each.

The long mat dominance of Oklahoma and Iowa is largely due to tradition, one that began with the remarkable men who blazed the path for others to follow. There have been others: Billy Sheridan, a native of Scotland who became a legend in the East while coaching at Lehigh University; Oregon State's Dr. Dale Thomas, the nation's all-time winningest wrestling coach; Arnold "Swede" Umbach of Auburn University, a man called the "father of wrestling in the South"; and many others who had a large regional and national impact. But the collegiate sport has existed largely as an Oklahoma-Iowa enterprise for most of the century.

Perhaps as many as 100,000 men have participated in college wrestling since the first NCAA Tournament in 1928. Yet, only 10 wrestlers completed their collegiate eligibilities with three NCAA titles and no losses or ties. The first was Oklahoma A&M heavyweight Earl McCready (final year, 1931).

Matching his example were six other Oklahoma State champions: Conrad Caldwell (1931), Jack Van Bebber (1931), Rex Peery (1935), Joe McDaniel (1939), David Arndt (1946), and Yojiro Uetake (1966). Iowa State Teachers College stars Bill Koll (1948) and Keith Young (1951) also finished undefeated with three NCAA titles. One of the last to do so was Oklahoma's Dan Hodge (1957), whose pinning percentage of .738 is the highest recorded in a full college career.

Richard DiBatista came very close to joining that august group and probably would have had it not been for World War II. The rugged Ardmore, Pennsylvania, product never lost in high school and was undefeated throughout his college career, winning three Eastern Conference titles and two NCAA championships at (175 pounds). He was set to battle for his third NCAA title in 1943, but the meet was canceled by the war. DiBatista reportedly closed out his mat career with an overall mark of 133-0.

The fact that no college wrestler between the years of 1966 and 1988 was able to complete his career undefeated can be primarily attributed to the increase in the number of matches wrestled. Although Uetake wrestled 52 times in his entire collegiate career, many wrestlers now exceed that figure in a single season, crisscrossing the nation to enter tournaments of all kinds. Wade Hughes of George Washington University wrestled 57 matches in the 1985 season alone and took part in 192 matches during his entire college career. Both figures are considered NCAA records.

However, it was reported that Ed Sernoski, who competed at Simon Fraser University (an NAIA-affiliated school located in Burnaby, British Columbia, Canada), posted a 73-3 record in 1988 and actually competed in an incredible 234 matches (197-36-1 record) during his college career.

Six wrestlers have gained the championship finals of the NCAA Tournament four times. The first was Oklahoma State heavyweight Dick Hutton (1947 to 1950, three titles). He was followed by Pat Milkovich of Michigan State (1972 to 1976, two titles), Lee Kemp of Wisconsin (1975 to 1978, three titles), Darryl Burley of Lehigh (1979 to 1983, two titles), Ed Banach of Iowa (1980 to 1983, three titles), and Duane Goldman of Iowa (1983 to 1986, one title).

Winning the NCAA Tournament as a legitimate freshman has proven to be very difficult through the years, partially because freshmen have not been eligible for long periods of time under NCAA rules. Men who have won titles as legitimate freshmen are Dick Hutton of Oklahoma State (1947), Dick Hauser and Lowell Lange of Cornell College (1947), Bill Nelson of Iowa State Teachers College (1947), Pat Milkovich of Michigan State (1972), Don Rohn of Clarion State (1973), and Darryl Burley of Lehigh (1979).

Koll was the first wrestler to garner two Outstanding Wrestler awards, heading an elite group of five. Only Tommy Evans of Oklahoma, Elliott "Gray" Simons of Lock Haven, Dan Hodge, and Yojiro Uetake have done likewise.

Dan Gable holds the all-time record for consecutive wins and pins. He pinned 25 in a row during his junior season of 1969 and won 117 straight at Iowa State, although the NCAA limits the record at 100 because 17 of the foes had exhausted their collegiate eligibilities.

The second-longest pinning streak is 22, by Hodge, and the second-longest winning streak is 90, by Oklahoma State's John Smith, concluding at the NCAA finals in 1988. Iowa's Jim Zalesky won 89 straight, whereas Simons and Mike Land of Iowa State each racked up 84 in a row.

Wade Hughes of George Washington University never captured an NCAA title, but he holds the distinction of the most career victories in history, winning 174 matches between 1982 and 1985. The all-time pinning record is the 110 compiled by Al Sears of Southern Illinois at Edwardsville from 1982 to 1985.

No family has been able to match the unique success of the Peerys. Rex Peery captured three NCAA titles for Oklahoma A&M, the last coming in 1935. He then coached two sons, Hugh and Ed, to three NCAA titles each at the University of Pittsburgh. The Peerys entered nine NCAA tournaments among them and came away with nine NCAA titles!

Ed closed out the remarkable string by coming from behind to nip Oklahoma State's Harmon Leslie in 1957. Their 123-pound battle finished at 7-7, then 2-2 in overtime. "When the extensions ended in a 2-2 draw, Ed Peery was voted national champion by the judges, and wrestling owned a family legend without precedent in the world of sport," Bob Dellinger, curator of the National Wrestling Hall of Fame, wrote in the official program the year of Peery's induction.

Five brothers from the Carr family of Pennsylvania have earned all-American status. Fletcher (Tampa), Joe (Kentucky), Jimmy (Kentucky), Nate (Iowa State), and Mike (West Virginia) all placed in the NCAA Division I Tournament from 1972 through 1988.

Wrestling programs were offered in 427 colleges across the nation by the end of 1988. There were 132 in Division I, 51 in Division II, 130 in Division III, 68 in the NAIA, and 90 in the junior college ranks (including 27 in California). For a comprehensive overview of the NCAA Division I Tournament champions, see Table 8.1 on p. 172, Table 8.2 on p. 176, and Table 8.3 on p. 178.

The NCAA Tournament: Divisions II and III

Although the NCAA Division I Tournament is considered the pinnacle of the college wrestling world and attracts the lion's share of the attention, there are four other national collegiate titles to be won. The NCAA has splintered twice since 1963, forming two additional divisions for schools with smaller programs. In 1958 the NAIA was created. In addition, the junior colleges created a national tournament in 1960.

In 1963, the NCAA created the Division II Tournament, and the first champion was Western State of Colorado, coached by Tracy Borah. Western State repeated the following season, but California schools have dominated since.

California Poly State, under coach Vaughan Hitchcock, won eight titles between 1966 and 1974. California State College, Bakersfield, under coach Joe Seay, won seven titles in the 8 years between 1976 and 1983. In 1987, under new coach T.J. Kerr, California State, Bakersfield, came back to win the title again, breaking a 3-year string by Larry Kristoff's Southern Illinois at Edwardsville team.

Tim Wright of Southern Illinois at Edwardsville made history in 1987 when he won the 118-pound Division II title with a 12-4 victory over Roger Singleton of Grand Valley State in the finals. That performance made Wright a four-time Division II champion, the only four-time NCAA wrestling champion in history.

The North Central Conference crowned its fourth Division II team champion in 1988 when North Dakota State, many times a top-five finisher, captured its first national title. Nebraska at Omaha was second, giving the North Central Conference 12 runner-up spots since the tourney began. For a comprehensive overview of NCAA Division II Tournament champions, see Table 8.4 on p. 235.

In 1974, the Division III Tournament was established for even smaller colleges. Wilkes College in Pennsylvania took that team title, led by coach John Reese. Trenton State in New Jersey, coached by Dave Icenhower, had won more titles (five) than any other team by the end of 1988. The 1988 champion was St. Lawrence University in Canton, New York. It was the first national title for the Saints, whose previous claim to fame had come 50 years earlier, when film star Kirk Douglas served as wrestling captain in 1938. For a comprehensive overview of NCAA Division III Tournament champions, see Table 8.5 on p. 275.

The NAIA Tournament

The NAIA Tournament was 31 years old in 1988. Although Mankato State in Minnesota, coached by Rummy Macias, claimed the first two titles, Adams State in Alamosa, Colorado, and Central State in Edmonds, Oklahoma, each had seven titles by the end of 1988. The title left the country in 1988 when Simon Fraser University in Burnaby, British Columbia, ended Central State's 4-year run by a 104.5-89 margin.

The brightest star of the NAIA is Lock Haven's Elliott "Gray" Simons, who won four titles at 115 pounds and was voted the tourney's Outstanding Wrestler all 4 years (1959 through 1962). Simons then moved on to win the NCAA three times and to win two Outstanding Wrestler awards there as well.

Other four-time NAIA champions are Lock Haven's Jerry Swope at 177 (1963 to 1966), St. Cloud State's Jim Hazewinkel at 115 and 123 (1963 to 1967), and Simon Fraser's Bob Molle at heavyweight (1983 to 1986). Chuck Jean won two NAIA titles at 177 for Adams State (1972 and 1973) after transferring from Iowa State, where he had captured two NCAA titles. For a comprehensive overview of NAIA Tournament champions, see Table 8.6 on p. 297.

Gray Simons (top), four-time NAIA champion, in action. (Courtesy of National Wrestling Hall of Fame)

The Junior College National Wrestling Tournament

The first Junior College National Wrestling Tournament took place at Long Island, New York. Lamar Junior College of Colorado ran away with the team title, scoring 98 points to 55 for second-place Long Island. Lamar won five titles in all, but by the end of the 1988 season the power base had shifted to the Northwest. At the 29th annual tournament in 1988, North Idaho College, situated in Coeur d'Alene, won its ninth title and its fourth in a row.

Among junior college champions who went on to win NCAA crowns are Chris Taylor, Darrell Keller, Ron Ray, and Eddie Urbano. Taylor won the heavyweight title for Muskegon, Michigan (1969), and two NCAA titles at Iowa State. Keller took the 123-pound title for Columbia Basin, Washington (1967), and then won the NCAA at 142 for Oklahoma State.

Ron Ray won two junior college titles at 167 for Wright Junior College in Chicago (1972 and 1973) and took the same weight at the NCAA Tournament for Oklahoma State. Urbano was a 150-pound champ for Pima Junior College in Arizona (1982) before winning the same weight class in the NCAA Tournament for Arizona State. For a comprehensive overview of Junior College Tournament champions, see Table 8.7 on p. 331.

Chris Taylor, junior college national champion. (From the Chapman collection)

Table 8.1
NCAA Tournament History, 1928-1988

Three-time NCAA Champions

Name	School	Weight	Year
David Arndt	Oklahoma State	145	1941, 1942
		146	1946
Ed Banach	Iowa	177	1980, 1981
		190	1983
Rick Bonomo	Bloomsburg State	118	1985, 1986, 1987
Conrad Caldwell	Oklahoma State	165	1929
		175	1930, 1931
Nate Carr	Iowa State	150	1981, 1982, 1983

Three-time NCAA Champions

Name	School	Weight	Year
Mike Caruso	Lehigh	123	1965, 1966, 1967
Mark Churella	Michigan	150	1977, 1978
		167	1979
Barry Davis	Iowa	118	1982
		126	1983, 1985
Ross Flood	Oklahoma State	126	1933, 1934, 1935
Larry Hayes	Iowa State	137	1959
		147	1960, 1961
Stanley Henson	Oklahoma State	145	1937, 1938
		155	1939
Dan Hodge	Oklahoma	177	1955, 1956, 1957
Richard Hutton	Oklahoma State	Heavyweight	1947, 1948, 1950
Jimmy Jackson	Oklahoma State	Heavyweight	1976, 1977, 1978
Greg Johnson	Michigan State	118	1970, 1971, 1972
Lee Kemp	Wisconsin	158	1976, 1977, 1978
William Koll	Northern Iowa	145	1946, 1947
		147.5	1948
Lowell Lange	Cornell C	136	1947, 1949, 1950
Wayne Martin	Oklahoma	135	1934
		145	1935
		134	1936
Earl McCready	Oklahoma State	Heavyweight	1928, 1929, 1930
Joe McDaniels	Oklahoma State	118	1937, 1938
		121	1939
William Nelson	Northern Iowa	165	1947
		155	1949, 1950
Ed Peery	Pittsburgh	123	1955, 1956, 1957
Hugh Peery	Pittsburgh	115	1952, 1953, 1954
Rex Peery	Oklahoma State	118	1933, 1934, 1935
Myron Roderick	Oklahoma State	137	1954
		130	1955, 1956
Mark Schultz	Oklahoma	167	1981
		177	1982, 1983
Elliott Simons	Lock Haven	115	1960, 1961, 1962
Yojiro Uetake	Oklahoma State	130	1964, 1965, 1966
Jack Van Bebber	Oklahoma State	155	1929
		165	1930, 1931
Keith Young	Northern Iowa	145	1949, 1950
		147	1951
Jim Zalesky	Iowa	158	1982, 1983, 1984

Amateur Wrestling News Selections for
Unofficial National Collegiate Wrestling Team Championship

Year	*School*
1905	Yale
1906	Yale
1907	Yale
1908	Yale
1909	Yale
1910	Cornell U
1911	Princeton, Penn State
1912	Cornell U
1913	Penn State
1914	Penn State
1915	Navy
1916	Yale
1917	Penn State
1918	Penn State
1919	Navy
1920	Navy
1921	Navy
1922	Iowa State, Navy
1923	Cornell U, Iowa State
1924	Iowa State, Nebraska
1925	Oklahoma State
1926	Oklahoma State
1927	Oklahoma State
1928	Oklahoma State
1929-1930	Tournaments held
1931	Oklahoma State
1932	Indiana
1933	Iowa State, Oklahoma State
1934-1942	Tournaments held
1943	Navy
1944	Navy
1945	Navy

Team Champions

Year	*Champion*	*Points*	*Runner-up*	*Points*
1929	Oklahoma State	26	Michigan	18
1930	Oklahoma State	27	Illinois	14
1934	Oklahoma State	29	Indiana	19
1935	Oklahoma State	36	Oklahoma	18

Team Champions

Year	*Champion*	*Points*	*Runner-up*	*Points*
1936	Oklahoma	16	Central State (OK)	10
1937	Oklahoma State	31	Oklahoma	13
1938	Oklahoma State	19	Illinois	15
1939	Oklahoma State	33	Lehigh	12
1940	Oklahoma State	24	Indiana	14
1941	Oklahoma State	37	Michigan State	26
1942	Oklahoma State	31	Michigan State	26
1946	Oklahoma State	25	Northern Iowa	24
1947	Cornell C	32	Northern Iowa	19
1948	Oklahoma State	33	Michigan State	28
1949	Oklahoma State	32	Northern Iowa	27
1950	Northern Iowa	30	Purdue	16
1951	Oklahoma	24	Oklahoma State	23
1952	Oklahoma	22	Northern Iowa	21
1953	Penn State	21	Oklahoma	15
1954	Oklahoma State	32	Pittsburgh	17
1955	Oklahoma State	40	Penn State	31
1956	Oklahoma State	65	Oklahoma	62
1957	Oklahoma State	73	Pittsburgh	66
1958	Oklahoma State	77	Iowa State	62
1959	Oklahoma State	73	Iowa State	51
1960	Oklahoma	59	Iowa State	40
1961	Oklahoma State	82	Oklahoma	63
1962	Oklahoma State	82	Oklahoma	45
1963	Oklahoma	48	Iowa State	45
1964	Oklahoma State	87	Oklahoma	58
1965	Iowa State	87	Oklahoma State	86
1966	Oklahoma State	79	Iowa State	70
1967	Michigan State	74	Michigan	63
1968	Oklahoma State	81	Iowa State	78
1969	Iowa State	104	Oklahoma	69
1970	Iowa State	99	Michigan State	84
1971	Oklahoma State	94	Iowa State	66
1972	Iowa State	103	Michigan State	72.50
1973	Iowa State	85	Oregon State	72.50
1974	Oklahoma	69.50	Michigan	67
1975	Iowa	102	Oklahoma	77
1976	Iowa	123.25	Iowa State	85.75
1977	Iowa State	95.50	Oklahoma State	88.75
1978	Iowa	94.50	Iowa State	94
1979	Iowa	112.50	Iowa State	88
1980	Iowa	110.75	Oklahoma State	87
1981	Iowa	129.75	Oklahoma	100.25

Team Champions

Year	*Champion*	*Points*	*Runner-up*	*Points*
1982	Iowa	131.75	Iowa State	111
1983	Iowa	155	Oklahoma State	102
1984	Iowa	123.75	Oklahoma State	98
1985	Iowa	145.25	Oklahoma	98.50
1986	Iowa	158	Oklahoma	84.25
1987	Iowa State	133	Iowa	108
1988	Arizona State	93	Iowa	85.50

Table 8.2

NCAA Division I Outstanding Wrestler Awards

Year	Name	School	Weight
1932	Edwin Belshaw	Indiana	135
1933	Allan Kelley	Oklahoma State	145
	Pat O. Johnson	Harvard	135
1934	Ben Bishop	Lehigh	155
1935	Ross Flood	Oklahoma State	126
1936	Wayne Martin	Oklahoma	134
1937	Stan Henson	Oklahoma State	145
1938	Joe McDaniel	Oklahoma State	118
1939	Dale Hanson	Minnesota	128
1940	Don Nichols	Michigan	175
1941	Alfred Whitehurst	Oklahoma State	136
1942	David Arndt	Oklahoma State	145
1943-1945	No tournaments held		
1946	Gerry Leeman	Northern Iowa	128
1947	William Koll	Northern Iowa	145
1948	William Koll	Northern Iowa	147.5
1949	Charles Hetrick	Oklahoma State	128
1950	Anthony Gizoni	Waynesburg State	121
1951	Walt Romanowski	Cornell C	130
1952	Tommy Evans	Oklahoma	147

Year	Name	School	Weight
1953	Frank Bettucci	Cornell U	147
1954	Tommy Evans	Oklahoma	147
1955	Ed Eichelberger	Lehigh	147
1956	Dan Hodge	Oklahoma	177
1957	Dan Hodge	Oklahoma	177
1958	Dick Delgado	Oklahoma	115
1959	Ron Gray	Iowa State	147
1960	Dave Auble	Cornell U	123
1961	Elliott Simons	Lock Haven	115
1962	Elliott Simons	Lock Haven	115
1963	Mickey Martin	Oklahoma	130
1964	Dean Lahr	Colorado	177
1965	Yojiro Uetake	Oklahoma State	130
1966	Yojiro Uetake	Oklahoma State	130
1967	Richard Sanders	Portland State	115
1968	Dwayne Keller	Oklahoma State	123
1969	Dan Gable	Iowa State	137
1970	Larry Owings	Washington	142
1971	Darrell Keller	Oklahoma State	142
1972	Wade Schalles	Clarion State	150
1973	Greg Strobel	Oregon State	190
1974	Floyd Hitchcock	Bloomsburg State	177
1975	Mike Frick	Lehigh	134
1976	Chuck Yagla	Iowa	150
1977	Nick Gallo	Hofstra	126
1978	Mark Churella	Michigan	150
1979	Bruce Kinseth	Iowa	150
1980	Howard Harris	Oregon State	Heavyweight
1981	Gene Mills	Syracuse	118
1982	Mark Schultz	Oklahoma	177
1983	Mike Sheets	Oklahoma State	167
1984	Jim Zalesky	Iowa	158
1985	Barry Davis	Iowa	126
1986	Marty Kistler	Iowa	167
1987	John Smith	Oklahoma State	134
1988	Scott Turner	North Carolina State	150

Table 8.3
NCAA Tournament Records
Division I—1928-1988

1928 (at Iowa State University, Ames, IA)

(No team scoring kept)

Place winners

115-lb class
1. Harold DeMarsh (Oklahoma A&M)
2. Leach (Oklahoma)
3. Higgins (Iowa State)

125-lb class
1. Ralph Lupton (Northwestern)
2. Hewett (Michigan)
3. Paxson (Kansas)

135-lb class
1. Arthur Holding (Iowa State)
2. Moore (Oklahoma A&M)
3. Thomas (Michigan)

145-lb class
1. Melvin Clodfelter (Oklahoma A&M)
2. Swain (Indiana)
3. Campbell (Illinois)

158-lb class
1. Leslie Beers (Iowa)
2. Donohoe (Michigan)
3. Blaire (Iowa State)

175-lb class
1. George Rule (Oklahoma A&M)
2. Hammonds (Texas)
3. Helgerson (Ohio)

Heavyweight
1. Earl McCready (Oklahoma A&M)
2. Webster (Illinois)
3. Freese (Kansas)

1929 (at Ohio State University, Columbus, OH)

Team	*Points*
1. Oklahoma A&M	26
2. Michigan	18
3. Oklahoma	13
4. Illinois	11

Place winners

115-lb class
1. Joe Sapora (Illinois)
2. Leach (Oklahoma)
3. Shockley (Oklahoma A&M)

125-lb class
1. Lawrence Mantooth (Oklahoma)
2. Hewitt (Michigan)
3. Hesser (Oklahoma A&M)

135-lb class
1. George Minot (Illinois)
2. Miller (Oklahoma)
3. Cox (West Virginia)

145-lb class
1. George Bancroft (Oklahoma A&M)
2. Kelly (Michigan)
3. Montgomery (Iowa)

155-lb class
1. Jack Van Bebber (Oklahoma A&M)
2. Parker (Michigan)
3. Hammer (Wisconsin)

165-lb class
1. Conrad Caldwell (Oklahoma A&M)
2. Hooker (Purdue)
3. Warren (Michigan)

175-lb class
1. Glenn Stafford (Cornell U)
2. Dougovito (Michigan)
3. Heywood (Wisconsin)

Heavyweight
1. Earl McCready (Oklahoma A&M)
2. Swenson (Wisconsin)
3. Fairall (Ohio State)

1930 (at Ohio State University, Columbus, OH)

Team	*Points*
1. Oklahoma A&M	27
2. Illinois	14
3. Oklahoma	12

Team	*Points*
4. Iowa State	7
5. Michigan	6
6. Kansas State, MIT	5
8. Edmond (OK) STC, Cornell College, Kansas, Ohio State	4
12. Chicago, Harvard	2
14. Indiana, Rochester (NY), Mechanics Institute, Michigan State, Missouri, Northwestern	1

Place winners

115-lb class
1. Joe Sapora (Illinois
2. Axford (MIT)
3. Leach (Oklahoma)

125-lb class
1. Lawrence Mantooth (Oklahoma)
2. Morford (Cornell C)
3. Cline (Oklahoma A&M)

135-lb class
1. Hugh Linn (Iowa State)
2. Bauerle (Illinois)
3. Stevenson (Oklahoma A&M)

145-lb class
1. Hardie Lewis (Oklahoma)
2. Tomlinson (Oklahoma A&M)
3. Dyer (Chicago)

155-lb class
1. Otto Kelley (Michigan)
2. Watkins (Edmond STC)
3. Berry (Oklahoma)

165-lb class
1. Jack Van Bebber (Oklahoma A&M)
2. Church (Kansas)
3. Solano (Harvard)

175-lb class
1. Conrad Caldwell (Oklahoma A&M)
2. Helgerson (Ohio State)
3. Robbins (Missouri)

Heavyweight
1. Earl McCready (Oklahoma A&M)
2. Burdick (Illinois)
3. Errington (Kansas State)

1931 (at Brown University, Providence, RI)

(No team prizes awarded, thus placing the emphasis on individual performance)

Place winners

118-lb class
1. John Engel (Lehigh)
2. Jesse Arends (Iowa State Teachers)
3. Andrew Hesser (Oklahoma A&M)

126-lb class
1. Robert Pearce (Oklahoma A&M)
2. Lyle Morford (Cornell C)
3. Joe Fickel (Kansas State)

135-lb class
1. Richard Cole (Iowa State)
2. J.W. Divine (Oklahoma A&M)
3. H.S. Byam (Michigan State)

145-lb class
1. William Doyle (Kansas State)
2. Walter Thomas (Iowa State)
3. Walter Young (Oklahoma A&M)

155-lb class
1. LeRoy McGuirk (Oklahoma A&M)
2. John Richardson (Kansas State)
3. Orville Orr (Iowa State Teachers)

165-lb class
1. Jack Van Bebber (Oklahoma A&M)
2. R.W. Hess (Iowa State)
3. M.W. Shanker (Lehigh)

175-lb class
1. Conrad Caldwell (Oklahoma A&M)
2. C.J. Dougovito (Michigan)
3. A.W. Brown Jr. (Northwestern)

Heavyweight
1. Jack Riley (Northwestern)
2. Harry Fields (Haverford)
3. C.H. Errington (Kansas State)

Heavyweight
1. Jack Riley (Northwestern)
2. Harry Fields (Haverford)
3. C.H. Errington (Kansas State)

1932 (at Indiana University, Bloomington, IN)

(No team points awarded)

Place winners

123-lb class
1. Joseph Puerta (Illinois)
2. Pearce (Oklahoma A&M)
3. Ball (Michigan State)

134-lb class
1. Edwin Belshaw (Indiana)
2. Rasor (Oklahoma A&M)
3. Lyle Morford (Cornell C)

145-lb class
1. Hardie Lewis (Oklahoma)
2. Goings (Indiana)
3. Harman (Iowa State Teachers)

158-lb class
1. Carl Dougovito (Michigan)
2. Silverstein (Navy)
3. Martin (Iowa State)

174-lb class
1. Robert Hess (Iowa State Teachers)
2. McGuirk (Oklahoma A&M)
3. Rascher (Indiana)

191-lb class
1. Kermit Blosser (Ohio)
2. Teague (Weatherford STC)
3. Jones (Indiana)

Heavyweight
1. Jack Riley (Northwestern)
2. Mehringer (Kansas)
3. Gerber (Iowa State Teachers)

1933 (at Lehigh University, Bethlehem, PA)

(No team points awarded)

Place winners

118-lb class
1. Rex Peery (Oklahoma A&M)
2. Joe Puerta (Illinois)
3. Milo Meixell (Lehigh)

126-lb class
1. Ross Flood (Oklahoma A&M)
2. R.L. Emmons (Illinois)
3. Oliver Cellini (Indiana)

135-lb class
1. Patrick H. Devine (Indiana)
2. W.R. Phillips (Franklin and Marshall)
3. Pat Johnson (Harvard)

145-lb class
1. Alan Kelley (Oklahoma A&M)
2. Roy Stout (Weatherford STC)
3. Dale Goings (Indiana)

155-lb class
1. Merrill Frevert (Iowa State)
2. Warren Landis (Virginia Military Institute)
3. Gus Kremer (Lehigh)

165-lb class
1. George Martin (Iowa State)
2. Clarence J. Peck (Lehigh)
3. Orville England (Weatherford STC)

175-lb class
1. Robert Hess (Iowa State)
2. Richard Voliva (Indiana)
3. Gordon Dupree (Oklahoma A&M)

Heavyweight
1. Ralph Teague (Weatherford STC)
2. Robert Jones (Indiana)
3. Ernest Zeller (Indiana STC)

1934 (at University of Michigan, Ann Arbor, MI)

Team	*Points*
1. Oklahoma A&M	29
2. Indiana	19
3. Oklahoma	14
4. Weatherford (OK) STC	12
5. Lehigh	7
6. Springfield (MA)	4
7. Michigan, Iowa State Teachers, Edmond (OK) STC	3
10. Washington and Lee, Cornell College, Illinois	2
13. Temple, Rochester (NY) Mechanics Institute, Iowa	1

Place winners

118-lb class
1. Rex Peery (Oklahoma A&M)
2. Alvie Natvig (Iowa State Teachers)
3. Howard T. Bush (Indiana)

126-lb class
1. Ross Flood (Oklahoma A&M)
2. Oliver G. Cellini (Indiana)
3. Eldon Stout (Weatherford STC)

135-lb class
1. Wayne Martin (Oklahoma)
2. Roger Leathers (Springfield C)
3. Patrick H. Devine (Indiana)

145-lb class
1. Alan Kelley (Oklahoma A&M)
2. Arthur Mosier (Michigan)
3. Charles Pritchard (Washington and Lee)

155-lb class
1. Ben L. Bishop (Lehigh)
2. Frank Lewis (Oklahoma A&M)
3. Foy Stout (Weatherford STC)

165-lb class
1. Marion Foreman (Oklahoma)
2. Steve England (Weatherford STC)
3. Gordon Ellison (Cornell C)

175-lb class
1. Richard Voliva (Indiana)
2. Emil Schellstede (Edmond STC)
3. Gordon Dupree (Oklahoma A&M)

Heavyweight
1. Ralph Teague (Weatherford STC)
2. Otto R. Kuss (Indiana)
3. Barney Cosneck (Illinois)

1935 (at Lehigh University, Bethlehem, PA)

Team	*Points*
1. Oklahoma A&M	36
2. Oklahoma	18
3. Indiana, Illinois	15
5. Lehigh, Penn State	8
7. Weatherford (OK) STC, Iowa	6

Place winners

118-lb class
1. Rex Peery (Oklahoma A&M)
2. Duffy (Indiana)
3. Ledbetter (Illinois)

126-lb class
1. Ross Flood (Oklahoma A&M)
2. Gott (Weatherford STC)
3. Pakutinsky (Illinois)

135-lb class
1. Vernon Sisney (Oklahoma)
2. Rasor (Oklahoma A&M)
3. Hanks (Weatherford STC)

145-lb class
1. Wayne Martin (Oklahoma)
2. Tomlinson (Edmond STC)
3. McIlvoy (Illinois)

155-lb class
1. Frank Lewis (Oklahoma A&M)
2. McGrath (Cornell C)
3. Kalpin (Oklahoma)

165-lb class
1. Howard Johnston (Penn State)
2. Kiehorn (Iowa)
3. Robertson (Oklahoma)

175-lb class
1. Ralph Silverstein (Illinois)
2. Ricks (Oklahoma A&M)
3. Nickerson (Weatherford STC)

Heavyweight
1. Charles McDaniel (Indiana)
2. Scobey (Lehigh)
3. Bonino (Washington and Lee)

1936 (at Washington and Lee University, Lexington, VA)

(No team scoring kept)

Place winners

123-lb class
1. Ted Anderson (Edmond STC)
2. D.C. Matthews (Oklahoma)
3. Joe Parkey (Weatherford STC)
4. Willard Duffy (Indiana)

134-lb class
1. Wayne Martin (Oklahoma)
2. Dale Brand (Cornell C)
3. Earl Thomas (Michigan)
4. George Hanks (Weatherford STC)

145-lb class
1. H.D. Strong (Oklahoma)
2. Carl Kitt (Weatherford STC)
3. Byron Guernsey (Iowa)
4. Joe Kalpin (Oklahoma)

158-lb class
1. Walter Jacob (Michigan State)
2. Bill Keas (Oklahoma)
3. Earl Kielhorn (Iowa)
4. (tie) Hugh Bishop (Lehigh) and Caifson Johnson (Minnesota)

174-lb class
1. Harry Broadbent (Oklahoma)
2. Dormer Browning (Oklahoma A&M)
3. Raymond Vogel (Navy)
4. McCullough (Weatherford STC)

191-lb class
1. Duke Clemons (Edmond STC)
2. Charles McDaniel (Indiana)
3. Willard Loretti (Oklahoma A&M)
4. Richard Landis (Temple)

Heavyweight
1. Howell Scobey (Lehigh)
2. Hugo Bonino (Washington and Lee)
3. Gordon Dupree (Oklahoma A&M) (only three contestants in this class)

1937 (at Indiana State Teachers College, Terre Haute, IN)

Team	Points
1. Oklahoma A&M	31
2. Oklahoma	13
3. Iowa State Teachers, Minnesota	9
5. Illinois	8
6. Cornell College	7
7. Kansas State	5
8. Central State Teachers (OK), Indiana	4
10. Iowa State College	3
11. Michigan	2
12. Chicago, Haverford, Southwest Teachers (OK), St. Lawrence, West Virginia	1

Place winners

118-lb class
1. Joe McDaniel (Oklahoma A&M)
2. Davis Natvig (Iowa State Teachers)
3. William Carr (Oklahoma)

126-lb class
1. Dale Brand (Cornell C)
2. Ted A. Anderson (Central State Teachers)
3. D.C. Matthews (Oklahoma)

135-lb class
1. Raymond Cheyney (Iowa State Teachers)
2. Fred Parkey (Oklahoma A&M)
3. M.W. Villa Real (Central State Teachers)

145-lb class
1. Stanley Henson (Oklahoma A&M)
2. Jack C. McIlvoy (Illinois)
3. Charles Carson (Oklahoma)

155-lb class
1. Bill Keas (Oklahoma)
2. Ernest Jessup (Kansas State)
3. Dale Scrivens (Oklahoma A&M)

165-lb class
1. Harvey Base (Oklahoma A&M)
2. Marshall Word (Oklahoma)
3. Marvin E. Farrell (Iowa State)

175-lb class
1. John Whitaker (Minnesota)
2. John J. Ginay (Illinois)
3. Willard Lorette (Oklahoma A&M)

Heavyweight
1. Lloyd Ricks (Oklahoma A&M)
2. Bob Haak (Indiana)
3. Clifton Gustafson (Minnesota)

1938 (at Penn State, State College, PA)

Team	Points
1. Oklahoma A&M	19
2. Illinois	15
3. Indiana	12
4. Southwest Teachers (OK), Oklahoma	8
6. Minnesota	6
7. Lehigh, Harvard, Cornell College	5
10. Chicago	4
11. Franklin and Marshall, Princeton, Iowa State, Iowa State Teachers	3
15. City College of New York	2
16. Nebraska, Syracuse	1

Place winners

118-lb class
1. Joe McDaniels (Oklahoma A&M)
2. Duffy (Indiana)
3. Natvig (Iowa State Teachers)

126-lb class
1. Allen Sapora (Illinois)
2. Murray (Cornell C)
3. Stone (Oklahoma)

135-lb class
1. David Matthews (Oklahoma)
2. Deutschman (Illinois)
3. Parkey (Oklahoma A&M)

145-lb class
1. Stanley Henson (Oklahoma A&M)
2. Finwall (Chicago)
3. Linn (Iowa State)

155-lb class
1. Dale Scrivens (Oklahoma A&M)
2. Knight (Southwest Teachers)
3. Loucks (Iowa State)

165-lb class
1. John Ginay (Illinois)
2. Ford (Lehigh)
3. Wittenberg (CCNY)

175-lb class
1. John Harkness (Harvard)
2. Olsen (Southwest Teachers)
3. Traicoff (Indiana)

Heavyweight
1. Charley McDaniel (Indiana)
2. Gustafson (Minnesota)
3. Kygar (Southwest Teachers)

1939 (at Franklin and Marshall College, Lancaster, PA)

Team	*Points*
1. Oklahoma A&M	33
2. Lehigh	12
3. Illinois	11
4. Franklin and Marshall	10
5. Michigan, Indiana, Minnesota	9
8. Penn State	5
9. City College of New York	4
10. Appalachian	3
11. Cornell College, Kent State	2
13. Navy, Colorado Normal, Illinois Normal	1

Place winners

121-lb class
1. Joe McDaniel (Oklahoma A&M)
2. Burgess (Franklin and Marshall)
3. Parks (Appalachian)

128-lb class
1. Dale Hanson (Minnesota)
2. Rorex (Oklahoma A&M)
3. Petry (Illinois)

136-lb class
1. Archie Deutschman (Illinois)
2. Roman (Indiana)
3. Culbertson (Minnesota)

145-lb class
1. Harold Nichols (Michigan)
2. Scalzo (Penn State)
3. Logan (Oklahoma A&M)

155-lb class
1. Stanley Henson (Oklahoma A&M)
2. Combs (Michigan)
3. King (Lehigh)

165-lb class
1. Henry Matthews (Lehigh)
2. Nelson (Oklahoma A&M)
3. Bachman (Penn State)

175-lb class
1. Chris Traicoff (Indiana)
2. Wittenberg (CCNY)
3. Williams (Oklahoma A&M)

Heavyweight
1. Johnny Harrell (Oklahoma A&M)
2. Sikich (Illinois)
3. Falcone (Kent State)

1940 (at University of Illinois, Champaign, IL)

Team	*Points*
1. Oklahoma A&M	24
2. Indiana	14
3. Michigan	10
4. Colorado State, Lehigh, Ohio State	7
7. Iowa State Teachers, Minnesota	6
9. Iowa State, Oklahoma	5
11. Franklin and Marshall, Illinois	4
13. Kansas State, Kent State	2
15. Dubuque, Lafayette, Michigan State, Southwest Teachers (OK), Purdue, Syracuse, Temple	1

Place winners

121-lb class
1. Robert Antonacci (Indiana)
2. Calvin Melhorn (Oklahoma A&M)
3. Delbert Jensen (Iowa State Teachers)

128-lb class
1. Harold Byrd (Oklahoma)
2. Dale Hanson (Minnesota)
3. Bob Kitt (Oklahoma A&M)

136-lb class
1. Alfred Whitehurst (Oklahoma A&M)
2. Roger Issacson (Iowa State Teachers)
3. Joseph Roman (Indiana)

145-lb class
1. Harold Masem (Lehigh)
2. Bill Combs (Michigan)
3. A.C. Schacheman (Franklin and Marshall)

155-lb class
1. Vernon Logan (Oklahoma A&M)
2. Marvin Farrell (Iowa State)
3. Harland Danner (Michigan)

165-lb class
1. Crawford Grenard (Colorado State)
2. Clay Albright (Oklahoma A&M)
3. Chauncey McDaniel (Indiana)

175-lb class
1. Don Nichols (Michigan)
2. Garnet Inman (Indiana)
3. Leon Reynard (Kansas State)

Heavyweight
1. George Downes (Ohio State)
2. George Chiga (Oklahoma A&M)
3. John Sikich (Illinois)

1941 (at Lehigh University, Bethlehem, PA)

Team	*Points*
1. Oklahoma A&M	37
2. Michigan State	26
3. Minnesota	12
4. Yale	8
5. Wisconsin, Kent State, Appalachian STC	7
8. Kansas State, Pennsylvania	6
10. Iowa State Teachers, Iowa, Franklin and Marshall	5
13. Illinois, Iowa State College, Lafayette, Penn State	3
17. Dubuque, Michigan, Ohio State, Temple	2
21. Rutgers, Springfield, Virginia Military Institute, Wyoming	1

Place winners

121-lb class
1. Merle Jennings (Michigan State)
2. Calvin Melhorn (Oklahoma A&M)
3. William Sherman (Iowa State College)
4. Charles Parks (Appalachian)

128-lb class
1. Burl Jennings (Michigan State)
2. Michael Slcpecky (Kent State)
3. Dillard Talbutt (Oklahoma A&M)
4. Roy Julius (Iowa State College)

136-lb class
1. Alfred Whitehurst (Oklahoma A&M)
2. William Maxwell (Michigan State)
3. Frank Gleason (Penn State)
4. John Gastles (Yale)

145-lb class
1. David Arndt (Oklahoma A&M)
2. Vernon Hassman (Iowa State Teachers)
3. Al Schacheman (Franklin and Marshall)
4. Alphonse Janesko (Minnesota)

155-lb class
1. Earl Van Bebber (Oklahoma A&M)
2. Leland Porter (Kansas State)
3. Ted Seabrooke (Illinois)
4. Frank Osinski (Temple)

165-lb class
1. Virgil Smith (Oklahoma A&M)
2. John Roberts (Wisconsin)
3. Charles Hutson (Michigan State)
4. Sam Linn (Iowa State)

175-lb class
1. Richard DiBattista (Pennsylvania)
2. Al Crawford (Appalachian)

3. James Galles (Michigan)
4. Earl Hager (Wisconsin)

Heavyweight
1. Leonard Levy (Minnesota)
2. Larry Pickett (Yale)
3. Lloyd Arms (Oklahoma A&M)
4. John Thomas (Lafayette)

1942 (at Michigan State University, East Lansing, MI)

Team	*Point*
1. Oklahoma A&M	31
2. Michigan State	26
3. Penn State	10
4. Michigan	8
5. Purdue, Navy, Kent State	7
8. Pennsylvania, Illinois	6
10. Iowa State Teachers	5
11. Cornell College	4
12. Kansas State, Nebraska	2
14. Princeton	1

Place winners

121-lb class
1. Merle "Cut" Jennings (Michigan State)
2. Malcolm MacDonald (Purdue)
3. Charles Ridenour (Penn State)
4. Richard Kopel (Michigan)

128-lb class
1. Burl "Bo" Jennings (Michigan State)
2. Sidney Marks (Oklahoma A&M)
3. Samuel Harry (Penn State)
4. Mark Matovina (Purdue)

136-lb class
1. William Maxwell (Michigan State)
2. Fred Bishop (Cornell C)
3. Dillard Talbutt (Oklahoma A&M)
4. Warren Taylor (Princeton)

145-lb class
1. David "Buddy" Arndt (Oklahoma A&M)
2. Manly Johnson (Michigan)
3. Glen Alexander (Penn State)
4. Newton Copple (Nebraska)

155-lb class
1. Vernon Logan (Oklahoma A&M)
2. Theodore Seabrooke (Illinois)
3. Leland Merrill (Michigan State)
4. Milton Bennett (Navy)

165-lb class
1. Virgil Smith (Oklahoma A&M)
2. William Carmichael (Navy)
3. William Courtright (Michigan)
4. Robert Bader (Kent State)

175-lb class
1. Richard DiBattista (Pennsylvania)
2. Leon Martin (Iowa State Teachers)
3. Paul Chronister (Kansas State)
4. Kenneth Berry (Illinois)

Heavyweight
1. Lloyd Arms (Oklahoma A&M)
2. Walter Porowski (Kent State)
3. Frank Ruggieri (Purdue)
4. Shuford Switt (Navy)

(No tournaments held, 1943-1945)

1946 (at Oklahoma A&M, Stillwater, OK)

Team	*Points*
1. Oklahoma A&M	25
2. Iowa State Teachers	24
3. Illinois	17
4. Indiana	13
5. Michigan	8
6. Ohio State, Iowa State	6
8. Michigan State	5
9. Colorado State, Nebraska, Penn State	2
12. Kent State	1

Place winners

121-lb class
1. Cecil Mott (Iowa Sate)
2. M. Rolak (Indiana)

3. B. Tomaras (Illinois)
4. C. Fletcher (Michigan State)

128-lb class
1. Gerald Leeman (Iowa State Teachers)
2. L. Kachiroubas (Illinois)
3. S. Harry (Penn State)
4. I. Konrad (Michigan State)

136-lb class
1. David Arndt (Oklahoma A&M)
2. R. Bush (Illinois State)
3. E. George (Indiana)
4. L. Smith (Michigan)

145-lb class
1. William Koll (Iowa State Teachers)
2. E. Welch (Oklahoma A&M)
3. G. Mikles (Michigan State)
4. T. Yamasawi (Northern Colorado)

155-lb class
1. William Courtright (Michigan)
2. J. St. Clair (Oklahoma A&M)
3. R. Ditsworth (Illinois State)
4. K. Marlin (Illinois)

165-lb class
1. David Shapiro (Illinois)
2. G. Walker (Oklahoma A&M)
3. H. Boker (Nebraska)
4. G. Glass (Kent State)

175-lb class
1. George Dorsch (Oklahoma A&M)
2. N. Antounsen (Illinois)
3. S. Golonka (Indiana)
4. J. Klune (Northern Colorado)

Heavyweight
1. George Bollas (Ohio State)
2. M. Chittwood (Indiana)
3. G. Brand (Iowa State)
4. L. Arms (Oklahoma A&M)

1947 (at University of Illinois, Champaign, IL)

Team	*Points*
1. Cornell College	32
2. Iowa State Teachers	19
3. Oklahoma A&M	15
4. Michigan State	11
5. Oklahoma	10
6. Illinois	9
7. Iowa	6
8. Iowa State College, Purdue	5
10. Michigan, Minnesota	4
12. Navy	3
13. Colorado A&M, Colorado State	1

Place winners

121-lb class
1. Richard Hauser (Cornell C)
2. B. Jernigan (Oklahoma A&M)
3. G. Lappin (Minnesota)
4. R. Gibbs (Oklahoma)

128-lb class
1. Russell Bush (Iowa State Teachers)
2. L. Kachiroubas (Illinois)
3. L. Thomsen (Cornell C)
4. P. McDaniels (Oklahoma A&M)

136-lb class
1. Lowell Lange (Cornell C)
2. N. Bauer (Oklahoma A&M)
3. D. Johnson (Michigan State)
4. K. Watson (Oklahoma)

145-lb class
1. William Koll (Iowa State Teachers)
2. R. Snook (Cornell C)
3. J. Fletcher (Navy)
4. D. Anderson (Michigan State)

155-lb class
1. Gail Mikles (Michigan State)
2. W. Courtright (Michigan)
3. L. Stecker (Oklahoma)
4. K. Marlin (Illinois)

165-lb class
1. William Nelson (Iowa State Teachers)
2. J. Eagleton (Oklahoma)
3. F. Dexter (Cornell C)
4. D. Sapiro (Illinois)

175-lb class
1. Joe Scarpello (Iowa)
2. G. Brand (Iowa State)
3. D. Thomas (Cornell C)
4. W. Van Cott (Purdue)

Heavyweight
1. Richard Hutton (Oklahoma A&M)
2. R. Gunkel (Purdue)
3. V. Gagne (Minnesota)
4. C. Gottfried (Illinois)

1948 (at Lehigh University, Bethlehem, PA)

Team	Points
1. Oklahoma A&M	33
2. Michigan State	28
3. Illinois	23
4. Iowa State Teachers, Purdue, Iowa	15
7. Minnesota	12
8. Waynesburg	11
9. Navy, Colorado A&M, Iowa State	9
12. Lock Haven	7
13. Nebraska	5
14. Franklin and Marshall, Lehigh	3
16. Penn State, Rutgers, Indiana, Hofstra, Syracuse	2
21. Kansas State, Williams College, Colorado College	1

Place winners

114.5-lb class
1. Arnold Plaza (Purdue)
2. Mann (Illinois)
3. Jernigan (Oklahoma A&M)
4. Deaugustine (Lock Haven)

125.5-lb class
1. George Lewis (Waynesburg)
2. Macias (Iowa)
3. McDaniel (Oklahoma A&M)
4. McDonald (Michigan State)

136.5-lb class
1. Richard Dickenson (Michigan State)
2. Bauer (Oklahoma A&M)
3. Verga (Lock Haven State)
4. Garcia (Illinois)

147.5-lb class
1. William Koll (Iowa State Teachers)
2. Fletcher (Navy)
3. Copple (Nebraska)
4. Anderson (Michigan State)

160.5-lb class
1. George St. Clair (Oklahoma A&M)
2. Mikles (Michigan State)
3. Mullison (Colorado A&M)
4. Thomas (Waynesburg)

174-lb class
1. Glen Brand (Iowa State)
2. Van Cott (Purdue)
3. Scarpello (Iowa)
4. Gaumer (Illinois)

191-lb class
1. Verne Gagne (Minnesota)
2. Gottfried (Illinois)
3. Geigel (Iowa)
4. Allitz (Iowa State Teachers)

Heavyweight
1. Dick Hutton (Oklahoma A&M)
2. Maldegan (Michigan State)
3. McGraw (Colorado A&M)
4. Archer (Illinois)

1949 (at Colorado A&M, Fort Collins, CO)

Team	Points
1. Oklahoma A&M	32
2. Iowa State Teachers	27
3. Cornell College	22
4. Michigan State	13
5. Minnesota	11
6. Purdue	9
7. Nebraska, Iowa	5
9. Syracuse	4
10. Colorado A&M, Illinois	3
12. Navy, Penn State	2
14. Indiana, Ithaca, Wheaton, Iowa State, Utah State, Kansas State	1

Place winners

121-lb class
1. Arnold Plaza (Purdue)
2. Penninger (Oklahoma A&M)
3. Hauser (Cornell C)
4. Lappin (Minnesota)

128-lb class
1. Charles Hetrick (Oklahoma A&M)
2. Thomsen (Cornell C)
3. Bush (Iowa State Teachers)
4. Rice (Minnesota)

136-lb class
1. Lowell Lange (Cornell C)
2. Dickenson (Michigan State)
3. Klar (Iowa State Teachers)
4. Meeker (Oklahoma A&M)

145-lb class
1. Keith Young (Iowa State Teachers)
2. Anderson (Michigan State)
3. Lange (Cornell C)
4. George (Oklahoma A&M)

155-lb class
1. William Nelson (Iowa State Teachers)
2. Hunte (Syracuse)
3. Mullison (Colorado A&M)
4. Snook (Cornell C)

165-lb class
1. William Smith (Iowa State Teachers)
2. Flessner (Oklahoma A&M)
3. Gaumer (Illinois)
4. Lyons (Kansas State)

175-lb class
1. James Gregson (Oklahoma A&M)
2. Scarpello (Iowa)
3. Reese (Nebraska)
4. Van Cott (Purdue)

Heavyweight
1. Verne Gagne (Minnesota)
2. Hutton (Oklahoma A&M)
3. Maldegan (Michigan State)
4. Barr (Penn State)

1950 (at University of Northern Iowa, Cedar Falls, IA)

Team	*Points*
1. Iowa State Teachers	30
2. Purdue	16
3. Cornell College	14
4. Oklahoma A&M, Syracuse	10
6. Iowa	7
7. Ithaca, Waynesburg	6
9. Penn State	5
10. Navy, Illinois	3
12. Wyoming, Oklahoma, Wheaton, Michigan State	2
16. Auburn, Lock Haven	1

Place winners

121-lb class
1. Anthony Gizoni (Waynesburg)
2. Plaza (Purdue)
3. Altman (Iowa State Teachers)
4. Borders (Oklahoma)

128-lb class
1. Joe Patacsil (Purdue)
2. Romanowski (Cornell C)
3. Blubaugh (Oklahoma)
4. Klar (Iowa State Teachers)

136-lb class
1. Lowell Lange (Cornell C)
2. Oglesby (Iowa State Teachers)
3. Smith (Navy)
4. Farina (Purdue)

145-lb class
1. Keith Young (Iowa State Teachers)
2. Moreno (Purdue)
3. Maurey (Penn State)
4. Snook (Cornell C)

155-lb class
1. William Nelson (Iowa State Teachers)
2. Hunte (Syracuse)

3. Todd (Oklahoma A&M)
4. Mason (Wyoming)

165-lb class
1. William Smith (Iowa State Teachers)
2. LaRoch (Ithaca)
3. Gibbons (Michigan State)
4. Nardini (Cornell C)

175-lb class
1. Joe Scarpello (Iowa)
2. Gebhardt (Syracuse)
3. Vohaska (Illinois)
4. Mantrone (Auburn)

Heavyweight
1. Dick Hutton (Oklahoma A&M)
2. Stoeker (Iowa State Teachers)
3. Barr (Penn State)
4. Simmons (Wheaton)

1951 (at Lehigh University, Bethlehem, PA)

Team	*Points*
1. Oklahoma	24
2. Oklahoma A&M	23
3. Penn State	15
4. Iowa State Teachers	10
5. Princeton	8
6. Ohio State, Michigan State, Toledo	7
9. Cornell College, Waynesburg	6
11. Yale	4
12. Lehigh, Wyoming, Navy, Colorado State	3
16. Auburn	2
17. Army, Washington State, Ursinus, Wisconsin, San Francisco State, Columbia, Mankato State, California	1

Place winners

123-lb class
1. Anthony Gizoni (Waynesburg)
2. Borders (Oklahoma)
3. Kevs (Oklahoma A&M)
4. Dragoin (Auburn)

130-lb class
1. Walter Romanowski (Cornell C)
2. Moore (Oklahoma A&M)
3. Lybbert (Iowa State Teachers)
4. Blubaugh (Oklahoma)

137-lb class
1. George Layman (Oklahoma A&M)
2. Evans (Oklahoma)
3. Maurey (Penn State)
4. Hartman (Columbia)

147-lb class
1. Keith Young (Iowa State Teachers)
2. Fry (Penn State)
3. Todd (Oklahoma A&M)
4. Jackson (Oklahoma)

157-lb class
1. Phil Smith (Oklahoma)
2. McLean (Ohio State)
3. Govoni (Colorado State)
4. Mason (Wyoming)

167-lb class
1. Gene Gibbons (Michigan State)
2. Graveson (Yale)
3. Thomas (Navy)
4. Prihodo (Mankato State)

177-lb class
1. Grover Rains (Oklahoma A&M)
2. Rubino (Penn State)
3. Torio (Toledo)
4. Lyon (California)

Heavyweight
1. Bradley Glass (Princeton)
2. Barr (Penn State)
3. Lanzi (Toledo)
4. Miller (Ohio State)

1952 (at Colorado A&M, Fort Collins, CO)

Team	*Points*
1. Oklahoma	22
2. Iowa State Teachers	21
3. Oklahoma A&M	20
4. Toledo	10

Team	*Points*
5. Penn State	8
6. Illinois, Waynesburg, Colorado	7
9. Pittsburgh, Indiana, California	6
12. Michigan State, Oregon State	5
14. Denver, Iowa	4
16. Michigan, Rutgers, Kansas State, Princeton	3
20. Colorado State, Cornell College, Maryland, Wyoming	2
24. Harvard, Yale, South Dakota	1

Place winners

115-lb class
1. Hugh Peery (Pittsburgh)
2. Howard (Denver)
3. Meeks (Illinois)
4. Carlin (Indiana)

123-lb class
1. Bill Borders (Oklahoma)
2. Arthur (Indiana)
3. Kachiroubas (Illinois)
4. Lee (Harvard)

130-lb class
1. Gene Lybbert (Iowa State Teachers)
2. D. Reece (Oklahoma)
3. Lemyre (Penn State)
4. Lewis (Waynesburg)

137-lb class
1. George Layman (Oklahoma A&M)
2. Morris (Iowa State Teachers)
3. H. Reece (Oklahoma)
4. Compton (Illinois)

147-lb class
1. Tommy Evans (Oklahoma)
2. Harmon (Iowa State Teachers)
3. Lee (Michigan)
4. Todd (Oklahoma A&M)

157-lb class
1. Bill Weick (Iowa State Teachers)
2. Titsworth (Oklahoma A&M)
3. Govoni (Colorado State)
4. Perona (Rutgers)

167-lb class
1. Joe Lemyre (Penn State)
2. Bender (Michigan State)
3. Schneider (Waynesburg)
4. Sonneman (Cornell C)

177-lb class
1. Bentley Lyon (California)
2. Skinner (Colorado)
3. Weaver (Kansas State)
4. Vohden (Rutgers)

191-lb class
1. Harry Lanzi (Toledo)
2. Meyers (Iowa)
3. Glass (Princeton)
4. Butler (Oklahoma)

Heavyweight
1. Gene Nicks (Oklahoma A&M)
2. Witte (Oregon State)
3. Valtoney (Waynesburg)
4. Torio (Toledo)

1953 (at Penn State, State College, PA)

Team	*Points*
1. Penn State	21
2. Oklahoma	15
3. Cornell College	13
4. Oklahoma A&M, Iowa State Teachers	11
6. Pittsburgh	9
7. Michigan	8
8. Michigan State, Minnesota	7
10. Lock Haven, Illinois, Colorado A&M	6
13. Northwestern, Army, West Chester	5
16. Toledo	4

Team	Points
17. Brown, UCLA	3
19. Ithaca, Iowa State, Washington State	2
22. Colorado, Columbia, Indiana, Lehigh, Franklin and Marshall, Harvard, Syracuse	1

Place winners

115-lb class
1. Hugh Peery (Pittsburgh)
2. Christensen (Northwestern)
3. Meeks (Illinois)
4. Helf (Franklin and Marshall)

123-lb class
1. Dick Mueller (Minnesota)
2. D. Reece (Oklahoma)
3. McCarron (Iowa State Teachers)
4. Lee (Harvard)

130-lb class
1. Snip Nalan (Michigan)
2. R. Lemyre (Penn State)
3. Howard (Ithaca)
4. Casalicchio (Michigan State)

137-lb class
1. Len DeAugustino (Lock Haven)
2. Compton (Illinois)
3. Maurey (Penn State)
4. Scott (Oklahoma)

147-lb class
1. Frank Bettucci (Cornell C)
2. Hoke (Michigan State)
3. Don Frey (Penn State)
4. Uram (Pittsburgh)

157-lb class
1. James Harmon (Iowa State Teachers)
2. Sniff (Colorado A&M)
3. Eagleton (Oklahoma)
4. Perrone (Michigan State)

167-lb class
1. Don Dickason (Cornell C)
2. Marks (Oklahoma)
3. J. Lemyre (Penn State)
4. Eastham (Brown)

177-lb class
1. Ned Blass (Oklahoma A&M)
2. Paulekas (Army)
3. Wirds (Iowa State)
4. Lanzi (Toledo)

191-lb class
1. Hud Samson (Penn State)
2. Weber (West Chester)
3. Torio (Toledo)
4. Gatto (Iowa State Teachers)

Heavyweight
1. Dan McNair (Auburn)
2. Nicks (Oklahoma A&M)
3. Kraemer (Pittsburgh)
4. Ellena (UCLA)

1954 (at University of Oklahoma, Norman, OK)

Team	Points
1. Oklahoma A&M	32
2. Pittsburgh	17
3. Penn State	13
4. Navy, Iowa	12
6. Michigan State	11
7. Oklahoma, Michigan	10
9. Lehigh	9
10. Syracuse	6
11. Purdue, Illinois, Minnesota	5
14. Ithaca, Maryland, Nebraska, Wisconsin, Colorado	4
19. Kansas State	3
20. Kent State, Cornell College	2
22. Colorado State, Springfield, Toledo, Brigham Young, Texas A&M	1

Place winners

115-lb class
1. Hugh Peery (Pittsburgh)
2. Ofsthun (Minnesota)

3. McCann (Iowa)
4. Love (Kent State)

123-lb class
1. Richard Govig (Iowa)
2. Lobaugh (Oklahoma A&M)
3. Vega (Purdue)
4. Anderson (Minnesota)

130-lb class
1. Snip Nalan (Michigan)
2. Howard (Ithaca)
3. Sinadinos (Michigan State)
4. Kozy (Pittsburgh)

137-lb class
1. Myron Roderick (Oklahoma A&M)
2. Eichelberger (Lehigh)
3. Maurey (Penn State)
4. Kaul (Michigan)

147-lb class
1. Tommy Evans (Oklahoma)
2. Thompson (Oklahoma A&M)
3. Corwin (Cornell C)
4. Bronstein (Colorado State)

157-lb class
1. Robert Hoke (Michigan State)
2. Rooney (Syracuse)
3. TenPas (Illinois)
4. Eagleton (Oklahoma)

167-lb class
1. Joseph Solomon (Pittsburgh)
2. Fischer (Maryland)
3. Cattuso (Navy)
4. Davis (Oklahoma A&M)

177-lb class
1. Ned Blass (Oklahoma A&M)
2. Smith (Colorado)
3. Krufka (Penn State)
4. Weaver (Kansas State)

191-lb class
1. Peter Blair (Navy)
2. Comly (Lehigh)
3. Oberly (Penn State)
4. Shining (Iowa)

Heavyweight
1. Gene Nicks (Oklahoma A&M)
2. Konovsky (Wisconsin)
3. Kitzelman (Nebraska)
4. Ellis (Kansas State)

1955 (at Cornell University Ithaca, NY)

Team	*Points*
1. Oklahoma A&M	40
2. Penn State	31
3. Pittsburgh	28
4. Oklahoma	26
5. Lehigh	25
6. Iowa	24
7. Michigan	23
8. Navy	21
9. Illinois	19
10. Colorado	15
11. Iowa State Teachers	14
12. West Virginia	13
13. Cornell College	11
14. Colorado A&M	10
15. Michigan State	9
16. Rutgers	8
17. Wisconsin	7
18. Syracuse, Indiana	6
20. Temple, Springfield	5
22. Cornell University, Cortland State, Army, Toledo	3
26. Hofstra, Nebraska, Oregon State, Purdue, Washington State, Wheaton	2
32. Harvard, Ohio, Wyoming, Knox, Loyola College, San Jose State, Waynesburg	1

Place winners

115-lb class
1. Terrance McCann (Iowa)
2. David Bowlin (Oklahoma A&M)
3. Edward Amerantes (Springfield)
4. Robert Perry (West Virginia)

123-lb class
1. Ed Peery (Pittsburgh)
2. Lewis Guidi (West Virginia)
3. Richard Meeks (Illinois)
4. Daniel Deppe (Michigan)

130-lb class
1. Myron Roderick (Oklahoma A&M)
2. Robert Lyons (Oklahoma)
3. Linn Long (Colorado)
4. Ronald Day (Colorado A&M)

137-lb class
1. Lawrence Fornicola (Penn State)
2. Andrew Kaul (Michigan)
3. Jim Sinadinos (Michigan State)
4. William Simmons (Temple)

147-lb class
1. Edward Eichelberger (Lehigh)
2. Lloyd Corwin (Cornell C)
3. Douglas Blubaugh (Oklahoma A&M)
4. George Mulligan (Rutgers)

157-lb class
1. Bill Weick (Iowa State Teachers)
2. Mike Rodriguez (Michigan)
3. Ed DeWitt (Pittsburgh)
4. Edwin Rooney (Syracuse)

167-lb class
1. Fred Davis (Oklahoma A&M)
2. Larry TenPas (Illinois)
3. Joseph Gattuso (Navy)
4. Joe Solomon (Pittsburgh)

177-lb class
1. Dan Hodge (Oklahoma)
2. Joseph Krufka (Penn State)
3. Frank Rosenmayer (Colorado)
4. Don Wem (Toledo)

191-lb class
1. Peter Blair (Navy)
2. Kenneth Leuer (Iowa)
3. Richard Anthony (Indiana)
4. Gus Gatto (Iowa State Teachers)

Heavyweight
1. William Oberly (Penn State)
2. Werner Seel (Lehigh)
3. Robert Konovsky (Wisconsin)
4. Willis Holland (Colorado A&M)

1956 (at Oklahoma A&M, Stillwater, OK)

Team	Points
1. Oklahoma A&M	65
2. Oklahoma	62
3. Pittsburgh	51
4. Iowa	43
5. Penn State	27
6. Lehigh	25
7. Colorado A&M	24
8. Michigan State, Illinois	20
10. Purdue	13
11. Wisconsin	12
12. Michigan	11
13. Iowa State Teachers, Mankato State	10
15. Indiana	8
16. Wyoming	7
17. Lafayette, Maryland	6
19. Virginia Polytechnic, Kansas State	5
21. Navy, Minnesota, Iowa State, Franklin and Marshall	4
25. Springfield, Ohio, Lock Haven Colorado	3
29. Kent State, Oregon, Cornell College, Coast Guard	2
33. Virginia Military Institute, San Diego State, Toledo, Ohio State	1

Place winners

115-lb class
1. Terrance McCann (Iowa)
2. Bill Hulings (Pittsburgh)
3. Dick Delgado (Oklahoma)
4. David Bowlin (Oklahoma A&M)

123-lb class
1. Ed Peery (Pittsburgh)
2. Harmon Leslie (Oklahoma A&M)
3. Vernon Whitney (Purdue)
4. Don Stroud (Michigan State)

130-lb class
1. Myron Roderick (Oklahoma A&M)
2. Bobby Lyons (Oklahoma)
3. Victor DeFelice (Pittsburgh)
4. Frank Hirt (Michigan)

137-lb class
1. Jim Sinadinos (Michigan State)
2. Ron Day (Colorado A&M)
3. John Pepe (Ohio)
4. Joseph Gratto (Lehigh)

147-lb class
1. Ed Eichelberger (Lehigh)
2. David Adams (Penn State)
3. Dick Heaton (Iowa State Teachers)
4. Paul Weinhold (Colorado A&M)

157-lb class
1. Larry TenPas (Illinois)
2. Doug Blubaugh (Oklahoma A&M)
3. Jerry Bross (Oklahoma)
4. LaRue Dillon (Lafayette)

167-lb class
1. Edward DeWitt (Pittsburgh)
2. Fred Davis (Oklahoma A&M)
3. Harlan Jenkinson (Iowa)
4. Jim Ellis (Indiana)

177-lb class
1. Dan Hodge (Oklahoma)
2. Roy Minter (Mankato State)
3. Gary Kurdelmeier (Iowa)
4. Edward Zabrycki (Navy)

191-lb class
1. Kenneth Leuer (Iowa)
2. Jim Gregson (Oklahoma A&M)
3. Ronald Schirf (Pittsburgh)
4. Ahmet Senol (Purdue)

Heavyweight
1. Gordon Roesler (Oklahoma)
2. Bob Konovsky (Wisconsin)
3. William Oberly (Penn State)
4. Willis Holland (Colorado A&M)

1957 (at University of Pittsburgh, Pittsburgh, PA)

Team	Points
1. Oklahoma	73
2. Pittsburgh	66
3. Iowa State	38
4. Oklahoma A&M	37
5. Penn State	33
6. Michigan, Illinois	30
8. Iowa	27
9. Lehigh	19
10. Minnesota, Virginia	13
12. Mankato State	12
13. Maryland, Waynesburg, Franklin and Marshall, Navy	11
17. Oregon State	8
18. Colorado	7
19. Williams, Wyoming	6
21. Iowa State Teachers, Michigan State, Oregon	5
24. Colorado A&M, Cortland, Indiana, Kansas State, Northwestern	4
29. Carleton, Colorado State, Drexel, Kent State, Ohio, Rutgers	2
35. Brown, Columbia, Lewis and Clark, Southern Illinois	1

Place winners

115-lb class
1. Dick Delgado (Oklahoma)
2. Bill Hulings (Pittsburgh)
3. Dick Gillihan (Oklahoma A&M)
4. Dave Moore (Illinois)

123-lb class
1. Ed Peery (Pittsburgh)
2. Harmon Leslie (Oklahoma A&M)
3. Dick Mueller (Minnesota)
4. Leonard Shelton (Oklahoma)

130-lb class
1. John Johnston (Penn State)
2. Max Pearson (Michigan)
3. Dean Corner (Iowa State)
4. Vic DeFelice (Pittsburgh)

137-lb class
1. Joe Gratto (Lehigh)
2. John Pepe (Penn State)
3. Ralph Rieks (Iowa)
4. Paul Aubrey (Oklahoma)

147-lb class
1. Simon Roberts (Iowa)
2. Ron Gray (Iowa State)
3. Werner Holzer (Illinois)
4. Jack Anderson (Mankato State)

157-lb class
1. Doug Blubaugh (Oklahoma A&M)
2. Mike Rodriguez (Michigan)
3. Dale Ketelson (Iowa State Teachers)
4. Robert Koster (Williams)

167-lb class
1. Tom Alberts (Pittsburgh)
2. Ralph Schneider (Waynesburg)
3. Rex Edgar (Oklahoma)
4. Roy Minter (Mankato State)

177-lb class
1. Dan Hodge (Oklahoma)
2. Ron Flemming (Franklin and Marshall)
3. Gene Franks (Iowa State)
4. John Dustin (Oregon State)

191-lb class
1. Ron Schirf (Pittsburgh)
2. Anthony Stremic (Navy)
3. Bernard Sullivan (Oklahoma)
4. Jack Himmelwright (Colorado)

Heavyweight
1. Robert Norman (Illinois)
2. Henry Jordan (Virginia)
3. Gordon Roesler (Oklahoma)
4. Mike Sandusky (Maryland)

1958 (at University of Wyoming, Laramie, WY)

Team	*Points*
1. Oklahoma State	77
2. Iowa State	62
3. Oklahoma	50
4. Michigan State	35
5. Iowa	26
6. Illinois	22
7. Wyoming, Cornell University	16
9. Pittsburgh	15
10. Lehigh, Mankato State	13
12. Colgate	11
13. Michigan	10
14. Iowa State Teachers, Penn State, Oregon	8
17. Lock Haven, Nebraska, Oregon State, Western Colorado	7
21. Colorado State College, Maryland	6
23. California Poly, Colorado, Indiana	5
26. Minnesota	4
27. Kansas State, San Jose State, Utah State	3
30. Colorado State University, Colorado Mines, Southern Illinois, Springfield	2
34. Brigham Young, Cornell College, Dartmouth, Kent State, Portland State	1

Place winners

115-lb class
1. Dick Delgado (Oklahoma)
2. Bob Taylor (Oklahoma State)
3. Jim Williams (Western State)
4. Frank Altman (Iowa State)

123-lb class
1. Paul Powell (Pittsburgh)
2. Bob Herald (Oklahoma State)
3. John Johnston (Penn State)
4. Don Bernard (Iowa State)

130-lb class
1. Les Anderson (Iowa State)
2. Max Pearson (Michigan)
3. Stan Abel (Oklahoma)
4. Ted Pierce (Oklahoma State)

137-lb class
1. Paul Aubrey (Oklahoma)
2. Shelby Wilson (Oklahoma State)
3. Dick Santoro (Lehigh)
4. Joe Hammaker (Lock Haven)

147-lb class
1. Ron Gray (Iowa State)
2. Dick Vincent (Cornell U)
3. Jack Anderson (Mankato State)
4. Nick Petronka (Indiana)

157-lb class
1. Dick Beattie (Oklahoma State)
2. Dave Ketelsen (Iowa State)
3. William Gabberd (Illinois)
4. Dick Heaton (Iowa State Teachers)

167-lb class
1. Duane Murty (Oklahoma State)
2. Dick Ballinger (Wyoming)
3. Jim Ferguson (Michigan State)
4. Roy Minter (Mankato State)

177-lb class
1. Gary Kurdelmeier (Iowa)
2. Tim Woodin (Michigan State)
3. Frank Powell (Iowa State)
4. John Dustin (Oregon State)

191-lb class
1. Kenneth Maidlow (Michigan State)
2. Pete Newell (Colgate)
3. Jim Craig (Iowa)
4. Adnan Kaisy (Oklahoma State)

Heavyweight
1. Bob Norman (Illinois)
2. Gordon Roesler (Oklahoma)
3. Earl Lynn (Oklahoma State)
4. Dan Brand (Nebraska)

1959 (at University of Iowa, Iowa City, IA)

Team	*Points*
1. Oklahoma State	73
2. Iowa State	51
3. Oklahoma	41
4. Iowa	33
5. Pittsburgh	30
6. Wyoming	25
7. Mankato State	21
8. Lehigh	20
9. Michigan State, Minnesota	17
11. Yale	16
12. Cornell University	14
13. Syracuse	13
14. Toledo	12
15. Colorado State College	11
16. Ithaca	10
17. Colorado State University	9
18. Northwestern	8
19. Kansas State, Kent State, Virginia Tech	7
22. Cornell College, Oregon State, Maryland	5
25. Indiana, Penn State, Western State, Illinois	4
29. Washington State, Utah, Portland State, Colorado Mines	3
33. Bloomsburg State, Harvard, Ohio State, Northern Illinois, Lock Haven, Southern Illinois	2
39. Nebraska, North Carolina, Northwest Missouri, Purdue, Rochester Tech, Colorado, Bowling Green, Bradley, Carleton	1

Place winners

115-lb class
1. Andy Fitch (Yale)
2. Dick Wilson (Toledo)
3. Bob Taylor (Oklahoma State)
4. Jack Thamert (Mankato State)

123-lb class
1. Dave Auble (Cornell U)
2. Larry Lauchle (Pittsburgh)
3. Vince Garcia (Iowa)
4. Herbert Karcher (Wyoming)

130-lb class
1. Stanley Abel (Oklahoma)
2. Les Anderson (Iowa State)
3. Brandon Glover (Virginia Tech)
4. Clarence McNair (Kent State)

137-lb class
1. Larry Hayes (Iowa State)
2. Shelby Wilson (Oklahoma State)
3. Paul Aubrey (Oklahoma)
4. Charles Coffee (Minnesota)

147-lb class
1. Ron Gray (Iowa State)
2. Jerry Frude (Wyoming)
3. Bob Wilson (Oklahoma State)
4. Bob Bubb (Pittsburgh)

157-lb class
1. Dick Beattie (Oklahoma State)
2. Sid Terry (Oklahoma)
3. Ellie Watkins (Iowa State)
4. Arthur Kraft (Northwestern)

167-lb class
1. Ed Hamer (Lehigh)
2. Tom Alberts (Pittsburgh)
3. Duane Murty (Oklahoma State)
4. Dick Ballinger (Wyoming)

177-lb class
1. Jim Craig (Iowa)
2. Al Blanshan (Mankato State)
3. Bill Wright (Minnesota)
4. Ed Rath (Colorado State U)

191-lb class
1. Arthur Baker (Syracuse)
2. Tim Woodin (Michigan State)
3. Gordon Trapp (Iowa)
4. Adnan Kaisy (Oklahoma State)

Heavyweight
1. Ted Ellis (Oklahoma State)
2. Bob Marella (Ithaca)
3. Walter Goltl (Colorado State U)
4. Don Darter (Kansas State)

1960 (at University of Maryland, College Park, MD)

Team	*Points*
1. Oklahoma	59
2. Iowa State	40
3. Wyoming	36
4. Iowa	32
5. Oklahoma State	29
6. Lock Haven	25
7. Penn State	23
8. Pittsburgh	21
9. Northwestern	20
10. Cornell University, Northern Illinois	17
12. Lehigh	16
13. Purdue	14
14. Ithaca, Syracuse	11
16. Rutgers, Toledo	10
18. Indiana, Michigan, Michigan State	9
21. Oregon State, Waynesburg	8
23. Army	7
24. Kent State, Minnesota, Portland State	6
27. Cornell College, Oregon, West Chester, Yale	5
31. Colorado State College, Mankato State, Utah	4
34. Rochester Tech, Southern Illinois, Springfield	3
37. Brown, Iowa State Teachers, Kansas State, Maryland, Ohio State, Ohio, South Dakota State, Washington State	2

Team	*Points*
45. Bowling Green, Coast Guard, Colorado Mines, Knox, Nebraska	1

Place winners

115-lb class
1. Elliott Simons (Lock Haven)
2. Dick Wilson (Toledo)
3. Dennis Friedericks (Iowa State)
4. Mits Tamura (Oregon State)

123-lb class
1. Dave Auble (Cornell U)
2. Masaaki Hatta (Oklahoma State)
3. Dave Hansen (Wyoming)
4. Tony Macias (Oklahoma)

130-lb class
1. Stanley Abel (Oklahoma)
2. Larry Lauchle (Pittsburgh)
3. John Kelly (Iowa)
4. Ronald Hutcherson (Indiana)

137-lb class
1. Les Anderson (Iowa State)
2. Lester Austin (Syracuse)
3. Mike Leta (Rutgers)
4. Patrick Semary (Kent State)

147-lb class
1. Larry Hayes (Iowa State)
2. Jerry Frude (Wyoming)
3. Ralph Clark (Lock Haven)
4. Dominia Fatta (Purdue)

157-lb class
1. Art Kraft (Northwestern)
2. Thad Turner (Lehigh)
3. Almer Marshall (Purdue)
4. Ronald Pifer (Penn State)

167-lb class
1. Dick Ballinger (Wyoming)
2. Ronnie Clinton (Oklahoma State)
3. Dennis Fitzgerald (Michigan)
4. Bob Koehen (Minnesota)

177-lb class
1. Roy Conrad (Northern Illinois)
2. Dave Campbell (Oklahoma)
3. Al Rushatz (Army)
4. Bruce Campbell (Oklahoma State)

191-lb class
1. George Goodner (Oklahoma)
2. Jack Stanboro (Ithaca)
3. Paul Eckley (Waynesburg)
4. Gordon Trapp (Iowa)

Heavyweight
1. Dale Lewis (Oklahoma)
2. Sherwin Thorson (Iowa)
3. Johnston Oberly (Penn State)
4. Roy Weber (Northwestern)

1961 (at Oregon State University, Corvallis, OR)

Team	*Points*
1. Oklahoma State	82
2. Oklahoma	63
3. Iowa State	29
4. Oregon State	28
5. Pittsburgh	26
6. Lehigh	24
7. Penn State	20
8. Michigan State, Iowa State Teachers	19
10. Michigan	18
11. Colorado State University	17
12. Lock Haven, Colorado State College	13
14. Toledo, Purdue	10
16. Northwestern, Southern Illinois	9
18. Utah	7
19. Mankato State	6
20. Portland State	4
21. Western State, Illinois, Nebraska	3
24. Army, Kansas State, Wyoming, The Citadel	2
28. Washington, San Jose State, South Dakota State, Springfield, Navy, Coast Guard, Ohio State, Colorado, Rochester Tech, Bowling Green, Kent State, Cornell College	1

Place winners

115-lb class
1. Elliott Simons (Lock Haven)
2. Dick Wilson (Toledo)
3. Wally Curtis (Oklahoma)
4. Don Webster (Iowa State)

123-lb class
1. Duwane Miller (Oklahoma)
2. Masaaki Hatta (Oklahoma State)
3. Richard Martin (Pittsburgh)
4. Francis Freeman (Iowa State Teachers)

130-lb class
1. Larry Lauchle (Pittsburgh)
2. David Jensen (Iowa State Teachers)
3. Mickey Martin (Oklahoma)
4. Al DeLeon (Mankato State)

137-lb class
1. Norman Young (Michigan State)
2. Ron Finley (Oregon State)
3. Bill Carter (Oklahoma)
4. Doug Wilson (Oklahoma State)

147-lb class
1. Larry Hayes (Iowa State)
2. Ron Pifer (Penn State)
3. Bob Wilson (Oklahoma State)
4. James Blaker (Michigan)

157-lb class
1. Phil Kinyon (Oklahoma State)
2. Kirk Pendleton (Lehigh)
3. Don Corriere (Michigan)
4. Virgil Carr (Iowa State)

167-lb class
1. Don Conway (Oregon State)
2. Bruce Campbell (Oklahoma State)
3. Elmer Marshall (Purdue)
4. Frank Hankin (Utah)

177-lb class
1. Bob Johnson (Oklahoma State)
2. Wayne Baughman (Oklahoma)
3. Kenneth Houston (Southern Illinois)
4. Bob Burge (Colorado State C)

191-lb class
1. Len Lordino (Colorado State C)
2. Nick Kohls (Colorado State U)
3. Ron Clinton (Oklahoma State)
4. Dave Angell (Lehigh)

Heavyweight
1. Dale Lewis (Oklahoma)
2. Ted Ellis (Oklahoma State)
3. Rory Weber (Northwestern)
4. Johnson Oberly (Penn State)

1962 (at Oklahoma State University, Stillwater, OK)

Team	*Points*
1. Oklahoma State	82
2. Oklahoma	45
3. Iowa	34
4. Lehigh	27
5. State College of Iowa	23
6. Southern Illinois, Pittsburgh, Wisconsin	19
9. Nebraska, Michigan State	18
11. Lock Haven	16
12. Wyoming, Minnesota	15
14. Colorado State College, Army	14
16. Air Force, Penn State, Colorado	11
19. Mankato State	10
20. Colorado Mines, Colorado State University	7
22. Northwestern	6
23. Lewis and Clark, Purdue	5
25. Ithaca, Maryland, Lycoming, Oregon State, Wheaton	3
30. Kansas State, Iowa State, Virginia Tech, Toledo, Navy, Western State, Illinois, South Dakota State, Springfield (MA), Rutgers	2
40. Coast Guard, Washington, Coe, Miami (OH), Fresno State, Ohio	1

Place winners

115-lb class
1. Elliott Simons (Lock Haven)
2. Mark McCracken (Oklahoma State)
3. Okla Johnson (Michigan State)
4. Fran McCann (Iowa)

123-lb class
1. Masaaki Hatta (Oklahoma State)
2. Frank Freeman (State College of Iowa)
3. Mike Nissen (Nebraska)
4. Richard Martin (Pittsburgh)

130-lb class
1. Mickey Martin (Oklahoma)
2. Al DeLeon (Mankato State)
3. Tom Huff (Iowa)
4. Lewis Kennedy (Minnesota)

137-lb class
1. Bill Carter (Oklahoma)
2. Bill Dotson (State College of Iowa)
3. Doug Wilson (Oklahoma State)
4. Dan Fix (Colorado Mines)

147-lb class
1. Mike Natvig (Army)
2. Kirk Pendleton (Lehigh)
3. Harold Thompson (Nebraska)
4. George Kelvington (Pittsburgh)

157-lb class
1. Jack Flasche (Colorado State C)
2. Phil Kinyon (Oklahoma State)
3. Ron Pifer (Penn State)
4. Jim Reifstock (Minnesota)

167-lb class
1. Ronnie Clinton (Oklahoma State)
2. Terry Isaacson (Air Force)
3. James Harrison (Pittsburgh)
4. Don Millard (Southern Illinois)

177-lb class
1. Bob Johnson (Oklahoma State)
2. Dean Lahr (Colorado)
3. Ronald Paar (Wisconsin)
4. Jim Detrixhe (Lehigh)

191-lb class
1. Wayne Baughman (Oklahoma)
2. Joe James (Oklahoma State)
3. Ken Houston (Southern Illinois)
4. Pat Clock (Lewis and Clark)

Heavyweight
1. Sherwyn Thorson (Iowa)
2. Roger Pillath (Wisconsin)
3. John Baum (Michigan State)
4. Rory Weber (Northwestern)

1963 (at Kent State University, Kent, Ohio)

Team	*Points*
1. Oklahoma	48
2. Iowa State	45
3. Michigan	36
4. Syracuse, Pittsburgh, Oklahoma State	32
7. Iowa	25
8. Lehigh	24
9. Colorado State University	23
10. Minnesota	18
11. Navy, Moorhead State	17
13. State College of Iowa, Nebraska	16
15. Army	14
16. Ohio, Colorado	13
18. UCLA, Penn State	12
20. Southern Illinois	11
21. West Liberty State, Michigan State, Colorado State College	10
24. Toledo, Northwestern, Wisconsin	9
27. Lock Haven, Air Force, Washington, Ohio State, Bloomsburg State	8
32. Kansas State, Purdue	5
34. Adams State, Cornell College	4
36. Wyoming, Oregon, Springfield, Rutgers	3
40. Illinois, Maryland	2
42. Miami (OH), Bowling Green, Cincinnati, New Mexico, South Dakota State	1

Place winners

115-lb class
1. Arthur Maugham (Moorhead State)
2. Gilbert Sanchez (Colorado State U)
3. Tom Balenz (Penn State)
4. Lowell Stewart (Iowa State)
5. Wallace Curtis (Oklahoma)
6. Okla Johnson (Michigan State)

123-lb class
1. Mike Nissen (Nebraska)
2. Mike Johnson (Pittsburgh)
3. Mark McCracken (Oklahoma State)
4. Fred Powell (Lock Haven)
5. Gary Joseph (Ohio State)
6. Donald Neff (Colorado State C)

130-lb class
1. Mickey Martin (Oklahoma)
2. Robert Douglas (West Liberty State)
3. David Dozeman (Michigan)
4. Lewis Kennedy (Minnesota)
5. Ron Jones (Iowa State)
6. James Smartt (Lehigh)

137-lb class
1. Bill Dotson (State College of Iowa)
2. Tom Huff (Iowa)
3. Mike Harman (Navy)
4. Larry Bewley (Iowa State)
5. Charles White (Oklahoma)
6. Gary Wilcox (Michigan)

147-lb class
1. Mike Natvig (Army)
2. Lonnie Rubis (Minnesota)
3. Veryl Long (Iowa State)
4. Richard Slutzky (Syracuse)
5. Jim Crider (Colorado State C)
6. David Gibson (Purdue)

157-lb class
1. Kirk Pendleton (Lehigh)
2. Phil Kinyon (Oklahoma State)
3. Virgin Carr (Iowa State)
4. Rahim Javanmard (UCLA)
5. Rick Bay (Michigan)
6. Timothy Gay (Pittsburgh)

167-lb class
1. James Harrison (Pittsburgh)
2. Steve Combs (Iowa)
3. Gordon Hassman (Iowa State)
4. Terry Isaacson (Air Force)
5. Robert Hall (Bloomsburg State)
6. William Roy (Illinois)

177-lb class
1. Dean Lahr (Colorado)
2. Harry Houska (Ohio)
3. Tommy Edgar (Oklahoma)
4. Richard Bell (Washington)
5. Kenneth Barr (Pittsburgh)
6. Gerald Franzen (Navy)

191-lb class
1. Jack Barden (Michigan)
2. Richard Baughman (Oklahoma)
3. Ronald Carr (Wisconsin)
4. Allan Jaklich (Northwestern)
5. Kenneth Hines (Colorado State U)
6. Gerald Everling (Syracuse)

Heavyweight
1. James Nance (Syracuse)
2. Larry Kristoff (Southern Illinois)
3. Joe James (Oklahoma State)
4. Merrell Solowin (Toledo)
5. Robert Spaly (Michigan)
6. John Illengwarth (Lehigh)

1964 (at Cornell University, Ithaca, NY)

Team	*Points*
1. Oklahoma State	87
2. Oklahoma	58
3. Iowa State	46
4. Colorado, Southern Illinois	31
6. Michigan	29
7. Lock Haven	23
8. Penn State	19
9. Maryland, Ohio	18
11. Lehigh	17
12. Iowa, Oregon State	15
14. Bloomsburg State, Cornell University, Syracuse	14
17. Mankato State	12
18. Indiana, Moorhead State, UCLA	11

Team	*Points*
21. Purdue	9
22. Colorado Mines, Colorado State College, Minnesota, Toledo, Wisconsin	8
27. Army, Pittsburgh	7
29. Navy, Rutgers, Temple	6
32. Pennsylvania, Yale	5
34. Air Force, Arizona State, Duke	4
37. Cornell College, East Stroudsburg, West Virginia	3
40. CW Post, Ithaca, Kansas State, New Mexico, Ohio State, State College of Iowa	2
46. Adams State, Colorado State University, Illinois, Luther, Lycoming, Notre Dame, Wyoming	1

Place winners

115-lb class
1. Terry Finn (Southern Illinois)
2. Roger Sebert (Iowa State)
3. Jerry Tanner (Oklahoma)
4. Larry Lloyd (Minnesota)
5. Charles Bush (Cornell U)
6. Morris Barnhill (Iowa)

123-lb class
1. Fred Powell (Lock Haven)
2. Howard Gangestad (Mankato State)
3. William Fuller (Iowa)
4. Bobbie Janko (UCLA)
5. Dennis Dutsch (Oklahoma State)
6. none awarded

130-lb class
1. Yojiro Uetake (Oklahoma State)
2. Jim Hanson (Colorado)
3. Mark Piven (Penn State)
4. William Robb (Bloomsburg State)
5. Ted Lansky (Pennsylvania)
6. Robert Campbell (Indiana)

137-lb class
1. Mike Sager (Oklahoma)
2. Gary Wilcox (Michigan)
3. Dan Fix (Colorado Mines)
4. Bob Buzzard (Iowa State)
5. Jim Rogers (Oklahoma State)
6. Richard Scorese (Bloomsburg State)

147-lb class
1. Jerry Stanley (Oklahoma)
2. Mike Reding (Oklahoma State)
3. Doug Koch (Lehigh)
4. Veryl Long (Iowa State)
5. George Edwards (Penn State)
6. Jim Crider (Colorado State C)

157-lb class
1. Gordon Hassman (Iowa State)
2. Richard Slutzky (Syracuse)
3. Bill Lam (Oklahoma)
4. Wayne Miller (Michigan)
5. Robert Kopnisky (Maryland)
6. Geoffrey Stephens (Cornell U)

167-lb class
1. Donald Millard (Southern Illinois)
2. Bob Zweiacher (Oklahoma State)
3. Leonard Kauffman (Oregon State)
4. Tim Geiger (Maryland)
5. Tom Peckham (Iowa State)
6. Terry Isaacson (Air Force)

177-lb class
1. Dean Lahr (Colorado)
2. Bill Harlow (Oklahoma State)
3. Jerry Swope (Lock Haven)
4. Marshall Dauberman (Maryland)
5. Gerald Franzen (Navy)
6. Robert Hannah (Yale)

191-lb class
1. Harry Houska (Ohio)
2. Jack Brisco (Oklahoma State)
3. Robert Spaly (Michigan)
4. Sven Holm (Oklahoma)
5. Ronald Paar (Wisconsin)
6. John Gladish (Lehigh)

Heavyweight
1. Joe James (Oklahoma State)
2. Bob Billberg (Moorhead State)
3. Merrell Solowin (Toledo)

4. Robert Hopp (Purdue)
5. Richard Conaway (Indiana)
6. Edward Scharer (Rutgers)

1965 (at University of Wyoming, Laramie, WY)

Team	*Points*
1. Iowa State	87
2. Oklahoma State	86
3. Lehigh	45
4. Oklahoma	44
5. Michigan	39
6. Arizona State	30
7. Oregon State, Syracuse	17
9. Maryland	16
10. Army, Navy, Wisconsin	15
13. Gettysburg, Penn State	12
15. Michigan State, Utah State	11
17. Lock Haven, Notre Dame	10
19. California, Colorado State University, Yale	7
22. Brigham Young, Illinois, Minnesota, Moorhead State, Western State	6
27. Colorado	5
28. Adams State, Cornell University	4
30. Bloomsburg State, Colorado State College, Mankato State, San Jose State, Washington State	3
35. Kansas State, Lycoming, Miami (OH), Nebraska, Ohio State, Oregon, San Francisco State, Temple, Utah, Wilkes	2
45. Harvard, Indiana, Northwestern, Pittsburgh, South Dakota State, Southern Illinois, Waynesburg, Wyoming	1

Place winners

115-lb class
1. Tadaaki Hatta (Oklahoma State)
2. Glenn McMinn (Arizona State)
3. Ernie Gillum (Iowa State)
4. Rich Warnke (Lehigh)
5. John Windfelder (Penn State)
6. James Garcia (Colorado)

123-lb class
1. Mike Caruso (Lehigh)
2. Robert Fehrs (Michigan)
3. Roger Sebert (Iowa State)
4. Dennis Dutsch (Oklahoma State)
5. Richard Kelvington (Moorhead State)
6. Allen Peterson (Washington State)

130-lb class
1. Yojiro Uetake (Oklahoma State)
2. Joe Peritore (Lehigh)
3. Donald Behm (Michigan State)
4. Ron Jones (Iowa State)
5. Alan Siegel (California)
6. Bill Johannesen (Michigan)

137-lb class
1. Bill Stuart (Lehigh)
2. Wayne Hicks (Navy)
3. Bob Buzzard (Iowa State)
4. Gene Davis (Oklahoma State)
5. Mike Sager (Oklahoma)
6. Bob Robbins (Army)

147-lb class
1. Veryl Long (Iowa State)
2. Joe Bavaro (Gettysburg)
3. Mark Scureman (Army)
4. Buzz Hays (Arizona State)
5. Lee Deitrick (Michigan)
6. Jim Crider (Colorado State C)

157-lb class
1. Bob Kopnisky (Maryland)
2. Bill Lam (Oklahoma)
3. Gordon Hassman (Iowa State)
4. Clayton Beattie (Illinois)
5. Mike Reding (Oklahoma State)
6. Jeff Stephens (Cornell U)

167-lb class
1. Greg Ruth (Oklahoma)
2. Len Kauffman (Oregon State)
3. Vic Marcucci (Iowa State)

4. Ken Haltenhoff (Yale)
5. Martin Strayer (Penn State)
6. Bob Anderson (Adams State)

177-lb class
1. Tom Peckham (Iowa State)
2. Bill Harlow (Oklahoma State)
3. Charles Tribble (Arizona State)
4. Roger Mickisk (Oklahoma)
5. Jerry Swope (Lock Haven)
6. Chris Stowell (Michigan)

191-lb class
1. Jack Brisco (Oklahoma State)
2. Dan Pernat (Wisconsin)
3. Robert Spaly (Michigan)
4. Allan Keller (Colorado State U)
5. Al Rozman (Western State)
6. Lenard Hansen (Utah State)

Heavyweight
1. Jim Nance (Syracuse)
2. Russ Winer (Oklahoma State)
3. Richard Arrington (Notre Dame)
4. Robert Broughton (Utah State)
5. Ted Tuinstra (Iowa State)
6. Mike Koeller (Michigan)

1966 (at Iowa State University, Ames, IA)

Team	*Points*
1. Oklahoma State	79
2. Iowa State	70
3. Oklahoma	69
4. Lehigh	48
5. Michigan	47
6. Michigan State	32
7. Lock Haven	22
8. East Stroudsburg, Portland State	21
10. Army	17
11. Ohio State	16
12. Gettysburg, Moorhead State	13
14. Colorado State College	11
15. Indiana, Oregon, Utah State, Wilkes	9
19. Navy	8
20. Kansas State, Temple,	
23. Albany State, California Poly (Pomona), Indiana State, Lycoming, Penn State, Oregon State	6
29. UCLA, Washington State	5
31. Moravian, Western Colorado, Wyoming	4
34. Bloomsburg State, Georgia Tech, Mankato State, Nebraska, North Carolina State	3
39. Arizona State, Coast Guard, Colorado, Ohio, San Jose State, Southern Illinois	2
45. Adams State, Arizona, California, Gustavus Adolphus, Kent State, Marquette, Northwestern, Pittsburgh, Rutgers, State College of Iowa	1

Place winners

115-lb class
1. Rich Sanders (Portland State)
2. Ernie Gillum (Iowa State)
3. Tadaaki Hatta (Oklahoma State)
4. Ted Remer (California Poly, SLO)
5. Ron Iwasaki (Oregon State)
6. Consantine Lambros (Michigan)

123-lb class
1. Mike Caruso (Lehigh)
2. Bob Fehrs (Michigan)
3. Bob Steenlage (Army)
4. Warren Crow (Albany State)
5. Rich Leichtman (Iowa State)
6. Bobby Guzzo (East Stroudsburg)

130-lb class
1. Yojiro Uetake (Oklahoma State)
2. Joe Peritore (Lehigh)
3. Bob Campbell (Indiana)
4. Curtis Scott (Oregon)
5. Dale Anderson (Michigan State)
6. Dom Milone (Temple)

137-lb class
1. Gene Davis (Oklahoma State)
2. Mike Sager (Oklahoma)
3. Bill Stuart (Lehigh)
4. Bill Johannsen (Michigan)
5. Masaru Yatabe (Portland State)
6. Jerry Cheynet (Kansas State)

145-lb class
1. Bill Blacksmith (Lock Haven)
2. Dale Bahr (Iowa State)
3. Jerry Stanley (Oklahoma)
4. Jim Rogers (Oklahoma State)
5. Bob Robbins (Army)
6. Jim Pond (Georgia Tech)

152-lb class
1. Dick Cook (Michigan State)
2. Joe Bavaro (Gettysburg)
3. Jim Kamman (Michigan)
4. Mike Reding (Oklahoma State)
5. Alan Frude (Wyoming)
6. Bill Brown (Kansas State)

160-lb class
1. Greg Ruth (Oklahoma)
2. Vic Marcucci (Iowa State)
3. John Carr (Wilkes)
4. Elmer Beale (Wisconsin)
5. Chester Dalgewicz (East Stroudsburg)
6. Dan Hensley (Washington State)

167-lb class
1. Dave Reinbolt (Ohio State)
2. Roger Mickish (Oklahoma)
3. Jon Rushatz (Lehigh)
4. Bill Bachardy (Lycoming)
5. Bill Byers (Colorado State C)
6. Bob Drebenstedt (Oklahoma State)

177-lb class
1. Tom Peckham (Iowa State)
2. Fred Fozzard (Oklahoma State)
3. Jerry Swope (Lock Haven)
4. Gary Cook (East Stroudsburg)
5. Dave Mucka (Moravian)
6. Gordon Fisher (Colorado State C)

191-lb class
1. Bill Harlow (Oklahoma State)
2. Don Buzzard (Iowa State)
3. Tom Foster (Utah State)
4. Rich Whittington (UCLA)
5. John Nichols (Navy)
6. Tony Bennett (Oklahoma)

Heavyweight
1. Dave Porter (Michigan)
2. Bob Billberg (Moorhead State)
3. Luke Sharpe (Oklahoma)
4. Steve Shippos (Iowa State)
5. Jeff Richardson (Michigan State)
6. Tom Beeson (Western State)

1967 (at Kent State University, Kent, OH)

Team	*Points*
1. Michigan State	74
2. Michigan	63
3. Iowa State	51
4. Oklahoma	48
5. Portland State	41
6. Oklahoma State	40
7. Lehigh	36
8. Arizona State	27
9. Navy	20
10. Air Force	18
11. Syracuse, Wyoming	17
13. East Stroudsburg, Stanford	16
15. Adams State, Colorado	15
17. Minnesota, Oregon State, UCLA	14
20. Fresno State, Wisconsin	13
22. Penn State	12
23. Brigham Young	11
24. Army, Cornell University, Toledo, Winona State	8
28. Mankato State, Northwestern, Ohio State, Southern Illinois, Washington State	7
33. Colorado State College, Illinois State, Indiana, Moorhead State	6
37. Cortland State, Indiana State, Lock Haven, Ohio, State College of Iowa, Western Colorado, Wilkes	4

Team	*Points*
44. Albany, Bloomsburg, Coast Guard, Kent State, Kings Points, Marquette, Maryland, Miami (OH), Princeton, Virginia Tech, Washington (MO)	2
55. Colorado Mines, Arizona, Colorado State University, Franklin and Marshall, Fairleigh-Dickinson, Illinois, Missouri, MIT, Montana State, Seton Hall, Utah, Wesleyan, Yale	1

Place winners

115-lb class
1. Richard Sanders (Portland State)
2. Jim Anderson (Minnesota)
3. Roy McMinn (Arizona State)
4. Ray Sanchez (Wyoming)
5. Bob Rhodes (Colorado)
6. Ron Iwasaki (Oregon State)

123-lb class
1. Mike Caruso (Lehigh)
2. Bob Fehrs (Michigan)
3. Gary Burger (Navy)
4. Gary Wallman (Iowa State)
5. Ed Parker (Indiana State)
6. Bill Desario (Cortland State)

130-lb class
1. Harold McGuire (Oklahoma)
2. Don Behm (Michigan)
3. Joe Peritore (Lehigh)
4. Jim Hanson (Colorado)
5. Tim McCall (Indiana)
6. John Hansen (Iowa State)

137-lb class
1. Dale Anderson (Michigan State)
2. Masaru Yatabe (Portland State)
3. Gene Davis (Oklahoma State)
4. Russ McAdams (Brigham Young)
5. Don Neu (Cornell U)
6. Rick Stuyvesant (Moorhead State)

145-lb class
1. Don Henderson (Air Force)
2. Mike Gluck (Wisconsin)
3. Dale Bahr (Iowa State)
4. Jim Rogers (Oklahoma State)
5. Pete Vendelofske (Navy)
6. Dale Carr (Michigan State)

152-lb class
1. Jim Kamman (Michigan)
2. Wayne Wells (Oklahoma)
3. Charles Seal (Portland State)
4. Len Borcher (Stanford)
5. Jim Tanniehill (Winona State)
6. Phil McCartney (Toledo)

160-lb class
1. Vic Marcucci (Iowa State)
2. Cleo McGlory (Oklahoma)
3. Lee Ehrler (UCLA)
4. Fred Stehman (Michigan)
5. John Kent (Navy)
6. Jerry Stone (Oklahoma State)

167-lb class
1. George Radman (Michigan State)
2. Mike Gallego (Fresno State)
3. Pete Cornell (Michigan)
4. Jeff Smith (Oregon State)
5. Fred Fairbanks (Washington State)
6. Don Miller (Wyoming)

177-lb class
1. Fred Fozzard (Oklahoma State)
2. Mike Bradley (Michigan State)
3. Gary Cook (East Stroudsburg)
4. Jim Harter (Army)
5. Allen Bulow (Southern Illinois)
6. Dave Mucka (Moravian)

191-lb class
1. Tom Schlendorf (Syracuse)
2. Don Buzzard (Iowa State)
3. Jack Zindel (Michigan State)
4. Jerry Crenshaw (Stanford)
5. Willie Williams (Illinois State)
6. Don Parker (State College of Iowa)

Heavyweight
1. Curley Culp (Arizona State)
2. Dom Carollo (Adams State)
3. Dave Porter (Michigan)

4. Jeff Richardson (Michigan State)
5. Tom Beeson (Western Colorado)
6. Granville Liggins (Oklahoma)

1968 (at Penn State University, University Park, PA)

Team	Points
1. Oklahoma State	81
2. Iowa State	78
3. Oklahoma	74
4. Michigan State	55
5. Navy	35
6. Portland State, California Poly (SLO), Lock Haven	28
9. Michigan	27
10. Northwestern	25
11. Oregon State	24
12. Penn State	23
13. East Stroudsburg, Colorado, UCLA	22
16. Brigham Young	21
17. Adams State, Indiana	19
19. Fresno State	18
20. Maryland	16
21. Central Washington, Colorado State College, Mankato State	14
24. Toledo, Hofstra	12
26. Oregon	11
27. Cortland State	10
28. Arizona State, MIT, Utah	9
31. Iowa	8
32. Army, Cornell University, Indiana State, Stanford	7
36. Bloomsburg State, Temple	6
38. Northwest Missouri, Washington	5
40. Nebraska, Ohio, Southern Illinois, Utah State	4
44. Arizona, Clarion State, Georgia Tech, Lehigh, Miami (OH), West Chester, Western Colorado, Wisconsin	3
52. Ashland, Colgate, Colorado State University, Davidson, Delaware, Kent State, Marquette, Northern Iowa, Ohio State, Pittsburgh, South Dakota State, Washington State, Wilkes, Winona State, Yale	2
67. Air Force, Bowling Green, California, The Citadel, Franklin and Marshall, Luther, MacMurray, North Carolina State, North Central Illinois, Northern Illinois, Pennsylvania, Syracuse, Virginia Tech	1

Place winners

115-lb class
1. Ken Melchior (Lock Haven)
2. Sergio Gonzales (UCLA)
3. Tommy Green (Oklahoma State)
4. Dave Keller (Toledo)
5. John Miller (Oregon)
6. Dave Unik (Ohio)

123-lb class
1. Dwayne Keller (Oklahoma State)
2. Rich Sanders (Portland State)
3. Tim McCall (Indiana)
4. Bill DeSario (Cortland State)
5. Ed Parker (Indiana State)
6. Gary Wallman (Iowa State)

130-lb class
1. Dan Gable (Iowa State)
2. Dave McGuire (Oklahoma)
3. Mike McAdams (Brigham Young)
4. Dennis Crowe (Oklahoma State)
5. Peter Nord (Colorado)
6. John Hahn (UCLA)

137-lb class
1. Dale Anderson (Michigan State)
2. Masaru Yatabe (Portland State)
3. Pete Vanderlofske (Navy)
4. Martin Willigan (Hofstra)
5. Ron Murphy (Oklahoma State)
6. Ron Russo (Bloomsburg State)

145-lb class
1. Dale Bahr (Iowa State)
2. Mike Grant (Oklahoma)
3. Kent Wyatt (California Poly, SLO)
4. Dale Carr (Michigan State)
5. Russ McAdams (Brigham Young)
6. Wayne Carlson (Utah State)

152-lb class
1. Wayne Wells (Oklahoma)
2. John Kent (Navy)
3. Russ Schneider (Northwestern)
4. Gobel Kline (Maryland)
5. Hal Sneed (Oklahoma State)
6. Jim Blacksmith (Lock Haven)

160-lb class
1. Reg Wicks (Iowa State)
2. Cleo McGlory (Oklahoma)
3. Jim Alexander (Colorado State C)
4. Matt Kline (Penn State)
5. Otto Zeman (Northwestern)
6. Mike Nardotti (Army)

167-lb class
1. Mike Gallego (Fresno State)
2. Lamoin Merkley (Central Washington)
3. Jason Smith (Iowa State)
4. Bob Drebenstedt (Oklahoma State)
5. Les Cornell (Michigan)
6. Rod Ott (Michigan State)

177-lb class
1. Bob Justice (Colorado)
2. Larry Amundson (Mankato State)
3. Fred Fozzard (Oklahoma State)
4. Charles Shivers (Oklahoma)
5. Dick Minekime (Cornell U)
6. Wally Podgurski (Miami of Ohio)

191-lb class
1. Nick Carollo (Adams State)
2. Tom Kline (California Poly SLO)
3. Gary Cook (East Stroudsburg)
4. Rich Lorenzo (Penn State)
5. John Schneider (Michigan State)
6. Gary Seymour (Arizona State)

Heavyweight
1. Dave Porter (Michigan)
2. Jess Lewis (Oregon State)
3. Jeff Smith (Michigan State)
4. Fred Andree (MIT)
5. Richard Schumaker (East Stroudsburg)
6. Al Borkowski (Northwest Missouri)

1969 (at Brigham Young University, Provo, UT)

Team	*Points*
1. Iowa State	104
2. Oklahoma	69
3. Oregon State	58
4. Michigan State	57
5. California Poly (SLO)	52
6. Oklahoma State	51
7. Iowa	38
8. UCLA	28
9. Michigan	27
10. Temple	22
11. Hofstra	21
12. Maryland	20
13. Colorado State College, Washington	18
15. Indiana State	17
16. Oregon	16
17. Arizona, San Diego State	15
19. Navy	14
20. Lehigh, Northern Iowa, Penn State, San Francisco State	13
24. Bloomsburg State, Minnesota, Winona State	11
27. Brigham Young	10
28. Pittsburgh	9
29. Moorhead State, Lock Haven, Northwestern	8
32. Colorado, Utah, Wilkes, Southern Illinois	7

Team	*Points*
36. California, Clarion State, Drake, Colorado State University, Indiana, Missouri	5
42. Buffalo, Harvard, Ohio State, Northern Illinois, Portland State	4
47. Adams State, Army, Long Beach State, Kent State, New York Maritime, Northwest Missouri, Ohio, Wisconsin	3
55. Air Force, Arizona State, East Stroudsburg, Idaho State, Ithaca, Kansas State, North Central, Old Dominion, Oswego State, South Dakota State	2
65. CW Post, Montana State, Nebraska, New Hampshire, Pennsylvania, Stanford, Washington State, West Chester	1

Place winners

115-lb class
1. John Miller (Oregon)
2. Sergio Gonzales (UCLA)
3. Terry Hall (California Poly, SLO)
4. Ray Stapp (Oklahoma State)
5. John Morley (Moorhead State)
6. Steve Lampe (Iowa State)

123-lb class
1. Wayne Boyd (Temple)
2. Stanley Keeley (Oklahoma)
3. Randy Berg (Washington)
4. David Waters (Lehigh)
5. Mike Schmauss (Iowa State)
6. Wes Caine (Northern Illinois)

130-lb class
1. David McGuire (Oklahoma)
2. Leo Groom (Colorado State C)
3. John Hahn (UCLA)
4. Reid Lamphere (Minnesota)
5. Mike Riley (Oklahoma State)
6. Marv Reiland (Northern Iowa)

137-lb class
1. Dan Gable (Iowa State)
2. Marty Willigan (Hofstra)
3. Keith Lowrance (Michigan State)
4. Ron Busso (Bloomsburg State)
5. Bob Hawkins (Oregon State)
6. Richard Humphries (Indiana State)

145-lb class
1. Mike Grant (Oklahoma)
2. Ray Murphy (Oklahoma State)
3. Clyde Franz (Penn State)
4. Phil Frey (Oregon State)
5. Conard Metcalf (Colorado)
6. Clarence Seal (Portland State)

152-lb class
1. Gobel Kline (Maryland)
2. Richard Mihal (Iowa)
3. Jim Tanniehill (Winona State)
4. Robert Ferraro (Indiana State)
5. Carl Adams (Iowa State)
6. Kim Snider (Oregon State)

160-lb class
1. Cleo McGlory (Oklahoma)
2. Dave Martin (Iowa State)
3. Gary Rushing (Arizona)
4. Tom Muir (Michigan State)
5. Joe Wiendl (Wilkes)
6. Doug Niebel (Clarion State)

167-lb class
1. Jason Smith (Iowa State)
2. John Woods (California Poly, SLO)
3. Jesse Rawls (Michigan)
4. Jim Vandehey (Oregon State)
5. Ben Welch (Navy)
6. Bill Laursen (Northwestern)

177-lb class
1. Chuck Jean (Iowa State)
2. Peter Cornell (Michigan)
3. Verlyn Strellner (Iowa)
4. Ken Bos (California Poly, SLO)
5. John Sorochinsky (Brigham Young)
6. Jack Zindel (Michigan State)

191-lb class
1. Tom Kline (California Poly, SLO)
2. Robert Grimes (San Diego State)
3. Robert Buehler (San Francisco State)
4. John Schneider (Michigan State)
5. Jim Duschen (Iowa State)
6. Geoff Baum (Oklahoma State)

Heavyweight
1. Jess Lewis (Oregon State)
2. Jeff Smith (Michigan State)
3. John Ward (Oklahoma State)
4. Ralph Cindrick (Pittsburgh)
5. Wayne Beske (Iowa State)
6. Kent Osboe (Northern Iowa)

1970 (at Northwestern University, Evantston, IL)

Team	*Points*
1. Iowa State	99
2. Michigan State	84
3. Oregon State	80
4. Oklahoma State	79
5. Iowa	45
6. Oklahoma	44
7. Washington	27
8. Pittsburgh	22
9. Ohio	21
10. Michigan	19
11. Toledo, Lehigh	18
13. Portland State, Indiana State	17
15. Northwestern	16
16. Oregon, Southern Illinois, Syracuse	13
19. Kent State, Minnesota, Penn State, Utah	12
23. Navy	11
24. Idaho State	10
25. Texas El Paso	9
26. Central Michigan	8
27. Air Force	7
28. Wyoming	6
29. Bloomsburg State, Princeton, Wisconsin	5
32. Colorado State, Nebraska, Gettysburg, Missouri	4
36. Ball State, Harvard, Purdue, West Chester	3
40. Arizona, Army, Brown, Clarion State, Cornell University, Illinois, Kansas State, Lock Haven, Montana State, New York University, Buffalo, Ohio State, Temple, Virginia Tech, Washington State	2
55. Alabama, Auburn, UCLA, Colorado, Drake, Fresno State, Louisiana State, Miami (OH), San Jose State, Tennessee, Western Michigan	1

Place winners

118-lb class
1. Greg Johnson (Michigan State)
2. Ray Stapp (Oklahoma State)
3. Mike Cachero (Oklahoma)
4. John Miller (Oregon)
5. Greg Schmidt (South Dakota State)
6. Jerry Hoddy (Michigan)

126-lb class
1. Dwayne Keller (Oklahoma State)
2. Randy Payne (Pittsburgh)
3. Roger Weigel (Oregon State)
4. Larry Wagner (Colorado State)
5. Richard Meyer (Lehigh)
6. Mike Milkovich (Kent State)

134-lb class
1. Darrell Keller (Oklahoma State)
2. Joe Carstensen (Iowa)
3. Phil Parker (Iowa State)
4. Tom Milkovich (Michigan State)

5. Wydell Boyd (Northwestern)
6. Ron Junko (Toledo)

142-lb class
1. Larry Owings (Washington)
2. Dan Gable (Iowa State)
3. Keith Lowrance (Michigan State)
4. Lester Bright (Old Dominion)
5. Bill Beakley (Oklahoma)
6. Dan Silbaugh (Wyoming)

150-lb class
1. Mike Grant (Oklahoma)
2. Robert Ferraro (Indiana State)
3. Stan Dziedzic (Slippery Rock)
4. Bob Tomasovic (Oregon State)
5. Tom Minkel (Central Michigan)
6. Jay Arneson (Oklahoma State)

158-lb class
1. Dave Martin (Iowa State)
2. Bruce Trammell (Ohio)
3. Kim Snider (Oregon State)
4. James Axtell (Minnesota)
5. Charles Shepherd (Utah)
6. Bob Kuhn (Pittsburgh)

167-lb class
1. Jason Smith (Iowa State)
2. Phil Henning (Iowa)
3. Pat Karslake (Michigan State)
4. John Caccia (Idaho State)
5. Jim Vandehey (Oregon State)
6. Jesse Rawls (Michigan)

177-lb class
1. Chuck Jean (Iowa State)
2. Jim Crumley (Oregon State)
3. Ben Cooper (Southern Illinois)
4. Gerald Malecek (Michigan State)
5. Steve Shields (Lehigh)
6. Tom Corbin (Oklahoma)

190-lb class
1. Geoff Baum (Oklahoma State)
2. Robert Rust (Syracuse)
3. Jack Zindel (Michigan State)
4. Ben Peterson (Iowa State)
5. Paul Zander (Iowa)
6. Emil Deliere (Princeton)

Heavyweight
1. Jess Lewis (Oregon State)
2. Greg Wojciechowski (Toledo)
3. Wayne Karney (Portland State)
4. Vic Mittleberg (Michigan State)
5. Rich Schumacher (East Stroudsburg)
6. Mike Edwards (Iowa)

1971 (at Auburn University, Auburn, AL)

Team	*Points*
1. Oklahoma State	94
2. Iowa State	66
3. Michigan State	44
4. Oregon State, Penn State	43
6. Oklahoma	39
7. Lehigh	32
8. Washington	30
9. Navy, Portland State	26
11. Ohio	24
12. Air Force	21
13. Toledo	17
14. Michigan	14
15. Brigham Young, Colorado, Lock Haven, Syracuse	13
19. Northwestern, UCLA	10
21. New Mexico	9
22. Harvard	8
23. Arizona, Illinois State, Kent State, Western Michigan	7
27. Clarion State, West Chester	6
29. Army	5
30. Idaho State, Iowa, Utah	4
33. Nebraska, Notre Dame	3
35. California, Indiana, Kansas State, Minnesota, Massachusetts, Pittsburgh, Stanford, Weber State, Wyoming	2
44. Auburn, Brown, Drake, California (PA), East Carolina, Gettysburg, Indiana State, Fresno State, Louisiana State,	

Team	*Points*
Maryland, Missouri, Princeton, Purdue, Utah State, Wisconsin	1

Place winners

118-lb class
1. Greg Johnson (Michigan State)
2. Tom Schuler (Navy)
3. Gary Breece (Oklahoma)
4. Ray Stapp (Oklahoma State)
5. Kirt Donaldson (Air Force)
6. Dale Brumit (Arizona)

126-lb class
1. Yoshiro Fujita (Oklahoma State)
2. Ken Donaldson (Air Force)
3. Greg Surenian (Lehigh)
4. John Meikle (UCLA)
5. Mark Massery (Northwestern)
6. Jim Hagen (Michigan)

134-lb class
1. Roger Weigel (Oregon State)
2. Dwayne Keller (Oklahoma State)
3. Phil Parker (Iowa State)
4. Larry Rippey (Lock Haven)
5. Laron Hansen (Brigham Young)
6. Bill James (Army)

142-lb class
1. Darrell Keller (Oklahoma State)
2. Larry Owings (Washington)
3. Leando Torres (California Poly, SLO)
4. Lloyd Keaser (Navy)
5. Timothy Whitaker (Kent State)
6. Richard Bacon (Western Michigan)

150-lb class
1. Stan Dziedzic (Slippery Rock)
2. Jay Arneson (Oklahoma State)
3. Dave Stone (Penn State)
4. Jarrett Hubbard (Michigan)
5. Don Pleasant (Washington)
6. Paul Gillespie (West Chester)

158-lb class
1. Carl Adams (Iowa State)
2. Mike Jones (Oregon State)
3. Bruce Trammell (Ohio)
4. John Finch (California Poly, SLO)
5. Larry Laush (Oklahoma)
6. Hajime Sinjo (Washington)

167-lb class
1. Andrew Matter (Penn State)
2. Steve Shields (Lehigh)
3. Junior Johnson (Portland State)
4. Tom Corbin (Oklahoma)
5. Eric Bates (Illinois State)
6. Joe George (Nebraska)

177-lb class
1. Geoff Baum (Oklahoma State)
2. Al Nacin (Iowa State)
3. Russ Johnson (Ohio)
4. Dave Van Meveren (New Mexico)
5. Jim Crumley (Oregon State)
6. Bill Demarey (North Dakota State)

190-lb class
1. Ben Peterson (Iowa State)
2. Vince Paolano (Syracuse)
3. Bill Bragg (Colorado)
4. Dave Ciolek (Michigan State)
5. Ritchie Starr (Harvard)
6. Tom Hutchinson (Lehigh)

Heavyweight
1. Greg Wojciechowski (Toledo)
2. Dave Joyner (Penn State)
3. Jim Shields (Oklahoma State)
4. Wayne Karney (Portland State)
5. Ben Lewis (Michigan State)
6. Bill Luttrell (Oklahoma)

1972 (at University of Maryland, College Park, MD)

Team	*Points*
1. Iowa State	103
2. Michigan State	72.5
3. Oklahoma State	57
4. Washington	54
5. Oklahoma	45.5
6. Clarion State	36
7. Oregon State	28
8. Penn State	26.5
9. Navy, Ohio	26
11. Idaho State	24.5
12. Iowa	24

Team	*Points*
13. Minnesota	23.5
14. Arizona	21.5
15. Portland State	21
16. Illinois State	20
17. Michigan	19
18. Princeton, Toledo	16
20. Slippery Rock	14.5
21. California Poly (SLO)	13.5
22. New Mexico	13
23. Northern Iowa	12.5
24. Brigham Young, Northern Illinois, Ohio State	10
27. Washington State	8.5
28. Indiana State, Southern Illinois	8.5
30. Arizona State, Lehigh	7.5
32. Western Michigan	7
33. Tampa	6.5
34. Boise State, Mankato State, West Chester	6
37. Drake	5.5
38. Massachusetts, Oregon, Wisconsin	5
41. Colorado	4.5
42. Georgia Tech, Maryland, Miami (OH), Missouri	4
46. Louisiana State	3.5
47. Army, Fresno State, Yale, Hofstra, Nebraska, San Jose State, Northwestern	3
54. Brockport State	2.5
55. Cincinnati, Cleveland State, East Carolina, Humboldt State, Indiana, Florida, Franklin and Marshall, Gettysburg, Pennsylvania, Purdue, William and Mary	2
66. Pittsburgh	1.5
67. Auburn, Buffalo, New York University, Central Michigan, UCLA, Notre Dame, Utah, Cornell University	1

Place winners

118-lb class
1. Greg Johnson (Michigan State)
2. Gary Breece (Oklahoma)
3. Dale Brumit (Arizona)
4. Tom Schuler (Navy)
5. Tom Phillips (Oregon State)
6. Dan Sherman (Iowa)

126-lb class
1. Pat Milkovich (Michigan State)
2. Chris Quigley (Illinois State)
3. Eddie Webb (Oklahoma)
4. Joe Zychowicz (Ohio)
5. Bill Fjetland (Iowa State)
6. Jeff Lamphere (Minnesota)

134-lb class
1. Gary Barton (Clarion State)
2. Phil Parker (Iowa State)
3. Mike Riley (Oklahoma State)
4. Jim Humphrey (Ohio State)
5. Larry Morgan (California Poly, SLO)
6. Jim Cook (Southern Illinois at Carbondale)

142-lb class
1. Tom Milkovich (Michigan State)
2. Larry Owings (Washington)
3. Lloyd Keaser (Navy)
4. Bobby Stites (Oklahoma State)
5. Kelly Trujillo (Arizona State)
6. Bob Bergen (Portland State)

150-lb class
1. Wade Schalles (Clarion State)
2. Jarrett Hubbard (Michigan)
3. Hajime Shinjo (Washington)
4. Jay Arneson (Oklahoma State)
5. Ron Fehlberg (Brigham Young)
6. Bill Beakley (Oklahoma)

158-lb class
1. Carl Adams (Iowa State)
2. Stan Dziedzic (Slippery Rock)
3. Alan Albright (Oklahoma State)
4. Rick Hadman (Michigan State)
5. Larry Johnson (Northern Illinois)
6. Jan Sanderson (Iowa)

167-lb class
1. Andy Matter (Penn State)
2. Keith Abens (Iowa State)
3. John Caccia (Idaho State)
4. Gerald Malecek (Michigan State)
5. Doug Wyn (Western Michigan)
6. Jim Woods (Washington)

177-lb class
1. Bill Murdock (Washington)
2. John Panning (Minnesota)
3. Rich Binek (Iowa State)
4. Albert Sye (Arizona)
5. Warren Reid (Oklahoma)
6. Eric Bates (Illinois State)

190-lb class
1. Ben Peterson (Iowa State)
2. Emil Deliere (Princeton)
3. Barry Reighard (Ohio)
4. Paul Zander (Iowa)
5. Greg Strobel (Oregon State)
6. Fletcher Carr (Tampa)

Heavyweight
1. Chris Taylor (Iowa State)
2. Greg Wojciechowski (Toledo)
3. Mike McCready (Northern Iowa)
4. Harry Geris (Oklahoma State)
5. Wayne Karney (Portland State)
6. Jim Hagen (Oregon State)

1973 (at University of Washington, Seattle, WA)

Team	*Points*
1. Iowa State	85
2. Oregon State	72.5
3. Michigan	59.5
4. Brigham Young	42.5
5. Oklahoma State	42
6. Oklahoma	38
7. Washington, Iowa	34
9. Ohio	25.5
10. Navy, Penn State	24.5
12. Wisconsin	20.5
13. Northern Illinois, Northwestern	19
15. Western Michigan	17.5
16. Michigan State, Arizona	14
18. Hofstra	13
19. Southern Illinois	12
20. Ball State	10
21. Nebraska	9.5
22. Portland State, San Jose State, Auburn	9
25. Stanford, Minnesota, Lehigh	8
28. Colorado State	7
29. Central Michigan	6.5
30. California, Oregon	5.5
32. Ohio State, New Mexico, East Carolina	5
35. Columbia, UCLA	4.5
37. Alabama, Rhode Island, William and Mary	4
40. Indiana State	3.5
41. Buffalo, Florida, Kent State, Massachusetts, Pennsylvania, Utah State, Yale	3
48. Colorado, Cornell University, Duke, Kansas State, Pittsburgh, Virginia	2
54. Boston, Montana State	1.5
56. Boise State, Drake, Fresno State, Idaho State, Illinois State, Indiana, Maryland, Army, Missouri, Rider, Air Force, Utah, Washington State	1

Place winners

118-lb class
1. Dan Sherman (Iowa)
2. Tom Phillips (Oregon State)
3. Jim Brown (Michigan)
4. Dale Brumit (Arizona)
5. Dan Kida (San Jose State)
6. Gary Breece (Oklahoma)

126-lb class
1. Mark Massery (Northwestern)
2. Ron Glass (Iowa State)
3. John Fritz (Penn State)
4. Bill David (Michigan)
5. Billy Martin (Oklahoma State)
6. John Smith (Ball State)

134-lb class
1. Don Rohn (Clarion State)
2. Bobby Stites (Oklahoma State)
3. Laron Hansen (Brigham Young)
4. Bill Fjetland (Iowa State)
5. Jeff Guyton (Michigan)
6. Conrad Calendar (Michigan State)

142-lb class
1. Dan Muthler (Navy)
2. Reed Fehlberg (Brigham Young)
3. Tom Brown (Washington)
4. Lee Peterson (North Dakota State)
5. Tim Williams (Colorado State)
6. Tom Milkovich (Michigan State)

150-lb class
1. Jarrett Hubbard (Michigan)
2. Rick Lawinger (Wisconsin)
3. Dan Holm (Iowa)
4. Brian Oswald (Ohio)
5. Chris Horpel (Stanford)
6. Mike Fitzpatrick (Washington)

158-lb class
1. Wade Schalles (Clarion State)
2. Mike Jones (Oregon State)
3. Rod Kilgore (Oklahoma)
4. Allyn Cooke (California Poly, SLO)
5. Bob Tscholl (Ohio)
6. Hajime Shinjo (Washington)

167-lb class
1. Bill Simpson (Clarion State)
2. Doug Wyn (Michigan)
3. Jeff Callard (Oklahoma)
4. Keith Abens (Iowa State)
5. Donnie Stumph (Southern Illinois)
6. Terry DeStito (Lehigh)

177-lb class
1. Rich Binek (Iowa State)
2. Gene Barber (Trenton State)
3. Bill Knippel (Seattle Pacific)
4. Warren Reid (Oklahoma)
5. Jim Crumley (Oregon State)
6. Bill Reinbolt (Ohio State)

190-lb class
1. Greg Strobel (Oregon State)
2. Johnny Johnson (Northern Illinois)
3. Ben Ohai (Brigham Young)
4. Fletcher Carr (Tampa)
5. Al Nacin (Iowa State)
6. Russ Johnson (Ohio)

Heavyweight
1. Chris Taylor (Iowa State)
2. Jim Hagen (Oregon State)
3. Joel Kislin (Hofstra)
4. Gary Ernst (Michigan)
5. Charles Getty (Penn State)
6. Tom Hazell (Oklahoma State)

1974 (at Iowa State University, Ames, IA)

Team	Points
1. Oklahoma	69.5
2. Michigan	67
3. Oklahoma State	64
4. Iowa State	63
5. Iowa	48.5
6. Washington	44.5
7. Penn State	43
8. Oregon State	39.5
9. Lehigh	35
10. Slippery Rock	33.5
11. Clarion State	31.5
12. Brigham Young	30.5
13. Wisconsin	26
14. Michigan State	24
15. Western Michigan	22
16. Minnesota	20
17. Navy	19
18. Pittsburgh	15
19. West Chester	13
20. Northwestern, Oregon	12
22. San Jose State	11.5
23. Ohio	9
24. East Carolina, William and Mary	8
26. Indiana State, Utah	6
28. Central Michigan, Cornell University	5.5

Team	*Points*
30. Northern Colorado, Portland State	5
32. Illinois	4
33. Miami (OH)	3.5
34. Auburn, Buffalo, Hofstra, Kansas State, Northern Illinois, UCLA, Washington State	3
41. Delaware, Southern Illinois	2.5
43. Colorado, Fresno State, Idaho State, Missouri, New Mexico, California–Santa Barbara, Syracuse, Toledo	2
51. Air Force, California, Cincinnati, Maryland, Massachusetts, Tennessee	1.5
57. Boston, Bowling Green, Drake, Kent State, Long Beach State, Rhode Island State, Rutgers, Utah State, Virginia, Wyoming	1
67. Ball State, Duke, Northern Arizona	.5

Place winners

118-lb class
1. Gary Breece (Oklahoma)
2. Jack Spates (Slippery Rock)
3. Dan Mallinger (Iowa State)
4. Dan Kida (San Jose State)
5. George Bryant (Pittsburgh)
6. Rick Dawson (Colorado State)

126-lb class
1. Pat Milkovich (Michigan State)
2. Billy Martin (Oklahoma State)
3. John Fritz (Penn State)
4. Mike Frick (Lehigh)
5. Bob Antonacci (Iowa State)
6. Rande Stottlemeyer (Pittsburgh)

134-lb class
1. Tom Sculley (Lehigh)
2. Jim Miller (Northern Iowa)
3. Don Rohn (Clarion State)
4. Billy Davids (Michigan)
5. Mark Belknap (William and Mary)
6. Fred Hahndorf (Navy)

142-lb class
1. Rick Lawinger (Wisconsin)
2. Steve Randall (Oklahoma State)
3. Ken Synder (Northern Iowa)
4. Paul Gillespie (West Chester)
5. Gordon Ilams (Oregon State)
6. Brian Beatson (Oklahoma)

150-lb class
1. Jarrett Hubbard (Michigan)
2. Bob Holland (Iowa State)
3. Tom Brown (Washington)
4. Chuck Yagla (Iowa)
5. Mike Waller (Slippery Rock)
6. Roger Warner (California Poly, SLO)

158-lb class
1. Rod Kilgore (Oklahoma)
2. Larry Zilverberg (Minnesota)
3. Dan Holm (Iowa)
4. Jerry Villeco (Penn State)
5. Duane Stutzman (Oregon)
6. Ron Ray (Oklahoma State)

167-lb class
1. Doug Wyn (Western Michigan)
2. Jeff Callard (Oklahoma)
3. Jan Sanderson (Iowa)
4. Dave Froehlich (Northwestern)
5. Bill Simpson (Clarion State)
6. Jon Jackson (Oklahoma State)

177-lb class
1. Floyd Hitchcock (Bloomsburg State)
2. Mel Renfro (Washington)
3. Rob Huizenga (Michigan)
4. Mike Hansen (Brigham Young)
5. Bill Hill (East Carolina)
6. Kurt Blank (Ohio)

190-lb class
1. Greg Strobel (Oregon State)
2. Ben Ohai (Brigham Young)
3. Al Nacin (Iowa State)
4. Rich Calderon (Washington)
5. Jeff Simons (Navy)
6. Bill Shuffstahl (Slippery Rock)

Heavyweight
1. Jim Woods (Western Illinois)
2. Gary Ernst (Michigan)
3. Charlie Getty (Penn State)
4. Tim Karpoff (Yale)
5. Larry Bielenberg (Oregon State)
6. Tom Hazell (Oklahoma State)

1975 (at Princeton University, Princeton, NJ)

Team	Points
1. Iowa	102
2. Oklahoma	77
3. Oklahoma State	68
4. Iowa State	66.5
5. Lehigh	54
6. Wisconsin	41
7. Oregon State	36.5
8. California Poly (SLO)	36
9. Purdue	34.5
10. Penn State	33
11. Northwestern	32
12. Oregon, Michigan	25.5
14. Yale	24
15. Michigan State	23.5
16. Syracuse	19.5
17. William and Mary	18.5
18. Kentucky	18
19. Hofstra, Minnesota	16.5
21. Washington	15.5
22. Brigham Young	14
23. Boise State	13.5
24. Toledo	12.5
25. Slippery Rock	10
26. Air Force, Clarion State	9
28. Tennessee	8.5
29. Northern Illinois	7.5
30. New Mexico, Pittsburgh	6.5
32. Stanford	6
33. Arizona State, UCLA	5.5
35. Delaware, Navy, Portland State	5
38. East Carolina	4.5
39. Boston, Indiana State	4
41. Buffalo, Colorado State, Missouri, Northern Colorado	3.5
45. Kent State, Nebraska, Ohio State	3
48. Central Michigan	2.5
49. Arizona, Long Beach State, Duke, Rhode Island, Tampa, Utah State, Virginia, Wyoming, Princeton	2
58. California, Connecticut	1.5
60. Cleveland State, Drake, Florida, Miami (OH), North Carolina State, Ohio, Pennsylvania, Weber State, Western Michigan	1
69. Kansas State, Maryland	.5

Place winners

118-lb class
1. Shawn Garel (Oklahoma)
2. Jim Brown (Michigan)
3. Myron Shapiro (Toledo)
4. Nick Gallo (Hofstra)
5. Nabil Guketiov (Montclair State)
6. Mike Land (Iowa State)

126-lb class
1. John Fritz (Penn State)
2. Pat Milkovich (Michigan State)
3. Joe Corso (Purdue)
4. Jack Reinwand (Wisconsin)
5. Bob Antonacci (Iowa State)
6. Toshi Oonishi (Washington)

134-lb class
1. Mike Frick (Lehigh)
2. Brian Beatson (Oklahoma)
3. Mark Belknap (William and Mary)

4. Jim Miller (Northern Iowa)
5. Steve Barrett (Oklahoma State)
6. Rande Stottlemeyer (Pittsburgh)

142-lb class

1. Jim Bennett (Yale)
2. Andre Allen (Northwestern)
3. Roger Warner (California Poly, SLO)
4. Steve Randall (Oklahoma State)
5. Ken Snyder (Northern Iowa)
6. Alan Housner (Purdue)

150-lb class

1. Chuck Yagla (Iowa)
2. Lee Kemp (Wisconsin)
3. Paul Martin (Oklahoma State)
4. Peter Galea (Iowa State)
5. Doug Ziebert (Oregon State)
6. Randall Watts (Bloomsburg State)

158-lb class

1. Dan Holm (Iowa)
2. John Janiak (Syracuse)
3. Larry Zilverberg (Minnesota)
4. Rod Kilgore (Oklahoma)
5. Dave Chandler (Boise State)
6. Dan Brink (Michigan)

167-lb class

1. Ron Ray (Oklahoma State)
2. Cliff Hatch (California Poly, SLO)
3. Joe Carr (Kentucky)
4. Bernie Barrile (Purdue)
5. Jeff Callard (Oklahoma)
6. Jerry Villecco (Penn State)

177-lb class

1. Mike Lieberman (Lehigh)
2. Chris Campbell (Iowa)
3. Willie Gadson (Iowa State)
4. Scott Klippert (Northwestern)
5. David McQuaig (Oklahoma State)
6. Bill Shuffstall (Slippery Rock)

190-lb class

1. Al Nacin (Iowa State)
2. Greg Stevens (Iowa)
3. Laurent Soucie (Wisconsin)
4. Brad Rheingans (North Dakota State)
5. Bob Orwig (Air Force)
6. Mark Tiffany (Northern Illinois)

Heavyweight

1. Larry Bielenberg (Oregon State)
2. Greg Gibson (Oregon)
3. John Bowlsby (Iowa)
4. Bill Kalkbrenner (Oklahoma)
5. Terry DeStito (Lehigh)
6. Larry Avery (Michigan State)

1976 (at University of Arizona, Tucson, AZ)

Team	*Points*
1. Iowa	123.25
2. Iowa State	85.25
3. Oklahoma State	64.50
4. Wisconsin	64
5. Lehigh	55.25
6. California Poly (SLO)	53
7. Minnesota	43
8. Michigan	36.50
9. Oklahoma	34.50
10. Penn State	23.25
11. Kentucky	22.50
12. Yale	21.75
13. Navy	21.50
14. Oregon State	20.25
15. Oregon, Clarion State	19.50
17. Washington	17.75
18. Slippery Rock	17.50
19. Michigan State, California (Santa Barbara)	17
21. Arizona State, Brigham Young	16.50
23. Colorado, Tennessee, Toledo	12.25
26. Indiana	12
27. Southern Illinois at Carbondale	9.50
28. Rhode Island	9
29. Portland State, Syracuse	7
31. East Carolina	6.50
32. Wyoming	6
33. Indiana State	5.50
34. UCLA	5

Team	*Points*
35. North Carolina State, Fullerton State	4
37. The Citadel	3.75
38. Pittsburgh, Northwestern, Northern Colorado	3.50
41. Bucknell, Drake, Northern Illinois, Ohio, Weber State, William and Mary	3
47. Ball State	2.75
48. Nebraska	2.50
49. Alabama, Eastern Michigan, Florida, Illinois, Kent State, Princeton, West Chester	2
56. Hofstra	1.75
57. Boise State, Colorado State	1.50
59. Arizona, Boston, Idaho State, California, Central Michigan, Maryland, Notre Dame, Missouri, Shippensburg State, Utah, Utah State, Virginia, Wilkes	1
72. Illinois State, Virginia Military Institute	.50

Place winners

118-lb class
1. Mark DiGirolamo (California Poly, SLO)
2. John Jones (Iowa State)
3. Mike McArthur (Minnesota)
4. Chuck Davis (Colorado)
5. Sam Orme (Brigham Young)
6. Mark Costello (Navy)

126-lb class
1. Jack Reinwand (Wisconsin)
2. Harold Wiley (California, Santa Barbara)
3. Ken Nelson (Oklahoma)
4. Bob Sloand (Lehigh)
5. Scott Pucino (Rhode Island)
6. Joe Goldsmith (Southern Illinois at Carbondale)

134-lb class
1. Mike Frick (Lehigh)
2. Pat Milkovich (Michigan State)
3. Tim Cysewski (Iowa)
4. Sam Komar (Indiana)
5. Mark Hawald (John Carroll)
6. Kurt Mock (Kentucky)

142-lb class
1. Brad Smith (Iowa)
2. Gene Costello (Slippery Rock)
3. Steve Barrett (Oklahoma State)
4. Brad Smith (Toledo)
5. Tihamer Toth-Fejel (Lehigh)
6. Don Rohn (Clarion State)

150-lb class
1. Chuck Yagla (Iowa)
2. Pete Galea (Iowa State)
3. Mark Churella (Michigan)
4. Jim Bennett (Yale)
5. Roye Oliver (Arizona State)
6. Ken Wilson (Syracuse)

158-lb class
1. Lee Kemp (Wisconsin)
2. Tom Brown (Washington)
3. Joe Zuspann (Iowa State)
4. John Althans (Navy)
5. Ethan Reeve (Tennessee)
6. Jim Weir (John Carroll)

167-lb class
1. Pat Christenson (Wisconsin)
2. Dan Wagemann (Iowa)
3. Joe Carr (Kentucky)
4. Jerry Villecco (Penn State)
5. Kim Wasick (California Poly, SLO)
6. Larry Zilverberg (Minnesota)

177-lb class
1. Chris Campbell (Iowa)
2. Mark Johnson (Michigan)
3. Mike Lieberman (Lehigh)
4. Sythell Thompson (California Poly, SLO)
5. Dave McQuaig (Oklahoma State)
6. Willie Gadson (Iowa State)

190-lb class
1. Evan Johnson (Minnesota)
2. Frank Santana (Iowa State)
3. Bud Palmer (Iowa)
4. Neal Brendel (Yale)
5. Mark Neumann (Oklahoma)
6. Daryl Monasmith (Oklahoma State)

Heavyweight
1. Jimmy Jackson (Oklahoma State)
2. Greg Gibson (Oregon)
3. Larry Bielenberg (Oregon State)
4. Chuck Coryea (Clarion State)
5. Doug Benschoter (Iowa)
6. Bob Fouts (Iowa State)

1977 (at University of Oklahoma, Norman, OK)

Team	*Points*
1. Iowa State	95.50
2. Oklahoma State	88.75
3. Iowa	84
4. Minnesota	66
5. Oregon State	52.25
6. Wisconsin	50.75
7. Oklahoma	49
8. Lehigh	48.75
9. Michigan	45.50
10. Kentucky	41.50
11. Arizona State	35.25
12. Brigham Young	27.25
13. Syracuse	26.75
14. Hofstra	24.50
15. Tennessee	20.75
16. Indiana	20
17. Michigan State	19
18. Penn State	18
19. Missouri	17.75
20. Ohio State	13.50
21. Oregon	12.75
22. California Poly (SLO)	12.50
23. Navy	12
24. Notre Dame	11.50
25. Princeton	10
26. Portland State	7.25
27. California, Wilkes	6
29. Arizona, Rhode Island	5.50
31. Ohio, UCLA	5
33. William and Mary	4.25
34. Boston, Illinois State, North Carolina	3.75
37. Utah State, Wyoming	3.50
39. Alabama, Lock Haven, Toledo, West Chester	3
43. Bucknell, Pittsburgh	2
45. Clarion State, Colorado, California (Long Beach), Rutgers, Slippery Rock State, Southern Illinois at Carbondale	1.50
51. Appalachian State, Army, Bloomsburg State, Boise State, Cleveland State, Florida, California State (Fresno), California State (Fullerton), Rider, Northern Colorado, Virginia Military Institute, Shippensburg State, St. Lawrence, Virginia Tech, Washington	1

Place winners

118-lb class
1. Jim Haines (Wisconsin)
2. Mike McArthur (Minnesota)
3. Gene Mills (Syracuse)
4. Johnnie Jones (Iowa State)
5. Billy Rosado (Arizona State)
6. Pat Plourd (Oregon State)

126-lb class
1. Nick Gallo (Hofstra)
2. Keith Mourlam (Iowa)
3. Mike Land (Iowa State)
4. Ricky Reed (Arizona State)
5. Jim Carr (Kentucky)
6. Billy Martin (Oklahoma State)

134-lb class
1. Pat Neu (Minnesota)
2. Dennis Brighton (Michigan State)
3. Franc Affentranger (California, Bakersfield)
4. Kurt Mock (Kentucky)
5. Lee Roy Smith (Oklahoma State)
6. George Medina (Syracuse)

142-lb class
1. Steve Barrett (Oklahoma State)
2. Sam Komar (Indiana)
3. Andy DiSabato (Ohio State)
4. John Mecham (Brigham Young)
5. Dick Knorr (Oregon State)
6. Tim Mousetis (Kentucky)

150-lb class
1. Mark Churella (Michigan)
2. Joe Zuspann (Iowa State)
3. Paul Martin (Oklahoma State)
4. Terril Williams (Missouri)
5. Roye Oliver (Arizona State)
6. Buddy Walker (Tennessee)

158-lb class
1. Lee Kemp (Wisconsin)
2. Kelly Ward (Iowa State)
3. Ethan Reeve (Tennessee)
4. Mike McGivern (Iowa)
5. Keith Stearnes (Oklahoma)
6. John Althans (Navy)

167-lb class
1. Rod Kilgore (Oklahoma)
2. Mark Lieberman (Lehigh)
3. Mike DeAnna (Iowa)
4. Florencio Rocha (California State, Bakersfield)
5. Dave Powell (Iowa State)
6. Steve Lawinger (Wisconsin)

177-lb class
1. Chris Campbell (Iowa)
2. Mark Johnson (Michigan)
3. Jerry White (Penn State)
4. Eric Wais (Oklahoma State)
5. Mike Brown (Lehigh)
6. Marty Ryan (Oregon State)

190-lb class
1. Frank Santana (Iowa State)
2. Evan Johnson (Minnesota)
3. Don McCorkle (Lehigh)
4. Bob Bragg (Oregon)
5. Mark Neumann (Oklahoma)
6. Howard Harris (Oregon State)

Heavyweight
1. Jimmy Jackson (Oklahoma State)
2. Larry Bielenberg (Oregon State)
3. Harold Smith (Kentucky)
4. Bob Golic (Notre Dame)
5. John Bowlsby (Iowa)
6. John Sefter (Princeton)

1978 (at University of Maryland, College Park, MD)

Team	*Points*
1. Iowa	94.50
2. Iowa State	94
3. Oklahoma State	86.25
4. Wisconsin	77.25
5. Oklahoma	52.25
6. Brigham Young	41.50
7. Lehigh	37.50
8. Oregon State	33.25
9. California Poly (SLO)	32.50
10. Michigan	29.25
11. Syracuse	27
12. Arizona State	26.75
13. Ohio	24.75
14. Princeton	21.75
15. Penn State	19.25
16. Florida	17.50
17. Louisiana State	16
18. Notre Dame	15.50
19. Kent State	13
20. Pittsburgh	12.50
21. Oregon	11.75
22. Shippensburg State	11.50
23. Franklin and Marshall	10.50
24. Lock Haven	10.25
25. Kentucky	9.50
26. UCLA	7.75
27. California	7
28. Cleveland State	6.50
29. Columbia, Drake, Missouri	6
32. Nevada at Las Vegas	5.50

Team	*Points*
33. Rhode Island	5
34. Washington, Auburn	4
36. Navy	3.75
37. Michigan State, William and Mary, Illinois, Virginia	3.50
41. Clarion State, Washington State, Arizona, Minnesota, Wilkes	3
46. North Carolina	2.50
47. California State (Long Beach), East Stroudsburg, Cortland State, Boise State, Hobart, Connecticut, Tennessee at Chattanooga, Hofstra	2
55. Western Michigan, Bowling Green	1.75
57. Wyoming, West Chester, Indiana, Nebraska	1.50
61. Ohio State, Miami (OH), Rutgers, North Carolina State, Rider, Northern Colorado, Ball State, Idaho State	1
69. Colorado, Maryland	.50

Place winners

118-lb class
1. Andy Daniels (Ohio)
2. John Azevedo (California State, Bakersfield)
3. Dan Glenn (Iowa)
4. Gene Mills (Syracuse)
5. Gary Fisher (California Poly, SLO)
6. Mike Deaugustino (Penn State)

126-lb class
1. Mike Land (Iowa State)
2. Randy Lewis (Iowa)
3. Kenny Nelson (Oklahoma)
4. Jim Hanson (Wisconsin)
5. Glenn Burket (Shippensburg State)
6. Jerry Reid (Columbia)

134-lb class
1. Ken Mallory (Montclair State)
2. Frank Deangelis (Oklahoma)
3. Franc Affentranger (California State, Bakersfield)
4. Brian Brown (Franklin and Marshall)
5. Mike Chinn (Louisiana State)
6. Rande Stottlemeyer (Pittsburgh)

142-lb class
1. Dan Hicks (Oregon State)
2. Andy Rein (Wisconsin)
3. Scott Trizzino (Iowa)
4. John Mecham (Brigham Young)
5. Donald Moore (William and Mary)
6. Randy Nielson (Iowa State)

150-lb class
1. Mark Churella (Michigan)
2. Bruce Kinseth (Iowa)
3. David Schultz (Oklahoma State)
4. Joe Zuspann (Iowa State)
5. Kim Jefferies (Arizona State)
6. Scott Bliss (Oregon)

158-lb class
1. Lee Kemp (Wisconsin)
2. Kelly Ward (Iowa State)
3. John Janiak (Syracuse)
4. Ron Michaels (Kent State)
5. Dave Becker (Penn State)
6. William Smith (Morgan State)

167-lb class
1. Keith Stearns (Oklahoma)
2. Paul Martin (Oklahoma State)
3. Scott Heaton (California Poly, SLO)
4. Jim Weir (John Carroll)
5. Brad Hansen (Brigham Young)
6. Mike DeAnna (Iowa)

177-lb class
1. Mark Lieberman (Lehigh)
2. Eric Wais (Oklahoma State)
3. Charles Gadson (Iowa State)
4. Don Shuler (Arizona State)
5. Bill Teutsch (Florida)
6. Steve Fraser (Michigan)

190-lb class
1. Ron Jeidy (Wisconsin)
2. Frank Santana (Iowa State)

3. Mike Brown (Lehigh)
4. Daryl Monasmith (Oklahoma State)
5. Howard Harris (Oregon State)
6. Kirk Myers (Northern Iowa)

Heavyweight
1. Jimmy Jackson (Oklahoma State)
2. John Sefter (Princeton)
3. Bob Golic (Notre Dame)
4. Gary Peterson (Brigham Young)
5. John Bowlsby (Iowa)
6. Jeff Blatnick (Springfield)

1979 (at Iowa State University, Ames, IA)

Team	*Points*
1. Iowa	122.50
2. Iowa State	88
3. Lehigh	69.75
4. Oregon State	60.50
5. Wisconsin	56.50
6. Oklahoma State	52.75
7. Minnesota	43.75
8. Arizona State	34.50
9. Oklahoma	31.50
10. Michigan	25
11. Syracuse	23.75
12. UCLA	21.75
13. Clarion State	20
14. Brigham Young	18.50
15. California Poly	16.75
16. Missouri	15.50
17. North Carolina	14.50
18. Oregon, Portland State	13.75
20. Arizona	13
21. Louisiana State	11.50
22. Kentucky	11
23. Cleveland State	10.50
24. Illinois, Franklin and Marshall	9.50
26. Bloomsburg	9.25
27. Wilkes	8.50
28. Navy, Marquette	8
30. North Carolina State	7
31. Michigan State, Toledo	6.25
33. Colorado State	6
34. Colorado	5.75
35. Central Michigan, Utah State, Florida, Slippery Rock	5.50
39. Wyoming	5
40. Temple	4.50
41. West Virginia	4
42. Yale	3.50
43. Kent State	3
44. Rhode Island, San Jose State	2.75
46. California State (Fullerton), East Stroudsburg, Georgia, Miami (OH), Nevada at Las Vegas, Northern Illinois	2
52. Alabama	1.75
53. Clemson	1.50
54. Ball State, Bowling Green, Drake, Hofstra, Indiana, Middle Tennessee, New Mexico, Ohio State, Pittsburgh, Weber State, West Chester, William and Mary, Western Michigan	1
67. East Carolina, Notre Dame	.50

Place winners

118-lb class
1. Gene Mills (Syracuse)
2. Joe Gonzales (California State, Bakersfield)
3. Dan Glenn (Iowa)
4. Bill DePaoli (California of Pennsylvania)
5. Dan Finnegan (Iowa State)
6. Jim Zenz (North Carolina State)
7. Randy Hoffman (Arizona State)
8. Chris Wents (Louisiana State)

126-lb class
1. Randy Lewis (Iowa)
2. John Azevedo (California State, Bakersfield)

3. C.D. Mock (North Carolina)
4. Rick Dellagatta (Kentucky)
5. Kevin Puebla (Illinois)
6. Keith Whelan (Missouri)
7. Steve Perdew (Slippery Rock)
8. Mike Bauer (Oregon State)

134-lb class
1. Darryl Burley (Lehigh)
2. Mike Land (Iowa State)
3. Jim Martinez (Minnesota)
4. Joe Romero (Arizona State)
5. Brian Brown (Franklin and Marshall)
6. Ed Maisey (Brigham Young)
7. Randy Miller (Clarion State)
8. Mark Cagle (West Virginia)

142-lb class
1. Dan Hicks (Oregon State)
2. Scott Trizzino (Iowa)
3. Mike Mathies (Portland State)
4. Lee Roy Smith (Oklahoma State)
5. Andre Metzger (Oklahoma)
6. Andy Rein (Wisconsin)
7. Bill Cripps (Arizona)
8. Dan Boos (Luther)

150-lb class
1. Bruce Kinseth (Iowa)
2. Dick Knorr (Oregon State)
3. Tom Coffing (Arizona)
4. Ces Shelton (Oklahoma State)
5. Mike Terry (Wisconsin)
6. Larry Kihlstadius (Navy)
7. Chuck Biggert (Toledo)
8. Steve Suder (Wyoming)

158-lb class
1. Kelly Ward (Iowa State)
2. Dan Zilverberg (Minnesota)
3. Dave Evans (Wisconsin)
4. Bob Holland (Eastern Illinois)
5. Tobey Matney (Cleveland State)
6. Mark Evenhus (Oregon State)
7. Rick Stewart (Oklahoma State)
8. Roye Oliver (Arizona State)

167-lb class
1. Mark Churella (Michigan)
2. Mike DeAnna (Iowa)
3. Dave Powell (Iowa State)
4. Brad Hansen (Brigham Young)
5. Dom DiGiaocchino (Bloomsburg State)
6. Mike Abrams (Grand Valley State)
7. Dave Miller (Missouri)
8. Jim Hall (Oklahoma)

177-lb class
1. Mark Lieberman (Lehigh)
2. Bud Palmer (Iowa)
3. Dave Allen (Iowa State)
4. Russ Pickering (Miami, OH)
5. Dave Severn (Arizona State)
6. Don Brown (Oregon)
7. Brian Parlet (Augustana)
8. Mark Hattendorf (Southern Illinois at Edwardsville)

190-lb class
1. Eric Wais (Oklahoma State)
2. Mike Brown (Lehigh)
3. Kirk Meyers (Northern Iowa)
4. Mitch Hull (Wisconsin)
5. Howard Harris (Oregon State)
6. Edgar Thomas (Oklahoma)
7. Mike Mann (Iowa State)
8. Geno Savegnago (Eastern Illinois)

Heavyweight
1. Fred Bohna (UCLA)
2. Dave Klemm (Eastern Illinois)
3. Jeff Blatnick (Springfield, MA)
4. Jack Campbell (Clarion State)
5. Fred McGaver (Marquette)
6. Steve Williams (Oklahoma)
7. Tom Waldon (Iowa State)
8. Shawn Whitcomb (Michigan State)

1980 (at Oregon State University, Corvallis, OR)

Team	*Points*
1. Iowa	110.75
2. Oklahoma State	87
3. Iowa State	81.75
4. Oklahoma	67.50
5. Arizona State	56.50
6. Lehigh	56.25
7. Wisconsin	55
8. California State (Bakersfield)	51.75

Team	*Points*
9. North Carolina State	37.25
10. Oregon State	32.50
11. Kentucky	24.75
12. Oregon	22.75
13. California Poly	21.50
14. Colorado	20.50
15. Clemson	20
16. Indiana State, UCLA	19
18. Clarion State	17.25
19. Morgan State	16.75
20. Rider	14.50
21. Minnesota, Navy	14
23. Auburn, Tennessee	13
25. Old Dominion, Michigan State, Rhode Island	11.50
28. Temple	11.25
29. Missouri	10.50
30. Michigan	9.50

Place winners

118-lb class
1. Joe Gonzales (California State, Bakersfield)
2. Dan Glenn (Iowa)
3. Jim Zenz (North Carolina State)
4. Gary Fischer (California Poly)
5. Mike Picozzi (Iowa State)
6. Rich Santoro (Lehigh)
7. Tony Leonino (Auburn)
8. Mark Zimmer (Wisconsin)

126-lb class
1. John Azevedo (California State, Bakersfield)
2. Jerry Kelly (Oklahoma State)
3. Rick Dellagatta (Kentucky)
4. Eddie Ortiz (Arizona State)
5. Byron McGlathery (Tennessee at Chattanooga)
6. Mike Giustizia (Tennessee)
7. Chris Whelan (Missouri)
8. Jeff Thomas (Michigan State)

134-lb class
1. Randy Lewis (Iowa)
2. Darryl Burley (Lehigh)
3. Derek Glenn (Colorado)
4. Buddy Lee (Old Dominion)
5. Thomas Landrum (Oklahoma State)
6. Harlan Kistler (UCLA)
7. Jim Gibbons (Iowa State)
8. Mike Bauer (Oregon State)

142-lb class
1. Lee Roy Smith (Oklahoma State)
2. Andre Metzger (Oklahoma)
3. Bill Cripps (Arizona State)
4. Lenny Zalesky (Iowa)
5. Doug Parise (Temple)
6. Dave Brown (Iowa State)
7. Denis Reed (Lehigh)
8. Jeff Barksdale (California Poly)

150-lb class
1. Andy Rein (Wisconsin)
2. Scott Bliss (Oregon)
3. King Mueller (Iowa)
4. Roger Frizzell (Oklahoma)
5. Mike Elliott (California State, Fullerton)
6. Fred Boss (Central Michigan)
7. Anthony Surage (Rutgers)
8. Tony Caravella (Bloomsburg State)

158-lb class
1. Ricky Stewart (Oklahoma State)
2. William Smith (Morgan State)
3. Isreal Sheppard (Oklahoma)
4. Tom Pickard (Iowa State)
5. Dan Zilverberg (Minnesota)
6. Mike Terry (Wisconsin)
7. Mark Stevenson (Iowa)
8. Jim Reilly (Lehigh)

167-lb class
1. Matt Reiss (North Carolina State)
2. Perry Hummel (Iowa State)
3. Dave Evans (Wisconsin)
4. John Reich (Navy)
5. Lee Spiegel (Rhode Island)
6. Brad Bitterman (Northern Michigan)
7. Jamie Milkovich (Auburn)
8. Doug Anderson (Iowa)

177-lb class
1. Ed Banach (Iowa)
2. Dave Allen (Iowa State)
3. Colin Kilrain (Lehigh)
4. Charles Heller (Clarion State)

5. Steve Fraser (Michigan)
6. Ben Hill (Tennessee)
7. Gary Germundson (Oklahoma State)
8. Dave Severn (Arizona State)

190-lb class
1. Noel Loban (Clemson)
2. Dan Severn (Arizona State)
3. Lou Diserafino (Rider)
4. Mike Mann (Iowa State)
5. Geno Savegnago (Eastern Illinois)
6. Mitch Hull (Wisconsin)
7. Mike Brown (Lehigh)
8. Joe Atiyeh (Louisiana State)

Heavyweight
1. Howard Harris (Oregon State)
2. Bruce Baumgartner (Indiana State)
3. Dean Phinney (Iowa)
4. Mike Haschak (UCLA)
5. Steve Williams (Oklahoma)
6. Harold Smith (Kentucky)
7. Ron Essink (Grand Valley)
8. Jeff Golz (Ohio State)

1981 (at Princeton University, Princeton, NJ)

Team	*Points*
1. Iowa	129.75
2. Oklahoma	100.25
3. Iowa State	84.75
4. Oklahoma State	68.50
5. Lehigh	38
6. Penn State	31.75
7. Syracuse	30.50
8. Central Michigan	28.75
9. Auburn	25.75
10. Oregon State	25.25
11. Arizona State	24.50
12. Northern Iowa	22.25
13. North Carolina	22
14. Indiana State, Kent State	20.75
16. Clarion State	19.50
17. Temple	16.75
18. Kentucky, Minnesota	16.50
20. North Carolina State	15.75

Place winners

118-lb class
1. Gene Mills (Syracuse)
2. John Hartupee (Central Michigan)
3. Randy Willingham (Oklahoma State)
4. Tom Reed (Southern Illinois at Edwardsville)
5. Joe McFarland (Michigan)
6. Chris Wentz (North Carolina State)
7. Barry Davis (Iowa)
8. Tony Calderaio (Slippery Rock)

126-lb class
1. Dan Cuestas (California State, Bakersfield)
2. Dave Cook (North Carolina)
3. Jerry Kelly (Oklahoma State)
4. Ed Pidgeon (Hofstra)
5. John Ianuzzi (Wisconsin)
6. Gary Lefebvre (Minnesota)
7. Tim Riley (Iowa)
8. Mark Galyan (Indiana)

134-lb class
1. Jim Gibbons (Iowa State)
2. Darryl Burley (Lehigh)
3. Ricky Dellagatta (Kentucky)
4. Dalen Wasmund (Minnesota)
5. Eddie Boza (San Jose State)
6. Clar Anderson (Auburn)
7. Randy Lewis (Iowa)
8. not awarded

142-lb class
1. Andre Metzger (Oklahoma)
2. Lennie Zalesky (Iowa)
3. Dave Brown (Iowa State)
4. Shawn White (Michigan State)
5. Ken Gallagher (Northern Iowa)
6. Bernie Fritz (Penn State)
7. Gene Nighman (Cornell U)
8. Al Freeman (Nebraska)

150-lb class
1. Nate Carr (Iowa State)
2. Scott Trizzino (Iowa)
3. Roger Frizzell (Oklahoma)
4. Fred Boss (Central Michigan)

5. Jackson Kistler (Arizona State)
6. Brad Swartz (Oregon State)
7. Roger Randall (Old Dominion)
8. Charlie Lucas (Portland State)

158-lb class
1. Ricky Stewart (Oklahoma State)
2. Dave Schultz (Oklahoma)
3. Perry Shea (California State, Bakersfield)
4. Dion Cobb (Northern Iowa)
5. Jim Zalesky (Iowa)
6. Kevin Benson (Portland State)
7. Jim Reilly (Lehigh)
8. Jan Michaels (North Carolina)

167-lb class
1. Mark Schultz (Oklahoma)
2. Mike DeAnna (Iowa)
3. John Hanrahan (Penn State)
4. Perry Hummel (Iowa State)
5. Jamie Milkovich (Auburn)
6. Steve Reedy (Kent State)
7. Mike Sheets (Oklahoma State)
8. Matt Reiss (North Carolina State)

177-lb class
1. Ed Banach (Iowa)
2. Charlie Heller (Clarion State)
3. Colin Kilrain (Lehigh)
4. Marty Ryan (Oregon State)
5. Dave Young (Missouri)
6. Jim Hall (Oklahoma)
7. Eli Blazeff (Auburn)
8. Dave Brouhard (San Jose State)

190-lb class
1. Tom Martucci (Trenton State)
2. Tony Mantella (Temple)
3. Geno Savegnago (Eastern Illinois)
4. Ryan Kelly (Oregon)
5. Craig Blackman (Franklin and Marshall)
6. John Forshee (Iowa State)
7. Henry Milligan (Princeton)
8. Pat McKay (Michigan)

Heavyweight
1. Lou Banach (Iowa)
2. Bruce Baumgartner (Indiana State)
3. Steve Williams (Oklahoma)
4. Dan Severn (Arizona State)
5. Ray Wagner (Kent State)
6. Steve Sefter (Penn State)
7. Mike Evans (Louisiana State)
8. Mike Howe (Northern Michigan)

1982 (at Iowa State University, Ames, IA)

Team	Points
1. Iowa	131.75
2. Iowa State	111
3. Oklahoma	109
4. Oklahoma State	71.75
5. North Carolina	47
6. Nebraska	40.25
7. Indiana State	33
8. Lehigh	31.75
9. San Jose State	27.75
10. Northern Iowa	26
11. North Carolina State	24.75
12. Missouri	23.50
13. Bloomsburg State	23.25
14. Penn State	20.25
15. Boise State	20
16. Minnesota	17.75
17. Navy	17
18. Oregon	16.50
19. Eastern Illinois	15.75
20. Louisiana State	14.50

Place winners

118-lb class
1. Barry Davis (Iowa)
2. Kevin Darkus (Iowa State)
3. Bobby Weaver (Lehigh)
4. Bob Monaghan (North Carolina)
5. Randy Willingham (Oklahoma State)
6. Joe McFarland (Michigan)
7. Bob Dickman (Indiana State)
8. Charlie Heard (Tennessee at Chattanooga)

126-lb class
1. Dan Cuestas (California State, Bakersfield)
2. Scott Barrett (Boise State)

3. Wayne Jones (San Jose State)
4. Joe Gibbons (Iowa State)
5. Frank Famiano (Brockport State)
6. Scott Lynch (Penn State)
7. Dave Cooke (North Carolina)
8. Derek Porter (Eastern Illinois)

134-lb class

1. C.D. Mock (North Carolina)
2. Don Reese (Bloomsburg)
3. Jim Gibbons (Iowa State)
4. Eddie Boza (San Jose State)
5. Jim Edwards (Louisiana State)
6. Jeff Kerber (Iowa)
7. Buddy Lee (Old Dominion)
8. Mike Barfuss (California Poly)

142-lb class

1. Andre Metzger (Oklahoma)
2. Lennie Zalesky (Iowa)
3. Jim Martinez (Minnesota)
4. Bill Nugent (Oregon)
5. Johnnie Selmon (Nebraska)
6. Randy Conrad (Iowa State)
7. Ken Gallagher (Northern Iowa)
8. Lenny Nelson (Wilkes)

150-lb class

1. Nate Carr (Iowa State)
2. Kenny Monday (Oklahoma State)
3. Roger Frizzell (Oklahoma)
4. Wes Roper (Missouri)
5. Frank Castrignano (North Carolina State)
6. Mark Schmitz (Wisconsin)
7. Mike Elinsky (North Carolina)
8. Dave Goldi (Columbia)

158-lb class

1. Jim Zalesky (Iowa)
2. Perry Shea (California State, Bakersfield)
3. Ricky Stewart (Oklahoma State)
4. Isreal Sheppard (Oklahoma)
5. Chris Catalfo (Syracuse)
6. Bill Dykeman (Louisiana State)
7. Jackson Kistler (Arizona State)
8. Louis Montano (California Poly)

167-lb class

1. Dave Schultz (Oklahoma)
2. Mike Sheets (Oklahoma State)
3. John Reich (Navy)
4. Brad Bitterman (New Mexico)
5. John Hanrahan (Penn State)
6. Colin Grissom (Yale)
7. Dave Fitzgerald (Iowa)
8. Jan Michaels (North Carolina)

177-lb class

1. Mark Schultz (Oklahoma)
2. Ed Banach (Iowa)
3. Charlie Heller (Clarion State)
4. Perry Hummel (Iowa State)
5. Dave Young (Missouri)
6. Jim Scherr (Nebraska)
7. Joe Gormally (Northern Iowa)
8. Ed Potokar (Ohio State)

190-lb class

1. Pete Bush (Iowa)
2. Mike Mann (Iowa State)
3. Colin Kilrain (Lehigh)
4. Bill Scherr (Nebraska)
5. Kirk Myers (Northern Iowa)
6. Geno Savegnago (Eastern Illinois)
7. Greg Hawkins (Oklahoma State)
8. Mike Potts (Michigan State)

Heavyweight

1. Bruce Baumgartner (Indiana State)
2. Steve Williams (Oklahoma)
3. Lou Banach (Iowa)
4. Wayne Cole (Iowa State)
5. Mike Holcomb (Miami, OH)
6. Mark Rigatuso (Nebraska at Omaha)
7. Gary Albright (Nebraska)
8. Tab Thacker (North Carolina State)

1983 (at Myriad Center, Oklahoma City, OK)

Team	*Points*
1. Iowa	155
2. Oklahoma State	102
3. Iowa State	94.25
4. Oklahoma	64.75
5. Lehigh	49
6. Nebraska	46
7. Penn State	33.75

Team	Points
8. Louisiana State	30.50
9. California Poly	28.50
10. Northern Iowa	28
11. Navy	26
12. Michigan State	24.75
13. Ohio State	24.50
14. Arizona State, Tennessee at Chattanooga	20.25
16. North Carolina State	16
17. Illinois State, North Carolina	15
19. Harvard	14.50
20. Missouri	14.25

Place winners

118-lb class
1. Adam Cuestas (California State, Bakersfield)
2. Charlie Heard (Tennessee at Chattanooga)
3. Bob Dickman (Indiana State)
4. John Thorn (Iowa State)
5. Tim Riley (Iowa)
6. Anthony Calderaio (Slippery Rock)
7. Mike Erb (Oregon)
8. Al Guiterrez (California Poly)

126-lb class
1. Barry Davis (Iowa)
2. Gary Bohay (Arizona State)
3. Randy Majors (Northern Iowa)
4. Scott Lynch (Penn State)
5. Kevin Darkus (Iowa State)
6. Frank Famiano (Brockport State)
7. Rich Santoro (Lehigh)
8. Don Stevens (Southern Illinois at Edwardsville)

134-lb class
1. Clar Anderson (Oklahoma State)
2. Clint Burke (Oklahoma)
3. Pete Schuyler (Lehigh)
4. Kris Whelan (Missouri)
5. Jeff Kerber (Iowa)
6. Rick Burton (Ohio State)
7. Bill Marino (Penn State)
8. Gary Scriven (Weber State)

142-lb class
1. Darryl Burley (Lehigh)
2. Al Freeman (Nebraska)
3. Harlan Kistler (Iowa)
4. Andrew McNerney (Harvard)
5. Randy Conrad (Iowa State)
6. Leo Bailey (Oklahoma State)
7. Anthony Surage (Rutgers)
8. John Giura (Wisconsin)

150-lb class
1. Nate Carr (Iowa State)
2. Kenny Monday (Oklahoma State)
3. Roger Frizzell (Oklahoma)
4. Jim Heffernan (Iowa)
5. Dave Holler (Illinois State)
6. Wes Gasner (Wyoming)
7. Pat O'Donnell (California Poly)
8. Ron Winnie (Brockport State)

158-lb class
1. Jim Zalesky (Iowa)
2. Lou Montano (California Poly)
3. Kevin Jackson (Louisiana State)
4. Matt Skove (Oklahoma State)
5. Chris Catalfo (Syracuse)
6. Fred Worthem (Michigan State)
7. Chris Mondragon (North Carolina State)
8. Murray Crews (Iowa State)

167-lb class
1. Mike Sheets (Oklahoma State)
2. John Reich (Navy)
3. Jan Michaels (North Carolina)
4. Ray Oliver (Nebraska)
5. Sylvester Carter (California State, Fresno)
6. Jim Truedau (Minnesota)
7. Pete Capone (Hofstra)
8. Mike Jones (Illinois State)

177-lb class
1. Mark Schultz (Oklahoma)
2. Duane Goldman (Iowa)
3. Ed Potokar (Ohio State)
4. Clare Richardson (Louisiana State)
5. Eli Blazeff (Michigan State)
6. Bob Harr (Penn State)

7. Wayne Catan (Syracuse)
8. Scott Mansur (Portland State)

190-lb class
1. Ed Banach (Iowa)
2. Mike Mann (Iowa State)
3. Bill Scherr (Nebraska)
4. Jim Baumgardner (Oregon State)
5. Tim Morrison (Rider)
6. Dan Chaid (Oklahoma)
7. Doug Perkins (Stanford)
8. Jeff Dillman (Eastern Illinois)

Heavyweight
1. Lou Banach (Iowa)
2. Wayne Cole (Iowa State)
3. Mitch Shelton (Oklahoma State)
4. Mark Rigatuso (Nebraska at Omaha)
5. John Kriebs (Northern Iowa)
6. Tab Thacker (North Carolina State)
7. George Fears (Navy)
8. Kahlan O'Hara (Nevada at Las Vegas)

1984 (at Byrne Arena, East Rutherford, NJ)

Team	*Points*
1. Iowa	123.75
2. Oklahoma State	98
3. Penn State	70.50
4. Nebraska	61
5. Oklahoma	51.50
6. Wisconsin	49.50
7. Iowa State	40.25
8. Louisiana State	38.75
9. Michigan State	29.25
10. Missouri	29
11. Northern Iowa	28.75
12. North Carolina State	25.50
13. Oregon State	23.25
14. San Jose State	22.25
15. Lehigh	20.50
16. Arizona State	19
17. Princeton	18.25
18. Michigan	18
19. Temple	16.75
20. Miami (OH)	16.25

Place winners

118-lb class
1. Carl DeStefanis (Penn State)
2. Bob Hallman (Northern Iowa)
3. Mike Clevenger (Louisiana State)
4. Joe Spinazzola (Missouri)
5. Tim Riley (Iowa)
6. Mark Perry (Oklahoma State)
7. Charlie Heard (Tennessee at Chattanooga)
8. Jim Peters (Navy)

126-lb class
1. Kevin Darkus (Iowa State)
2. Joe McFarland (Michigan)
3. John Loomis (California State, Bakersfield)
4. Mark Trizzino (Iowa)
5. Rich Santoro (Lehigh)
6. Robbie Johnson (Louisiana State)
7. Mark Zimmer (Oklahoma)
8. Don Stevens (Southern Illinois at Edwardsville)

134-lb class
1. Scott Lynch (Penn State)
2. Greg Randall (Iowa)
3. Clint Burke (Oklahoma)
4. Chris DeLong (California Poly)
5. Clar Anderson (Oklahoma State)
6. Jim Jordan (Wisconsin)
7. Jim Mason (Michigan State)
8. Doug Castellari (Temple)

142-lb class
1. Jesse Reyes (California State, Bakersfield)
2. John Orr (Princeton)
3. John Giura (Wisconsin)
4. Joe Gibbons (Iowa State)
5. Luke Skove (Oklahoma State)

6. Jeff Kerber (Iowa)
7. Eric Childs (Penn State)
8. David Lundskog (Weber State)

150-lb class
1. Kenny Monday (Oklahoma State)
2. Marty Kistler (Iowa)
3. Eddie Urbano (Arizona State)
4. John Sonderegger (Missouri)
5. Darren Abel (Oklahoma)
6. Mike Langlais (North Dakota State)
7. Ben Ward (Old Dominion)
8. Chris Bevilacqua (Penn State)

158-lb class
1. Jim Zalesky (Iowa)
2. Mark Schmitz (Wisconsin)
3. Kevin Jackson (Louisiana State)
4. Bill Dykeman (Oklahoma State)
5. Darryl Pope (San Jose State)
6. Johnny Johnson (Oklahoma)
7. Greg Elinsky (Penn State)
8. Dave Grant (Northern Iowa)

167-lb class
1. Mike Sheets (Oklahoma State)
2. Lindley Kistler (Iowa)
3. Sylvester Carter (California State, Fresno)
4. Chris Edmond (Tennessee)
5. Jeff Jelic (Pittsburgh)
6. Rudy Isom (Wisconsin)
7. Greg Williams (Utah State)
8. Eric Brugel (Penn State)

177-lb class
1. Jim Scherr (Nebraska)
2. Duane Goldman (Iowa)
3. Booker Benford (Southern Illinois at Edwardsville)
4. Dan Chaid (Oklahoma)
5. Bob Harr (Penn State)
6. Dennis Limmex (Wisconsin)
7. Jeff Wilson (Stanford)
8. Marvin Jones (San Jose State)

190-lb class
1. Bill Scherr (Nebraska)
2. Jim Baumgardner (Oregon State)
3. Eli Blazeff (Michigan State)
4. Karl Lynes (Oklahoma State)
5. Jim Biechner (Clarion State)
6. Paul Diekel (Lehigh)
7. Bob Shriner (North Carolina)
8. Tod Giles (Boston)

Heavyweight
1. Tab Thacker (North Carolina State)
2. Gary Albright (Nebraska)
3. Mike Holcomb (Miami, OH)
4. Bill Hyman (Temple)
5. Kahlan O'Hara (Nevada at Las Vegas)
6. John Kriebs (Northern Iowa)
7. Mike Blaske (California State, Bakersfield)
8. Mike Potts (Michigan State)

1985 (at Myriad Center, Oklahoma City, OK)

Team	*Points*
1. Iowa	145.25
2. Oklahoma	98.50
3. Iowa State	70
4. Oklahoma State	56
5. Michigan	52
6. Arizona State	50.75
7. Penn State	46.75
8. Tennessee	32.50
9. Lehigh	31.50
10. Bloomsburg State	30.75
11. California Poly	30
12. Wisconsin	29.25
13. Syracuse	29
14. Kent State	27.50
15. Temple	26.50
16. Princeton	23.75
17. Louisiana State	22
18. Northern Iowa	21.50
19. North Carolina	19
20. Hofstra	18.25

Place winners

118-lb class
1. Ricky Bonoma (Bloomsburg State)
2. Matt Egeland (Iowa)
3. Don Horning (Kent State)
4. Joe Melchiore (Oklahoma)

5. Mark Perry (Oklahoma State)
6. Paul Kreimeyer (Northern Iowa)
7. Alfred Castro (Utah State)
8. Dave Crisanti (Princeton)

126-lb class

1. Barry Davis (Iowa)
2. Joe McFarland (Michigan)
3. Wade Hughes (George Washington)
4. John Lucerne (Rider)
5. Steve DePetro (Northwestern)
6. Cordel Anderson (Utah State)
7. Rob Johnson (Louisiana State)
8. Gary Bairos (Arizona State)

134-lb class

1. Jim Jordan (Wisconsin)
2. John Smith (Oklahoma State)
3. Alan Grammer (Southern Illinois at Edwardsville)
4. John Fisher (Michigan)
5. Greg Randall (Iowa)
6. Mark Ruettiger (Eastern (Illinois)
7. Tim Cochran (Tennessee)
8. Terry Lauver (Shippensburg State)

142-lb class

1. Joe Gibbons (Iowa State)
2. John Orr (Princeton)
3. Pete Yozzo (Lehigh)
4. Kevin Dresser (Iowa)
5. Lew Sondgeroth (Northern Iowa)
6. Jack Effner (Indiana State)
7. John Giura (Wisconsin)
8. Scott Wiggen (Stanford)

150-lb class

1. Eddie Urbano (Arizona State)
2. Jim Heffernan (Iowa)
3. Darrin Higgins (Oklahoma)
4. Chris Bevilacqua (Penn State)
5. Dave Holler (Indiana State)
6. Ken Haselrig (Clarion)
7. Luke Skove (Oklahoma State)
8. Rob Koll (North Carolina)

158-lb class

1. Marty Kistler (Iowa)
2. Greg Elinsky (Penn State)
3. Dave Ewing (Iowa State)
4. Dave Lilovich (Purdue)
5. Ernie Blazeff (Michigan State)
6. Tom Draheim (Arizona State)
7. Bill Dykeman (Oklahoma State)
8. Glenn Lanham (Tennessee)

167-lb class

1. Chris Edmond (Tennessee)
2. Pete Capone (Hofstra)
3. John Laviolette (Oklahoma)
4. Jon Monaco (Montclair State)
5. Lindley Kistler (Iowa)
6. Mike VanArsdale (Iowa State)
7. Kevin Jackson (Louisiana State)
8. Tod Wilson (North Carolina)

177-lb class

1. Melvin Douglas (Oklahoma)
2. Wayne Catan (Syracuse)
3. Booker Benford (Southern Illinois at Edwardsville)
4. Roger Sayles (California Poly)
5. Rico Chiapparelli (Iowa)
6. Tom Klopus (Arizona State)
7. Doug Dake (Kent State)
8. Bob McCurdy (Shippensburg State)

190-lb class

1. Dan Chaid (Oklahoma)
2. Duane Goldman (Iowa)
3. Paul Diekel (Lehigh)
4. Kolin Knight (Augustana, SD)
5. Mark Cody (Missouri)
6. Jim Beichner (Clarion State)
7. Mark Tracey (California Poly)
8. Ryan Western (Weber State)

Heavyweight

1. Bill Hyman (Temple)
2. Kirk Trost (Michigan)
3. Rick Brunot (Youngstown)
4. Steve Sefter (Penn State)
5. Darryl Peterson (Iowa State)
6. Kahlan O'Hara (Oklahoma State)
7. Rod Severn (Arizona State)
8. Al Sears (Southern Illinois at Edwardsville)

1986 (at University of Iowa, Iowa City, IA)

Team	*Points*
1. Iowa	158
2. Oklahoma	84.75
3. Oklahoma State	77.25
4. Iowa State	71
5. Penn State	47.25
6. North Carolina	38.75
7. Bloomsburg State	37.75
8. Arizona State	36.50
9. Lehigh	32.75
10. Michigan	32
11. Wisconsin	30.50
12. Nebraska	28.25
13. Army	27.75
14. Syracuse	26
15. North Carolina State	25.50
16. Ohio State	22.75
17. Northern Iowa	20.50
18. Utah State	19
19. Northwestern	17
20. Clemson	15.50

Place winners

118-lb class
1. Ricky Bonomo (Bloomsburg State)
2. Al Palacio (North Carolina)
3. Ed Geise (Minnesota)
4. Jim Martin (Penn State)
5. Mark Schwab (Northern Iowa)
6. Eddie Woodburn (Oklahoma State)
7. Joe Melchiore (Oklahoma)
8. Alfred Catro (Utah State)

126-lb class
1. Brad Penrith (Iowa)
2. Dennis Semmel (Army)
3. Steve DePetro (Northwestern)
4. Brad Gustafson (Brigham Young)
5. Alan Grammer (Southern Illinois at Edwardsville)
6. Cordel Anderson (Utah State)
7. Don Horning (Kent State)
8. Rocky Bonomo (Bloomsburg State)

134-lb class
1. Jim Jordan (Wisconsin)
2. Greg Randall (Iowa)
3. David Ray (Edinboro)
4. Leo Bailey (Oklahoma State)
5. Tim Cochran (Tennessee)
6. Phil Callahan (Illinois)
7. Dan Matauch (Michigan State)
8. Kyle Nellis (Pittsburgh)

142-lb class
1. Kevin Dresser (Iowa)
2. Pete Yozzo (Lehigh)
3. Joe Gibbons (Iowa State)
4. Luke Skove (Oklahoma State)
5. Jack Effner (Indiana State)
6. Pat Santoro (Pittsburgh)
7. Darrel Nerove (Army)
8. Dave Zahoransky (Cleveland State)

150-lb class
1. Jim Heffernan (Iowa)
2. Adam Cohen (Arizona State)
3. Scott Turner (North Carolina State)
4. Joey McKenna (Clemson)
5. Tim Krieger (Iowa State)
6. Jeff Cardwell (Oregon State)
7. Vince Silva (Oklahoma State)
8. Jeff Mills (Central Michigan)

158-lb class
1. Jude Skove (Ohio State)
2. Greg Elinsky (Penn State)
3. Rob Koll (North Carolina)
4. Johnny Johnson (Oklahoma)
5. Royce Alger (Iowa)
6. Ardeshir Asgari (California State, Fullerton)
7. Dave Lilovich (Purdue)
8. Jeff Clutter (Northern Iowa)

167-lb class
1. Marty Kistler (Iowa)
2. Mark VanTine (Oklahoma State)
3. Mike VanArsdale (Iowa State)
4. John Laviolette (Oklahoma)
5. Dave Lee (Stanford)
6. Darryl Pope (California State, Bakersfield)

7. Brad Lloyd (Lock Haven)
8. Fred Little (Fresno State)

177-lb class
1. Melvin Douglas (Oklahoma)
2. Wayne Catan (Syracuse)
3. Marvin Jones (California State, Bakersfield)
4. Rico Chiapparelli (Iowa)
5. Dave Mariola (Michigan State)
6. Reggie Wilson (Oklahoma State)
7. Mark Tracey (California Poly)
8. John Ginther (Arizona State)

190-lb class
1. Duane Goldman (Iowa)
2. Dan Chaid (Oklahoma)
3. Kolin Knight (Augustana, SC)
4. Mark Coleman (Miami, OH)
5. Paul Diekel (Lehigh)
6. Scott Rechsteinner (Michigan)
7. Dave Dewalt (Delaware)
8. Wade Ayala (Montana State)

Heavyweight
1. Kirk Trost (Michigan)
2. John Heropoulos (Iowa State)
3. Gary Albright (Nebraska)
4. Tom Erikson (Oklahoma State)
5. John Potts (Toledo)
6. Dean Hall (Edinboro)
7. Rocco Liace (Arizona State)
8. Emanuel Yarbrough (Morgan State)

1987 (at University of Maryland, College Park, MD)

Team	*Points*
1. Iowa State	133
2. Iowa	108
3. Penn State	97.75
4. Oklahoma State	85.25
5. Bloomsburg State	47.25
6. Clarion State, North Carolina	46
8. Edinboro	38.24
9. Arizona State	35.75
10. Lehigh	32.25
11. Wisconsin	28.50
12. Oklahoma	28.25
13. Northern Iowa	25.50
14. Nebraska	24.50
15. Pittsburgh, Purdue	23.50
17. Maryland	22
18. Northwestern	20.50
19. Michigan, Minnesota	20

Place winners

118-lb class
1. Ricky Bonomo (Bloomsburg State)
2. Jim Martin (Penn State)
3. Tim Wright (Southern Illinois, Edwardsville)
4. Dave Rowan (Edinboro)
5. Jack Cuvo (East Stroudsburg)
6. Roger Singleton (Grand Valley State)
7. Al Palacio (North Carolina)
8. Dennis Mejias (Wilkes)

126-lb class
1. Bill Kelly (Iowa State)
2. Brad Penrith (Iowa)
3. Ken Chertow (Penn State)
4. Rock Bonomo (Bloomsburg State)
5. Matt Treaster (Navy)
6. Marc Sodano (North Carolina State)
7. Scott Hinkel (Purdue)
8. Mike Schwab (Northern Iowa)

134-lb class
1. John Smith (Oklahoma State)
2. Gil Sanchez (Nebraska)
3. Jeff Gibbons (Iowa State)
4. John Fisher (Michigan)
5. Paul Clark (Clarion State)
6. Rob Johnson (Ohio)
7. Tim Flynn (Penn State)
8. Andre Miller (Wilkes)

142-lb class
1. Pete Yozzo (Lehigh)
2. Pat Santoro (Pittsburgh)

3. Mike Cole (Clarion State)
4. Len Bernstein (North Carolina)
5. Nick Neville (Oklahoma)
6. Joe Hadge (Penn State)
7. Sean O'Day (Edinboro)
8. Jeff Castro (Montana)

150-lb class

1. Tim Krieger (Iowa State)
2. Jim Heffernan (Iowa)
3. Darrin Higgins (Oklahoma)
4. Jeff Jordan (Wisconsin)
5. Vince Silva (Oklahoma State)
6. Sean Finkbeiner (Penn State)
7. Scott Cook (Utah State)
8. Jim Akerly (West Virginia)

158-lb class

1. Stewart Carter (Iowa State)
2. Ken Haslerig (Clarion State)
3. Rob Koll (North Carolina)
4. Paul McShane (Wisconsin)
5. Glen Lanham (Oklahoma State)
6. John Heffernan (Iowa)
7. Jeff Cardwell (Oregon State)
8. Brian Kurlander (James Madison)

167-lb class

1. Royce Alger (Iowa)
2. Kevin Jackson (Louisiana State)
3. Greg Elinsky (Penn State)
4. Mike Farrell (Oklahoma State)
5. Craig Martin (Missouri)
6. Joe Urso (Purdue)
7. Jerry Umin (Eastern Michigan)
8. Curt Scovel (Maryland)

177-lb class

1. Rico Chiapparelli (Iowa)
2. Darryl Pope (California State, Bakersfield)
3. Dan Mayo (Penn State)
4. Mike Funk (Northwestern)
5. Reggie Wilson (Chicago)
6. Fred Little (Fresno State)
7. Steve Peperak (Maryland)
8. John Ginther (Arizona State)

190-lb class

1. Eric Voelker (Iowa State)
2. Dave Dean (Minnesota)
3. Mike Davies (Arizona State)
4. Andy Voit (Penn State)
5. Jeff Weatherman (Northern Iowa)
6. Dan Catigan (Army)
7. Eric Middlestead (California State, Bakersfield)
8. Ken Hackman (California, PA)

Heavyweight

1. Carlton Haselrig (Pittsburgh, Johnstown)
2. Dean Hall (Edinboro)
3. Tom Erickson (Oklahoma State)
4. Mark Sindlinger (Iowa)
5. Tom Reese (Maryland)
6. Rod Severn (Arizona State)
7. Jim Neilsen (Brigham Young)
8. Demetrius Harper (Eastern Illinois)

1988 (at Iowa State University, Ames, IA)

Team	*Points*
1. Arizona State	93
2. Iowa	85.50
3. Iowa State	83.75
4. Oklahoma State	80.50
5. Penn State	71.50
6. Michigan	62.50
7. Edinboro	53.50
8. Oklahoma	45
9. Ohio State	39.75
10. North Carolina State	36
11. Wisconsin	34.75
12. Lock Haven	34
13. Northern Iowa	31
14. Bloomsburg State	29
15. Pittsburgh	26.25
16. Minnesota, North Carolina	26
18. East Stroudsburg	23.25
19. Missouri, Oregon State	19.50

Place winners

118-lb class

1. Jack Cuvo (East Stroudsburg)
2. Keith Nix (Minnesota)

3. Ken Chertow (Penn State)
4. Craig Corbin (Lock Haven)
5. Cory Baze (Oklahoma State)
6. Zeke Jones (Arizona State)
7. Gary McCall (Iowa State)
8. Greg Gascon (New Mexico)

126-lb class
1. Jim Martin (Penn State)
2. Brad Penrith (Iowa)
3. Chip Park (Arizona State)
4. Craig Walters (Wyoming)
5. Steve Knight (Iowa State)
6. Kendall Cross (Oklahoma State)
7. Pete Gonzales (Montclair State)
8. John Epperly (Lehigh)

134-lb class
1. John Smith (Oklahoma State)
2. Joe Melchoire (Iowa)
3. John Fisher (Michigan)
4. Dan Willaman (Edinboro)
5. Joei Bales (Northwestern)
6. Jeff Gibbons (Iowa State)
7. T.J. Sewell (Oklahoma)
8. Pat Dorn (South Dakota State)

142-lb class
1. Pat Santoro (Pittsburgh)
2. Sean O'Day (Edinboro)
3. Karl Monaco (Montclair State)
4. Tom Ortiz (Arizona State)
5. Larry Gotcher (Michigan)
6. Laurence Jackson (Oklahoma State)
7. Kirk Azinger (Illinois)
8. Dave Zahoransky (Cleveland State)

150-lb class
1. Scott Turner (North Carolina State)
2. Tim Krieger (Iowa State)
3. Dave Morgan (Bloomsburg State)
4. Jeff Jordan (Wisconsin)
5. Terry Kennedy (Edinboro)
6. Wes White (Oklahoma State)
7. Junior Taylor (Oklahoma)
8. Brian Dolph (Indiana)

158-lb class
1. Rob Koll (North Carolina)
2. Joe Pantaleo (Michigan)
3. Dan St. John (Arizona State)
4. John Heffernan (Iowa)
5. Chris Lemback (Northern Iowa)
6. Andrew Skove (Ohio State)
7. Mike Carr (West Virginia)
8. Kenny Fischer (Oklahoma)

167-lb class
1. Mike VanArsdale (Iowa State)
2. Mike Amine (Michigan)
3. Jim Gressley (Arizona State)
4. Eric Osborne (California Poly)
5. Mike Farrell (Oklahoma State)
6. Dave Lee (Wisconsin)
7. Rod Sande (Minnesota)
8. Joe DeCamillis (Wyoming)

177-lb class
1. Royce Alger (Iowa)
2. Dan Mayo (Penn State)
3. Brad Lloyd (Lock Haven)
4. Chris Barnes (Oklahoma State)
5. Chuck Kearney (Oregon)
6. R.J. Nebe (Nebraska at Omaha)
7. Pat Johannes (North Dakota State)
8. Ron Gharbo (Ohio State)

190-lb class
1. Mark Coleman (Ohio State)
2. Mike Davies (Arizona State)
3. Eric Voelker (Iowa State)
4. Kyle Richards (Wisconsin)
5. Andy Voit (Penn State)
6. Carlton Kinkade (Central Michigan)
7. Junior Meek (Oklahoma)
8. Charlie Scheretz (Missouri)

Heavyweight
1. Carlton Haselrig (Pittsburgh Johnstown)
2. Dave Orndorff (Oregon State)
3. Mark Tatum (Oklahoma)
4. Joel Greenlee (Northern Iowa)
5. Rod Severn (Arizona State)
6. Mark Sindlinger (Iowa)
7. Dean Hall (Edinboro)
8. Mike Lombardo (North Carolina State)

Table 8.4
Division II, 1963-1988

1963 (at State College of Iowa, Cedar Falls, IA)

Team	Points
1. Western State	62
2. Southern Illinois	57
3. State College of Iowa	47
4. South Dakota State	31
5. Cornell College	27
6. Wheaton	22
7. Mankato State	12
8. Luther	11
9. University of the South	9
10. Hiram	8
11. Lycoming, Wartburg	6
13. Colorado Mines	5
14. California State (Long Beach), Rochester Tech	4
16. North Central	3

Place winners

115-lb class
1. Van Doughty (Western State)
2. Don Brown (Cornell C)
3. Gary Pollard (State College of Iowa)
4. Dale Deffner (California State, Long Beach)

123-lb class
1. Terry Finn (Southern Illinois)
2. Jim Schonauer (Hiram)
3. Dave Drake (Rochester Tech)
4. Al Rende (Western State)

130-lb class
1. Dee Brainerd (South Dakota State)
2. Bob Hollingshead (Western State)
3. Jim Mueller (Wartburg)
4. Ron Knoebel (Lycoming)

137-lb class
1. Bill Dotson (State College of Iowa)
2. Jim Perkins (South Dakota State)
3. Joe Oldfield (Western State)
4. Ken Droegemuller (Mankato State)

147-lb class
1. Jim Sanford (State College of Iowa)
2. Truman Sandelin (Western State)
3. Eric Felock (Southern Illinois)
4. John Novak (North Central)

157-lb class
1. Tom Jarman (Wheaton)
2. Dick Austin (State College of Iowa)
3. Lyle Voss (South Dakota State)
4. Leonard Erdahl (Luther)

167-lb class
1. Jim Gass (Cornell C)
2. Dave Skonberg (Wheaton)
3. Dave Schreiber (Luther)
4. Ron Mehlin (State College of Iowa)

177-lb class
1. Ken Houston (Southern Illinois)
2. Frank Pinney (University of the South)
3. Dave Hrouda (Cornell C)
4. Steve Hoemann (State College of Iowa)

191-lb class
1. Roger Plapp (Southern Illinois)
2. Al Rozman (Western State)
3. Roger Eischens (South Dakota State)
4. Joe Confer (Lycoming)

Heavyweight
1. Larry Kristoff (Southern Illinois)
2. Joe Kuhn (Western State)
3. Dick Zeyen (Mankato State)
4. Hugh Wentz (Colorado Mines)

1964 (at State College of Iowa, Cedar Falls, IA)

Team	Points
1. Western State	51
2. Colorado Mines	49
3. Southern Illinois	46
4. Mankato State	37
5. West Chester	23
6. State College of Iowa	17
7. Eastern Illinois	16

Team	*Points*
8. California Poly (San Luis Obispo)	15
9. Northwest Missouri	14
10. Wheaton, St. Olaf	12
12. CW Post, Lycoming	11
14. Wilkes, Cornell College	9
16. Luther	8
17. Augustana (IL), California State (Fresno)	7
19. Morgan State	6
20. Montclair State	5
21. Northern Illinois, South Dakota State, Oswego State	3
24. Macalester, Loras, New York University, Idaho State, Hiram	2
29. Grinnell, Sewanee	1

Place winners

115-lb class
1. Terry Finn (Southern Illinois)
2. Ray Coca (Western State)
3. Don Brown (Cornell C)
4. Mike McNamara (Mankato State)

123-lb class
1. Howard Gangestad (Mankato State)
2. Brooke Yeager (Wilkes)
3. Roy Stuckey (California State, Fresno)
4. Van Doughty (Western State)

130-lb class
1. Dave Linder (Colorado Mines)
2. Ken Droegemuller (Mankato State)
3. Don Schneider (Southern Illinois)
4. Jim Teem (California Poly, Pomona)

137-lb class
1. Bob Hollingshead (Western State)
2. Dan Fix (Colorado Mines)
3. Ron Semetis (Eastern Illinois)
4. Bob Trautman (State College of Iowa)

147-lb class
1. Richard Hickman (Colorado Mines)
2. Pete Parlett (West Chester)
3. Bruce Strom (Eastern Illinois)
4. Eldorado Vancy (Morgan State)

157-lb class
1. Roger Sanders (West Chester)
2. Richard Duffy (CW Post)
3. Lonny Wieland (Northwest Missouri)
4. Tom Jarman (Wheaton)

167-lb class
1. Don Millard (Southern Illinois)
2. Jim Monroe (State College of Iowa)
3. Dave Schreiber (Luther)
4. Allan Packer (Northwest Missouri)

177-lb class
1. Dave Schmidt (St. Olaf)
2. Art Oraschin (Lycoming)
3. Dave Skonberg (Wheaton)
4. Mel Schmidt (Northern Illinois)

191-lb class
1. Al Rozman (Western State)
2. Bill Fife (California Poly, Pomona)
3. Al Russ (Mankato State)
4. Fred Johnson (Augustana)

Heavyweight
1. Larry Kristoff (Southern Illinois)
2. DeWayne Schroeder (Colorado Mines)
3. Joe Kuhn (Western State)
4. Larry Sciacchetano (Montclair State)

1965 (at Colorado School of Mines, Golden, CO)

Team	*Points*
1. Mankato State	57
2. California Poly (SLO)	54
3. Western State	44
4. Northern Illinois	30
5. South Dakota State	18
6. Lycoming	17
7. MacMurray	16
8. San Francisco State	15
9. Wilkes	14
10. Colorado Mines, California State (Fresno), Gettysburg	12
13. Augustana (IL)	10

Team	Points
14. Monmouth	9
15. Northwest Missouri	8
16. Ball State, Denison	7
18. Akron, West Chester	6
20. Coe, Cornell College, Gustavus Adolphus	5
23. Hiram, State College of Iowa	4
25. CW Post, Oswego State	3
27. Lebanon Valley	2
28. Albany State, Luther, San Fernando State	1

Place winners

115-lb class
1. Steve Johansen (California State, Fresno)
2. Mike McNamara (Mankato State)
3. Frank Murphy (South Dakota State)
4. Michael Remer (California Poly, SLO)

123-lb class
1. Howard Gangestad (Mankato State)
2. John Lambert (Augustana)
3. John Garcia (California Poly, SLO)
4. James Schonauer (Hiram)

130-lb class
1. Dale Stryker (Western State)
2. Wayne Paulsen (South Dakota State)
3. Lennis Cowell (California Poly, SLO)
4. Curtis Ashman (Ball State)

137-lb class
1. Ronald Knoebel (Lycoming)
2. Jim Rush (Western State)
3. Doug Ebeling (Mankato State)
4. Steve McCormick (Cornell C)

147-lb class
1. Joe Bavaro (Gettysburg)
2. Jim Teem (California Poly, SLO)
3. Bob Furlan (Northern Illinois)
4. Bob Wendel (Mankato State)

157-lb class
1. Jim Burke (San Francisco State)
2. Rich Hickman (Colorado Mines)
3. Paul Tillman (West Chester)
4. Bill Bachardy (Lycoming)

167-lb class
1. John Carr (Wilkes)
2. Sam Cereceres (California Poly, SLO)
3. John Alexis (Mankato State)
4. George Dyche (Coe)

177-lb class
1. Phillip Sullivan (California Poly, SLO)
2. Mel Schmidt (Northern Illinois)
3. Robert Gibson (Denison)
4. Syd LaMore (MacMurray)

191-lb class
1. Al Rozman (Western State)
2. Gary Storm (Mankato State)
3. Pete Guthrie (Akron)
4. Ted Mays (Gustavus Adolphus)

Heavyweight
1. Neal McDonald (Northern Illinois)
2. Robert Kellogg (MacMurray)
3. Rich Paasch (Monmouth)
4. Mike Pierro (Mankato State)

1966 (at Mankato State College, Mankato, MN)

Team	Points
1. California Poly (SLO)	55
2. Wilkes	51
3. Portland State	47
4. Mankato State	42
5. Augustana (IL)	29
6. South Dakota State	28
7. Western Colorado, Gettysburg	26
9. California State (Fresno)	24
10. State College of Iowa	23
11. Montana	21
12. Eastern Michigan	19
13. Gustavus Adolphus, Luther, Lycoming	17
16. Albany State, Northern Illinois	15
18. West Chester	14

Team	*Points*
19. Old Dominion, Springfield (MA), Wheaton	12
22. Moravian, CW Post, Colorado Mines, Northwest Missouri	10
26. Central Missouri, Southeast Missouri	9
28. Massachusetts, North Dakota State	8
30. California (Davis)	7
31. MacMurray	6
32. Beloit, Cornell College, Western Illinois	4
35. Denison, Illinois State, South Dakota	3
38. California State (Chico), Eastern Illinois, Monmouth (IL), North Dakota, Wabash	2
43. Coe, Knox, Merchant Marine, Parsons, St. Olaf, Wooster	1

Place winners

115-lb class
1. Michael Remer (California Poly, SLO)
2. James Johansen (California State, Fresno)
3. Gerald Gipp (Luther)
4. Al Ogdie (Mankato State)
5. Lance Smith (Cornell C)
6. Steve Tipton (Colorado Mines)

123-lb class
1. Warren Crow (Albany State)
2. John Lambert (Augustana)
3. Richard Sanders (Portland State)
4. Glenn Younger (Western Colorado)
5. Everette Hill (Wheaton)
6. Davis Johnson (Luther)

130-lb class
1. Bob Soulek (Mankato State)
2. Carl Ragland (Old Dominion)
3. Rich Green (Portland State)
4. Lennis Cowell (California Poly, SLO)
5. Billy Paddock (Colorado Mines)
6. Dan Ingegno (CW Post)

137-lb class
1. Robert Palmer (Montana)
2. Joe Keifer (Wilkes)
3. Masaru Yatabe (Portland State)
4. Steve Boozell (Central Missouri)
5. Jesse Brogen (Massachusetts)
6. Cyril Faulkner (Wheaton)

145-lb class
1. Dennis Downing (California Poly, SLO)
2. Scott Higgins (Gettysburg)
3. Robert Furlan (Northern Illinois)
4. Joe McCormick (North Dakota State)
5. William Trenz (CW Post)
6. Ron James (Northwest Missouri)

152-lb class
1. Joe Bavaro (Gettysburg)
2. John Miller (California Poly, SLO)
3. Freeman Garrison (Portland State)
4. Joe Weindl (Wilkes)
5. Bob Wendel (Mankato State)
6. Michael Gallego (California State, Fresno)

160-lb class
1. John Carr (Wilkes)
2. Rick Evans (Gustavus Adolphus)
3. Larry Amundson (Mankato State)
4. Fred Siebenthal (Portland State)
5. Neal Skaar (Luther)
6. Dave Steinkamp (State College of Iowa)

167-lb class
1. William Bachardy (Lycoming)
2. Robert Ray (Eastern Michigan)
3. Paul Tillman (West Chester)
4. Jim Riesselman (Mankato State)
5. John Kain (South Dakota State)
6. Dick Cook (Wilkes)

177-lb class
1. Don Parker (State College of Iowa)
2. Dave Mucha (Moravian)
3. Joe Cerra (Springfield)

4. Tom Buckalew (Eastern Michigan)
5. Dennis Sager (Gustavus Adolphus)
6. Francis Olexy (Wilkes)

191-lb class
1. Fred Johnson (Augustana)
2. Paul Thomas (South Dakota State)
3. Grover Ford (California, Davis)
4. Barry Gold (Wilkes)
5. Tony Costello (Montana)
6. Gary Wintjen (Eastern Illinois)

Heavyweight
1. Tom Beeson (Western Colorado)
2. Walter Fuller (Southeast Missouri)
3. Richard Birbeck (California State, Fresno)
4. Mick Hurlbut (South Dakota State)
5. Charles Ellis (Beloit)
6. Earl Paasch (Monmouth)

1967 (at Wilkes College, Wilkes-Barre, PA)

Team	Points
1. Portland State	86
2. Mankato State	57
3. State College of Iowa	40
4. Colorado Mines, Illinois State, Western Colorado	35
7. California Poly (SLO)	34
8. South Dakota State, Wilkes	26
10. Springfield	23
11. Wisconsin (Milwaukee)	22
12. Northwest Missouri	20
13. MacMurray	17
14. California State (Fresno)	15
15. Albany State	13
16. Gustavus Adolphus, Wheaton	12
18. Augustana (IL)	11
19. Denison, King's Point, Old Dominion, Oneonta State	9
23. Ashland	8
24. Luther, West Chester	7
26. CW Post, Eastern Michigan, Moravian, Morningside, San Francisco State	6
31. California State (Chico), Drexel Tech	4
33. Hampden-Sydney, Indiana (PA), Lincoln (PA), South Dakota	3
37. Allegheny, Augustana (SD), Ball State, Brockport State, Lycoming, Wooster	2
43. Clarkson, Cleveland State, Eastern Illinois, Elizabethtown, Fort Lewis, John Carroll, California State (Long Beach), Maryville, Oswego State, California (Davis), Western Maryland	1

Place winners

115-lb class
1. Richard Sanders (Portland State)
2. John Garcia (California Poly, SLO)
3. David Eberhard (Illinois State)
4. Al Ogdie (Mankato State)
5. Everette Hill (Wheaton)
6. Steve Tipton (Colorado Mines)

123-lb class
1. Warren Crow (Albany State)
2. Glen Younger (Western Colorado)
3. Les Kempf (Kings Point)
4. James Burch (Ashland)
5. Mike Howe (Mankato State)
6. Billy Paddock (Colorado Mines)

130-lb class
1. Bob Soulek (Mankato State)
2. Dale Stryker (Western Colorado)
3. Gerry Smith (South Dakota State)
4. Rich Green (Portland State)
5. David King (Indiana)
6. Ken Frus (Illinois State)

137-lb class
1. Masaru Yatabe (Portland State)
2. Jerry Bond (State College of Iowa)
3. Gene Morrison (Colorado Mines)
4. Paul Stehman (Northwest Missouri)
5. Tom Sowles (Mankato State)
6. Dave Mentzer (Drexel Tech)

145-lb class
1. Bob Wendel (Mankato State)
2. Robert Waligunda (Springfield)
3. Freeman Garrison (Portland State)
4. David Lindhjem (Old Dominion)
5. Bill Rex (Northwest Missouri)
6. Kent Wyatt (California Poly, SLO)

152-lb class
1. Clarence Seal (Portland State)
2. Frank Paraino (Springfield)
3. Ron James (Northwest Missouri)
4. Bryan Lambe (Oneonta State)
5. John Miller (California Poly, SLO)
6. Gordy Frisch (Gustavus Adolphus)

160-lb class
1. Don Morrison (Colorado Mines)
2. Joe Wiendl (Wilkes)
3. Curtis Sexton (Illinois State)
4. Jim Soulek (Mankato State)
5. Rick Evans (Gustavus Adolphus)
6. Neal Skaar (Luther)

167-lb class
1. Mike Gallego (California State, Fresno)
2. Jon McNitt (South Dakota State)
3. Hal Gritzmacher (Wisconsin, Milwaukee)
4. Dick Cook (Wilkes)
5. Bob Ray (Eastern Michigan)
6. William Miller (Hampden-Sydney)

177-lb class
1. Don Parker (State College of Iowa)
2. Robert Flayter (Wisconsin, Milwaukee)
3. Robert Gibson (Denison)
4. Dave Mucka (Moravian)
5. Tony Campbell (Portland State)
6. Denny Sager (Gustavus Adolphus)

191-lb class
1. Willie Williams (Illinois State)
2. Mike McKeel (Portland State)
3. Tom Kline (California Poly, SLO)
4. Fred Johnson (Augustana)
5. Peter Middleton (Morningside)
6. Barry Gold (Wilkes)

Heavyweight
1. Bob Kellogg (MacMurray)
2. Kent Osboe (State College of Iowa)
3. Tom Beeson (Western Colorado)
4. David McDowell (Wheaton)
5. Storm Goranson (San Francisco State)
6. Don Huffer (CW Post)

1968 (at Mankato State College, Mankato, MN)

Team	*Points*
1. California Poly (SLO)	91
2. Portland State	62
3. South Dakota State	46
4. Mankato State	44
5. Wilkes	39
6. Western Colorado	37
7. West Chester	34
8. Northern Iowa, Upper Iowa	29
10. California State (Fresno), Illinois State, Northeast Missouri	25
13. Idaho State	23
14. Luther, Northwest Missouri	20
16. Eastern Illinois	18
17. MacMurray, Oswego State	16
19. Old Dominion	15
20. Ball State, Norfolk State	14
22. Southwest Missouri, Ashland, CW Post, Gustavus Adolphus, North Central 13	

Team	*Points*
27. California State (Long Beach)	12
28. San Francisco State	9
29. Morningside, Brockport State	8
31. Elizabethtown, Oneonta State	6
33. Seattle Pacific, Wisconsin (Milwaukee)	5
35. Central Missouri, Cornell College, Baltimore, Colorado Mines	4
39. Cleveland State, Howard, North Dakota State, St. Olaf, Wayne State, John Carroll	3
45. Augustana (IL), Central Michigan, Nevada, Western Maryland, Carleton, California State (Chico), New York Maritime	2
52. Springfield, Wartburg, Monmouth (NJ), Lincoln (PA), Lake Forest, Drexel, Augustana (SD), Wheaton, Beloit	1

Place winners

115-lb class
1. Curt Alexander (Northeast Missouri)
2. Greg Schmidt (South Dakota State)
3. Frank Carrozza (West Chester)
4. Andy Matviak (Wilkes)
5. Lou Curra (Old Dominion)
6. Bill Simpson (Morningside)

123-lb class
1. Rich Sanders (Portland State)
2. John Walter (Oswego State)
3. Sam King (California Poly, SLO)
4. Scott Evans (Mankato State)
5. Craig Campbell (Upper Iowa)
6. Bill Neumeister (St. Olaf)

130-lb class
1. Glen Younger (Western Colorado)
2. Jerry Smith (South Dakota State)
3. Ed Jackson (North Central)
4. Jerry Smith (Southwest Missouri)
5. John Marfia (Wilkes)

137-lb class
1. Masaru Yatabe (Portland State)
2. Ron Otto (MacMurray)
3. Rich Yates (Idaho State)
4. John Geyer (California State, Long Beach)
5. Paul Stehman (Northwest Missouri)
6. Tom Baker (Colorado Mines)

145-lb class
1. Kent Wyatt (California Poly, SLO)
2. Clarence Seal (Portland State)
3. John DeMarco (West Chester)
4. Gerald Bond (Northern Iowa)
5. Wayne Franks (North Dakota)
6. Steve Stachelski (Ball State)

152-lb class
1. John Finch (California Poly, SLO)
2. Dave Nerothin (Gustavus Adolphus)
3. Bob Emerick (Ball State)
4. Gary Neist (Luther)
5. Bryan Lambe (Oneonta State)
6. Earl Brinser (Elizabethtown)

160-lb class
1. Joe Wiendl (Wilkes)
2. Curtis Sexton (Illinois State)
3. Neal Skaar (Luther)
4. Ken Biles (West Chester)
5. Harry Oliphant (Idaho State)
6. Ashley Sherman (San Francisco State)

167-lb class
1. Mike Gallego (California State, Fresno)
2. John Woods (California Poly, SLO)
3. Don Ryland (Mankato State)
4. Jon McNitt (South Dakota State)
5. Bruce Turner (Brockport State)
6. Dick Cook (Wilkes)

177-lb class
1. Larry Amundson (Mankato State)
2. James Lee (Norfolk State)
3. Ken Bos (California Poly, SLO)
4. Larry Kanke (Eastern Illinois)
5. Del Hughes (Upper Iowa)
6. William Todd (Old Dominion)

191-lb class
1. Tom Kline (California Poly, SLO)
2. Dave Sanger (Upper Iowa)
3. Chris Feder (CW Post)
4. Herman Pettigrew (Ashland)
5. Carlton Tanka (Idaho State)
6. Allen Baxter (Morningside)

Heavyweight
1. Kent Osboe (Northern Iowa)
2. Tom Beeson (Western Colorado)
3. Al Borkowski (Northwest Missouri)
4. Richard Beard (Northeast Missouri)
5. Fred Beifuss (Illinois State)
6. Lonn Ipsen (Eastern Illinois)

1969 (at California Poly, San Luis Obispo, CA)

Team	Points
1. California Poly (SLO)	127
2. Colorado State College	81
3. Northern Iowa	49
4. Portland State	45
5. Moorhead State	36
6. Old Dominion, San Francisco State	33
8. East Stroudsburg	31
9. Oswego State	29
10. South Dakota State	26
11. Northwest Missouri	22
12. Mankato State	21
13. California (Davis)	19
14. Wilkes	18
15. Western Illinois	16
16. Humboldt State	14
17. CW Post, Western Colorado	13
19. Central Michigan	12
20. New York Maritime, North Dakota State	11
22. Illinois State, Colorado Mines	10
24. Oneonta State, Ithaca, Springfield	9
27. North Park, Northern Michigan	8
29. Morningside	7
30. Nevada	6
31. Augustana (IL), Luther	5
33. Ashland, Lycoming, Central Missouri	4
36. California State (Chico), North Central, Seattle Pacific	3
39. Elizabethtown, John Carroll, Cortland State, Southwest Missouri	2
43. Cleveland State, Cornell College, Denison, Northeast Missouri, California State (Sacramento), Wheaton, Worcester Poly	1

Place winners

115-lb class
1. Terry Hall (California Poly, SLO)
2. John Morley (Moorhead State)
3. Greg Schmidt (South Dakota)
4. Ted Pease (East Stroudsburg)
5. Lou Curra (Old Dominion)
6. John Anderson (San Francisco State)

123-lb class
1. John Walter (Oswego State)
2. Scott Clark (Western Illinois)
3. Sam Kucenic (North Dakota State)
4. Mike Tello (Northern Michigan)
5. Art Chavez (San Francisco State)
6. Darwin Popow (Lycoming)

130-lb class
1. Len Groom (Colorado State C)
2. Marv Reiland (Northern Iowa)
3. Tom Best (East Stroudsburg)
4. Brian McGann (Oswego State)
5. Jesse Flores (California Poly, SLO)
6. Chuck Gipp (Luther)

137-lb class
1. Paul Stehmann (Northwest Missouri)
2. Mike Rogers (Colorado State C)
3. John Rembold (South Dakota State)
4. Terry Habecker (Ithaca)

5. Lester Bright (Old Dominion)
6. Angelo Testone (Western Illinois)

145-lb class
1. Chuck Seal (Portland State)
2. John Fern (Humboldt State)
3. Steve Johnson (California Poly, SLO)
4. Mike Fitzgerald (Moorhead State)
5. Stan Zeamer (Northwest Missouri)
6. Bob Smith (Colorado State C)

152-lb class
1. Carl Ragland (Old Dominion)
2. John Finch (California Poly, SLO)
3. Mel Crider (Colorado State C)
4. Sam Uhrick (Western Colorado)
5. Jim Warren (Nevada at Reno)
6. Bob DeVore (East Stroudsburg)

160-lb class
1. Joe Weindl (Wilkes)
2. Rick Arnold (California Poly, SLO)
3. Jim Guyer (Northern Iowa)
4. Jim Gildersleeve (Moorhead State)
5. Art Ziegler (Springfield)
6. Eric Bates (Illinois State)

167-lb class
1. John Woods (California Poly, SLO)
2. Richard Wright (Portland State)
3. Jim Alexander (Colorado State C)
4. John Amicucci (New York Maritime)
5. Tim Dodge (Augustana)
6. Skip Bellock (Northern Iowa)

177-lb class
1. Ken Bos (California Poly, SLO)
2. Kemper Chafin (California, Davis)
3. Mike Patterson (Colorado State C)
4. Gary Lehr (Oswego State)
5. Tony Campbell (Portland State)
6. Mike Hack (Central Missouri)

191-lb class
1. Tom Kline (California Poly, SLO)
2. Chris Feder (CW Post)
3. Bob Buehler (San Francisco State)
4. Walt Kummerow (North Park)
5. Brad Martin (Central Michigan)
6. Bill Henderson (Moorhead State)

Heavyweight
1. Kent Osboe (Northern Iowa)
2. Al Blanshan (Mankato State)
3. Dennis Petracek (California Poly, SLO)
4. Richard Schumacher (East Stroudsburg)
5. Dave Bush (Colorado Mines)
6. Wayne Karney (Portland State)

1970 (at Ashland College, Ashland OH)

Team	Points
1. California Poly (SLO)	82
2. Northern Iowa	58
3. New York Maritime	48
4. South Dakota State	43
5. Mankato State	41
6. Central Michigan	40
7. Western Colorado	38
8. Springfield	35
9. Wilkes, East Stroudsburg	34
11. Northern Michigan	32
12. Illinois State	31
13. Old Dominion, Chico State	30
15. Slippery Rock	29
16. Augustana (IL)	26
17. Colorado State College	23
18. Northwest Missouri	22
19. Seattle Pacific	17
20. Ashland, Brockport State	16
22. Cleveland State, Northeast Missouri, North Dakota State	11
25. Oswego State	10
26. Amherst	9
27. Moorhead State	8
28. Elizabethtown, John Carroll, CW Post, Rochester Tech	6
32. Akron, Wisconsin (Milwaukee), San Francisco State	5
35. St. Lawrence, Luther, Lycoming	4
38. Humboldt State, Union Ithaca, MacMurray, North Park	3

Team	*Points*
43. Boise State, Eastern Illinois, Montclair State, Ohio Wesleyan, Coast Guard	2
48. California (PA), Central Connecticut, Cornell College, Denison, Howard, Marietta, Moravian, Oneonta State, Thiel, Wayne State, Wesleyan, Westminster	1

Place winners

118-lb class
1. Terry Hall (California Poly, SLO)
2. Greg Schmidt (South Dakota State)
3. Andrew Matviak (Wilkes)
4. Luciana Curra (Old Dominion)
5. Wally Jaskot (Oswego State)
6. Ron Hinderliter (Western Colorado)

126-lb class
1. Larry Wagner (Northern Colorado)
2. John Morfia (Wilkes)
3. Glen Anderson (California Poly, SLO)
4. Mike Tello (Northern Michigan)
5. Tom Cheshner (Central Michigan)
6. Ed Kochachii (CW Post)

134-lb class
1. Stan Zeamer (Northwest Missouri)
2. Robert Sinclair (Springfield)
3. John Norris (California State, Chico)
4. Marvin Reilan (Northern Iowa)
5. Ken Jackson (Seattle Pacific)
6. Clarence Ross (Northern Colorado)

142-lb class
1. Lester Bright (Old Dominion)
2. Dale Richter (Mankato State)
3. Larry Hulbert (Central Michigan)
4. Larry Johnson (Western Colorado)
5. Lee Barylski (Cleveland State)
6. Keith Engle (South Dakota State)

150-lb class
1. Stan Dziedzic (Slippery Rock)
2. Leandro Torres (California Poly, SLO)
3. Tom Minkle (Central Michigan)
4. Dan Weck (New York Maritime)
5. Rich Hornbeck (Western Colorado)
6. Steve Durian (Augustana)

158-lb class
1. Don Dixon (New York Maritime)
2. John Finch (California Poly, SLO)
3. Art Ziegler (Springfield)
4. Clinton Young (Northern Iowa)
5. Russ Holland (Northern Michigan)
6. Bill DeMary (North Dakota State)

167-lb class
1. Eric Bates (Illinois State)
2. Vince Bellock (Northern Iowa)
3. Tim Dodge (Augustana)
4. Ted Hart (Western Colorado)
5. Bill Schellhorn (Slippery Rock)
6. Ken Hagen (Seattle Pacific)

177-lb class
1. Don Trapp (South Dakota State)
2. Rich Simmons (California Poly, SLO)
3. Bob Boeck (Northern Iowa)
4. John Reid (New York Maritime)
5. John Sigfrid (Moorhead State)
6. Ron Woodie (Ashland)

190-lb class
1. Regen Beers (Brockport State)
2. Brian Hage (Mankato State)
3. Mike Forini (Illinois State)
4. Gary Sklaver (Amherst)
5. George Enos (Slippery Rock)
6. Evan Weier (California State, Chico)

Heavyweight
1. Rich Schumacker (East Stroudsburg)
2. Ron Fandrick (Northern Michigan)
3. Mike McCready (Northern Iowa)
4. Doug Dressler (California State, Chico)
5. Len Pettigrew (Ashland)
6. Richard Beard (Northeast Missouri)

1971 (at North Dakota State University, Fargo, ND)

Team	Points
1. California Poly, SLO	118
2. Slippery Rock State	58
3. Mankato State	51
4. North Dakota State	46
5. East Stroudsburg, Wilkes	42
7. Northern Iowa	41
8. Franklin and Marshall	35
9. Ashland, Northern Colorado, Seattle Pacific	30
12. Western Illinois	24
13. Oswego State	22
14. California State (Chico)	21
15. Central Michigan	20
16. John Carroll	18
17. Eastern Illinois, Northern Michigan, South Dakota State	16
20. Eastern Michigan	14
21. Humboldt State, Luther, Southern Illinois	8
24. Colorado Mines, Western State	7
26. Cleveland State, Coast Guard, Moorhead State, San Francisco State	6
30. Akron, Sonoma State, Springfield	5
33. Central Missouri, Fullerton State, Rochester Tech, Shippensburg State	4
37. Augustana (IL), California Poly (Pomona), Hiram, Illinois at Chicago Circle, Northeast Missouri, South Dakota	3
43. Amherst, U California (Davis), New York Maritime, St. Cloud State, Southwest Missouri	2
48. Coe, Cornell College, Delaware Valley, Kalamazoo, King's Point, Northwest Missouri, Oneonta State, Potsdam State, Puget Sound, Valparaiso, Wayne State	1

Place winners

118-lb class
1. Gary McBride (California Poly, SLO)
2. Stan Opp (South Dakota State)
3. Ted Pease (East Stroudsburg)
4. Wally Joskot (Oswego State)
5. Paul MacArthur (Northern Colorado)
6. Ron Hinderliter (Western Colorado)

126-lb class
1. Chris Black (Franklin and Marshall)
2. Mark Davids (Eastern Michigan)
3. Glenn Anderson (California Poly, SLO)
4. Sam Myers (Seattle Pacific)
5. Duayne Nyckel (Eastern Illinois)
6. Phil Janeteas (Southern Illinois)

134-lb class
1. Ken Stockdale (Mankato State)
2. Larry Morgan (California Poly, SLO)
3. Kemble Matter (East Stroudsburg)
4. Rod Irwin (Slippery Rock)
5. John Norris (California State, Chico)
6. Lynn Forde (North Dakota State)

142-lb class
1. Jim Guizzotti (Ashland)
2. Tom Cox (Slippery Rock)
3. Leaandro Torres (California Poly, SLO)
4. Tony Ptak (East Stroudsburg)
5. Joe Protsman (Western Illinois)
6. Dave Alitz (Luther)

150-lb class
1. Stan Dziedzic (Slippery Rock)
2. Mike Medchill (Mankato State)
3. Tom Minkel (Central Michigan)
4. Drake Lemm (Seattle Pacific)
5. Allyn Cooke (California Poly, SLO)
6. Jerry Seifert (North Dakota State)

158-lb class
1. Clint Young (Northern Iowa)
2. Jerry Strauman (Western Illinois)
3. John Finch (California Poly, SLO)
4. Ralph Pizzo (Oswego State)
5. Pat Miller (Humboldt State)
6. James Gildersleeve (Moorhead State)

167-lb class
1. John Stevenson (Franklin and Marshall)
2. Gerry Willetts (Wilkes)
3. Bill Schellhorn (Slippery Rock)
4. Ken Hagen (Seattle Pacific)
5. Ron England (Northern Colorado)
6. Steve Johnson (Mankato State)

177-lb class
1. Bill Demaray (North Dakota State)
2. Pat Farner (California Poly, SLO)
3. Dave Alexander (Northern Colorado)
4. Tom Corbo (John Carroll)
5. Richard Ceccoli (Wilkes)
6. Dan McGrath (Akron)

190-lb class
1. Bob Backlund (North Dakota State)
2. Gary Maiolfi (California Poly, SLO)
3. Dennis Scott (California State, Chico)
4. Brian Hage (Mankato State)
5. Randy Omvig (Northern Iowa)
6. Larry Dunlay (John Carroll)

Heavyweight
1. Tim Kopitar (California Poly, SLO)
2. Herman Pettigrew (Ashland)
3. Ron Fandrick (Northern Michigan)
4. Alain Arnold (Wilkes)
5. Dennis Pierro (Mankato State)
6. Paul Azzaniti (Cleveland State)

1972 (at New York State University at Oswego, NY)

Team	Points
1. California Poly (SLO)	94
2. North Dakota State, Northern Iowa	64.5
4. Slippery Rock	56
5. Clarion State	49.5
6. Wilkes	47
7. Seattle Pacific	44
8. Northern Colorado	41.5
9. Franklin and Marshall	37.5
10. Western Illinois	34
11. Mankato State	28.5
12. South Dakota State	28
13. Cleveland State	24.5
14. California State (Fullerton)	24
15. Brockport State, Northern Michigan	23.5
17. San Francisco State, Shippensburg State	21.5
19. Illinois at Chicago Circle	20
20. Tampa, Trenton State	19
22. Eastern Illinois	18.5
23. Eastern Michigan	16.5
24. Humboldt State	15.5
25. Potsdam State	15
26. Springfield	14
27. Cortland State	13
28. Ashland, John Carroll, Western Colorado	12
31. Akron	10
32. U California (Davis), East Stroudsburg	9
34. St. Cloud State	8.5
35. York	8
36. Binghamton State, Mount Union	7
38. Hiram, Lock Haven, St. Lawrence	6.5
41. Chattanooga	6

Team	*Points*
42. California State (Chico), Southwest Missouri	5.5
44. Indiana Central, Merchant Marine, Oswego State	5
47. Augustana (IL), Howard, Old Dominion, Rochester, Sonoma State, Central (IA)	4
53. Coast Guard, Lebanon Valley, Lincoln (PA), Luther, Millersville State, Moorhead State, Northwest Missouri, Puget Sound, Rochester Tech	3
62. Baltimore	2.5
63. Amherst, Case Western, CW Post, Elizabethtown, Elmhurst, Lake Superior State, Lycoming, Moravian, Montclair State, St. Joseph's (IN)	2
73. Bowdoin, Lake Forest, North Park, Towson, Wabash, Washington and Jefferson	1

Place winners

118-lb class
1. Bruce Biondi (Brockport State)
2. Ray Hernandez (San Francisco State)
3. Lee Allen (Seattle Pacific)
4. Gary McBride (California Poly, SLO)
5. Stan Opp (South Dakota State)
6. Bruce Thompson (St. Cloud State)

126-lb class
1. Chris Black (Franklin and Marshall)
2. Sam Myers (Seattle Pacific)
3. Bob Roberts (Wilkes)
4. John Wassum (California Poly, SLO)
5. John Maestas (Western Colorado)
6. Joe Siprut (Illinois at Chicago Circle)

134-lb class
1. Rod Irwin (Slippery Rock)
2. Larry Morgan (California Poly, SLO)
3. Gary Barton (Clarion State)
4. Kent Tinquist (North Dakota State)
5. Jon Moeller (Northern Iowa)
6. Tony DeGiovanni (Cleveland State)

142-lb class
1. Glenn Anderson (California Poly, SLO)
2. Tom Cox (Slippery Rock)
3. Frank Yoo (Cleveland State)
4. Mark Fox (Northern Iowa)
5. Doug Willer (Eastern Michigan)
6. Bob Manley (California State, Fullerton)

150-lb class
1. Wade Schalles (Clarion State)
2. Mike Engels (South Dakota State)
3. Mike Lee (Wilkes)
4. Stan Sotherden (Springfield)
5. Dave Toth (Ashland)
6. Bill Dowbiggin (St. Lawrence)

158-lb class
1. Stan Dziedzic (Slippery Rock)
2. Mike Medchill (Mankato State)
3. Al Cooke (California Poly, SLO)
4. Al Zellner (Wilkes)
5. John Corman (Shippensburg State)
6. Jerry Strauman (Western Illinois)

167-lb class
1. John Stevenson (Franklin and Marshall)
2. Don Dixon (Northern Michigan)
3. Doug Stone (Humboldt State)
4. Geza Vella (Illinois at Chicago Circle)
5. Bob Johnston (Potsdam State)
6. Bill Simpson (Clarion State)

177-lb class
1. Bill Demaray (North Dakota State)
2. Dave Alexander (Northern Colorado)
3. Gene Barber (Trenton State)
4. Mike O'Brien (California, Davis)
5. Bob Perez (Eastern Illinois)
6. Jim Kulpa (Western Illinois)

190-lb class

1. Fletcher Carr (Tampa)
2. Joe Hatchett (Northern Iowa)
3. Jim Schlueter (Northern Colorado)
4. Keith Leland (California Poly, SLO)
5. Joe Kurtz (Seattle Pacific)
6. Brad Rheingans (North Dakota State)

Heavyweight

1. Mike McCready (Northern Iowa)
2. Jim Woods (Western Illinois)
3. Dennis Pierro (Mankato State)
4. Len Schlacter (Cortland State)
5. Bob Backlund (North Dakota State)
6. Paul Britcher (Clarion State)

1973 (at South Dakota State University, Brookings, SD)

Team	Points
1. California Poly (SLO)	108
2. Clarion State	80
3. North Dakota State	59.5
4. Northern Iowa	50.5
5. Wilkes	41.5
6. South Dakota State	40.5
7. Mankato State	34
8. Cleveland State	33
9. Ashland	30.5
10. Northern Colorado, Western Illinois	27
12. Central Missouri	26
13. Eastern Illinois, California State (Fullerton)	25.5
15. Slippery Rock	23.5
16. Northern Michigan	20.5
17. Lock Haven	20
18. Tampa	19
19. Springfield	18.5
20. Trenton	17.5
21. Humboldt State	16.5
22. Brockport, Western Colorado	16
24. Seattle Pacific	13
25. St. Cloud State	10.5
26. Akron	10
27. Northwest Missouri	8.5
28. Puget Sound	8
29. St. John's (MN)	7.5
30. Glassboro	7
31. Central Connecticut, San Francisco	6.5
33. John Carroll, Luther, Tennessee at Martin	5.5
36. Augustana (IL), California (Davis), Franklin and Marshall, Potsdam State	5
40. Hiram	4.5
41. Sonoma State, Monmouth, North Dakota, Towson	4
45. Coe, Indiana State (PA), Old Dominion, Binghamton State, Chattanooga	3.5
50. Baltimore, California State (Chico), Ohio Northern, Kalamazoo, Rochester Tech, Swarthmore, Oswego State	3
57. Augustana (SD), CW Post, Sacramento State, Cornell College, Coast Guard, De Pauw, Indiana Central, King's, MacMurray, Millersville, Missouri Rolla, Mount Union, Moorhead State, North Park, Shippensburg State, South Dakota, Geneseo State	2
74. Northeast Missouri, Albany	1.5
76. California State (Bakersfield), Delaware Valley, Hartford, Merchant Marine, Missouri at St. Louis, Montclair State, Ohio Wesleyan, Rochester, Washington and Lee	1

Place winners

118-lb class
1. Jack Spates (Slippery Rock)
2. Stan Opp (South Dakota State)
3. Bruce Biondi (Brockport State)
4. Brad Thompson (Mankato State)
5. Bruce Thompson St. Cloud State)
6. Craig Turnbull (Clarion State)

126-lb class
1. Phil Reimnitz (North Dakota State)
2. Harold Wiley (California State, Fullerton)
3. Bob Roberts (Wilkes)
4. Dave Nicol (Northern Iowa)
5. Gary McBride (California Poly, SLO)
6. Duayne Nyckel (Eastern Illinois)

134-lb class
1. Larry Morgan (California Poly, SLO)
2. Greg Maestas (Western Colorado)
3. Don Rohn (Clarion State)
4. Jim Miller (Northern Iowa)
5. Tony DeGiovanni (Cleveland State)
6. Tom Svendson (St. John's)

142-lb class
1. Lee Petersen (North Dakota State)
2. Ken Synder (Northern Iowa)
3. Dave Toth (Ashland)
4. Larry Reed (Northern Colorado)
5. Art Trovei (Wilkes)
6. Rick Brua (Mankato State)

150-lb class
1. Glenn Anderson (California Poly, SLO)
2. Tom Cavanaugh (Cleveland State)
3. Al Ordonez (Eastern Illinois)
4. Randy Hughell (Central Missouri)
5. Mark Hugh (North Dakota State)
6. Rich Munroe (Springfield)

158-lb class
1. Wade Schalles (Clarion State)
2. Allyn Cooke (California Poly, SLO)
3. Bert Dalton (Northern Colorado)
4. Larry Goodnature (Mankato State)
5. Joseph Carr (Ashland)
6. Dennis Bishop (Kalamazoo)

167-lb class
1. Bill Simpson (Clarion State)
2. Doug Stone (Humboldt State)
3. Gerry Person (South Dakota State)
4. Doug LeRoy (Springfield)
5. Dave Cummings (Mankato State)
6. Mark Bauerly (St. Cloud State)

177-lb class
1. Jim Kulpa (Western Illinois)
2. Bill Knippel (Seattle Pacific)
3. Gene Barber (Trenton)
4. Gary West (California Poly, SLO)
5. Elijah Whitten (Ashland)
6. Lloyd Teasley (San Francisco State)

190-lb class
1. Fletcher Carr (Temple)
2. Keith Leland (California Poly, SLO)
3. Tom Loew (North Dakota State)
4. Duane Fritchie (Central Missouri)
5. Rich Maras (Seattle Pacific)
6. Dick Vliem (South Dakota State)

Heavyweight
1. Gil Domiani (Northern Michigan)
2. Chuck Coryea (Clarion State)
3. Frank Barnhart (California Poly, SLO)
4. Randy Omvig (Northern Iowa)
5. Jim Schuster (Lock Haven)
6. Jim Woods (Western Illinois)

1974 (at Fullerton State, Fullerton, CA)

Team	*Points*
1. California Poly, SLO	131.5
2. Northern Iowa	95.5
3. Southern Illinois at Edwardsville	72
4. North Dakota State	56.5
5. Bloomsburg State	53.5
6. Mankato State	52.5
7. East Stroudsburg	39.5
8. Old Dominion	36
9. California State (Bakersfield), San Francisco State	31
11. Eastern Illinois	30

Team	*Points*
12. Western Illinois	29.5
13. Humboldt State	25.5
14. Tennessee at Chattanooga, Akron	22.5
16. Springfield, CW Post	18
18. South Dakota State	17.5
19. California State (Chico)	12.5
20. California State (Fullerton), Seattle Pacific	11
22. Western Colorado	9.5
23. St. Cloud State	6.5
24. Maryland at Baltimore	4.5
25. Central Connecticut, California (Davis)	4
27. Northern Michigan	3.5
28. Central Missouri, Indiana Central	3
30. Moorhead State, Florida Tech	2.5
32. Lincoln, Puget Sound, South Dakota, Southeast Missouri	2
36. California State (Sacramento)	1.5
37. North Dakota	1
38. Towson State, Augustana (SD) Southwest Missouri, Wayne State	.5

Place winners

118-lb class

1. Terrence Perdew (Old Dominion)
2. Brad Thompson (Mankato State)
3. Greg Kesserling (Akron)
4. Rick Molina (California State, Bakersfield)
5. Guy Greene (California Poly, SLO)
6. Dave Cunningham (Northern Iowa)

126-lb class

1. Tom Garcia (Northern Iowa)
2. Bill Burnside (Tennessee at Chattanooga)
3. Phil Reimnitz (North Dakota State)
4. Leon Iannarelli (California Poly, SLO)
5. Jack Eustice (Mankato State)
6. Mike Dahlheimer (St. Cloud State)

134-lb class

1. Jim Miller (Northern Iowa)
2. Grant Arnold (California Poly, SLO)
3. Larry Pruitt (Southern Illinois, Edwardsville)
4. Percy Martinez (San Francisco State)
5. Wade Davey (CW Post)
6. Cliff Maze (California State, Bakersfield)

142-lb class

1. Ken Snyder (Northern Iowa)
2. Lee Peterson (North Dakota State)
3. Ray Pond (Old Dominion)
4. Ruben Ramos (California State, Chico)
5. Steve Gardner (California Poly, SLO)
6. disqualified

150-lb class

1. Bill Luckenbaugh (East Stroudsburg)
2. Rodger Warner (California Poly, SLO)
3. Mike Taylor (Southern Illinois, Edwardsville)
4. Al Ordonez (Eastern Illinois)
5. Steve Tirapelle (Humboldt State)
6. Rich Munroe (Springfield)

158-lb class

1. Cliff Hatch (California Poly, SLO)
2. Mike Engles (South Dakota State)
3. Bob Stetler (East Stroudsburg)
4. Mike Turnbull (Akron)
5. Dennis Byrne (Southern Illinois at Edwardsville)
6. Larry Goodnature (Mankato State)

167-lb class

1. Ron Sheehan (Bloomsburg State)
2. Bruce Lynn (California Poly, SLO)
3. Lloyd Teasley (San Francisco State)
4. Dan Keller (Northern Iowa)
5. Bill Kalivas (California, Bakersfield)
6. Rick Nelson (Western Illinois)

177-lb class
1. Floyd Hitchcock (Bloomsburg State)
2. Brad Rheingans (North Dakota State)
3. Sytehll Thompson (California Poly, SLO)
4. Frank Savegnago (Southern Illinois at Edwardsville)
5. Gary Christensen (Mankato State)
6. Rich Erickson (Northern Iowa)

190-lb class
1. Keith Leland (California Poly, SLO)
2. Jerry Washington (Southern Illinois at Edwardsville)
3. Kurt Keuhl (Mankato State)
4. Rick Maras (Seattle Pacific)
5. Doug Hilliard (Fullerton State)
6. John Hohman (Bloomsburg State)

Heavyweight
1. Jim Woods (Western Illinois)
2. Bill Van Worth (Humboldt State)
3. Gene Pouliot (Eastern Illinois)
4. Randy Omvig (Northern Iowa)
5. Barry Walsh (Southern Illinois at Edwardsville)
6. Tim Smith (Springfield)

1975 (at East Stroudsbourg State, East Stroudsburg, PA)

Team	Points
1. Northern Iowa	112
2. Southern Illinois at Edwardsville	71.5
3. Tennessee at Chattanooga	67.5
4. North Dakota State	66.5
5. San Francisco State	59
6. Mankato State	58.5
7. Bloomsburg State	53.5
8. East Stroudsburg, California State (Bakersfield)	47
10. St. Cloud State	44
11. Nebraska at Omaha, Western Colorado	30.5
13. Northern Michigan	25
14. Western Illinois	23.5
15. Eastern Illinois	21.5
16. Springville	20.5
17. CW Post	17
18. Central Missouri, Southeast Missouri	16
20. South Dakota	10.5
21. Old Dominion	10
22. Akron	9
23. North Dakota	8.5
24. Wright State, Seattle Pacific, South Dakota State	6.5
27. Morgan State	6
28. Augustana (SD), Indiana Central	5
30. Tennessee at Martin	4
31. Evansville, Florida Tech, Southwest Missouri	3
34. California (Davis), Lincoln (MO), Salisbury State	2.5
37. Moorhead State, Valparaiso, Northwest Missouri	2
40. Virginia State, Missouri at St. Louis	1.5
42. George Mason, Towson State	1

Place winners

118-lb class
1. Randy Batten (Tennessee at Chattanooga)
2. Dave Cunningham (Northern Iowa)
3. Richard Molina (California State, Bakersfield)
4. Tom Fink (Bloomsburg State)
5. Doug Gruber (St. Cloud State)
6. Bruce Kesserling (Akron)

126-lb class
1. Alex Gonzales (San Francisco State)
2. Jack Eustice (Mankato State)
3. Mike Dahlheimer (St. Cloud State)
4. Terry Mulrenin (Southern Illinois at Edwardsville)

5. Mike McCarthy (Old Dominion)
6. John Niebur (Western Illinois)

134-lb class
1. Jim Miller (Northern Iowa)
2. Larry Pruitt (Southern Illinois at Edwardsville)
3. John Kalvelage (Tennessee at Chattanooga)
4. Russell Waag (Western Colorado)
5. Dave Keller (Mankato State)
6. Jeff Andvik (North Dakota State)

142-lb class
1. Ken Snyder (Northern Iowa)
2. Harvey Dalton (Western Colorado)
3. Brad Dodds (North Dakota State)
4. Tony Defendis (CW Post)
5. James Haub (Central Missouri)
6. Nehemiah Jackson (Morgan State)

150-lb class
1. Randy Watts (Bloomsburg State)
2. Gary Kessel (East Stroudsburg)
3. Mike Taylor (Southern Illinois at Edwardsville)
4. Rodney Hines (South Dakota)
5. Rich Munroe (Springfield)
6. Dan Houtchens (Southern Illinois, Bakersfield)

158-lb class
1. Joe Jackson (Tennessee at Chattanooga)
2. Bob Stetler (East Stroudsburg)
3. Craig Artist (Nebraska at Omaha)
4. Al Ordonez (Eastern Illinois)
5. William Kalivas (California State, Bakersfield)
6. Jerry Schmitz (St. Cloud State)

167-lb class
1. Lloyd Teasley (San Francisco State)
2. Rick Nelson (Western Illinois)
3. Steve Wenker (St. Cloud State)
4. John Hittler (Northern Michigan)
5. Dennis Byrne (Southern Illinois at Edwardsville)
6. Nick Porillo (Springfield)

177-lb class
1. Gary Christensen (Mankato State)
2. Dick Erickson (Northern Iowa)
3. Steve Scheib (Bloomsburg State)
4. David Weeks (Tennessee at Chattanooga)
5. Rick Lee (North Dakota)
6. Robert Wilson (Northern Michigan)

190-lb class
1. Brad Rheingans (North Dakota State)
2. Frank Savegnago (Southern Illinois at Edwardsville)
3. Kurt Kuehl (Mankato State)
4. Mike Bull (California State, Bakersfield)
5. Matt Tydor (Bloomsburg State)
6. Scott Johnson (Western Colorado)

Heavyweight
1. Randy Omvig (Northern Iowa)
2. Bruce Thomas (Southeast Missouri)
3. Dalfin Blaske (Norther Dakota State)
4. Glenn Maiolino (San Francisco State)
5. Gene Pouliot (Eastern Illinois)
6. Fred Swanson (East Stroudsburg)

1976 (at North Dakota State, Fargo, ND)

Team	*Points*
1. California State (Bakersfield)	92.50
2. Tennessee at Chattanooga	88.25
3. Northern Iowa	83
4. Mankato State	60
5. North Dakota State	59.50
6. Southern Illinois at Edwardsville, Augustana (SD)	49
8. St. Cloud State	45.25
9. South Dakota State	35.50
10. East Stroudsburg	34.50
11. Central State (OK)	30.50
12. Eastern Illinois	28
13. Springfield	25.25
14. California State (Chico)	24.25
15. Nebraska at Omaha	22.75
16. San Francisco State	18.25
17. Grand Valley State	15.75
18. North Dakota	13.50

Team	Points
19. Northern Michigan	12
20. Old Dominion	10.50
21. Western Illinois, Southeast Missouri	8.50
23. Florida International	7.75
24. Lincoln (MO), Baltimore	7.50
26. South Dakota, California (Davis)	7
28. Tampa	6.25
29. Akron	6
30. Western State	4.50
31. Central Missouri, Salisbury State	3.50
33. Indiana Central	3.25
34. Michigan Tech	3
35. Livingston	2.50
36. Moorhead State, Central Connecticut, Maryland (Baltimore)	2
39. Madison	1.50
40. Youngstown State, CW Post, Puget Sound, Northeast Missouri	1
44. Evansville	.50

Place winners

118-lb class
1. Randy Batten (Tennessee at Chattanooga)
2. Brent Hagen (Mankato State)
3. Rich Molina (California State, Bakersfield)
4. Jene Burris (California State, Chico)
5. Dave Cunningham (Northern Iowa)
6. Randy Rillman (East Stroudsburg)

126-lb class
1. Rich Jensen (South Dakota State)
2. Alex Gonzales (San Francisco State)
3. Mark Mangianti (Grand Valley State)
4. Mike McCarthy (Old Dominion)
5. John Niebur (Western Illinois)
6. Fred Frimmelt (Baltimore)

134-lb class
1. Jack Eustice (Mankato State)
2. Dave Robinson (Southern Illinois at Edwardsville)
3. John Kalvelage (Tennessee at Chattanooga)
4. Bruce McClure (Northern Iowa)
5. Bernie Anderson (Northern Michigan)
6. Lon Brew (North Dakota State)

142-lb class
1. Gary Bentrim (Northern Iowa)
2. Russell Clark (St. Cloud State)
3. Rex Branum (Eastern Illinois)
4. Pat Flaherty (Augustana)
5. Gary Kessel (East Stroudsburg)
6. Kirk Simet (South Dakota State)

150-lb class
1. Dan Houtchens (California State, Bakersfield)
2. Dave Scherer (North Dakota State)
3. Jim Blasingame (Northern Iowa)
4. Dave Cain (Augustana)
5. Ken Gabriel (North Dakota)
6. Dick Munroe (Springfield)

158-lb class
1. Turner Jackson (Tennessee at Chattanooga)
2. Ed Torrejon (Eastern Illinois)
3. Nick Porillo (Springfield)
4. Myron Feist (North Dakota State)
5. Larry Goodnature (Mankato State)
6. Bob Rinehart (California State, Chico)

167-lb class
1. Bill Mitchell (Central State)
2. Jerome Schmitz (St. Cloud State)
3. Flor Rocha (California State, Bakersfield)
4. Keith Poolman (Northern Iowa)
5. Mark Hattendorf (Southern Illinois at Edwardsville)
6. Tim Brennan (Tennessee Chattanooga)

177-lb class
1. David Weeks (Tennessee Chattanooga)
2. Dan Keller (Northern Iowa)

3. Kurt Kuehl (Mankato State)
4. Scott Ecklund (Augustana)
5. Kevin Burgess (Lincoln)
6. David Byrne (Southern Illinois at Edwardsville)

190-lb class
1. Mike Bull (California State, Bakersfield)
2. Frank Savegnago (Southern Ilinois at Edwardsville)
3. Clare Duda (Augustana)
4. Darwin Brodt (East Stroudsburg)
5. Steven Lovrien (South Dakota)
6. Charles Siefert (St. Cloud State)

Heavyweight
1. Bill Van Worth (California State, Bakersfield)
2. Don Meyer (North Dakota State)
3. Jim Gregory (Nebraska at Omaha)
4. Richard Long (Central State)
5. Bruce Thomas (Southeast Missouri)
6. Mike Stambaugh (East Stroudsburg)

1977 (at Northern Iowa, Cedar Falls, IA)

Team	Points
1. Bakersfield State	107.25
2. Augustana (SD)	78
3. Northern Iowa	74.75
4. Eastern Illinois	71.25
5. North Dakota State	71
6. Southern Illinois at Edwardsville	63
7. Central State (OK)	45.75
8. South Dakota State	38.50
9. Tennessee at Chattanooga	36
10. Mankato State	35.75
11. South Dakota	32.25
12. Springfield	30.50
13. Northern Michigan	29.50
14. St. Cloud State	26.50
15. San Francisco State	19.50
16. Nebraska at Omaha	18.25
17. Morgan State	17
18. Florida Tech	15
19. Chico State	14
20. Western Illinois	13.75
21. Wright State	7.75
22. Central Missouri	7.50
23. Western State	6.50
24. CW Post	6
25. Indiana Central, Youngstown State	4
27. Oakland, Puget Sound, Towson State	3.50
30. Southeast Missouri	3
31. Evansville, George Mason	2.50
33. North Dakota	2
34. Central Connecticut, Minnesota at Duluth, Northeast Missouri, Southwest Missouri	1
38. Florida International, King's, Michigan Tech	.50

Place winners

118-lb class
1. Brent Hagen (Mankato State)
2. Ken Bellmard (Augustana)
3. Kent Taylor (Central State)
4. Doug Weisz (North Dakota State)
5. Haruki Kawamukai (Florida Tech)
6. Dave Prehm (Northern Iowa)

126-lb class
1. Randy Batten (Tennessee at Chattanooga)
2. Neal Seagren (Northern Michigan)
3. David James (Central State)
4. Sam Herriman (Augustana)
5. Jeff Melvin (Northern Iowa)
6. Terry Mulrenin (Southern Illinois at Edwardsville)

134-lb class
1. Franc Affentranger (California State, Bakersfield)
2. Rick Jensen (South Dakota State)

3. Jack Eustice (Mankato State)
4. Steve Martinson (North Dakota State)
5. Dave Nelson (San Francisco State)
6. Scott Kollings (Northern Iowa)

142-lb class
1. Gary Bentrim (Northern Iowa)
2. Rich Clark (St. Cloud State)
3. Ray Yocum (California State, Bakersfield)
4. Lon Brew (North Dakota State)
5. Dru Meshes (Southern Illinois at Edwardsville)
6. Ralph McCausland (Eastern Illinois)

150-lb class
1. Mark Reimnitz (North Dakota State)
2. Rod Balch (California State, Bakersfield)
3. Pat Flaherty (Augustana)
4. Dick Briggs (Northern Iowa)
5. Barry Hintze (Eastern Illinois)
6. Ron Weller (St. Cloud State)

158-lb class
1. Ed Torrejon (Eastern Illinois)
2. William Smith (Morgan State)
3. Bob Rinehart (California State, Chico)
4. Jerry Esses (San Francisco State)
5. John Newell (Nebraska at Omaha)
6. William Ewing (CW Post)

167-lb class
1. Florencio Rocha (California State, Bakersfield)
2. Brian Parlet (Augustana)
3. Dave Byrne (Southern Illinois at Edwardsville)
4. Keith Poolman (Northern Iowa)
5. Bob Stout (Eastern Illinois)
6. Tim Neumann (Northern Michigan)

177-lb class
1. Jeff Hoherts (South Dakota State)
2. Mike Anderson (California State, Bakersfield)
3. Mark Hattendorf (Southern Illinois at Edwardsville)
4. John Mulligan (Springfield)
5. Don Lubbert (Augustana)
6. Jack Weisenborn (Western Illinois)

190-lb class
1. Jerry Washington (Southern Illinois at Edwardsville)
2. Mike Bull (California State, Bakersfield)
3. Steve Lovrien (South Dakota)
4. Scott Ecklund (Augustana)
5. Don Cahill (Nebraska at Omaha)
6. Ed Herman (Northern Iowa)

Heavyweight
1. Dave Klemm (Eastern Illinois)
2. Jeff Blatnick (Springfield)
3. Glen Geraets (South Dakota)
4. Richard Long (Central State)
5. Ralph Zinger (Tennessee at Chattanooga)
6. Don Meyer (North Dakota State)

1978 (at University of Northern Iowa, Cedar Falls, IA)

Team	*Points*
1. Northern Iowa	124
2. Bakersfield State	100.50
3. Eastern Illinois	68
4. Augustana (SD)	66.25
5. Southern Illinois at Edwardsville	50.25
6. Northern Michigan	46.50
7. Nebraska at Omaha	43.25
8. North Dakota State	36.50
9. South Dakota State	34.50
10. Springfield	26.50
11. Morgan State, Western Illinois	25
13. Mankato State	24.50
14. California State (Chico)	21.50
15. California State (Sacramento)	20
16. St. Cloud State	18.50
17. Central Missouri	18.25
18. Southern Connecticut	18
19. Puget Sound	17
20. Central Connecticut	16.50

Team	*Points*
21. California Poly (Pomona)	16
22. San Francisco State	14.50
23. CW Post, Moorhead State	13
25. Northeast Missouri, Northwest Missouri	9.50
27. Florida Tech	8.50
28. Western State	8
29. Youngstown State	7.50
30. Florida International	4.50
31. Michigan Tech	4
32. Towson State	3.50
33. Akron, Oakland	3
35. Lowell	2.50
36. Indiana Central	2

Place winners

118-lb class
1. John Azevedo (California State, Bakersfield)
2. Dave Prehm (Northern Iowa)
3. Bill DiPaoli (California Poly, Pomona)
4. Tom Reed (Southern Illinois at Edwardsville)
5. Steve Fontana (CW Post)
6. Curtis Ellis (Morgan State)

126-lb class
1. Sam Herriman (Augustana)
2. Jene Burris (California State, Chico)
3. Rhett Hilzendeger (Moorhead State)
4. Neal Seagren (Northern Michigan)
5. Mark Anderson (North Dakota State)
6. Paul Bulzomi (Southern Connecticut)

134-lb class
1. Frank Gonzales (Nebraska at Omaha)
2. Franc Affentranger (California State, Bakersfield)
3. Matt Long (South Dakota State)
4. Kevin Finn (Northern Iowa)
5. Doug Robinson (Southern Illinois at Edwardsville)
6. Bob McGuinn (Eastern Illinois)

142-lb class
1. Ralph McCausland (Eastern Illinois)
2. Dru Meshes (Southern Illinois at Edwardsville)
3. Mark Salge (Central Connecticut)
4. Fred Madigan (Mankato State)
5. Rod Balch (California State, Bakersfield)
6. Lon Kvanli (Augustana)

150-lb class
1. Kirk Simet (South Dakota State)
2. Steve Spangenberg (Northern Michigan)
3. Dick Briggs (Northern Iowa)
4. Tom Gongora (California State, Bakersfield)
5. Jerry Huls (St. Cloud State)
6. Andy Wilson (California State, Sacramento)

158-lb class
1. Gary Bentrim (Northern Iowa)
2. William Smith (Morgan State)
3. Ed Egan (Northern Michigan)
4. Dan Reichenberg (California State, Sacramento)
5. Steve Cook (San Francisco State)
6. Jim Harstad (St. Cloud State)

167-lb class
1. Keith Poolman (Northern Iowa)
2. Brian Parlet (Augustana)
3. Rick Lafnitzgegger (Western Illinois)
4. Ken Lewis (Eastern Illinois)
5. Ron Marker (Central Missouri)
6. Ron Hilgart (North Dakota State)

177-lb class
1. Steve Draper (California State, Bakersfield)
2. Mark Hattendorf (Southern Illinois at Edwardsville)
3. Sean Bilodeau (Southern Connecticut)
4. Joe Gormally (Northern Iowa)
5. Rick Waggoner (Western State)
6. Glenn Zenor (Northwest Missouri)

190-lb class
1. Kirk Myers (Northern Iowa)
2. Robin Ayres (Eastern Illinois)
3. Pete Kozlowski (North Dakota State)
4. Mike Johnson (California State, Bakersfield)
5. Ray Barker (Florida Tech)
6. Les Gatrel (Central Missouri)

Heavyweight
1. Jeff Blatnick (Springfield)
2. Joe Williams (Nebraska at Omaha)
3. Jeff Grier (Augustana)
4. Bill Stout (Puget Sound)
5. John Pasholk (Western Illinois)
6. Joe Johnson (Mankato State)

1979 (at South Dakota State University, Brookings, SD)

Team	*Points*
1. California State (Bakersfield)	112.75
2. Eastern Illinois	112.50
3. Northern Iowa	87.50
4. Southern Illinois at Edwardsville	83.50
5. Augustana (SD)	68.25
6. Northern Michigan	65
7. Nebraska at Omaha	35
8. Springfield	32.75
9. South Dakota State	31.75
10. Grand Valley State, North Dakota State	24.75
12. Mankato State	21.50
13. Lake Superior State	20.75
14. California (PA)	17
15. Central Missouri	14.25
16. Wisconsin (Parkside)	13.75
17. Morgan State	12.50
18. Western State	12
19. St. Cloud State	10.75
20. Southern Connecticut	10.50
21. California State (Sacramento)	10
22. Oakland University	8.50
23. Southwest Missouri	8.25
24. Pittsburgh (Johnstown)	7.75
25. CW Post	7
26. Central Florida	6.50
27. California (Davis)	5.50
28. Moorhead State	5
29. Northeast Missouri	4.75
30. Central Connecticut	4.50
31. Southeast Missouri	4
32. Western Illinois	3
33. Youngstown State	2.50
34. Towson State	2
35. San Francisco State	1.50
36. California State (Chico)	1

Place winners

118-lb class
1. Joe Gonzales (California State, Bakersfield)
2. Bill DePaoli (California, PA)
3. Tom Reed (Southern Illinois at Edwardsville)
4. Greg Anderson (Central Missouri)
5. Phil Lieblang (Oakland)
6. Curt Ellis (Morgan State)
7. Matt Hawes (Springfield College)
8. Randy Blackman (Eastern Illinois)

126-lb class
1. John Azevedo (California State, Bakersfield)
2. Sam Herriman (Augustana)
3. Neal Seagren (Northern Michigan)
4. Paul Bulzomi (Southern Connecticut)
5. Terry Mulrenin (Southern Illinois at Edwardsville)
6. Steve Fontana (CW Post)
7. Fred Jenkins (California State, Davis)
8. David Stredig (Central Missouri)

134-lb class
1. Bob McGuinn (Eastern Illinois)
2. Gary Baldwin (Nebraska at Omaha)
3. Lon Kvanli (Augustana)
4. Kevin Finn (Northern Iowa)
5. Tim Ervin (Southern Illinois at Edwardsville)

6. Joe Lopez (California State, Bakersfield)
7. Keith Lawn (Northern Michigan)
8. Don Stinewalt (California State, Sacramento)

158-lb class
1. Bob Holland (Eastern Illinois)
2. Roger Dallas (Lake Superior State)
3. Kevin Dugan (California State, Bakersfield)
4. Ed Egan (Northern Michigan)
5. Barry Gresh (Pittsburgh, Johnstown)
6. Rich Dombrowski (Central Florida)
7. Andy Wilson (California State, Sacramento)
8. Dave Stilgenbauer (Youngstown)

167-lb class
1. Mike Abrams (Golden Valley State)
2. Bob Stout (Eastern Illinois)
3. Greg Waggoner (Western State)
4. Keith Poolman (Northern Iowa)
5. William Smith (Morgan State)
6. John Newell (Nebraska at Omaha)
7. Brad Bitterman (Northern Michigan)
8. Phil Herbold (St. Cloud State)

177-lb class
1. Mark Hattendorf (Southern Illinois)
2. Joe Gormally (Northern Iowa)
3. Brian Parlet (Augustana)
4. Steve Draper (California State, Bakersfield)
5. Ron Zmuda (Wisconsin, Parkside)
6. Gerald Conklin (Southeast Missouri)
7. Rolf Turner (St. Cloud State)
8. Tim Harris (Northern Michigan)

190-lb class
1. Kirk Myers (Northern Iowa)
2. Geno Savegnago (Eastern Illinois)
3. Norm Mitchell (Southern Illinois at Edwardsville)
4. Al Minor (South Dakota)
5. Randy Waggoner (Southern Missouri State)
6. Ed King (Grand Valley State)
7. John Linda (Moorhead State)
8. Herb Alamed (Springfield)

Heavyweight
1. Jeff Blatnick (Springfield)
2. Jeff Grier (Augustana)
3. Dave Klemm (Eastern Illinois)
4. Bob How (Northern Michigan)
5. Kevin Kurth (Northern Iowa)
6. Joe Williams (Nebraska at Omaha)
7. Chris Weers (California State, Bakersfield)
8. George Nikolopolus (Wisconsin—Parkside)

1980 (at University of Nebraska at Omaha, NE)

Team	*Points*
1. California State (Bakersfield)	110.50
2. Northern Iowa	89
3. Eastern Illinois	75
4. Augustana (SD)	64.75
5. Northern Michigan	64
6. Southern Illinois at Edwardsville	44.75
7. Mankato State	39.50
8. Morgan State	37
9. South Dakota State	26.50
10. San Francisco State	23.25
11. Grand Valley State	22.50
12. Nebraska at Omaha	22.25
13. Northern Colorado	20.75
14. Wisconsin—Parkside	20
15. Ashland College	18.50
16. Springfield, Central Missouri	18.25
18. Southern Connecticut	18
19. North Dakota	16
20. Florida International	15
21. Chicago State	13
22. California State (Chico)	12.25
23. California State (Sacramento)	11.75
24. CW Post	10.75
25. Minnesota at Duluth	10
26. Pittsburgh (Johnstown)	9.50

Team	*Points*
27. North Dakota State	9
28. Pembroke State	8
29. Wright State	6.75
30. Livingstone	5.75
31. Northeast Missouri	5.50
32. Indiana Central	3.50
33. Southwest Missouri	2.50
34. Northwest Missouri, California (Davis)	2
35. St. Cloud State, Fort Lewis	1.50
37. Colorado School of Mines, Jacksonville State, Southeast Missouri, Western Illinois	1

Place winners

118-lb class

1. Joe Gonzales (California State, Bakersfield)
2. Matt Hawes (Springfield)
3. Tom Reed (Southern Illinois at Edwardsville)
4. Eddie Franco (California State, Sacramento)
5. Reggie Johnson (Ashland)
6. Randy Blackman (Eastern Illinois)
7. Guy Kimball (North Dakota State)
8. Robert Wimberly (Central Florida)

126-lb class

1. John Azevedo (California State, Bakersfield)
2. Brent Hagen (Northern Iowa)
3. Paul Bulzomi (Southern Connecticut)
4. Brad Morton (California State, Chico)
5. Steve Fontana (CW Post)
6. Brent Means (Southern Illinois at Edwardsville)
7. Harvey Kruckenberg (North Dakota)
8. Willie Dye (Pembroke)

134-lb class

1. Craig Jordan (Mankato State)
2. Douglas House (Florida International)
3. Bob McGuinn (Eastern Illinois)
4. Jessie Reyes (California State, Bakersfield)
5. Doug Peters (Central Florida)
6. Jay Swanson (South Dakota State)
7. Dan Winter (Wisconsin—Parkside)
8. Bob Melfi (Southern Connecticut)

142-lb class

1. Steve Spangenberg (Northern Michigan)
2. D.J. West (Northern Colorado)
3. Tim Ervin (Southern Illinois at Edwardsville)
4. John Monolakis (San Francisco State)
5. Lee Noble (California State, Bakersfield)
6. Craig Miller (Wright State)
7. Paul Marquart (North Dakota)
8. Randy Goette (South Dakota State)

150-lb class

1. Ken Gallagher (Northern Iowa)
2. Scott Madigan (Mankato State)
3. Marty Maciel (Southern California, Bakersfield)
4. Jim Paddock (Minnesota at Duluth)
5. Phil Brown (Morgan State)
6. Mike Duffy (Northeast Missouri)
7. Tony Starks (Indiana Central)
8. Bruce Wilson (Fort Lewis)

158-lb class

1. William Smith (Morgan State)
2. Kevin Dugan (California State, Bakersfield)
3. Bob Gruner (Wisconsin—Parkside)
4. Kevin Newsome (San Francisco State)
5. Ed Egan (Northern Michigan)
6. Rich Dombrowski (Central Florida)
7. Tim Homan (Augustana)
8. Cliff Verron (Southern Connecticut)

167-lb class

1. Jon Lundberg (Augustana)
2. Bob Stout (Eastern Illinois)
3. Bob Bitterman (Northern Michigan)
4. John Newell (Nebraska at Omaha)
5. Mark Hall (California State, Bakersfield)
6. Dion Cobb (Northern Iowa)
7. Kent Haake (Southern Dakota State)
8. Scott Lowery (Southwest Missouri)

177-lb class

1. Brian Parlet (Augustana)
2. Efonda Sproles (Northern Iowa)
3. Norm Mitchell (Southern Illinois at Edwardsville)
4. Derrick Hardy (Chicago State)
5. Jeff Hohertz (South Dakota State)
6. Dan Revesz (Pittsburgh, Johnstown)
7. Tim Harris (Northern Michigan)
8. Sam Carson (Eastern Illinois)

190-lb class

1. Kirk Myers (Northern Iowa)
2. Geno Savegnano (Eastern Illinois)
3. Les Gatrel (Central Missouri)
4. Tim Cahill (Nebraska at Omaha)
5. Jeff Esmont (Ashland)
6. Greg Shealy (Pembroke State)
7. Willard Crews (Morgan State)
8. Herb Alamed (Springfield)

Heavyweight

1. Ron Essink (Grand Valley State)
2. Dave Klemm (Eastern Illinois)
3. Jeff Grier (Augustana)
4. Mike Howe (Northern Michigan)
5. Jerry Larson (North Dakota)
6. Kevin Kurth (Northern Iowa)
7. Josh Bryant (Livingstone)
8. Jeff Schanhals (Northern Colorado)

1981 (at University of California, Davis)

Team	*Points*
1. California State (Bakersfield)	144.50
2. Eastern Illinois	98
3. Nebraska at Omaha	53.25
4. Humboldt State	45.25
5. North Dakota State	43
6. Ashland College	42
7. Southern Illinois at Edwardsville	36
8. Augustana (SD), Morgan State	32.75
10. South Dakota State	24.75
11. Northern Michigan	23.75
12. Central Connecticut	21.50
13. California State (Chico)	21.25
14. CW Post	21
15. Pittsburgh (Johnstown)	20.25
16. Lake Superior State	18.50
17. Northern Colorado	16.50
18. Jacksonville State, Wisconsin—Parkside	15.50
20. Pembroke State	15.25

Place winners

118-lb class

1. Adam Cuestas (California State, Bakersfield)
2. Tom Reed (Southern Illinois at Edwardsville)
3. Reggie Johnson (Ashland)
4. Jones (Pembroke State)
5. Smesler (Ferris State)
6. Murphy (Eastern Illinois)
7. Gonzales (California State, Sacramento)
8. Ellis (Morgan State)

126-lb class

1. Dan Cuestas (California State, Bakersfield)
2. Marty Nellis (Humboldt State)
3. Fontana (CW Post)
4. Porter (Eastern Illinois)
5. Halloran (North Dakota State)
6. Arrante (Springfield)
7. Valerian (Central Connecticut)
8. Lopez (California State, Sacramento)

134-lb class

1. Mark Bower (Augustana)
2. Bob Hoffman (Nebraska at Omaha)
3. Winter (Wisconsin—Parkside)
4. Garcia (CW Post)
5. Smith (California, Davis)
6. Shafer (Eastern Illinois)
7. Pringle (Morgan State)
8. Gaughan (Moorhead State)

142-lb class
1. Ryan Kaufman (Nebraska at Omaha)
2. Tim Ervin (Southern Illinois at Edwardsville)
3. Granger (Grand Valley State)
4. Langlais (North Dakota State)
5. Monolakis (San Francisco State)
6. Williams (California State, Chico)
7. Nickell (California State, Bakersfield)
8. Williams (Winona State)

150-lb class
1. Glenn Cooper (California State, Bakersfield)
2. Gary Erwin (Jacksonville State)
3. Moe (Winona State)
4. Black (Ashland)
5. Husar (Nebraska at Omaha)
6. Yoder (Lake Superior State)
7. Kuintzle (California State, Chico)
8. Brown (Morgan State)

158-lb class
1. Perry Shea (California State, Bakersfield)
2. Mike Polz (Eastern Illinois)
3. Smedley (Humboldt State)
4. Jones (North Dakota)
5. Paulson (Northern Colorado)
6. Davis (Morgan State)
7. McLaughlin (California State, Chico)
8. Bonk (St. Cloud State)

167-lb class
1. Mark Gronowski (Eastern Illinois)
2. Rich Sykes (Humboldt State)
3. Veal (Morgan State)
4. Gritz (California, Davis)
5. Cribbs (Lakes Superior State)
6. Carter (Western Illinois)
7. Rothman (Central Connecticut)
8. Tescher (North Dakota State)

177-lb class
1. Jeff Hohertz (South Dakota State)
2. Dennis McCormick (Eastern Illinois)
3. Loomis (California State, Bakersfield)
4. Dyer (Western Illinois)
5. Homan (Augustana)
6. Glowacki (Central Connecticut)
7. Herbold (St. Cloud State)
8. Luckage (Youngstown State)

190-lb class
1. Geno Savegnago (Eastern Illinois)
2. Jeff Esmont (Ashland)
3. Hall (California State, Bakersfield)
4. Cameron (Central Connecticut)
5. Wilcox (Nebraska at Omaha)
6. Heisick (Minnesota at Duluth)
7. Christian (Northern Colorado)
8. Harris (Norfolk State)

Heavyweight
1. Mike Howe (Northern Michigan)
2. Sean Isgan (Pittsburgh, Johnstown)
3. Schoene (California State, Bakersfield)
4. Brunot (Youngstown State)
5. Pfiefer (North Dakota State)
6. Schanhals (Northern Colorado)
7. Zastrow (South Dakota State)
8. Lee (California State, Sacramento)

1982 (at Wisconsin—Parkside, Kenosha, WI)

Team	*Points*
1. California State (Bakersfield)	166.50
2. North Dakota State	78.75
3. Southern Illinois at Edwardsville	61.75
4. Nebraska at Omaha	51.25
5. Ashland	49.50
6. Northern Michigan	48.50
7. Morgan State	38.50
8. Augustana (SD)	32.50
9. Lake Superior State	29
10. San Francisco State	26.75
11. California State (Chico)	23.75
12. California (Davis), Central Missouri	22.50
14. Jacksonville State	22
15. Minnesota at Duluth	19

Team	*Points*
16. Northern Colorado, Southern Connecticut	17.75
18. Portland State	17
19. California State (Sacramento)	16
20. North Dakota	15.50

Place winners

118-lb class
1. Adam Cuestas (California State, Bakersfield)
2. Jerry Hoy (Minnesota at Duluth)
3. Tim Schultz (Northern Michigan)
4. Reggie Johnson (Ashland)
5. Tim Smelzer (Ferris State)
6. Dave McGowan (Pittsburgh, Johnstown)

126-lb class
1. Dan Cuestas (California State, Bakersfield)
2. Don Stevens (Southern Illinois at Edwardsville)
3. Lyle Clem (North Dakota State)
4. Kirt Strand (Northwest Missouri)
5. Willie Ingold (Northern Michigan)
6. Jim Kattleman (Southwest Missouri)

134-lb class
1. Mike Garcia (Central Missouri)
2. Charlie Cheney (California State, Bakersfield)
3. Pete Dalaker (Southern Connecticut)
4. Ted Navare (Eastern Washington)
5. Dan Winter (Wisconsin—Parkside)
6. George Stone (Northern Michigan)

142-lb class
1. Mike Langlais (North Dakota State)
2. Steve Nickell (California State, Bakersfield)
3. Ryan Kaufman (Nebraska at Omaha)
4. Charlie Lucas (Portland State)
5. Dorr Granger (Grand Valley State)
6. Don Williams (California State, Chico)

150-lb class
1. Gary Erwin (Jacksonville State)
2. Craig Noble (California State, Bakersfield)
3. Mark Black (Ashland)
4. Randy Mieir (Northern Michigan)
5. D.J. West (Northern Colorado)
6. Robert Kuintzle (California State, Chico)

158-lb class
1. Perry Shea (California State, Bakersfield)
2. Kevin Newsome (San Francisco State)
3. John Davis (Morgan State)
4. Bill Wofford (Nebraska at Omaha)
5. Tim Jones (North Dakota State)
6. Glenn Jarvis (Mansfield)

167-lb class
1. Mike Cribbs (Lake Superior State)
2. Eric Gritz (California, Davis)
3. Greg Veal (Morgan State)
4. Gregg Stensgard (North Dakota State)
5. Booker Benford (Southern Illinois at Edwardsville)
6. Scott Teuscher (California State, Bakersfield)

177-lb class
1. Mark Loomis (California State, Bakersfield)
2. Koln Knight (Augustana)
3. Joe Loose (Mankato State)
4. Bill Leveille (California State, Sacramento)
5. Kyle Heaton (Lake Superior State)
6. Dave Iverson (Northern Michigan)

190-lb class
1. Jeff Esmont (Ashland)
2. Dave Hass (North Dakota State)
3. Mark Young (Augustana)
4. Joe Glasder (Southern Illinois at Edwardsville)
5. Garen McDonald (California State, Bakersfield)
6. Karl Pope (Portland State)

Heavyweight
1. Mark Rigituso (Nebraska at Omaha)
2. Al Sears (Southern Illinois at Edwardsville)
3. Jerome Larson (North Dakota)
4. Robert Herrera (California State, Bakersfield)
5. Wade Hall (Indiana Central)
6. Bill Kropoq (California State, Chico)

1983 (at North Dakota State University, Fargo, ND)

Team	Points
1. California State (Bakersfield)	107.50
2. North Dakota State	103.75
3. Nebraska at Omaha	93.75
4. Southern Illinois	91.50
5. Portland State	54.25
6. Morgan State	47
7. St. Cloud State	38.75
8. Ashland	38.50
9. Augustana (SD)	33.25
10. Wisconsin—Parkside	21.25
11. North Dakota	21
12. Northern Colorado	19.25
13. Northern Michigan	19
14. San Francisco State	18.50
15. Pembroke State	17.50
16. Pfeifer	12.50
17. Ferris State	12.25
18. Minnesota at Duluth	11
19. Pittsburgh (Johnstown)	10.50
20. California (Davis)	10

Place winners

118-lb class
1. Adam Cuestas (California State, Bakersfield)
2. Reggie Johnson (Ashland)
3. Willie Ingold (Northern Michigan)
4. Jose Martinez (California, Davis)
5. Steve Werner (North Dakota State)
6. Ray Garcia (Southern Illinois at Edwardsville)
7. Scott Knowlen (North Dakota)
8. Darrell Burchfield (Sagin)

126-lb class
1. Don Stevens (Southern Illinois at Edwardsville)
2. Lyle Clem (North Dakota State)
3. John Loomis (California State, Bakersfield)
4. Mike Vania (Wisconsin—Parkside)
5. Kraig Pressler (Augustana)
6. Craig Kosinksi (Springfield)
7. Brad Wilkerson (Oakland)
8. Dave Morel (Ashland)

134-lb class
1. Steve Carr (North Dakota State)
2. Nick Karantinos (Augustana)
3. Steve Stearns (Southern Illinois at Edwardsville)
4. Bob Hoffman (Nebraska at Omaha)
5. Dave Navaree (Humboldt State)
6. Randy Dowden (Central Missouri)
7. Pat Hughes (Springfield)
8. Mario Decaro (San Francisco State)

142-lb class
1. Jesse Reyes (California State, Bakersfield)
2. Mike Langlais (North Dakota State)
3. Charlie Lucas (Portland State)
4. Freddie Richardson (Pembroke State)
5. Gary Rucinski (St. Cloud State)
6. D.J. West (Northern Colorado)
7. Jeff Schumacher (North Dakota)
8. Rick Babbitts (Southern Connecticut)

150-lb class
1. Mark Manning (Nebraska at Omaha)
2. Mark Black (Ashland)
3. Mark Kristoff (Southern Illinois at Edwardsville)
4. Mike Muckerheide (Wisconsin—Parkside)
5. Phil Sowers (Minnesota at Duluth)
6. Alan Davis (Pembroke State)

7. Dave Wiklund (Augustana)
8. Mike McGrath (St. Cloud State)

158-lb class
1. John Davis (Morgan State)
2. John Barrett (St. Cloud State)
3. Lanny Paulson (Northern Colorado)
4. Craig Noble (California State, Bakersfield)
5. Tim Jones (North Dakota State)
6. Terry Schumacker (Ferris State)
7. Mike Specht (Augustana)
8. Johnny Haynes (Winston-Salem)

167-lb class
1. Greg Veal (Morgan State)
2. Kevin Benson (Portland State)
3. Jim Kimsey (Nebraska at Omaha)
4. John Revesz (Pittsburgh, Johnstown)
5. John Morgan (North Dakota State)
6. Dave Cornemann (South Dakota State)
7. Stephen Scott (Elizabeth)
8. Sam Williams (Central Missouri)

177-lb class
1. Scott Mansur (Portland State)
2. Booker Benford (Southern Illinois at Edwardsville)
3. Mark Loomis (California State, Bakersfield)
4. Phil Herbold (St. Cloud State)
5. Steve Hammers (North Dakota State)
6. Rick Heckendorn (Nebraska at Omaha)
7. Dave Rothman (Central Connecticut)
8. Craig McManaman (Grand Valley State)

190-lb class
1. Greg Wilcox (Nebraska at Omaha)
2. Mike Blaske (California State, Bakersfield)
3. Joe Gladser (Southern Illinois at Edwardsville)
4. Dave Hass (North Dakota State)
5. Forrest Brown (Ferris State)
6. Russ Jones (California State, Sacramento)
7. Willard Crews (Morgan State)
8. Wayne Beaman (Bemidji State)

Heavyweight
1. Mark Rigatuso (Nebraska at Omaha)
2. Morris Johnson (San Francisco State)
3. Herome Larson (North Dakota)
4. Bruce Lambert (Pfeifer)
5. Wade Hall (Indiana Central)
6. Rogelio Herrera (California State, Bakersfield)
7. Al Sears (Southern Illinois at Edwardsville)
8. Emanuel Yarbough (Morgan State)

1984 (at Morgan State University, Baltimore, MD)

Team	*Points*
1. Southern Illinois at Edwardsville	141.50
2. California State (Bakersfield)	93
3. North Dakota State	79.25
4. Morgan State	56
5. Northern Michigan	37.50
6. South Dakota State	36.50
7. Nebraska at Omaha	31
8. Humboldt State	28.50
9. St. Cloud State	28.25
10. Springfield	28
11. Augustana (SD)	27.50
12. Northwest Missouri	22.50
13. Ferris State	21.50
14. San Francisco State	20
15. Portland State	17.50
16. North Dakota	17.25
17. Pembroke State	15
18. Ashland	14.50
19. Grand Valley State	14
20. Pittsburgh (Johnstown)	13.50

Place winners

118-lb class
1. Tim Wright (Southern Illinois at Edwardsville)
2. Chuck Kennedy (Morgan State)
3. Willie Ingold (Northern Michigan)
4. Jose Martinez (California, Davis)
5. Mark Weston (Nebraska at Omaha)
6. Darryl Arroyo (Springfield)
7. Scott Knowlen (North Dakota)
8. Mike Brown (Northwest Missouri)

126-lb class
1. Don Stevens (Southern Illinois at Edwardsville)
2. John Loomis (California State, Bakersfield)
3. Kyle Presler (Augustana)
4. Dave Morell (Ashland)
5. Tim Begley (Wright State)
6. Jack Maughn (North Dakota State)
7. Craig Kosinski (Springfield)
8. Gorge Acosta (California State, Chico)

134-lb. class
1. Steve Markey (California State, Bakersfield)
2. Pat Hughes (Springfield)
3. Alan Grammer (Southern Illinois at Edwardsville)
4. Steve Carr (North Dakota State)
5. Dave Navarre (Humboldt State)
6. Rick Sielhamer (Liberty Baptist)
7. Tom Churchard (Grand Valley State)
8. John Craig (Oakland)

142-lb class
1. Jesse Reyes (California State, Bakersfield)
2. Maurice Brown (Southern Illinois at Edwardsville)
3. Boyd Goodpaster (Portland State)
4. Mike Frazier (North Dakota State)
5. Jon Groskreutz (Augustana)
6. Eric Lessley (Humboldt State)
7. Rich Friberg (Northern Michigan)
8. Trent Smith (Central Florida)

150-lb class
1. Mike Langlais (North Dakota State)
2. Mark Kristoff (Southern Illinois at Edwardsville)
3. Jeff Schumacher (North Dakota State)
4. Rob Yahner (Pittsburgh, Johnstown)
5. Mark Manning (Nebraska at Omaha)
6. Troy Osborne (California State, Bakersfield)
7. Glenn Sartorelli (Northern Michigan)
8. Dan Wilson (Liberty Baptist)

158-lb class
1. John Davis (Morgan State)
2. John Barrett (St. Cloud State)
3. Don Cox (South Dakota State)
4. Don Dodds (Humboldt State)
5. Jerry Umin (Oakland)
6. Mike Specht (Augustana)
7. John Scott (Portland State)
8. Russ Schenk (Central Florida)

167-lb class
1. Dave Cornemann (South Dakota State)
2. Tim Jones (Northern Michigan)
3. John Morgan (North Dakota State)
4. Todd Yde (Wisconsin—Parkside)
5. Doug Hassell (Nebraska at Omaha)
6. Dale Delaney (Springfield)
7. Randy Strayer (Indiana, PA)
8. Pat Allen (Springfield)

177-lb class
1. Booker Benford (Southern Illinois at Edwardsville)
2. Wayne Love (Northwest Missouri)
3. Dave Hammers (North Dakota State)
4. Graig McManaman (Grand Valley State)
5. Bob Button (California State, Bakersfield)
6. Rick Heckendorn (Nebraska at Omaha)

7. Dave Bonifas (Ferris State)
8. Rich Bonaccorsi (Indiana, PA)

190-lb class

1. Ernie Badger (Southern Illinois at Edwardsville)
2. Jay Stainback (Pembroke State)
3. Paul Jungck (Ferris State)
4. Noel Nemitz (St. Cloud State)
5. Russ Jones (California State, Sacramento)
6. John Vorrice (Morgan State)
7. Dave Maiorana (Ashland)
8. Bill Eaton (Northwest Missouri)

Heavyweight

1. Morris Johnson (San Francisco State)
2. Mike Blaske (California State, Bakersfield)
3. Jeff Green (Morgan State)
4. Al Sears (Southern Illinois at Edwardsville)
5. Bruce Lambert (Pfiefer)
6. Ronnie Locust (Winston-Salem)
7. Frank Shepard (California State, Chico)
8. Al Holleman (South Dakota State)

1985 (at University of Dayton, Dayton, OH)

Team	*Points*
1. Southern Illinois at Edwardsville	132.75
2. Nebraska at Omaha	84.25
3. Augustana	57
4. Ashland	50.75
5. Edinboro	48.75
6. North Dakota State	43.50
7. California State (Bakersfield)	43
8. Humboldt State	39.50
9. South Dakota State	32.50
10. Wright State	31.25
11. Portland State	30.50
12. Northern Michigan	22.50
13. Liberty Baptist	19.25
14. North Dakota	19
15. Wisconsin—Parkside	16.75
16. Lake Superior State, San Francisco State, Northwest Missouri	14.50
19. Oakland	13.50
20. Pittsburgh (Johnstown)	12

Place winners

118-lb class

1. Tim Wright (Southern Illinois at Edwardsville)
2. Mark Weston (Nebraska at Omaha)
3. Rick Dicola (Ashland)
4. Brett McNama (California State, Chico)
5. Eddie Woodburn (California State, Bakersfield)
6. Steve Anderson (North Dakota State)
7. John Tau (Liberty Baptist)
8. Pat Ingold (Northern Michigan)

126-lb class

1. Anthony Amado (Portland State)
2. Kyle Presler (Augustana)
3. Steve Stearns (Southern Illinois at Edwardsville)
4. Tim Begley (Wright State)
5. Morteza Abedi (California State, Bakersfield)
6. Rick Travis (California, PA)
7. Perry Ainscough (Liberty Baptist)
8. Tony Molchak (Ashland)

134-lb class

1. Alan Grammer (Southern Illinois at Edwardsville)
2. Vince McCullough (South Dakota State)
3. Bill O'Connor (Northwest Missouri)
4. Steve Meckel (Humboldt State)
5. Calvin Clay (Livingston)
6. Jack Maughan (North Dakota State)

7. Richard Ellingsen (San Francisco State)
8. Skip Goerner (Lake Superior State)

142-lb class
1. Eric Lessley (Humboldt State)
2. Maurice Brown (Southern Illinois at Edwardsville)
3. Todd Winter (Ashland)
4. Shawn Murdock (Lake Superior State)
5. Mike Frazier (North Dakota State)
6. Dave Witgen (Oakland)
7. Shawn Knudsen (Nebraska at Omaha)
8. Jim Strande (South Dakota State)

150-lb class
1. Mark Manning (Nebraska at Omaha)
2. Jim Martinson (North Dakota)
3. Rob Yahner (Pittsburgh, Johnstown)
4. Brian McTague (Southern Illinois at Edwardsville)
5. Chuck Justice (California State, Bakersfield)
6. Boyd Goodpaster (Portland)
7. Jack Thomas (Wright State)
8. Todd Geerts (California, Davis)

158-lb class
1. Mike Hahesy (Edinboro)
2. Ken Davis (Wright State)
3. Curt Ramsey (Nebraska at Omaha)
4. Jerry Umin (Oakland)
5. Mike Muckerheide (Wisconsin—Parkside)
6. Noel Hygelund (Portland)
7. Ardeshir Asgari (California State, Bakersfield)
8. Dan McGinnis (Southern Illinois at Edwardsville)

167-lb class
1. Matt Furey (Edinboro)
2. Howard Lawson (California State, Bakersfield)
3. Andrew Steffen (San Francisco State)
4. Pat Johannes (North Dakota State)
5. Todd Yde (Wisconsin—Parkside)
6. Tim Jones (Northern Michigan)
7. William Wamsley (Virginia State)
8. Brent Hoffner (North Dakota)

177-lb class
1. Booker Benford (Southern Illinois at Edwardsville)
2. Paul Jones (Nebraska at Omaha)
3. John Morgan (North Dakota State)
4. Jim Zachar (Ashland)
5. Pat Bussey (Liberty Baptist)
6. Dave Held (Edinboro)
7. Dave Iverson (Northern Michigan)
8. Jeff Leuders (South Dakota State)

190-lb class
1. Koln Knight (Augustana)
2. Ernie Badger (Southern Illinois at Edwardsville)
3. R.J. Nebe (Nebraska at Omaha)
4. Dave Maiovana (Ashland)
5. John Kroez (CW Post)
6. Paul Jungck (Ferris State)
7. Derrick Munos (Northern Michigan)
8. Jay Stainbeck (Pembroke State)

Heavyweight
1. Keith Hanson (Augustana)
2. Al Sears (Southern Illinois at Edwardsville)
3. Al Holleman (South Dakota State)
4. Rod Prnjak (Humboldt State)
5. Duane Lutgring (Indiana Central)
6. Joe Buelt (Northern Michigan)
7. Mike Monroe (California State, Bakersfield)
8. Derek Edmonds (Pembroke)

1986 (at Southern Illinois University at Edwardsville)

Team	*Points*
1. Southern Illinois at Edwardsville	119
2. Edinboro	106.50
3. California State (Bakersfield)	81.75
4. North Dakota State	53.75
5. Liberty Baptist	36.75

Team	*Points*
6. Augustana (SD)	33.25
7. Nebraska at Omaha	31.25
8. St. Cloud State	26
9. South Dakota State	25.50
10. San Francisco State	25
11. Northern Michigan	23.50
12. Portland State	22
13. North Dakota	21
14. California (PA)	20.75
15. Northwest Missouri	20.50
16. Central Missouri	20
17. Lake Superior State	19
18. Oakland	17.50
19. Pembroke State, Norfolk State, Ashland	17

Place winners

118-lb class

1. Tim Wright (Southern Illinois at Edwardsville)
2. Perry Ainscough (Liberty Baptist)
3. John Christen (North Dakota)
4. Brett McNamar (California State, Chico)
5. Roger Singleton (Grand Valley State)
6. Pat Ingold (Northern Michigan)
7. Brian Guzzo (South Dakota State)
8. Rick Goodwin (San Francisco State)

126-lb class

1. Alan Grammer (Southern Illinois at Edwardsville)
2. Anthony Amado (Portland State)
3. Joe Stukes (Pembroke State)
4. Paul Anderson (St. Cloud State)
5. Tim Begley (Wright State)
6. Rick Travis (California, PA)
7. Rick Goeb (North Dakota State)
8. Allen Paradise (California State, Bakersfield)

134-lb class

1. Steve Stearns (Southern Illinois at Edwardsville)
2. David Ray (Edinboro)
3. Ira Cheatham (Norfolk State)
4. Bill O'Connor (Northwest Missouri)
5. Rich Ellingsen (San Francisco State)
6. Tony Molchak (Ashland)
7. Tony Trabucco (California State, Chico)
8. Robert Burrows (Central Missouri)

142-lb class

1. Greg Wright (Edinboro)
2. Mark Danner (Central Missouri)
3. Shawn Murdock (Lake Superior State)
4. Mike Frazier (North Dakota State)
5. John Sanderson (Grand Valley State)
6. Perry Fink (South Dakota State)
7. Kip Kristoff (Southern Illinois at Edwardsville)
8. Bill Newton (California State, Bakersfield)

150-lb class

1. Bob Kauffman (Edinboro)
2. Brian McTague (Southern Illinois at Edwardsville)
3. Vinnie Hanlon (California, PA)
4. Matt Olejnik (California State, Bakersfield)
5. Lance Rogers (North Dakota State)
6. Jim Martinson (North Dakota)
7. Gerry Bell (Lake Superior State)
8. Keith Lawver (Northern Michigan)

158-lb class

1. Pat Huyck (California State, Bakersfield)
2. Mike Hahesy (Edinboro)
3. Gene Green (North Dakota State)
4. Todd Kendle (Augustana)
5. Bob Dahm (Southern Illinois at Edwardsville)
6. Ken Davis (Wright State)
7. Darrin Arberry (Indiana Central)
8. Brad Hildebrandt (Nebraska at Omaha)

167-lb class

1. Darryl Pope (California State, Bakersfield)
2. Mark Kristoff (Southern Illinois at Edwardsville)
3. John Barrett (St. Cloud State)
4. John Morgan (North Dakota State)
5. John Solomonson (Oakland)
6. Mike Wood (Norfolk State)
7. Fred Meyer (Southern Connecticut)
8. Dave Held (Edinboro)

177-lb class

1. Marvin Jones (California State, Bakersfield)
2. Paul Jones (Nebraska at Omaha)
3. Ray Porter (Ashland)
4. Wayne Love (Northwest Missouri)
5. Matt Furey (Edinboro)
6. Pat Bussey (Liberty Baptist)
7. Pat Johannes (North Dakota State)
8. Dean Wygal (Portland State)

190-lb class

1. Koln Knight (Augustana)
2. Derrick Munos (Northern Michigan)
3. R.J. Nebe (Nebraska at Omaha)
4. Tim Gleeson (San Francisco State)
5. Ernie Badger (Southern Illinois at Edwardsville)
6. Jay Stainback (Pembroke State)
7. Mike Arnold (Lake Superior State)
8. Matt Palmer (North Dakota State)

Heavyweight

1. Dean Hall (Edinboro)
2. Mike Hatch (Liberty Baptist)
3. Carlton Haselrig (Pittsburgh, Johnstown)
4. Al Holleman (South Dakota State)
5. Craig Brooks (Oakland)
6. Alex Koehler (San Francisco State)
7. Ed Christensen (St. Cloud State)
8. William Martin (Norfolk State)

1987 (at Southern Illinois University at Edwardsville)

Team	*Points*
1. California State (Bakersfield)	90.50
2. Southern Illinois at Edwardsville	69.50
3. North Dakota State	62.25
4. North Dakota	56.75
5. Nebraska at Omaha	49.50
6. Liberty Baptist	46
7. Ferris State	42.50
8. Portland State	32
9. San Francisco State	31.50
10. South Dakota State	30.50
11. California (PA)	29
12. Pittsburgh, Johnstown	28.50
13. Lake Superior State	24
14. Wright State	18.25
15. Southern Connecticut	18
16. Ashland	17
17. Grand Valley State	15.75
18. Pembroke State	15.50
19. Central Missouri	14
20. St. Cloud State	13.75

Place winners

118-lb class

1. Tim Wright (Southern Illinois at Edwardsville)
2. Roger Singleton (Grand Valley State)
3. Mark Piterski (Southern Connecticut)
4. John Christen (North Dakota)
5. Loren Baum (Liberty Baptist)
6. Don Vanmourik (Ferris State)
7. Tony Ramirez (California State, Chico)
8. Rick Goodwin (San Francisco State)

126-lb class
1. Haig Brown (Portland State)
2. Mike Dallas (California State, Bakersfield)
3. Cliff Lentz (San Francisco State)
4. Joe Stukes (Pembroke State)
5. Rick Goeb (North Dakota State)
6. Chris Gelvin (Wright State)
7. Paul Anderson (St. Cloud State)
8. Dennis Duechen (Wisconsin—Parkside)

134-lb class
1. Pat Dorn (South Dakota State)
2. Andy Leier (North Dakota)
3. Rick Travis (California, PA)
4. Skip Smith (Wright State)
5. Dan Collins (North Dakota State)
6. Bob Burrows (Central Missouri)
7. Dean Branstetter (Indianapolis)
8. Walter Ulrich (California State, Chico)

142-lb class
1. Junior Saunders (California State, Bakersfield)
2. Brian McTague (Southern Illinois at Edwardsville)
3. Rick Lapaglia (Ashland)
4. Jeff Ocel (North Dakota State)
5. Mark Danner (Central Missouri)
6. Bob Ray (Pittsburgh, Johnstown)
7. John Wachsmuth (Portland State)
8. Dwane Maue (Colorado Mines)

150-lb class
1. Kip Kristoff (Southern Illinois at Edwardsville)
2. Carlos Levexier (San Francisco State)
3. Tim Morris (Liberty Baptist)
4. Brad Solberg (North Dakota)
5. Lance Rogers (North Dakota State)
6. Hazen Bye (South Dakota State)
7. Wayne Trosino (Portland State)
8. Rich Shaffer (Pittsburgh, Johnstown)

158-lb class
1. Kory Mosher (North Dakota)
2. Lloyd Hygelund (Portland State)
3. Bob Dahm (Southern Illinois at Edwardsville)
4. Darren Arberry (Indianapolis)
5. Brad Hildebrandt (Nebraska at Omaha)
6. Kevin Frame (Liberty Baptist)
7. Joe Juliar (Mankato State)
8. Craig Settles (San Francisco State)

167-lb class
1. Marty Morgan (North Dakota State)
2. Brad Morris (Ferris State)
3. Jeff Randall (Nebraska at Omaha)
4. Robert Watkins (Humboldt State)
5. Ted Price (Wisconsin—Parkside)
6. William Johnson (Northern Colorado)
7. Willie Mays (Pembroke State)
8. Mike Root (Lake Superior State)

177-lb class
1. Darryl Pope (California State, Bakersfield)
2. R.J. Nebe (Nebraska at Omaha)
3. Pat Johannes (North Dakota State)
4. James Solomonson (Ferris State)
5. Danzil Forrester (Southern Connecticut)
6. Steve Miller (Ashland)
7. Kip Fennelly (Liberty Baptist)
8. Phil Scott (California State, Chico)

190-lb class
1. Eric Mittlestead (California State, Bakersfield)
2. Ken Hackman (California, PA)
3. Doug Chapman (Ferris State)
4. Mike Arnold (Lake Superior State)
5. Craig Whitaken (West Chester)
6. Dave Pippin (Nebraska at Omaha)
7. Nate Toedter (St. Cloud State)
8. Antonio Kilpatrick (Pembroke State)

Heavyweight
1. Carlton Haselrig (Pittsburgh, Johnstown)
2. Mike Hatch (Liberty Baptist)
3. Mike Monroe (California State, Bakersfield)
4. Clark Schnepel (Nebraska at Omaha)
5. Randy Sieler (Lake Superior State)
6. Ed Christensen (St. Cloud State)
7. Kyle Jensen (South Dakota State)
8. Tim Lajcik (California, Davis)

1988 (at University of Nebraska at Omaha)

Team	Points
1. North Dakota State	88
2. Nebraska at Omaha	81.75
3. Southern Illinois at Edwardsville	75
4. Ferris State	60
5. North Dakota	50.75
6. South Dakota State	41.75
7. Portland State	40.75
8. Pittsburgh (Johnstown)	38.75
9. Liberty Baptist	35
10. Pembroke State	29.25
11. Southern Connecticut	27.50
12. Springfield	26.50
13. California (PA)	26.25
14. Northern Michigan	23.50
15. Grand Valley State	23.25
16. Ashland	21
17. Lake Superior State	20.50
18. Colorado Mines	17.50
19. California State (Chico)	17
20. Central Missouri	11

Place winners

118-lb class
1. Roger Singleton (Grand Valley State)
2. Dave Calliguri (North Dakota State)
3. Mark Piterski (Southern Connecticut)
4. Dan VanMourik (Ferris State)
5. Rick DiCola (Ashland)
6. Brian Guzzo (South Dakota State)
7. Steve Jakl (Nebraska at Omaha)
8. Loren Baum (Liberty Baptist)

126-lb class
1. Rick Goeb (North Dakota State)
2. Joe Stukes (Pembroke State)
3. Haig Brown (Portland State)
4. Philip Johns (Southern Illinois at Edwardsville)
5. Tony Ramirez (California State, Chico)
6. Robert Lilly (Central Missouri)
7. Sean Haight (Gannon)
8. Mike Centanni (Lake Superior State)

134-lb class
1. Pat Dorn (South Dakota State)
2. Bob Berceau (Northern Michigan)
3. Tim Failing (Springfield)
4. Walter Ulrich (California State, Chico)
5. Duane Barnhart (North Dakota)
6. Kirwyn Adderly (Norfolk)
7. Larry Robey (Pittsburgh, Johnstown)
8. Mike Bruner (Lake Superior State)

142-lb class
1. Warren Stewart (Liberty Baptist)
2. Duane Maue (Colorado Mines)
3. Bob Ray (Pittsburgh, Johnstown)
4. Jeff Ocel (North Dakota State)
5. Andy Leier (North Dakota)
6. Eric Morgan (Southern Illinois at Edwardsville)
7. Brian Thomas (Nebraska at Omaha)
8. Tom Paveglio (Ferris State)

150-lb class
1. Dan Russell (Portland State)
2. Kip Kristoff (Southern Illinois at Edwardsville)
3. Shaun O'Hearn (Springfield)
4. Perry Fink (South Dakota State)
5. Bourck Cashmore (North Dakota State)
6. Ben Dagley (Ashland)

7. Mike Curley (Grand Valley State)
8. Rich Shaffer (Pittsburgh, Johnstown)

158-lb class
1. Kory Mosher (North Dakota)
2. Brad Hildebrandt (Nebraska at Omaha)
3. Kurt Johnson (Ferris State)
4. Gene Green (North Dakota State)
5. Steve Harmon (Southern Illinois at Edwardsville)
6. John Mansfield (California, PA)
7. Andre Taylor (Portland State)
8. Willis Mouzon (Winston-Salem)

167-lb class
1. Mark Kirstoff (Southern Illinois at Edwardsville)
2. Jeff Randall (Nebraska at Omaha)
3. Kevin Frame (Liberty Baptist)
4. Brad Morris (Ferris State)
5. Todd Kendle (Augustana)
6. Chris Mihlfeld (Central Missouri)
7. Brent Hoffner (North Dakota)
8. William Johnson (Northern Colorado)

177-lb class
1. R.J. Nebe (Nebraska at Omaha)
2. Denzil Forrester (Southern Connecticut)
3. Doug Mooney (Ferris State)
4. Pat Johannes (North Dakota State)
5. Dwight Downs (Southern Illinois at Edwardsville)
6. Steve Miller (Ashland)
7. Joe Wypiszenski (Northern Michigan)
8. Don Zeman (California, Davis)

190-lb class
1. Ken Hackman (California, PA)
2. Matt Palmer (North Dakota State)
3. Antonio Kilpatrick (Pembroke State)
4. Doug Chapman (Ferris State)
5. Paul Koenig (South Dakota State)
6. Dave Pippen (Nebraska at Omaha)
7. Nate Toedter (St. Cloud State)
8. Russ Witzig (Southern Illinois at Edwardsville)

Heavyweight
1. Carlton Haselrig (Pittsburgh, Johnstown)
2. Randy Seiler (Lake Superior State)
3. Clark Schnepel (Nebraska at Omaha)
4. Jair Toedter (North Dakota)
5. Tim Lajcik (California, Davis)
6. Kurt Bednar (Southern Illinois at Edwardsville)
7. Craig Brooks (Northern Michigan)
8. Tim Pennie (Virginia State)

Table 8.5
Division III—1974-1988

1974 (at Wilkes College, Wilkes-Barre, PA)

Team	Points
1. Wilkes	135.5
2. John Carroll	86.5
3. Montclair State	78
4. Brockport State	71.5
5. Ashland	52
6. Millersville State	48.5
7. Lake Superior State	43.5
8. Trenton State	39.5
9. Mount Union	28.5
10. Franklin and Marshall	28
11. Potsdam State	26.5
12. Elizabethtown, Delaware Valley	24.5
14. Ripon	20
15. Augustana (IL)	17
16. Ithaca, Binghamton State, Coast Guard	15
19. Kutztown State	14
20. Coe	11.5

Team	*Points*
21. MIT, Wabash	11
23. Albany State	9
24. MacMurray, Mansfield State	8.5
26. Oswego State	8
27. Olivet	6
28. Lebanon Valley	4.5
29. Ohio Northern, Sonoma State	4
31. DePauw	3.5
32. Luther	3
33. CCNY, Wooster, Colorado Mines, St. John's (MN)	2.5
37. Washington (MD), Washington and Jefferson, Maryville	2
40. Western Maryland, Moravian, Rochester Tech, Rochester	1.5
44. Susquehanna	1

Place winners

118-lb class
1. Eric Mast (Elizabethtown)
2. Rick Mahonski (Wilkes)
3. Ed Alber (Montclair State)
4. Dave Whare (Millersville State)
5. Ron Angello (Ashland)
6. Peter Berti (Binghamton State)

126-lb class
1. Nabil Guketlov (Montclair State)
2. Alana Evangilista (John Carroll)
3. Lon Balum (Wilkes)
4. Jim Leyndyke (Lake Superior State)
5. Jim Craddox (Trenton State)
6. Ed Hanley (MIT)

134-lb class
1. John Chakmakas (Wilkes)
2. Rae McDonald (Mount Union)
3. Mark Cale (John Carroll)
4. Dave Foxen (Brockport State)
5. Craig Spencer (Montclair State)
6. Ken Glueck (MacMurray)

142-lb class
1. Art Trovei (Wilkes)
2. John Martellucci (Brockport State)
3. Jim Pazyniak (John Carroll)
4. Rich Zinek (Millersville State)
5. Larry Mims (Albany State)
6. Dave Jirikovic (Lake Superior State)

150-lb class
1. Mike Lee (Wilkes)
2. Charles Beck (John Carroll)
3. Kevin McCleary (Franklin and Marshall)
4. Rich Tschantz (Mount Union)
5. Steve Wagner (Wabash)
6. Oscar Zavala (Montclair State)

158-lb class
1. Jim Fallis (Lake Superior State)
2. Gene Ashley (Wilkes)
3. Lou Demyan (Kutztown State)
4. Clayton Barnard (Ashland)
5. Andy Fairle (Coe)
6. Mark Sassani (Mansfield State)

167-lb class
1. Mike Van Boxel (Ripon)
2. Bill Hays (Trenton State)
3. Paul Bruns (Brockport State)
4. Jim Grant (Franklin and Marshall)
5. Jim Weisenfluh (Wilkes)
6. Fran Campbell (Delaware Valley)

177-lb class
1. Frank Calabria (Brockport State)
2. Pat Cavanaugh (Augustana)
3. Elijah Whitten (Ashland)
4. Steve Strellner (Montclair State)
5. Doug Cope (Delaware Valley)
6. Tom Corbo (John Carroll)

190-lb class
1. Rich Molbury (Potsdam State)
2. Jim Zoschg (Millersville State)
3. Glen Carson (Trenton State)
4. Paul Iacovelli (Ithaca)
5. John Reid (Montclair State)
6. Dennis Luzon (Oswego State)

Heavyweight
1. Joe Bertolone (John Carroll)
2. Al Scharer (Wilkes)
3. Jim Murray (Coast Guard)
4. Al Bartlebaugh (Delaware Valley)
5. Greg Low (Ashland)
6. Dave Schrey (Millersville State)

1975 (at John Carroll, Cleveland, OH)

Team	Points
1. John Carroll	111
2. Montclair State	96
3. Wilkes	92
4. Potsdam State	57
5. Binghamton State	51.5
6. Ashland	51
7. Millersville	45.5
8. Brockport State	45
9. Humboldt State	36.5
10. Gettysburg	28.5
11. Oswego State	24.5
12. Mansfield State	21.5
13. Coe	19.5
14. Trenton State	17.5
15. St. Lawrence, Elizabethtown	16.5
17. Coast Guard, Massachusetts Maritime	15
19. Mount Union, York (PA)	14.5
21. Albany State	13.5
22. Augustana (IL)	13
23. Ripon	12
24. Delaware Valley	10.5
25. Luther	10
26. MIT	9.5
27. Lebanon Valley, Washington and Jefferson, Oberlin	9
30. RPI	7.5
31. Cortland State	7
32. Baldwin-Wallace	6.5
33. Ithaca	6
34. Rochester Tech, Olivet, MacMurray	5.5
37. Ohio Northern, Thiel	5
39. California State (Chico)	4.5
40. Lycoming	4
41. Amherst, Kalamazoo	3.5
43. Plymouth State, Washington and Lee	3
45. Kutztown State, Geneseo State	2.5
47. Adrian, Allegheny	2
49. Maryville, Hiram	1.5
51. Alma, Calvin, Glassboro State, Rochester, Grove City, Heidelberg, Moravian, Case Western, Muskingham	1
60. Nebraska Wesleyan, Williams, Union	.5

Place winners

118-lb class
1. Nabil Guketlov (Montclair State)
2. Jack Mulhall (John Carroll)
3. Roy Preefer (Wilkes)
4. Dwight Miller (Humboldt State)
5. Bob Daschbach (Washington and Jefferson)
6. James Aquilo (Mount Union)

126-lb class
1. Crag Helmuth (Gettysburg)
2. Tim Borshoff (Binghamton State)
3. Andy Zook (Millersville State)
4. Rich Numa (Montclair State)
5. Mike Rossetti (Trenton State)
6. Greg Rotell (Thiel)

134-lb class
1. Mark Hawald Cale (John Carroll)
2. Vince Tundo (Montclair State)
3. Abe Lang (Brockport State)
4. John Chakmakas (Wilkes)
5. Brian Smith (Gettysburg)
6. Rae McDonald (Mount Union)

142-lb class
1. John Martellucci (Brockport State)
2. Nick Hobbs (Coe)
3. Larry Mims (Albany State)
4. Mike Fiamingo (Mansfield State)
5. Kevin Welter (Montclair State)
6. Rick Zink (Millersville State)

150-lb class
1. Charles Becks (John Carroll)
2. Tony Peraza (Potsdam State)
3. Greg DiGioacchino (Montclair State)
4. Walt Weller (Binghamton State)
5. Jim Friedrich (Oberlin)
6. Dave Gardner (Mansfield State)

158-lb class
1. Gene Ashley (Wilkes)
2. Ed Pucci (Oswego State)
3. Mitch Brown (St. Lawrence)
4. Raleigh Clemons (Ashland)
5. Greg Reilly (Binghamton State)
6. Al Garber (Mansfield State)

167-lb class
1. Jim Weisenfiuh (Wilkes)
2. Joe Galea (Potsdam State)
3. Clayton Bernard (Ashland)
4. Ricardo Bailey (Elizabethtown)
5. Mike Van Boxel (Ripon)
6. Tim True (RPI)

177-lb class
1. Brad Bowman (John Carroll)
2. Tom McCue (Potsdam State)
3. Joe Borsa (York)
4. Mike Polakoff (Binghamton State)
5. Allen Grinde (Luther)
6. Ron King (Ithaca)

190-lb class
1. Brend Wissenback (Humboldt State)
2. Skip Fair (Ashland)
3. Leon Dunnam (Massachusetts Maritime)
4. Fred Penrod (Augustana)
5. Steve Sanko (Lebanon Valley)
6. Eric Guyll (Millersville State)

Heavyweight
1. Joe Bertolone (John Carroll)
2. Steve Caldwell (Montclair State)
3. Jim Murray (Coast Guard)
4. Al Scharer (Wilkes)
5. Al Bartlebaugh (Delaware Valley)
6. Erland Van Lidth de Jeude (MIT)

1976 (at Coe College, Cedar Rapids, IA)

Team	Points
1. Montclair State	143
2. John Carroll	112.25
3. Ashland	51
4. St. Lawrence	44.50
5. Millersville State	42
6. Massachusetts Maritime	39.50
7. Lycoming	36
8. Gettysburg, Potsdam State	29
10. Humboldt State	28.50
11. Coe	24.50
12. Binghamton State	23.75
13. Brockport State	22.50
14. Luther	22
15. Upper Iowa	21.50
16. Wheaton	21
17. MacMurray	20
18. Trenton State	19
19. Cortland State, MIT	18
21. Hiram	15
22. Delaware Valley	14
23. Stanislaus State	13.75
24. Maryville	12
25. Grove City	11.50
26. Kutztown State	11
27. Olivet	9.75
28. Wartburg	9.25
29. Cornell College	9
30. Simpson	8.75
31. Ohio Northern	8.50
32. Thiel	7.50
33. Coast Guard	5
34. Lake Superior State	3.50
35. Merchant Marine, York (PA)	3.25
37. Kalamazoo, Oswego State	3
39. California Lutheran, Widener,	

Team	*Points*
Elizabethtown, Rhode Island, Loras	2.50
44. Adrian, Alma, Amherst, Baldwin-Wallace, Millikin, Glassboro State, Oberlin, Monmouth (IL)	2
52. Augustana (IL)	1.75
53. Oneonta State	1.50
54. Mansfield State, Rochester Tech, St. Thomas, Washington and Jefferson	1
58. Hamline, Wabash	.50

Place winners

118-lb class
1. Jack Mulhall (John Carroll)
2. Pete Berti (Binghamton State)
3. George Kacavas (Montclair State)
4. Scott Puzia (Trenton State)
5. Mike Tobin (Massachusetts Maritime)
6. Bob Ortenzio (Gettysburg)

126-lb class
1. Vince Tundo (Montclair State)
2. Graig Helmuth (Gettysburg)
3. Andy Zook (Millersville State)
4. Mike Rossetti (Trenton State)
5. John Ciotoli (Cortland State)
6. Al Evangelista (John Carroll)

134-lb class
1. Mark Hawald (John Caroll)
2. Mike Blakely (Montclair State)
3. Abe Lang (Brockport State)
4. Mel Harris (Stanislaus State)
5. Gil Waterman (Wheaton)
6. Gerald Bouchard (Potsdam State)

142-lb class
1. Rick Freitas (Montclair State)
2. Nick Hobbs (Coe)
3. Harold Shaw (Lycoming)
4. Alex Massiello (Hiram)
5. John Bittenbender (Kutztown State)
6. Mike Harr (Humboldt State)

150-lb class
1. Tony Peraza (Potsdam State)
2. Fred Wideman (MacMurray)
3. Greg DiGioacchino (Montclair State)
4. Graig Savitsky (Lycoming)
5. Doug Burton (Ohio Northern)
6. Rory Whipple (Cortland State)

158-lb class
1. Jim Weir (John Carroll)
2. Robert Harris (Massachusetts Maritime)
3. Mitch Brown (St. Lawrence)
4. Steve Boria (Lycoming)
5. Jerome Stewart (Simpson)
6. Mike Karges (Humboldt State)

167-lb class
1. Dante Caprio (Montclair State)
2. Clay Barnard (Ashland)
3. Ken Meditz (John Carroll)
4. Kris Henry (Humboldt State)
5. David Bauchman (Grove City)
6. Wayne Dunn (Maryville)

177-lb class
1. Dom DiGioacchino (Montclair State)
2. Brad Bowman (John Carroll)
3. Doug Cope (Delaware Valley)
4. Allen Grinde (Luther)
5. Skip Fair (Ashland)
6. Ronald Bates (Olivet)

190-lb class
1. Eric Guyll (Millersville State)
2. Frank Kuennen (Upper Iowa)
3. Ed Hissa (Ashland)
4. Leon Dunnam (Massachusetts Maritime)
5. Kevin Hinkel (John Carroll)
6. Robert Valentine (Maryville)

Heavyweight
1. Ron Pelligra (St. Lawrence)
2. Erland Van Lidth de Jeude (MIT)
3. Steve Caldwell (Montclair State)
4. Steve McRoberts (Wheaton)
5. Steve Riess (Luther)
6. Joe Collins (Ashland)

1977 (at Binghamton State, Binghamton, NY)

Team	*Points*
1. Brockport State	99.25
2. Humboldt State	93
3. Millersville State	65.25
4. Montclair State	61.50
5. John Carroll	57
6. Cortland State	50
7. St. Lawrence	41.50
8. Lycoming	39.75
9. Elizabethtown	39.50
10. Maryville	37.50
11. Coe	37.25
12. Binghamton State	36.75
13. Wartburg	35
14. Upper Iowa	33.75
15. Trenton State	32.50
16. Ashland	30.25
17. Oswego State	28.25
18. Massachusetts Maritime	24.50
19. Hiram	16
20. Cornell College	14.50
21. William Penn	12.50
22. Olivet, Swarthmore	12.25
24. Gettysburg	11.75
25. Augustana (IL)	11.50
26. Union	10.75
27. Mansfield State	10
28. Wheaton	9
29. Salisbury State	8.50
30. Plymouth State	8
31. Hamline, Kutztown State, Ursinus	7.50
34. Lebanon Valley, York (PA), New York Maritime	6.50
37. Glassboro State	6
38. Rochester Tech	5.50
39. St. Thomas	5
40. Washington and Jefferson	4.75
41. Allegheny	4
42. Case Western Reserve	3.50
43. Adrian, Delaware Valley, Ferris State, Luther, North Central, Western New England	3
49. California State College (Stanislaus)	2.75
50. Capital, Grove City, Moravian	2.50
53. SUNY at Albany, Amherst, Lynchburg, Marietta, St. John Fisher, Oberlin, Ohio Northern, Oneonta State, Postsdam State, Washington and Lee	2
63. Baldwin-Wallace, MacMurray, Mount Union, Ripon, Thiel	1.50
68. Coast Guard, Geneseo State	1
70. Buena Vista, Lawrence, Lowell	.50

Place winners

118-lb class
1. Eric Mast (Elizabethtown)
2. Scott Puzia (Trenton State)
3. Joe Smith (Upper Iowa)
4. Jerome Goodfellow (Brockport State)
5. Bob Ortenzio (Gettysburg)
6. Keith Fabrizi (Hiram)

126-lb class
1. Andy Zook (Millersville State)
2. Jeff Mase (Montclair State)
3. Steve Cella (Brockport State)
4. Ralph Melia (Maryville)
5. Doug Englert (Cornell College)
6. Mike Arnold (Ashland)

134-lb class
1. Ken Mallory (Montclair State)
2. Pete Rossi (Cortland State)
3. Steve Deike (Wartburg)
4. Steve Holley (Augustana of South Dakota)
5. Gary Heim (Elizabethtown)
6. Dan Ireland (Millersville State)

142-lb class
1. Steve Cavayero (Binghamton State)
2. Jim Luster (Humboldt State)
3. Gary wood (William Penn)
4. Harold Shaw (Lycoming)
5. Scott Hill (Brockport State)
6. Charles Breithoff (Trenton State)

150-lb class
1. Fran Presley (Millersville State)
2. Craig Savitsky (Lycoming)
3. Bob Brenton (Brockport State)
4. Mike Harr (Humboldt State)
5. Dick Krueger (Upper Iowa)
6. Kevin Brandenburg (Hiram)

158-lb class
1. Mitch Brown (St. Lawrence)
2. Mike Karges (Humboldt State)
3. Jeff Freedman (Ashland)
4. Bill Rawdings (Swarthmore)
5. Steve Borja (Lycoming)
6. Rick Armstrong (Cortland State)

167-lb class
1. Jim Weir (John Carroll)
2. Kris Henry (Humboldt State)
3. Jim Bruck (Coe)
4. Mike Carra (Binghamton State)
5. Matt Staples (Plymouth State)
6. Bill Benthert (St. Lawrence)

177-lb class
1. Rich Sippel (Brockport State)
2. Brad Bowman (John Carroll)
3. Wayne Dunn (Maryville)
4. Mike Paquette (Union)
5. Tom Littauer (Wheaton)
6. Alan Callahan (Ursinus)

190-lb class
1. Eric Woolsey (Humboldt State)
2. Bob Menz (Cortland State)
3. Paul Guillaume (Wartburg)
4. Bob Valentine (Maryville)
5. Leon Dunnam (Massachusetts Maritime)
6. John Truscello (Lebanon Valley)

Heavyweight
1. Mackey Tindall (Brockport State)
2. Gary Long (Coe)
3. Bill Kahl (John Carroll)
4. Art Sopelsa (Montclair State)
5. Kevin Andrew (Upper Iowa)
6. James Hauptfleisch (Oswego State)

1978 (at Wheaton College, Wheaton, IL)

Team	*Points*
1. Buffalo	91.75
2. Millersville State	90
3. Humboldt State	71.50
4. Cortland State	64.50
5. Binghamton State	63.50
6. St. Lawrence	51.25
7. Brockport State	50
8. Montclair State	48
9. Concordia (MN)	46.25
10. Minnesota (Morris)	36
11. John Carroll	34.75
12. Salisbury State	29.25
13. Trenton State	28.75
14. Hiram, Wartburg	27.75
16. Ohio Northern	25
17. Baldwin-Wallace	24.75
18. Ashland	24
19. Luther	20.75
20. Mount Union	20
21. Upper Iowa	19
22. Coe	17.25
23. Gettysburg	15.75
24. Mansfield State	15.50
25. Maryville	13.50
26. Potsdam State	12.50
27. Lycoming	11.75
28. St. Thomas	11
29. Coast Guard	10.25
30. Ursinus	8
31. Wheaton	7.50
32. Swarthmore	7
33. Cornell College, Kalamazoo, Muskingum, York (PA)	6.50
37. Grove City, Hamline	6
39. Oswego State	5.50
40. Delaware Valley, North Central	5
42. Central of Iowa	4.50
43. Capital, Union (NY)	4

Team	*Points*
45. Albany State, St. John Fisher	.75
47. Olivet, Thiel	3.50
49. Augustana (IL)	3
50. Alma, Elizabethtown, MacMurray, Washington and Jefferson	2.50
54. Allegheny, Massachusetts Maritime, New York Maritime, Ripon, Williams, Worcester Tech	2
60. DePauw, Kutztown State, Oneonta State, Rochester, Pomona-Pitzer, Nebraska Wesleyan, Washington (MO)	1.50
67. Dubuque, Geneseo State, Lynchburg, Wabash, Washington and Lee, Wesleyan	1

Place winners

118-lb class
1. Henry Callie (Millersville State)
2. Kirby Frank (Minnesota-Morris)
3. Joe Smith (Upper Iowa)
4. George White (Humboldt State)
5. Raymond Porteus (Brockport State)
6. James Pecori (St. Lawrence)

126-lb class
1. Michael Rossetti (Trenton State)
2. Michael Jacoutot (Buffalo)
3. Steven Darling (Binghamton State)
4. Mike Arnold (Ashland)
5. Craig Helmuth (Gettysburg)
6. John Little (Millersville State)

134-lb class
1. Ken Mallory (Montclair State)
2. Pete Rossi (Cortland State)
3. Andrew Zook (Millersville State)
4. Steve Deike (Wartburg)
5. Barry Barone (St. Lawrence)
6. Steve Crooks (Kalamazoo)

142-lb class
1. Steven Cavayero (Binghamton State)
2. Dan Boos (Luther)
3. Rafael Soto (Brockport State)
4. Mike Blakely (Montclair State)
5. Stephen Hohl (Ohio Northern)
6. Chris Donaldson (Coe)

150-lb class
1. Francis Presley (Millersville State)
2. Mark Jensen (Concordia)
3. Kirk Anderson (Buffalo)
4. Doug Burton (Ohio Northern)
5. Kevin Brandenburg (Hiram)
6. Mike Sickles (Montclair State)

158-lb class
1. Rick Armstrong (Cortland State)
2. Ronald Reedy (Binghamton State)
3. Mitch Brown (St. Lawrence)
4. Tom Pender (Humboldt State)
5. Bruce Hadsell (Buffalo)
6. Kevin McNamer (St. Thomas)

167-lb class
1. Jim Weir (John Carroll)
2. Ken Berry (Hiram)
3. Roy Pikulski (Mansfield State)
4. Wayne Dunn (Maryville)
5. Mark Jarosz (Salisbury State)
6. David Baugham (Grove City)

177-lb class
1. Paul Petrella (Baldwin-Wallace)
2. Wayne Nickerson (Humboldt State)
3. Charles White (Millersville State)
4. David Mitchell (Buffalo)
5. Joseph Jarosz (Salisbury State)
6. Rich Sippel (Brockport State)

190-lb class
1. Eric Woolsey (Humboldt State)
2. Robert Menz (Cortland State)
3. Dan Harmon (Brockport State)
4. Jeff Wheeler (Buffalo)
5. Dennis Koslowski (Minnesota at Morris)
6. Mike Broghammer (Wartburg)

Heavyweight
1. Barry Bennett (Concordia)
2. Ken Wilcox (Mount Union)

3. Paul Curka (Buffalo)
4. Loren Hacker (Minnesota at Morris)
5. David Hudson (St. Lawrence)
6. John Patt (Potsdam State)

1979 (at Humboldt State University, Arcata, CA)

Team	*Points*
1. Trenton State	77.75
2. Brockport State	77.50
3. Salisbury State	75
4. Minnesota at Morris	56.75
5. Montclair State	54.75
6. Millersville State	48.25
7. Buffalo	48
8. Ashland	45.75
9. Humboldt State	44.75
10. William Penn	31
11. Cortland State	29
12. John Carroll	28.25
13. Lycoming	25
14. St. Lawrence, Upper Iowa	24
16 Baldwin-Wallace	23.75
17 Luther	23.50
18 Dubuque	21.50
19 Allegheny	16.50
20. California State (Stanislaus), York (PA)	14.50
22. Gettysburg	13.50
23. Western New England	12.50
24. Wheaton	11
25. Kutztown State	10.25
26. Delaware Valley	10
27. Potsdam	9
28. Concordia, Kalamazoo	8
30. Mansfield State	7.50
31. Ursinus	7
32. Juniata	6
33. Muskingum State	5.75
34. Hiram, Massachusetts Maritime	5.50
36. Case Western Reserve	5.25
37. Binghamton State, Ithaca	5
39. Coast Guard	4.75
40. Milliken	4.50
41. Hunter	4.25
42. St. John's (MN), Washington and Jefferson	4
44. Alma, Worchester Plymouth	3.50
46. Mount Union	3
47. Carthage	2.75
48. Central, Ohio Northern, Glassboro State, Marietta, Coe, Oswego State, Rhode Island, Scranton, Wabash, Wartburg	2
58. Elizabethtown	1.75
59. Fairleigh-Dickerson	1.50
60. Ripon, Adrian, Claremont-Mudd, Hamline, St. Thomas, Oneonta State, Plymouth, Swarthmore	1

Place winners

118-lb class
1. Ed Bailey (Salisbury State)
2. Henry Callie (Millersville State)
3. Thomas Jacoutot (Buffalo State)
4. Kirby Frank (Minnesota at Morris)
5. Andy Zuckerman (Trenton State)
6. Marty Nelis (Humboldt State)
7. Dan Stefancin (John Carroll)
8. George Werling (Ashland)

126-lb class
1. Mike Rossetti (Trenton State)
2. Edward Tyrrell (Buffalo)
3. Robert Ortenzio (Gettysburg)
4. Steve Fernandes (Western New England)
5. Jerry McGinty (Salisbury State)
6. Erick Rea (Ursinus)

7. Mike Arnold (Ashland)
8. Chris Moberly (Wheaton)

134-lb class

1. Kenny Mallory (Montclair State)
2. Mike Jacoutot (Trenton State)
3. John Ciotoli (Cortland State)
4. Doug Calhoun (Upper Iowa)
5. Barry Barone (St. Lawrence)
6. Steve Crooks (Kalamazoo)
7. Mark Hettinger (Ashland)
8. Chris Meyer (St. John's)

142-lb class

1. Dan Boos (Luther)
2. Mike Fredenburg (Humboldt State)
3. Mike Sickles (Montclair State)
4. Wilbur Borrero (Minnesota State)
5. John Parisella (Brockport State)
6. Glenn Jarvis (Mansfield State)
7. Brad Keith (California State, Stanislaus)
8. Pete Rossi (Cortland)

150-lb class

1. Gary Wood (William Penn)
2. Jon Sylvia (Humboldt State)
3. Joe Giani (Brockport State)
4. Tom Elcott (Allegheny)
5. Mark Jensen (Concordia)
6. Joe Paskill (Juniata)
7. Kelvin LeClair (Minnesota at Morris)
8. John Parreira (California State, Stanislaus)

158-lb class

1. Jeff Freedman (Ashland)
2. Lynwood Vandenberg (Brockport State)
3. Kevin Ruhnke (Upper Iowa)
4. Rick Armstrong (Cortland State)
5. Alex Martello (Montclair State)
6. Dave DePasquale (Millersville State)
7. Don Mason (Muskingum State)
8. Tom Lynn (Hunter)

167-lb class

1. Tom Beyer (Minnesota at Morris)
2. Britt Mock (Trenton State)
3. Prince Greene (Brockport State)
4. Brett Stamm (Wheaton)
5. Mark Johnson (Baldwin-Wallace)
6. Rick Roberts (St. Lawrence)
7. Tim Spruill (Lycoming)
8. Mike Danis (Delaware Valley)

177-lb class

1. Mark Jarosz (Salisbury State)
2. Chris Termel (Lycoming)
3. Paul Petrella (Baldwin-Wallace)
4. Mark Miller (York)
5. Rick Sipple (Brockport State)
6. Ralph Salem (Ithaca)
7. Andy Davidson (William Penn)
8. Mario Alemagno (John Carroll)

190-lb class

1. Joe Jarosz (Salisbury State)
2. Tony Smith (Brockport State)
3. Chuck Bronder (Montclair State)
4. Mike Trautman (John Carroll)
5. Dale Derr (Kutztown State)
6. Mike Burggraaf (William Penn)
7. Bill Francke (Binghamton State)
8. Jesse Canayaggia (Washington and Jefferson)

Heavyweight

1. Gene Rowell (Dubuque)
2. Paul Curka (Buffalo)
3. Wayne Witmer (Millersville State)
4. Eric Templin (Allegheny)
5. Micky Aikens (Trenton State)
6. J. Patt (Potsdam)
7. Tom Hanson (Minnesota at Morris)
8. Joel Chenevey (Ashland)

1980 (at U.S. Coast Guard Academy, State University of New York)

Team	*Points*
1. Brockport State	111.25
2. Trenton State	88.75
3. Salisbury State	80.50
4. Humboldt State	78.50
5. Millersville State	64
6. Minnesota at Morris	57.50
7. John Carroll	37.50
8. Binghamton State	31.50
9. Oswego State	30.50

Team	*Points*
10. Rochester Tech	28.50
11. Elizabethtown, Luther	26.50
13. Buffalo	24.50
14. Allegheny	23
15. Lycoming	21.75
16. Wheaton	21.25
17. Rutgers-Newark	21
18. Cornell College	18.75
19. St. Lawrence	18.50
20. Montclair State	17.50
21. Delaware Valley, Swarthmore	16.50
23. Wabash, Worcester Tech	14
25. Cortland State	13.25
26. Hiram	11.75
27. Muskingum State	11
28. Mansfield State	10.25
29. California State (Stanislaus)	9.50
30. Albany State	7
31. Buena Vista, Clarkson	6.50
33. Concordia (MN)	6
34. Oneonta State	5.25
35. Central of Iowa, Wesleyan	5
37. St. Olaf, Washington and Jefferson	4.50
39. William Penn	4.25
40. Augustana (IL)	4
41. Western New England	3.50
42. Simpson, Ursinus	3
44. Rhode Island College	2.50
45. Ripon	2.25
46. Baldwin-Wallace, Kalamazoo, Marietta, New York Maritime, Scranton, Wartburg	2
52. Juniata, North Part	1.50
54. Lebanon Valley, Ohio Northern, Susquehanna, St. John's (MN), St. Thomas, Thiel, Coe	1
61. Boston State, Capital, Case Western Reserve, Kutztown State	.50

Place winners

118-lb class
1. Jacoutot (Buffalo)
2. Bailey (Salisbury State)
3. Nellis (Humboldt State)
4. Parise (Oswego State)
5. Callie (Millersville State)
6. Tafoya (California State, Stanislaus)
7. Famiano (Brockport State)
8. Sullivan (Western New England)

126-lb class
1. Richard (Brockport State)
2. Jacoutot (Trenton State)
3. Wilson (Worcester Tech)
4. Batanian (John Carroll)
5. Benanti (Binghamton State)
6. Rod Smith (Montclair State)
7. Colwell (Cornell College)
8. Zehnder (Humboldt State)

134-lb class
1. Dolch (Salisbury State)
2. Holmes (Swarthmore)
3. Carbo (Oswego State)
4. Bervinchak (Elizabethtown)
5. Browning (Hiram)
6. Barone (St. Lawrence)
7. Battoglia (Cortland State)
8. Soares (Rhode Island C)

142-lb class
1. Fredenburg (Humboldt State)
2. Parisella (Brockport State)
3. Lazzari (Rutgers)
4. Leslie (Rochester Tech)
5. Johnson (Trenton State)
6. Maurer (Elizabethtown)
7. Dawson (Buena Vista)
8. Bowman (Oswego State)

150-lb class
1. Elcott (Allegheny)
2. Giani (Brockport State)
3. LeClair (Minnesota at Morris)
4. Hozella (Millersville State)
5. Misita (Trenton State)
6. Anderson (Elizabethtown)
7. Shaner (Lycoming)
8. Boos (Luther)

158-lb class
1. Bouslog (Luther)
2. Breithoff (Trenton State)
3. Smedley (Humboldt State)
4. Catanzarite (John Carroll)
5. Jarvis (Mansfield State)
6. Taylor (Cornell C)
7. Steele (Wesleyan)
8. Cook (Clarkson)

167-lb class
1. Stamm (Wheaton)
2. Mock (Trenton State)
3. Smith (Rochester Tech)
4. Beyer (Minnesota at Morris)
5. Vandenberg (Brockport State)
6. Antosiewicz (Montclair State)
7. DeJesus (Oneonta State)
8. Coudright (Humboldt State)

177-lb class
1. Jarosz (Salisbury State)
2. Martucci (Trenton State)
3. Greene (Brockport State)
4. Conner (Millersville State)
5. Sykes (Humboldt State)
6. Sawyer (Lycoming)
7. Robertson (Delaware Valley)
8. Hornbach (Albany State)

190-lb class
1. Koslowski (Minnesota at Morris)
2. Smith (Brockport State)
3. Lanzatella (St. Lawrence)
4. Jarosz (Salisbury State)
5. Malkovich (Humboldt State)
6. Roth (John Carroll)
7. Allen (Lycoming)
8. Burggraaf (William Penn)

Heavyweight
1. Wagner (Millersville State)
2. Ware (Binghamton State)
3. Sopelsa (Montclair State)
4. Rust (Wabash)
5. Bartholomew (Delaware Valley)
6. McLeod (Concordia)
7. Grimes (Muskingum State)
8. Ryan (Rochester Tech)

1981 (at John Carroll University, Cleveland, OH)

Team	Points
1. Trenton State	111.75
2. Brockport State	100
3. Minnesota at Morris	75.25
4. John Carroll	68.75
5. Salisbury State	57.50
6. SUNY at Binghamton	44
7. Wisconsin—Platteville, Wheaton	28
9. Wisconsin—Whitewater	26.50
10. Oswego State	26
11. Luther Iowa	24
12. California State (Stanislaus)	23.75
13. Washington and Jefferson	23
14. Elmhurst	20
15. SUNY at Albany, St. Lawrence	19
17. Buffalo University	18.75
18. Allegheny	18.50
19. Buena Vista	18
20. Muskingum State	17.25

Place winners

118-lb class
1. Dan Stefancin (John Carroll)
2. David Parisi (Oswego State)
3. Craig Gifford (Ursinus)
4. Dick Grube (Wisconsin—Oshkosh)
5. Curt Cawley (Buena Vista)
6. Tom Shiels (Minnesota at Morris)

126-lb class
1. Mike Jacoutot (Trenton State)
2. Jay McGinty (Salisbury State)
3. Jeff Merritt (Minnesota at Morris)
4. Frank Famiano (Brockport State)
5. Joe Benenati (SUNY at Binghamton)
6. Bob Eddy (Cortland State)

134-lb class
1. Chad Gross (John Carroll)
2. Andy Seras (SUNY at Albany)
3. Ron Bussey (Trenton State)
4. Pat Holmes (Swarthmore)
5. Kai Togami (Wheaton)
6. Kevin Brockway (Glass)

142-lb class
1. John Dolch (Salisbury State)
2. Dave Krivus (Washington and Jefferson)
3. Brett Wyss (Hiram)
4. Mike Morone (SUNY at Binghamton)
5. Darrel Leslie (RIT)
6. Shawn Hall (Coe)

150-lb class
1. Joe Giani (Brockport State)
2. Tom Elcott (Allegheny)
3. Mike Keogh (Minnesota at Morris)
4. Dave Schmacht (Augustana)
5. Tom Gallagher (John Carroll)
6. Martin Butler (Amherst)

158-lb class
1. Jeff Bouslog (Luther)
2. Vertis Elmore (California State, Stanislaus)
3. Mike McInerney (Salisbury State)
4. Derek Bigford (Brockport State)
5. Eric Vance (Amherst)
6. Doug Jewett (Muskingum State)

167-lb class
1. Woody Vandenburg (Brockport State)
2. Scott Slade (Buffalo)
3. Brett Mock (Trenton State)
4. Lowell Davis (Wisconsin—Platteville)
5. Dennis Hareza (John Carroll)
6. John Antosiewicz (Montclair State)

177-lb class
1. Kevin Walzac (Trenton State)
2. Tom Beyer (Minnesota at Morris)
3. Phil Lanzatella (St. Lawrence)
4. Brett Stamm (Wisconsin—Whitewater)
5. Tony Conetta (Brockport State)
6. Warren Robertson (Delaware Valley)

190-lb class
1. Tom Martucci (Trenton State)
2. Tony Smith (Brockport State)
3. Jeff Eastlick (Wisconsin—Platteville)
4. Stacy Bandy (Iowa Central)
5. Bill Francke (SUNY at Binghamton)
6. Paul Lancaster (Wheaton)

Heavyweight
1. Duane Koslowski (Minnesota at Morris)
2. Mike Jorgenson (Elmhurst)
3. Tim Carmin (Wisconsin—Whitewater)
4. Mickey Aikins (Trenton State)
5. Lester Ware (SUNY at Binghamton)
6. Greg Sattergen (Coast Guard)

1982 (at Corland State, Cortland, NY)

Team	Points
1. Brockport State	111.50
2. Trenton State	93.50
3. Oswego State	62.25
4. John Carroll	62
5. Augustana	54.50
6. Wisconsin—Oshkosh	46
7. Minnesota at Morris	42.50
8. St. Lawrence	39.50
9. Wheaton	33.50
10. Wisconsin—Whitewater	32.25

Place winners

118-lb class
1. David Parisi (Oswego State)
2. Rich Gruber (Wisconsin—Oshkosh)
3. Greg Evans (Upsala)

4. Curt Cawley (Buena Vista)
5. Greg Lanning (Luther)
6. Gary Reegor (Lebanon Valley)

126-lb class
1. Frank Famiano (Brockport State)
2. Jeff Merritt (Minnesota at Morris)
3. Orlando Caceres (Trenton State)
4. Jim Cornick (Buena Vista)
5. Tim Hardy (Wisconsin—Whitewater)
6. John Novinksa (Wisconsin—Platteville)

134-lb class
1. Steve Gernandez (Trenton State)
2. Robert Corbo (Oswego State)
3. Pat McMahon (Augustana)
4. Kai Togami (Wheaton)
5. Ron Headlee (Messiah)
6. Tony Novak (Delaware Valley)

142-lb class
1. Randy Viviani (John Carroll)
2. Ron Bussey (Trenton State)
3. Darrell Leslie (RIT)
4. Andrew Seras (SUNY at Albany)
5. Shawn Hall (Coe)
6. Mike Marone (SUNY at Binghamton)

150-lb class
1. Ron Winnie (Brockport State)
2. Martin Butler (Amherst)
3. Dale Schmacht (Augustana)
4. Todd Read (Clarkson)
5. Jeff Ill (North Central)
6. John Misita (Trenton State)

158-lb class
1. Bob Glaberman (Trenton State)
2. Derek Bigford (Brockport State)
3. Chris Casey (Augustana)
4. Mike McInerney (Salisbury State)
5. Bryan Soloman (Western New England)
6. Tod Northrup (St. Lawrence)

167-lb class
1. Jeff Cox (Brockport State)
2. Sean McCarthy (Wisconsin—Oshkosh)
3. Scott Slade (Buffalo)
4. Juan DeJesus (Oneonta State)
5. Tom Pilari (SUNY at Binghamton)
6. Pat Murphy (Trenton State)

177-lb class
1. Brett Stamm (Wheaton)
2. Anthony Connetta (Brockport State)
3. Ken Bringe (Augustana)
4. Ken Tashjy (Susquehanna)
5. Dan Coon (Alma)
6. Mark Schell (John Carroll)

190-lb class
1. Phil Lanzatella (St. Lawrence)
2. Doug Morse (Oswego State)
3. Nick D'Angelo (John Carroll)
4. David Chute (Elizabeth)
5. Randy Graves (Allegheny)
6. John Brown (Buena Vista)

Heavyweight
1. Dennis Koslowski (Minnesota at Morris)
2. Tim Carmin (Wisconsin—Whitewater)
3. Sal D'Angelo (John Carroll)
4. Malcolm McLeod (Concordia)
5. Chris Haley (Brockport State)
6. Michael Connors (St. Lawrence)

1983 (at Wheaton College, Wheaton, IL)

Team	Points
1. Brockport State	85.75
2. Trenton State	80.75
3. Augsburg	74.50
4. St. Lawrence	71
5. Augustana	52.50
6. Oswego State	38.75
7. SUNY at Albany, Luther	31.50
9. Buena Vista	28.50
10. John Carroll	28.25
11. Hunter	23.50
12. Allegheny, RIT	21
14. Ithaca	20.50
15. Concordia, Lycoming	18.50
17. Glassboro State	17.75
18. Minnesota at Morris	17.50

Team	*Points*
19. Wisconsin—Whitewater	16.75
20. Cornell College	15

Place winners

118-lb class
1. Greg Lonning (Luther)
2. John Barna (Trenton State)
3. Rick Gruber (Wisconsin—Oshkosh)
4. Bob Panariello (Ithaca)
5. Steve Gliva (Augsburg)
6. Ryan Haines (Upper Iowa)
7. Dave Averill (SUNY at Albany)
8. John Leo (SUNY at Binghamton)

126-lb class
1. Frank Famiano (Brockport State)
2. Greg Davis (Minnesota at Morris)
3. Curt Cawley (Buena Vista)
4. Orlando Caceres (Trenton State)
5. Bob Spagnolia (SUNY at Albany)
6. John Pecora (Whitehead)
7. Jim Kerr (Baldwin-Wallace)
8. Gary Reesor (Lebanon Valley)

134-lb class
1. Bob Adams (Augsburg)
2. Pat McMahon (Augustana)
3. Steve Fernandes (Trenton State)
4. Steve Miller (Cornell C)
5. Bart Morrow (Ithaca)
6. Bob Pennotti (Montclair State)
7. Ken Shull (MIT)
8. Mark Howard (Oswego State)

142-lb class
1. Darryl Leslie (RIT)
2. Ron Bussey (Trenton State)
3. Andrew Seras (SUNY at Albany)
4. Kevin Brockway (Glassboro State)
5. Dan Pantaleo (Olivet)
6. Perry Graehling (Hiram)
7. Tom Hall (Augsburg)
8. Marty Joseph (John Carroll)

150-lb class
1. Ron Winnie (Brockport State)
2. Shea Kennedy (Augsburg)
3. Dale Schmacht (Augsburg)
4. Dave Reifsteck (Wisconsin—Whitewater)
5. Ed Trizzino (Mount Union)
6. Dave Krivus (Washington and Jefferson)
7. Mike Truncale (SUNY at Binghamton)
8. Dave Alemi (York)

158-lb class
1. Chris Casey (Augsburg)
2. Mark Bowman (Oswego State)
3. Bob Glaberman (Trenton State)
4. Scott Bouslog (Luther)
5. Dennie Giaimo (SP)
6. Jon Beuter (Lycoming)
7. Don Valesky (Theil)
8. Bruce Stajnrajh (Delaware)

167-lb class
1. Todd Northrup (St. Lawrence)
2. Bruce Arvold (Augsburg)
3. Jeff Cox (Brockport State)
4. Guy Ventura (Hunter)
5. Matt Skalla (Wesleyan)
6. Mark Morgan (Lycoming)
7. Tom Stanbro (Oswego State)
8. Jim Andrich (Rutgers)

177-lb class
1. Anthony Conetta (Brockport State)
2. Leland Rogers (St. Lawrence)
3. Kevin Troche (Hunter)
4. Paul Lancaster (Wheaton)
5. Dan Coons (Alma)
6. Kurt Searvogel (Ripon)
7. Brian Bedard (Buena Vista)
8. Paul Newman (Oswego State)

190-lb class
1. Nick D'Angelo (John Carroll)
2. Phil Lanzatella (St. Lawrence)
3. Doug Morse (Oswego State)
4. James Maurer (Lycoming)
5. Brad Ellis (Glassboro State)
6. Bill Mays (York)
7. Bob Henig (Trenton State)
8. Guy Lucas (Buffalo)

Heavyweight
1. Bob Muth (Allegheny)
2. Malcolm McLeod (Concordia)

3. Mike Connors (St. Lawrence)
4. Scott Becker (Wartburg)
5. Jim Viaene (UW-State at Stout)
6. Scott Nichols (Brockport State)
7. Vic Herman (SUNY at Albany)
8. Steve Harter (Mount Union)

1984 (at SUNY at Binghamton, Binghamton, NY)

Team	Points
1. Trenton State	96.50
2. Augsburg	68.50
3. SUNY at Binghamton	62.50
4. John Carroll	58.75
5. Ithaca	58.50
6. Augustana	43
7. Oswego State	33.75
8. St. Lawrence	32.25
9. SUNY at Albany, Olivet	31
11. Wisconsin—River Falls	27.50
12. Wheaton	25.50
13. Brockport State	25
14. Western New England	23.75
15. Central of Iowa	23.50
16. Salisbury State	20.50
17. Glassboro State	20
18. Lycoming	19.50
19. Buffalo	18.50
20. Chicago	18.25

Place winners

118-lb class
1. Steve Gilva (Augsburg)
2. Bob Panariello (Ithaca)
3. John Leo (SUNY at Binghamton)
4. Scott Jehle (Cornell C)
5. Rich Gruber (Wisconsin—Oshkosh)
6. Shawn Sheldon (SUNY at Albany)
7. Bryant Hancock (Iowa Central)
8. Ed Morales (Brockport State)

126-lb class
1. Dave Averill (SUNY at Albany)
2. Orlando Caceres (Trenton State)
3. Keith Crowingshield (St. Lawrence)
4. Glenn Cogswell (Ithaca)
5. Rich Wileczek (York)
6. Tim Hardy (Wisconsin—Whitewater)
7. Murray Anderson (Central of Iowa)
8. Dan Canale (Buena Vista)

134-lb class
1. Pat McMahon (Augustana)
2. Bart Morrow (Ithaca)
3. Paul VanOosbree (Buena Vista)
4. Bob Yilek (Coe)
5. Pat Whitteking (Oswego State)
6. Tom Bennett (Augsburg)
7. Bill McHugh (Ohio Northern)
8. John Egitto (SUNY at Binghamton)

142-lb class
1. Don Pantaleo (Olivet)
2. Marty Joseph (John Carroll)
3. Larry Disimone (Trenton State)
4. Andy Komarek (Buffalo)
5. Dave Recor (Brockport State)
6. Tom Hall (Augsburg)
7. John Parry (Salisbury State)
8. Fred McColl (Glassboro State)

150-lb class
1. Shea Kennedy (Augsburg)
2. Ron Bussey (Trenton State)
3. Mike Truncale (SUNY at Binghamton)
4. Daryl Strumph (Hiram)
5. John Leone (Brockport State)
6. Ed Trizzino (Mount Union)
7. Kelly McGovern (Central of Iowa)
8. Dennis McNamara (Wisconsin—River Falls)

158-lb class
1. Bob Glaberman (Trenton State)
2. Bruce Arvold (Augsburg)
3. Mike McInerney (Salisbury State)
4. Terry Keller (Rutgers-Newark)
5. Scott Bouslog (Luther)
6. Don Valesky (Chicago)
7. Tom Diamond (Mount Union)
8. Dave VanTine (Montclair State)

167-lb class

1. Chris Casey (Augustana)
2. Brian Solomon (Western New England)
3. Keith Cavayero (SUNY at Binghamton)
4. Dave Labrecque (Olivet)
5. Tom Jobin (Buffalo)
6. Karl Lietzen (Chicago)
7. Brian Keller (Wisconsin—River Falls)
8. Brian Stamm (Wheaton)

177-lb class

1. Tom Pillari (SUNY at Binghamton)
2. Paul Lancaster (Wheaton)
3. Dave Kittay (Ithaca)
4. Mark Morgan (Lycoming)
5. John Scesa (Cortland)
6. Dave Brandvold (Wisconsin—River Falls)
7. Don Elfstrom (Wisconsin—Whitewater)
8. Duane Stanbridge (Trenton State)

190-lb class

1. Doug Morse (Oswego State)
2. Nick D'Angelo (John Carroll)
3. Bob Henig (Trenton State)
4. Gene Shin (Chicago)
5. Gary Solomon (Western New England)
6. Rob Klime (Wheaton)
7. Dale Lawrence (Central of Iowa)
8. Bill Condon (Ithaca)

Heavyweight

1. Mike Connors (St. Lawrence)
2. Mark Sullivan (John Carroll)
3. Mike Suk (Glassboro State)
4. Mike Baker (Ohio)
5. Rick Ruhm (Simpson)
6. Larry Stern (Lycoming)
7. Jay Bean (Wartburg)
8. Greg Chemlik (Augsburg)

1985 (at Augustana College, Rock Island, IL)

Team	*Points*
1. Trenton State	67
2. Iowa Central	59.50
3. Wisconsin—River Falls	58.50
4. John Carroll	52.75
5. Brockport State	52
6. Montclair State	48.50
7. Buffalo	45.25
8. Buena Vista	38
9. Augsburg	34
10. Wisconsin—Whitewater	33.50
11. Olivet	30.50
12. Ithaca	29.50
13. SUNY at Albany	26.50
14. Cornell College	25.25
15. SUNY at Binghamton	24
16. Luther	23.50
17. St. Lawrence	22
18. Thiel	19
19. Mount Union	16.50
20. Delaware Valley	15.25

Place winners

118-lb class

1. Tim Jacoutot (Trenton State)
2. Steve Gliva (Augsburg)
3. Tony Auletta (John Carroll)
4. Scott Arneson (Wisconsin—Platteville)
5. Dan Pippenger (Coast Guard)
6. Randy Cook (Mt. Union)
7. Steve Bird (Wisconsin—Whitewater)
8. Glay Hathaway (Widener)

126-lb class
1. Nick Milonas (Montclair State)
2. John Pecora (Wisconsin—Whitewater)
3. Mike Pantaleo (Olivet)
4. Tom Kessler (York)
5. Jay VanCleve (Cornell C)
6. Lee McFerren (SUNY at Albany)
7. Bob Carr (Luther)
8. Mike Sessor (Mount Union)

134-lb class
1. Scott DeTore (Brockport State)
2. Bart Morrow (Ithaca)
3. Ed Ergenbright (Iowa Central)
4. Dean Miller (Cornell C)
5. Ralph Venuto (Trenton State)
6. Phil Corbet (St. Thomas)
7. Jerry Tennant (Mount Union)
8. Tom Dowler (SUNY at Albany)

142-lb class
1. Shawn Smith (Delaware Valley)
2. Dan Pantaleo (Olivet)
3. Tom Bennett (John Carroll)
4. Paul VanOosbree (Buena Vista)
5. Tom Hall (Augsburg)
6. Ed Brady (Wisconsin—Whitewater)
7. Dave Recor (Brockport State)
8. Andy Komarek (Buffalo)

150-lb class
1. Larry DiSimone (Trenton State)
2. Mike Truncale (SUNY at Binghamton)
3. Daryl Stumph (Hiram)
4. Mike Schimp (Buena Vista)
5. John Leone (Brockport State)
6. Dave Hickson (Buffalo)
7. Joe Crispo (Wisconsin—Platteville)
8. Jason Barnett (John Carroll)

158-lb class
1. Andy Seras (SUNY at Albany)
2. Scott Bouslog (Luther)
3. Todd Slade (Brockport State)
4. Dwayne Standridge (Trenton State)
5. Dan Dresser (Buena Vista)
6. Paul Wyman (Wisconsin—Platteville)
7. Pete Rao (Buffalo)
8. Kevin Troche (Hiram)

167-lb class
1. John Monaco (Montclair State)
2. Rod Wilt (Thiel)
3. Steve Klein (Buffalo)
4. Brian Keller (Wisconsin—River Falls)
5. Karl Leitzan (Chicago)
6. Keith Cavayero (SUNY at Binghamton)
7. Jeff Bryner (Ohio Northern)
8. Mike Price (Potsdam State)

177-lb class
1. Dave Brandvold (Wisconsin—River Falls)
2. Tom Jobin (Buffalo)
3. Dave Kittay (Ithaca)
4. Sam Walker (John Carroll)
5. Duane Lawrence (Iowa Central)
6. Todd Peterson (Montclair State)
7. Tim Kemp (Bethel)
8. Terry Schuler (Wisconsin—Whitewater)

190-lb class
1. Leland Rogers (St. Lawrence)
2. Dale Lawrence (Central of Iowa)
3. Steve Deckard (Susquehanna)
4. Gary Solomon (Western New England)
5. Terry Burnat (Potsdam State)
6. Doyle Naig (Buena Vista)
7. Kevin Wolff (Milliken)
8. Mark Gaspich (Montclair State)

Heavyweight
1. Matt Renn (Wisconsin—River Falls)
2. Scott Storjohann (Central of Iowa)
3. Jim O'Halloran (Salisbury State)
4. Sal D'Angelo (John Carroll)
5. Tim Hessing (Augustana)
6. Greg Chmelik (Ausburg)
7. Larry Stern (Lycoming)
8. Mark Lickman (Oswego State)

1986 (at Trenton State, Trenton, NJ)

Team	*Points*
1. Montclair State	87.75
2. Brockport State	78
3. Buena Vista	60.25
4. John Carroll	55.25
5. Trenton State	53.50
6. Ithaca	52.75
7. SUNY at Albany	51.75
8. Iowa Central	42
9. St. Lawrence	37.75
10. Delaware State	34.25
11. Glassboro State	33.75
12. Buffalo	29.50
13. Cornell College, St. Olaf, Upper Iowa	22
16. SUNY at Binghamton	21
17. Augsburg	20.75
18. Wisconsin—Whitewater	18.50
19. Chicago	17.50
20. Wisconsin—River Falls	15.50

Place winners

118-lb class
1. Shawn Shedlon (SUNY at Albany)
2. Pete Gonzales (Montclair State)
3. Tim Jacoutot (Trenton State)
4. Rick Williams (Delaware State)
5. Guy Bowers (Cortland State)
6. Paul Schuman (Ithaca)
7. Tim Ebrehard (Concordia)
8. Pete Regalado (Augustana)

126-lb class
1. Nick Milonas (Montclair State)
2. Tim Hackel (Iowa Central)
3. Randy Simpson (Capital)
4. Pete Hayek (John Carroll)
5. Glenn Cogwell (Ithaca)
6. Keith Gliva (Augustana)
7. Jay Van Cleve (Cornell C)
8. Pat Hart (SUNY at Binghamton)

134-lb class
1. Mark Shortsleeve (St. Lawrence)
2. Scott DeTore (Brockport State)
3. Ralph Venuto (Trenton State)
4. Dean Miller (Cornell C)
5. Darren Scott (Ohio Northern)
6. Greg Roehrick (St. Olaf)
7. Dail Fellin (Buena Vista)
8. Phil Corbett (St. Thomas)

142-lb class
1. Shaun Smith (Delaware Valley)
2. Mark Gumble (SUNY at Binghamton)
3. Paul VanOosbree (Buena Vista)
4. Pete Mankowich (Ithaca)
5. Rob Allison (Brockport State)
6. Mark Nace (Montclair State)
7. Karl Monaco (Trenton State)
8. Roy Wilt (Thiel)

150-lb class
1. Brian Barrett (Glassboro State)
2. John Leone (Brockport State)
3. Kevin Azinger (Iowa Central)
4. Joe Darling (Oswego State)
5. Daryl Stumph (Hiram)
6. Jim Fox (SUNY at Albany)
7. Jeff Payne (Allegheny)
8. Mike Schimp (Buena Vista)

158-lb class
1. Todd Slade (Brockport State)
2. Dan Dresser (Buena Vista)
3. Dwayne Standridge (Trenton State)
4. Rick Spaulding (St. Lawrence)
5. Kelly McGovern (Iowa Central)
6. Jason Barnett (John Carroll)
7. Dave Zariczny (Cortland State)
8. Roger Forystek (St. Olaf)

167-lb class
1. Steve Klein (Buffalo)
2. Steve Hile (Ithaca)
3. Rod Wilt (Thiel)
4. Brian Keller (Wisconsin—River Falls)
5. Jeff Schlieff (Augsburg)
6. Willie Lake (Olivet)

7. Tony DeCarlo (John Carroll)
8. Jay Hines (Mount Union)

177-lb class

1. John Moncao (Montclair State)
2. Sam Walker (John Carroll)
3. Kevin Besch (Buena Vista)
4. Rick Kichman (Lebanon Valley)
5. Terry Schuler (Wisconsin—Whitewater)
6. Joe Adam (Trinity)
7. Tom Tuomi (Concordia)
8. Steve Goodall (Cornell C)

190-lb class

1. Mike Himes (Upper Iowa)
2. Gene Shin (Chicago)
3. Dwayne Fischer (Wisconsin—Oshkosh)
4. Steve Kopecky (Wisconsin—Whitewater)
5. Dan Dugan (Glassboro State)
6. Greg Finnan (John Carroll)
7. Todd McArdell (Cortland State)
8. Dean Gavin (Wartburg)

Heavyweight

1. Chris Tironi (SUNY at Albany)
2. Jim Petty (Montclair State)
3. Rusty Middlebrook (Brockport State)
4. Rich Kane (Ithaca)
5. Rolf Carlson (St. Olaf)
6. Dave Witt (Stout)
7. Craig Hanson (Buena Vista)
8. Russ Sutherland (Buffalo)

1987 (at University of Buffalo, Buffalo, NY)

Team	*Points*
1. Trenton State	107.50
2. Brockport State	70.75
3. SUNY at Albany	70.50
4. Montclair State	60.50
5. Buffalo	57
6. John Carroll	52
7. Wisconsin—Whitewater	46.50
8. Iowa Central	40.75
9. St. Lawrence	36.50
10. Delaware Valley	35
11. Ohio Northern	25.75
12. Ithaca	24.50
13. St. Olaf	24.25
14. St. Thomas	22.25
15. Olivet	18.75
16. Upper Iowa	18.50
17. Augsburg, Buena Vista	17.50
19. Oneonta State	17.25
20. Glassboro State	17

Place winners

118-lb class

1. Tim Jacoutot (Trenton State)
2. Shawn Sheldon (SUNY at Albany)
3. Bob Panariello (Ithaca)
4. John Canty (St. Lawrence)
5. Dan Franch (North Central)
6. Rich Williams (Delaware Valley)
7. Matt Diehl (Iowa Central)
8. Rob Beck (Buffalo)

126-lb class

1. Tim Hackel (Iowa Central)
2. John Beatty (Augsburg)
3. Pete Gonzales (Montclair State)
4. Pete Hayek (John Carroll)
5. Keith Crowingshield (St. Lawrence)
6. Mike Pantaleo (Olivet)
7. Jose Munoz (Brockport State)
8. Rich Widmer (Trenton State)

134-lb class

1. Darren Scott (Ohio Northern)
2. Ralph Venuto (Trenton State)
3. Desmond Basnight (Oneonta State)
4. Greg Roehrick (St. Olaf)
5. Paul Veak (Iowa Central)
6. Steve Irving (Buffalo)
7. Andy Lonning (Luther)
8. Keith Peavy (Brockport State)

142-lb class

1. Karl Monaco (Montclair State)
2. Shawn Smith (Delaware Valley)
3. Mark Gumbel (SUNY at Binghamton)

4. Rodney Smith (Western New England)
5. Dean Salvaggio (Buffalo)
6. Shawn Voight (Cornell C)
7. Dan Donahue (Ursinus)
8. Todd Hibbs (Mount Union)

150-lb class
1. Ed Brady (Wisconsin—Whitewater)
2. Brian Barratt (Glassboro State)
3. Dave Ricor (Brockport State)
4. Dave Hickson (Buffalo)
5. Ed Fogarty (St. Thomas)
6. Tom Bennett (John Carroll)
7. Jay Peichel (Swarthmore)
8. John Verdes (Heidelberg)

158-lb class
1. John Leone (Brockport State)
2. Dwayne Standridge (Millikin)
3. State Raczek (Wisconsin—Platteville)
4. Ken Mansell (MacMurray)
5. Dale Massop (St. Thomas)
6. Tom Mankowich (Ithaca)
7. Jay McGovern (Iowa Central)
8. Dave McLaughlin (William Penn)

167-lb class
1. John Monaco (Montclair State)
2. Matt Ryan (SUNY at Albany)
3. Todd Slade (Brockport)
4. Jason Barnett (John Carroll)
5. Jeff Hoing (Buena Vista)
6. Randy Worrell (Delaware Valley)
7. Jay Hines (Mount Union)
8. Dennis McNamara (St. Thomas)

177-lb class
1. Greg McDonald (Trenton State)
2. Terry Schuler (Wisconsin—Whitewater)
3. Marty Pidel (SUNY at Albany)
4. Tim Servies (Wabash)
5. Joe Errigo (Buffalo)
6. Jim Hunter (Cortland State)
7. Kevin Besch (Buena Vista)
8. Garth Lakitsky (Delaware Valley)

190-lb class
1. Vic Pozsonyi (Trenton State)
2. Mike Himes (Upper Iowa)
3. Paul Bailey (Buffalo)
4. John Raut (Olivet)
5. Tom Tuomi (Concordia)
6. Steve Kopecky (Wisconsin—Whitewater)
7. Ed Smith (Montclair State)
8. Brad Eggers (Iowa Central)

Heavyweight
1. Chris Tironi (SUNY at Albany)
2. Mark Sullivan (John Carroll)
3. Pat Conners (St. Lawrence)
4. Rolf Carlson (St. Olaf)
5. Jon Buhner (Oswego State)
6. Russ Sutherland (Buffalo)
7. Rusty Middlebrook (Brockport State)
8. Al Nardone (Kean)

1988 (at Wheaton College, Wheaton, IL)

Team	*Points*
1. St. Lawrence	71
2. Montclair State	66.75
3. Ithaca	56.25
4. Trenton State	55.25
5. Buffalo	43.50
6. SUNY at Binghamton	39.50
7. Buena Vista	33
8. Augsburg	28.25
9. Wisconsin—Whitewater	27.50
10. Delaware Valley	26.50
11. Cornell College	25.75
12. John Carroll	25
13. St. Thomas	23.50
14. Loras	23
15. Chicago	22.75
16. Upper Iowa	21.50
17. Muskingum State	20.50
18. Millikin	17.75
19. William Penn	16.50
20. Kean	15

Place winners

118-lb class
1. Tim Jacoutot (Trenton State)
2. John Conty (St. Lawrence)
3. Joe Dasti (Kean)
4. Scott Martin (Rhode Island)
5. Rob Beck (Buffalo)
6. Dave Jordan (Buena Vista)
7. Chris Hoffman (Iowa Central)
8. Ryan Burns (Wisconsin, Stevens Point)

126-lb class
1. Pete Gonzales (Montclair State)
2. Brad Brosdahl (Buena Vista)
3. Rick Fioro (SUNY at Albany)
4. John Fagen (Trenton State)
5. Scott Arneson (Wisconsin—Platteville)
6. Brad Rogers (Ohio Northern)
7. Bob Carrigan (Chicago)
8. Stan Rhodes (John Carroll)

134-lb class
1. John Beatty (Augsburg)
2. Joe Boehenski (Chicago)
3. Kevin Bishop (St. Lawrence)
4. Scott Sondergren (Coast Guard)
5. Tony Pendolino (Allegheny)
6. Tim Cotter (Ithaca)
7. Jeff Bakken (Buena Vista)
8. Scott Kaye (Ohio Northern)

142-lb class
1. Karl Monaco (Montclair State)
2. Dean Salvaggio (Buffalo)
3. Shawn Voight (Cornell C)
4. Todd Bender (Wisconsin—Whitewater)
5. Rodney Smith (Western New England)
6. Brian Reed (St. Lawrence)
7. Larry Pilcher (Buena Vista)
8. Rich Venuto (Trenton State)

150-lb class
1. Mark Gumble (SUNY at Binghamton)
2. Dave McLaughlin (William Penn)
3. Dan Keating (St. Lawrence)
4. Bob Kays (Salisbury State)
5. Scott Miller (Case)
6. Marty Nichols (Ithaca)
7. Dave Zariczny (Cortland State)
8. Matt Kretlow (Augsburg)

158-lb class
1. Mike Cronmiller (Ithaca)
2. Mark Ambrose (Delaware Valley)
3. Jim Capone (Buffalo)
4. Mickey Best (Wheaton)
5. Tony Guinones (Loras)
6. Bill Cioffi (Glassboro State)
7. Tom Beeman (Luther)
8. Dave Berg (St. Thomas)

167-lb class
1. Mark Hoppel (Muskingum State)
2. Joe Schmidt (John Carroll)
3. Dana Spires (Thiel)
4. Matt Parmely (Cornell C)
5. Gary Ridout (Simpson)
6. Chris LaBrecque (Susquehanna)
7. Jim Gorman (Hunter)
8. Brian Glatz (William Penn)

177-lb class
1. Pete Georgeoutsos (Montclair State)
2. Dennis McNamara (St. Thomas)
3. Blair Early (Loras)
4. Brett Larson (Concordia, MN)
5. Dan Beiller (Ithaca)
6. Garth Lakitsky (Delaware Valley)
7. Jack Denholm (Wartsburg)
8. Joe Errigo (Buffalo)

190-lb class
1. Mike Himes (Upper Iowa)
2. Vic Pozsonyi (Trenton State)
3. Terry Schuler (Wisconsin—Whitewater)
4. Tom Tuomi (Concordia, MN)
5. Todd McArdle (Cortland State)
6. Mike Fusilli (Ithaca)
7. Dean Gavin (Wartburg)
8. Larry Danko (Kings)

Heavyweight
1. Pat Conners (St. Lawrence)
2. Kip Crandall (Millikin)
3. Greg Geisenhof (SUNY at Binghamton)

4. John Buhner (Oswego State)
5. Steve Lacher (Mount Union)
6. Mike Gilmore (Lycoming)
7. Bob Bentz (Carthage)
8. Rich Kane (Ithaca)

Table 8.6
NAIA Tournament

1958 (at Mankato State University, Mankato, MN)

Team	Points
1. Mankato State	97
2. Iowa State Teachers	69
3. Northern Illinois	45
4. South Dakota State	30
5. St. Cloud State	20
6. Wartburg	19
7. Illinois State, St. John's (MN), Winona State	14
10. Indiana Central	11
11. St. Thomas	10
12. Eastern Illinois, Gustavus Adolphus	7
14. Luther	5
15. Bemidji State	3

Place winners

115-lb class
1. Jack Thamert (Mankato State)
2. Allen Morgan (Indiana Central)
3. Gulberg (Iowa State Teachers)
4. Fredericks (Wartburg)

123-lb class
1. Dale Tessler (Northern Illinois)
2. John DeLozier (Winona State)
3. Sauer (St. John's)
4. Lundholm (Mankato State)

130-lb class
1. Jerry Lane (Iowa State Teachers)
2. Jerry Sharp (Mankato State)
3. Semetis (Eastern Illinois)
4. Chellevold (Wartburg)

137-lb class
1. John Vovos (Iowa State Teachers)
2. Robert Juarez (Illinois Normal)
3. Dravis (Mankato State)
4. Brown (Bemidji State)

147-lb class
1. Jack Anderson (Mankato State)
2. Jerry Ray (Iowa State Teachers)
3. Grach (Northern Illinois)
4. Betzler (St. John's)

157-lb class
1. Dick Heaton (Iowa State Teachers)
2. Guss Gleiter (South Dakota State)
3. Kelly (Mankato State)
4. L. Fretheim (Luther)

167-lb class
1. Dick Anderson (St. Cloud State)
2. Gerry Geinger (Iowa State Teachers)
3. Young (Northern Illinois)
4. Hess (Illinois Normal)

177-lb class
1. Al Blanshan (Mankato State)
2. Roy Conrad (Northern Illinois)
3. Alfredson (South Dakota State)
4. L. Peipers (Winona State)

191-lb class
1. Roy Minter (Mankato State)
2. Richard Gurtek (St. Thomas)
3. Jensen (South Dakota State)
4. Hudson (Northern Illinois)

Heavyweight
1. Dick Kubes (Mankato State)
2. Bruce Brye (Wartburg)
3. Sponberg (Gustavus Adolphus)
4. McHugh (St. Cloud State)

1959 (at Northern Illinois University, Dekalb, IL)

Team	Points
1. Mankato State	64
2. Southern Illinois	52
3. Lock Haven	41
4. Northern Illinois	23
5. St. Cloud State	19
6. Wartburg	18
7. Winona State	16
8. Illinois State	14
9. Central Michigan	13
10. Indiana Central	12
11. Luther, Lycoming	11
13. Moorhead State	9
14. Findlay	7
15. Fort Hays	5

Place winners

115-lb class
1. Gray Simons (Lock Haven)
2. Jack Thamert (Mankato State)
3. Dale Votapka (Fort Hays)
4. Al Morgan (Indiana Central)

123-lb class
1. Maynard Nelson (Mankato State)
2. Dan Welliever (Indiana Central)
3. Jack Bronner (Luther)
4. Rufus Bankole (Moorhead State)

130-lb class
1. Jim Bledsoe (Southern Illinois)
2. Dave Frame (Mankato State)
3. Bill Sushak (Findlay)
4. Charles Burman (Wartburg)

137-lb class
1. John Rollins (Central Michigan)
2. Henry Shaw (Lock Haven)
3. Ray Mueller (Northern Illinois)
4. Harry Romig (Lycoming)

147-lb class
1. Ralph Clark (Lock Haven)
2. Lee Grubbs (Southern Illinois)
3. Bill Lewis (Mankato State)
4. Robert Pac (Lycoming)

157-lb class
1. Herman Ayres (Southern Illinois)
2. Bob Klick (St. Cloud State)
3. John Kreamer (Lock Haven)
4. Bill Young (Northern Illinois)

167-lb class
1. Lowell Glynn (Mankato State)
2. Dick Anderson (St. Cloud State)
3. Ron Fretheim (Luther)
4. Paul Evenson (Winona State)

177-lb class
1. Wally Hess (Illinois State)
2. Roy Conrad (Northern Illinois)
3. Jerry Slattery (Mankato State)
4. Al Hassman (Wartburg)

191-lb class
1. Marion Rushing (Southern Illinois)
2. Al Blanshan (Mankato State)
3. Tom Seeman (Northern Illinois)
4. Henry Hettwer (Moorhead State)

Heavyweight
1. Jerry Wedemeier (Winona State)
2. Bruce Brye (Wartburg)
3. Houston Antwine (Southern Illinois)
4. Ron Wiger (Moorhead State)

1960 (at Lock Haven State College, Lock Haven, PA)

Team	Points
1. Bloomsburg State	79
2. Southern Illinois	73
3. Lock Haven	62
4. Wilkes	23
5. Lycoming	21
6. Winona State	18
7. Appalachian	16
8. Baldwin-Wallace	13
9. Central Michigan, Fort Hays, Moorhead State	10
12. Findlay	7
13. Edinboro	6
14. Shippensburg State	5
15. Oregon College	2

Place winners

118-lb class
1. Gray Simons (Lock Haven)
2. Votapka (Fort Hays)
3. Yeager (W)
4. Hughes (Bloomsburg State)

123-lb class
1. Bledsoe (Southern Illinois)
2. Gorant (Bloomsburg State)
3. Walker (Lock Haven)
4. Wolfe (Lycoming)

130-lb class
1. Sullivan (Bloomsburg State)
2. Cook (Appalachian)
3. Lynch (Lock Haven)
4. Kehrig (Lycoming)

137-lb class
1. Romig (Lycoming)
2. Rollins (Central Michigan)
3. Rimple (Bloomsburg State)
4. Morrace (Winona State)

147-lb class
1. Ralph Clark (Lock Haven)
2. Crider (Southern Illinois)
3. Rider (Bloomsburg State)
4. Dellapina (Findlay)

157-lb class
1. Rohm (Bloomsburg State)
2. Lewis (Southern Illinois)
3. Cox (Appalachian)
4. Sinibaldi (Lock Haven)

167-lb class
1. Kreamer (Lock Haven)
2. Cronen (Moorhead State)
3. Plapp (Southern Illinois)
4. Dixon (Bloomsburg State)

177-lb class
1. Antinnes (Wilkes)
2. Houston (Southern Illinois)
3. Elinsky (Bloomsburg State)
4. Manning (Edinboro)

191-lb class
1. Moore (Southern Illinois)
2. Poust (Bloomsburg State)
3. Herman (Wilkes)
4. Lewis (Baldwin-Wallace)

Heavyweight
1. Antwine (Southern Illinois)
2. Wedemeier (Winona State)
3. Sprague (Baldwin-Wallace)
4. Garson (Bloomsburg)

1961 (at Colorado Mines, Golden CO)

Team	*Points*
1. Lock Haven	50
2. Colorado Mines	35
3. Northern Illinois	34
4. Winona State	32
5. Bloomsburg State, Eastern Illinois	30
7. Indiana Central	22
8. Moorhead State	21
9. St. Cloud State, Luther	17
11. Central Michigan	13
12. Graceland	11
13. Augustana, Valley City, River Falls	10

Place winners

115-lb class
1. Gray Simons (Lock Haven)
2. Banks Swan (Moorhead State)
3. Beltch (Fort Hays)
4. Seery (Colorado State)

123-lb class
1. Earl Stottler (Moorhead State)
2. Don Welliever (Indiana Central)
3. Tisone (Colorado Mines)
4. Willis (Winona State)

130-lb class
1. Charles Walizer (Lock Haven)
2. Terry Shockley (Augustana)
3. Hasse (Colorado Mines)
4. Kontos (Northern Illinois)

137-lb class
1. John Rollins (Central Michigan)
2. John Day (Lock Haven)
3. Moracco (Winona State)
4. Auxier (Graceland)

147-lb class
1. Monte Sinner (St. Cloud State)
2. William Bailey (Lock Haven)
3. Haworth (Winona State)
4. Fix (Colorado Mines)

157-lb class
1. Gene Dixon (Bloomsburg State)
2. Ralph Cundiff (Eastern Illinois)
3. Frank (Bemidji State)
4. Martin (Indiana Central)

167-lb class
1. Ray Guzak (Northern Illinois)
2. Chuck Peterson (Luther)
3. Gardner (Eastern Illinois)
4. Johnson (Indiana Central)

177-lb class
1. Roy Conrad (Northern Illinois)
2. Don Meyers (Colorado Mines)
3. Stauffer (Wisconsin—Superior)
4. Stephenson (Wisconsin—Stout)

191-lb class
1. Bill Garson (Bloomsburg State)
2. Jack Ramey (Valley City)
3. Stracke (Eastern Illinois)
4. St. Marie (St. Cloud State)

Heavyweight
1. Jerry Wedemeier (Winona State)
2. Larry Julien (Wisconsin—River Falls)
3. Pruisner (Luther)
4. Wagner (Dickinson State)

1962 (at Winona State College, Winona, MN)

Team	*Points*
1. Bloomsburg State	56
2. Lock Haven	47
3. Lycoming	39
4. Moorhead State	28
5. Winona State	27
6. Eastern Illinois	24
7. Fort Hays, Nebraska at Omaha, Graceland	17
10. Western Illinois	16
11. Millersville State, Wisconsin—Superior	15
13. West Liberty State	14
14. St. John's (MN)	13
15. Dickinson State	12

Place winners

115-lb class
1. Gray Simons (Lock Haven)
2. Jim Beltch (Fort Hays)
3. Bill McCreary (Wisconsin—Superior)
4. Bud Schmitz (Valley City)

123-lb class
1. Bucky Maughan (Moorhead State)
2. Fred Powell (Lock Haven)
3. Bill Hughes (Bloomsburg State)
4. Lee Wolfe (Lycoming)

130-lb class
1. Robert Douglas (West Liberty State)
2. Bill Kehrig (Lycoming)
3. Charles Walizer (Lock Haven)
4. Ed Taylor (Bloomsburg State)

137-lb class
1. Jack Day (Lock Haven)
2. Dick Scorese (Bloomsburg State)
3. Harlan Leopole (Concordia)
4. Grant Nelson (St. Cloud State)

147-lb class
1. Bill Gutermuth (Lycoming)
2. Jim Shipp (Western Illinois)
3. Laverne Alton (Portland State)
4. Charles Ginther (Hillsdale)

157-lb class
1. Walt Kottmeyer (Millersville State)
2. George Crenshaw (Nebraska at Omaha)
3. Roger Saunders (West Chester)
4. Maurice Rogers (Indiana State)

167-lb class
1. Robert Hall (Bloomsburg State)
2. Gary Moyer (Fairmont State)
3. Gary Sage (Graceland)
4. Ron Wynne (Western Illinois)

177-lb class
1. Jim Gardner (Eastern Illinois)
2. Gary Collins (Graceland)
3. Tim Stauffer (Wisconsin—Superior)
4. Pat Flaherty (Winona State)

191-lb class
1. Bill Garson (Bloomsburg State)
2. Ben Pulkrabek (St. John's)
3. Larry Sciacchetano (Montclair State)
4. Don Neece (Eastern Illinois)

Heavyweight
1. Jerry Wedemeier (Winona State)
2. Charles Wagner (Dickinson State)
3. John Dano (Moorhead State)
4. Joe Confer (Lycoming)

1963 (at Lock Haven State College, Lockhaven, PA)

Team	*Points*
1. Lock Haven	61
2. Bloomsburg State	60
3. St. Cloud State	49
4. Indiana State	35
5. Wisconsin, Superior	32
6. CW Post	29
7. Wisconsin—River Falls	25
8. Moorhead State	22
9. Graceland	18
10. Hillsdale	16
11. West Chester, Nebraska at Omaha	14

Place winners

115-lb class
1. D. Hazewinkle (St. Cloud State)
2. Hughes (Bloomsburg State)
3. McGinley (Wilkes)
4. Welliever (Indiana State)

123-lb class
1. Maughan (Moorhead State)
2. Powell (Lock Haven)
3. Guzzo (East Stroudsburg)
4. Caslow (Clarion State)

130-lb class
1. Walizer (Lock Haven)
2. Douglas (West Liberty State)
3. McCreary (Wisconsin—Superior)
4. Hill (Indiana State)

137-lb class
1. Scorese (Bloomsburg State)
2. Mrotek (Wisconsin—River Falls)
3. Leopold (Concordia, MN)
4. Blacksmith (Bloomsburg)

147-lb class
1. Nelson (St. Cloud State)
2. Shipp (Western Illinois)
3. Culver (Wisconsin—River Falls)
4. Paule (Bloomsburg State)

157-lb class
1. Dick Duffy (CW Post)
2. Getgen (Wisconsin—Superior)
3. Marshall (Findlay)
4. Lawrey (Hillsdale)

167-lb class
1. Crenshaw (Nebraska at Omaha)
2. Ingarozza (CW Post)
3. Hall (Bloomsburg State)
4. Moyer (Fairmont)

177-lb class
1. Swope (Lock Haven)
2. Beckham (Indiana State)
3. Collikns (Graceland)
4. Washington (Lincoln U, PA)

191-lb class
1. G. Smith (St. Cloud State)
2. G. Sage (Graceland)
3. Relyea (Eastern Michigan)
4. H. Sage (West Chester)

Heavyweight
1. Garsoni (Bloomsburg State)
2. Jones (Hillsdale)

3. Zimmerman (Wisconsin—Superior)
4. Sisak (Lock Haven)

1964 (at Black Hills State Teachers College, Spearfish, SD)

Team	Points
1. Moorhead State	65
2. Lock Haven	62
3. Indiana State	46
4. Bloomsburg State	44
5. St. Cloud State	31
6. Waynesburg	24
7. East Stroudsburg	20
8. Dickinson State	17
9. Lewis and Clark, Winona State, Findlay	16
12. Arizona State College	15
13. Lincoln University (PA)	14
14. Eastern Oregon	13
15. St. Thomas	12

(Only winners available)

115-lb class
1. Jim Hazewinkel (St. Cloud State)

123-lb class
1. Fred Powell (Lock Haven)

130-lb class
1. Jim Dreitzler (Moorhead State)

137-lb class
1. Dean Bachmeier (Dickinson State)

147-lb class
1. Adam Waltz (Lock Haven)

157-lb class
1. Rollin Schimmel (Eastern Oregon)

167-lb class
1. Frank Mosier (Moorhead State)

177-lb class
1. Jerry Swope (Lock Haven)

191-lb class
1. Gary Smith (St. Cloud State)

Heavyweight
1. Bob Billberg (Moorhead State)

1965 (at Indiana State College, Terre Haute, IN)

Team	Points
1. Bloomsburg State	60
2. Lock Haven	50
3. St. Cloud State	48
4. Moorhead State, Waynesburg	46
6. Portland State	35
7. Adams State	34
8. Eastern Illinois	27
9. Indiana State	23
10. Westmar	20
11. Concordia (MN), Eastern Oregon	17
13. Findlay	16
14. Illinois State, Lewis and Clark	15

Place winners

115-lb class
1. Rick Sanders (Portland State)
2. Dave Hazewinkel (St. Cloud State)
3. Welliever (Indiana State)
4. Mooley (Moorhead State)
5. Weaver (Westmar)
6. Marquardt (Eastern Illinois)

123-lb class
1. Jim Hazewinkel (St. Cloud State)
2. Bill Robb (Bloomsburg State)
3. Severson (Adams State)
4. Kelvington (Moorhead State)

130-lb class
1. James Rolley (Bloomsburg State)
2. Doug Dufty (Concordia)
3. Trulock (Westmar)
4. Cheatwood (Eastern Illinois)

137-lb class
1. Tony Gusic (Waynesburg)
2. Ed Taylor (Bloomsburg State)
3. Johnson (Dickinson State)
4. Graves (Hillsdale)
5. Yatabe (Portland State)
6. Stuyvesant (Moorhead State)

147-lb class
1. Bill Blacksmith (Lock Haven)
2. Raphael Gonshorowski (Moorhead State)
3. Brown (Portland State)
4. Leopold (Concordia)
5. Burkhart (Indiana State)
6. Brunson (Eastern Michigan)

157-lb class
1. Frank Eisenhower (Lock Haven)
2. Floyd Marshall (Findlay)
3. Friestad (Valley City)
4. Paule (Bloomsburg State)
5. Schimmel (Eastern Oregon)
6. Deutsch (Adams State)

167-lb class
1. Mike Zrimm (Waynesburg)
2. Chuck Holliday (Eastern Oregon)
3. Vargo (Bloomsburg State)
4. Anderson (Adams State)
5. Lovelack (Western Illinois)
6. Miller (Moorhead State)

177-lb class
1. Jerry Swope (Lock Haven)
2. Bob Gary (Waynesburg)
3. Dolce (Adams State)
4. Toedman (Fort Hays)
5. Heinemi (St. Cloud State)
6. McCauley (Western Illinois)

191-lb class
1. Don Neece (Eastern Illinois)
2. Willie Williams (Illinois State)
3. Flygare (Minot)
4. Miller (East Stroudsburg State)
5. Freese (Indiana State)
6. Elling (Lock Haven)

Heavyweight
1. Harold Weight (Lewis and Clark)
2. Bob Kruse (Wayne State)
3. Billberg (Moorhead State)
4. Winters (Westmar)
5. Jackson (Fairmont State)
6. Avery (North Central)

1966 (at St. Cloud State College, St. Cloud, MN)

Team	Points
1. Lock Haven	107
2. Moorhead State	64
3. Central Washington	55
4. Adams State	52
5. St. Cloud State	33
6. Winona State	26
7. Fort Hays, Wisconsin—Superior	22
9. Minot	21
10. Clarion State	20
11. Eastern Oregon	18
12. Wisconsin—LaCrosse	15
13. Wisconsin—River Falls	14
15. East Stroudsburg, Valley City	13

Place winners

115-lb class
1. Darl Weaver (Westmar)
2. Dave Hazewinkel (St. Cloud State)
3. Ken Melchior (Lock Haven)
4. Curlee Alexander (Nebraska at Omaha)
5. Rich Kuzminski (Wisconsin—Superior)
6. Rich Tamble (Adams State)

123-lb class
1. Bob Guzzo (East Stroudsburg)
2. Ralph Adamson (Waynesburg)
3. Bob Ruedy (St. Cloud State)
4. Bob Larson (Lock Haven)
5. Ken Vandver (Western Wisconsin)
6. Dick Bane (West Liberty State)

130-lb class
1. Mike Stanley (Adams State)
2. Ken Warnick (Clarion State)

3. Bill Germann (Moorhead State)
4. Tom Thompson (Wisconsin—Superior)
5. Bil McCollum (Minot)
6. Tom Pugliese (West Liberty)

137-lb class
1. Rick Stuyvesant (Moorhead State)
2. Bob Johnson (Fort Hays)
3. Dick Rhoades (Lock Haven)
4. Leo Kinsella (Minot)
5. Don Huggins (Westmar)
6. Jim Whitmer (Appalachian)

145-lb class
1. Dennis Warren (Central Washington)
2. Howard Leopold (Concordia)
3. Nash Tillman (Adams State)
4. Adam Waltz (Lock Haven)
5. Mike Garside (Wisconsin—Superior)
6. Raphael Gonshorowski (Moorhead State)

152-lb class
1. Bill Blacksmith (Lock Haven)
2. Merle Sovereign (Winona State)
3. Dick Redfoot (Moorhead State)
4. Tom Ott (Wisconsin—Stout)
5. Jerry Kemp (Clarion State)
6. Dave Youngbluth (Linfield)

160-lb class
1. Jim Blacksmith (Lock Haven)
2. Rollin Schimmel (Eastern Oregon)
3. Jim Tanniehill (Winona State)
4. Bob Anderson (Adams State)
5. Carl Olson (St. Cloud State)
6. Vern Non Merkley (Central Washington)

167-lb class
1. Lamoin Merkley (Central Washington)
2. John Smith (Lock Haven)
3. Del Schwartz (Valley City)
4. Frank Mosier (Moorhead State)
5. Ray Wicks (Winona State)
6. Chuck Holliday (Eastern Oregon)

177-lb class
1. Jerry Swope (Lock Haven)
2. Charles Toedman (Fort Hays)
3. Paul Reedy (Graceland)
4. Al Gross (Wisconsin—River Falls)
5. Darren Sipe (Central Washington)
6. Dennie Sager (Gustavus Adolphus)

191-lb class
1. Alan Poser (Wisconsin—LaCrosse)
2. Dallas Delay (Central Washington)
3. Roger Behm (Minot)
4. Ron Hampton (Adams State)
5. Tom Elling (Lock Haven)
6. Peter Seller (Wisconsin—Stevens Point)

Heavyweight
1. Bob Billberg (Moorhead State)
2. Bob McDermott (Lock Haven)
3. Bob Kruse (Wayne State)
4. Wade Winter (Westmar)
5. LeRoy Werkhoven (Central Washington)
6. Roy Jackson (Fairmont State)

1967 (at Lock Haven State College, Lock Haven, PA)

Team	*Points*
1. Lock Haven	80
2. Adams State	69
3. Moorhead State	56
4. Central Washington	47
5. St. Cloud State	44
6. Winona State	38
7. Waynesburg	35
8. Wisconsin—Superior	32
9. Eastern Oregon	28
10. Bloomsburg State	24

Place winners

115-lb class
1. Ken Melchior (Lock Haven)
2. Rick Engh (Bemidji State)

3. Art Simoni (Adams State)
4. Dick Tressler (Wisconsin—Superior)
5. Raymond Day (Clarior State)
6. Curlee Alexander (Nebraska at Omaha)

123-lb class
1. Jim Hazewinkel (St. Cloud State)
2. Ralph Adamson (Waynesburg)
3. Shane Foley (Lock Haven)
4. Rick Kelvington (Moorhead State)
5. Mike Hernandez (Adams State)
6. Tony Leonardo (Wisconsin—Superior)

130-lb class
1. Mike Stanley (Adams State)
2. Jeff Lorson (Lock Haven)
3. Cecil Austin (Wisconsin—Whitewater)
4. Bill Germann (Moorhead State)
5. Gene Nagy (Waynesburg)
6. Tom Thompson (Wisconsin—Superior)

137-lb class
1. Rick Stuyvesant (Moorhead State)
2. Mike Garside (Wisconsin—Superior)
3. Don McCollim (Clarion State)
4. Tom Sprigler (Black Hills State)
5. Jim Thitmer (Appalachian)
6. Dennis Killion (Lock Haven)

145-lb class
1. Dennis Warren (Central Washington)
2. Roy Washington (Nebraska at Omaha)
3. Jim Chapman (Western Washington)
4. Mike Fitzgerald (Moorhead State)
5. Leo Kinsella (Minot)
6. Robert Teagarden (Clarion State)

152-lb class
1. Joe Gerst (Bloomsburg State)
2. Jack Klingaman (Lock Haven)
3. Merle Sovereign (Winona State)
4. Carl Olson (St. Cloud State)
5. Alan Johnson (Central Washington)
6. Steve Larson (Bemidji State)

160-lb class
1. Rollin Schimmel (Eastern Oregon)
2. Jim Blacksmith (Lock Haven)
3. Jim Tanniehill (Winona State)
4. Tom Karpency (Waynesburg)
5. Tom Ott (Wisconsin—Stout)
6. Mike Ross (Wisconsin—Superior)

167-lb class
1. Lamoin Merkley (Central Washington)
2. John Smith (Lock Haven)
3. Ray Wicks (Winona State)
4. Don Apodaca (Adams State)
5. Jim Grieco (Montclair State)
6. Fares Washington (Lincoln U, PA)

177-lb class
1. Frank Mosier (Moorhead State)
2. Tom Kusleika (Adams State)
3. Leonard Phelan (Eastern Oregon)
4. Rudy Ross (Midland)
5. Paul Reedy (Graceland)
6. Steve Melchior (Dakota Wesleyan)

191-lb class
1. Mike Rybak (St. Cloud State)
2. Pete Middleton (Morningside)
3. Dallas Delay (Central Washington)
4. Ron Hampton (Adams State)
5. Jeff Rosen (Montclair State)
6. Jim Henderson (Moorhead State)

Heavyweight
1. Nick Carollo (Adams State)
2. Wade Winters (Westmar)
3. Steve Schmidt (Wisconsin—River Falls)
4. Joe Righette (Waynesburg)
5. John Zwolinski (Winona State)
6. Craig Maddox (Western Illinois)

1968 (at Adams State College, Alamosa, CO)

Team	*Points*
1. Adams State	106
2. Nebraska at Omaha	77
3. Central Washington	56
4. Wayne State	48
5. Bloomsburg State	38
6. Eastern Oregon	34
7. Lock Haven	33
8. Westmar	27
9. Bemidji State	24
10. Clarion State	23
11. St. Cloud State	22
12. Morningside	21
13. Wisconsin—River Falls, Winona State	18
15. Waynesburg, Northern State	17

Place winners

115-lb class
1. Ken Melchior (Lock Haven)
2. Rich Tamble (Adams State)
3. Curlee Alexander (Nebraska at Omaha)
4. John Krusei (Eastern Oregon)
5. Kestle (Eastern Michigan)
6. Heim (Bloomsburg State)

123-lb class
1. Cullen Carey (Wisconsin—Platteville)
2. Dick Tressler (Wisconsin—Superior)
3. Rich Engh (Bemidji State)
4. Bill Schwartz (Wayne State)
5. Sansone (Appalachian)
6. Adamson (Waynesburg)

130-lb class
1. Doug Neuharth (Northern State)
2. Craig Swenson (Wisconsin—River Falls)
3. Larry Brown (Central Washington)
4. Curt Grabfelter (Bloomsburg State)
5. Meineke (Wayne State)
6. Pollock (Waynesburg)

137-lb class
1. Mike Stanley (Adams State)
2. Ron Russo (Bloomsburg State)
3. John Casebeer (Central Washington)
4. Randy Stine (Clarion State)
5. Johnson (Fort Hays)
6. Ellsworth (Eastern Washington)

145-lb class
1. Roy Washington (Nebraska at Omaha)
2. Rick Stuyvesant (Moorhead State)
3. Larry Miele (Eastern Michigan)
4. Gary Mogensen (Central Washington)
5. Levy (Adams State)
6. Jehlicka (Winona State)

152-lb class
1. Larry Michelson (Wayne State)
2. Joe Gerst (Bloomsburg State)
3. Charles Eckert (Bemidji State)
4. Ross Brown (Westmar)
5. Williams (Nebraska at Omaha)
6. Tresner (Fort Hays)

160-lb class
1. Wendell Hakanson (Nebraska at Omaha)
2. Jim Blacksmith (Lock Haven)
3. Dwight Fritz (Adams State)
4. Paul Kendle (Huron)
5. Wicks (Winona State)
6. Braine (Appalachian)

167-lb class
1. Lamoin Merkley (Central Washington)
2. Don Apodaca (Adams State)
3. Craig Woodward (Eastern Oregon)
4. Mike Ross (Superior)
5. Riccotta (Clarion State)
6. Lasley (Graceland)

177-lb class
1. Glen Engle (Adams State)
2. Dennis Christensen (Morningside)
3. Mel Washington (Nebraska at Omaha)
4. Steve Drange (Winona State)
5. Byrnes (Central Washington)
6. Hoge (Dickinson State)

191-lb class
1. Nick Carollo (Adams State)
2. Mike Rybak (St. Cloud State)
3. Bill Henderson (Moorhead State)
4. Pete Middleton (Morningside)
5. Melcher (Nebraska at Omaha)
6. Stamp (Concordia, MN)

Heavyweight
1. Wade Winters (Westmar)
2. Tom Firestack (Wayne State)
3. Tom Kusleika (Adams State)
4. Joe Righetti (Waynesburg)
5. Halbert (St. Cloud State)
6. Ives (Minot)

1969 (at University of Nebraska, Omaha, NE)

Team	*Points*
1. Adams State	98
2. Nebraska at Omaha	84
3. Lock Haven	60
4. Wayne State	57
5. Upper Iowa	44
6. Eastern Oregon	43
7. Bloomsburg State	38
8. Waynesburg	34
9. Clarion State	27
10. Winona State	24
11. Augsburg	23
12. Bemidji State	20
13. North Central, Appalachian State	19
15. Northern Arizona	15

Place winners

115-lb class
1. Curlee Alexander (Nebraska at Omaha)
2. John Kreusi (Eastern Oregon)
3. Don Fay (Lock Haven)
4. Pat Fernandez (Mayville)
5. Larry Harrington (Edinboro)
6. Hector Cruz (Wisconsin—Stout)

123-lb class
1. Ken Melchior (Lock Haven)
2. Rich Engh (Bemidji State)
3. Bill Schwartz (Wayne State)
4. Dennis Cozad (Nebraska at Omaha)
5. Bob Flint (Waynesburg)
6. Craig Campbell (Upper Iowa)

130-lb class
1. Ed Jackson (North Central)
2. Mike Good (Augsburg)
3. Shane Foley (Lock Haven)
4. Jody Thompson (Adams State)
5. Herb Singerman (Appalachian)
6. Cullen Carey (Wisconsin—Platteville)

137-lb class
1. Ron Russo (Bloomsburg State)
2. Roger Vigil (Adams State)
3. Dick Pollack (Waynesburg)
4. Steve Callson (Macalester)
5. Randy Stine (Clarion State)
6. Larry Rippey (Lock Haven)

145-lb class
1. Roy Washington (Nebraska at Omaha)
2. Gordon Levy (Adams State)
3. Mark Janicki (Wisconsin—Eau Claire)
4. Mike Ketchum (Wartburg)
5. Wes Bressler (Clarion State)
6. Pete Sandberg (Winona State)

152-lb class
1. Leland Tresner (Fort Hays)
2. Larry Michelson (Wayne State)
3. Jim Tanniehill (Winona State)
4. Arnold Thompson (Bloomsburg State)
5. Marlowe Mullen (Indiana Central)
6. Art Holden (Wisconsin—Whitewater)

160-lb class
1. Eric Woodward (Eastern Oregon)
2. Fred Lett (Adams State)
3. Wendell Hakanson (Nebraska at Omaha)

4. John Yoder (Wayne State)
5. Doug Niebel (Clarion State)
6. Charles Eckert (Bemidji State)

167-lb class

1. Mickey Carroll (Northern Arizona)
2. Charles Schroeder (Adams State)
3. Larry Hoge (Dickinson State)
4. Craig Woodward (Eastern Oregon)
5. Bill Hitesman (Winona State)
6. Daryl Miller (Augsburg)

177-lb class

1. Mel Washington (Nebraska at Omaha)
2. Mike Fisher (Biola)
3. Craig Long (Southern Oregon)
4. Glen Engle (Adams State)
5. Del Hughes (Upper Iowa)
6. Howard Hellickson (Macalester)

191-lb class

1. Dave Sanger (Upper Iowa)
2. Harvey Gray (Adams State)
3. Rollie Canham (Valley City)
4. Hank Hawkins (Lock Haven)
5. Bill Buchanan (Waynesburg)
6. Allen Beagle (California Tech)

Heavyweight

1. Tom Firestack (Wayne State)
2. Mike Carr (Whitworth)
3. Steve Exline (Upper Iowa)
4. Jim McCue (Bloomsburg State)
5. Tom Kusleika (Adams State)
6. Bruce Schlegel (Appalachian State)

1970 (at Wisconsin State University, Superior, WI)

Team	*Points*
1. Nebraska at Omaha	86
2. Adams State	58
3. Winona State	57
4. Upper Iowa	55
5. Bemidji State	51
6. Clarion State	43
7. Lock Haven	36
8. Wayne State	33
9. Bloomsburg State	30
10. Central Washington	29
11. Ohio Northern	27
12. Wisconsin—River Falls	25
13. Wisconsin—Oshkosh	24
14. Wisconsin—Superior	21
15. Westmar	18

Place winners

118-lb class

1. Don Fay (Lock Haven)
2. Ron Aglesby (Winona State)
3. Kenichi Kanno (Central Washington)
4. Art Simoni (Adams State)
5. Ken Flouro (Wisconsin—River Falls)
6. George Garrett (Westmar)

126-lb class

1. Craig Campbell (Upper Iowa)
2. LeRoy Polkowski (Adams State)
3. Rick Engh (Bemidji State)
4. Bill Murdock (Clarion State)
5. Bruce Williams (Ohio Northern)
6. John Stephenson (Fairmont State)

134-lb class

1. Larry Rippey (Lock Haven)
2. Pete Saxe (Bemidji State)
3. Landy Waller (Nebraska at Omaha)
4. Max Branum (Wayne State)
5. Bob Ward (Black Hills State)
6. Jody Thompson (Adams State)

142-lb class

1. Thurman Landers (Central Washington)
2. Mike Niemczk (Bemidji State)
3. Rich Pollack (Waynesburg)
4. Robert Coniam (Ohio Northern)
5. Mike Garside (Wisconsin—Superior)
6. Tom McClusky (Westmar)

150-lb class

1. Roy Washington (Nebraska at Omaha)
2. Jim Tanniehill (Winona State)

3. Edward Thompson (Bloomsburg State)
4. Mark Janicki (Wisconsin—Eau Claire)
5. Mike Young (Fort Lewis)
6. Ken Taylor (Adams State)

158-lb class
1. Les Bressler (Clarion State)
2. Lyndell Johnson (Wisconsin—River Falls)
3. Gregzie White (Lincoln U, PA)
4. Bill Hitesman (Winona State)
5. John Villecco (Glassboro State)
6. Chuck Eckert (Bemidji State)

167-lb class
1. Ken Monroe (Wayne State)
2. Santo Ricotto (Clarion State)
3. Mickey Carroll (Northern Arizona)
4. Curt Foulks (Ohio Northern)
5. Mark Mulqueen (Wisconsin—Oshkosh)
6. Robert Rynesburger (Hillsdale)

177-lb class
1. Harvey Grey (Adams State)
2. Mel Washington (Nebraska at Omaha)
3. Floyd Hitchcock (Bloomsburg State)
4. Fletcher Carr (Tampa)
5. Mike Weede (Eastern Michigan)
6. Jim Kovacs (Westmar)

190-lb class
1. Bernard Hospodka (Nebraska at Omaha)
2. Dave Sanger (Upper Iowa)
3. Ron Moen (Winona State)
4. Dale Jensen (Wisconsin—Superior)
5. Richard Edwards (Oregon C)
6. Ron Sheehan (Bloomsburg State)

Heavyweight
1. Steve Exline (Upper Iowa)
2. Bruce Schlegel (Appalachian State)
3. Gary Kipfmiller (Nebraska at Omaha)
4. Vern Soeldner (Wisconsin—Oshkosh)
5. Steve Gremm (Chadron)
6. Tom Jackson (Eastern Michigan)

1971 (at Appalachian State College, Boone, NC)

Team	*Points*
1. Central Washington	56
2. Bloomsburg State	49
3. Bemidji State, Nebraska at Omaha	46
5. Upper Iowa	44
6. U.S. International	35
7. Augsburg	27
8. Eastern Oregon	26
9. Wayne State	25
10. Appalachian State	23
11. Oregon College, Waynesburg	20
13. Graceland, Lincoln University (PA), Valley City	18

Place winners

118-lb class
1. Kanichi Kanno (Central Washington)
3. Mike Shull (Bloomsburg State)
4. Dwayne Burkholder (Upper Iowa)

126-lb class
1. Ricardo Ortega (U.S. International)
2. Larry Bolanos (Morningside)
3. Craig Campbell (Upper Iowa)
4. Bob Davis (North Park)

134-lb class
1. Craig Skeesicks (Central Washington)
2. Ken Martin (Wisconsin—Parkside)
3. Doug Willer (Eastern Michigan)
4. Mike Good (Augsburg)

142-lb class
1. Wayne Smythe (Bloomsburg State)
2. Pete Saxe (Bemidji State)

3. Ron Johnson (Augsburg)
4. Dick Pollock (Waynesburg)

150-lb class
1. Bob Dettmer (Bemidji State)
2. Mike McCoy (Eastern Oregon)
3. Jim Jensen (Northern State)
4. Steve Magruder (California Lutheran)

158-lb class
1. Gregzie White (Lincoln U)
2. James Fallis (Lake Superior State)
3. Mike Young (Fort Lewis)
4. Lee Anderson (Western Washington)

167-lb class
1. Tom Tomlinson (U.S. International)
2. Ken Monroe (Wayne State)
3. Brick Woodward (Eastern Oregon)
4. Gary Stevenson (Central Washington)

177-lb class
1. Mel Washington (Nebraska at Omaha)
2. Floyd Hitchcock (Bloomsburg State)
3. Tom Heizer (Earlham)
4. Mike Panarella (Millersville State)

190-lb class
1. Rich Edwards (Oregon C)
2. Bernie Hospodka (Nebraska at Omaha)
3. Ron Schmuck (Bemidji State)
4. Jay DeBoer (Southern State, SD)

Heavyweight
1. Steve Exline (Upper Iowa)
2. Bruce Schlegel (Appalachian State)
3. Toby Ackerman (Wisconsin—Whitewater)
4. Bill Ehlers (Huron)

1972 (at Oregon Tech, Klamath Falls, OR)

Team	*Points*
1. Adams State	64
2. Nebraska at Omaha	53.5
3. U.S. International	51
4. Central Washington	41
5. Bemidji State	38.5
6. Oregon College	38
7. St. John's (MN), Wayne State	34.5
9. Southern Oregon	33
10. Wisconsin—Superior	22.5
11. Chadron State	21
12. Northland	19.5
13. Winona State	19
14. West Liberty	18
15. Eastern Washington, Wisconsin—Parkside	17.5

Place winners

118-lb class
1. Scott Casper (Northland)
2. Paul Martinez (Nebraska at Omaha)
3. James Steiger (U.S. International)
4. Richard Vaughn (Grand Valley State)
5. Henry Wilk (Anderson, IN)
6. Scott Miller (Winona State)

126-lb class
1. Phil Gonzales (Nebraska at Omaha)
2. James Leyendyke (Lake Superior State)
3. Ricardo Ortega (U.S. International)
4. Dirk Sorenson (Wisconsin—Superior)
5. Dan Speasl (Southern Oregon)
6. William Gibson (Colorado Mines)

134-lb class
1. Gary Svendsen (St. John's)
2. Craig Skeesick (Central Washington)
3. Ken Martin (Wisconsin—Parkside)
4. Dale Evans (Wisconsin—Stout)
5. Kani Rowland (Oregon College)
6. Mike Pickford (Morningside)

142-lb class
1. Doug Moses (Adams State)
2. Pete Saxe (Bemidji State)
3. Ron Johnson (Augsburg)
4. Jarrett Williams (Biola)

5. Dennis Daker (Upper Iowa)
6. Gabriel Ruz (U.S. International)

150-lb class
1. Pat Marcy (Augsburg)
2. Ken Taylor (Adams State)
3. Lee Adams (Carthage)
4. Dana Sorensen (Tayor)
5. Lee Anderson (Western Washington)
6. Bill McFadden (Oregon C)

158-lb class
1. Bob Lynch (Chadron)
2. John Craig (West Liberty State)
3. Bob Dettmer (Bemidji State)
4. James Fallis (Lake Superior State)
5. Steve Zawacki (Wisconsin—Superior)
6. Bob Stetler (Huron)

167-lb class
1. Ken Monroe (Wayne State)
2. Tom Tomlinson (U.S. International)
3. Bill Hitesman (Winona State)
4. Roger Duvall (Southern Oregon)
5. Leslie Jackson (Mayville)
6. Chuck Robinson (North Central)

177-lb class
1. Chuck Jean (Adams State)
2. Richard Jay (Biola)
3. Jim Herold (Pacific)
4. Vard Jenks (Eastern Washington)
5. John Herzog (Southern Oregon)
6. Ray Blondin (Central Washington)

190-lb class
1. Richard Edwards (Oregon C)
2. Tom Omli (Central Washington)
3. Tom Miller (St. John's)
4. Bob Whelan (Bemidji State)
5. Bill Spieker (Wisconsin—Superior)
6. Ray Larson (Linfield)

Heavyweight
1. Gary Kipfmiller (Nebraska at Omaha)
2. Bob Maresh (Valley City)
3. Ron Coles (Wayne State)
4. Leonard Peavy (Graceland)
5. Greg Nelson (Eastern Oregon)
6. Bill Larsen (Dakota State)

1973 (at Morningside College, Sioux City, IA)

Team	Points
1. Adams State	62.5
2. Central Washington	48.5
3. Huron	46
4. Central Oklahoma	40
5. U.S. International	39
6. Wayne State	38.5
7. Southern Oregon	35.5
8. Nebraska at Omaha	33.5
9. Wisconsin—Parkside	32.5
10. Bemidji State	32
11. Lake Superior State	31.5
12. Waynesburg	29.5
13. St. John's (MN)	26.5
14. Winona State, Wisconsin—LaCrosse	25.5

Place winners

118-lb class
1. Jim Steiger (U.S. International)
2. Henry Wilk (Anderson, IN)
3. Paul Martinez (Nebraska at Omaha)
4. Barry Casper (Northland)
5. Randy Ross (Central Oklahoma)
6. Tom Cortez (Wayne State)

126-lb class
1. Phil Gonzales (Nebraska at Omaha)
2. Bill West (Wisconsin—Parkside)
3. Dan Speasl (Southern Oregon)
4. Dan Yoder (Adams State)
5. Dave Turner (Central Oklahoma)
6. David Storey (Warner Pacific)

134-lb class
1. Ken Martin (Wisconsin—Parkside)
2. Tom Svendsen (St. John's)
3. Greg Gowens (Central Washington)
4. Paul Hoover (Waynesburg)
5. Jerry Weyer (Wisconsin—LaCrosse)
6. Rodney Patterson (California, PA)

142-b class
1. Kit Shaw (Central Washington)
2. Gabe Ruz (U.S. International)

3. Dale Evans (Wisconsin—Stout)
4. Roger DeMarais (Bemidji State)
5. Ron Dworak (Wisconsin—Oshkosh)
6. Steve Randall (Central Oklahoma)

150-lb class
1. Tom Adams (Carthage)
2. Pat McCaffery (York)
3. Bob Dettmer (Bemidji State)
4. Bill Schmidt (Augsburg)
5. John Sappington (Oregon C)
6. Daniel Holwegner (Minot)

158-lb class
1. Jim Falls (Lake Superior State)
2. Tom Kubiak (Wisconsin—River Falls)
3. Curtis Saiki (Pacific U)
4. Phil Mueller (Wisconsin—Stevens Point)
5. Tom Luth (Wayne State)
6. Mike Briggs (Wisconsin—La Crosse)

167-lb class
1. Ken Monroe (Wayne State)
2. Tom Carter (Central Oklahoma)
3. Ruben Rios (Eastern Washington)
4. Randy Haught (California, PA)
5. Leslie Jackson (Mayville)
6. B.D. LaProd (Wisconsin—La Crosse)

177-lb class
1. Chuck Jean (Adams State)
2. Gary Keck (Huron)
3. Steven Newhard (Morningside)
4. Craig Halverson (Winona State)
5. Bob Hudkins (Pembroke State)
6. Scott Davis (Augsburg)

190-lb class
1. Mike Allison (Adams State)
2. Lowell Romfo (Minot)
3. Jerry Stidham (Southern Oregon)
4. Ernest Middleton (Winona State)
5. Tom Omli (Central Washington)
6. Bob Whelen (Bemidji State)

Heavyweight
1. Tom Herr (Edinboro)
2. Bill Ehlers (Huron)
3. Henry Banke (Upper Iowa)
4. Curtis Niederbaumer (Northern State)
5. Vern Dulany (Southern Oregon)
6. Rick Doran (Fort Hays)

1974
(at University of Wisconsin—River Falls)

Team	*Points*
1. Central Washington	102
2. Central State (OK)	80.5
3. Wisconsin—Parkside	66
4. York (PA)	46.5
5. Augsburg	46
6. Eastern Washington	43
7. Wisconsin—Whitewater	40.5
8. Southern Oregon	38.5
9. Winona State	35.5
10. Bemidji State	35
11. Adams State	34
12. Grand Valley State	28
13. Wisconsin—River Falls	27.5
14. Minot	25.5
15. Lake Superior State	24

Place winners

118-lb class
1. Mark Mangianti (Grand Valley State)
2. Todd Keady (Southern Oregon)
3. Fiorella (Loras)
4. Zizzo (Wisconsin—Whitewater)
5. Draper (Eastern Washington)
6. Hutchinson (Upper Iowa)

126-lb class
1. Terry Henry (Central State)
2. Gerry Brusletten (Wisconsin—Superior)
3. Bland (Chicago State)
4. Solem (Augsburg)
5. Pierce (Central Washington)
6. Speasl (Southern Oregon)

134-lb class
1. Bill West (Wisconsin—Parkside)
2. Charles Blixt (Augsburg)
3. Svendsen (St. John's)
4. Pope (Wisconsin—River Falls)
5. Papa (York)
6. Gowens (Central Washington)

142-lb class
1. Kit Shaw (Central Washington)
2. Ken Martin (Wisconsin—Parkside)
3. Dworak (Wisconsin—Oshkosh)
4. Cleveland (Bemidji State)
5. White (Lewis)
6. Crenshaw (Southern Oregon)

150-lb class
1. Randy Skarda (Wisconsin—Parkside)
2. Dan Holwegner (Minot)
3. Burkholder (Central Washington)
4. Moe (Wisconsin—Whitewater)
5. Schmidt (Augsburg)
6. Lindsey (York)

158-lb class
1. Jim Fallis (Lake Superior State)
2. Phil Mueller (Wisconsin—Stevens Point)
3. Kubiak (Wisconsin—River Falls)
4. Sullivan (Central State)
5. Parrish (Central Washington)
6. Daly (Western Washington)

167-lb class
1. Joe Waltemyer (York)
2. Dan Older (Central Washington)
3. Dickey (Central State)
4. Harn (Bemidji State)
5. Keck (Huron)
6. Peterson (Westmar)

177-lb class
1. Billy Mitchell (Central State)
2. Lanny Davidson (Eastern Washington)
3. Halvorson (Winona State)
4. Hosford (Grand Valley State)
5. Millard (Cedarville)
6. Everhart (Chicago State)

190-lb class
1. Mike Allison (Adams State)
2. Rockey Isley (Central Washington)
3. Middleton (Winona State)
4. Kenny (Eastern Washington)
5. Stidham (Southern Oregon)
6. Kendall (Valley City)

Heavyweight
1. Lynn Crawn (William Penn)
2. Curt Niederbaumer (Northern State)
3. Herr (Edinboro)
4. Law (Hillsdale)
5. Ladick (Alderson Broaddus)
6. Coles (Wayne State)

1975 (at Morningside College, Sioux City, IA)

Team	*Points*
1. Adams State	61
2. Augsburg	56
3. Central State	46
4. Wisconsin—Whitewater	45.5
5. Wisconsin—Parkside	36
6. Westmar	35
7 Wisconsin—La Crosse	34.5
8 Eastern Michigan	32
9 Southern Oregon	31
10 Upper Iowa	30.5
11 Wisconsin—Oshkosh	29
12 Wisconsin—River Falls	28.5
13 Peru State	28
14 Winona State	27.5
15 Huron	.5

Place winners

118-lb class
1. Sam Fiorell (Loras)
2. Gary Zizzo (Wisconsin—Whitewater)
3. Tom Cortez (Adams State)

4. Murry Herstein (Augsburg)
5. Bob Fullerton (Westmar)
6. Kevin Anderson (Kearney State)

126-lb class

1. Terry Henry (Central State)
2. Gerry Bruesletten (Wisconsin—Superior)
3. Alan Betcher (Southern Oregon)
4. Jim Meyer (Wayne State)
5. Glenn Guerin (Taylor)
6. Joe Landers (Wisconsin—Parkside)

134-lb class

1. Bill West (Wisconsin—Parkside)
2. Gene Pope (Wisconsin—River Falls)
3. Mike Kirby (Fairmont State)
4. Geno Zucaro (California, PA)
5. Randal Donovan (Huron)
6. Chuck Blixt (Augsburg)

142-lb class

1. Bob Bassuener (Wisconsin—La Crosse)
2. Joe Bold (Southern Oregon)
3. Dean Kennedy (Augsburg)
4. Paul LeBlanc (Southern California C)
5. Ray Roth (Findlay)
6. Ken Better (Minot)

150-lb class

1. Bud Frohling (Peru State)
2. Bil Schmidt (Augsburg)
3. Ray Luna (Adams State)
4. Cecil Bergen (Taylor)
5. Kerry Feekes (Westmar)
6. Steve Rogland (Johnstown)

158-lb class

1. Rick DeMarais (Wisconsin—Oshkosh)
2. Steve LaPrade (Pembroke State)
3. Jerome Stewart (Simpson)
4. Ron Haldinger (Wisconsin—Whitewater)
5. Lee Garboden (Pacific U)
6. Steve Stoute (Rutgers-Newark)

167-lb class

1. Larry McCoy (Indiana, PA)
2. Gary Keck (Huron)
3. Stan Peterson (Westmar)
4. Dan Older (Central Washington)
5. Ron Buffo (Adams State)
6. Gary Chopp (Grand Valley State)

177-lb class

1. Lanny Davidson (Eastern Washington)
2. Bill Mitchell (Central State)
3. Vic Millard (Cedarville)
4. Jamie Hosford (Grand Valley State)
5. Gary Marshall (Upper Iowa)
6. Deryll Rohda (Defiance)

190-lb class

1. Craig Kelso (Adams State)
2. Ernest Middleton (Winona State)
3. Frank Kuennen (Upper Iowa)
4. Todd Johnson (Taylor)
5. Lowell Kuecker (Wartburg)
6. Bob Christopherson (Wisconsin—La Crosse)

Heavyweight

1. Bob Whelan (Bemidji State)
2. Mark Law (Hillside)
3. Steve Bollenbeck (Grand Valley State)
4. Joe Johnson (Wisconsin—Stevens Point)
5. Jerry Reker (Southwest State)
6. Dan Malm (Winona State)

1976 (at Edinboro College, Edinboro, PA)

Team	Points
1. Adams State	83.50
2. Eastern Washington	70.25
3. Central State (OK)	60.50
4. Grand Valley State	51.50
5. Wisconsin—Whitewater	48.50
6. Taylor	43.75
7. Bemidji State	42.50
8. California (PA)	41.25
9. Wisconsin—Parkside	38.75
10. Pacific University	34.25
11. Winona State	33.50
12. Concordia (MN)	32
13. Edinboro	31.50

Team	*Points*
14. Indiana (PA)	30.50
15. Southern Oregon	29.25

Place winners

118-lb class
1. Kevin Kish (Bemidji State)
2. Doug McHenry (Central State)
3. William DePaoli (California, PA)
4. Jim Walters (Edinboro)
5. Steve Muterspaw (Taylor)
6. Bob Motooka (Pacific U)

126-lb class
1. Glenn Guerin (Taylor)
2. Darwin Stalnaker (California, PA)
3. Mark Mangianti (Grand Valley State)
4. Jerry Lorton (Eastern Washington)
5. Doug Stoll (Anderson, IN)
6. Henry Flores (Adams State)

134-lb class
1. Joe Landers (Wisconsin—Parkside)
2. John Harris (Grand Valley State)
3. David Miller (Pembroke State)
4. John Flores (Adams State)
5. Dan Mason (Pacific U)
6. Mark Carter (Mayville)

142-lb class
1. Jim Wood (Adams State)
2. Marlow Burton (Winona State)
3. Joe Bold (Southern Oregon)
4. Greg Greeno (Jamestown)
5. Tom Hutchison (Edinboro)
6. Pete Hartzheim (Wisconsin—Whitewater)

150-lb class
1. Robert McDowell (Graceland)
2. Randy LeBlanc (Mesa)
3. Bill Linthicum (Central Washington)
4. Bob Gruner (Wisconsin—Parkside)
5. Tony Byrne (Eastern Washington)
6. Cecil Bergen (Taylor)

158-lb class
1. Mike Reed (Eastern Washington)
2. Ron Haidinger (Wisconsin—Whitewater)
3. Rick DeMarais (Wisconsin—Oshkosh)
4. Ken Baird (Fairmont State)
5. Roger Rowbotham (Bemidji State)
6. Rich Wagner (Lewis)

167-lb class
1. Larry McCoy (Indiana, PA)
2. Mike Stanek (Wisconsin—Whitewater)
3. Tom Moeggenberg (Lake Superior State)
4. Tom Jean (Adams State)
5. Kevin Lindberg (Concordia)
6. Corky Hanson (Bemidji State)

177-lb class
1. Lanny Davidson (Eastern Washington)
2. Bill Mitchell (Central State)
3. Charlie Lemke (Pacific U)
4. Deryll Rohda (Defiance)
5. Theopolis Williams (Whitman)
6. Dennis Baker (Malone)

190-lb class
1. Craig Kelso (Adams State)
2. Mike Riedmann (Wayne State)
3. Jamie Hosford (Grand Valley State)
4. Kevin Smith (Central State)
5. Rod Hampton (Livingstone)
6. Rick Link (West Liberty State)

Heavyweight
1. Barry Bennett (Concordia)
2. Bruce Tonsor (Wisconsin—River Falls)
3. Dan Malm (Winona State)
4. Jerome Huck (Valley City)
5. Mark Newburg (Findlay)
6. Fred Marisett (Peru State)

1977 (at Eastern Washington University, Cheney, WA)

Team	*Points*
1. Eastern Washington	90.75
2. Grand Valley State	89
3. Adams State	81.25
4. Southern Oregon	45.25
5. Wisconsin—Parkside	35.25
6. Pacific University	33.50
7. Augsburg	32
8. Wisconsin—Whitewater	29.75
9. Simon Fraser	28.75
10. Tayor	27.75

Place winners

118-lb class
1. Bill DePaoli (California, PA)
2. Ken Foss (Eastern Washington)
3. Fred Townsend (Wisconsin—Whitewater)
4. Randy Hoffman (Messiah)
5. Bob Motooka (Pacific U)
6. Lindsey Johnson (Adams State)

126-lb class
1. Glen Guerin (Taylor)
2. Doug Stoll (Anderson, IN)
3. Henry Flores (Adams State)
4. Wayne Petterson (Graceland)
5. Dave Motta (Westmar)
6. Mark Yori (Peru State)

134-lb class
1. John Flores (Adams State)
2. John Harris (Grand Valley State)
3. Roger Rolen (Oregon C)
4. Dan Reina (Southern Oregon)
5. Joel Stolzmann (Wisconsin—Oshkosh)
6. Dave Sauter (St. Olaf)

142-lb class
1. Bill Roersma (Grand Valley State)
2. Jeff Carroll (West Liberty State)
3. Dominic Todaro (Edinboro)
4. Jim Wood (Adams State)
5. Mark Poletti (Lake Superior State)
6. Greg Greeno (Jamestown)

150-lb class
1. Rick Hensel (Southern Oregon)
2. Steve Luth (Wisconsin—Platteville)
3. Roger Dallas (Lake Superior State)
4. Bob Gruner (Wisconsin—Parkside)
5. Tom Sypien (not available)
6. John Gruzke (Bemidji State)

158-lb class
1. Mike Reed (Eastern Washington)
2. Rodney Baird (Fairmont State)
3. Steve Stoute (Rutgers-Camden)
4. Michael Abrams (Grand Valley)
5. Steve LaPrad (Pembroke State)
6. David Wygant (Augsburg)

167-lb class
1. Mark Mongeon (Simon Fraser)
2. Staff Polk (Adams State)
3. Ralph Roberts (Saginaw Valley)
4. Jeff Swenson (Augsburg)
5. Pat Rohlik (South Dakota at Springfield)
6. Scott Yerrick (Grand Valley State)

177-lb class
1. Lanny Davidson (Eastern Washington)
2. Steve Kilwein (Dickinson State)
3. Derryl Rohda (Defiance)
4. Jeff Blixt (Augsburg)
5. Steve Behl (Wisconsin—Platteville)
6. Jim Blagg (Biola)

190-lb class
1. Jamie Hosford (Grand Valley State)
2. Dennis Baker (Malone)
3. Bob Eckerd (Bemidji State)
4. John Gale (Wisconsin—Parkside)
5. Jeff Bradshaw (Edinboro)
6. Rodney Hampton (Livingstone)

Heavyweight
1. Barry Bennett (Concordia, MN)
2. Don Wilson (Eastern Washington)
3. Jerome Huck (Valley City)
4. Charles Taylor (Pacific U)
5. Blaine Felsman (Wisconsin—Oshkosh)
6. Doug Noetzel (Northland)

1978 (at University of Wisconsin—Whitewater)

Team	*Points*
1. Southern Oregon	81.50
2. Grand Valley State	78.75
3. Eastern Washington	75
4. Central State (OK)	60.50
5. Wisconsin—Whitewater	53
6. Adams State	51.75
7. Taylor	45.50
8. Lake Superior State	41.75
9. Central Washington	41
10. Saginaw Valley	37.50
11. Bemidji State	33.75
12. Edinboro	31.75
13. Wisconsin—Oshkosh	29.25
14. Simon Fraser	29
15. Biola	26.75

Place winners

118-lb class
1. Kevin Kish (Bemidji State)
2. Ken Foss (Eastern Washington)
3. James Walters (Edinboro)
4. Larry Winslow (Westmar)
5. Jeff Robinett (Central State)
6. Ron Jones (Rutgers-Newark)

126-lb class
1. Fred Townsend (Wisconsin—Whitewater)
2. Jerry Lorton (Eastern Washington)
3. Terry Nicholson (Saginaw Valley)
4. Ted Yachanin (Lake Superior State)
5. Steve Scotten (Maryland Eastern Shore)
6. Pete Cassanos (Hanover)

134-lb class
1. James Shutich (Grand Valley State)
2. David James (Central State)
3. Larry Nugent (Southern Oregon)
4. Carmelo Flores (Wisconsin—Whitewater)
5. Roger Rolen (Oregon C)
6. Doug Herher (Northern State)

142-lb class
1. Rick Franklin (Pacific U)
2. Lynn Taylor (Eastern Washington)
3. Danny Cruze (Central State)
4. Dennis Dixon (Southern Oregon)
5. David Miller (Pembroke State)
6. Rich Lopez (Adams State)

150-lb class
1. Joe Sanford (Central Washington)
2. Dave Adams (Southern Oregon)
3. Dave LaMotte (West Liberty State)
4. Gary Ader (Wisconsin—Oshkosh)
5. Jerry Wollen (Eastern Washington)
6. John Duffy (Loras)

158-lb class
1. Michael Abrams (Grand Valley State)
2. Roger Dallas (Lake Superior State)
3. Monte Griffith (Mesa, CO)
4. Kevin Frohling (Graceland)
5. Harvey Adams (Central State)
6. Lane Kinna (Kearney State)

167-lb class
1. Marc Mongeon (Simon Fraser)
2. Staff Polk (Adams State)
3. Ralph Roberts (Saginaw Valley)
4. Jeff Swenson (Augsburg)
5. Pat Rohlik (South Dakota at Springfield)
6. Jeff Culp (Waynesburg)

177-lb class
1. Darrel Landers (Southern Oregon)
2. Robert LaFollette (Taylor)
3. Theopolis Williams (Whitman)
4. William Kinkle (Fairmont State)
5. John Stroble (Central State)
6. Corky Hanson (Bemidji State)

190-lb class
1. Jim Blagg (Biola)
2. Drew Whitfield (Taylor)
3. Kurt Bledsoe (Central Washington)
4. Rodney Hampton (Livingstone)
5. Greg Barreto (Southern Oregon)
6. Wade Fletcher (Wisconsin—Whitewater)

Heavyweight
1. Herb Stanley (Adams State)
2. Ron Essink (Grand Valley State)
3. Jerome Huck (Valley City)
4. Blaine Felsman (Wisconsin—Oshkosh)
5. Henry Harmony (Huron)
6. Mark Harvey (Linfield)

1979 (at Wheeling, WV)

Team	Points
1. Central State (OK)	99.50
2. Adams State	69
3. Augsburg	59.25
4. Grand Valley State	54.25
5. Wisconsin—Parkside	48.25
6. Fairmont State	47.75
7. Fort Hays	41.50
8. Southern Oregon	41
9. Central Washington	40
10. Taylor	37.50
11. Messiah, Edinboro	32.50
13. Wisconsin—Oshkosh	31.75
14. West Liberty State	31
15. St. Cloud State	28.25

Place winners

118-lb class
1. Bill DePaoli (California, PA)
2. Jeff Robinett (Central State)
3. Art Aragon (Adams State)
4. Greg Sirb (Edinboro)
5. Ron Schaulis (Midland Lutheran)
6. Andy Jirik (St. Cloud State)
7. Troy Owens (West Liberty State)
8. Frank Hart (Malone)

126-lb class
1. Scott Whirley (Augsburg)
2. Ron Ellis (Central Washington)
3. Dan Winter (Wisconsin—Parkside)
4. Ken Taylor (Central State)
5. Scott Giese (Wisconsin—Whitewater)
6. Les Plumby (Southwest State)
7. Blake Sohn (St. Cloud State)
8. Jim Stewart (Malone)

134-lb class
1. David James (Central State)
2. Larry Nugent (Southern Oregon)
3. Pat Sheridan (Biola)
4. Stan Kellenberger (Wisconsin—Oshkosh)
5. Steve Olson (Huron)
6. Carmelo Flores (Wisconsin—Whitewater)
7. Todd Kriewall (St. Cloud State)
8. Wayne Peterson (Fort Hays)

142-lb class
1. John Powell (Central State)
2. Joel Stolzmann (Wisconsin—Oshkosh)
3. Rick Lopez (Adams State)
4. Dan Mechtenberg (South Dakota at Springfield)
5. Greg Gerdes (Bemidji State)
6. Steve Bryan (Lake Superior State)
7. Rick Langer (Wisconsin—Parkside)
8. Dave Dawson (Pacific U)

150-lb class
1. Dave LaMotte (West Liberty State)
2. Paul Neumann (Grand Valley State)
3. Dave Remnitz (Eastern Washington)
4. Brian Arvold (Augsburg)
5. Mark Poletti (Lake Superior State)
6. Dave Adams (Southern Oregon)
7. Jerry Klonowski (Wisconsin—Stout)
8. Todd Simmons (Adams State)

158-lb class
1. Bob Gruner (Wisconsin—Parkside)
2. Dan Morrison (Messiah)
3. Harvey Adams (Central State)
4. Daryl Henning (Fort Hays)
5. John Finn (Central State)
6. Roger Dallas (Lake Superior State)
7. Barry Gresh (Pittsburgh-Johnstown)
8. Greg Dixon (Adams State)

167-lb class
1. Jeff Sewnson (Augsburg)
2. Randy Hill (Fort Hays)
3. Mike Abrams (Grand Valley State)
4. Virgil Watson (Dana)
5. Tim Morrison (Messiah)
6. Ron Zeno (Central State)

7. Todd Whitfield (Taylor)
8. Monty Griffith (Mesa, CO)

177-lb class

1. Bruce Hinkle (Fairmont State)
2. Steve Behl (Wisconsin—Platteville)
3. Ray Yeager (Edinboro)
4. Darrel Landers (Southern Oregon)
5. Jay Tyree (Taylor)
6. Mike Stolp (Eastern Washington)
7. Theopolis Williams (Witmar)
8. Jim Louwagie (Southwest State)

190-lb class

1. Tony Huck (Valley City)
2. Drew Witfield (Taylor)
3. Bob Eckert (Bemidji State)
4. Phil Gifford (Fairmont State)
5. Ed King (Grand Valley State)
6. Mark Elliott (Franklin)
7. Daryl Yohn (Adams State)
8. Mike Wilsey (Pacific U)

Heavyweight

1. Herb Stanley (Adams State)
2. Mike Wilson (Central Washington)
3. Josh Bryant (Livingstone)
4. Chandler Mackey (Chicago)
5. Steve Foster (Central State)
6. Tom Kruger (Kearney State)
7. Greg Ganyo (St. Cloud State)
8. Joe Gayan (Wisconsin—Superior)

1980 (at Fort Hays State, Hays, KS)

Team	*Points*
1. Adams State	86
2. Huron	76.50
3. Central State (OK)	62.25
4. Grand Valley State, Wisconsin—Parkside	51.50
6. Wisconsin—Superior, Fairmont State	38.50
8. Chicago State, Simon Fraser	37.25
10. Wisconsin—River Falls	33.25
11. Central Washington	33
12. Southern Oregon	30
13. Kearney State	28.25
14. Wisconsin—Whitewater	27.50
15. Pacific University	26.75

Place winners

118-lb class

1. Rudy Glur (Huron)
2. Mike Vania (Pacific U)
3. Kent Taylor (Central State)
4. Ken Jordan (Bemidji State)
5. Chuck Jones (Pembroke State)
6. Jeff Henderson (Grand Valley State)
7. Rob Lagerquist (Central Washington)
8. Bob Erickson (Wisconsin—River Falls)

126-lb class

1. Scott Ritzen (Adams State)
2. Ronald Ellis (Central Washington)
3. Jeff Robinet (Central State)
4. Andy Mora (Western State)
5. Ted Yachinin (Lake Superior State)
6. Willie Dye (Pembroke State)
7. Don Donar (Wisconsin—Platteville)
8. Jed Dobberstein (Kearney State)

134-lb class

1. David James (Central State)
2. Lawrence MacErnie (Adams State)
3. Dan Winter (Wisconsin—Parkside)
4. Pat Sheridan (Biola)
5. Greg Bristol (Mesa)
6. Dorr Granger (Grand Valley State)
7. Paul Giovannini (Pacific Lutheran)
8. Walt Maslem (Kearney State)

142-lb class

1. Genaro Zamudio (Southern Oregon)
2. John Sheridan (Adams State)
3. Tim Horn (Grand Valley State)
4. Joseph White (Fairmont State)
5. Andy Johnson (Wisconsin—River Falls)
6. Rick Halverson (Augsburg)
7. Sandy Spero (St. JF)
8. Romar Gutierrez (Western State)

150-lb class
1. James Morkel (Huron)
2. Bob Pekarske (Wisconsin—Parkside)
3. Glenn Zipperer (Wisconsin—Superior)
4. Brian Arvold (Augsburg)
5. Gary Erwin (Jax)
6. Everitt Neal (Pembroke State)
7. Michael Daniels (Western State)
8. William Allen (Central State)

158-lb class
1. Daniel Morrison (Messiah)
2. Bob Gruner (Wisconsin—Parkside)
3. Harvey Adams (Central Ohio)
4. Lane Kinnan (Kearney)
5. Barry Gresh (Pittsburgh-Johnstown)
6. Tony Ledbetter (Central Washington
7. Tim Hardyman (Wisconsin—Platteville)
8. Randy McKinney (Edinboro)

167-lb class
1. John Dwyer (Simon Fraser)
2. Tom Conlon (Wisconsin—Parkside)
3. Ken Beyer (Loras)
4. David Miller (Huron)
5. John Revesz (Pittsburgh-Johnstown)
6. Jerry Prusha (Kearney State)
7. Gary Astle (Central Oklahoma)
8. Rick Holub (Southern Oregon)

177-lb class
1. Jeff Laube (Wisconsin—Superior)
2. Mike Quinsey (Simon Fraser)
3. Derrick Hardy (Chicago)
4. Jim Louwagie (Southwest State)
5. Craig Foster (Eastern Washington)
6. Jody Van Laanen (Wisconsin—Whitewater)
7. Ronelio Galas (Pacific U)
8. William Hinkel (Fairmont State)

190-lb class
1. Tony Huck (Valley City)
2. Philip Clifford (Fairmont State)
3. Jim Koslowski (Huron)
4. Robert Valentine (Carson-Newman)
5. Bob LaFollette (Taylor)
6. Rick Rabensdorf (Wisconsin—Whitewater)
7. Kurt Bledsoe (Central Washington)
8. Jeff Eastlick (Wisconsin—Platteville)

Heavyweight
1. Ron Essink (Grand Valley State)
2. Herb Stanley (Adams State)
3. Josh Bryant (Livingstone)
4. Chandler Mackey (Chicago)
5. Kike Jorgenson (Elmhurst)
6. Lyle Lundgren (Northwestern College, IA)
7. Tom Hanson (Minnesota at Morris)
8. Keith Seals (Southern U)

1981 (at Central State University, Edmond, OK)

Team	Points
1. Central State (OK)	155.25
2. Adams State	69.50
3. Wisconsin—River Falls	55.75
4. Western State	52.75
5. Augsburg	49.50
6. Fort Hays	42.75
7. Pacific University	42.50
8. Waynesburg	36
9. Pittsburgh-Johnstown	34.75
10. Bemidji State	32
11. Dickinson State	30.75
12. Southern Oregon, West Liberty State	30
14. Biola	27.75
15. Grand Valley State	25

Place winners

118-lb class
1. Dennis Kendrick (Central State)
2. Chuck Jones (Pembroke State)
3. Ken Jordan (Bemidji State)
4. Mike Vania (Pacific U)
5. Tim Smelser (Ferris State)
6. Greg Sirb (Edinboro)

7. Hal Fabrycki (Southern Oregon)
8. Richard Barron (Augsburg)

126-lb class

1. Todd Osborn (Central State)
2. Scott Whirley (Augsburg)
3. Stan Seffensen (Huron)
4. Andy Mora (Western State)
5. Pat Sheridan (Biola)
6. Scott Ritzen (Adams State)
7. Lee Plumley (Southwest State)
8. Ron Ellis (Central Washington)

134-lb class

1. Ronnie James (Central State)
2. Tony Ippolito (Biola)
3. Dan Winter (Wisconsin—Parkside)
4. Joe Ore (Adams State)
5. Paul Giovannini (Pacific Lutheran)
6. Matthew Mark (Pacific U)
7. Bob Hirsch (Northern State)
8. Tony Algiers (Wisconsin—Eau Claire)

142-lb class

1. Alan Maddox (Central State)
2. C.D. Hoiness (Central Washington)
3. John Sheridan (Adams State)
4. Jesse Castro (Liberty Baptist)
5. Ron Vorpahl (Wisconsin—La Crosse)
6. Greg Astorino (Edinboro)
7. Bob Arvold (Augsburg)
8. Dorr Granger (Grand Valley State)

150-lb class

1. Jack Garrison (Western State)
2. Greg Gerdes (Bemidji State)
3. Paul Frandsen (Wisconsin—River Falls)
4. Charles Ekey (Fort Hays)
5. Harvey Adams (Central State)
6. John Lower (West Liberty State)
7. Dave McKay (Simon Fraser)
8. Dan Yoder (Lake Superior State)

158-lb class

1. Darryl Henning (Fort Hays)
2. Jeff Stoks (Augsburg)
3. Dave Newman (Wisconsin—River Falls)
4. Will Allen (Central State)
5. John Revesz (Johnstown)
6. Mike Muckerheide (Wisconsin—Parkside)
7. Dave Ellison (Pacific U)
8. Bill Fox (Liberty Baptist)

167-lb class

1. Benny Coleman (Central State)
2. Rick Diemert (Waynesburg)
3. Mike Bertram (Adams State)
4. Tony Diola (Grand Valley State)
5. Andy Decoteau (Mayville)
6. Mike Cribbs (Lake Superior State)
7. Ken Beyer (Loras)
8. David Veal (Huron)

177-lb class

1. Bill Ameen (Central State)
2. Brian Edison (West Liberty State)
3. Paul Delmonico (Western State)
4. Dan Revesz (Johnstown)
5. Dan Lee (Southwest State)
6. Jerry Prusha (Kearney State)
7. Mike Hunter (Wisconsin—Stout)
8. Chris Goete (Fort Hays)

190-lb class

1. Jim Meyer (Wisconsin—River Falls)
2. Phil Gifford (Waynesburg)
3. Darrell Yohn (Adams State)
4. Jeff Eastlick (Wisconsin—Platteville)
5. Forrest Brown (Ferris State)
6. Kim Hogan (Pacific U)
7. Scott Dogg (Taylor)
8. Ronnie Hawkins (Central State)

Heavyweight

1. Kurt Lesser (Dickinson State)
2. Rick Chandler (Southern Oregon)
3. Lyle Lundgren (Northwestern, IA)
4. Sean Isgan (Johnstown)
5. Ed Ritt (Pacific U)
6. Tom Brutscher (Southwest State)
7. Nick Kiniski (Simon Fraser)
8. Chris Lund (Northern State)

1982 (at Forest Grove, OR)

Team	*Points*
1. Central State (OK)	105.50
2. Adams State	88.75
3. Wisconsin—River Falls	60
4. Southern Oregon	56.25
5. Pacific University	54.25
6. Simon Fraser	52.75
7. Augsburg	51.25
8. Central Washington	50.50
9. Fort Lewis	46
10. Fort Hays	34.75
11. Kearney State	30.25
12. Carson-Newman	28
13. West Liberty State	25.25
14. Huron	23.50
15. Wisconsin—Platteville	17.75

Place winners

118-lb class
1. Bill Hoglund (Central Washington)
2. Ryan Foley (Wisconsin—La Crosse)
3. Rudy Glur (Huron)
4. Ken Crenshaw (Fort Lewis)
5. Steve Gliva (Augsburg)
6. Allan Koors (Carson-Newman)

126-lb class
1. Scott Ritzen (Adams State)
2. Kevin Binkard (Pacific U)
3. Joe Starzenski (Central State)
4. Scott Whirley (Augsburg)
5. Scott Stansbury (Kearney State)
6. Jay Lineberry (Elon)

134-lb class
1. Brent Lofstedt (Southern Oregon)
2. Darrin Huff (Central State)
3. Wayne Peterson (Fort Hays)
4. Tony Algiers (Wisconsin—Eau Claire)
5. John Kranz (Loras)
6. Mike Holmes (Mayville)

142-lb class
1. Ronnie James (Central State)
2. John Sheridan (Adams State)
3. Maury Vanderpool (Carson-Newman)
4. Dan Pitsch (Dickinson State)
5. Bob Arvold (Augsburg)
6. Charlie Hicks (Central Washington)

150-lb class
1. Paul Frandsen (Wisconsin—River Falls)
2. Rich Exparza (Central Washington)
3. Shea Kennedy (Augsburg)
4. Rick Scheuermann (Waynesburg)
5. Mimmo Marello (Simon Fraser)
6. Rick Morkel (Huron)

158-lb class
1. Chas Ekey (Fort Hays)
2. Terry Keller (Wisconsin—River Falls)
3. Mike Clark (Central State)
4. Gilbert Lucero (New Mexico Highlands)
5. Tim Vogel (Kearney State)
6. John Revesz (Pittsburgh-Johnstown)

167-lb class
1. Shane Palmer (Adams State)
2. Duane Groshek (Wisconsin—Platteville)
3. Howard Johnson (Liberty Baptist)
4. Benny Coleman (Central State)
5. Russell Hanson (Southern Oregon)
6. Brett Corsentino (Fort Lewis)

177-lb class
1. Bill Ameen (Central State)
2. Brian Edison (West Liberty State)
3. Chris Rinke (Simon Fraser)
4. John Curtis (Fort Hays)
5. Mike Agostini (Pacific Lutheran)
6. Kim Hogan (Pacific U)

190-lb class
1. Darrell Yohn (Adams State)
2. James Meyer (Wisconsin—River Falls)
3. Steve Marshall (Simon Fraser)

4. Greg Haga (Southern Oregon)
5. Joel Huffman (Westminister)
6. Tom Boerger (Jamestown)

Heavyweight
1. Ed Ritt (Pacific U)
2. Jim Viaene (Wisconsin—Superior)
3. Jim Etzler (Fort Lewis)
4. Chris Ruterbusch (Saginaw Valley)
5. Tom Hanson (Minnesota at Morris)
6. Kevin DesPlanques (Adams State)

1983 (at Minot, ND)

Team	*Points*
1. Southern Oregon	98.50
2. Simon Fraser	89.75
3. Augsburg	72
4. Jamestown	66.75
5. Central State (OK)	62.50
6. Huron	60.75
7. Adams State	57
8. Pacific University	43.50
9. Wisconsin—River Falls	43.25
10. Dickinson State	41.50
11. Carson-Newman	36.50
12. Central Washington	34
13. Southwest State	27.50
14. Loras	25.50
15. Liberty Baptist	22.75

Place winners

118-lb class
1. Randy Burwick (Dickinson State)
2. Alan Koors (Carson-Newman)
3. Jay Lineberry (Elon)
4. Rick Herrin (Pacific U)
5. Steve Gliva (Augsburg)
6. Darrell Burchfield (Saginaw)
7. Hal Fabrycki (Southern Oregon)
8. Jerry Marshall (Huron)

126-lb class
1. Keith Colsch (Loras)
2. Robin MacAlpine (Central Washington)
3. Doug Samarron (Southern Oregon)
4. Stan D'Andrea (Augsburg)
5. Mike Niccum (Anderson, IN)
6. Randy Pryor (West Liberty)
7. Eddie Baker (Jamestown)
8. Cyrus Winn (Carson-Newman)

134-lb class
1. Brent Lofstedt (Southern Oregon)
2. Bob Adams (Augsburg)
3. Les Plumley (Southwest State)
4. Jack Nishikawa (Fort Hays)
5. Jeff Vance (Northwestern, IA)
6. Tom Hershberger (Fort Hays)
7. Bob Hirsch (Northern State)
8. Keith Harpster (Malone)

142-lb class
1. Ron James (Central State)
2. Nathan Winner (Southern Oregon)
3. Lynn Plumley (Southwest State)
4. Merrick Wiles (Huron)
5. Mike Holmes (Mayville)
6. Tom Hall (Augsburg)
7. Dave Delande (West Liberty State)
8. Rick Willits (Adams State)

150-lb class
1. Dave McKay (Simon Fraser)
2. Gene Noce (Huron)
3. Paul Syvrud (Jamestown)
4. C.D. Hoiness (Central Washington)
5. Eric Dean (Adams State)
6. Maury Vanderpool (Carson-Newman)
7. Noel Hygelund (Pacific U)
8. Bob Stroh (Oregon Institute of Technology)

158-lb class
1. Jaime Armento (Adams State)
2. Paul Frandsen (Wisconsin—River Falls)
3. Mike Rouse (Pacific U)
4. Dan Stepleton (Huron)
5. Jim Fitterer (Southern Oregon)
6. Scott Weber (Jamestown)
7. Mark Allen (Central State)
8. Don Studer (St. Thomas)

167-lb class
1. Bruce Arvold (Augsburg)
2. Shane Palmer (Adams State)
3. Brian Hilts (Northern Montana)
4. Gabe Damiani (James)
5. Tony Ramsey (Simon Fraser)
6. Gary Astle (Central State)
7. Steve Behrns (Liberty Baptist)
8. Tom Mikalson (Biola)

177-lb class
1. Chris Rinke (Simon Fraser)
2. Bennie Coleman (Central State)
3. Dave Shoemaker (Liberty Baptist)
4. Dan Barent (Chadron State)
5. Russell Hanson (Southern Oregon)
6. Dave Veal (Huron)
7. Brian Ross (Wayne State)
8. Greg Krueger (Hanover)

190-lb class
1. David Marshall (Jamestown)
2. Jim Meyer (Wisconsin—River Falls)
3. Phil Gifford (Waynesburg)
4. Greg Haga (Southern Oregon)
5. Greg Herman (Huron)
6. Rich Schoene (West Liberty)
7. Keith Vogel (Siena)
8. Dean Reicks (Kearney State)

Heavyweight
1. Bob Molle (Simon Fraser)
2. Kurt Lesser (Dickinson State)
3. James Etzler (Fort Lewis)
4. Bruce Lambert (Pfeiffer)
5. Malcolm McLeod (Concordia)
6. Ed Ritt (Pacific U)
7. Rick Chandler (Southern Oregon)
8. Bob Pearce (Western Montana)

1984 (at Edmond, OK)

Team	Points
1. Central State (OK)	122.25
2. Jamestown	89.25
3. Southern Oregon	73.50
4. Simon Fraser	63.50
5. Adams State	49.75
6. Pacific University	44.25
7. Central Washington	40.50
8. Southwest State	37.25
9. Wisconsin—Parkside	36.75
10. Wisconsin—River Falls, Carson-Newman	32.25
12. West Liberty State	28.50
13. Northern Montana, Huron	27.25
15. Kearney State	25.25

Place winners

118-lb class
1. Greg Ford (Central Washington)
2. Mike Arnold (Adams State)
3. Mickey McGowan (Central State)
4. Randy Burwick (Dickinson State)
5. Duane Possail (Southwest State)
6. Darryl Strait (Jamestown)
7. Mike Romero (Southern Oregon)
8. Jerry Marshall (Huron)

126-lb class
1. Robin MacAlpine (Central Washington)
2. Doug Samarron (Southern Oregon)
3. Joe Klein (Pacific U)
4. Mike Vania (Wisconsin—Parkside)
5. Keith Colsch (Loras)
6. Cyrus Wynn (Carson-Newman)
7. Andy Mora (Western State)
8. Mike Niccum (Anderson, IN)

134-lb class
1. Clay Holly (Adams State)
2. Darren Huff (Central State)
3. David Perea (Western Colorado)
4. Tom Gallagher (Wisconsin—River Falls)
5. Matt Kluge (Wisconsin—Parkside)
6. Nike Nelson (Southern Oregon)
7. Brian Nelson (Carson-Newman)
8. Rich Gaudi (Jamestown)

142-lb class
1. Nathan Winner (Southern Oregon)
2. Merrick Wiles (Huron)
3. Ronnie James (Central State)
4. Tom Molitor (Southwest State)

5. Mike Holmes (Mayville)
6. Bret Corner (Wisconsin—La Crosse)
7. Mike Winter (Wisconsin—Parkside)
8. Mike Jozwowski (Wisconsin—Platteville)

150-lb class
1. Paul Syvrud (Jamestown)
2. Mark Allen (Central State)
3. Dale Krzmarzick (Pacific U)
4. Eric Dean (Adams State)
5. Joseph Aline (Northern Montana)
6. Alan Noce (Huron)
7. Maury Vanderpool (Carson-Newman)
8. Greg Rojas (Kearney State)

158-lb class
1. Jack O'Connor (Central State)
2. Terry Keller (Wisconsin—River Falls)
3. Lionel Keys (Chicago)
4. Don Zellner (Pacific U)
5. Rick Crosier (West Liberty State)
6. Art Willden (Fort Lewis)
7. Chris Moore (Carson-Newman)
8. Tim DeLarm (Westmar)

167-lb class
1. Tony Ramsay (Simon Fraser)
2. Scott Dubbelde (Southwest State)
3. Gregg Moore (Jamestown)
4. Gary Astle (Central State)
5. Steve Klock (Olivet Nazarene)
6. Alan Brown (Carson-Newman)
7. Ron Yde (Wisconsin—La Crosse)
8. Steve Tekander (Southern Oregon)

177-lb class
1. Benny Coleman (Central State)
2. Russ Hanson (Southern Oregon)
3. Mike Guenther (Southern Colorado)
4. Gabe Damiani (Jamestown)
5. Wesley Robinson (Northern Montana)
6. Ted Keyes (Wisconsin—Parkside)
7. Mike Agostini (Pacific Lutheran)
8. Tim Kemp (Bethel)

190-lb class
1. Lari Mertens (Mesa)
2. Tom Boerger (Jamestown)
3. Rich Schoene (West Liberty State)
4. Lou Kok (Simon Fraser)
5. Gary Solomon (Western New England)
6. Bary Voycheske (Chadron State)
7. Kirk Humphrey (Loras)
8. Jay Graham (Northern Montana)

Heavyweight
1. Bob Molle (Simon Fraser)
2. Ted Reehl (Kearney State)
3. George Fraher (Jamestown)
4. James Viaene (Wisconsin—Superior)
5. Dave Wiane (Wisconsin—Platteville)
6. George McDuffie (Findlay)
7. Lary Wooten (Fort Hays)
8. Bruce Lambert (Pfeiffer)

1985 (at Jamestown, ND)

Team	*Points*
1. Central State	124.25
2. Southern Colorado	80.50
3. Northern State	77.50
4. Simon Fraser	62.50
5. Southern Oregon	58.50
6. Wisconsin—River Falls	51.75
7. West Liberty State	41.75
8. Dickinson State	32.50
9. Central Washington	31
10. Western State	30
11. Carson-Newman	28.75
12. Jamestown	28
13. Adams State	25
14. New Mexico Highlands	24.50
15. Moorhead State	22.50

Place winners

118-lb class
1. Dave Harvey (Northern State)
2. Billy Reid (Central State)
3. Randy Burwick (Dickinson State)
4. Bryan Bunch (West Liberty State)
5. Troy Humphrey (Valley City)
6. Pete Eagle (Pacific U)
7. Justin Birikelo (Moorhead State)
8. Randy Henderson (Simon Fraser)

126-lb class
1. Bryan Hawkins (Southern Colorado)
2. Doyle Everson (Northern State)
3. Adrian Rodriquez (Biola)
4. Mike Ritchey (Southern Oregon)
5. Mike Miller (Malone)
6. Mark Peterson (Central Washington)
7. Darryl Stevens (Wisconsin—River Falls)
8. Darryl Strait (Jamestown)

134-lb class
1. Brain Nelson (Carson-Newman)
2. Joe Starzenski (Central State)
3. David Perea (Western State)
4. Bill Bradley (Northern Montana)
5. Greg Stalnaker (Fort Lewis)
6. Allen Foltz (Moorhead)
7. Jack Neshikawa (Simon Fraser)
8. Mike LaBrosse (Dickinson State)

142-lb class
1. Ricky Bollenback (Central State)
2. Dennis Lucero (New Mexico Highlands)
3. Chris Wolfe (Pacific U)
4. LeRoy McCormick (Dickinson State)
5. Brent Corner (Wisconsin—La Crosse)
6. John Blangor (West Liberty State)
7. Jeff Nelson (Minot)
8. Don Rachel (Minnesota at Morris)

150-lb class
1. Rick Willits (Adams State)
2. Kevin Freeman (Central State)
3. Kris Morgan (Central Washington)
4. Dave Delande (West Liberty State)
5. Todd Carey (Southern Colorado)
6. Tim Molitor (Southwest State)
7. Scott Miller (Malone)
8. Vince Jones (Jamestown)

158-lb class
1. Paul Syvrud (Jamestown)
2. Jack O'Connor (Central State)
3. Eric Lujan (Southern Colorado)
4. Kevin Vandyke (Mayville)
5. Rick Crosier (West Liberty)
6. Daniel Stapleton (Northwestern, IA)
7. Mick Mazzuca (Western State)
8. Mike Muckerheide (Wisconsin—Parkside)

167-lb class
1. Steve Tekander (Southern Oregon)
2. Howard Seay (Central State)
3. Brian Keller (Wisconsin—River Falls)
4. Greg Edgelow (Simon Fraser)
5. Todd Yde (Wisconsin—Parkside)
6. Kerry Ast (Huron)
7. Bob Meszaros (Siena)
8. Jeff Walker (West Liberty State)

177-lb class
1. Mike Guenther (Southern Colorado)
2. Dave Brandvold (Wisconsin—River Falls)
3. John Deaton (Central State)
4. Mark Kissell (Waynesburg)
5. Leonard Hawkins (Chadron State)
6. Jeff Lipp (Pacific Lutheran)
7. Bill Bussey (Dana)
8. Jeff Pratt (Carson-Newman)

190-lb class
1. Greg Haga (Southern Oregon)
2. Blaine McCance (Northern State)
3. Peter Banicevic (SM)
4. Tom Harris (Northwestern, IA)
5. Tim Olson (Wisconsin—Superior)
6. Joe Brown (Southern Colorado)
7. Michael Zerr (Western State)
8. Doug Pfeiffer (Siena)

Heavyweight
1. Bob Molle (Simon Fraser)
2. Matt Renn (Wisconsin—River Falls)
3. Jim Fryer (Northern State)
4. Jim Williamson (Minnesota at Morris)
5. Daryl Tysdal (Moorhead State)
6. Rod Tickle (Kearney State)
7. Randy Penrose (Central Washington)
8. Mike Max (Chadron State)

1986 (at Minot, ND)

Team	*Points*
1. Central State (OK)	98.50
2. Southern Oregon	91.25
3. Simon Fraser	83.25
4. West Liberty State	55.25
5. Fort Hays	54.25
6. Minnesota at Duluth	49.75
7. Northern State	47
8. Dickinson State	44
9. Southern Colorado	42.25
10. Southwest State	41.75
11. Adams State	37.50
12. Minnesota at Morris	36.50
13. Central Washington, Jamestown	34.75
15. Western State	34

Place winners

118-lb class
1. Greg Davis (Minnesota at Morris)
2. Billy Johnson (Fort Hays)
3. Bryan Bunch (West Liberty State)
4. Peter Eagle (Pacific U)
5. Steve Wright (Carson-Newman)
6. Mike Wiley (Northern State)
7. Rodney Romero (Adams State)
8. Kurt Snyder (Dickinson State)

126-lb class
1. Dave Harvey (Northern State)
2. Bill Reid (Central State)
3. Blaine Dravis (Minnesota at Duluth)
4. Mike Fitzgerald (Southern Colorado)
5. Mike LaBrosse (Dickinson State)
6. Mike Richey (Southern Oregon)
7. Dennis Oliver (Kearney State)
8. Mike Hendrickson (Minnesota at Morris)

134-lb class
1. Joe Starzenski (Central State)
2. Tim Satre (Southern Oregon)
3. Marc Hull (Fort Hays)
4. Lee Braaten (Southwest State)
5. Ken Nelson (Western State)
6. Tad Thorstenson (Northern State)
7. Thad O'Donnell (Dickinson State)
8. Jim LaBrosse (Adams State)

142-lb class
1. Jeff Kloetzer (Northern Montana)
2. Bret Corner (Wisconsin—La Crosse)
3. Kevin Freeman (Central State)
4. Chris Wolfe (Pacific Lutheran)
5. Jeff Dravis (Minnesota at Duluth)
6. Pat Hogan (Loras)
7. Steve Giadone (Southern Colorado)
8. David Venem (Adams State)

150-lb class
1. Ed Sernoski (Simon Fraser)
2. Stoney Wright (Central State)
3. Randi Talvi (Central Washington)
4. Rich Wilson (Adams State)
5. Blain Schutzler (Southern Oregon)
6. Tim Delarm (Westmar)
7. Scott Thompson (Northern State)
8. Bill McDonald (Southwest State)

158-lb class
1. Paul Syvrud (Jamestown)
2. Dave Delande (West Liberty State)
3. Kris Morgan (Central Washington)
4. Wayne Simons (Fort Hays)
5. Rick Dove (Simon Fraser)
6. Jack O'Connor (Central State)
7. Brad Simon (Wisconsin—Superior)
8. Brian Rognholt (Adams State)

167-lb class
1. Steve Tekander (Southern Oregon)
2. Chuck Pipher (Southern Colorado)
3. Brian Keller (Wisconsin—River Falls)
4. Arthur Willden (Fort Lewis)
5. Howard Seay (Central State)
6. Ken Parshall (Pacific U)
7. Jeff Bratt (Carson-Newman)
8. Duain Woodruff (Jamestown)

177-lb class
1. Greg Edgelow (Simon Fraser)
2. Scott Schenerlein (West Liberty State)
3. Ted Bullerman (Southwest State)
4. Vince Dawson (Southern Oregon)
5. Kelly McNary (Dickinson State)
6. Richard Harding (Stevenson)
7. Dan Laurent (Adams State)
8. Scott Pickert (Mesa)

190-lb class
1. Mike Zerr (Western State)
2. Paul Dodson (Southern Oregon)
3. Gary Solomon (Western New England)
4. Tim Olson (Wisconsin—Superior)
5. Ab Brown (Mesa)
6. Mark Kissell (Wayne State)
7. John Trevett (Northern State)
8. Bob Kipp (Defiance)

Heavyweight
1. Bob Molle (Simon Fraser)
2. Dave Viaene (Minnesota at Duluth)
3. Mike Max (Chadron State)
4. Dean Reicks (Kearney State)
5. Jody Walsh (Northwestern, IA)
6. Don Verbruggen (Wisconsin—Parkside)
7. Frank Shepard (Chicago State)
8. Hector Hernandez (New Mexico Highlands)

1987 (at Wheeling, WV)

Team	*Points*
1. Central State (OK)	92.50
2. Alaska Pacific	71.50
3. Southern Oregon	64.25
4. Adams State	62.75
5. Fort Hays	54
6. West Liberty State	52
7. Carson-Newman	51.25
8. Southern Colorado	43
9. Dickinson State	42
10. Minnesota at Duluth	41.50
11. Kearney State	40
12. Southwest State	38.75
13. Simon Fraser	37
14. Central Washington	31
15. Western State	28

Place winners

118-lb class
1. Bill Johnson (Fort Hays)
2. Calvin Matutina (Pacific U)
3. Steve Wright (Carson-Newman)
4. Rodney Romero (Adams State)
5. Ernie Jimenez (Western State)
6. Jason Kordus (Southern Oregon)
7. Shawn Fleming (Central State)
8. Mike Mueller (Wisconsin—River Falls)

126-lb class
1. Lenal Brinson (Central Washington)
2. Adrian Rodriguez (Pacific Lutheran)
3. Bryan Bunch (West Liberty State)
4. Michael Pontoya (Fort Lewis)
5. Mike Mazurkeiwicz (Northern Montana)
6. Mike Ritchey (Southern Oregon)
7. Dale Hall (Wisconsin—Parkside)
8. Greg Phannenstie (Fort Hays)

134-lb class
1. Marc Hull (Fort Hays)
2. Thad O'Donnell (Dickinson State)
3. Jeff Wallace (Alaska Pacific)
4. Ken Wharry (Southern Oregon)
5. Jerry Goss (Central State)
6. Jeff Yearous (Adams State)
7. Jim Jenkins (Waynesburg)
8. Warren Dumas (Pembroke State)

142-lb class
1. Todd Steidley (Central State)
2. Jeff Dravis (Minnesota at Duluth)
3. Jim LaBrosse (Adams State)
4. Steve Giadone (Southern Colorado)
5. Mark Jenkins (Waynesburg)
6. Derrik Sych (Simon Fraser)
7. Greg Kay (Wisconsin—River Falls)
8. Don Rachel (Minnesota at Morris)

150-lb class
1. Johnny Nimmo (Central State)
2. Ed Sernoski (Simon Fraser)
3. Randy Halvi (Alaska Pacific)
4. Roy Heverly (Pembroke State)
5. Bill McDonald (Southwest State)
6. Trent Gutschenritter (Dana)
7. Eddie Crocker (Carson-Newman)
8. John Metz (Northern Montana)

158-lb class
1. Michael Hirschey (Minnesota at Duluth)
2. Ray Birden (Huron)
3. Jeff Steele (Alaska Pacific)
4. Steve Roberts (Kearney State)
5. Darren Peaster (Central State)
6. Todd Ponick (Wisconsin—River Falls)
7. Geoff Marsh (Simon Fraser)
8. Mark Hensey (Adams State)

167-lb class
1. Chuck Pipher (Southern Colorado)
2. Brett Beams (Central State)
3. Trevor Wilson (Dickinson State)
4. Bryan Driscoll (West Liberty State)
5. Joe Swanson (Olivet)
6. Duain Woodruff (James)
7. Lawrence Owen (Pacific U)
8. Wayne Simons (Fort Hays)

177-lb class
1. John Fredrickson (Alaska Pacific)
2. Scott Schenerlein (West Liberty State)
3. Dan Laurent (Adams State)
4. Hugh Meek (Carson-Newman)
5. Ted Bullerman (Southwest State)
6. Eugene Martinez (Southern Colorado)
7. Jeff Parke (Chadron State)
8. Larry Denn (Southern Oregon)

190-lb class
1. Paul Dodson (Southern Oregon)
2. Mike Zerr (Western State)
3. John Sterner (Southwest State)
4. Rob Trayner (Adams State)
5. Bob Manville (Olivet)
6. Bill Ogilvie (Central State)
7. Tim Oson (Wisconsin—Superior)
8. Keith Eager (Pacific Lutheran)

Heavyweight
1. Hector Hernandez (New Mexico Highlands)
2. Dean Reicks (Kearney State)
3. Jim Wiliamson (Minnesota at Morris)
4. Tom Theilig (Carson-Newman)
5. Don Ver Bruggen (Wisconsin—Parkside)
6. Jay Stainbeck (Pembroke State)
7. Craig Danielson (Central Washington)
8. Bradley Steward (Alaska Pacific)

1988 (at Pacific Lutheran University, Tacoma, WA)

Team	*Points*
1. Simon Fraser	104.50
2. Central State (OK)	89
3. Southern Oregon	79.75
4. Alaska Pacific	78.25
5. Southern Colorado	73.25
6. Carson-Newman	70
7. Pacific University	50.75
8. Northern Montana, Western Montana	42
10. Minnesota at Duluth	39
11. Mesa	36.25
12. Adams State	35.50
13. Southwest State	33
14. Olivet Nazarene	27
15. Wisconsin—Parkside	24.75

Place winners

118-lb class
1. Jeffrey Wright (Carson-Newman)
2. Shawn Fleming (Central State)
3. Calvin Matutino (Pacific U)
4. Billy Johnson (Fort Hays)
5. Rodney Romero (Adams State)
6. Chol An (Northern Montana)
7. Norm Spence (Simon Fraser)
8. Dan Harms (Southwest State)

126-lb class
1. Troy Humphrey (Western Montana)
2. Torey McCully (Alaska Pacific)
3. Mike Mazurkiewicz (Northern Montana)
4. Michael Pantoya (Fort Lewis)
5. Mike Ritchey (Adams State)
6. Tracy Ping (Northwest State)
7. Larry Stanbrough (Huron)
8. Chooper Shrull (Southern Colorado)

134-lb class
1. Ken Wharry (Southern Oregon)
2. Craig Roberts (Simon Fraser)
3. Jeff Wallace (Alaska Pacific)
4. Jeff Dravis (Minnesota at Duluth)
5. Eddie Clark (Northern State)
6. Warren Dumas (Pembroke State)
7. James Jenkins (Wayne State)
8. Jack Danner (Wisconsin—Parkside)

142-lb class
1. Chuck Ahsmuhs (Pacific U)
2. Todd Steidley (Central State)
3. Trevor Londgren (Minnesota at Duluth)
4. Roy Heverly (Pembroke State)
5. Greg Kay (Wisconsin—River Falls)
6. Mark Jenkins (Wayne State)
7. Jim Labrosse (Adams State)
8. Tad Thorstenson (Western Montana)

150-lb class
1. Ed Sernowski (Simon Fraser)
2. Kevin Freeman (Central State)
3. Jim Zeigler (Southern Colorado)
4. Tim Blatter (Western Montana)
5. Scott Barker (Mesa)
6. Bob Freund (Pacific Lutheran)
7. Brad Christensen (Southern Oregon)
8. Larry Evens (Adams State)

158-lb class
1. Johnny Nimmo (Central State)
2. Bill McDonald (Southwest State)
3. Chris Wilson (Simon Fraser)
4. Jeff Marshall (Southern Oregon)
5. Jeff Steele (Alaska Pacific)
6. Ray Birden (Huron)
7. Maurice Harrison (Carson-Newman)
8. Marty Boday (North Idaho)

167-lb class
1. Chuck Pipher (Southern Colorado)
2. Gianni Buono (Simon Fraser)
3. Bryan Driscoll (West Liberty State)
4. Mark Hemauer (Wisconsin—Parkside)
5. Larry Denn (Southern Oregon)
6. Lawrence Owen (Pacific)
7. Brad Simon (Minnesota at Duluth)
8. Philip Farley (Black Hills State)

177-lb class
1. John Fredrickson (Alaska Pacific)
2. Hugh Meek (Carson-Newman)
3. Eugene Martinez (Southern Colorado)
4. Bob Waldner (Chadron State)
5. Richard Agee (Central State, OK)
6. Jerry Nagel (Mary)
7. Mike Nansel (Fort Hays)
8. Mark French (Northern Montana)

190-lb class
1. Bob Manville (Olivet)
2. Scott Pickert (Mesa)
3. Paul Neuner (Carson-Newman)
4. Bob Wozniak (Wisconsin—Eau Claire)
5. Kevin Colvin (Southern Colorado)
6. Tom Upchurch (Alaska Pacific)
7. Scott Bianco (Simon Fraser)
8. Dan Stifter (Minnesota at Morris)

Heavyweight
1. Dan Payne (Simon Fraser)
2. Jim Williamson (Minnesota at Morris)
3. J.D. Alley (Southern Oregon)
4. John Richburg (Adams State)
5. Jeff Russell (Mesa)
6. Fred Maroschek (Mayville)
7. Tim Leuer (Westmar)
8. Shawn Hughes (Alaska Pacific)

Table 8.7
Junior Colleges Tournament (1960-1988)

1960 (at Farmingdale, Long Island, NY)

Team	*Points*
1. Lamar (CO)	98
2. Long Island	55
3. Mesa (CO)	37
4. SUNY A&T at Alfred	29
5. Paul Smith's	28
6. Orange County	24

Place winners

115-lb class
1. Sanchez (Lamar)
2. Leonhardt (Long Island)
3. Simko (Orange County)

123-lb class
1. Archuleta (Lamar)
2. Nebbia (Paul Smith's)
3. Factora (Long Island)

130-lb class
1. Terronez (Lamar)
2. Ferrari (Paul Smith's)

137-lb class
1. Apodaca (Lamar)
2. Erickson (Long Island)
3. Durham (Paul Smith's)

147-lb class
1. Rath (Lamar)
2. Wheeler (Alfred)
3. Lee (Long Island)

157-lb class
1. Hines (Mesa)
2. Coronato (Long Island)
3. Ross Lamar)

167-lb class
1. Schauer (Lamar)
2. Kasperski (Long Island)
3. Lind (Paul Smith's)

177-lb class
1. Barton (Mesa)
2. Collins (Long Island)
3. Franco (Lamar)

191-lb class
1. Crothers (Alfred)
2. Curtis (Orange County)
3. Alderman (Lamar)

Heavyweight
1. Rush (Mesa)
2. Baker (Lamar)
3. Shay (Orange County)

1961 (at Farmingdale, Long Island, NY)

Team	*Points*
1. Lamar (CO)	122
2. Mesa (CO)	76
3. Orange County (NY)	36
4. Paul Smith's	27
5. Rockland	26
6. SUNY A&T at Alfred	22
7. New York Aggies	17

Team	Points
8. Nassau	16
9. SUNY A&T at Delhi	10
10. Wright (IL)	1

Place winners

115-lb class
1. Lensky (Lamar)
2. Svenson (Rockland)
3. Sintzonich (Paul Smith's)
4. Martinez (New York Aggies)

123-lb class
1. Madden (Lamar)
2. Ward (Rockland)
3. Clubb (Mesa)
4. Mostowsky (Orange County)

130-lb class
1. Boydston (Lamar)
2. Normoyle (Orange County)
3. Huff (Alfred)
4. Baldwin (Mesa)

137-lb class
1. Crider (Mesa)
2. Ross (Lamar)
3. Hicks (Alfred)
4. Scalire (Wright)

147-lb class
1. Anderson (Lamar)
2. Lee (New York Aggies)
3. Peterson (Mesa)
4. Dupree (Paul Smith's)

157-lb class
1. Hines (Mesa)
2. Beitz (Lamar)
3. Wheeler (Alfred)
4. Parshley (Paul Smith's)

167-lb class
1. Schauer (Lamar)
2. Mutchler (Mesa)
3. Robinson (Rockland)
4. Cowen (Alfred)

177-lb class
1. Jacobsen (Lamar)
2. Miller (Mesa)
3. Board (Orange County)
4. Glur (Paul Smith's)

191-lb class
1. Traynor (Mesa)
2. Miller (Nassau)
3. Linn (Lamar)
4. Toth (Paul Smith's)

Heavyweight
1. Kuhn (Lamar)
2. Gawden (Delhi)
3. Shay (Orange County)
4. Baker (New York Aggies)

1962 (at Lamar, CO)

Team	Points
1. Lamar (CO)	67
2. Worthington	61
3. Mesa (ICO)	53
4. Trinidad	43
5. Northeastern	25
6. Ricks	23
7. Nassau	15
8. Lower Columbia	8
9. Sheridan	6
10. Fort Lewis	5
11. Otero	0

Place winners

115-lb class
1. Gallegos (Northeastern)
2. Velasquez (Trinidad)
3. Trantham (Lamar)
4. Houk (Mesa)

123-lb class
1. Gangestad (Worthington)
2. Clugston (Mesa)
3. Yost (Ricks)
4. Manzanares (Trinidad)

130-lb class
1. Derryberry (Mesa)
2. Boydston (Lamar)
3. Paulsen (Worthington)
4. Cerrone (Trinidad)

137-lb class
1. Lorenz (Worthington)
2. A. Ruckman (Mesa)

3. Christiansen (Ricks)
4. Wallesen (Sheridan)

147-lb class
1. Beitz (Lamar)
2. Seery (Trinidad)
3. Tow (Lower Columbia)
4. Jardine (Ricks)

157-lb class
1. Sampson (Trinidad)
2. Hinton (Mesa)
3. Leonard (Lamar)
4. Fairbanks (Ricks)

167-lb class
1. Jacobsen (Lamar)
2. Bays (Mesa)
3. Voss (Worthington)
4. Pruett (Sheridan)

177-lb class
1. Tuin (Worthington)
2. Alnwick (Northeastern)
3. Lynn (Lamar)
4. W. Ruckman (Mesa)

191-lb class
1. Keller (Northeastern)
2. Rider (Lamar)
3. John (Fort Lewis)
4. Miller (Nassau)

Heavyweight
1. Karstens (Worthington)
2. Brookhart (Lamar)
3. Brown (Trinidad)
4. Nugent (Nassau)

1963 (at Lamar, CO)

Team	*Points*
1. Lamar (CO)	74
2. Northeastern (CO)	58
3. Phoenix	43
4. Worthington	38
5. Joliet	35
6. Boise	31
7. Nassau	23
8. Paul Smith's	12
9. Mesa (CO), Rochester (MN)	10
11. Bismarck	8
12. Ricks	5
13. LeTourneau	3
14. Centerville, Wentworth (MO)	2

Place winners

115-lb class
1. Graves (Phoenix)
2. Murphy (Mor)
3. R. Pontius (Lamar)
4. Sandoval (Northeastern)

123-lb class
1. Henry (Lamar)
2. Free (Mesa)
3. Vance (Boise)
4. Ingalls (Rochester)

130-lb class
1. Carcia (Phoenix)
2. Epps (Joliet)
3. Paulsen (Worthington)
4. Oretega (Northeastern)

137-lb class
1. Walker (Lamar)
2. Furlan (Joliet)
3. Carrasco (Northeastern)
4. Lorenz (Worthington)

147-lb class
1. Bauchman (Phoenix)
2. T. Pontius (Lamar)
3. Heinz (Northeastern)
4. Moors (Nassau)

157-lb class
1. Edwards (Northeastern)
2. Butler (Lamar)
3. Jacobsen (Rochester)
4. Tuin (Worthington)

167-lb class
1. Leonard (Lamar)
2. Hagaman (Northeastern)
3. Biondolillo (Paul Smith's)
4. Schuler (Bismarck)

177-lb class
1. Johnson (Boise)
2. Alles (Northeastern)
3. Urban (Lamar)
4. Voss (Joliet)

191-lb class
1. Pederson (Boise)
2. McDonald (Joliet)
3. Keller (Northeastern)
4. Rider (Lamar)

Heavyweight
1. Karsten (Worthington)
2. Nugent (Nassau)
3. Bell (Phoenix)
4. Bowers (LeTourneau)

1964 (at Worthington, MN)

Team	*Points*
1. Northeastern (CO), Joliet	56
3. Lamar (CO)	37
4. Ricks	34
5. Bismarck	33
6. Mesa (CO), Rochester (MN)	29
8. SUNY A&T at Alfred	26
9. Phoenix	19
10. Paul Smith's	15
11. SUNY A&T at Farmingdale, SUNY A&T at Cobleskill	13
13. Rockland, Arizona Western	7
15. Suffolk County	5

Place winners

115-lb class
1. Ulibarri (Northeastern)
2. Schaff (Bismarck)
3. Edwards (Joliet)
4. Bolognini (Rockland)

123-lb class
1. Ceplecha (Rochester)
2. Clegg (Joliet)
3. Dietz (Bismarck)
4. Meador (Phoenix)

130-lb class
1. Henry (Lamar)
2. Austin (Northeastern)
3. Manwaring (Ricks)
4. Free (Mesa)

137-lb class
1. Furlan (Joliet)
2. Staudenbaur (Farmingdale)
3. Abel (Lamar)
4. Miller (Ricks)

147-lb class
1. Thomas (Joliet)
2. Bower (Paul Smith's)
3. Pontious (Lamar)
4. Schurtz (Ricks)

157-lb class
1. Keller (Bismarck)
2. Heinz (Northeastern)
3. Fairbanks (Ricks)
4. Butler (Lamar)

167-lb class
1. Groski (Cobleskill)
2. Aadahl (Rochester)
3. Hutchings (Northeastern)
4. Eddy (Lamar)

177-lb class
1. Rowley (Mesa)
2. Templin (Phoenix)
3. Anna (Alfred)
4. Patterick (Mesa)

191-lb class
1. Walker (Alfred)
2. Patterick (Mesa)
3. Voss (Joliet)
4. Gardner (Suffolk County)

Heavyweight
1. Christensen (Ricks)
2. Hastings (Northeastern)
3. Colmenero (Arizona Western)
4. Wright (Paul Smith's)

1965 (at Worthington, MN)

Team	*Points*
1. Lamar (CO)	93
2. Phoenix	58
3. Rochester (MN)	51
4. Joliet, Ricks	35
6. Northeastern (CO), Paul Smith's	24
8. Worthington	18
9. North Dakota Science	15
10. Bismarck, SUNY A&T at Delhi, Hershey	14
13. Mesa (CO)	12
14. Corning	11
15. Cobleskill, SUNY A&T at Snow	10

Place winners

115-lb class
1. Wayne Watson (Joliet)
2. Tackabury (Cobleskill)
3. Ghormley (Ricks)
4. Rondeau (Phoenix)
5. Wandrow (Rochester)
6. Ulibarri (Northeastern)

123-lb class
1. Gene Parrish (Lamar)
2. Bakke (Austin)
3. Schaff (Bismarck)
4. Wolf (North Dakota Science)
5. McBride (Rochester)
6. Romack (Mesa)

130-lb class
1. Don Mullenbach (Rochester)
2. Thomas (Lamar)
3. Townsend (Joliet)
4. Dunham (Mesa)
5. Jochim (Bismarck)
6. Axtell (Itasca)

137-lb class
1. Al Freeman (Paul Smith's)
2. Lorenz (Worthington)
3. Abel (Lamar)
4. Kinney (Northeastern)
5. Brewer (Delhi A&T)
6. Ellis (Itasca)

147-lb class
1. Jerry Lattimore (Lamar)
2. Jouett (Northeastern)
3. Iverson (Rochester)
4. Norskog (Worthington)
5. Sukle (Mesa)
6. Roberson (Joliet)

157-lb class
1. Juis Baiz (Phoenix)
2. Eddie (Lamar)
3. Newman (Snow)
4. Johnson (Rochester)
5. Schulze (Worthington)
6. Dillman (North Dakota Science)

167-lb class
1. Matt Kline (Hershey)
2. Antrim (Lamar)
3. Patterson (Phoenix)
4. Fairbanks (Ricks)
5. Kohm (North Dakota Science)
6. Aadahl (Rochester)

177-lb class
1. Mike DuMas (Lamar)
2. Gillespie (Ricks)
3. Templin (Phoenix)
4. Wetzel (Willmar)
5. Mackey (Joliet)
6. Nicol (Farmingdale)

191-lb class
1. Floyd Schade (Lamar)
2. Middleton (Rochester)
3. Clark (Corning)
4. Cook (Dawson)
5. Haug (York)
6. Ostergaard (Dixie)

Heavyweight
1. Gil Lilienthal (Phoenix)
2. Knout (Delhi)
3. Christensen (Ricks)
4. Wright (Paul Smith's)
5. Kuntz (Bismarck)
6. Richards (Northeastern)

1966 (at Worthington, MN)

Team	Points
1. Northeastern (CO)	93
2. Lamar (CO)	73
3. Joliet	67
4. Phoenix	36
5. Arizona Western	26
6. Bismarck	23
7. Willmar	21
8. Mesa (CO)	20
9. SUNY A&T at Morrisville	15
10. Suffolk County	14
11. Itasca, Worthington	13
13. Austin (MN), Ricks	11
15. Garden City	9

Place winners

118-lb class
1. Bob Shines (Joliet)
2. Stinson (Lamar)
3. Bingham (Ricks)
4. Matias (Orange County)
5. Montana (Auburn)
6. Engquist (Rochester)

123-lb class
1. Carlos Fontanez (Lamar)
2. Varra (Northeastern)
3. Bakke (Austin)
4. Watson (Joliet)
5. Evans (Broome Tech)
6. Wergin (Mesa)

130-lb class
1. Don Mullenbach (Rochester)
2. Jensen (Phoenix)
3. Brown (Northeastern)
4. Ward (New York Aggies)
5. St. Clair (Lamar)
6. Schild (Broome Tech)

137-lb class
1. Jack Radabaugh (Rochester)
2. Sheppard (Joliet)
3. Kinney (Northeastern)
4. Grim (York)
5. Holland (Phoenix)
6. Watson (Itasca)

145-lb class
1. Jerry Lattimore (Lamar)
2. Mihal (Rochester)
3. Jouett (Northeastern)
4. Stachelski (Joliet)
5. Murphy (Arizona Western)
6. Tresner (Garden City)

152-lb class
1. Jim Johnson (Rochester)
2. Sadrazdeh (Phoenix)
3. Kettleson (Bismarck)
4. Weber (Joliet)
5. Buckner (Northeastern)
6. Kenyon (Paul Smith's)

160-lb class
1. Jim Sukle (Mesa)
2. Rudzek (Northeastern)
3. Carroll (Arizona Western)
4. Lechtenberg (Rochester)
5. Roberson (Joliet)
6. Biggs (Garden City)

167-lb class
1. Robert Hough (Suffolk County)
2. Herring (Arizona Western)
3. Strand (Joliet)
4. Howard (Itasca)
5. Hawkins (Northeastern)
6. Nelson (Worthington)

177-lb class
1. Dave Wetzel (Willmar)
2. Notario (Northeastern)
3. Henderson (Lamar)
4. Gordon (Worthington)
5. Middleton (Rochester)
6. Wilinsky (Phoenix)

190-lb class
1. Gary Seymour (Morrisville)
2. Schade (Lamar)
3. Pachello (Northeastern)
4. Wintersteen (Joliet)
5. Parker (Ricks)
6. Eckerman (Rochester)

Heavyweight
1. Tom Firestack (Northeastern)
2. Kuntz (Bismarck)
3. Brown (Lamar)
4. Gerdel (Joliet)
5. Hudson (Phoenix)
6. Kallevig (Willmar)

1967 (at Worthington, MN)

Team	*Points*
1. Northeastern (CO)	61
2. Lamar (CO)	58
3. Trinidad	55
4. Phoenix	54
5. Rochester (MN)	53
6. Arizona Western	41
7. Garden City	34
8. Big Bend	28
9. SUNY A&T at Farmingdale	27
10. Columbia Basin, Itasca	25
12. Joliet	23
13. Keystone	18
14. SUNY A&T at Morrisville	17
15. Bismarck	15

Place winners

118-lb class
1. Ray Stapp (Trinidad)
2. Sprouse (Northeastern)
3. Lodge (Rochester)
4. Clinton (Arizona Western)
5. Oglesby (Joliet)
6. Grant (Morrisville)

123-lb class
1. Darrell Keller (Columbia Basin)
2. Sprhr (Nassau)
3. Steinson (Lamar)
4. Padilla (Northeastern)
5. Kitt (Arizona Western)
6. Gee (Joliet)

130-lb class
1. Bob Smith (Northeastern)
2. Kemp (Delhi)
3. Jenson (Phoenix)
4. Serrano (Mesa, CO)
5. Hartle (Rochester)
6. Baumgardt (Willmar)

137-lb class
1. Dick Keefe (Keystone)
2. Groom (Lamar)
3. Johnson (Northeastern)
4. Davilla (Orange County)
5. Murphy (Trinidad)
6. Tewksburg (Rochester)

145-lb class
1. Ed Adams (Farmingdale)
2. James (Columbia Basin)
3. Suzuki (Garden City)
4. Thompson (Trinidad)
5. Thorpe (Fulton-Montgomery)
6. Ruoho (Phoenix)

152-lb class
1. Jon Lane (Big Bend)
2. Mazzitelli (Itasca)
3. Sandrzadeh (Phoenix)
4. Johnson (Rochester)
5. Hosack (Arizona Western)
6. Stancel (Austin)

160-lb class
1. Rich Mihal (Rochester)
2. Johnston (Rockland)
3. Long (Mesa, AZ)
4. Kettleson (Bismarck)
5. Seibel (Big Bend)
6. Rawls (Trinidad)

167-lb class
1. Mickey Carroll (Arizona Western)
2. Biggs (Garden City)
3. Warren (Big Bend)
4. Conley (Lamar)
5. Pierce (Ricks)
6. Ask (Rochester)

177-lb class
1. John Lightner (Garden City)
2. Reinhardt (Itasca)
3. Notario (Northeastern)
4. Wolinsky (Phoenix)
5. Herring (Arizona Western)
6. Franckowiak (Trinidad)

191-lb class
1. Mike Sparaco (Trinidad)
2. Seymour (Morrisville)
3. Smith (Lamar)
4. Wintersteen (Joliet)
5. Engler (Phoenix)
6. Parker (Ricks)

Heavyweight
1. Jack Hudson (Phoenix)
2. Brown (Lamar)
3. Snyder (Farmingdale)
4. Aaland (Rochester)
5. Ives (Bismarck)
6. Lindquist (Fergus Falls)

1968 (at Worthington, MN)

Team	*Points*
1. Phoenix	96
2. Trinidad	81
3. Lamar (CO)	71
4. Joliet	70
5. Northeastern (CO)	54
6. Rochester (MN)	46
7. Big Bend	32
8. Orange County, SUNY A&T at Morrisville	30
10. Itasca	26
11. Blue Mountain (OR)	25
12. Grand Rapids Junior, Garden City	24
14. North Iowa	20
15. Ricks	18

Place winners

115-lb class
1. Tom Clardy (Trinidad)
2. Lodge (Rochester)
3. Cachero (Phoenix)
4. Froehle (Itasca)
5. Oglesby (Joliet)
6. Smith (Lamar)

123-lb class
1. Ed Maze (Lamar)
2. Sato (Northeastern)
3. Arnold (Trinidad)
4. Stockdale (Rochester)
5. Tonn (North Iowa)
6. Dana (Ricks)

130-lb class
1. Gayle Tollifson (Phoenix)
2. Lambson (Mesa)
3. Brown (Morrisville)
4. Moses (Lamar)
5. Melchoir (Orange County)
6. Dextor (Big Bend)

137-lb class
1. Eddie Wells (Blue Mountain)
2. Johnson (Northeastern)
3. Doddy (Joliet)
4. Stevens (North Iowa)
5. Morgan (Morrisville)
6. Thone (Arizona Western)

145-lb class
1. Terry Anders (Trinidad)
2. McHenry (Blackhawk)
3. Ault (Phoenix)
4. Cleveland (Itasca)
5. Munson (Mohawk Valley)
6. Zerba (Blue Mountain)

152-lb class
1. Darrel Hartle (Rochester)
2. Hornbeck (Phoenix)
3. Adams (Long Island)
4. Dawson (Big Bend)
5. Spohr (Morrisville)
6. Lott (Grand Rapids Junior)

160-lb class
1. Ralph Gambin (Phoenix)
2. Carey (North Dakota Science)
3. Handy (Joliet)
4. Maher (Orange County)
5. Long (Mesa)
6. Coon (Northeastern)

167-lb class
1. Jesse Rawls (Trinidad)
2. Bell (Joliet)
3. Schroeder (Lamar)
4. Crook (Grand Rapids Junior)
5. Jacobs (Phoenix)
6. McCann (Miles)

177-lb class
1. John Lightner (Garden City)
2. Ciaccia (Fulton)
3. Galloway (Grand Rapids Junior)
4. Hudson (Trinidad)
5. Van Meveren (Worthington)
6. Parenteau (Anoka)

191-lb class
1. Larry Paul (Big Bend)
2. Smith (Lamar)
3. Mosch (Corning)
4. Moudry (Willmar)
5. Busnuck (Phoenix)
6. Gladwin (Rochester)

Heavyweight
1. Harry Geris (Joliet)
2. Collins (Northeastern)
3. Jacques (Orange County)
4. Carta (Lamar)
5. Davis (Trinidad)
6. Wager (Fulton-Montgomery)

1969 (at Worthington, MN)

Team	*Points*
1. Phoenix, Joliet	66
3. Mesa (AZ)	49
4. Black Hawk, Northeastern (CO)	47
6. Trinidad	44
7. Big Bend, Orange County, Muskegon	40
10. North Iowa	36
11. Northern Oklahoma	34
12. Keystone	33
13. Ricks, McCook	31
15. Worthington, North Dakota Science	30

Place winners

115-lb class
1. Mike Cachero (Phoenix)
2. Paul MacArthur (Northeastern)
3. Ed Homan (Worthington)
4. Steve McGoffin (Mesa, AZ)
5. John Coleman (Delhi)
6. William Scott (Ocean County)

123-lb class
1. Mike Shearer (Muskegon)
2. Robert Williams (Phoenix)
3. Don Evans (Trinidad)
4. Mark Beckerman (Cobleskill)
5. Vic Campbell (Colby)
6. Val Bravo (Black Hawk)

130-lb class
1. Terry Stuehrenberg (North Dakota Science)
2. Tony Stevens (North Iowa)
3. Ken Stockdale (Rochester)
4. Wydell Boyd (Black Hawk)
5. George Dugan (Boyce Campus)
6. Steve Arnold (Trinidad)

137-lb class
1. Eddie Wells (Blue Mountain, OR)
2. Charles Heene (North Iowa)
3. Gary Baker (Itasca)
4. Dale Samuelson (Colby)
5. Richard Estrada (Phoenix)
6. David Holker (Ricks)

145-lb class
1. Mike Medchill (Mesa, AZ)
2. Nate Phillips (Northern Oklahoma)
3. Tom Pierson (Joliet)
4. Robert Waller (Delhi)
5. Mike Childers (Northeastern)
6. Wayne Gordon (Mesa, CO)

152-lb class
1. Robert Pomplum (Mesa, AZ)
2. Randy Ault (Phoenix)
3. Errol Wilson (Trinton)
4. Gary Ventimiglia (Orange County)
5. Al Hodgdon (Rochester)
6. Dan Meyer (Black Hawk)

160-lb class
1. Rich Maher (Orange County)
2. Bill Bell (Joliet)
3. Bill Thornton (Northern Oklahoma)
4. Ron Queen (Keystone)
5. Gary Coley (Glendale)
6. Ron Gresham (Black Hawk)

167-lb class
1. Terry Dawson (Big Bend)
2. Vern Jacobs (Phoenix)
3. Kevin Hazard (Keystone)
4. Mark Mulqueen (McCook)
5. David Hammons (Ricks)
6. Greg Freehauf (Thornton)

177-lb class
1. Les Armes (Black Hawk)
2. Jack Yorgensen (Ricks)
3. Bob Shelby (Trinidad)
4. Dave VanMeveren (Worthington)
5. Bill Schellhorn (Nassau)
6. Frank Howell (Itasca)

191-lb class
1. Mike Bay (Joliet)
2. Larry Paull (Big Bend)
3. Bob Backlund (Waldorf)
4. Bill Coleman (Grand Rapids Junior)
5. John Tkalcevic (Arizona Western)
6. Ron Soden (Northeastern)

Heavyweight
1. Chris Taylor (Muskegon)
2. Harry Geris (Joliet)
3. Alan Petersen (McCook)
4. Mike Atchley (Arizona Western)
5. Paul Azzariti (Lorain County)
6. Dan Froiland (Rochester)

1970 (at Worthington, MN)

Team	*Points*
1. Muskegon	77
2. North Iowa	49
3. Triton	48
4. Northern Oklahoma	43
5. SUNY A&T at Delhi	42
6. Colby	27
7. Orange County	26
8. Boyce Campus, Luzerne County, Willmar	24
11. Worthington	23
12. Black Hawk	22
13. McCook	21
14. Fergus Falls, William Rainey Harper, Joliet, Lake County, Mesa (CO)	20

Place winners

118-lb class
1. Bill Vail (Joliet)
2. Doug Lee (Muskegon)
3. Paul Graham (Eastern IA)
4. Bob Roberts (Luzerne County)
5. Bob Hanes (Rochester)
6. Cisco Martinez (Mesa, CO)

126-lb class
1. John Scanlon (Orange County)
2. Dave Turner (Northern Oklahoma)
3. error in reporting
4. Tom Dahlsheid (Willmar)
5. Jim Sanders (Trinidad)
6. Hugh Wigginton (Colby)

134-lb class
1. Neil Duncan (Keystone)
2. Bob Young (Cuyahoga)
3. Bob Knoll (Muskegon)
4. Dale Samuelson (Colby)
5. Chuck Heene (North Iowa)
6. Rod Crawford (Mesa, CO)

142-lb class
1. Bobby Waller (Delhi)
2. Larry Arnold (Muskegon)
3. Bruce Hedlund (Fergus Falls)
4. Phil Lengerich (Rangely)
5. Ray Deidel (Bismarck)
6. Quentin Horning (McCook)

150-lb class
1. Tom Neuses (Harper)
2. Roger Duty (Muskegon)
3. Stan Faulkender (Colby)
4. Nate Phillips (Northern Oklahoma)

5. Wayne Palow (Worthington)
6. error in reporting

158-lb class
1. George Beene (Triton)
2. Roger Ingalls (Delhi)
3. Randy Ballinger (Big Bend)
4. Jay Schmidt (Miles)
5. Gary Ventimiglia (Orange County)
6. Don Rocky (Boyce Campus)

167-lb class
1. Clem DeLane (Triton)
2. Bill Thornton (Northern Oklahoma)
3. Bill Sweet (Rockland)
4. Warren Reid (Phoenix)
5. Matt Clarke (North Iowa)
6. Dave Biel (Wahpeton)

177-lb class
1. Les Armes (Black Hawk)
2. Al Sye (Gloucester)
3. Curt Van Meveren (Worthington)
4. Doug Moundry (Willmar)
5. Jim Davis (Glendale)
6. Ken House (Ricks)

190-lb class
1. Joe Hatchett (North Iowa)
2. Bob Backlund (Waldorf)
3. John Pinion (McCook)
4. Jim LeClair (Minnesota Tech at Crookston)
5. Fred Marcello (Broome Tech)
6. Frank Johnson (Meramec)

Heavyweight
1. Tom Murrey (Lake County)
2. Joe Kislin (Luzerne County)
3. Chris Taylor (Muskegon)
4. Paul Wager (Fulton-Montgomery)
5. Harris Butler (Forest Park)
6. Barry Williams (Boyce Campus)

1971 (at Worthington, MN)

Team	*Points*
1. Clackamas	75
2. North Iowa	66
3. Triton	40
4. Grand Rapids Junior	34
5. Lake County	32
6. SUNY A&T at Delhi	31
7. Muskegon	30
8. Northern Oklahoma	29
9. Keystone	27
10. McCook	22
11. SUNY A&T at Farmingdale	20

Place winners

118-lb class
1. Doug Lee (Muskegon)
2. Biondi (Farmingdale)
3. Allison (North Iowa)
4. Calarco (Cuyahoga)
5. Graham (Delhi)
6. Lewis (Colby)

126-lb class
1. Jim Welter (Lake County)
2. Elmada (Trinton)
3. Turner (Northern Oklahoma)
4. Rutter (Farmingdale)
5. Gustin (Alfred)
6. Soco (Clackamas)

134-lb class
1. Jim McCloe (Delhi)
2. Shetsinger (Grand Rapids)
3. Owens (Big Bend)
4. DeMarais (Wahpeton)
5. Stockdale (North Iowa)
6. Cardinel (Grand Rapids Junior)

142-lb class
1. Tim Williams (Clackamas)
2. Hedlund (Fergus Falls)
3. Loeb (Keystone)
4. Parker (Lake County)
5. Waller (Delhi)
6. Smith (Triton)

150-lb class
1. Gale Epp (McCook)
2. Arnold (Muskegon)
3. Jones (Clackamas)

4. Hobson (Grand Rapids Junior)
5. Cuomo (Trinidad)
6. Wille (Keystone)

158-lb class
1. George Beene (Triton)
2. Smith (Ricks)
3. Irvine (Blackhawk)
4. Jackson (Miami-Dade)
5. Nowakowski (Boyce)
6. Kargel (Grand Rapids)

167-lb class
1. Tom Carter (Northern Oklahoma)
2. Barber (Camden)
3. Clarke (North Iowa)
4. Gabel (Northeastern)
5. Arndt (Worthington)
6. Tracy (Alfred)

177-lb class
1. Glenn Snowley (Clackamas)
2. Hamilton (Erie)
3. Kerr (Triton)
4. Schneider (Keystone)
5. Witham (Bloomington)
6. Urquhart (Farmingdale)

190-lb class
1. Joe Hatchett (North Iowa)
2. Fye (Gloucester)
3. Trachel (Grand Rapids Junior)
4. Baumgardner (Rangely)
5. Marsello (Broome)
6. Devalos (Orange County)

Heavyweight
1. Joel Kislin (Luzerne County)
2. Ludlow (Clackamas)
3. Banke (North Iowa)
4. Schroeder (Florissant Valley)
5. Murray (Blackhawk)
6. Slay (Trinidad)

1972 (at Worthington, MN)

Team	*Points*
1. SUNY A&T at Farmingdale	49.5
2. North Iowa	49
3. Northern Oklahoma	48.5
4. Middlesex	47
5. North Idaho	44
6. Clackamas	43
7. Cuyahoga West	37.5
8. Boyce Campus	?
9. Florissant Valley, Grand Rapids Junior	27.5
11. Northeastern (CO)	26
12. William Rainey Harper	23.5
13. Oscar Rose	22
14. Anoka-Ramsey, Corning	18

Place winners

118-lb class
1. Everett Gomez (Oscar Rose)
2. Tom Singleton (Oakland)
3. Rick Dawson (Northern Oklahoma)
4. Ed Albers (Farmingdale)
5. Joe Corso (North Iowa)
6. Julio Dimarco (Behrend)

126-lb class
1. Henry Flores (Northeastern)
2. Jim Young (Middlesex)
3. Mike Dahlheimer (Anoka)
4. Gary Richardson (North Idaho)
5. Terry Niblett (Florissant Valley)
6. Richard Norton (Alfred)

134-lb class
1. Tom Garcia (North Iowa)
2. Gary Wilson (Genesee)
3. Sam McCollum (Boyce Campus)
4. Don Langham (Florissant Valley)
5. Dan Anderson (Iowa Central)
6. Bill Jacoutot (Middlesex)

142-lb class
1. Tim Williams (Clackamas)
2. Tom Rigdon (Muskegon)
3. Bruce Ahmes (Farmingdale)
4. Bill Williams (North Iowa)
5. John McCloskey (Boyce Campus)
6. Steve Borders (Brainerd)

150-lb class
1. Ron Adams (Farmingdale)
2. Mark Gillespie (Corning)

3. Andy Reimnitz (Bismarck)
4. Dan Lease (Cuyahoga West)
5. Charles Becks (Lakeland)
6. Dan Graham (Ellsworth)

158-lb class
1. Gary Hosta (Cuyahoga West)
2. Chuck Woolery (North Idaho)
3. Bob Wilson (Grand Rapids Junior)
4. Gary Plosser (Pratt)
5. Jerry Nowakowski (Boyce Campus)
6. Raleigh Clemens (Cuyahoga Metro)

167-lb class
1. Ron Ray (Wilbur Wright)
2. Jim Stone (Northern Oklahoma)
3. Frank Clark (Ricks)
4. Charles Alley (Keystone)
5. Jim Urquhart (Farmingdale)
6. Keith Gates (Florissant Valley)

177-lb class
1. Steve Bonsall (Middlesex)
2. Scott Ravan (William Rainey Harper)
3. Tom Trachsel (Grand Rapids Junior)
4. Bruce Bora (Cuyahoga West)
5. Paul Janzewski (Behrend)
6. Tyrone Everhart (Kennedy-King)

190-lb class
1. Ken Vogt (Willmar)
2. Jim Hindricks (North Idaho)
3. Ted Petty (Middlesex)
4. Art Mohorn (Triton)
5. Dick Zietler (Alfred State)
6. Steve Eidness (North Iowa)

Heavyweight
1. Dave Graves (Northern Oklahoma)
2. Barry Walsh (Schoolcraft)
3. Bill Scott (Clackamas)
4. Rich Mosch (Broward)
5. Pete Clark (Eastern Utah)
6. Charles Bragg (Northeastern)

1973 (at Worthington, MN)

Team	*Points*
1. North Iowa	72.5
2. North Idaho	44.5
3. SUNY A&T at Farmingdale, Grand Rapids Junior	41
5. Middlesex (NJ)	37.5
6. Northern Oklahoma	35.5
7. Bismarck	33
8. Keystone (PA)	30
9. Joliet	27.5
10. Muskegon	23.5
11. Gloucester	23
12. Corning	22.5
13. Nassau	20
14. William Rainey Harper, Willmar	19

Place winners

118-lb class
1. Rick Dawson (Northern Oklahoma)
2. Charles Gomez (Rose)
3. Tom Singleton (Oakland)
4. Howard Strick (Schoolcraft)
5. Joe Corso (North Iowa)
6. Don Heller (Keystone)

126-lb class
1. Vince Tundo (Alfred)
2. Dedrick Doolin (North Iowa)
3. Greg Henning (Southwestern Oregon)
4. Tony Houle (Joliet)
5. Hans Van Brill (Gloucester)
6. Paul Ostentoski (Schoolcraft)

134-lb class
1. Charlie Wells (Grand Rapids Junior)
2. Jim Young (Middlesex)
3. Rex Branum (Joliet)
4. Bob Tribble (Suffolk County)
5. Rick Campbell (Northern Oklahoma)
6. Scott Hinz (Mesa, CO)

142-lb class
1. Bill Kametz (Keystone)
2. Bruce Ahmes (Farmingdale)
3. Pat Kelley (Fond du Lac)
4. Duane McKaney (Central Arizona)

5. Tim McDonald (Muskegon)
6. Bob Nearing (North Idaho)

150-lb class
1. John Welter (Lake County)
2. Paul Morris (William Rainey Harper)
3. Scott Turkel (Farmingdale)
4. Bruce Wilson (North Iowa)
5. Van Graham (Ellsworth)
6. Brad Gillespie (Corning)

158-lb class
1. Gary Hoffman (Bismarck)
2. Marc Gillespie (Corning)
3. Thom Kostrzewski (Lansing)
4. Chuck Woolery (North Idaho)
5. Steve Wenker (Willmar)
6. Frank Penn (Central Arizona)

167-lb class
1. Ron Ray (Wright)
2. Dan Brink (Muskegon)
3. Steve Gannon (North Idaho)
4. Chuck Alley (Keystone)
5. Tony Grimmel (Glendale)
6. John Rawley (Broward)

177-lb class
1. Bob Ankney (Grand Rapids Junior)
2. Ed Herman (North Iowa)
3. Steve Bonsall (Middlesex)
4. Jerry Skiles (Clackamas)
5. Mark Uselman (Ricks)
6. Jerry Abrams (Claremore)

190-lb class
1. Willie Gadson (Nassau)
2. Dave Krepel (McHenry)
3. Henry Jackson (Miami-Dade North)
4. Gary Nelson (Willmar)
5. Harold King (Grand Rapids Junior)
6. Eric Stevens (Glendale)

Heavyweight
1. Bob Fouts (North Iowa)
2. Willard Bryant (Gloucester)
3. Ray Miro (Farmingdale)
4. Dalfin Blaske (Bismarck)
5. Bob Georger (Meramec)
6. Ray King (North Idaho)

1974 (at Worthington, MN)

Team	*Points*
1. North Idaho	72.5
2. Bismarck	64
3. Clackamas	47.5
4. Schoolcraft	46
5. Blackhawk	44.5
6. Nassau, Northern Oklahoma	39
8. Forest Park	36.5
9. Middlesex (NJ)	31.5
10. Claremore, SUNY A&T at Farmingdale	31
12. Joliet	30.5
13. Jamestown (NY), Phoenix	28.5
15. North Iowa	26

Place winners

118-lb class
1. Johnnie Jones (Schoolcraft)
2. John Phillips (Claremore)
3. Bernie Kleiman (William Rainey Harper)
4. Rod Buttry (Canton)
5. Charles Gomez (Rose)
6. Bill Rosada (Phoenix)

126-lb class
1. Rhett Hilzendager (Bismarck)
2. Howard Strick (Schoolcraft)
3. Mike Hanlon (Minnesota Tech at Crookston)
4. Marty Barcus (Mesa, CO)
5. Tim Banks (Forest Park)
6. Mel Perez (Northern Oklahoma)

134-lb class
1. Kerry Bolen (Clackamas)
2. Rick Campbell (Northern Oklahoma)
3. Dave Robinson (Forest Park)
4. Art VanNote (Middlesex)
5. Tom Flores (Northeastern)
6. Glen Reed (Nassau)

142-lb class
1. Steve Dummett (Waldorf)
2. Roger Williams (Northern Oklahoma)
3. Mel Johnston (Clackamas)
4. Rick Pope (Lorain)
5. Dan Elliott (North Idaho)
6. Mike McGinnis (Blackhawk)

150-lb class
1. Tim MacDonald (Muskegon)
2. Steve Boothe (Phoenix)
3. Floyd Coburn (Claremore)
4. Viggo Worum (Jamestown)
5. Rory Whipple (Farmingdale)
6. Chris Moffa (Gloucester)

158-lb class
1. Gary Hoffman (Bismarck)
2. Marc Buchanen (Cuyahoga)
3. Dan Breedlove (Blackhawk)
4. Ken Smith (Clackamas)
5. Nate Johnson (Lorain)
6. Paul Berry (Forest Park)

167-lb class
1. Steve Gannon (North Idaho)
2. Steve Migliaccio (Union)
3. Ken Moore (Mott)
4. Steve Fladeboe (Willmar)
5. Bray Day (Joliet)
6. George Schaus (Jamestown)

177-lb class
1. Ted Petty (Middlesex)
2. Bob Ankney (Grand Rapids Junior)
3. Steve Day (Blackhawk)
4. Steve Pawlak (Jamestown)
5. Mike Maculuso (North Idaho)
6. Paul Guillaume (Kirkwood)

190-lb class
1. Willie Gadson (Nassau)
2. Sam Allen (Gloucester)
3. Harold King (Grand Rapids Junior)
4. Ed Herman (North Iowa)
5. Ray Greeley (Triton)
6. Lewis Green (Central Arizona)

Heavyweight
1. Ray King (North Idaho)
2. Mitch Marsicano (Farmingdale)
3. Dalfin Blaske (Bismarck)
4. Tom Burns (North Iowa)
5. Mike Kettman (Joliet)
6. Bob Georger (Meramec)

1975 (at Worthington, MN)

Team	*Points*
1. North Idaho	69
2. Blackhawk	66
3. Joliet	57
4. Phoenix	56.5
5. Schoolcraft	49.5
6. North Iowa	42.5
7. Bismarck	41
8. Jamestown (NY), Cuyahoga West, Parma	39
10. Oscar Rose, Midwest City	31.5
11. Grand Rapids Junior	28.5
12. Northern Oklahoma, Tonkawa	28
13. Claremore	25.5
14. Nassau, Garden City	24
15. Forest Park, St. Louis	23.5

Place winners

118-lb class
1. John Phillips (Claremore)
2. Bobby Parra (Phoenix)
3. John Beaune (Cuyahoga West)
4. Mark Jordine (Blackhawk)
5. Terry Durland (North Idaho)
6. Matt Boyle (Joliet)

126-lb class
1. Johnnie Jones (Schoolcraft)
2. Tim Banks (Forest Park)
3. Ron Gray (Blackhawk)
4. Jim Shutich (Grand Rapids Junior)
5. Rhett Hilzendeger (Bismarck)
6. Vern Louden (Central IA)

134-lb class
1. Bill Karpowicz (Cuyahoga West)
2. Lynn Taylor (North Idaho)
3. Dave Polsinelli (Jamestown)
4. Don Logan (Phoenix)
5. Randy Baker (Worthington)
6. DeWayne Martin (Oscar Rose)

142-lb class
1. Roger Williams (Northern Oklahoma)
2. Jeff Nelson (Rochester)
3. John Roberts (Grand Rapids Junior)
4. Dan Elliott (North Idaho)
5. Kerry Bolen (Clackamas)
6. Mike Dolan (Northeast Tech)

150-lb class
1. Mike Mirick (Schoolcraft)
2. Casey Welter (Lake County)
3. Bob Sanders (Niagara County)
4. Ed Moody (Broward)
5. Joe Milligan (Alfred)
6. Edwin Beeks (Florissant Valley)

158-lb class
1. Dan Breedlove (Blackhawk)
2. John White (Umpqua)
3. Bill Edmondson (North Iowa)
4. Ed Torrijon (Phoenix)
5. Mike Reed (North Idaho)
6. Jerry Shaw (Mesa, CO)

167-lb class
1. Jim O'Connel (North Idaho)
2. Ken Lewis (Joliet)
3. Tom Thias (Lansing)
4. Bruce Passe (Clackamas)
5. John Stockberger (North Idaho)
6. Randy Wyss (Madison Area Tech)

177-lb class
1. Lee Guzzo (Jamestown)
2. Gregg Barreto (Southwestern Oregon)
3. Jeff Vapp (Colby)
4. Cliff Thurman (Joliet)
5. Mike Dekker (Mesa, AZ)
6. Dennis Gajos (Macomb County)

190-lb class
1. Bob Bragg (Northeastern of Colorado)
2. Robin Ayres (Bismarck)
3. Steve Day (Blackhawk)
4. Paul Schmidt (Nassau)
5. Mark Erickson (Joliet)
6. Mark Angle (Central Arizona)

Heavyweight
1. Rick Long (Oscar Rose)
2. Mark Booth (Lane, OR)
3. Bob Fouts (North Iowa)
4. James Mitchell (Phoenix)
5. Albert Williams (Joliet)
6. Tom Schmidt (Mesa, AZ)

1976 (at Worthington, MN)

Team	Points
1. Cuyahoga West	61
2. Grand Rapids Junior	53
3. Muskegon	50.25
4. Monroe	48.75
5. North Dakota Science	37.75
6. Bismarck	36
7. Phoenix	34
8. Rochester (MN)	32.50
9. SUNY A&T at Farmingdale, Joliet	29.50
11. North Idaho	29.25
12. Clackamas	26.50
13. Nassau	26.25
14. Waldorf (IA)	24
15. Jamestown (NY)	23.25

Place winners

118-lb class
1. John Olson (Clackamas)
2. Bob Parra (Phoenix)
3. Dan Mannion (Nassau)
4. Doug Weisz (Bismarck)
5. Ken Ross (North Idaho)
6. Masa Kwanishi (Southwestern Oregon)

126-lb class
1. Jim Polsinelli (Monroe)
2. Joe Davidson (Suffolk County)

3. Mike Walsh (Cuyahoga West)
4. Keith Burks (Rochester)
5. Neil Gilbert (Ricks)
6. Mark Starr (Muskegon)

134-lb class
1. Bill Karpowicz (Cuyahoga West)
2. Les Standerfer (Northern Oklahoma)
3. Joe Romero (Phoenix)
4. Eric Filer (Jamestown)
5. Greg Pressler (Muskegon)
6. Joe Calantjis (Delhi)

142-lb class
1. Bill Roersma (Grand Valley State)
2. Paul Georgeades (Delhi)
3. Glenn Schneider (Nassau)
4. Brad Carr (North Dakota Science)
5. Ray Swidan (Southwestern Michigan)
6. Johnny Brown (Miami-Dade North)

150-lb class
1. Karl Jefferson (Forest Park)
2. Fred Schmitt (Muskegon)
3. Phil Roblee (Jamestown)
4. Panch Doherty (Montgomery)
5. Jim Diemer (North Iowa)
6. Randy James (Northern Oklahoma)

158-lb class
1. Jan Anderson (Waldorf)
2. Tim Corner (Grand Rapids Junior)
3. Guy Redinger (Muskegon)
4. Paul Hamilton (North Idaho)
5. Marshall Oliver (Mesa, AZ)
6. Ed Krager (Southwestern Michigan)

167-lb class
1. Ken Lewis (Joliet)
2. Max Tafaya (McCook)
3. Rick Benz (Blackhawk)
4. Rick Moore (Cuyahoga Metro)
5. Craig Cody (Monroe)
6. Ray Barrett (Cuyahoga West)

177-lb class
1. Charles Gadson (Farmingdale)
2. Ron Varga (Cuyahoga West)
3. Mark Yerrick (Grand Rapids Junior)
4. Jack Dreyer (Iowa Central)
5. David Mitchell (Monroe)
6. Cliff Thurman (Joliet)

190-lb class
1. Robin Ayres (Bismarck)
2. Greg Moe (Rochester)
3. Perry Keller (Colby)
4. Brian Plank (Northeastern of Colorado)
5. Bruce Putman (Macomb County)
6. Bob Menz (Monroe)

Heavyweight
1. Mark Booth (Lane)
2. Chris Weeres (North Dakota Science)
3. Brian Davis (Waubonsee)
4. Paul Curka (Middlesex)
5. John Nino (Triton)
6. Jerry Hill (Muskegon)

1977 (at Worthington, MN)

Team	*Points*
1. Triton	71.25
2. North Idaho	64.50
3. Iowa Central	52
4. Grand Rapids	49.50
5. Cuyahoga West	45.25
6. Phoenix	42.75
7. Broward	41.75
8. Ricks	40
9. Muskegon	39.50
10. SUNY A&T at Farmingdale	34
11. Willmar	30.50
12. Jamestown (NY)	24.75
13. Clackamas	24.25
14. Colby, Nassau	23.50

Place winners

118-lb class
1. Russ Swanson (Muskegon)
2. Mike Inghram (Lakeland)
3. Mike Fuller (Alfred)
4. Brett Means (Labette)

5. Jerome Watts (Florissant Valley)
6. George King (North Idaho)

126-lb class
1. Tom Alexander (Broward Central)
2. Lou Dionisio (Nassau)
3. Dan Owen (Waldorf)
4. Kent Ness (Bismarck)
5. John Ciotoli (Delhi)
6. Mark Starr (Muskegon)

134-lb class
1. Willie Moore (Niagra)
2. Joe Romero (Phoenix)
3. Jeff Powell (North Idaho)
4. Jim Shutich (Grand Rapids Junior)
5. Wilbur Borrero (Lake County)
6. Jim White (Delhi)

142-lb class
1. Dave Morgan (Iowa Central)
2. Lon Kvanli (Willmar)
3. Steve Morris (Clackamas)
4. Herb Fisher (Claremore)
5. Greg Worthem (Muskegon)
6. Larry Buckner (Garden City)

150-lb class
1. Phil Robles (Jamestown)
2. Ron Grubaugh (Monroe)
3. Don Owen (North Idaho)
4. Mike Ripplinger (Ricks)
5. Jim LeDoux (North Dakota Science)
6. Dirk Palmer (Blackhawk)

158-lb class
1. Greg Moore (Triton)
2. Rick Prousch (Broward)
3. Tom Joseph (Grand Rapids Junior)
4. Howard Printer (Phoenix)
5. Chuck Broderick (Farmingdale)
6. John Dobbie (McHenry)

167-lb class
1. Jim McReady (Ricks)
2. Bob Nolan (Miami-Dade North)
3. Charlie Kox (Cuyahoga West)
4. Mike Garcia (Phoenix)
5. Gordy Molenaar (Willmar)
6. Lee Schechinger (Iowa Central)

177-lb class
1. Noel Loban (Farmingdale)
2. Dave Van Holstyne (Grand Rapids Junior
3. Dan Pfautz (Keystone)
4. Jamie Kurtz (Cuyahoga West)
5. Bob Ruzich (Triton)
6. Joe Davis (Clackamas)

190-lb class
1. Gary Germundson (North Idaho)
2. Perry Keller (Colby)
3. Sam Carson (Triton)
4. Russell Koz (Cuyahoga West)
5. Mark Helling (Waldorf)
6. Scott Schmitz (Rochester)

Heavyweight
1. John Nino (Triton)
2. Bruce Eastman (Iowa Central)
3. Paul Curka (Middlesex)
4. Jeff Gillman (DuPage)
5. Pat Copenhaver (North Dakota Science)
6. Joe Williams (Garden City)

1978 (at Worthington, MN)

Team	*Points*
1. North Idaho	68
2. Triton	65.25
3. Bismarck	56.50
4. Cuyahoga West	42.50
5. Nassau	39.25
6. North Dakota Science	37.25
7. Grand Rapids Junior	35.25
8. Muskegon	35
9. Iowa Central	33
10. Colby, Waldorf	31.50
12. Joliet	29.50
13. Claremore	28.75
14. Arizona Western	27.50
15. Corning	26.50

Place winners

118-lb class
1. Ernanio DeAngelis (Corning)
2. Rick Zamorano (Pima)
3. Gifford Owens (Grand Rapids Junior)
4. Mike Fuller (Alfred)
5. Keith Whelan (St. Louis)
6. Brian Ricks (Ricks)

126-lb class
1. Kent Ness (Bismarck)
2. Ed Snook (North Idaho)
3. Russ Swanson (Muskegon)
4. Dan Schmidt (Colby)
5. Rich Wilson (Iowa Central)
6. John Horsley (Northwestern Colorado)

134-lb class
1. Jeff Powell (North Idaho)
2. Willie Staples (Triton)
3. Roger McCausland (DuPage)
4. Bob Williams (Mesa)
5. Robert Weiner (Westchester)
6. Irwin Valesquez (Middlesex)

142-lb class
1. David Reimnitz (Bismarck)
2. Paul Newman (Grand Rapids Junior)
3. Bob Hilfiger (Delhi)
4. Jeff Hoss (Triton)
5. Robert Ludlum (Brevard)
6. John Ognibene (Jamestown)

150-lb class
1. Isreal Sheppard (Claremore)
2. Frank Imbriano (Suffolk County)
3. Dave Bulmer (Rochester)
4. Jim LeDoux (North Dakota Science)
5. Al Grimes (Niagara County)
6. Joel Thone (Waldorf)

158-lb class
1. Gregg Moore (Triton)
2. Avery Cockrel (Nassau)
3. Stan Garey (Cuyahoga West)
4. Tim Jones (Clackamas)
5. Brad Schneider (Colby)
6. Darrell LaFountaine (North Dakota Science)

167-lb class
1. Tom Rankin (Arizona Western)
2. Chuck Giordano (Monroe)
3. Jim Thomas (Triton)
4. Bill Pavlak (Middlesex)
5. Clay Nagle (Bismarck)
6. Glen Spies (Waukesha)

177-lb class
1. Paul Nooyen (Wisconsin—Richland Center)
2. John Karcher (Nassau)
3. Morit Curtis (North Idaho)
4. Nick Moenkedick (North Dakota Science)
5. Grant Honis (Mohawk Valley)
6. Chris Albers (Colby)

190-lb class
1. Mark Helling (Waldorf)
2. Charles Hageman (Cuyahoga West)
3. Mike Evans (Joliet)
4. Keith Steffens (Ellsworth)
5. Ryan Kelly (North Idaho)
6. Jim Walker (Blackhawk)

Heavyweight
1. Greg Byrne (Lakeland)
2. Bruce Eastman (Iowa Central)
3. Rod Chamberlin (Joliet)
4. J.L. Coon (Ricks)
5. Dan Holt (Muskegon)
6. Kelly Aalfs (Willmar)

1979 (at Worthington, MN)

Team	*Points*
1. Lakeland	95.50
2. Joliet	81.25
3. Cuyahoga West	62.75
4. Grand Rapids Junior	58.75
5. Phoenix	51
6. Westchester	50.25
7. Triton	37
8. Claremore	35.50
9. Colby	32.25
10. McCook Area Tech	31
11. Middlesex (NJ)	30.25
12. Labette	25.25
13. Rochester (MN)	24.50
14. Broward	24
15. Muskegon	22.50

Place winners

118-lb class
1. Gifford Owens (Grand Rapids)
2. Mike Jones (Claremore)
3. Rudy Glur (McCook)
4. Doug Unger (Westchester)
5. Erminio DeAngelis (Corning)
6. Jerry Shorey (Umpqua)

126-lb class
1. Eldon Edwards (Labette)
2. John Mulligan (Middlesex, NJ)
3. Kerry Welling (Cuyahoga West)
4. Kevin Bellis (Joliet)
5. Mike Barfuss (Arizona West)
6. Jeff Virkler (Morrisville)

134-lb class
1. Johnnie Selmon (Grand Rapids Junior)
2. Terry Jackson (Claremore)
3. Rich Brown (Triton)
4. Robert Weiner (Westchester)
5. John McNulty (Cuyahoga West)
6. Bob Taylor (Sauk Valley)

142-lb class
1. Mike Reif (William Rainey Harper)
2. Brian Palcko (Cuyahoga West)
3. Bob Hilfiger (Delhi)
4. Billy Selmon (Grand Rapids Junior)
5. Jeff Hoss (Triton)
6. Mark Early (Middlesex, NJ)

150-lb class
1. Tom Gagliardi (Lakeland)
2. Ron Mascia (Cuyahoga West)
3. Rory Cahoj (Colby)
4. Jim Morkel (McCook Northeast)
5. Joe Solario (Phoenix)
6. Tim Johnson (Diablo Valley)

158-lb class
1. Glen Sumpter (Westchester)
2. John Ohly (Rochester)
3. Dan Hary (Nassau)
4. Mark Howard (Broward)
5. George Dergo (Joliet)
6. Mark Parrott (Madison Area Tech)

167-lb class
1. Jeff Dillman (Joliet)
2. Pat Day (Lakeland)
3. Rom Rankin (Phoenix)
4. Mike Prosby (North Dakota Science)
5. Richard Sykes (Diablo Valley)
6. Edic Anderson (Forest Park)

177-lb class
1. John Zele (Lakeland)
2. Bob McDaniels (Colby)
3. Clay Nagel (Bismarck)
4. Chuck Gentry (Northeastern of Colorado)
5. Chuck Giordano (Monroe)
6. Randy Gevora (Muskegon)

190-lb class
1. Mike Evans (Joliet)
2. Steve Mallernee (Phoenix)
3. Robert Stelle (Snow)
4. Dean Johnson (Alfred)
5. Mark Wilson (Broward)
6. Don Dahl (Rochester)

Heavyweight
1. Greg Byrne (Lakeland)
2. Rod Chamberlain (Joliet)
3. Dan Holt (Muskegon)
4. Mike Carter (Triton)
5. Tom Brown (Iowa Central)
6. Howard Evans (Cuyahoga Metro)

1980 (at Worthington, MN)

Team	*Points*
1. Lakeland	76
2. Muskegon	67.75
3. Iowa Central	59.75
4. Grand Rapids Junior	47
5. Northern Oklahoma	40
6. Ricks	39.50
7. Chowan	38.25
8. Joliet	37.25
9. Nassau	36.25
10. Pima	28.25
11. Colby	25.50
12. Columbia Basin, North Idaho	25.25
14. Phoenix	25
15. Cuyahoga Metro	23.75

Place winners

118-lb class
1. Tim Smelser (Muskegon)
2. John Duncan (DuPage)
3. Shelby Bullard (Northern Oklahoma)
4. Richard Ortiz (Pima)
5. Jeff Schumacher (Bismarck)
6. Dave Fisher (Cuyahoga West)

126-lb class
1. Tony Bass (Cuyahoga Metro)
2. Steve Groce (Cayuga County)
3. Dwayne Smith (Grand Rapids Junior)
4. Jerry Johnson (Brevard, FL)
5. Dwayne Lobdell (Delhi)
6. Chris Jackson (Nassau)

134-lb class
1. Doug Saunders (Chowan)
2. Rick Anderele (Columbia Basin)
3. Otis Calvin (Yuma)
4. Tom Wade (Nassau)
5. Jim Aumick (Bethany Lutheran)
6. Tony Henry (Muskegon)

142-lb class
1. Jerry Trainor (Grand Rapids Junior)
2. Rick Horton (Lakeland)
3. Mark Ostranger (Eagle Grove)
4. Ron Winnie (Corning)
5. Wade Finch (Ellsworth)
6. Colin Roetman (Worthington)

150-lb class
1. Rory Cahoj (Colby)
2. Jack Nicholson (North Idaho)
3. Dan Yoder (Muskegon)
4. Al Frost (Iowa Central)
5. Chuck Koestler (Rochester)
6. John Cheney (Randolph Township)

158-lb class
1. John Schaumburg (Iowa Central)
2. James Shough (Phoenix)
3. Todd Sumter (Westchester)
4. Tom Hren (Lakeland)
5. Steve Fario (Newton)
6. Randy Demo (Delhi)

167-lb class
1. Jeff Dillman (Joliet)
2. Pat Day (Lakeland)
3. Dan Harvey (Nassau)
4. Charles Wood (Pima)
5. Keith Elgin (Phoenix)
6. Shepard Pittman (Forest Park)

177-lb class
1. John Zele (Lakeland)
2. Mike Cribbs (Muskegon)
3. Jeff Cocco (Joliet)
4. Rob Rechsteiner (Grand Rapids Junior)
5. Dave Poppinga (Eagle Grove)
6. Melvin Gatewood (Northeastern Oklahoma State)

190-lb class
1. Karl Lynes (Northern Oklahoma)
2. Robert Steele (Snow)
3. Stefanois Miltsakakis (Chowan)
4. Layne Evans (Ricks)
5. Kent Brown (Garden City)
6. Greg Wilcox (McCook)

Heavyweight
1. Henry Williams (Ricks)
2. Keith Beard (Garden City)
3. Mitch Shelton (Meramec)
4. Kurt Lesser (North Dakota Science)

5. Dave Kofoed (Willmar)
6. John Lucas (Muskegon)

1981 (at Worthington, MN)

Team	*Points*
1. Iowa Central	85.50
2. Cuyahoga West	74.75
3. North Idaho	63.25
4. Northern Oklahoma	54.75
5. Phoenix	51
6. Middlesex (NJ)	41.50
7. Meramec	40.25
8. Forcst Park	36.50
9. Waldorf	26.50
10. SUNY A&T at Delhi, Grays Harbor	26
12. Suffolk County	25.50
13. Lincoln College	24.50
14. Bismarck, Colby	24

Place winners

118-lb class
1. Mike Ryba (Cuyahoga West)
2. Steve Krause (Northern Oklahoma)
3. Bill Adkins (Lakeland)
4. John Duncan (DuPage)
5. Tom Graham (Glendale)
6. Jeff Mallet (Forest Park)
7. Matt Latoni (Monroe)
8. Terry Gerding (Linn-Benton)

126-lb class
1. Kevin Russell (Iowa Central)
2. Ken Karl (Middlesex, NJ)
3. John Scholtz (Cuyahoga West)
4. Perry Byrd (Meramec)
5. John Wyshenski (Gloucester)
6. John DeBeniditts (Nassau)
7. Jeff Schumacher (Bismarck)
8. Randy Manchester (Fulton-Montgomery)

134-lb class
1. Robert Gray (Lincoln C)
2. Mike Kelner (Bismarck)
3. Bob Kirgan (Meramec)
4. Bob Siegwarth (North Idaho)
5. Tim Anderson (Willmar)
6. Brad Root (Minnesota Teach at Waseca)
7. Domonic Morino (Suffolk County)
8. Dave Mauser (Waldorf)

142-lb class
1. Pete Yee (Colby)
2. Mark Ostrander (Iowa Central)
3. Mejo Hernandez (North Idaho)
4. John Sonderegger (Forest Park)
5. Lance Wilson (Clackamas)
6. Wade Finch (Ellsworth)
7. Larry Biundo (Muskegon)
8. Jim Aumick (Bethany)

150-lb class
1. Rick Horton (Cuyahoga West)
2. Jaime Armenta (Phoenix)
3. Craig Noble (Arizona Western)
4. Danny Wilson (Oscar Rose)
5. Jeff Richardson (Columbia Basin)
6. Phil Mattern (Delhi)
7. Jack Woltjer (Grand Rapids Junior)
8. Tim Schwindt (Labette)

158-lb class
1. Brad Anderson (Middlesex, NJ)
2. Steve Swan (Jamestown)
3. John Schaumburg (Iowa Central)
4. Brent Barnes (North Idaho)
5. Randy Wirtjes (Rochester, MN)
6. Tom Overbay (Clackamas)
7. Dave Mason (Cuyahoga West)
8. Tom Suter (Gloucester)

167-lb class
1. Keith Elgin (Phoenix)
2. Alan Lauchner (Northeastern Oklahoma Tech)
3. Jim McCready (Ricks)
4. Brad Cast (Northern Oklahoma)
5. Curt Pacha (Iowa Central)
6. Gary Emzer (North Dakota)
7. Drew Lance (Keystone)
8. Pat Summerville (DuPage)

177-lb class
1. Mike Hogaboam (Gray's Harbor)
2. Shane Palmer (Labette)
3. Shep Pittman (Forest Park)
4. Mark Cody (Delhi)

5. Roger Sayler (Mount Hood)
6. Freddie Wilson (Triton)
7. Rusty Daily (North Idaho)
8. Joe Franza (Nassau)

190-lb class
1. Karl Lynes (Northern Oklahoma)
2. Kevin Morris (Suffolk County)
3. John Whitehead (Cuyahoga)
4. Dave Schumpert (Grand Rapids Junior)
5. Ron Weaver (Pima)
6. John Carpenter (Phoenix)
7. Hal Graber (Gloucester)
8. Chris Blake (Columbia Basin)

Heavyweight
1. Keith Beard (Garden City)
2. Wayne Cole (Iowa Central)
3. Darryl Peterson (North Idaho)
4. Mitch Shelton (Meramec)
5. Dwain Clark (Waldorf)
6. John Lucas (Muskegon)
7. Greg Dabrowski (Cuyahoga West)
8. Sifto Rosales (Mesa), AZ

1982 (at Worthington, MN)

Team	*Points*
1. North Idaho	87.25
2. Cuyahoga West	81.75
3. Phoenix	51.25
4. Ellsworth	50.75
5. Triton	48.50
6. Bismarck	47.50
7. Joliet	42.50
8. SUNY A&T at Delhi	31.75
9. Colby	31
10. Middlesex (NJ)	30.75
11. Waldorf	27.50
12. North Dakota Science	25.25
13. Pima	25
14. Mt. Hood	24
15. Rochester (MN)	23.50

Place winners

118-lb class
1. Mike Ryba (Cuyahoga)
2. Vic Montalvo (Delhi)
3. Scott Knolen (Bismarck)
4. George Hara (Big Bend)
5. Mike Arnold (Colby)
6. Mike Duhigg (Middlesex, NJ)
7. Jim Lefebvre (Mesa)
8. Tony Deggue (Grays Harbor)

126-lb class
1. John Scholtz (Cuyahoga)
2. Ken Karl (Middlesex, NJ)
3. Fred King (Phoenix)
4. Pat Spain (Alford)
5. Matt Latona (Monroe)
6. Todd Gaston (North Idaho)
7. Brad Wilkenson (Grand Rapids Junior)
8. Vince Stout (Labette)

134-lb class
1. Steve Carr (North Dakota Science)
2. Tom Thompson (Iowa Central)
3. George Patterson (North Idaho)
4. Robert Garn (Northwest, WY)
5. Dave Savron (Cuyahoga)
6. Robert Gray (Lincoln C)
7. Mike Morley (Niagara)
8. Jonathon Love (Joliet)

142-lb class
1. Ignacio Garcia (Colby)
2. Nathan Winner (Clackamas)
3. Mitch Brinlee (Northwest, WY)
4. Allen Aires (Gloucester)
5. Rick Dorn (Willmar)
6. Tim Siekmann (Meramec)
7. Perry Graehling (Lakeland)
8. Lars Imhoff (Bismarck)

150-lb class
1. Eddie Urbano (Pima)
2. Larry Jackson (Ellsworth)

3. Wes Gasner (Northwestern Colorado)
4. Bruce Wilson (North Dakota Science)
5. Jaime Armenta (Phoenix)
6. Joe Mignano (Middlesey, NJ)
7. Jack Nicholsen (North Idaho)
8. Gene Noce (Labette)

158-lb class
1. Brent Barnes (North Idaho)
2. Lionell Keys (Triton)
3. Sam Jolly (Joliet)
4. Don Zellner (Umpqua)
5. Kevin Sistrunk (Nassau)
6. Rob Young (Bergen)
7. Tom Draheim (Phoenix)
8. Dave Mason (Cuyahoga)

167-lb class
1. Randy Wirtjes (Rochester, MN)
2. Pat Delaney (Anoka)
3. Danny Romero (Arizona Western)
4. Bob Toben (Meramec)
5. Daryl Brophy (Suffolk County)
6. Mike Thomas (Chowan)
7. Fred Meyer (Nassau)
8. Steve Swan (Jamestown)

177-lb class
1. Roger Sayles (Mount Hood)
2. Clarence Richardson (Joliet)
3. Tom Harris (North Idaho)
4. Todd Kohl (Dodge City)
5. Doug Brookes (Grand Rapids Junior)
6. Mark Cody (Delhi)
7. Curt Paccha (Iowa Central)
8. Wayne Love (Ellsworth)

190-lb class
1. Mike Blaske (Bismarck)
2. John Carpenter (Phoenix)
3. Todd Smith (Ellsworth)
4. Tony Cotrupi (Cobleskill)
5. Carl Davis (Waldorf)
6. Tim Stapleton (Waldorf)
7. Monte Crozier (Garden City)
8. Bruce Carroll (Muskegon)

Heavyweight
1. Darryl Peterson (North Idaho)
2. Greg Dabrowski (Cuyahoga)
3. George Fraher (Triton)
4. Duane Clark (Waldorf)
5. Dave Patton (Bismarck)
6. Joe Kuras (Alfred)
7. Daryl Tysdal (Fergus Falls)
8. Bob McMorris (Herkimer)

1983 (at Worthington, MN)

Team	*Points*
1. Triton	109.75
2. Phoenix	66.75
3. North Idaho	59.75
4. Middlesex (NJ)	52.75
5. Colby	46.25
6. Arizona Western, Ellsworth	43.50
8. Willmar	36
9. Iowa Central	35.25
10. Ricks	34.25
11. Lakeland	34
12. Big Bend	29.50
13. Rochester (MN)	28
14. Muskegon	27.50
15. North Dakota Science	26.25

Place winners

118-lb class
1. Bill Adkins (Lakeland)
2. George Hara (Big Bend)
3. Mike Duhigg (Middlesex, NJ)
4. Kyle Presler (Willmar)
5. Mike Provenzano (Arizona Western)
6. Mike Wiley (Bismarck)
7. Jay Gegenheimer (Triton)
8. Marty Foote (Muskegon)

126-lb class
1. Mitch Powers (Phoenix)
2. Scott Beach (Arizona Western)

3. Jim Smith (Middlesex, NJ)
4. Jeff Dawes (Muskegon)
5. Tim Jones (Northwest, WY)
6. Chris Richards (Colby)
7. Joe Johnson (Triton)
8. Curt Scott (Lincoln C)

134-lb class

1. George Patterson (North Idaho)
2. Dave Apedaca (Pima)
3. Russell Jackson (Triton)
4. Gene Staulters (Fulton-Montgomery)
5. Tommy Thompson (Iowa Central)
6. Brian Nelson (Richland)
7. Vince McCullough (Johnson)
8. Cory Conallis (Oscar Rose)

142-lb class

1. Mark Terrill (Phoenix)
2. Mark Tracy (Arizona Western)
3. Ignacio Garcia (Colby)
4. Sam Pruitt (Lincoln C)
5. Mike Bolf (Clackamas)
6. Hank Roney (Northwest, WY)
7. Scott Harney (Suffolk County)
8. Steve Camp (Ricks)

150-lb class

1. Larry Jackson (Ellsworth)
2. Brian Rognholt (Phoenix)
3. Mark Woitalla (Willmar)
4. Pete Comes (Altoona)
5. Jim Martinson (Bismarck)
6. Jeff Steele (Muskegon)
7. John Kabanuk (North Dakota Science)
8. Dennis Wunderlich (Waldorf)

158-lb class

1. John Mineo (Middlesex, NJ)
2. Sid Richard (Northwestern Colorado)
3. Jon Cook (Iowa Central)
4. Dave Johnson (Rochester)
5. Al Schmidt (North Dakota Science)
6. Dan Martin (Clackamas)
7. Howard Seay (Northwestern Oklahoma)
8. Pat Laskey (Joliet)

167-lb class

1. Reggie Wilson (Triton)
2. Mike Thomas (Chowan)
3. Eric Koehler (Garden City)
4. Duane Zamora (Big Bend)
5. John Deaton (Oscar Rose)
6. John Carlson (North Dakota Science)
7. Wes Robinson (Glendale)
8. Ken Nielsen (Northwest, WY)

177-lb class

1. Mike Guenther (Colby)
2. Wayne Love (Ellsworth)
3. Fred Wilson (Triton)
4. Todd Praska (Rochester, MN)
5. Mike Harter (Iowa Central)
6. Joe Rigous (Bucks)
7. Wade Ayala (Bismarck)
8. Dwayne Seals (Lakeland)

190-lb class

1. Carl Davis (Triton)
2. Doyle Naig (Waldorf)
3. Jeff Clark (Ricks)
4. John Johnson (Southwestern Michigan)
5. Tim Doherty (Bergen)
6. Kyle Jensen (Bismarck)
7. Steve Voss (Willmar)
8. Dave Grube (Lincoln C)

Heavyweight

1. Jamie Weber (North Idaho)
2. Dave Orndorff (Ricks)
3. Dave Besser (Triton)
4. Steve Burton (Mesa)
5. Dave West (Keystone)
6. Garrett Keith (Delhi)
7. Tom Dole (Rochester, MN)
8. Daryl Tysdal (Fergus Falls)

1984 (at Glen Ellyn, IL)

Team	*Points*
1. Triton	145.25
2. North Idaho	96
3. SUNY A&T at Delhi	58
4. Bismarck	51
5. Phoenix	47.75
6. Northwest (WY)	46.50
7. Iowa Central	43.50
8. Lincoln College	34.75
9. Waldorf	31
10. Northwestern Colorado	29.50
11. Arizona Western	26.75
12. SUNY A&T at Alfred	26.50
13. Fulton-Montgomery	24
14. Willmar	21.50
15. Muskegon	21

Place winners

118-lb class
1. Anthony Bellai (Delhi)
2. Randy Sandoval (Northwestern Colorado)
3. Raul Rodriguez (Lincoln C)
4. Julioi Tores (Northwest, WY)
5. Mark McKenna (North Idaho)
6. Sonny Bachicha (Garden City)
7. Dan Matos (Cuyahoga)
8. Mike Wiley (Bismarck)

126-lb class
1. Scott Beach (Arizona Western)
2. Lenal Brinson (Triton)
3. Dave Singletary (North Idaho)
4. Steve Chevalier (Bismarck)
5. Jim Smith (Middlesex, NJ)
6. Gus Sosa (Dodge City)
7. Phil Ratten (Northeastern Oklahoma State U)
8. Sam Cribb (Forest Park)

134-lb class
1. Gene Staulters (Fulton-Montgomery)
2. Mike Gilsdorf (Triton)
3. Jeff Songeroth (Northwestern Colorado)
4. Mark Indrelie (Waseca)
5. Al Bastain (Willmar)
6. Boby Garcia (Phoenix)
7. Randy LaPardus (Granite City)
8. Kevin Bonin (Garden City)

142-lb class
1. Dave Heatherlington (Iowa Central)
2. Hank Roney (Northwest, WY)
3. Darren Peaster (Northeastern Oklahoma State U)
4. Dave Meirick (Rochester, MN)
5. Chris Salisbury (Muskegon)
6. Dave Venem (Minnesota Tech at Crookston)
7. Todd Ahrenstroff (Waldorf)
8. Charles Monroe (Forest Park)

150-lb class
1. Maurice Harrison (Triton)
2. Randi Talvi (North Idaho)
3. Kevin Parrott (Delhi)
4. Darren Cannon (Lakeland)
5. Art Castillo (Phoenix)
6. Thaine Fischer (Northwest, WY)
7. Dan Cox (Iowa Central)
8. Jim Tieman (Granite City)

158-lb class
1. Steve Kluver (North Idaho)
2. Daryl Rogers (Alfred)
3. Chuck Updergraft (Meramec)
4. John Bonello (Triton)
5. Steve Klein (Monroe)
6. Bryan Wilson (Northwest, WY)
7. Bill Benson (Worthington)
8. John Richter (Bismarck)

167-lb class
1. Tom Phelan (North Idaho)
2. Leroy Murray (Phoenix)
3. Bruce Hammel (Waldorf)
4. Scott Dyer (Willmar)
5. Joe Vadina (Cuyahoga West)
6. Tim Ruppert (Worthington)
7. Tim Rathbun (Herkimer)
8. Ken Jensen (Bismarck)

177-lb class
1. Reggie Wilson (Triton)
2. Joey Rigous (Bucks)
3. Mike Harter (Iowa Central)

4. Wade Ayala (Bismarck)
5. Matt Begger (Lincoln C)
6. Roy Oeser (North Idaho)
7. Ron DeBolt (Alfred)
8. Vic Pozsonyi (Middlesex, NJ)

190-lb class
1. Derrick Waldroup (Triton)
2. Stan Williams (Morrisville)
3. Doyle Naig (Waldorf)
4. Kyle Jensen (Bismarck)
5. Demetrius Harper (Lincoln C)
6. Scott Ames (Clackamas)
7. Roger Rahm (Anoka)
8. Jim Petty (Middlesex, NJ)

Heavyweight
1. Tom Erikson (Triton)
2. Garrett Keith (Delhi)
3. Tom Reese (Frederick)
4. Steve Whelan (Nassau)
5. Jeff Horton (Phoenix)
6. Myron Keppy (Ellsworth)
7. Chris Mast (Muskegon)
8. Larry Juern (Forest Park)

1985 (at Glen Ellyn, IL)

Team	*Points*
1. North Idaho	110.50
2. Triton	74.75
3. SUNY A&T at Delhi	72.50
4. Lincoln College	72.25
5. Iowa Central	70.50
6. Middlesex (NJ)	46.75
7. Bismarck	43.25
8. SUNY A&T at Morrisville	42.75
9. SUNY A&T at Alfred	30.50
10. Northeastern Oklahoma	30
11. Madison Area Tech	26.50
12. Muskegon	26.25
13. Forest Park, Gloucester, Pima	25.50

Place winners

118-lb class
1. Anthony Bellai (Delhi)
2. Bobby Thompson (Iowa Central)
3. Joe Arminas (Lincoln C)
4. Mike Stilson (Waldorf)
5. Chris Riley (Triton)
6. Don Van Mourik (Muskegon)
7. Tom Openhoff (Alfred)
8. Mike Schmitz (Willmar)

126-lb class
1. Rene Nunez (Pima)
2. Tom Muttal (Muskegon)
3. Jamie Nichols (L & B)
4. Zane Jones (Northwest)
5. Duane Schmuecker (Iowa Central)
6. Tory McCully (North Idaho)
7. Sam Cribb (Forest Park)
8. Joe Williams (Lincoln C)

134-lb class
1. James Agee (Lincoln C)
2. Angelo DeAngelis (Alfred)
3. Mike Seymour (Iowa Central)
4. Ken Sroka (Triton)
5. Jeff Semrad (North Idaho)
6. Barry Mahon (GS)
7. Tom Mannen (CLMS)
8. Tim Bergloff (North Dakota Science)

142-lb class
1. Mike Gilsdorf (Triton)
2. Wayne Sharp (North Idaho)
3. Bruce Basaraba (Bismarck)
4. Rich Zele (Lakeland)
5. Mark Toarming (Grand Rapids Junior)
6. Bruce Holt (Ricks)
7. Dave Venem (Minnesota Tech at Crookston)
8. Dean Salvaggio (Monroe)

150-lb class
1. Mike Barna (Middlesex, NJ)
2. Bryce Hall (North Idaho)
3. Dan Peterson (Delhi)
4. Mike Reavis (Northeastern Oklahoma)
5. Tim Morriss (GS)
6. Charles Monroe (Forest Park)
7. Tim Ressler (Bismarck)
8. Bill Peters (Iowa Central)

158-lb class
1. Dan Niebuhr (Madison Area Teach)
2. Pete Dibendetto (GS)
3. Don Peterson (Delhi)
4. Kevin Frame (North Idaho)
5. John Purceilli (Forest Park)
6. Anthony Wilheims (Iowa Central)
7. William Woods (Dodge City)
8. Nick Grevelding (Morrisville)

167-lb class
1. Alonzo Nalls (Lincoln C)
2. Bob Vredenburgh (Delhi)
3. John Fredrickson (North Idaho)
4. Braden Atkinson (Cuyahoga West)
5. Andrew Boyd (NAS)
6. Dave Christianson (Willmar)
7. Greg McClure (Northwest, WY)
8. Mat Clark (Ricks)

177-lb class
1. Ken Rucker (North Idaho)
2. Ted Bullerman (Worthington)
3. Fritz Stratton (Iowa Central)
4. Wade Willis (Ricks)
5. Dave Attaway (Joliet)
6. Ron DaBolt (Alfred)
7. Kevin Pesch (Waldorf)
8. Tom Hoy (Triton)

190-lb class
1. Stan Williams (Morris)
2. Joel Ralfs (Ellsworth)
3. Tom Thelig (Bismarck)
4. C.J. Dominick (Monroe)
5. Jim Gill (Northeastern Oklahoma)
6. John Johnson (SWM)
7. Bryan Hagen (Worthington)
8. Ab Brown (Northwest, WY)

Heavyweight
1. Tom Erickson (Triton)
2. Emanuel Yarbrough (Middlesex, NJ)
3. Larry Grieve (Colby)
4. Curtis Freeman (Morrisville)
5. Rawley Alger (Kirkwood)
6. Demetrius Harper (Lincoln C)
7. Tom Haney (LaBette)
8. Mike Thomas (Arizona Western)

1986 (at Glen Ellyn, IL)

Team	*Points*
1. North Idaho	131
2. Bismarck	62.50
3. Triton	56.25
4. Middlesex (NJ)	54.50
5. Iowa Central	48.50
6. SUNY A&T at Delhi	47.75
7. Lakeland (OH)	46.75
8. Ricks	44.75
9. Muskegon	41
10. Northeastern Oklahoma, Waldorf	39
12. Phoenix	36.75
13. Garden City	33.75
14. SUNY A&T at Morrisville	29
15. Kirkwood	27.50

Place winners

118-lb class
1. Jerry Garcia (Phoenix)
2. Fernando Cota (Pima)
3. Bobby Thompson (Iowa Central)
4. Bobby Crawford (Northeastern Oklahoma)
5. John Pauley (Delhi)
6. Joe Arminas (Triton)
7. Micky Wright (Meramec)
8. Steve Meuer (North Idaho)

126-lb class
1. Torey McCully (North Idaho)
2. Shawn Flowers (Morrisville)

3. Tim Jones (Northwest, WY)
4. Joe Williams (Triton)
5. Rich Florio (Fulton-Montgomery)
6. Luis Palacio (Delhi)
7. Stacy Weiland (Meramec)
8. Mike Schmitz (Willmar)

134-lb class
1. Anibel Nieves (Delhi)
2. Trevor Clark (Bismarck)
3. John Kinchen (Middlesex, NJ)
4. Jeff Goss (Northwestern Oklahoma)
5. Ram Echeverria (Phoenix)
6. Antonio Parker (Garden City)
7. Dave Ryan (William Rainey Harper)
8. Brain Jones (Muskegon)

142-lb class
1. Mark Toarmina (Grand Rapids Junior)
2. Bobby Jones (Lakeland)
3. Reid Diehl (DuPage)
4. Doug Bomk (Willmar)
5. Jim Daniels (Muskegon)
6. Jeff Kingland (Waldorf)
7. Larry Thompson (Garden City)
8. Paul Peterson (Monroe)

150-lb class
1. Darren Cannon (Lakeland)
2. Kevin Frame (North Idaho)
3. Tim Blatter (Ricks)
4. Jim Zeigler (LaBette)
5. Glen Barker (Ellsworth)
6. Mike Barna (Middlesex, NJ)
7. Kevin Bos (Niagara)
8. Dennis McNamara (Rochester, MN)

158-lb class
1. Jeff Steele (Muskegon)
2. Bill Butteris (Kirkwood)
3. Bob Codden (North Idaho)
4. Kory Taylor (Garden City)
5. Randy Bock (Northwest, WY)
6. Frank Rey (Morrisville)
7. Don Peterson (Delhi)
8. Jeff Harris (Lincoln C)

167-lb class
1. Dan Niebuhr (Madison ARea Tech)
2. Alonzo Nalls (Triton)
3. Vincent Walker (Garden City)
4. John Richter (Bismarck)
5. Dave Nicolson (Ricks)
6. Bill Scott (Middlesex, NJ)
7. Darrel Hoogendoorn (Worthington)
8. Andy Conant (Muskegon)

177-lb class
1. Kenny Rucker (North Idaho)
2. Les Kvien (Bismarck)
3. Scott McCabe (Waldorf)
4. John Ybarra (Clackamas)
5. Roger Koppes (Iowa Central)
6. Mark Kumpula (North Dakota Science)
7. Rick Valli (Willmar)
8. Greg McDonald (Gloucester)

190-lb class
1. Pat Whitcomb (North Idaho)
2. Copache Tyler (Triton)
3. Vic Pozsonyi (Middlesex, NJ)
4. Jim Gill (Northwestern Oklahoma)
5. Tod Smith (Iowa Central)
6. Bryan Hagen (Worthington)
7. Terry Gibbons (Cuyahoga)
8. C.J. Dominick (Monroe Heavyweight)

Heavyweight
1. Robbie Benjamin (North Idaho)
2. Dan Stephani (Iowa Central)
3. Dave Orndorff (Ricks)
4. Kevin Mettler (Waldorf)
5. Jim Baker (Cuyahoga)
6. Dennis Cannon (Chowan)
7. Joey Nagel (Bismarck)
8. Chris Piatt (Big Bend)

1987 (at Glen Ellyn, IL)

Team	*Points*
1. North Idaho	132
2. Clackamas	63.75

3.	Cuyahoga West	60
4.	Nassau	52.50
5.	SUNY A&T at Morrisville	50.75
6.	Monroe (NY), Worthington	38.50
8.	Wimar	37.50
9.	Lakeland (OH)	35.25
10.	Lincoln College	35
11.	Middlesex (NJ)	30
12.	Phoenix	28.75
13.	William Rainey Harper	28.50
14.	Grand Rapids Junior	27.50
15.	Waldorf	26.75

Place winners

118-lb class
1. Anthony Washington (Cuyahoga West)
2. Mickey Wright (Meramec)
3. Doug Harper (Clackamas)
4. Terry Schmuecker (Kirkwood)
5. Tim Elphick (Chowan)
6. Ralph Godshall (Stevens)
7. Bret Penrith (Broome)
8. Tony McCall (Northeastern Oklahoma)

126-lb class
1. Gene McNeil (Nassau)
2. Anthony Crater (Grand Rapids Junior)
3. Chuck Pearson (Kirkwood)
4. Shawn Flowers (Morrisville)
5. Stacy Weiand (Meramec)
6. Al Neikirk (Lakeland)
7. Tim McCall (Northeastern Oklahoma)
8. Kevin Byrd (Lincoln C)

134-lb class
1. Sam Parker (North Idaho)
2. Jon Kinchen (Middlesex County)
3. Benny Bright (Cuyahoga West)
4. Matt Whelan (Forest Park)
5. Steve Bradish (Morrisville)
6. Duane Barnhardt (Bismarck)
7. Robert Young (Triton)
8. Ronnie Higdon (Granite City)

142-lb class
1. Charles Royer (Morrisville)
2. Bret Racicot (North Idaho)
3. Antoine Parker (Granite City)
4. Rob Gallagher (Lakeland)
5. Jeff Nokes (Waldorf)
6. Jim Gloudeman (Triton)
7. Frank Croce (Middlesex, NJ)
8. Alex Castrejon (Lincoln C)

150-lb class
1. William Taylor (Clackamas)
2. Mike Cronmiller (Monroe)
3. Jay Barrientes (Kirkwood)
4. Kannon Kares (Grand Rapids Junior)
5. Phil McClean (North Idaho)
6. Doug Youngs (Morrisville)
7. Scott Lewison (Rochester)
8. Bob Brown (Gloucester)

158-lb class
1. Marty Boday (North Idaho)
2. Jeff Sparrow (Phoenix)
3. Mike Hruska (William Rainey Harper)
4. Charles Parker (Chowan)
5. Kevin Akin (Muskegon)
6. Kelvin Wever (Worthington)
7. Steve Baumbach (Stevens)
8. Nick Jennissen (Willmar)

167-lb class
1. Drew Jackson (North Idaho)
2. Rick Vali (Willmar)
3. Darrell Hoogendoorn (Worthington)
4. Steve Keiser (Forest Park)
5. Craig Cameron (Pima)
6. Phil St. George (Monroe)
7. Blake Ford (Northwestern, WY)
8. Mike Simon (Nassau)

177-lb class
1. Juan Ybarra (Clackamas)
2. John Deinhart (Worthington)
3. Mike Janosko (Nassau)
4. Jim Putman (North Idaho)
5. Doug Krukowski (Muskegon)

6. Mike Carey (Highline)
7. Dave Rowden (William Rainey Harper)
8. Eric Napier (LaBette)

190-lb class
1. Pat Whitcomb (North Idaho)
2. Brian Jackson (Forest Park)
3. Norris Richardson (Cuyahoga West)
4. Rich Legrett (Monroe)
5. Jay Leo (Mohawk Valley)
6. Sam Thomas (Nassau)
7. James Kozuki (Ellsworth)
8. Steve Spencer (Phoenix)

Heavyweight
1. Copache Tyler (Lincoln C)
2. Anthony Jefferson (Granite City)
3. Kevin Mettler (Waldorf)
4. Terry Ullom (Willmar)
5. Rick Hufnus (William Rainey Harper)
6. Rick Loveland (Lakeland)
7. Kelly Cole (North Idaho)
8. John Ritchburg (LaBette)

1988 (at Glen Ellyn, IL)

Team	*Points*
1. North Idaho	84.25
2. Ricks	76.50
3. Northwest (WY)	72
4. Lincoln College	64.25
5. Gloucester	57.50
6. Northeastern Oklahoma	54.75
7. Garden City	49.25
8. Cuyahoga	41.25
9. Worthington	39
10. Willmar	38.25
11. Lakeland (OH)	38
12. Kirkwood	36.50
13. SUNY A&T at Delhi	32.75
14. North Dakota Science	30.75
15. DuPage	23.75

Place winners

118-lb class
1. Steve Kasza (Delhi)
2. Gabe Mendez (Garden City)
3. Zen Braggs (Waldorf)
4. Tony McCall (Northeastern Oklahoma)
5. Chris Caskey (Cuyahoga)
6. Rich Barron (Lakeland)
7. Wes Askew (Niagara)
8. Greg Schmitz (Willmar)

126-lb class
1. Tim McCall (Northeastern Oklahoma)
2. Gene McNeil (Nassau)
3. Sam Parker (Belleville)
4. Gordi LaCroix (North Idaho)
5. Curtis Crims (Lincoln C)
6. Kris Presler (Willmar)
7. Brian Carter (Cuyahoga)
8. Mike Morgan (North Dakota Science)

134-lb class
1. Scott Ruff (Northwest, WY)
2. Joe Hollywood (Gloucester)
3. Alex Castrejon (Lincoln C)
4. Jason Aarhus (Kirkwood)
5. Troy Almeter (Alfred)
6. Brett Gray (Northeastern Oklahoma)
7. Reggie Foston (Lakeland)
8. Brian Pearl (Cuyahoga)

142-lb class
1. Derrick Asbell (Kirkwood)
2. Bruce Holt (Ricks)
3. Bob Gallagher (Lakeland)
4. Chad Johnson (Garden City)
5. Lawrence Davis (LaBette)
6. Terry Murphy (Lincoln C)
7. Brian Schiller (Clackamas)
8. Jeff Flynn (Grand Rapids Junior)

150-lb class
1. Andy Howington (Ricks)
2. Maurice Fields (Lincoln C)

3. Mike Lamb (Gloucester)
4. Mike Garner (Phoenix)
5. Dave Haas (Willmar)
6. John Duraksi (DuPage)
7. John Barlund (North Dakota Science)
8. Tom Henderson (Garden City)

158-lb class

1. Leon Bullerman (Worthington)
2. Bob Cooden (North Idaho)
3. Jessie Smith (Northwest, WY)
4. Frank Short (Lincoln C)
5. Jay Lorton (Northeastern Oklahoma)
6. Tom Richter (Bismarck)
7. Bill Templeton (Middlesex, NJ)
8. Jeff Thompson (Ellsworth)

167-lb class

1. Mitch Mansfield (Ricks)
2. Jim Bebeau (Anoka)
3. Scott Filius (North Idaho)
4. Joe Giacometto (Brainerd)
5. Scott Smith (Highline)
6. David Tawater (Dodge City)
7. Ernest Harris (Chowan)
8. Pat Gratziana (DuPage)

177-lb class

1. Lloyd Huyck (North Dakota Science)
2. Jim Putman (North Idaho)
3. Dennis Marconi (Cuyahoga)
4. Rob Young (Northwest, WY)
5. Albert Olsen (Ricks)
6. Dave Martin (Stevens)
7. Steve Copenhaver (Bismarck)
8. Nick Castiglia (Delhi)

190-lb class

1. Greg Vanbrill (Gloucester)
2. Pat Gentzler (Northwest, WY)
3. Robert Wilson (Garden City)
4. Greg Butteris (North Idaho)
5. Dale Herbst (Willmar)
6. Hank Inderlied (Lakeland)
7. Todd Elrod (Northeastern Oklahoma)
8. Rod Smart (Ricks)

Heavyweight

1. Brian Jackson (Forest Park)
2. Paul Weltha (Iowa Central)
3. Barnie Drenth (Worthington)
4. Jim Richardson (Rochester)
5. Dave Wanameker (Stevens)
6. Kelly Cole (North Idaho)
7. Jim Ellis (Ricks)
8. Mike Faulkner (Grand Rapids Junior)

Chapter 9

The Midlands Championships

Although the various collegiate national tournaments make up the focal point for nearly all young wrestlers in the United States, a number of other tournaments offer splendid opportunities for competition. Many of these tournaments have evolved into very successful events, attracting many of the nation's finest wrestlers and developing large fan followings.

One of the oldest is the Wilkes Tournament. It began in 1932 in Wilkes-Barre, Pennsylvania, just 4 years after the first NCAA Tournament, and has continued to flourish with a large support base in the East.

The Great Plains Tournament in Lincoln, Nebraska, dawned in 1960 and for nearly 20 years was one of the most important midwestern meets. For many years it served as a qualifying format for the prestigious Tbilisi Tournament in the Soviet Union. Sponsored by the AAU, the Great Plains dissolved when the AAU was replaced by USA Wrestling in 1982 as the sport's national governing body.

The Mountain Intercollegiate Wrestling Association Tournament is the largest tourney in the Rocky Mountain area. Debuting in 1962, it moves from site to site throughout the Rocky Mountain area. Other highly regarded meets include the Southern Open in Chattanooga, Tennessee; the Northern Open in Madison, Wisconsin; the Sunshine Open in Tampa, Florida; the Sunkist Open in Tempe, Arizona; the Hall of Fame Classic in Stillwater, Oklahoma; and the Las Vegas Open in Las Vegas, Nevada.

But the tournament generally regarded as the nation's premiere event behind the NCAA Tournament is the Midlands Championships. The tournament began at the West Suburban YMCA in LaGrange, Illinois, in 1963 and steadily grew to the point where it has no peer. Originally known as the West Suburban Open, it has been called wrestling's "Super Bowl." In the first 17 years of the tournament's existence, 10 team champions went on to win the NCAA team title that same season.

Ken Kraft, coach at Northwestern University in the 1960s, was the motivating force behind the Midlands. He felt the long drive to the Wilkes

Tournament was too demanding on midwestern teams, and he wanted to offer a strong early-season tourney situated in the Midwest.

The Midlands is held each December following Christmas and before New Year's Eve. As it attracts postgraduates, it provides the stiffest possible test for the college stars around the country. In fact, there is a long list of NCAA champions who have entered the Midlands but never won a title there.

The first Midlands Tournament attracted a field of 132. The University of Michigan, coached by Cliff Keen, captured the crown, as Mike Palmisano (118), Cal Jenkins (142), and Rick Bay (167) took titles back to Ann Arbor. Other champions that first year were Terry Finn (126), Don Schneider (134), and Larry Kristoff (heavyweight) of Southern Illinois; Jerry Torrence (150) of Northwestern; Dave Gibson (158) of Purdue; Roy Conrad (177) of the Irving Park YMCA; and Dennis McCabe (unattached).

In 1964, the tournament moved to the new south campus of LaGrange Lyons High School, and Michigan repeated as the team champion. In 1965 Iowa State University entered the field and captured its first of six titles. The following year, the Cyclones lost the team title to Michigan State but saw a legend born in Dan Gable.

Gable entered the 1966 Midlands as a highly touted freshman at Iowa State. He had fashioned a 64-0 record for West Waterloo High School in Iowa and had never tasted defeat. But at the tough Midlands, he was expected to lose his first match at some point. Instead, he made wrestling history.

The boyish-looking Gable scored five straight wins and shocked veteran fans and sportswriters with his performance. He decisioned former Michigan State star Don Behm in the semifinals, 9-5, and then upended former Oklahoma State NCAA champion Masaaki Hatta in the finals, 8-2. For his efforts, Gable was named the meet's Outstanding Wrestler.

The Midlands proved to be the kickoff for the Gable legend. Before he was through, he would run off 181 straight wins in high school and college competition. At the Midlands alone, he compiled a 31-0 record in 6 years and was named Outstanding Wrestler five times. He also holds the all-time pin mark of 22 at the tourney.

Continuing to grow in both stature and size, the Midlands was forced to change sites again. In 1972, it shifted to McGaw Hall on the campus of Northwestern University. That year saw a record 528 entrants, and the following year tourney officials put a cap on the entries list.

By 1987, a total of 49 Midlands competitors had competed in the Olympics, beginning with heavyweight Larry Kristoff in 1964. Among the brightest stars were Dan Gable; the Peterson brothers, John and Ben; Randy Lewis; Steve Fraser; the Schultz brothers, Dave and Mark; the Banach brothers, Ed and Lou; and the late Chris Taylor. The huge Taylor, who stands second on the all-time pin list with 18, was one of the tournament's most popular attractions.

Dan Gable, winner of six straight Midlands titles. (Courtesy of Iowa State University)

The most successful Midlands wrestler by 1988 was Bruce Baumgartner. He owned a record eight titles at heavyweight as well as tourney records for most wins (43) and most consecutive wins (40).

Iowa was the most successful team as the 1980s drew to a close. The Hawkeyes, under coaches Gary Kurdelmeier and Dan Gable, owned 10 team titles. In 1984, the Sunkist Kids of Arizona became the first noncollegiate team to win the Midlands.

For a comprehensive overview of Midland Tournament champions, see Table 9.1.

Table 9.1
The Midlands Championships

Outstanding Wrestler

1964	Masaaki Hatta, 130 (Michigan WC)
1965	Masaaki Hatta, 123 (Michigan WC)
	Tom Peckham, 177 (Iowa State)
1966	Dan Gable, 130 (Iowa State)
1967	Dan Gable, 137 (Iowa State)
1968	Dan Gable, 137 (Iowa State)
1969	Dan Gable, 142 (Iowa State)

1970 Yoshiro Fujita, 126 (Oklahoma State)
1971 Dan Gable, 150 (unat)
1972 Wade Schalles, 158 (Clarion State)
1973 Jimmy Carr, 126 (unat)
1974 Don Behm, 134 (Daley WC)
1975 Larry Zilverberg, 167 (Minnesota)
1976 Harold Smith, Heavyweight (Kentucky)
1977 Mike McArthur, 118 (unat)
1978 Wade Schalles, 167 (New York AC)
1979 Randy Lewis, 126 (Iowa)
1980 Lenny Zalesky, 142 (Iowa)
1981 Ed Banach, 177 (Iowa)
1982 Al Freeman, 142 (Nebraska)
1983 Bruce Baumgartner, Heavyweight (NYAC)
1984 Don Horning, 118 (unat)
1985 Duane Goldman, 190 (Iowa)
1986 Bruce Baumgartner, Heavyweight (NYAC)
1987 Ed Giese, 118 (Gopher WC)

(Selected by tournament referees and members of the media)

Art Kraft Champion of Champions

1980 Lenny Zalesky, 142 (Iowa)
1981 Darryl Burley, 134 (unat, Lehigh)
1982 Al Freeman, 142 (Nebraska)
1983 Jim Zalesky, 158 (Iowa)
1984 Bill Scherr, 190 (Sunkist Kids)
1985 Gene Mills, 142 (NYAC)
1986 Jim Heffernan, 150 (Iowa)
1987 Mike Sheets, 167 (Sunkist Kids)

(Selected by the champions; the man who best represents the highest ideals of wrestling)

Gorriaran Most Falls—Least Time Trophy

1968 Dan Gable, 4 (Iowa State)
1969 Dan Gable, 5 (Iowa State)
1970 Larry Owings, 4 (Washington)
1971 Chris Tayor, 5 (Iowa State)
1972 Wade Schalles, 3 (Clarion State)
1973 Joe Wells, 3 (Daley WC)
1974 Ben Peterson, 3 (unat)
1975 Wade Schalles, 3 (Mean Machine)
1976 John Bowlsby, 4 (Iowa)
1977 Jim Mitchell, 3 (Arizona State)
1978 Randy Lewis, 4 (Iowa)
1979 Jimmy Jackson, 3 (Sunkist Kids)
1980 Bruce Baumgartner, 3 (Indiana State)
1981 Israel Sheppard, 2 (Oklahoma)
1982 Mike Foy, 5 (Minnesota)
1983 Eli Blazeff, 3 (Michigan State)
1984 Wade Hughes, 3 (George Washington)
1985 Brandon O'Donahue, 5 (Michigan State)
1986 Michael Cole, 4 (unat, Clarion State)
1987 Mike Lingenfelter, 4 (Lock Haven)

Most Career Pins

1.	Dan Gable	22
2.	Chris Taylor	18
3.	Wade Schalles	16
4.	Chuck Yagla, Verlyn Strellner	13
6.	Mike McArthur	12
7.	Bruce Baumgartner, Joe Wells, Randy Lewis	11
10.	Pat Kelly, John Bowlsby	10

Coaches of Midlands Championship Teams

Outstanding Wrestler

1963 Cliff Keen (Michigan)
1964 Cliff Keen (Michigan)
1965 Harold Nichols (Iowa State)
1966 Grady Peninger (Michigan State)
1967 Harold Nichols (Iowa State)
1968 Grady Peninger (Michigan State)
1969 Grady Peninger (Michigan State)
1970 Harold Nichols (Iowa State)
1971 Harold Nichols (Iowa State)
1972 Harold Nichols (Iowa State)
1973 Tom Chesbro (Oklahoma State)
1974 Gary Kurdelmeier (Iowa)
1975 Gary Kurdelmeier (Iowa)
1976 Gary Kurdelmeier (Iowa)

1977 Dan Gable (Iowa)
1978 Dan Gable (Iowa)
1979 Dan Gable (Iowa)
1980 Dan Gable (Iowa)
1981 Harold Nichols (Iowa State)
1982 Dan Gable (Iowa)
1983 J Robinson (Iowa)
1984 Bobby Douglas (Sunkist Kids)
1985 Dan Gable (Iowa)
1986 Bill Lam (North Carolina)
1987 Bobby Douglas (Sunkist Kids)

(Selected by tournament referees and members of the media)

Most Career Victories

1. Bruce Baumgartner	43
2. Barry Davis	39
3. Chuck Yagla	38
4. Tim Cysewski, Ben Peterson	36
6. Pete Galea	35
7. Randy Lewis	34
8. John Peterson	33
9. Jim Scherr, Mike McArthur, Abdul Raheem Ali, Russ Hellickson	32
13. Dan Gable, Marty Kistler, Scott Trizzino	31
16. Larry Zilverberg, Joe Wells	30
18. Doug Moses, Verlyn Strellner	29

(Wrestlers competed for a variety of clubs during their careers)

1963 Midlands

Team	*Points*
1. Michigan	93
2. Southern Illinois	62
3. Northwestern	26
4. Joliet JC	19
5. Hazel Park WC	17
6. Boilermaker WC	15
7. Irving Park YMCA	12
8. Moorhead State, Northern Illinois	10
10. Wisconsin	4

Place winners

118-lb class
1. Mike Palmisano (Michigan)
2. Stan Korona (Northern Illinois)
3. Andy Duvall (unat)
4. Chuck Schuman (unat)

126-lb class
1. Terry Finn (Southern Illinois at Carbondale)
2. Dave Kreider (Northwestern)
3. Tino Lambros (Michigan)
4. Bill Anderson (unat)

134-lb class
1. Don Schneider (Southern Illinois at Carbondale)
2. Bill Johanaeson (Michigan)
3. Bill Riddle (Hazel Park WC)
4. Bob Cappettini (Toledo)

142-lb class
1. Cal Jenkins (Michigan)
2. Lee Grubbs (unat)
3. Norm Parker (unat)
4. Sam Epps (Joliet)

150-lb class
1. Jerry Torrence (Northwestern)
2. Dick Smith (unat)
3. Dan Divito (Southern Illinois at Carbondale)
4. Bob Furian (Joliet)

158-lb class
1. Dave Gibson (Purdue)
2. Sam Ward (unat)
3. Wayne Miller (Michigan)
4. Dave Post (Michigan)

167-lb class
1. Rick Bay (Michigan)
2. Stu Marshall (Northwestern)
3. Bill Waterman (unat)
4. Ray Matesevac (Joliet)

177-lb class
1. Roy Conrad (Irving Park Y)
2. Don Millard (Southern Illinois at Carbondale)
3. Steve Combs (unat)
4. Chris Stowell (Michigan)

190-lb class
1. Dennis McCabe (unat)
2. Joe Arcure (Michigan)
3. Breck Johnson (unat)
4. Joe Milek (Wisconsin)

Heavyweight
1. Larry Kristoff (Southern Illinois at Carbondale)
2. Bob Billberg (Moorhead State)
3. Ralph Spaly (Michigan)
4. John Manner (Joliet)

1964

Team	*Points*
1. Michigan	51
2. Michigan State	50
3. Northwestern	49
4. Indianapolis WC	25
5. Southern Illinois	24
6. Indiana	19
7. Illinois	17
8. Miami (OH)	15
9. Moorhead State	12
10. Joliet JC	10

Place winners

118-lb class
1. Dave Range (Miami)
2. Wayne Watson (Joliet)
3. Larry Katz (South Bend Y)
4. Bob Dietz (Lehigh)

126-lb class
1. Bob Fehrs (Michigan)
2. Tino Lambros (Michigan)
3. Dan Devine (Southern Illinois at Carbondale)
4. Bill Anderson (Northwestern)

134-lb class
1. Masaaki Hatta (Hazel Park WC)
2. Don Behm (Michigan)
3. Larry Baron (Southern Illinois at Carbondale)
4. Doug Horning (Michigan)

142-lb class
1. Pete Beevers (Northwestern)
2. Joe Ganz (Michigan State)
3. Stu Fonda (Navy)
4. Bob Campbell (Indiana)

150-lb class
1. Dick Cook (Michigan State)
2. Chuck Coffee (unat)
3. Jim Kamman (Michigan)
4. John Schael (Miami, OH)

158-lb class
1. Clayton Beattie (Illinois)
2. Lee Deitrick (Michigan)
3. Rudy Dotlick (Indianapolis WC)
4. Morey Villareal (Michigan State)

167-lb class
1. Stu Marshall (Northwestern)
2. Jim Ellis (Indianapolis WC)
3. Dave Reinboldt (Ohio State)
4. Don Bennett (Indiana)

177-lb class
1. Steve Combs (unat)
2. Dick Ernst (Northwestern)
3. Joe Domko (unat)
4. Chris Stowell (Michigan)

190-lb class
1. Pat Kelly (Daley WC)
2. Dan Gesky (Southern Illinois at Carbondale)
3. Dan Pernat (unat)
4. Emerson Boles (Michigan State)

Heavyweight
1. Larry Kristoff (unat)
2. Bob Billberg (Moorhead State)
3. Ralph Spaly (Michigan)
4. Dave Porter (unat)

1965

Team	*Points*
1. Iowa State	69
2. Mayor Daley WC	59
3. Michigan	56
4. Southern Illinois	43
5. Wisconsin	42
6. Michigan State	38
7. Michigan WC	28
8. Northwestern	19
9. Cyclone WC	17
10. Miami (OH)	15

Place winners

118-lb class
1. Ernie Gillum (Iowa State)
2. Terry Magoon (Southern Illinois at Carbondale)
3. Gary Bissel (Michigan State)
4. Drew Algase (Toledo)

126-lb class
1. Masaaki Hatta (Michigan WC)
2. Bob Fehrs (Michigan)
3. Wayne Lenhares (Southern Illinois at Carbondale)
4. Dave Monroe (Wisconsin)

134-lb class
1. Don Behm (Michigan State)
2. Dale Anderson (unat)
3. Chet Mirus (unat)
4. Gordie Weeks (Michigan)

142-lb class
1. Mike Gluck (Wisconsin)
2. Dale Carr (Michigan State)
3. Don Schneider (Southern Illinois at Carbondale)
4. Bill Johanneson (Michigan)

145-lb class
1. Cal Jenkins (Michigan)
2. Dick Smith (unat)
3. Jerry Bond (Northern Iowa)
4. Don Henning (unat)

152-lb class
1. Bob Buzzard (Iowa State)
2. Jim Kamman (Michigan)
3. Russ Schneider (Northwestern)
4. Leo Simon (Winona State)

158-lb class
1. Lee Deitrick (Michigan WC)
2. Werner Holzer (Daley WC)
3. Vic Marcucci (Iowa State)
4. George McCreery (Southern Illinois at Carbondale)

167-lb class
1. Gordon Hassman (Cyclone WC)
2. Elmer Beale (Wisconsin)
3. Dave Reinboldt (Ohio State)
4. Curt Sexton (Illinois State)

177-lb class
1. Tom Peckham (Iowa State)
2. Steve Combs (Daley WC)
3. Walt Podgursici (Miami, OH)
4. John Schneider (Michigan State)

190-lb class
1. Don Buzzard (Iowa State)
2. Pat Kelly (Daley WC)
3. Dan Pernat (Wisconsin)
4. Don Parker (Northern Iowa)

Heavyweight
1. Larry Kristoff (Daley WC)
2. Joe James (Daley WC)
3. Dave Porter (Michigan)
4. Bob Roop (Southern Illinois at Carbondale)

1966

Team	*Points*
1. Michigan State	92
2. Iowa State	79
3. Mayor Daley WC	72
4. Michigan	46
5. Toledo	37
6. Southern Illinois	33
7. Iowa, Wisconsin	21
9. Northwestern	19
10. Michigan WC	14

Place winners

118-lb class
1. Dave Keller (Toledo)
2. Ron Oglesby (Daley WC)
3. Dave Kestel (Eastern Michigan)
4. Steve Potter (Wisconsin)

126-lb class
1. Gary Wallman (Iowa State)
2. Wayne Watson (Northwestern)
3. Gary Bissel (Michigan State)
4. Abe Chamie (Eastern Michigan)

134-lb class
1. Dan Gable (Iowa State)
2. Masaaki Hatta (Michigan WC)
3. Don Behm (Michigan State)
4. Tom Tisone (Daley WC)

142-lb class
1. Dale Anderson (Michigan State)
2. Norm Parker (Daley WC)
3. Sam Epps (Iowa State)
4. Mike Nagel (Wisconsin)

145-lb class
1. Bert Merical (Michigan)
2. Jerry Vincent (Toledo)
3. Dale Carr (Michigan State)
4. Mike Gluck (Wisconsin)

152-lb class
1. Dale Bahr (Iowa State)
2. Jim Kamman (Michigan)
3. Fred Stehman (Michigan)
4. Al Sievertson (Wisconsin)

158-lb class
1. Reggie Wicks (Iowa State)
2. Dave Martin (Iowa State)
3. Werner Holzer (Daley WC)
4. Phil Buerk (Marquette)

167-lb class
1. George Radman (Michigan State)
2. Vic Marcucci (Iowa State)
3. Joe Domko (Southern Illinois at Carbondale)
4. Jim Schindhelm (Marquette)

177-lb class
1. Pat Kelly (Daley WC)
2. Mike Bradley (Michigan State)
3. Norm Lovelace (Western Illinois)
4. Verlyn Strellner (Iowa)

190-lb class
1. Jim Duschen (Iowa State)
2. Jack Zindell (Michigan State)
3. Willie Williams (Illinois State)
4. Alan Bulow (Southern Illinois at Carbondale)

Heavyweight
1. Larry Kristoff (Daley WC)
2. Joe James (Daley WC)
3. Dave Porter (Michigan)
4. Dale Stearns (Iowa)

1967

Team	*Points*
1. Iowa State	96
2. Michigan State	69
3. Northwestern	43
4. Mayor Daley WC	40
5. Michigan	33
6. Indiana	31
7. Michigan WC	28
8. Iowa	26
9. Toledo	25
10. Southern Illinois	23

Place winners

118-lb class
1. Greg Johnson (unat)
2. Dave Keller (Toledo)
3. Mike Sheer (Michigan)
4. Dale Kestel (Eastern Michigan)

126-lb class
1. Gary Wallman (Iowa State)
2. Ted Parker (Indiana State)
3. Dale Barnard (unat)
4. Steve Rubin (Michigan)

134-lb class
1. Don Behm (Daley WC)
2. Masaaki Hatta (Michigan WC)
3. Tom McCall (Indiana)
4. Lou Hudson (Michigan)

142-lb class
1. Dan Gable (Iowa State)
2. Dale Anderson (Michigan State)
3. Jack Dunn (Northwestern)
4. Angelo Testone (Western Illinois)

145-lb class
1. Dale Carr (Michigan State)
2. Bill Johanneson (Michigan WC)
3. Larry Miele (East Michigan)
4. Chet Mirus (Daley WC)

152-lb class
1. Russ Schneider (Northwestern)
2. Dave Martin (Iowa State)
3. Fred Stehman (Michigan)
4. Bob Loffredo (Illinois)

158-lb class
1. Jim Tanniehill (unat)
2. Reg Wicks (Iowa State)
3. Rich Mihal (Iowa)
4. Otto Zeman (Northwestern)

167-lb class
1. Jason Smith (Iowa State)
2. Gene Denisar (Indiana)
3. Seth Norton (Northwestern)
4. Rich Heinzelman (Wisconsin)

177-lb class
1. Mike Bradley (Michigan State)
2. Don Buzzard (Iowa State)
3. Steve Combs (Daley WC)
4. Bob Ahrens (Navy)

190-lb class
1. Tom Peckham (unat)
2. Ben Cooper (Southern Illinois at Carbondale)
3. John Schneider (Michigan State)
4. Dan Wintersteen (Ball State)

Heavyweight
1. Jeff Smith (Michigan State)
2. Paul Elzey (Toledo)
3. Mike Kelly (Indiana State)
4. Dale Stearns (Iowa)

1968

Team	*Points*
1. Michigan State	102
2. Iowa State	62
3. Iowa	46
4. Northwestern	39
5. Michigan	35
6. Northern Illinois	27
7. Miami (OH)	24
8. Winona State	21
9. Toledo	20
10. Mayor Daley WC	18

Place winners

118-lb class
1. Dave Keller (Toledo)
2. Bill Vail (unat)
3. Norm Wilkerson (Iowa State)
4. Steve Jeffries (Iowa State)

126-lb class
1. Tim Cech (Michigan)
2. Jim Greiner (Miami, OH)
3. Gary Bissel (Michigan State)
4. Dennis Terdy (Northwestern)

134-lb class
1. Wes Caine (Northern Illinois)
2. Lou Hudson (Michigan)
3. Mike Ellis (Michigan State)
4. Scott Clark (Western Illinois)

142-lb class
1. Dan Gable (Iowa State)
2. Keith Lowrence (Michigan State)
3. Ted Parker (Daley WC)
4. Geoff Henson (Michigan)

145-lb class
1. Joe Carstenson (Iowa)
2. Bill Viverette (Eastern Michigan)
3. Ron Ouellet (Michigan State)
4. Bob Murfin (Wheaton)

152-lb class
1. John Abajace (Michigan State)
2. Dave Campbell (Michigan State)
3. Pete Sandburg (Winona State)
4. John Podgurski (Miami, OH)

158-lb class
1. Rich Mihal (Iowa)
2. Jim Tanniehill (Winona State)
3. Otto Zeman (Northwestern)
4. Tom Muir (Michigan State)

167-lb class
1. Seth Norton (Northwestern)
2. Rick Heinselman (unat)
3. Pat Karslake (Michigan State)
4. Pat North (Northern Illinois)

177-lb class
1. Chuck Jean (Iowa State)
2. Jason Smith (Iowa State)
3. Walt Podgursici (Miami, OH)
4. Jack Zindel (Michigan State)

190-lb class
1. John Schneider (Michigan State)
2. Jim Duschen (Iowa State)
3. Mike Bay (Joliet)
4. Gene Libal (unat)

Heavyweight
1. Jeff Smith (Michigan State)
2. Mike Kelly (Daley WC)
3. Dale Stearns (Iowa)
4. Chris Taylor (Muskegon CC)

1969

Team	*Points*
1. Michigan State	79
2. Michigan	68
3. Iowa State	61
4. Oklahoma	58
5. Northwestern, Mayor Daley WC	23
7. Winona State	21
8. Muskegon JC	18
9. Iowa	15
10. Illinois, Central Michigan	14

Place winners

118-lb class
1. Jerry Hoddy (Michigan)
2. Norm Wilkerson (Iowa State)
3. Lon Hicks (Michigan State)
4. Ray Stapp (Oklahoma State)

126-lb class
1. Yoshiro Fujita (Oklahoma State)
2. Ted Parker (Daley WC)
3. Dwayne Keller (Oklahoma State)
4. Tim Cech (Michigan)

134-lb class
1. Mike Ellis (Michigan State)
2. Tom Milkovich (Michigan State)
3. Doug Moses (Iowa State)
4. Mike Riley (Oklahoma State)

142-lb class
1. Dan Gable (Iowa State)
2. Keith Lowrence (Michigan State)
3. Larry Hulburt (Central Michigan)
4. Mark King (Michigan)

150-lb class
1. Ron Ouellet (Michigan State)
2. Lane Headrick (Michigan)
3. Doug Campbell (Oklahoma State)
4. Don Yahn (Iowa)

158-lb class
1. Dave Martin (Iowa State)
2. Jim Tanniehill (Winona State)
3. Joe Wells (unat)
4. Bill Laursen (Northwestern)

167-lb class
1. Pat Karslake (Michigan State)
2. Gerry Malecek (Michigan State)
3. Pat North (Northern Illinois)
4. Bruce Kirkpatrick (Illinois)

177-lb class
1. Chuck Jean (Iowa State)
2. Jesse Rawls (Michigan)
3. Gerald Winnard (Oklahoma State)
4. Pete Leiskau (Wisconsin)

190-lb class
1. Geoff Baum (Oklahoma State)
2. Jack Zindell (Michigan State)

3. Willie Williams (Daley WC)
4. Paul Zander (unat)

Heavyweight
1. Tom Peckham (unat)
2. Greg Wojciechowski (Toledo)
3. Dale Stearns (unat)
4. Chris Taylor (Muskegon CC)

1970

Team	*Points*
1. Iowa State	86
2. Oklahoma State	66
3. Michigan State	60
4. Michigan	46
5. Iowa, Northwestern	37
7. Wisconsin	26
8. Mayor Daley WC	21
9. Muskegon JC, Minnesota WC	19

Place winners

118-lb class
1. Ron Thrasher (Oklahoma State)
2. Stan Lampe (Iowa State)
3. Dan Sherman (Iowa)
4. Chuck Rossetti (Northern Illinois)

126-lb class
1. Yoshiro Fujita (Oklahoma State)
2. Bill Knight (Iowa State)
3. Mark Massery (Northwestern)
4. Jan Gitcho (Southern Illinois at Carbondale)

134-lb class
1. Dwayne Keller (Oklahoma State)
2. Tom Milkovich (Michigan State)
3. Phil Parker (Iowa State)
4. Mike Shearer (Iowa State)

142-lb class
1. Darrell Keller (Oklahoma State)
2. Dave Pruzansky (Penn Grapplers)
3. Mike Riley (Oklahoma State)
4. Reid Lamphere (Minnesota)

150-lb class
1. Dan Gable (unat)
2. Clyde Smith (Northwestern)
3. Larry Owings (Washington)
4. Jerry Hubbard (Michigan)

158-lb class
1. Carl Adams (Iowa State)
2. Joe Wells (Daley WC)
3. Tom Muir (Michigan State)
4. George Beene (Triton)

167-lb class
1. Jim Tanniehill (Minnesota WC)
2. John Peterson (Wisconsin—Stout)
3. Keith Abens (Iowa State)
4. Tom Quinn (Michigan)

177-lb class
1. Steve Devries (Iowa)
2. Pete Leiskau (Wisconsin)
3. Bruce Zindel (Michigan State)
4. Bill Reinboldt (Ohio State)

190-lb class
1. Russ Hellickson (unat)
2. Ben Peterson (Iowa State)
3. Jack Zindell (Michigan WC)
4. Dave Ciolek (Michigan State)

Heavyweight
1. Chris Taylor (unat)
2. Greg Wojciechowski (Toledo)
3. Dale Stearns (unat)
4. Ron Fandrick (Northern Michigan)

1971

Team	*Points*
1. Iowa State	97
2. Michigan State	81
3. Oklahoma State	51
4. Michigan	42
5. Mayor Daley WC	41
6. Northwestern	31.5
7. Clarion State	26.5
8. Michigan WC	26
9. Northern Illinois	22.5
10. Wisconsin	19

Place winners

118-lb class
1. Dan Sherman (Iowa)
2. Jim Brown (Michigan)
3. Dale Brumet (Arizona)
4. Lon Hicks (Michigan State)

126-lb class
1. Yoshiro Fujita (Oklahoma State)
2. Jan Gitcho (Southern Illinois at Edwardsville)
3. Greg Johnson (Michigan State)
4. Bill Davids (Michigan)

134-lb class
1. Conrad Calender (Michigan State)
2. Bill Fjetland (Iowa State)
3. Linus Keunnen (Iowa State)
4. Dwayne Nyckel (Eastern Illinois)

142-lb class
1. Tom Milkovich (Michigan State)
2. Phil Parker (Iowa State)
3. Dave Dominick (Oklahoma State)
4. Rick Lawinger (Wisconsin)

150-lb class
1. Dan Gable (unat)
2. Clyde Smith (Northwestern)
3. Dave Maple (Northern Illinois)
4. Larry Hulburt (Michigan WC)

158-lb class
1. Keith Abens (Iowa State)
2. Wade Schalles (Clarion State)
3. Jim Tanniehill (Winona State)
4. Alan Albright (Oklahoma State)

167-lb class
1. Carl Adams (Iowa State)
2. Tom Muir (unat)
3. Gerry Malecek (Michigan State)
4. Doug Wyn (Western Michigan)

177-lb class
1. John Peterson (Wisconsin—Stout)
2. Mike Bradley (Michigan WC)
3. Rich Binek (Iowa State)
4. Bill Simpson (Clarion State)

190-lb class
1. Ben Peterson (Iowa State)
2. Russ Hellickson (Daley WC)
3. Dave Ciolek (Michigan State)
4. Jim Duschen (unat)

Heavyweight
1. Chris Taylor (Iowa State)
2. Mike Kelly (Daley WC)
3. Mike McCready (Northern Iowa)
4. Ben Lewis (Michigan State)

1972

Team	*Points*
1. Iowa State	108.5
2. Oklahoma State	94
3. Michigan State	58.5
4. Michigan	51.5
5. Northwestern	46.5
6. Clarion State	40
7. Washington	38.5
8. Michigan WC	34
9. Iowa	32.5
10. Wisconsin	32

Place winners

118-lb class
1. Jim Brown (Michigan)
2. Dan Sherman (Iowa)
3. Dan Mallinger (Iowa State)
4. John Hagen (Iowa State)
5. Paul Bartlett (Iowa State)
6. Randy Miller (Michigan State)

126-lb class
1. Billy Martin (Oklahoma State)
2. Ron Glass (Iowa State)
3. Mike Downer (Wisconsin)
4. Jeff Lamphore (Minnesota)
5. Mark Massery (Northwestern)
6. Rick Sofman (NYAC)

134-lb class
1. Bill Fjetland (Iowa State)
2. Bill Willets (Indiana)
3. Conrad Calender (Michigan State)
4. Don Glass (Iowa State)
5. Tony DiGiovanni (Cleveland State)
6. Bill Davids (Michigan)

142-lb class
1. Tom Milkovich (Michigan State)
2. Bob Stites (Oklahoma State)
3. Andre Allen (Northwestern)
4. Doug Willer (Eastern Michigan)
5. Dave Dominick (Oklahoma State)
6. Bill Schuck (Michigan)

150-lb class
1. Mike Fitzpatrick (Washington)
2. Pete Galea (Iowa State)
3. Rick Lawinger (Wisconsin)
4. Doug Lunt (Iowa State)
5. Chuck Yagla (Iowa)
6. Larry Hulburt (Michigan WC)

158-lb class
1. Wade Schalles (Clarion State)
2. Leo Kocher (Northwestern)
3. Mitch Mendrygal (Michigan)
4. Alan Albright (Oklahoma State)
5. Larry Johnson (Northern Illinois)
6. Jim Fallis (Lake Superior State)

167-lb class
1. Joe Wells (Daley WC)
2. Keith Abens (Iowa State)
3. Bill Simpson (Clarion State)
4. Doug Wyn (Western Michigan)
5. Brendt Noon (Oklahoma State)
6. Ron Ray (Wright State)

177-lb class
1. John Peterson (unat)
2. Mike Bradley (Michigan WC)
3. Clem DeLane (Oklahoma State)
4. Bill Reinboldt (Ohio State)
5. Jeff Zindel (Michigan State)
6. Jim Kulpa (Western Illinois)

190-lb class
1. Ben Peterson (unat)
2. Al Nacin (Iowa State)
3. Jack Zindell (Michigan WC)
4. Bill Knippel (Seattle Pacific)
5. Scott Wickard (Michigan State)
6. Verlyn Strellner (Daley WC)

Heavyweight
1. Chris Taylor (Iowa State)
2. Tom Hazell (Oklahoma State)
3. Gary Ernst (Michigan)
4. Jim Witzleb (Iowa)
5. Jim Woods (Western Illinois)
6. Bob Fouts (Northern Iowa)

1973

Team	*Points*
1. Oklahoma State	101.5
2. Michigan	83.5
3. Iowa	74
4. Wisconsin	67.5
5. Mayor Daley WC	62
6. Athletes in Action	56.5
7. Michigan State	40.5
8. Washington	38.5
9. Wisconsin	38
10. Iowa State	33

Place winners

118-lb class
1. Everett Gomez (Oklahoma State)
2. Rick Reed (Oklahoma State)
3. Dwain Burkholder (unat)
4. Jim Bissell (Michigan State)
5. Jim Haines (Wisconsin)
6. Mike Beining (Marquette)

126-lb class
1. Jim Carr (unat)
2. Mark Massery (Daley WC)
3. Rich Sofman (NYAC)
4. Tim Cysewski (Iowa)
5. Kevin Mathey (Northwestern)
6. Brad Jacot (Washington)

134-lb class
1. Tom Garcia (Northern Iowa)
2. Conrad Calender (Michigan State)
3. Bill Davids (Michigan)
4. Brad Smith (Iowa)
5. Ken Martin (Wisconsin—Parkside)
6. Jeff Guyton (Michigan)

142-lb class
1. Steve Randall (Oklahoma State)
2. Reid Lamphere (AIA)
3. Bill Schuck (Michigan)

4. Steve Evans (Wisconsin)
5. Doug Moses (unat)
6. Dale Evans (Wisconsin WC)

150-lb class
1. Jerry Hubbard (Michigan)
2. Rick Lawinger (Wisconsin)
3. Tom Brown (Washington)
4. Dave Maple (Oklahoma State)
5. Chuck Yagla (Iowa)
6. Bob Morris (unat)

158-lb class
1. Larry Zilverberg (Minnesota)
2. Leo Kocher (Daley WC)
3. Laare Pepenfuse (Washington)
4. John Matthews (Central Michigan)
5. Dan Holm (Iowa)
6. Jim Fallis (Lake Superior State)

167-lb class
1. Doug Wyn (Western Michigan)
2. Jan Sanderson (Iowa)
3. Joe Wells (Daley WC)
4. Ron Ray (Oklahoma State)
5. Rick Nelson (Western Illinois)
6. John Framsted (Oklahoma State)

177-lb class
1. John Peterson (AIA)
2. Ed Vatch (Wisconsin)
3. Bob Huizenga (Michigan)
4. Jeff Zindel (Michigan State)
5. Chris Campbell (Iowa)
6. Rich Binek (Iowa State)

190-lb class
1. Al Nacin (Iowa State)
2. Alex Macalusco (Oklahoma State)
3. Laurent Soucie (Wisconsin)
4. Dave Curby (Michigan)
5. Verlyn Strellner (Daley WC)
6. Pete Leiskau (Wisconsin)

Heavyweight
1. Russ Hellickson (Wisconsin WC)
2. Mike McCready (AIA)
3. Tom Hazell (Oklahoma State)
4. Gary Ernst (Michigan)
5. Jim Woods (Western Illinois)
6. Randy Omvig (Northern Iowa)

1974

Team	*Points*
1. Iowa	88.5
2. Iowa State	75.5
3. Wisconsin	57.5
4. Oklahoma State	49
5. Northern Iowa	47
6. Mayor Daley WC	45.5
7. Kentucky	33.5
8. Minnesota	32.5
9. Michigan	31
10. Athletes in Action	30.5

Place winners

118-lb class
1. Jim Brown (Michigan)
2. Mike McArthur (Minnesota)
3. Mike Land (Iowa State)
4. Bernie Kleiman (Portland State)
5. Jim Haines (Wisconsin)
6. Garrett Headley (Kentucky)

126-lb class
1. Tim Cysewski (Iowa)
2. Jack Reinwand (Wisconsin)
3. Bill Martin (Oklahoma State)
4. Bob Antonacci (Iowa State)
5. Joe Corso (Purdue)
6. Mark Massery (Daley WC)

134-lb class
1. Don Behm (Daley WC)
2. Jimmy Carr (Kentucky)
3. Jim Miller (Northern Iowa)
4. Steve Hunte (Iowa)
5. Dennis Brighton (Michigan State)
6. Craig Horswill (Wisconsin)

142-lb class
1. Andre Allen (Northwestern)
2. Brad Smith (Iowa)
3. Ken Snyder (Northern Iowa)
4. Bill Schuck (Michigan)
5. Tom Garcia (Northern Iowa)
6. Tim Mousetis (Kentucky)

150-lb class
1. Bob Holland (Iowa State)
2. Chuck Yagla (Iowa)
3. Pete Galea (Iowa State)
4. Dave Maple (Daley WC)
5. Jim Blasingame (Northern Iowa)
6. Lee Kemp (Wisconsin)

158-lb class
1. Larry Zilverberg (Minnesota)
2. Dan Holm (Iowa)
3. Tom Keeley (AIA)
4. Mike Taylor (Southern Illinois at Edwardsville)
5. John Matthews (Central Michigan)
6. Larry Johnson (Daley WC)

167-lb class
1. Carl Adams (unat)
2. Ron Ray (Oklahoma State)
3. Joe Carr (Kentucky)
4. Pat Christenson (Wisconsin)
5. Dan Wageman (Iowa)
6. Mark Lieberman (Lehigh)

177-lb class
1. John Peterson (AIA)
2. Joe Wells (Daley WC)
3. Steve Devries (Hawkeye WC)
4. Mike Lieberman (unat)
5. Ed Vatch (Wisconsin)
6. Bill Reinboldt (Ohio State)

190-lb class
1. Ben Peterson (unat)
2. Al Nacin (Iowa State)
3. Laurent Soucie (Wisconsin)
4. Frank Savenago (Southern Illinois at Edwardsville)
5. Verlyn Strellner (Daley WC)
6. Elijah Whitten (unat)

Heavyweight
1. Russ Helickson (Wisconsin WC)
2. Mike McCready (AIA)
3. John Bowlsby (Iowa)
4. Tom Hazell (unat)
5. Larry Avery (Michigan State)
6. Randy Omvig (Northern Iowa)

1975

Team	*Points*
1. Iowa	67.25
2. Iowa State	61
3. Wisconsin	59.25
4. Hawkeye WC	46.75
5. Minnesota	46
6. Oklahoma State	44.50
7. Wisconsin	35.25
8. Illinois	31.25
9. Mean Machine	30.50
10. Cyclone	25.25

Place winners

118-lb class
1. Johnny Jones (Iowa State)
2. John Azevedo (Oklahoma State)
3. Mike McArthur (Minnesota)
4. Gary Matlock (Illinois)
5. Randy Miller (Michigan State)
6. Dale Brumit (Stow WC)

126-lb class
1. Jack Reinwand (Wisconsin)
2. Joe Corso (Hawkeye WC)
3. Kevin Puebla (Illinois)
4. Mike Land (unat)
5. Amos Goodlow (Michigan)
6. Sam Fiorella (Daley WC)

134-lb class
1. Tim Cysewski (Iowa)
2. Jimmy Carr (unat)
3. Pat Milkovich (Michigan State)
4. Rick Jensen (South Dakota State)
5. John Powell (Oklahoma State)
6. Ted Parker (Colorado AC)

142-lb class
1. Dwayne Keller (unat)
2. Brad Smith (Iowa)
3. Steve Barrett (Oklahoma State)
4. Steve Hunte (unat)

5. Doug Moses (Hawkeye WC)
6. Ken Martin (Parkside WC)

150-lb class

1. Pete Galea (Iowa State)
2. Mike Frick (unat)
3. Chuck Yagla (Iowa)
4. Mark Churella (Michigan)
5. Steve Randall (unat)
6. Pete Dombrowski (Northwestern)

158-lb class

1. Lee Kemp (Wisconsin)
2. Bob Holland (unat)
3. Paul Martin (Oklahoma State)
4. John Matthews (Michigan WC)
5. Tom Keeley (AIA)
6. Dave Maple (Daley WC)

167-lb class

1. Larry Zilverberg (Minnesota)
2. Stan Dziedzic (NYAC)
3. Pat Christensen (Wisconsin)
4. Joe Carr (Kentucky)
5. Ron Ray (Daley WC)
6. Wade Schalles (Mean Machine WC)

177-lb class

1. John Peterson (AIA)
2. Mark Lieberman (Me Ma WC)
3. Willie Gadson (Iowa State)
4. Dan Holm (Hawkeye WC)
5. Jim Lunde (Minnesota)
6. Gordie Ashebrook (Wisconsin)

190-lb class

1. Ben Peterson (unat)
2. Mel Renfro (unat)
3. Chris Campbell (Iowa)
4. Mike Lieberman (unat)
5. Laurent Soucie (Wisconsin WC)
6. Evan Johnson (Minnesota)

Heavyweight

1. Russ Hellickson (Wisconsin WC)
2. Mike McCready (Hawkeye WC)
3. Tom Hazell (unat)
4. Jimmie Jackson (Oklahoma State)
5. Ken Levels (Allegheny)
6. Kevin Pancratz (Illinois)

1976

Team	Points
1. Iowa	94.75
2. Oklahoma State	92.25
3. Hawkeye WC	67.75
4. Wisconsin	63.50
5. Mayor Daley WC	46.25
6. Michigan	40.75
7. Minnesota	36
8. Kentucky	32.50
9. Northwestern	31
10. Bakersfield Express	27.50

Place winners

118-lb class

1. Jim Haines (Wisconsin)
2. Mike McArthur (Minnesota)
3. Dave Triveline (Northwestern)
4. Dan Glenn (Iowa)
5. Garrett Headley (unat)
6. Randy Batten (Tennessee at Chattanooga)

126-lb class

1. Mark Massery (Daley WC)
2. Kevin Puebla (Illinois)
3. Mark Mangianti (Michigan WC)
4. Keith Mourlam (Iowa)
5. Jay Swanson (South Dakota State)
6. Mike Walsh (Michigan State)

134-lb class

1. Tim Cysewski (Hawkeye WC)
2. Steve Hunte (Iowa)
3. Roger Roberts (Oklahoma State)
4. LeeRoy Smith (Oklahoma State)
5. Kurt Mock (Kentucky)
6. Craig Horswill (Wisconsin WC)

142-lb class

1. Steve Barrett (Oklahoma State)
2. Tihamer Toth-Fejel (unat)
3. Mike Terry (Wisconsin)
4. Doug Moses (Hawkeye WC)
5. Pete Dombrowski (Northwestern)
6. Mike Frick (unat)

150-lb class
1. Chuck Yagla (Hawkeye WC)
2. Mark Churella (Michigan)
3. Joe Tice (Spartan WC)
4. Larry Morgan (Bakersfield Express)
5. Robert Schandle (Minnesota)
6. Bruce Kinseth (Iowa)

158-lb class
1. Lee Kemp (Wisconsin)
2. Paul Martin (Oklahoma State)
3. Turner Jackson (Chattanooga TC)
4. Mike McGivern (Iowa)
5. Toby Mathey (Cleveland State)
6. Kirk Anderson (Buffalo)

167-lb class
1. Wade Schalles (Hawkeye WC)
2. Dan Holm (Daley WC)
3. Cliff Hatch (Bakersfield Express)
4. Doug Anderson (Iowa)
5. Dave McQuaig (Oklahoma State)
6. Ed Neiswender (Michigan)

177-lb class
1. Chris Campbell (Iowa)
2. Mark Johnson (Michigan)
3. Eric Wais (Oklahoma State)
4. Daryl Monasmith (Oklahoma State)
5. Gordie Ashebrook (Wisconsin)
6. Rick Johnson (Illinois)

190-lb class
1. Laurent Soucie (Wisconsin WC)
2. Ron Jeidy (Wisconsin)
3. Greg Stevens (Iowa)
4. Bud Palmer (unat)
5. Steve Day (unat)
6. Evan Johnson (Minnesota)

Heavyweight
1. Harold Smith (Kentucky)
2. Jimmy Jackson (Oklahoma State)
3. John Bowlsby (Iowa)
4. Tom Hazell (unat)
5. Barry Walsh (Michigan WC)
6. Jim Witzleb (Hawkeye WC)

1977

Team	*Points*
1. Iowa	88.50
2. Hawkeye WC	82.75
3. Iowa State	67.25
4. Wisconsin	61
5. California State (Bakersfield)	27.50
6. Kentucky	21.25
7. Northwestern	20.50
8. Sunkist Kids	20.25
9. Bakersfield Express, Mayor Daley WC	20

Place winners

118-lb class
1. Mike McArthur (unat)
2. John Azevedo (California State, Bakersfield)
3. Jim Haines (Wisconsin WC)
4. Tom Husted (Wisconsin)
5. Joe Gonzales (Bakersfield Express)
6. Gary Matlock (Illinois)

126-lb class
1. Mike Land (Iowa State)
2. Jim Hanson (Wisconsin)
3. Joe Corso (Hawkeye WC)
4. Jay Swanson (South Dakota State)
5. Randy Lewis (Iowa)
6. Scott DeAugustino (Penn State)

134-lb class
1. Tim Cysewski (Hawkeye WC)
2. Mike Chinn (Louisiana State)
3. Franc Affentranger (California State, Bakersfield)
4. Mike Walsh (Michigan State)
5. Bobby Sparks (Washington)
6. Mark Warner (Iowa State)

142-lb class
1. Tihamer Toth-Fejel (unat)
2. Scott Trizzino (Iowa)
3. Robert McDowell (San Jose State)
4. Randy Nielsen (Iowa State)
5. Brad Smith (Hawkeye WC)
6. Mike Terry (unat)

150-lb class
1. Chuck Yagla (Hawkeye WC)
2. Tony Digiovanni (unat)
3. Bruce Kinseth (Iowa)
4. Steve Egesdal (Minnesota)
5. Karl Briggs (Michigan)
6. Dan Zilverberg (Minnesota)

158-lb class
1. Lee Kemp (Wisconsin)
2. Joe Zuspann (Iowa State)
3. Roye Oliver (unat)
4. Mike Taylor (Bakersfield Express)
5. Mark Stevenson (Iowa)
6. Joe Tice (Oregon WC)

167-lb class
1. Dave Powell (unat)
2. Dave Evans (Wisconsin)
3. Mike Deanna (Iowa)
4. Joe Carr (unat)
5. Leo Kocher (Daley WC)
6. David Miller (Missouri)

177-lb class
1. Chris Campbell (Hawkeye WC)
2. Larry Zilverberg (unat)
3. Mark Lieberman (Lehigh)
4. Don Shuler (Arizona State)
5. Charlie Gadson (Iowa State)
6. Charlie Heller (Iowa State)

190-lb class
1. Willie Gadson (Cyclone WC)
2. Al Marzano (Northwestern)
3. Ron Jeidy (Wisconsin)
4. Steve Day (Illinois State)
5. Bud Palmer (Iowa)
6. Dave Severn (unat)

Heavyweight
1. Larry Bielenberg (Sunkist Kids)
2. Harold Smith (Kentucky)
3. John Bowlsby (Iowa)
4. Tom Burns (Hawkeye WC)
5. Tom Waldon (Iowa State)
6. Jim Mitchell (Arizona State)

1978

Team	*Points*
1. Iowa	93.50
2. Hawkeye WC	84.50
3. Wisconsin	71.50
4. Iowa State	54.75
5. Cyclone WC	49
6. Louisiana State	40.50
7. Athletes in Action	36.50
8. Minnesota	32.75
9. Lehigh	27
10. New York AC	24.50

Place winners

118-lb class
1. Mike McArthur (AIA)
2. Bill DePaoli (California State of Pennsylvania)
3. Joe Gonzales (California State, Bakersfield)
4. Dan Glenn (Iowa)
5. Khris Whelan (Missouri)
6. Chris Wentz (Louisiana State)

126-lb class
1. Randy Lewis (Iowa)
2. Jim Hanson (Wisconsin)
3. Mark Mangianti (Sunkist Kids)
4. Mike Rossetti (Trenton State)
5. Keith Mourlam (Hawkeye WC)
6. Jim Lord (Iowa State)

134-lb class
1. Tim Cysewski (Hawkeye WC)
2. Darryl Burley (Lehigh)
3. Jim Martinez (Minnesota)
4. Dave Goodspeed (Wisconsin)
5. Mike Walsh (Michigan State)
6. Randy Conrad (Iowa State)

142-lb class
1. Andy Rein (Wisconsin)
2. Brad Smith (Hawkeye WC)

3. Robert McDowell (San Jose State)
4. Vic Hargett (Louisiana State)
5. Dennis Reed (Lehigh)
6. Tihamer Toth-Fejel (NYAC)

150-lb class
1. Bruce Kinseth (Iowa)
2. Sam Komar (unat)
3. Scott Trizzino (Iowa)
4. Pete Galea (Cyclone WC)
5. King Mueller (Iowa)
6. Robert Schandle (unat)

158-lb class
1. Chuck Yagla (Hawkeye WC)
2. Kelly Ward (Iowa State)
3. Joe Zuspann (Cyclone WC)
4. Dan Zilverberg (Minnesota)
5. Jed Brown (Iowa)
6. Steve Kruchoski (Wisconsin)

167-lb class
1. Wade Schalles (NYAC)
2. Larry Zilverberg (unat)
3. Mark Churella (Michigan)
4. Joe Carr (unat)
5. Dave Powell (Iowa State)
6. Perry Hummel (unat)

177-lb class
1. Chris Campbell (Hawkeye WC)
2. Dave Severn (Arizona State)
3. Don Shuler (AIA)
4. Mark Lieberman (Lehigh)
5. Charlie Gadson (Cyclone WC)
6. Mark Johnson (Hawkeye WC)

190-lb class
1. Willie Gadson (Cyclone WC)
2. Mike Mann (Iowa State)
3. Mitch Hull (Wisconsin)
4. George Bowman (Minnesota)
5. Steve Fraser (Michigan)
6. Bud Palmer (Iowa)

Heavyweight
1. Ben Peterson (Wisconsin WC)
2. Harold Smith (unat)
3. John Bowlsby (Iowa)
4. Dave Klemm (Eastern Illinois)
5. Steve Day (Daley WC)
6. Shawn Whitcomb (Michigan State

1979

Team	*Points*
1. Iowa	87.25
2. Hawkeye WC	71.75
3. Wisconsin	61.50
4. Sunkist Kids	60
5. Iowa State	50.75
6. New York AC	46.50
7. Oklahoma	44
8. Oklahoma State	40
9. Cyclone WC	33
10. Minnesota	30.25

Place winners

118-lb class
1. Mike McArthur (AIA)
2. Dan Glenn (Iowa)
3. Mike Picozzi (Iowa State)
4. Tony Leonino (Auburn)
5. Bob Monaghan (North Carolina)
6. Brad Huckle (Minnesota)

126-lb class
1. John Azevedo (California State, Bakersfield)
2. Mark Mangianti (Sunkist Kids)
3. Ricky Dellagatta (Kentucky)
4. Brent Hagen (Northern Iowa)
5. Byron McGlathery (Tennessee at Chattanooga)
6. George Kacavas (Louisiana State)

134-lb class
1. Randy Lewis (Iowa)
2. Tim Cysewski (Hawkeye WC)
3. Nick Gallo (NYAC)
4. Frank DeAngelis (Oklahoma)
5. Kevin Puebla (Illinois WC)
6. Steve Carr (Iowa State)

142-lb class
1. LeeRoy Smith (Oklahoma State)
2. Andre Metzger (Oklahoma)
3. Brad Smith (Hawkeye WC)
4. Ralph McCausland (Eastern Illinois)

5. Lenny Zalesky (Iowa)
6. Sam Komar (unat)

150-lb class
1. Andy Rein (Wisconsin)
2. King Mueller (Iowa)
3. Roger Frizzell (Oklahoma)
4. Reggie Thompson (San Jose)
5. Jim Humphrey (Oklahoma WC)
6. Terril Williams (unat)

158-lb class
1. Wade Schalles (NYAC)
2. Dave Schultz (Oklahoma WC)
3. Dan Zilverberg (Minnesota)
4. Mike Terry (Wisconsin)
5. Pete Galea (Cyclone WC)
6. Tom Pickard (Iowa State)

167-lb class
1. Bruce Kinseth (Hawkeye WC)
2. Dave Evans (Wisconsin)
3. Perry Hummel (Iowa State)
4. David Brouhard (San Jose)
5. Lee Spiegel (Rhode Island)
6. Dave Fitzgerald (Iowa)

177-lb class
1. Ed Banach (Iowa)
2. Larry Zilverberg (unat)
3. John Forshee (Iowa State)
4. Dave Severn (Arizona State)
5. Gary Germundson (Oklahoma State)
6. Charles Gadson (Cyclone WC)

190-lb class
1. Ben Peterson (Wisconsin WC)
2. Mark Johnson (Hawkeye WC)
3. Willie Gadson (Cyclone WC)
4. Mike Mann (Iowa State)
5. Steve Fraser (Michigan)
6. Noel Loban (Clemson)

Heavyweight
1. Jimmy Jackson (Sunkist Kids)
2. Fred Bohna (Sunkist Kids)
3. Larry Bielenberg (Sunkist Kids)
4. John Bowlsby (Hawkeye WC)
5. Mike Weitzman (Northwestern)
6. Scott Jerabck (Wisconsin)

1980

Team	*Points*
1. Iowa	133.50
2. Wisconsin WC	48.75
3. Iowa State	47.75
4. Hawkeye WC	44.25
5. Louisiana State	39.50
6. Oklahoma State	36.50
7. Kentucky	33.25
8. San Jose State	33
9. Central Michigan	32.25
10. Indiana State	23.75

Place winners

118-lb class
1. Dan Glenn (Hawkeye WC)
2. John Hartupee (Central Michigan)
3. Randy Willingham (Oklahoma State)
4. Bob Monaghan (North Carolina)
5. Barry Davis (Iowa)
6. Bobby Weaver (Lehigh)

126-lb class
1. Mark Mangianti (Sunkist Kids)
2. Mark Trizzino (Iowa)
3. Tim Riley (Iowa)
4. Tom Husted (unat)
5. Dave Cooke (North Carolina)
6. Dan Foldsey (Cleveland State)

134-lb class
1. Randy Lewis (Iowa)
2. Ricky Dellagatta (Kentucky)
3. Nick Gallo (NYAC)
4. Jim Gibbons (Iowa State)
5. Pete Schuyler (Lehigh)
6. Eddie Baza (San Jose State)

142-lb class
1. Lennie Zaleksy (Iowa)
2. LeeRoy Smith (Cowboy WC)
3. Darryl Burley (unat)
4. Mike Land (Cyclone WC)
5. Steve Babyack (Ball State)
6. Gene Nighman (Cornell U)

150-lb class
1. Andy Rein (Wisconsin WC)
2. Fred Boss (Central Michigan)
3. Reggie Thompson (San Jose State)
4. Scott Trizzino (Iowa)
5. Nate Carr (Iowa State)
6. Greg Drenik (Cleveland State)

158-lb class
1. Roye Oliver (Maverick)
2. Ricky Stewart (Oklahoma State)
3. Bill Dykeman (Louisiana State)
4. Mike McGivern (Hawkeye WC)
5. Jim Farina (Iowa State)
6. Mike Phianis (Northern Illinois)

167-lb class
1. Dave Evans (Wisconsin WC)
2. Jeff Parker (Louisiana State)
3. Mike DeAnna (Iowa)
4. Bob McDaniel (Kentucky)
5. John Hanrahan (Penn State)
6. Jim Reilly (unat)

177-lb class
1. Ed Banach (Iowa)
2. Lanny Davidson (Hawkeye WC)
3. Dave Fitzgerald (unat)
4. Steve Foley (Michigan State)
5. David Bronhard (San Jose State)
6. Russ Pickering (unat)

190-lb class
1. Charlie Gadson (Cyclone WC)
2. Mike Mann (Iowa State)
3. Noel Loban (unat)
4. John Forshee (Iowa State)
5. Pete Bush (Iowa)
6. Steve Fraser (Michigan WC)

Heavyweight
1. Bruce Baumgartner (Indiana State)
2. Lou Banach (Iowa)
3. Mike Evans (Louisiana State)
4. Russ Hellickson (Wisconsin WC)
5. John Sefter (Penn State)
6. Rod Chamberlain (Indiana)

1981

Team	*Points*
1. Iowa State	91.5
2. Hawkeye WC	75.5
3. Iowa	57.5
4. Oklahoma	50.5
5. Oklahoma State	49
6. Minnesota, Nebraska	42.5
7. North Carolina	40.5
8. Penn State	32.5
9. Michigan State	29.5

Place winners

118-lb class
1. Randy Willingham (Oklahoma State)
2. Dan Glenn (Hawkeye WC)
3. Barry Davis (Iowa)
4. Joe McFarland (Michigan)
5. Bob Monaghan (North Carolina)
6. Randy Blackman (Eastern Illinois)

126-lb class
1. Joe Gibbons (Iowa State)
2. Mark Trizzino (Iowa)
3. Scott Lynch (Penn State)
4. Dave Cooke (North Carolina)
5. Don Stevens (Southern Illinois at Edwardsville)
6. Rich Santoro (unat)

134-lb class
1. Darryl Burley (unat)
2. Randy Lewis (Hawkeye WC)
3. Keith Mourlam (Hawkeye WC)
4. Mike Land (Cyclone WC)
5. Bill Marino (Penn State)
6. Jeff Kerber (Iowa)

142-lb class
1. Jim Martincz (Minnesota)
2. Tihamer Toth-Fejel (unat)

3. Randy Conrad (Iowa State)
4. Dalen Wasmund (Minnesota)
5. Steve Babyack (Clemson)
6. Ricky Delagatta (NYAC)

150-lb class
1. Nate Carr (Iowa State)
2. Mark Schmitz (Wisconsin)
3. Scott Trizzino (Hawkeye WC)
4. Al Freeman (unat)
5. Wes Roper (Missouri)
6. Fred Boss (Michigan WC)

158-lb class
1. Ricky Stewart (Oklahoma State)
2. Chuck Yagla (Hawkeye WC)
3. Fred Worthem (Michigan State)
4. Pete Galea (Wildcat WC)
5. Roye Oliver (Maverick WC)
6. Tim Brown (Iowa State)

167-lb class
1. Dave Schultz (Oklahoma)
2. Mark Gronowski (Eastern Illinois)
3. Ray Oliver (Nebraska)
4. Jan Michaels (North Carolina)
5. Mike Sheets (Oklahoma State)
6. Tom Pickard (Iowa State)

177-lb class
1. Ed Banach (Iowa)
2. Mark Schultz (Oklahoma)
3. Perry Hummel (Iowa State)
4. Jeff Parker (Louisiana State)
5. Dave Brouhard (Spartan WC)
6. Bill Petoskey (Michigan WC)

190-lb class
1. Mike Mann (Iowa State)
2. Bill Scherr (Nebraska)
3. Charlie Gadson (Cyclone WC)
4. Mitch Hull (Wisconsin WC)
5. Kirk Myers (Northern Iowa)
6. Drew Whitfield (AIA)

Heavyweight
1. Bruce Baumgartner (Indiana State)
2. John Dougherty (Syracuse)
3. Rod Chamberlain (Indiana)
4. Mike Holcomb (Miami)
5. Eric Klasson (Michigan)
6. Mark Miller (Minnesota)

1982

Team	*Points*
1. Iowa	99.25
2. Oklahoma State	80
3. Nebraska	73
4. Hawkeye WC	58.25
5. Cowboy WC	50.75
6. New York AC	47
7. Penn State	30.50
8. Wildcat WC	30.25
9. Michigan State	29.75
10. Missouri	27.50

Place winners

118-lb class
1. Randy Willingham (Oklahoma State)
2. Mike McArthur (Cowboy WC)
3. Don Horning (Kent State)
4. Tom Dursee (NYAC)
5. Carl DeStefanis (Penn State)
6. Gil Sanchez (Nebraska)

126-lb class
1. Joe McFarland (unat)
2. Gene Mills (NYAC)
3. Barry Davis (Iowa)
4. Ed Pidgeon (Hofstra)
5. Jim Mason (Michigan State)
6. Scott Lynch (Penn State)

134-lb class
1. Khris Whelan (Missouri)
2. Bill Marino (Penn State)
3. Jeff Kerber (Iowa)
4. Greg Randall (unat)
5. Pete Schuyler (Lehigh)
6. Wayne Jones (Spartan WC)

142-lb class
1. Al Freeman (Nebraska)
2. Darryl Burley (Lehigh)
3. Randy Lewis (Hawkeye WC)
4. Tihamer Toth-Fejel (Irish WC)
5. Harlan Kistler (unat)
6. Steve Babyak (unat)

150-lb class
1. Kenny Monday (Oklahoma State)
2. Lennie Zalesky (Hawkeye WC)
3. Marty Kistler (unat)
4. Gene Nighman (NYAC)
5. Rick Rindfuss (Kentucky)
6. Tom Minkel (Michigan WC)

158-lb class
1. Jim Zalesky (Iowa)
2. Matt Skove (Oklahoma State)
3. Scott Trizzino (Hawkeye WC)
4. Lou Montano (California Poly)
5. Pete Galea (Wildcat WC)
6. Kirby Kepner (unat)

167-lb class
1. Mike Sheets (Oklahoma State)
2. Ricky Stewart (Cowboy WC)
3. Sylvester Carter (California State, Fresno)
4. Jackson Kistler (unat)
5. Ray Oliver (Nebraska)
6. Mark Gronowski (Eastern Illinois)

177-lb class
1. Jim Scherr (Nebraska)
2. Dave Fitzgerald (Hawkeye WC)
3. Mike Foy (Minnesota)
4. Duane Goldman (Iowa)
5. Clarence Richardson (Louisiana State)
6. Dominic DiGiocchino (NYAC)

190-lb class
1. Bill Scherr (Nebraska)
2. Ed Banach (Iowa)
3. Joe Glasder (Southern Illinois at Edwardsville)
4. Drew Whitfield (AIA)
5. Bill Petoskey (unat)
6. Regis Durbin (Northwestern)

Heavyweight
1. Bruce Baumgartner (Cowboy WC)
2. Dan Severn (Sunkist Kids)
3. Harold Smith (Wildcat WC)
4. Lou Banach (Iowa)
5. James Phills (unat)
6. Matt Ghafari (Cleveland State)

1983

Team	*Points*
1. Iowa	122.50
2. Hawkeye WC	102
3. Nebraska	47
4. Minnesota	44
5. New York AC	43
6. Oklahoma	40.75
7. Penn State	38
8. San Jose State	30.75
9. Michigan State	29
10. Northwestern	27.25

Place winners

118-lb class
1. Charlie Heard (Tennessee at Chattanooga)
2. Carl DeStefanis (Penn State)
3. John Hartupee (Michigan WC)
4. Bob Weaver (NYAC)
5. Ed Giese (Minnesota)
6. Matt Campbell (Nebraska)

126-lb class
1. Joe McFarland (Michigan)
2. Barry Davis (Iowa)
3. Don Stevens (Southern Illinois at Edwardsville)
4. Mark Mangianti (Hawkeye WC)
5. Randy Majors (Hawkeye WC)
6. Rich Decatur (Northwestern)

134-lb class
1. Mark Trizzino (Iowa)
2. Greg Randall (Iowa)
3. Randy Lewis (Hawkeye WC)
4. Scott DePetro (Northwestern)
5. Bill Marino (NYAC)
6. Clint Burke (Oklahoma)

142-lb class
1. Harlan Kistler (Hawkeye WC)
2. Jesse Reyes (California State, Bakersfield)
3. Keith Mourlam (Hawkeye WC)

4. Jeff Kerber (Iowa)
5. Tihamer Toth-Fejel (Irish WC)
6. Nathan Winer (Southern Oregon)

150-lb class
1. Jim Heffernan (Hawkeye WC)
2. Andy Rein (Wisconsin WC)
3. Marty Kistler (Iowa)
4. Steve Martinez (Minnesota)
5. Ron Bussey (Trenton State)
6. Jim Martinez (Minnesota WC)

158-lb class
1. Jim Zalesky (Iowa)
2. Andre Metzger (Tarhell WC)
3. Bob Glaberman (Trenton State)
4. Greg Elinsky (Penn State)
5. Dave Lolich (Purdue)
6. Neil Winer (Wildcat WC)

167-lb class
1. Scott Trizzino (Hawkeye WC)
2. Melvin Douglas (Oklahoma)
3. Lindley Kistler (Iowa)
4. Bill Gaffney (North Carolina)
5. Roye Oliver (Sunkist Kids)
6. Jackson Kistler (Hawkeye WC)

177-lb class
1. Duane Goldman (Iowa)
2. Jim Scherr (Nebraska)
3. Mike Foy (Minnesota)
4. Marvin Jones (San Jose)
5. Dan Chaid (Oklahoma)
6. Scott Rechsteiner (Michigan)

190-lb class
1. Bill Scherr (Nebraska)
2. Pete Bush (Iowa)
3. Eli Blazeff (Michigan State)
4. Andy Tsarnas (San Jose State)
5. Paul Diekel (unat)
6. Mike Davies (Arizona State)

Heavyweight
1. Bruce Baumgartner (NYAC)
2. Harold Smith (Wildcat WC)
3. Mike Potts (Michigan State)
4. Morris Johnson (San Francisco State)
5. Matt Ghaffari (Cleveland State)
6. Bill Hyman (Temple)

1984

Team	*Points*
1. Sunkist Kids WC	95.25
2. Iowa	82.50
3. Arizona State	66.25
4. New York AC	59.50
5. Wisconsin	47.75
6. Penn State	40.75
7. Indiana State	40
8. Syracuse	35.50
9. Michigan	33.25
10. Lehigh, Southern Illinois at Edwardsville	31.25

Place winners

118-lb class
1. Don Horning (unat)
2. Randy Willingham (Sunkist Kids)
3. Chip Park (Arizona State)
4. Ken Chertow (Penn State)
5. Matt Egeland (Iowa)
6. John Regan (Iowa)

126-lb class
1. Charlie Heard (Sunkist Kids)
2. John Fisher (Michigan)
3. Barry Davis (Iowa)
4. Tim Flynn (Penn State)
5. Steve Stearns (Southern Illinois at Edwardsville)
6. Wade Hughes (George Washington)

134-lb class
1. Gary Bohay (Sunkist Kids)
2. Jim Jordan (Wisconsin)
3. Gene Mills (NYAC)
4. Chris Campbell (Indiana State)
5. Steve DePetro (Northwestern)
6. John Manotti (Penn State)

142-lb class
1. Darryl Burley (Lehigh)
2. John Giura (Wisconsin)
3. Mark Trizzino (Hawkeye WC)
4. Pete Yozzo (Lehigh)
5. Kevin Dresser (Iowa)
6. Greg Wright (unat)

150-lb class
1. Jim Heffernan (Iowa)
2. Al Freeman (Wildcat WC)
3. Patrick Welch (Cornell U)
4. Bill Marino (NYAC)
5. Marty Lynch (Syracuse)
6. Mike Schmidlin (California State, Fullerton)

158-lb class
1. Marty Kistler (Iowa)
2. Eddie Urbano (Arizona State)
3. Jim Gressley (Arizona State)
4. Tom Draheim (Arizona State)
5. Royce Alger (Iowa)
6. Andy Seras (SUNY at Albany)

167-lb class
1. Shawn McCarthy (Arizona State)
2. Darryl Pope (Roadrunners)
3. Rudy Isom (Wisconsin)
4. Steve Tekander (Southern Oregon)
5. Ken Sheets (NYAC)
6. Mike Craft (Northwestern)

177-lb class
1. Jim Scherr (Sunkist Kids)
2. Booker Benford (Southern Illinois at Edwardsville)
3. Tom Kolopus (Arizona State)
4. Marvin Jones (Roadrunners)
5. Eric Brugel (unat)
6. Terry Manning (Wisconsin)

190-lb class
1. Bill Scherr (Sunkist Kids)
2. Paul Diekel (Lehigh)
3. Regis Durbin (Northwestern)
4. Bill Elbin (Michigan)
5. Mike Davies (Arizona State)
6. Andy Voit (Penn State)

Heavyweight
1. Bruce Baumgartner (NYAC)
2. Harold Smith (Wildcat WC)
3. Andy Schwab (Syracuse)
4. Bill Hyman (Temple)
5. Matt Ghaffari (Sunkist Kids)
6. Kirk Trost (Michigan)

1985

Team	*Points*
1. Iowa	118.75
2. Sunkist Kids WC	95.50
3. New York AC	75.75
4. Syracuse	48.75
5. Penn State	44.25
6. Wisconsin	42
7. Oklahoma	39.75
8. North Carolina	36
9. Cleveland State, Wildcat WC	33.50

Place winners

118-lb class
1. Tony Cotroneo (Syracuse)
2. Jim Martin (Penn State)
3. Pablo Saenz (Sunkist Kids)
4. Paul Kapper (Cleveland State)
5. Al Palacio (North Carolina)
6. Tony Bellai (Oklahoma)

126-lb class
1. Barry Davis (Hawkeye WC)
2. Steve DePetro (Northwestern)
3. Joe Melchiore (Oklahoma)
4. Tim Flynn (Penn State)
5. Brad Penrith (unat)
6. John Aumiller (North Carolina)

134-lb class
1. Gary Bohay (Sunkist Kids)
2. Greg Randall (Iowa)
3. Steve Stearns (Southern Illinois at Edwardsville)
4. Brandon O'Donahue (Michigan State)
5. Nick Neville (Oklahoma)
6. Rich Bailey (Baker)

142-lb class
1. Gene Mills (NYAC)
2. Kevin Dresser (Iowa)
3. Jim Jordan (Wisconsin)

4. Dave Wlodarz (Cleveland State)
5. Dave Zahoransky (Cleveland State)
6. Jack Effner (Indiana State)

150-lb class

1. John Giura (Wisconsin WC)
2. Jim Heffernan (Iowa)
3. Jim Akerly (West Virginia)
4. Jeff Mills (Central Michigan)
5. Bill Nugent (Sunkist Kids)
6. Pete Yozzo (Lehigh)

158-lb class

1. Royce Alger (Iowa)
2. Andre Metzger (NYAC)
3. Greg Elinsky (Penn State)
4. Tom Draheim (Sunkist Kids)
5. Eddie Urbano (Sunkist Kids)
6. Rob Koll (North Carolina)

167-lb class

1. Marty Kistler (Iowa)
2. Darryl Pope (California at Bakersfield)
3. Lindley Kistler (Hawkeye WC)
4. Terry Manning (Wisconsin)
5. Craig McManaman (Wildcat WC)
6. John Laviolette (Oklahoma)

177-lb class

1. Jim Scherr (Wildcat WC)
2. Melvyn Douglas (Oklahoma Underdogs)
3. Booker Benford (Sunkist Kids)
4. Rico Chiapparelli (Iowa)
5. Kevin Hill (Michigan)
6. Dave Ruckman (Michigan WC)

190-lb class

1. Duane Goldman (Iowa)
2. Bill Scherr (Sunkist Kids)
3. Wayne Catan (Syracuse)
4. Scott Rechsteiner (Michigan)
5. Andy Voit (unat)
6. John Przybyla (Michigan State)

Heavyweight

1. Bruce Baumgartner (NYAC)
2. Bill Hyman (NYAC)
3. Andy Schwab (Syracuse)
4. Morris Johnson (unat)
5. Dean Hall (Edinboro)
6. Roger Mello (unat)

1986

Team	*Points*
1. North Carolina	57.25
2. Sunkist Kids	55.50
3. Wisconsin	45
4. Wildcat WC	39.25
5. Northwestern	38.25

Place winners

118-lb class

1. Al Palacio (North Carolina)
2. Jack Griffin (Northwestern)
3. Ed Giese (Gopher WC)
4. Jack Cuvo (East Stroudsburg)
5. Jeff Bowyer (James Madison)
6. Steve Martin (Iowa)

126-lb class

1. Wade Hughes (Superiorland)
2. Jim Martin (unat)
3. Brad Gustafson (Sunkist Kids)
4. Mark Sodano (North Carolina State)
5. Chip McArdle (North Carolina)
6. Chip Park (Arizona State)

134-lb class

1. Barry Davis (Hawkeye WC)
2. Scott DePetro (Wildcat WC)
3. Joel Bales (Northwestern)
4. Paul Clark (Clarion State)
5. Tim Flynn (unat)
6. Jeff Strauss (Iowa)

142-lb class

1. Jim Jordan (Buckeye WC)
2. Pat Santoro (Pittsburgh)
3. John Orr (NYAC)
4. Mike Cole (Clarion State)
5. Lenny Bernstein (North Carolina)
6. Dave Wlodarz (Cleveland State)

150-lb class

1. Jim Heffernan (Iowa)
2. Jim Akerly (West Virginia)
3. Mark Manning (Sunkist Kids)
4. Charlie Cheney (Ashland)

5. Jeff Jordan (Wisconsin)
6. Dave Zahoransky (Cleveland State)

158-lb class
1. Rob Koll (North Carolina)
2. Johnny Johnson (Gopher WC)
3. Marty Kistler (Hawkeye WC)
4. Paul McShane (Wisconsin)
5. Phil Brown (Maryland)
6. Jesse Reyes (Sunkist Kids)

167-lb class
1. Greg Elinsky (Penn State)
2. Dave Lee (Wisconsin)
3. Norm Dahm (Cougar WC)
4. Mike Tongel (unat)
5. Tony Evensen (Wisconsin)
6. Travis Fagen (Arizona State)

177-lb class
1. Darryl Pope (California State, Bakersfield)
2. Reggie Wilson (Chicago State)
3. Fred Little (California State, Fresno)
4. Steve Peperak (Maryland)
5. Ralph Liegel (Wisconsin)
6. Craig Costello (West Virginia)

190-lb class
1. Jim Scherr (Wildcat WC)
2. Eric Middlestead (California State, Bakersfield)
3. Jim Baumgardner (Sunkist Kids)
4. David Ruckman (Buckeye WC)
5. Lelan Rogers (Syracuse)
6. Mike Davies (Arizona State)

Heavyweight
1. Bruce Baumgartner (NYAC)
2. Carlton Haselrig (Pittsburgh-Johnstown)
3. Dean Hall (Edinboro)
4. Tom Reese (Maryland)
5. Rod Severn (Arizona State)
6. Kirk Trost (Keen)

1987

Team	*Points*
1. Sunkist Kids	105.75
2. Wisconsin	70.50
3. New York AC	67.25
4. Arizona State	59.75
5. Iowa	55.50

Place winners

118-lb class
1. Ed Giese (Gopher WC)
2. Joe Gonzales (Sunkist Kids)
3. Rich Moeggenberg (Central Michigan)
4. Craig Corbin (Lock Haven)
5. Jack Griffin (Northwestern)
6. Doug Harper (Eastern Michigan)

126-lb class
1. Jim Martin (Penn State)
2. Ken Chertow (Penn State)
3. Brad Penrith (Iowa)
4. Wade Hughes (Sunkist Kids)
5. Joe Melchiore (unat)
6. Brett Penager (Wisconsin)

134-lb class
1. John Fisher (Michigan)
2. Barry Davis (Hawkeye WC)
3. Tim Flynn (NYAC)
4. Tom Fitzpatrick (Wisconsin)
5. Mike Lingenfelter (Lock Haven)
6. Thierry Chaney (William and Mary)

142-lb class
1. Pat Santoro (Pittsburgh)
2. John Orr (NYAC)
3. Tom Ortiz (Arizona State)
4. Dave Zahoransky (Cleveland State)

5. Jeff Strauss (Iowa)
6. Mike Gilsdorf (Missouri)

150-lb class

1. Jeff Jordan (Wisconsin)
2. Eddie Urbano (Sunkist Kids)
3. Mike Schmidlin (California State, Fullerton)
4. Thane Turner (Lock Haven)
5. Kirk Aziner (Illinois)
6. Jim Akerly (West Virginia)

158-lb class

1. Dan St. John (Arizona State)
2. Phil Brown (Maryland)
3. Mike Carr (West Virginia)
4. Sam Amine (unat)
5. Tony Evensen (Wisconsin)
6. Jason Suter (Penn State)

167-lb class

1. Kenny Monday (Sunkist Kids)
2. David Lee (Wisconsin)
3. Rob Koll (North Carolina)
4. Jerry Umin (Eastern Michigan)
5. Greg Elinsky (NYAC)
6. Marty Kistler (Hawkeye WC)

177-lb class

1. Mike Sheets (Sunkist Kids)
2. Royce Alger (Iowa)
3. Booker Benford (Sunkist Kids)
4. Jim Hardy (Missouri)
5. Braden Atkinson (Cleveland State)
6. Ernie Sloan (unat)

190-lb class

1. Jim Scherr (Sunkist Kids)
2. Mark Coleman (Ohio State)
3. Mike Davies (Arizona State)
4. Reggie Wilson (unat)
5. Kyle Richards (Wisconsin)
6. Charlie Shererts (unat)

Heavyweight

1. Bruce Baumgartner (NYAC)
2. Tom Erikson (Sunkist Kids)
3. Carlton Haselrig (Pittsburgh-Johnstown)
4. Andy Schwab (NYAC)
5. Mark Sindlinger (Iowa)
6. Tom Reese (Maryland)

1988

Place winners

118-lb class

1. Steve Martin (Iowa)
2. Zeke Jones (Arizona State)
3. Ed Giese (Sunkist Kids)
4. Jack Griffin (Northwestern)
5. Terry Brands (Iowa)
6. Doug Harper (Eastern Michigan)

126-lb class

1. Jim Martin (Penn State)
2. Tom Brands (Iowa)
3. Jeff Husick (Lehigh)
4. Ken Chertow (Penn State)
5. Mark Perry (Sunkist Kids)
6. Matt Rizzo (Pittsburgh)

134-lb class

1. Mike Lingenfelter (Lock Haven)
2. Joe Melchiore (Iowa)
3. Joel Bales (Northwestern)
4. Andrew McNaughton (Arizona State)
5. Bob Truby (Penn State)
6. Chuck Toler (George Mason)

142-lb class

1. Pat Santoro (Pittsburgh)
2. Greg Randall (Hawkeye WC)
3. Junior Saunders (Arizona State)
4. Peter Horst (Penn State)
5. Steve Morris (Cal State-Bakersfield)
6. Stacy Richmond (Michigan State)

150-lb class

1. Thom Ortiz (Arizona State)
2. Mike Schmidlin (Cal State-Fullerton)
3. Rich Bailey (Cal State-Bakersfield)
4. Kurt Shedenhelm (Panther WC)
5. Mike Cole (unat)
6. Richard Townsell (Wildcat WC)

158-lb class

1. Dan St. John (Arizona State)
2. Joel Smith (Eastern Michigan)
3. Vince Silva (Sunkist Kids)
4. Steve Hankerson (Illinois)

5. Rob Yahner (unat)
6. John Leone (unat)

167-lb class
1. Eddie Urbano (Sunkist Kids)
2. Fran McKeon (Cleveland State)
3. Jerry Umin (Michigan WC)
4. Robbie Larimore (William & Mary)
5. Brad Morris (Ferris State)
6. Jody Karam (unat)

177-lb class
1. Royce Alger (Hawkeye WC)
2. Brad Lloyd (Lock Haven)
3. Craig Martin (Tiger WC)
4. Dave Yahner (Pitt-Johnstown)
5. Derek Capanna (Virginia)
6. Jim Gressley (Arizona State)

190-lb class
1. Jim Scherr (Wildcat WC)
2. Mark Whitehead (Northwestern)
3. Mike Davies (Sunkist Kids)
4. Andy Voit (Penn State)
5. Charlie Sherertz (Missouri)
6. John Ginther (Arizona State)

Heavyweight
1. Joel Greenlee (Northern Iowa)
2. Tom Reese (New York AC)
3. Matt Ghaffari (Sunkist Kids)
4. Pat McDade (Boise State)
5. Andy Haman (Iowa)
6. Tom Erikson (Sunkist Kids)

Chapter 10

The Junior Nationals

Whether it is called by its official name, the Junior Olympic Wrestling Championships, or by its more common name, the Junior Nationals, the fact remains that this tournament, held each summer and sponsored by USA Wrestling, has become the largest wrestling tournament in the United States and quite probably the world.

The first tournament was held in the old field house on the University of Iowa campus in Iowa City in 1971 and drew competitors mostly from around the Midwest. Only freestyle was included that year, but Greco-Roman was added the following year.

The tournament experienced phenomenal growth in the following decade and was moved to the University of Northern Iowa campus in Cedar Falls in 1983. There, in the huge UNI Dome, wrestlers competed in air-conditioned comfort, and the tournament experienced even more growth.

By 1988 the numbers were immense. A total of 1,836 wrestlers, representing 45 states, competed in 3,644 matches during a 5-day period. Nearly 1,000 volunteers are needed in all capacities to run the huge tournament.

The first freestyle winners were Nathaniel Byrd (105.5) of Michigan, Joe Corso (114.5) of Iowa, Jim Carr (123) of Pennsylvania, Kit Shaw (132) of Washington, Andre Allen (143) and Dan Holm (154) of Illinois, Chuck Berrier (165) of Iowa, Robin Richards (178) of Oregon, Dave Curby (191.5) of Michigan, and Jim Witzleb (heavyweight) of Illinois. The first Greco-Roman winners were Dan Cliffe (105.5) of Illinois, Richard Nuna (114.5) and Vince Tundo (123) of New York, Tim Cysewski (132) of Illinois, Jack Bryan (143) of Oregon, Bob Holland (154) of Illinois, Ken Williams (165) of Oregon, Dave Spector (178) of New York, Mike Bull (191.5) of California, and Chuck Coryea (heavyweight) of Pennsylvania.

By 1988 only one wrestler had managed to win as many as five Junior National titles. Andre Metzger of Grand Rapids, Michigan, captured freestyle titles in 1977 and 1978 and Greco-Roman titles in 1976, 1977, and 1978 to stand alone on the list of champions.

Ranking behind Metzger are three wrestlers who each earned four championships: Kris Whelan of Illinois, Leo Bailey of Oklahoma, and Mark Schwab

Andre Metzger, winner of a record five titles at the Junior Nationals, throws an opponent during one of his many victories. (Ken Merlin/Courtesy of *Amateur Wrestling News*)

of Iowa. One wrestler, Steve Knight of Iowa, was voted Outstanding Wrestler in both freestyle and Greco-Roman in the same year (1982).

Through 1988, host Iowa was the state with the most overall titles with 54. Illinois was second with 50 titles, and Oregon was third with 32. Illinois had won the most Greco-Roman titles with 34, and Iowa had the most freestyle titles with 43.

Many of the tournament's stars have moved on to great success in college and international styles. A 1987 survey showed that 80 percent of Division I NCAA place winners had competed in the Junior Nationals. Also, 27 of the Junior Nationals freestyle champions had claimed NCAA Division I titles, and 7 of the Greco-Roman champions had done the same.

In addition, nine tournament graduates—Chris Campbell, Lee Kemp, Bill Scherr, Bruce Baumgartner, Randy Lewis, Ed and Lou Banach, Dave Schultz, and John Smith—climbed the ultimate mountain, winning world and/or Olympic titles.

Table 10.1 gives a comprehensive overview of the National Junior champions.

Table 10.1
National Junior Championships
(USA Wrestling)

1971
Freestyle (Iowa City, IA)

Place winners

105.5-lb class
1. Nathaniel Byrd (Michigan)
2. Dan Cliffe (Illinois)
3. Jim Jeffries (Oklahoma)

114.5-lb class
1. Joe Corso (Iowa)
2. Joe Goldsmith (New York)
3. Lance Leonhart (Pennsylvania)

123-lb class
1. Jimmy Carr (Pennsylvania)
2. George Bryant (Pennsylvania)
3. Brad Jacet (Washington)

132-lb class
1. Kit Shaw (Washington)
2. Mark Sanderson (Utah)
3. Rick Little (Oklahoma)

143-lb class
1. Andre Allen (Illinois)
2. Dave Nicholson
3. Jack Bryan (Oregon)

154-lb class
1. Dan Holm (Illinois)
2. Jim Rizzutti (Iowa)
3. Bob Morris (Illinois)

165-lb class
1. Chuck Berrier (Iowa)
2. Bob Hoffman (Illinois)
3. Dan Wagemann (Illinois)

178-lb class
1. Robin Richard (Oregon)
2. Dave Dwyer (Illinois)
3. Steve Jenzten (Michigan)

191.5-lb class
1. Dave Curby (Michigan)
2. Mark Tiffany (Illinois)
3. Jeff Jentzen (Michigan)

Heavyweight
1. Jim Witzleb (Illinois)
2. George Reihner (Pennsylvania)
3. Gary Summers (Wisconsin)

Outstanding Wrestler: Robin Richard (Oregon)

1972
Freestyle (Iowa City, IA)

Place winners

105.5-lb class
1. Robert Longmire (Ohio)
2. John Roberts (Illinois)
3. Mark Mysnyk (New York)
4. Robbie Taylor (Ohio)

114.5-lb class
1. Richard Numa (New York)
2. Tom Cortez (Illinois)
3. Mike Boucher (Michigan)
4. Mickey Rossetti (Illinois)

123-lb class
1. Rande Stottlemyer (Pennsylvania)
2. John Tompkins (Oklahoma)
3. Mike Land (Iowa)
4. Dan Paswicz (Illinois)

132-lb class
1. Lorenzo Jones (Oregon)
2. Tim Cysewski (Illinois)
3. Gary Bentrim (Iowa)
4. Eugene Price (Michigan)

143-lb class
1. Joe Amore (Illinois)
2. Jim Bennett (Pennsylvania)
3. Brad Smith (Illinois)
4. Paul Martin (Iowa)

154-lb class
1. Tony Cordes (Iowa)
2. Bob Holland (Illinois)

3. Frank Woods (Illinois)
4. Jerry White (Pennsylvania)

165-lb class
1. Joe Carr (Pennsylvania)
2. Tad DeLuca (Illinois)
3. Pat Christiansen (Wisconsin)
4. Gary Janseck (Michigan)

178-lb class
1. Jim O'Connell (Illinois)
2. Jim Paulsen (Missouri)
3. Mark Neumann (Wisconsin)
4. Steve Gillette (New York)
5. Mark Mullins (Oregon) TIE

191.5-lb class
1. Mark Tiffany (Illinois)
2. Jeff Menard (Pennsylvania)
3. Dave Dwyer (Illinois)
4. Frank Savegeano (Illinois)

Heavyweight
1. Don Mayorga (Illinois)
2. Chuck Coryea (Pennsylvania)
3. Ames Martin (Illinois)
4. Charles Stacy (Illinois)

Outstanding Wrestler: Joe Amore (Illinois)

1972
Greco-Roman (Iowa City, IA)

Place winners

105.5-lb class
1. Dan Cliffe (Illinois)
2. Mike Arnold (New York)
3. Phil Montoya (Colorado)
4. Stewart Abbe (Oregon)

114.5-lb class
1. Richard Numa (New York)
2. Steve Hart (California)
3. Keith Nellis (Pennsylvania)
4. Tom Cortez (Illinois)

123-lb class
1. Vince Tundo (New York)
2. Randy Stottlemyer (Pennsylvania)
3. Keith Larsen (Illinois)
4. Dean Sherman (Illinois)

132-lb class
1. Tim Cysewski (Illinois)
2. Craig Mann (Illinois)
3. Rick Detkowski (Michigan)
4. David Nowakowski (Pennsylvania)

143-lb class
1. Jack Bryan (Oregon)
2. Brad Smith (Illinois)
3. Dan Barnard (Colorado)
4. Rod Holland (Illinois)

154-lb class
1. Bob Holland (Illinois)
2. Dave Powell (Illinois)
3. Chuck Yagla (Iowa)
4. Tim MacDonald (Michigan)

165-lb class
1. Ken Williams (Oregon)
2. Lonnie Seufer (Colorado)
3. Rory Whipple (New York)
4. Dan Monroe (Oregon)

178-lb class
1. Dave Spector (New York)
2. Mark Mullins (Oregon)
3. Bill Sedlicke (Oregon)
4. Maurice Stewart (Michigan)

191.5-lb class
1. Mike Bull (California)
2. Arnie Goldstein (New York)
3. Jeff Gilchrist (Pennsylvania)
4. Gary Siebert (Illinois)

Heavyweight
1. Chuck Coryea (Pennsylvania)
2. Bob Paul (Illinois)
3. John Bowlsby (Iowa)
4. Butch Hoagland (Oregon)

Outstanding Wrestler: Ken Williams (Oregon)

1973
Freestyle (Iowa City, IA)

Place winners

105.5-lb class
1. Pat Plourd (Oregon)
2. Mark Jordine (Illinois)
3. Mark Mysnyk (New York)
4. Jerry Mason (Illinois)

114.5-lb class
1. Mike McArthur (Minnesota)
2. Greg Maxey (Illinois)
3. John Phillips (Oklahoma)
4. Amos Goodlow (Michigan)

123-lb class
1. Mike Land (Iowa)
2. James Earl (New York)
3. Randy Nielsen (Iowa)
4. Gary Matlock (Illinois)

132-lb class
1. Rande Stottlemyer (Pennsylvania)
2. Lorenzo Jones (Oregon)
3. Roger Roberts (California)
4. Dean Smith (Tennessee)

143-lb class
1. Kevin Young (Oklahoma)
2. Steve Hunte (New York)
3. George Espinoza (California)
4. Joe Zuspann (Iowa)

154-lb class
1. Kevin Kramer (Oregon)
2. Paul Martin (Iowa)
3. Jeff Weisinger (Iowa)
4. Lou Giani (New York)

165-lb class
1. Mark Lieberman (New Jersey)
2. Jerry White (Pennsylvania)
3. Dan Breedlove (Illinois)
4. Darrell Hill (Ohio)

178-lb class
1. Mark Johnson (Illinois)
2. Chris Campbell (New Jersey)
3. Steve Day (Illinois)
4. Maurice Stewart (Michigan)

191.5-lb class
1. Larry Bielenberg (Oregon)
2. Greg Stevens (New York)
3. Ken Smith (Illinois)
4. Dan McCullough (New Jersey)

Heavyweight
1. Jimmy Jackson (Michigan)
2. Kevin Pancratz (Illinois)
3. John Nino (Illinois)
4. Gil Hense (Maryland)

Outstanding Wrestler: Rande Stottlemeyer (Pennsylvania)

1973
Greco-Roman (Iowa City, IA)

Place winners

105.5-lb class
1. Mark Mysnyk (New York)
2. Pat Plourd (Oregon)
3. Mark Jordine (Illinois)
4. Brad Botorff (Oregon)

114.5-lb class
1. Dick DeSoto (Oregon)
2. Amos Goodlow (Michigan)
3. Bill Fuller (New York)
4. Mike Fleming (California)

123-lb class
1. Michael Burns (California)
2. Jeff Fujiwara (Washington)
3. Tom Turnbull (Pennsylvania)
4. Nick Gallo (New York)

132-lb class
1. Gus Bendeck (California)
2. Tim Mousetis (Pennsylvania)
3. Frank DeAngelis (New York)
4. Ron McKinney (California)

143-lb class
1. George Espinoza (California)
2. Robert Angell (Illinois)
3. Gerald Sherrill (Michigan)
4. Ernie Krist (Illinois)

154-lb class
1. Kevin Kramer (Oregon)
2. Robert Sanders (New York)
3. Robert Woods (New York)
4. Bill Miron (New Jersey)

165-lb class
1. Dave Powell (Illinois)
2. Don Thompson (Oregon)
3. Mark Palombo (New York)
4. Darrell Hill (Ohio)

178-lb class
1. Roy Palm (Oregon)
2. Steve Day (Illinois)
3. James Smith (Ohio)
4. Maurice Stewart (Michigan)

191.5-lb class
1. Larry Bielenberg (Oregon)
2. Greg Stevens (New York)
3. David Gillaspie (Oregon)
4. Harold Smith (Ohio)

Heavyweight
1. Mike Dumin (Pennsylvania)
2. Brian Welsh (Illinois)
3. Jeff Ward (Oklahoma)
4. Mike Johnson (Illinois)

Outstanding Wrestler: Dave Powell (Illinois)

1974
Freestyle (Iowa City, IA)

Place winners

105.5-lb class
1. Phil Drenik (Ohio)
2. Mike Picozzi (New York)
3. Mike Farina (Illinois)
4. Ed Snook (Michigan)
5. Scott Sondgeroth (Colorado)
6. Charlie Amaya (Colorado)

114.5-lb class
1. Mark Mysnyk (New York)
2. John Azevedo (California)
3. Jim London (Oklahoma)
4. Randy Batten (Tennessee)
5. Chuck Davis (Ohio)
6. Kenneth Carmichael (Indiana)

123-lb class
1. Mike Land
2. LeeRoy Smith (Oklahoma)
3. James Earl (New York)
4. Joe Gonzales (California)
5. Amos Goodlow (Michigan)
6. Mike Terry (Wisconsin)

132-lb class
1. Roger Roberts (California)
2. Rick Morris (Illinois)
3. Denny Brighton (Michigan)
4. Kenny Nelson (Oklahoma)
5. Kevin Morin (Wisconsin)
6. Randy Nielsen (Iowa)

143-lb class
1. Joe Zuspann (Iowa)
2. Tim Mousetis (Pennsylvania)
3. John Eichenlaub (Pennsylvania)
4. David Nelson (Oklahoma)
5. Dennis Steffens (Iowa)
6. Scott Trizzino (Illinois)

154-lb class
1. LeRoy Kemp (Ohio)
2. Mark Churella (Michigan)
3. Paul Martin (Iowa)
4. Kevin Hejnal (California)
5. Marco Laney (Missouri)
6. David Welch (Ohio)

165-lb class
1. David McQuaig (Oklahoma)
2. Mark Harris (Iowa)
3. Steve Scheib (Pennsylvania)
4. Lonnie Peterson (Wisconsin)
5. Randolph Scott (Maryland)
6. Chris Pope (Missouri)

178-lb class
1. Daryl Monasmith (Colorado)
2. Carmel Marina, New Jersey)
3. Bill Bailey (Pennsylvania)
4. Robert Fleming (Illinois)
5. Brett Benson (Iowa)
6. Dave Wagner (Wisconsin)

191.5-lb class
1. Harold Smith (Ohio)
2. Shawn Whitcomb (Michigan)
3. Fred Bohna (California)
4. Jere Turbin (Wisconsin)
5. Ken Smith (Illinois)
6. Steve Pate (Iowa)

Heavyweight
1. John Bowlsby (Iowa)
2. Herb Calvert (New Jersey)
3. Al Marzano (Illinois)
4. John Nino (Illinois)
5. Mike Engwall (Iowa)
6. Haunce Hansen (Missouri)

Outstanding Wrestler: Roger Roberts (California)

1974
Greco-Roman (Iowa City, IA)

Place winners

105.5-lb class
1. Mike Farina (Illinois)
2. Tom Diamond (Pennsylvania)
3. George Kacavas (Massachusetts)
4. Tom Husted (New Jersey)
5. Roger Seemiller (Pennsylvania)
6. Doug Branigan (Wisconsin)

114.5-lb class
1. Rudy Perez (Texas)
2. Herb Patterson (Illinois)
3. Marvin Gasner (Colorado)
4. Tim Murphy (New York)
5. George Medina (New York)
6. (tie) Mike McIntosh (Illinois) and Terry Ariki (Colorado)

123-lb class
1. Amos Goodlow (Michigan)
2. Joe Davidson (New York)
3. Kevin Puebla (Illinois)
4. Mike Arnold (New York)
5. Mike Terry (Wisconsin)
6. Tim Rimpley (Nebraska)

132-lb class
1. Joel Hestrup (Illinois)
2. James Sondgeroth (Colorado)
3. Bill Parkinson (Illinois)
4. Kevin Morin (Wisconsin)
5. Doug Henderson (Pennsylvania)
5. Mark Preston (New Jersey)

143-lb class
1. Tim Mousetis (Pennsylvania)
2. Thomas Gongora (California)
3. Dale Eggert (Illinois)
4. Doug Hutsell (Indiana)
5. Ron McKinney (California)
6. Jerry Bignotti (Michigan)

154-lb class
1. Marco Laney (Missouri)
2. Dom DiGioacchino (New Jersey)
3. Scott Crowell (Pennsylvania)
4. Terry Fike (Pennsylvania)
5. Wayne Williams (Pennsylvania)
6. (tie) Kevin Anduik (Minnesota) and Lance McKelvy (Colorado)

165-lb class
1. Dave Powell (Illinois)
2. Lonnie Peterson (Wisconsin)
3. Bob Marcione (Illinois)
4. Antonio Crawford (New York)
5. Ron Standridge (New Jersey)
6. Steve Scheib (Pennsylvania)

178-lb class
1. William Palmer (Indiana)
2. Bill Bailey (Pennsylvania)
3. Dave Severn (Michigan)
4. David Mitchell (New York)
5. Greg Golsvig (Illinois)
6. Steve Witte (Colorado)

191.5-lb class
1. Jeff Dutton (California)
2. Dan Severn (Michigan)
3. Harold Smith (Ohio)
4. Gerard Iverson (Wisconsin)
5. Ken Roy (Oregon)
6. Mike DeGain (Michigan)

Heavyweight
1. John Bowlsby (Iowa)
2. Jimmy Jackson (Michigan)
3. Herb Calvert (New Jersey)
4. Chuck Stewart (Pennsylvania)
5. Ronnie Shuman (Michigan)
6. Tom Freeman (Illinois)

Outstanding Wrestler: Dave Powell (Illinois)

1975
Freestyle (Iowa City, IA)

Place winners

105.5-lb class
1. Dan Glenn (Iowa)
2. Keith Whelan (Illinois)
3. Paul Bolanos (California)
4. Jim Mathias (Wisconsin)
5. Randy Lewis (South Dakota)
6. Jim Gibbons (Iowa)

114.5-lb class
1. Joe Gonzales (California)
2. Mark Iacovelli (New York)
3. Bill DePaoli (Pennsylvania)
4. Charlie Amaya (Colorado)
5. Nestle Grimes (Minnesota)
6. Tom Husted (New Jersey)

123-lb class
1. John Azevedo (California)
2. Steve Maurey (Pennsylvania)
3. Carl Mangrum (Washington)
4. Dave Cartier (Michigan)
5. Eric Kriebel (Indiana)
6. Ed Snook (Michigan)

132-lb class
1. LeeRoy Smith (Oklahoma)
2. Dennis Reed (Pennsylvania)
3. Mike Walsh (Ohio)
4. Jim Monday (Oklahoma)
5. Doug Zastrow (Wisconsin)
6. James Slatter (New York)

143-lb class
1. Scott Bliss (Washington)
2. Bruce Kinseth (Iowa)
3. Al Sullivan (Illinois)
4. Ricky Wolfson (New York)
5. Dave Juergens (New York)
6. Mario Burton (Wisconsin)

154-lb class
1. Mark Churella (Michigan)
2. William Smith (New York)
3. Mark Schwettman (Colorado)
4. Jim Morris (Illinois)
5. Harold Ritchie (Missouri)
6. Gary Baker (Oregon)

165-lb class
1. Mike DeAnna (Ohio)
2. Dom DiGioacchino (New Jersey)
3. Drew Whitfield (Illinois)
4. Ricky Rabensdorf (Wisconsin)
5. Russ Zintak (Illinois)
6. Kelly Korth (Pennsylvania)

178-lb class
1. Ron Varga (Ohio)
2. Dave Severn (Michigan)
3. Kelly Carter (Michigan)
4. Brett Benson (Iowa)
5. Jody Van Loannen (Wisconsin)
6. Randy Hill (Wisconsin)

191.5-lb class
1. Mitch Hull (Wisconsin)
2. Eric Wais (California)
3. Scott Wagner (Colorado)
4. Norm Walker (Pennsylvania)
5. Mike Bressler (Washington)
6. Russ Synder (Ohio)

Heavyweight
1. Shawn Whitcomb (Michigan)
2. Brad Young (Washington)
3. Bob Taylor (Illinois)
4. Terry Palm (Oregon)
5. Mike McDowell (Michigan)
6. Steve Duerst (Wisconsin)

Outstanding Wrestler: Joe Gonzales (California)

1975
Greco-Roman (Iowa City, IA)

Place winners

105.5-lb class
1. Mike Farina (Illinois)
2. Lewis Sondgeroth (Colorado)
3. Jerry Kelley (Illinois)
4. Art Aragon (Colorado)
5. Jim Bicknell (Michigan)
6. Gary Milligan (Pennsylvania)

114.5-lb class
1. Herbert Patterson (Illinois)
2. John Smithson (California)
3. Andre Metzger (Michigan)
4. Ed Florvanti (New York)
5. Bill Middleton (Oregon)
6. Mike Knight (Iowa)

123-lb class
1. Carl Mangrum (Washington)
2. Kevin Cortez (Illinois)
3. Jerry Lorton (Washington)
4. Steve Cavayero (New York)
5. Dave Cartier (Michigan)
6. John Mousetis (Pennsylvania)

132-lb class
1. Kevin Puebla (Illinois)
2. Ken Mallory (Massachusetts)
3. Amos Goodlow (Michigan)
4. Craig Phillips (Pennsylvania)
5. Andy Rein (Wisconsin)
6. Rich Morris (Illinois)

143-lb class
1. Scott Bliss (Washington)
2. Al Sullivan (Illinois)
3. Dave Juergens (New York)
4. Don Zellner (Oregon)
5. Ed Hibbs (Oklahoma)
6. Mike Thomas (New York)

154-lb class
1. Gary Baker (Oregon)
2. Terry Fike (Pennsylvania)
3. Mark Schwettman (Colorado)
4. Mike Abrams (Michigan)
5. Dave Dickstein (New York)
6. William Smith (New York)

165-lb class
1. Dom DiGioacchino (New Jersey)
2. Jeff Kovalenko (Illinois)
3. Kelly Korth (Pennsylvania)
4. Pete Lucas (Oregon)
5. Jim Parker (Washington)
6. Chris Lawson (New York)

178-lb class
1. Dave Severn (Michigan)
2. Marty Ryan (Oregon)
3. Joe Lidowski (New York)
4. Howard Harris (Oregon)
5. Craig Herbert (Washington)
6. Dan Plautz (Pennsylvania)

191.5-lb class
1. Mitch Hull (Wisconsin)
2. Eric Wais (California)
3. Norm Walker (Pennsylvania)
4. Mark Simpson (Missouri)
5. Jon Schnurpel (Indiana)
6. Greg Williams (Pennsylvania)

Heavyweight
1. Shawn Whitcomb (Michigan)
2. Jack Campbell (Pennsylvania)
3. Brad Young (Washington)
4. Kevin Kurth (Iowa)
5. Steve Insalacco (New York)
6. Terry Palm (Oregon)

Outstanding Wrestler: Kevin Puebla (Illinois)

1976
Freestyle (Iowa City, IA)

Place winners

98-lb class
1. Don St. James (New York)
2. Khris Whelan (Illinois)
3. Mark Trizzino (Illinois)
4. Karl Glover (California)

5. Joe Swartz (Indiana)
6. Josh Youel (Iowa)

105.5-lb class
1. Jeff Kerber (Iowa)
2. Kirk Dabney (Pennsylvania)
3. Chas Richards (Oklahoma)
4. Glen Beverly (Indiana)
5. Randy Blackman (Illinois)
6. Bob Dickman (Wisconsin)

114.5-lb class
1. Dan Glenn (Iowa)
2. Tom Husted (New Jersey)
3. Randy Lewis (South Dakota)
4. Scott Grudzinski (Wisconsin)
5. Bill Porter (Illinois)
6. Tom Blanco (California)

123-lb class
1. Howard Aulleger (Oklahoma)
2. Mark Iacovelli (New York)
3. Kevin Benson (Pennsylvania)
4. Jay Swanson (South Dakota)

132-lb class
1. LeeRoy Smith (Oklahoma)
2. Andy Rein (Wisconsin)
3. Ralph Cortez (Illinois)
4. Craig Garvin (Iowa)
5. Kyle Grunwald (New York)
6. Ted Patacsil (Indiana)

143-lb class
1. Glenn Cooper (California)
2. Scott Trizzino (Illinois)
3. Phil Anglim (Ohio)
4. Ed Fracasso (Ohio)
5. Thomas Landrum (Oklahoma)
6. Phil Gevock (Iowa)

154-lb class
1. Scott Madigan (Minnesota)
2. Grant Smith (Wisconsin)
3. Marvin Wiley (Illinois)
4. Al Harris (Wyoming)
5. Brian Boyle (Maryland)
6. Chris Semary (Ohio)

165-lb class
1. Mike DeAnna (Ohio)
2. Jeff Stuebing (Oregon)
3. Dave Schultz (California)
4. Charlie Heller (Pennsylvania)
5. Kevin Dugen (California)
6. Jeff Parker (New Jersey)

178-lb class
1. Mark Redman (Iowa)
2. Kevin Fisher (Wisconsin)
3. Dave Fitzgerald (Iowa)
4. Chris Pease (Oregon)
5. Bruce Lunds (Pennsylvania)
6. Dan Plautz (Pennsylvania)

191.5-lb class
1. Dan Severn (Michigan)
2. Lon Gerrish (Illinois)
3. Bruce Woyan (Florida)
4. Eric Booth (Pennsylvania)
5. John Wix (Colorado)
6. Paul Marfiz (Minnesota)

Heavyweight
1. Dave Klemm (Illinois)
2. Bob Taylor (Illinois)
3. Dean Phinney (Iowa)
4. Eugene Roswell (Wisconsin)
5. Brad Young (Washington)
6. Doug Arthur (California)

Outstanding Wrestler: Dan Severn (Michigan)

1976
Greco-Roman (Iowa City, IA)

Place winners

98-lb class
1. Khris Whelan (Illinois)
2. Mitch Powers (Washington)
3. Bryan Brown (California)
4. Josh Youel (Iowa)
5. Ron Gutierrez (Iowa)
6. Ken Sauer (Colorado)

105.5-lb class
1. Randy Blackman (Illinois)
2. Tracy Moore (Iowa)
3. Charles Biagini (New York)
4. Kirk Dabney (Pennsylvania)
5. James Breen (Connecticut)
6. Wendell White (Michigan)

123-lb class
1. Andre Metzger (Michigan)
2. Tim Clark (Illinois)
3. Kevin Benson (Pennsylvania)
4. Jon LaFleur (South Dakota)
5. Bill Donnelly (Iowa)
6. Lewis Sondgeroth (Colorado)

132-lb class
1. Ralph Cortez (Illinois)
2. Carl Mangrum (Washington)
3. Rafael Soto (New York)
4. Steve Hill (Michigan)
5. Kenneth Brodmerkel (New York)
6. Gino Vaccaro (Wisconsin)

143-lb class
1. Glenn Cooper (California)
2. Thomas Landrum (Oklahoma)
3. Melvin Gray (Pennsylvania)
4. Asa Jones (Michigan)
5. Don Zeliner (Oregon)
6. John Hall (Indiana)

154-lb class
1. Mike Pheanis (Illinois)
2. Mathew Hampton (Indiana)
3. Larry Hall (Indiana)
4. Roger Peterson (Colorado)
5. William Dickson (Alaska)
6. Byron Walton (Illinois)

165-lb class
1. Jeff Stuebing (Oregon)
2. Gordie Steffensmeier (Iowa)
3. Mark Jarosz (Maryland)
4. Edward Banach (New York)
5. Gary Chadwick (Oregon)
6. Tim Dean (New York)

178-lb class
1. Marty Ryan (Oregon)
2. Steve Bennett (New Jersey)
3. Gehrig Dergo (Illinois)
4. Jeff Parker (New Jersey)
5. Rick Rabensdorf (Wisconsin)
6. Kevin Burke (Washington)

191.5-lb class
1. Dan Severn (Michigan)
2. Eric Wais (California)
3. James Johnson (North Carolina)
4. Eric Booth (Pennsylvania)
5. George Swan (New York)
6. Mark Severn (Michigan)

Heavyweight
1. Jack Campbell (Pennsylvania)
2. Doug Arthur (California)
3. Jeff Grier (Indiana)
4. Brad Young (Washington)
5. Doug Noetzel (Wisconsin)
6. Mike Ruff (New York)

Outstanding Wrestler: Khris Whelan (Illinois)

1977
Freestyle (Iowa City, IA)

Place winners

98-lb class
1. Mark Trizzino (Illinois)
2. Craig Sander (Oklahoma)
3. Dane Tussel (Ohio)
4. Kraig Nellis (Pennsylvania)
5. Adam Cuestas (California)
6. Kevin Darkus (Pennsylvania)

105.5-lb class
1. Mark Palzer (New York)
2. Karl Glover (California)
3. Dave Piro (South Dakota)
4. Steve Krause (Illinois)
5. Paul Tucker (California)
6. Joe Swartz (Indiana)

114.5-lb class
1. Kenny Monday (Oklahoma)
2. Keith Whelan (Illinois)
3. Jan Clark (Pennsylvania)
4. Jeff Kerber (Iowa)
5. Anthony Lee Ovalle (California)
6. Cohen (New York)

123-lb class
1. Randy Lewis (South Dakota)
2. Tom Husted (New Jersey)
3. Chas Richards (Oklahoma)
4. Richard Hone (New Jersey)
5. Lewis Sondgeroth (Colorado)
6. Mike Glustizia (New York)

132-lb class
1. Lennie Zalesky (Iowa)
2. Chuck Joseph (Michigan)
3. Mark Iacovelli (New York)
4. Randy Conrad (Illinois)
5. Ferron Anderson (Colorado)
6. Paul Schneller (New York)

143-lb class
1. Andre Metzger (Michigan)
2. Phil Anglim (Ohio)
3. Jim Farina (Illinois)
4. Roger Frizzel (Oklahoma)
5. Tim Welch (Ohio)
6. Chris Catalfo (New Jersey)

154-lb class
1. Grant Smith (Wisconsin)
2. Barry Boyles (California)
3. Ricky Stewart (Oklahoma)
4. Gary Jones (Washington)
5. Tony Damiani (New York)
6. Steve Peck (Kansas)

165-lb class
1. Richard Evans (Oklahoma)
2. Jeffrey Parker (New Jersey)
3. Richard Lentz (Florida)
4. Dave Young (New York)
5. Doug Gallaher (Pennsylvania)
6. Neal Neyer (Ohio)

178-lb class
1. Colin Kilrain (New Jersey)
2. Ed Banach (New York)
3. Charlie Heller (Pennsylvania)
4. Mike Breeden (Indiana)
5. Randy Beard (Colorado)
6. George Bowman (North Dakota)

191.5-lb class
1. Michael Evans (Illinois)
2. Mike Bardel (Illinois)
3. Mark Severn (Michigan)
4. Scott Martino (Wisconsin)
5. Joe Hurley (Illinois)
6. Mike Mann (Iowa)

Heavyweight
1. Dean Phinney (Iowa)
2. Kurt Bankson (Illinois)
3. John Carnes (Indiana)
4. Richard Chandler (Oregon)
5. Bruce Kittle (Iowa)
6. Gurnest Brown (North Carolina)

Outstanding Wrestler: Randy Lewis (South Dakota)

1977
Greco-Roman (Iowa City, IA)

Place winners

98-lb class
1. Ron Gutierrez (Iowa)
2. Todd Rosenthal (Illinois)
3. Leonard Bailey (Oklahoma)
4. Ken Sauer (Colorado)
5. Bob Brown (Wisconsin)
6. Lindley Kistler (California)

105.5-lb class
1. Khris Whelan (Illinois)
2. David Cooke (North Carolina)
3. Mike Steiner (Illinois)
4. Keith Dixon (Maryland)
5. Tim Antisdel (Colorado)
6. Wade Genova (New York)

114.5-lb class
1. Randy Blackman (Illinois)
2. Harlan Kistler
3. Ed Peterson (South Dakota)
4. Harrell Milhouse (Michigan)
5. Larry Cohen (New York)
6. Mitch Powers (Washington)

123-lb class
1. Harry Barnabae (Maryland)
2. John Dolch (Maryland)
3. Gary Stalko (Pennsylvania)
4. Gifford Owens (Michigan)
5. Ignacio Garcia (Colorado)
6. Jeff Knight (Iowa)

132-lb class
1. Ed Florvanti (New York)
2. Jerry Kelly (Illinois)
3. John Monolakis (California)
4. Randy Lewis (South Dakota)
5. Bill Marino (Pennsylvania)
6. Noel Carter (Illinois)

143-lb class
1. Andre Metzger (Michigan)
2. Kevin Benson (Oregon)
3. Gene Nighman (Pennsylvania)
4. Jim Farina (Illinois)
5. Kirt Lewis (Illinois)
6. Nate Carr (Pennsylvania)

154-lb class
1. Gary Jones (Washington)
2. Tim Catalfo (New Jersey)
3. Terry Jones (Oregon)
4. Wes Roper (Missouri)
5. Nelson Immamura (California)
6. Ron Woods (Alabama)

165-lb class
1. Jim Hall (Colorado)
2. Tim Dean (New York)
3. Craig Pittman (New York)
4. Perry Pittenger (New Jersey)
5. Kevin Egelston (New York)
6. Robin Whitaker (Indiana)

178-lb class
1. George Bowman (North Dakota)
2. Kevin Burke (Washington)
3. Quin Yorton (Wisconsin)
4. Mike Schwarzschild (New Jersey)
5. Dave Kampa (Minnesota)
6. (tie) Chuck Giordano (New York) and Tod Wieczorek (South Dakota)

191.5-lb class
1. Michael Evans (Illinois)
2. Bruce Kopitar (California)
3. Larry Cox (Pennsylvania)
4. Mark Anthony (Pennsylvania)
5. Joe Hurley (Illinois)
6. Mark Severn (Michigan)

Heavyweight
1. Richard Chandler (Oregon)
2. John Carnes (Indiana)
3. Kurt Bankson (Illinois)
4. Rod Chamberlin (Illinois)
5. Wally Frederick (Michigan)
6. Leo Wisniewski (Pennsylvania)

Outstanding Wrestler: Andre Metzger (Michigan)

1978
Freestyle (Iowa City, IA)

Place winners

98-lb class
1. Tim Schultz (Iowa)
2. Mel Proffitt (Oklahoma)
3. Larry Nicholson (California)
4. Trevor Graham (New York)
5. Ralph Harrison (New Mexico)
6. Joe McFarland (Ohio)

105.5-lb class
1. Adam Cuestas (California)
2. Wes Clevenger (Oklahoma)
3. Joe Gibbons (Iowa)
4. Chuck Jerkovich (Iowa)
5. John Ianuzzi (New York)
6. Leonard Bailey (Oklahoma)

114.5-lb class
1. Khris Whelan (Illinois)
2. Mark Trizzino (Illinois)
3. Robert Dickman (Wisconsin)
4. Jim Pasano (New Jersey)
5. Dave Cooke (North Carolina)
6. Brian McFarland (Ohio)

123-lb class
1. Bob Bury (New York)
2. Randy Majors (Iowa)
3. Jeff Kerber (Iowa)
4. Greg Peery (Maryland)
5. Jeff Tolbert (Illinois)
6. Mark Zimmer (Ohio)

132-lb class
1. Jerry Kelly (Illinois)
2. Bill Nugent (Oklahoma)
3. Kenny Monday (Oklahoma)
4. Randy Conrad (Illinois)
5. Jim Lord (Iowa)
6. Pete Schuyer (New Jersey)

143-lb class
1. Andre Metzger (Michigan)
2. Darryl Burley (New Jersey)

3. Chris Catalfo (New Jersey)
4. Jim Zalesky (Iowa)
5. Tim Berrier (Iowa)
6. Sam Perkins (Illinois)

154-lb class
1. Grant Smith (Wisconsin)
2. Jim Farina (Illinois)
3. Roger Frizzell (Oklahoma)
4. Alan Freeman (Iowa)
5. Chris Leichtweis (New York)
6. Nate Carr (Pennsylvania)

165-lb class
1. Scott Luschen (Kansas)
2. Steve Bessette (New Jersey)
3. Kevin Egleston (New York)
4. Rick Neitenbach (Colorado)
5. Brad Anderson (New Jersey)
6. Bill Boyd (Oklahoma)

178-lb class
1. Perry Hummel (Iowa)
2. Joe East (Ohio)
3. Ed Banach (New York)
4. Jerry Tesch (Minnesota)
5. Marty Loy (Wisconsin)
6. Karl Lynes (Oklahoma)

191-lb class
1. Rey Martinez (California)
2. Mike Mann (Iowa)
3. Mike Hayes (Iowa)
4. Ron Weaver (Oregon)
5. Darrick Campbell (Maryland)
6. Pete Bush (Iowa)

Heavyweight
1. Bruce Baumgartner (New Jersey)
2. Don Luaders (Illinois)
3. Dick Kamm (Iowa)
4. Doug Dyer (Tennessee)
5. Myke Miller (Washington)
6. Chris Hackbarth (Oklahoma)

Outstanding Wrestler: Andre Metzger (Michigan)

1978
Greco-Roman (Iowa City, IA)

Place winners

98-lb class
1. Bill Kelly (Illinois)
2. Victor Campo (California)
3. Grady Grisson (Colorado)
4. Alan Rivera (Illinois)
5. Dave Schutter (Indiana)
6. Daniel Smith (Connecticut)

105.5-lb class
1. Randy Ohta (Oregon)
2. Mike Steiner (Illinois)
3. Leonard Bailey (Oklahoma)
4. Joe Downey (New York)
5. Paul Cotton (Illinois)
6. John Gibson (Illinois)

114.5-lb class
1. Khris Whelan (Illinois)
2. Ray Gulmatico (California)
3. Dave Cooke (North Carolina)
4. Ken Sauer (Colorado)
5. Olie Johnson (Illinois)
6. Wade Genova (New York)

123-lb class
1. Jeff Kerber (Iowa)
2. Ferron Anderson (Colorado)
3. Robert Wimberly (Florida)
4. Steve Hoglund (Washington)
5. Pat Holloran (Minnesota)
6. Ken Shorts (Pennsylvania)

132-lb class
1. Bill Nugent (Oregon)
2. Lewis Songderoth (Colorado)
3. Lawrence Bowman (Virginia)
4. Jerry Kelly (Illinois)
5. Bill Marino (Pennsylvania)
6. Rick Whitehead (Iowa)

143-lb class
1. Andre Metzger (Michigan)
2. Noel Carter (Illinois)
3. Randy Steward (Iowa)
4. Sam Perkins (Illinois)
5. Jack Woltjec (Michigan)
6. Dick Combs (Oregon)

154-lb class
1. Kevin Benson (Oregon)
2. Jim Farina (Illinois)
3. John Galarnyk (Wisconsin)
4. Chris Fuertsch (California)
5. Nate Carr (Pennsylvania)
6. Leister Bowling (Colorado)

165-lb class
1. Jeff Dillman (Illinois)
2. John Hanrahan (Virginia)
3. Keith Fisher (Wisconsin)
4. Scott Luschen (Kansas)
5. Sergio Gaudix (Florida)
6. Mark Wray (Oregon)

178-lb class
1. Phil Lanzatella (New York)
2. Michael Robinson (California)
3. Larry Meierotto (Iowa)
4. Karl Lynes (Oklahoma)
5. Tim Dean (New York)
6. Dan Rowell (Oregon)

191.5-lb class
1. Ron Weaver (Oregon)
2. Quin Yorton (Wisconsin)
3. Pete Bush (Iowa)
4. John Selk (Iowa)
5. Ted Moreau (Pennsylvania)
6. Matt Boyle (New York)

Heavyweight
1. Keith Paloucek (Illinois)
2. Dave Kofoed (Minnesota)
3. Dan Cook (Oregon)
4. Jeff Golz (California)
5. Curt Olsen (Pennsylvania)
6. Brian Martin (Michigan)

Outstanding Wrestler: Kris Whelan (Illinois)

1979
Freestyle (Iowa City, IA)

Place winners

98-lb class
1. Leroy Murnane (Wisconsin)
2. John Papas (Illinois)
3. Jeff Leaf (Pennsylvania)
4. James Wallace (Indiana)

105.5-lb class
1. Greg Randall (Iowa)
2. John Thorn (Iowa)
3. Chris Medina (New Mexico)
4. Andy Golembeski (New York)

114.5-lb class
1. John Ianuzzi (New York)
2. Kevin Darkus (Pennsylvania)
3. Ramon Gulmatico (California)
4. Bruce Ralston (Iowa)

123-lb class
1. Leo Bailey (Oklahoma)
2. Alan Goldman (Colorado)
3. Barry Davis (Iowa)
4. Daniel Foldesy (Ohio)

132-lb class
1. Tim Riley (Iowa)
2. Tim Merzweller (New Mexico)
3. Clark Yoder (Iowa)
4. Glen Goodman (Florida)

143-lb class
1. Rudy Isom (New York)
2. Ken Carter (Oregon)

3. Mark Schmitz (Wisconsin)
4. Kenny Monday (Oklahoma)

154-lb class
1. Nate Carr (Pennsylvania)
2. Jim Farina (Illinois)
3. Jim Zalesky (Iowa)
4. Chris Bojanovic (New Jersey)

165-lb class
1. Jan Michaels (New Jersey)
2. Rick O'Shea (Oregon)
3. Terry Jones (Oregon)
4. Dennis Limmex (Wisconsin)

178-lb class
1. Joe East (Ohio)
2. Eli Blazeff (Ohio)
3. Clarence Richardson (New Jersey)
4. John Zito (New York)

191.5-lb class
1. Pete Bush (Iowa)
2. Mike Porcelli (New York)
3. Mike Severn (Michigan)
4. Chris Llewellyn (Illinois)

Heavyweight
1. Jon Schoeb (Minnesota)
2. Curt Olson (Pennsylvania)
3. Steve Wilber (Iowa)
4. Kevin Simmons (Indiana)

Outstanding Wrestler: Leo Bailey (California)

1979
Greco-Roman (Iowa City, IA)

<u>*Place winners*</u>

83.5-lb class
1. Bill Meyers (Nebraska)
2. Marcio White (Oklahoma)
3. Gary O'Bannon (Missouri)
4. John Palmer (Pennsylvania)

88-lb class
1. Robert Pender (New Jersey)
2. Steve Swiderski (Pennsylvania)
3. Ronny Pontious (Illinois)
4. Todd Archer (Oklahoma)

92.5-lb class
1. Earl Snyder (Pennsylvania)
2. Phil Ogan (Washington)
3. Kevin Fritz (Oklahoma)
4. Larry LeGrande (Illinois)

99-lb class
1. Glenn Hall (New Jersey)
2. Bill Starke (New York)
3. Dan Ray (Iowa)
4. Brian Folson (California)

105.5-lb class
1. Nick Neville (Texas)
2. Ken Taroli (Indiana)
3. Wayne Jackson (Michigan)
4. John Parr (New Jersey)

112-lb class
1. Todd Sterr (Illinois)
2. Jeff Songderoth (Colorado)
3. Mario Pyles (Kansas)
4. Vince Macri (Pennsylvania)

121-lb class
1. Ted DiPasquale (New York)
2. John Orr (Pennsylvania)
3. Paul Glynn (Iowa)
4. Peter Mankowich (New York)

130-lb class
1. Rich Lithgow (New York)
2. Greg Lobell (New Jersey)
3. Leonard Taylor (Maryland)
4. Chris Whittle (Florida)

138.5-class
1. Rico Chiapparelli (Maryland)
2. John Cappiello (Pennsylvania)
3. Paul Nord (Minnesota)
4. Troy Sporer (Kansas)

149.5-lb class
1. Ralph Liegel (Wisconsin)
2. Troy Osborne (California)
3. Monty Guidi (Pennsylvania)
4. Tom Thurgood (New Jersey)

160.5-lb class
1. Doug Haines (Pennsylvania)
2. Todd Northrup (New York)
3. Doug McClister (Illinois)
4. Keith Pitts (Colorado)

171.5-lb class
1. Jack Uppling (Pennsylvania)
2. Steve Berhns (New York)
3. Lee Lam Ho (Oklahoma)
4. Rod LeMarche (Wisconsin)

Heavyweight
1. Randy Taylor (Illinois)
2. Andy Schwab (New York)
3. Dennis Jacobs (Wisconsin)
4. Stan Hill (New Mexico)

Outstanding Wrestler: Bill Meyers (Nebraska)

1979
Greco-Roman (Iowa City, IA)

Place winners

98-lb class
1. Alan Rivera (Illinois)
2. Scott Palmer (Pennsylvania)
3. Steve Cram (Minnesota)
4. Paul Woods (New York)

105.5-lb class
1. Todd Nighman (Pennsylvania)
2. Michael Johnson (Illinois)
3. Grady Grissom (Colorado)
4. Wesley Gaston (California)

114.5-lb class
1. Ramon Guimatico (California)
2. Olie Johnson (Illinois)
3. Joe Spinazzola (New Jersey)
4. James Kloetzer (Washington)

123-lb class
1. Leo Bailey (Oklahoma)
2. John Warlick (Georgia)
3. Michael Mann (Wisconsin)
4. Clarence Wilson (Michigan)

132-lb class
1. Jeff Kerber (Iowa)
2. Tom Seamans (Colorado)
3. Steve Hoglund (Washington)
4. Kirkie Hampton (Michigan)

143-lb class
1. Sam Perkins (Illinois)
2. Jim Layer (Illinois)
3. Mike Mankowich (New York)
4. Darrel McNair (Illinois)

154-lb class
1. Dale Krzmarzick (Oregon)
2. Nate Carr (Pennsylvania)
3. David Massey (Oklahoma)
4. Charlie Lucas (Oregon)

165-lb class
1. Jay Llewellyn (Iowa)
2. Matt Reiss (Pennsylvania)
3. Neil Zimmerman (Wisconsin)
4. Roy Lobdell (New York)

178-lb class
1. Phil Lanzatella (New York)
2. Bill Scherr (South Dakota)
3. Derrick Waldroup (Illinois)
4. Kent Elliott (Michigan)

191.5-lb class
1. Bob Kopecky (Wisconsin)
2. Mike D'Ambrose (Illinois)
3. Chris Llewellyn (Illinois)
4. Karl Lynes (Oklahoma)

Heavyweight
1. Curt Olson (Pennsylvania)
2. Jeff Golz (Ohio)
3. Keith Paloucek (Illinois)
4. Kevin Simmons (Indiana)

Outstanding Wrestler: Jeff Kerber (Iowa)

1980
Freestyle (Iowa City, IA)

Place winners

98-lb class
1. Philip Ogan (Washington)
2. Steve Knight (Iowa)
3. Roger Burkett (Georgia)

4. Dave Buzza (Pennsylvania)
5. Earl Snyder (Pennsylvania)
6. Joe Pardo (Oregon)

105.5-lb class
1. Jeff Carter (Iowa)
2. Lou Hame (New York)
3. David Washington (Nebraska)
4. Kyle Nellis (Pennsylvania)
5. Mike Pierre (Illinois)
6. Dave Goeb (Minnesota)

114.5-lb class
1. Pat Pickford (Iowa)
2. Lenal Brinson (Illinois)
3. Joe Rabin (New York)
4. Bob DeProspero (Virginia)
5. John Thorn (Iowa)
6. Ken Taroli (Indiana)

123-lb class
1. Kevin Darkus (Pennsylvania)
2. Mark Perry (Oklahoma)
3. Todd Steidley (Oklahoma)
4. Barry Davis (Iowa)
5. Dave Martin (Oklahoma)
6. Paul Kreimeyer (Iowa)

132-lb class
1. Joe Gibbons (Iowa)
2. David Ray (Kansas)
3. John Ianuzzi (New York)
4. Scott Morningstar (Iowa)
5. Walt Markee (Oregon)
6. Dave Woltjer (Michigan)

143-lb class
1. Bill Moss (Florida)
2. Kenny Monday (Oklahoma)
3. Michael Mills (Georgia)
4. Mike Burch (California)
5. Chris Bevilacqua (Oklahoma)
6. Mark Baker (Iowa)

154-lb class
1. Louis Chiapparelli (Maryland)
2. Rick O'Shea (Oregon)
3. Kirby Kepner (Indiana)
4. Mike Sheets (Oklahoma)
5. Dean Perkins (Illinois)
6. Chris Mondragon (Colorado)

165-lb class
1. Bill Dykeman (New Jersey)
2. Ernie Vatch (Illinois)
3. Eric Brugel (Pennsylvania)
4. Mike Falcon (New York)
5. Duane Groshek (Wisconsin)
6. Dennis Limmex (Wisconsin)

178-lb class
1. Bill Scherr (South Dakota)
2. Dan Chaid (California)
3. Tom Kaiski (Ohio)
4. Kirk Butryn (New York)
5. Mike Guenther (Colorado)
6. Brett Hooper (Iowa)

191.5-lb class
1. Hugh Bohne (Wisconsin)
2. Bob Button (New York)
3. Mike Conners (New York)
4. Kahlan O'Hara (Nevada)
5. Jody Munch (Pennsylvania)
6. Tony Ellison (Oklahoma)

Heavyweight
1. Vaughn Broadnax (Ohio)
2. Henry Lavender (Alabama)
3. Tom Miller (Illinois)
4. Jeff Steffens (Wisconsin)
5. Jimmie Kimmel (New York)
6. Jay Bean (Iowa)

Outstanding Wrestler: Bill Moss (Florida)

1980
Greco-Roman (Iowa City, IA)

Place winners

98-lb class
1. Earl Snyder (Pennsylvania)
2. Peter Ogan (Washington)
3. Steve Knight (Iowa)
4. Dave Sherman (Illinois)
5. Phil Ogan (Washington)
6. Dave Buzza (Pennsylvania)

105.5-lb class
1. Alan Rivera (Illinois)
2. Wesley Gaston (California)

3. Nick Milonas (New Jersey)
4. Kyle Nellis (Pennsylvania)
5. Melton Hardee (North Carolina)
6. Glen Frank (Oregon)

114.5-lb class

1. Eric Seward (Washington)
2. Steve Stearns (Illinois)
3. Wayne Jackson (Michigan)
4. Brian Hall (Iowa)
5. Zane Jones (Idaho)
6. Carl Barday (Colorado)

123-lb class

1. Kevin Darkus (Pennsylvania)
2. Jon Gibson (Illinois)
3. Brad Gustafson (California)
4. Ramon Gulmatico (California)
5. Todd Nighman (Pennsylvania)
6. Orlando Caceres (New Jersey)

132-lb class

1. David Ray (Kansas)
2. Ted DiPasquale (New York)
3. Joey Throckmorton (Pennsylvania)
4. Don Parsley (Pennsylvania)
5. Trevor Graham (New York)
6. Randy O'Shea (Oregon)

143-lb class

1. Ignacio Garcia (Colorado)
2. Poppy Guerrero (Illinois)
3. Garvin Smith (Illinois)
4. Randy Anderson
5. Walter White (Illinois)
6. Jim Layer (Illinois)

154-lb class

1. Rick O'Shea (Oregon)
2. Doug Haines (Pennsylvania)
3. Jay Slivkoff (California)
4. Mike Specht (South Dakota)
5. John Bynum (North Carolina)
6. Andre Bullocks (Illinois)

165-lb class

1. Mike Falcon (New York)
2. Mike Farrahar (Georgia)
3. Michael Flanagan (Missouri)
4. Jim Scherr (South Dakota)
5. Keith Beutler (Oregon)
6. Scott Simmons (Michigan)

178-lb class

1. Dan Chaid (California)
2. Chris Llewellyn (Illinois)
3. Tom McEntee (Illinois)
4. Lloyd Johnson (Illinois)
5. Kent Elliott (Michigan)
6. Scott Crow (California)

191.5-lb class

1. Hugh Bohne (Wisconsin)
2. Curt Monnig (Missouri)
3. Brian Irek (Wisconsin)
4. Derrick Waldroup (Illinois)
5. Jody Munch (Pennsylvania)
6. Doug Brooks (Michigan)

Heavyweight

1. Talmadge Thacker (North Carolina)
2. Robert Kopecky (Wisconsin)
3. Mike Knox (Colorado)
4. Jamie Kimmel (New York)
5. John Gonzales (California)
6. Henry Lavender (Alabama)

Outstanding Wrestler: Kevin Darkus (Pennsylvania)

1981
Freestyle (Iowa City, IA)

Place winners

98-lb class

1. Hans Houser (New Jersey)
2. Jim Best (Pennsylvania)
3. Bob Panariello (New York)
4. Scott Parker (Michigan)
5. Mack Nace (New Jersey)
6. Philip Ogan (Washington)

105.5-lb class

1. Jeff Carter (Iowa)
2. Steve Knight (Iowa)
3. Bruce Garner (Oklahoma)

4. Mel Goree (Oklahoma)
5. Mike Green (Illinois)
6. David Green (Illinois)

114.5-lb class
1. Ed Giese (Illinois)
2. Todd Sterr (Illinois)
3. Al Palacio (New York)
4. Bill Starke (New York)
5. Kyle Nellis (Pennsylvania)
6. Ricky Palomino (California)

123-lb class
1. Pat Pickford (Iowa)
2. Ramon Gulmatico (Nevada)
3. Wayne Jackson (Michigan)
4. David Rynda (Oklahoma)
5. Bob DeProspero (Virginia)
6. Jeff Sondgeroth (Colorado)

132-lb class
1. Joe Gibbons (Iowa)
2. Steve DePetro (New Jersey)
3. Greg Randall (Iowa)
4. Pete Mankowich (New York)
5. Nick Neville (Texas)
6. Paul Glynn (Iowa)

143-lb class
1. Leonard Bailey (Oklahoma)
2. Jim Heffernan (Ohio)
3. Matt King (New York)
4. Karl Wolfenberger (Kansas)
5. Scott Cardwell (Oregon)
6. Gary Fishbein (New York)

154-lb class
1. Rico Chiapparelli (Maryland)
2. Mike Rosman (Illinois)
3. Duane Goldman (Colorado)
4. Kevin Jackson (Michigan)
5. Bub Lawson (Ohio)
6. Terry Manning (Wisconsin)

165-lb class
1. John Johnson (Oklahoma)
2. Chuck Kearney (Oregon)
3. Dave Palmer (Indiana)
4. Steve Hare (New Jersey)
5. Nick Henson (Iowa)
6. Erick Brugel (Pennsylvania)

178-lb class
1. Melvin Douglas (Kansas)
2. Keith Pitts (Colorado)
3. Randy Thompson (Iowa)
4. Joel Newman (Pennsylvania)
5. Dave Garner (Pennsylvania)
6. Wayne Catan (New York)

191.5-lb class
1. Kent Elliott (Michigan)
2. Brian McCracken (Iowa)
3. Nick Gouletas (Illinois)
4. Jerry Jackson (Indiana)
5. Gregg Stoel (Michigan)
6. Edward Lohr (South Dakota)

Heavyweight
1. Randy Taylor (Illinois)
2. Larry Eide (Missouri)
3. John Jay Howard (Maryland)
4. Erwin Lavender (Alabama)
5. George Davis (Iowa)
6. Joe Smiley (Washington)

Outstanding Wrestler: Joe Gibbons (Iowa)

1981
Greco-Roman (Iowa City, IA)

Place winners

98-lb class
1. Philip Ogan (Washington)
2. Pat Bloom (Florida)
3. Darrell Nerove (California)
4. Bret Penrith (New York)
5. Willie Warren (New York)
6. Danny Hicks (California)

105.5-lb class
1. Steve Knight (Iowa)
2. Glen Frank (Oregon)
3. Eugene Lumsdon (Florida)
4. Jesse Teplicki (Florida)
5. Rick Goeb (Minnesota)
6. Leandro Perez (California)

114.5-lb class
1. Bill Starke (New York)
2. Mitch Sheppard (Illinois)

3. Kirk Azinger (Iowa)
4. Ricky Palomino (California)
5. Tom Lofland (Oregon)
6. Eric Powers (Washington)

123-lb class
1. Steve Stearns (Illinois)
2. Dennis Kagey (Michigan)
3. Jeff Semrad (Wisconsin)
4. John Garcia (Colorado)
5. Vince Herr (Oregon)
6. Jim Semrad (Wisconsin)

132-lb class
1. David Ray (Kansas)
2. John Giura (Illinois)
3. Todd Nighman (Pennsylvania)
4. Rich Barron (Pennsylvania)
5. Paul Glynn (Iowa)
6. James Bobbitt (North Carolina)

143-lb class
1. Leonard Bailey (Oklahoma)
2. Ted DiPasquale (New York)
3. Lester Christmas (Illinois)
4. Bob Lacefield (Illinois)
5. Lance Milsap (Kansas)
6. Pat Tongue (Washington)

154-lb class
1. Marty Kistler (California)
2. Garvin Smith (Illinois)
3. Walter White (Illinois)
4. Boyd Long (Oregon)
5. Leslie Lewis (Illinois)
6. Duane Peoples (Pennsylvania)

165-lb class
1. Eric Brugel (Pennsylvania)
2. Doug McClister (Illinois)
3. John Johnson (Oklahoma)
4. Mike Kraft (Illinois)
5. Reginald Wilson (Illinois)
6. Mark Farrahar (Georgia)

178-lb class
1. Kent Elliott (Michigan)
2. Bruce Mulford (Oregon)
3. Wayne Catan (New York)
4. Dan Chaid (California)
5. David Martin (Washington)
6. Seann Henry (New Jersey)

191.5-lb class
1. Bill Reed (Iowa)
2. Edward Lohr (South Dakota)
3. Gerald Belton (Illinois)
4. Joseph Thompson (Ohio)
5. Greg Zwilling (North Carolina)
6. Robert Button (New York)

Heavyweight
1. Tony Lasalandra (New Jersey)
2. George McDuffie (Ohio)
3. Walt Dunayczan (Michigan)
4. Erwin Lavender (Alabama)
5. Scott Beenken (Iowa)
6. Ted Isais (Colorado)

Outstanding Wrestler: Philip Ogan (Washington)

1982
Freestyle (Iowa City, IA)

Place winners

98-lb class
1. Mark Schwab (Iowa)
2. Dan Buzza (Pennsylvania)
3. John Galkowski (California)
4. Dan Evenson (Illinois)
5. Bob Malatesta (New Jersey)
6. Ricardo Abeyta (New Mexico)

105.5-lb class
1. Hans Houser (New Jersey)
2. Mike O'Brien (Illinois)
3. Peter Ogan (Washington)
4. Ken Sheppard (Illinois)
5. Doug Stafford (Pennsylvania), won by a forfeit

114.5-lb class
1. Steve Knight (Iowa)
2. Tom Dickman (Wisconsin)

3. Rod Robinson (Indiana)
4. Jeff Gibbons (Iowa)
5. Melvin Goree (Oklahoma)
6. Chris Cramer (Florida)

123-lb class
1. Tim Balzeski (Michigan)
2. Al Palacio (New York)
3. Mark Clayton (Missouri)
4. Blake Bonjean (New Mexico)
5. Ron Ensign (Florida)
6. Chris Luttrell (New Mexico)

132-lb class
1. Greg Randall (Iowa)
2. Keith Walton (Oklahoma)
3. Steve DePetro (New Jersey)
4. John Smith (Oklahoma)
5. John Parr (New Jersey)
6. Pete Yozzo (New York)

143-lb class
1. Stoney Wright (Oklahoma)
2. Ed Brady (Wisconsin)
3. Karl Wolfenberger (Kansas)
4. Bill Ferrie (Minnesota)
5. Scott Wiggen (Illinois)
6. Jim Engler (Iowa)

154-lb class
1. Jim Heffernan (Ohio)
2. Mike Rosman (Illinois)
3. Kevin Jackson (Michigan)
4. Gary Fischbein (New York)
5. Nick Mazzuca (Colorado)
6. Brian Flack (Colorado)

165-lb class
1. Greg Elinsky (Ohio)
2. Chuck Kearney (Oregon)
3. Rico Chiapparelli (Maryland)
4. Jeff Weatherman (Iowa)
5. Solomon Carr (Pennsylvania)
6. Ron DaBolt (New York)

178-lb class
1. David Palmer (Indiana)
2. Dan Mayo (New York)
3. Bruce Mulford (Oregon)
4. Mike Kraft (Illinois)
5. Eric Mittlestead (California)
6. Barry Preslaski (Wisconsin)

191.5-lb class
1. Rod Lamarche (Wisconsin)
2. Paul Neuner (Florida)
3. Kyle Richards (Wisconsin)
4. Scott Ames (Oregon)
5. Mike Calvin (Michigan)
6. Brett Hamilton (Washington)

Heavyweight
1. Mark Sindlinger (Iowa)
2. Tony Lasalandra (New Jersey)
3. Art Zygman (Illinois)
4. Brian Raber (Georgia)
5. Walt Dunayczan (Michigan)
6. Tom Erickson (Illinois)

Outstanding Wrestler: Steve Knight (Iowa)

1982
Greco-Roman (Iowa City, IA)

Place winners

98-lb class
1. Philip Ogan (Washington)
2. Bob Malatesta (New Jersey)
3. Dan Buzza (Pennsylvania)
4. Steve Fischbein (New York)
5. Chris Martin (New Jersey)
6. Scott Beck (New York)

105.5-lb class
1. Willie Warren (New York)
2. Peter Ogan (Washington)
3. Bret Penrith (New York)
4. Kevin Huck (Illinois)
5. Craig Barker (California)
6. Jeff Husick (Pennsylvania)

114.5-lb class
1. Steve Knight (Iowa)
2. Bob Panariello (New York)
3. Lorne Garrett (Illinois), won by forfeit
5. Mark McKenna (Washington)
6. Tom Lofland (Oregon)

123-lb class
1. Bill Starke (New York)
2. Brad Penrith (New York)

3. Blake Bonjean (Minnesota)
4. Mitch Sheppard (Illinois)
5. Dennis Kagey (Minnesota)
6. Tim O'Brien (Illinois)

132-lb class
1. Jeff Seward (Wisconsin)
2. Keith Presley (Illinois)
3. Keath Healy (Illinois)
4. Kirk Azinger (Iowa)
5. Daryl MarcAurele (Connecticut)
6. David Olmsted (Washington)

143-lb class
1. William Taylor (Oregon)
2. Glen Lanham (New York)
3. Richard Barron (Pennsylvania)
4. Tad DeRousse (Illinois)
5. Mike Joswowski (Wisconsin)
6. Lenworth Green (Florida)

154-lb class
1. Kevin Jackson (Michigan)
2. Ozzie Porter (Illinois)
3. Paul Harrison (Washington)
4. Nate Carter (Pennsylvania)
5. Russ Schenk (Florida)
6. John Jensen (California)

165-lb class
1. Derrick Williams (Illinois)
2. Dave Wiklund (Minnesota)
3. Bill Beutler (Oregon)
4. Jose Gomez (Illinois)
5. Eugene Martinez (Colorado)
6. Pete Basic (Florida)

178-lb class
1. Bruce Mulford (Oregon)
2. Jack Uppling (Pennsylvania)
3. Fritz Stratton (Iowa)
4. Eric Mittlestead (California)
5. Ab Brown (Wyoming)
6. Dave Dean (Michigan)

191.5-lb class
1. Scott Ames (Oregon)
2. Rod Lamarche (Wisconsin)
3. Greg Zwilling (North Carolina)
4. Victor Ceja (California)
5. Gerald Belton (Illinois)
6. Stacy Davis (North Carolina)

Heavyweight
1. Tony Lasalandra (New Jersey)
2. Erwin Lavender (Alabama)
3. Walt Dunayczan (Michigan)
4. Dave Orndorff (Washington)
5. Mark Sindlinger (Iowa)
6. Larry Eide (Missouri)

Outstanding Wrestler: Joe Melchiore (New Jersey)

1983
Freestyle (Cedar Falls, IA)

Place winners

98-lb class
1. Jim Martin (Pennsylvania)
2. Ken Gaudreau (California)
3. Jim Sanchez (Wyoming)
4. Gene McNeil (New York)
5. Larry Jones (Michigan)
6. Adam Goldstein (New Jersey)

105.5-lb class
1. Mark Schwab (Iowa)
2. Chris Bollin (Kansas)
3. Bobby Malatesta (New Jersey)
4. Dan Buzza (Pennsylvania)
5. Laurence Jackson (California)
6. Mike Guthrie (Iowa)

114.5-lb class
1. Corey Mills (Iowa)
2. Cory Baze (Oklahoma)
3. Steve Martin (Virginia)
4. Hans Houser (New Jersey)
5. Mike O'Brien (Illinois)
6. William Waters (Michigan)

123-lb class
1. Joe Melchiore (New Jersey)
2. Tim Wright (Illinois)
3. Scott Pifer (Pennsylvania)
4. Tommy Ortiz (Arizona)
5. Jeff Gibbons (Iowa)
6. Rick Goeb (Minnesota)

132-lb class
1. Keith Walton (Oklahoma)
2. Tim Balzeski (Michigan)
3. Anthony Palomino (California)
4. John Smith (Oklahoma)
5. Mike Hampton (Oklahoma)
6. Lenny Bernstein (Maryland)

143-lb class
1. Pete Yozzo (New York)
2. Kurt Shedenhelm (Iowa)
3. Tim Krieger (Iowa)
4. Stoney Wright (Oklahoma)
5. Tim Manning (South Dakota)
6. Eddie Borror (Kansas)

154-lb class
1. Royce Alger (Iowa)
2. Gary Fischbein (New York)
3. Tony Evensen (Illinois)
4. Rob Koll (Pennsylvania)
5. Jeff Cardwell (Oregon)
6. Pete Mitchell (Ohio)

165-lb class
1. Mike VanArsdale (Iowa)
2. Jim Gressley (Arizona)
3. Dave Lee (California)
4. John Heffernan (Ohio)
5. Rod Sande (Minnesota)
6. Anthony Romero (New Mexico)

178-lb class
1. Dan Mayo (New York)
2. Chuck Kearney (Oregon)
3. Charlie Sherertz (Nebraska)
4. Mike Llewellyn (Iowa)
5. Dan Miller (Indiana)
6. Dave Cowen (New York)

191.5-lb class
1. Kyle Richards (Wisconsin)
2. John Place (New York)
3. Tony Savegnago (Illinois)
4. Jerry Curby (Michigan)
5. Mark Tatum (Oklahoma)
6. Mike Zerr (Colorado)

Heavyweight
1. Rod Severn (Michigan)
2. Tony Koontz (Pennsylvania)
3. Jeff Glenn (Illinois)
4. Mark Singlinger (Iowa)
5. Ken Kolthoff (Iowa)
6. Rick Pinter (Michigan)

Outstanding Wrestler: Joe Melchiore (New Jersey)

1983
Greco-Roman (Cedar Falls, IA)

Place winners

98-lb class
1. Jim Sanchez (Wyoming)
2. Pete Gomez (Colorado)
3. Bob Yochimowitz (Pennsylvania)
4. Martin Strmiska (California)
5. Jim Sloan (New Jersey)
6. Darryl Micou (Iowa)

105.5-lb class
1. Mark Schwab (Iowa)
2. John Galkowski (California)
3. Bobby Malatesta (New Jersey)
4. Dan Buzza (Pennsylvania)
5. Bob Sterriker (Minnesota)
6. Scott Arneson (Wisconsin)

114.5-lb class
1. Doug Stanford (Pennsylvania)
2. William Waters (Michigan)
3. Steve Waddell (Iowa)
4. Bret Penrith (New York)
5. Willie Warren (New York)
6. Lorne Garrett (Illinois)

123-lb class
1. Brad Penrith (New York)
2. John Fisher (Michigan)
3. Pat Fitzgerald (Ohio)
4. Won Kim (Illinois)
5. Ron Karns (Pennsylvania)
6. Walter Keller (New Mexico)

132-lb class
1. Blake BonJean (Minnesota)
2. David Olmsted (Washington)
3. Todd Nicholson (Oregon)
4. Joe Russell (Oregon)
5. Jerry Durso (New Jersey)
6. Bubba Strauss (Ohio)

143-lb class
1. Sean Finkbeiner (Pennsylvania)
2. Tad DeRousse (Illinois)
3. Eric Messner (Oregon)
4. Tom Salisbury (South Carolina)
5. Paul Mankowich (New York)
6. Jeff Kloetzer (Idaho)

154-lb class
1. Anthony Romero (New Mexico)
2. Jody Karam (Pennsylvania)
3. Kevin Kahl (Iowa)
4. Jake Baker (Oregon)
5. Dave Zariczny (New York)
6. Bob Morris (Illinois)

165-lb class
1. Dave Lee (California)
2. Scott Diveney (Iowa)
3. Jose Gomez (Illinois)
4. Chuck Martens (Iowa)
5. Daemon Knight (Oregon)
6. Chris Barnes (Oklahoma)

178-lb class
1. Seann Henry (New Jersey)
2. Darrin Ziemer (Oregon)
3. Tom Hoy (Illinois)
4. Dave Dean (Michigan)
5. Don Faye (Arizona)
6. Anthony Belew (California)

191.5-lb class
1. Brad Steward (Alaska)
2. Greg Zwilling (North Carolina)
3. Bob Gassman (Illinois)
4. Tony Villareale (New York)
5. Joe Malecek (Iowa)
6. Mark Buckley (Connecticut)

Heavyweight
1. Mark Sindlinger (Iowa)
2. Tony Koontz (Pennsylvania)
3. Rod Severn (Michigan)
4. Jeff Glenn (Illinois)
5. Ken Young (Washington)
6. Hector Hernandez (Texas)

Outstanding Wrestler: Brad Penrith (New York)

1984
Freestyle (Cedar Falls, IA)

Place winners

1. Ben Morris (Illinois)
2. Scott Bates (Oklahoma)
3. Matt Myers (Oklahoma)
4. Dain Barrett (Minnesota)
5. Jeff Austin (Pennsylvania)
6. Chris Hoffman (Iowa)

105.5-lb class
1. Chris Bollin (Kansas)
2. Chris Gelvin (Ohio)
3. Larry Jones (Michigan)
4. Don Heckel (Oklahoma)
5. Martin Strmiska (California)
6. Travis West (Oregon)

114.5-lb class
1. Laurence Jackson (California)
2. Mark Schwab (Iowa)
3. Jim Martin (Pennsylvania)
4. Cory Baze (Oklahoma)
5. Dan Knight (Iowa)
6. Steve Martin Virginia)

123-lb class
1. Ken Chertow (West Virginia)
2. John Epperly (Virginia)
3. Mike O'Brien (Illinois)
4. Joe Sloan (Oregon)
5. John Regan (Iowa)
6. Corey Mills (Iowa)

132-lb class
1. Jeff Gibbons (Iowa)
2. John Viola (New Jersey)
3. Mark Nace (New Jersey)
4. Mike Cole (Pennsylvania)
5. Jeff Mustari (Florida)
6. Roque Canderlaia (New Mexico)

143-lb class
1. Tim Krieger (Iowa)
2. Marty King (New York)

3. Terry Kennedy (Ohio)
4. Tom Ortiz (Arizona)
5. Kip Kristoff (Illinois)
6. Michael Arena (New York)

154-lb class
1. Sean Finkbeiner (Pennsylvania)
2. Guy Russo (New Jersey)
3. Jeff Coltvet (Iowa)
4. Aaron Peters (Ohio)
5. Brandon Dennington (California)
6. Jeff Harris (Illinois)

165-lb class
1. Christopher Rosman (Illinois)
2. Jim Gressley (Arizona)
3. John Heffernan (Ohio)
4. Chris Geneser (Iowa)
5. Mike Farrell (Minnesota)
6. Tom McGourty (New Jersey)

178-lb class
1. Chris Barnes (Oklahoma)
2. Hugh Meek (Georgia)
3. James Dye (Illinois)
4. David Williams (Iowa)
5. Dave Barbour (Illinois)
6. Steve Myers (Illinois)

191.5-lb class
1. Jeff Ellis (New York)
2. Charlie Sheretz (Nebraska)
3. Eric Voelker (Iowa)
4. Hank Inderlied (Ohio)
5. Shawn Johnson (Colorado)
6. Ken Hackman (Pennsylvania)

Heavyweight
1. Tony Koontz (Pennsylvania)
2. Carl Haselrig (Pennsylvania)
3. Tom Moxley (Ohio)
4. Curt Riley (Oklahoma)
5. Mike Wallace (North Carolina)
6. Dale Veatch (Iowa)

Outstanding Wrestler: Ken Chertow (West Virginia)

1984
Greco-Roman (Cedar Falls, IA)

Place winners

98-lb class
1. Franklin Beck (Minnesota)
2. Vin Inners (New York)
3. Chris Hoffman (Iowa)
4. John Godhino (Washington)
5. Dean Ritts (Illinois)
6. Bam Pustelnick (Illinois)

105.5-lb class
1. Kurt Howell (Delaware)
2. Jim Sanchez (Wyoming)
3. Martin Strmiska (California)
4. Keith Taylor (New Jersey)
5. Chris Green (California)
6. Jeff Shapiro (Illinois)

114.5-lb class
1. Dan Knight (Iowa)
2. Laurence Jackson (California)
3. Duaine Martin (Nebraska)
4. Kevin Harvey (California)
5. Pat Higa (Hawaii)
6. Jim Walker (California)

123-lb class
1. Ken Chertow (West Virginia)
2. Bobby Malatesta (New Jersey)
3. Steve Waddell (Iowa)
4. Chuck Pearson (Iowa)
5. Sean O'Day (Pennsylvania)
6. Paul Gemberling (Pennsylvania)

132-lb class
1. David Olmstead (Washington)
2. John Fisher (Michigan)
3. Andre Taylor (Washington)
4. Bubba Strauss (Ohio)
5. Ed Bonuchi (Missouri)
6. Mike Leaman (Nebraska)

143-lb class
1. Jerry Durso (New Jersey)
2. Larry Gotcher (Washington)
3. Joe Russell (Oregon)
4. Gary Vanderheyden (Illinois)
5. Steve Shone (New York)
5. Tim Obrochta (Illinois)

154-lb class
1. Sean Finkbeiner (Pennsylvania)
2. Eric Messner (Oregon)
3. Hazen Bye (South Dakota)
4. Kannon Kares (Michigan)
5. Jeff Kelly (Iowa)
6. Aaron Peters (Ohio)

165-lb class
1. Steve Lawrence (California)
2. Doug Downs (New Jersey)
3. Dan Niebuhr (Wisconsin)
4. Junior Meek (Oklahoma)
5. Les Kvien (Minnesota)
6. Craig Christensen (Pennsylvania)

178-lb class
1. Dave Dean (Michigan)
2. Todd Seiler (Wisconsin)
3. Don Frye (Arizona), won by disqualification
5. Chris Barnes (Oklahoma)
6. Bill Freeman (Pennsylvania)

191.5-lb class
1. Tim Stanley (Iowa)
2. Kevin Mottlowitz (Illinois)
3. Mark Buckley (Connecticut)
4. (tie) Joe Malecek (Iowa) and Willie Krantz (Nebraska)
5. Mike Young (Pennsylvania)
6. Erik Christensen (Pennsylvania)

Heavyweight
1. Ken Young (Washington)
2. Tim Moxley (Ohio)
3. Kelly Cole (Oregon)
4. Mike DeCapua (New York)
5. Brad Burklund (Illinois)
6. John Owens (Washington)

Outstanding Wrestler: Ken Young (Washington)

1985
Freestyle (Cedar Falls, IA)

<u>*Place winners*</u>

98-lb class
1. Erin Millsap (California)
2. Terry Brands (Iowa)
3. Keith Stanford (Pennsylvania)
4. Scott Davis (Idaho)
5. Tim Trimble (South Dakota)
6. Damon Johnson (Oklahoma)

105.5-lb class
1. Sean Watts (Iowa)
2. Don Heckel (Oklahoma)
3. Scott Bates (Oklahoma)
4. Chip Elderkin (Indiana)
5. Ben Morris (Illinois)
6. Scott Pergram (Ohio)

114.5-lb class
1. Mark Schwab (Iowa)
2. Chris Bollin (Kansas)
3. Andy Radenbaugh (Michigan)
4. Zeke Jones (Michigan)
5. Vicente Rodriguez (California)
6. Allen Daubert (Pennsylvania)

123-lb class
1. Laurence Jackson (California)
2. Steve Martin (Virginia)
3. Joe Sloan (Oregon)
4. Kendall Cross (Oklahoma)
5. Bobby Malatesta (New Jersey)
6. Dwaine Martin (Nebraska)

132-lb class
1. Reagon Hicks (Oklahoma)
2. John Epperly (Virginia)
3. Eric Pierson (Maryland)
4. Dave Kennedy (Pennsylvania)
5. Travis West (Oregon)
6. Brian Shaffer (Virginia)

143-lb class
1. Larry Gotcher (Washington)
2. Jerry Durso (New Jersey)
3. Kip Kristoff (Illinois)
4. Sean O'Day (Pennsylvania)
5. Tobin Roitsch (Colorado)
6. Mike Murdoch (Michigan)

154-lb class
1. Joe Russell (Oregon)
2. Brandon Dennington (California)
3. Mike Lamb (New Jersey)
4. George Johnston (Oregon)
5. Thane Turner (Pennsylvania)
6. Scott Schumm (California)

165-lb class
1. Eric Messner (Oregon)
2. Brett Beams (Oklahoma)
3. Scott Pierre (Illinois)
4. Wade Zimmerman (Nevada)
5. Derek Brophy (New York)
6. Sean Bentson (California)

178-lb class
1. Chris Barnes (Oklahoma)
2. Mike Farrell (Minnesota)
3. Chris Geneser (Iowa)
4. Rob Laramore (Virginia)
5. Eric Eggers (Iowa)
6. Glenn Amador (Idaho)

191.5-lb class
1. Jeffrey Ellis (New York)
2. Mark Whitehead (Indiana)
3. Steve Lawson (California)
4. Tim McEowen (Iowa)
5. Brian Jackson (Missouri)
6. Hak Inderlied (Ohio)

286-lb class
1. Mike Wallace (North Carolina)
2. Jim Richardson (Minnesota)
3. Brian Krasowski (Illinois)
4. Tim Rider (California)
5. Torrence Manning (Indiana)
6. John Bielenberg (Oregon)

Outstanding Wrestler: Mark Schwab (Iowa)

1985
Greco-Roman (Cedar Falls, IA)

Place winners

98-lb class
1. Bam Pustelnik (Illinois)
2. Erin Millsap (California)
3. Ernie McNeal (Minnesota)
4. Chris Hoffman (Iowa)
5. Eddie Lee (Iowa)
6. Jeff Vasquez (Georgia)

105.5-lb class
1. Martin Strmiska (California)
2. Vinny Innes (New York)
3. Eric Millsap (California)
4. Frank Beck (Michigan)
5. Scott Pergram (Ohio)
6. Kelly Brewster (Kansas)

114.5-lb class
1. Chris Bollin (Kansas)
2. Kurt Howell (Delaware)
3. Salem Yaffai (Michigan)
4. Chris Green (California)
5. Bryan Patterson (Illinois)
6. Jack Vantress (Oregon)

123-lb class
1. Laurence Jackson (California)
2. Dan Knight (Iowa)
3. Dwaine Martin (Nebraska)
4. Randy Headrick (Colorado)
5. Curtis Crim (Illinois)
6. Theirry Chaney (Virginia)

132-lb class
1. Paul Walker (Illinois)
2. Charlie Bass (Washington)
3. Travis West (Oregon)
4. Scott Ruff (Wyoming)
5. Haig Brown (Oregon)
6. Ray Downey (New York)

143-lb class
1. Bubba Strauss (Ohio)
2. Jerry Durso (New Jersey)
3. Kerry Ryan (Illinois)
4. Danny White (Colorado)
5. Pat Whitford (Michigan)
6. Shawn Ryan (Iowa)

154-lb class
1. Joe Russell (Oregon)
2. George Johnston (Oregon)
3. Dan Russell (Oregon)
4. Steve Duval (Minnesota)
5. Johnny Scott (Iowa)
6. John Groves (Iowa)

165-lb class
1. Eric Messner (Oregon)
2. Drew D'Augostino (New York)
3. Chris Short (Minnesota)
4. Steve Lander (Oregon)
5. Jace McKeighan (New York)
6. Von Hoehn (Massachusetts)

178-lb class
1. Craig Christensen (Pennsylvania)
2. Glenn Amador (Idaho)
3. Gavin Green (Wyoming)
4. Scott Benson (California)
5. Darrell Long (Iowa)
6. David Williams (Iowa)

191.5-lb class
1. Jeff Seaney (Oregon)
2. Steve Lawson (California)
3. Joe Malecek (Iowa)
4. Michael Young (Pennsylvania)
5. Scott Hamilton (Missouri)
6. Mark Meier (Minnesota)

286-lb class
1. Ben Lizama (California)
2. Olden Reese (Florida)
3. Mike Wallace (North Carolina)
4. Bob Karl (Wisconsin)
5. Randy Stuhr (Nebraska)
6. R.J. Updike (Arizona)

Outstanding Wrestler: Laurence Jackson (California)

1986
Freestyle (Cedar Falls, IA)

Place winners

98-lb class
1. Dan Vidlak (Oregon)
2. Glen Nyquist (Illinois)
3. Jason Buxton (South Dakota)
4. David Warnick (Pennsylvania)
5. Nick Purler (Missouri)
6. Tony Purler (Missouri)
7. (tie) Rod Heiser (Oregon) and Sam Henso (Missouri)

105.5-lb class
1. Alan Fried (Ohio)
2. Sean Watt (Iowa)
3. John Buxton (South Dakota)
4. Eric Akin (Kansas)
5. Erin Millsap (California)
6. Neil Kohlberg (Iowa)
7. (tie) Carey Falcone (New Jersey) and Scott Lathrop (Michigan)

114.5-lb class
1. Andy Radenbaugh (Michigan)
2. Jack Griffin (Illinois)
3. Scott Bates (Oklahoma)
4. Jeff Prescott (New York)
5. Terry Brands (Iowa)
6. Don Heckel (Oklahoma)
7. (tie) Keith Nix (Oklahoma) and Ben Mororis (Illinois)

123-lb class
1. Danny Knight (Iowa)
2. Danny Smith (New Jersey)
3. Paul Kuznik (Minnesota)
4. Thomas Brands (Iowa)
5. Salem Yaffai (Michigan)
6. Wayne McMinn (Minnesota)
7. (tie) Adam Disabato (Ohio) and Chol An (Washington)

132-lb class
1. Jeff Dernlan (Ohio)
2. T.J. Campbell (Montana)
3. Mark Marineleli (Ohio)
4. Tim Rothka (Pennsylvania)
5. Duaine Marati (Nebraska)
6. Troy Sunderland (Pennsylvania)
7. (tie) Eric Mendoza (Colorado) and T.J. Sewelel (Oklahoma)

143-lb class
1. Kenny Ramsey (Ohio)
2. Jimmy Sconce (Oklahoma)
3. Steve Hamilton (Iowa)
4. Eric Wilson (Oklahoma)
5. Gary Chaddock (Ohio)
6. Haig Brown (Oregon)
7. (tie) Jeff Gotcher (Washington) and Pat Smith (Oklahoma)

154-lb class
1. Mike Murdoch (Michigan)
2. Todd Chesbro (Oklahoma)
3. Brandon Dennington (California)
4. John Harms (Wisconsin)
5. Tim Briggs (California)
6. Mark Gerardi (California)
7. (tie) Scott Hovan (Pennsylvania) and Steve Yarbrough (New Mexico)

165-lb class
1. Derek Brophy (New York)
2. Marty Morgan (Minnesota)
3. Chris Kwortnick (Pennsylvania)
4. Greg Gardner (Illinois)
5. Sean Brunson (Oregon)
6. Tedd Russ (Georgia)
7. (tie) Mar Cheff (Montana) and Bryan Flint (Georgia)

178-lb class
1. Scott Chenoweth (Oklahoma)
2. Kurt York (Ohio)
3. Paul Keysaw (Pennsylvania)
4. Lance Markel (Pennsylvania)
5. Bob Hundertmark (Maryland)
6. Von Heohn (Massachusetts)
7. (tie) Greg Butteris (Iowa) and Pat Gentzler (Wyoming)

191.5-lb class
1. Billy Wagner (Virginia)
2. Fritz Lehrke (Wisconsin)
3. Scott Hamilton (Missouri)
4. Kirk Mamman (Illinois)
5. Mark Tice (California)
6. Perry Miller (Pennsylvania)
7. (tie) Eric Eggers (Iowa) and Don Finch (Iowa)

286-lb class
1. John Matyiko (Virginia)
2. Carl Presley (Illinois)
3. John Mororis (Virginia)
4. Dave Szott (New Jersey)
5. Tyler Cowans (Indiana)
6. Steve Lawso (California)
7. (tie) Jack Gallagher (Georgia) and Bart Lockward (New Jersey)

Outstanding Wrestler: Danny Knight (Iowa)

1986
Greco-Roman (Cedar Falls, IA)

Place winners

98-lb class
1. Sam Dollyhigh (Virginia)
2. Tony Purler (Missouri)
3. Nick Purler (Missouri)
4. Matt Bartett (Illinois)
5. Glen Nyquist (Illinois)
6. David Martinz (California)

105.5-lb class
1. Corey Jones (Kansas)
2. Erin Milsap (California)
3. Eric Akin (Kansas)
4. Eddie Lee (Iowa)
5. Ernie McNeal (Minnesota)
6. Jeff Vasquez (Georgia)

114.5-lb class
1. Bam Pustelnick (Illinois)
2. Keith Nix (Oklahoma)
3. Brett Dinovi (New Jersey)
4. Chuck Boyle (Connecticut)

5. Mike Pasdo (Illinois)
6. Scott Pegram (Ohio)

123-lb class
1. Danny Knight (Iowa)
2. Curtis Crims (Illinois)
3. Tom Best (Pennsylvania)
4. Patrick Higa (Hawaii)
5. Dennis Martinez (Illinois)
6. Mike Graham (Washington)

132-lb class
1. David Dameron (Michigan)
2. Phil Trimble (Indiana)
3. James Kennedy (Massachusetts)
4. Duaine Martin (Nebraska)
5. Lloyd Wurm (Minnesota)
6. Eric Trulock (Minnesota)

143-lb class
1. Jimmy Sconce (Oklahoma)
2. Shawn Critelli (Oregon)
3. Casey Graham (Virginia)
4. Mar Rogers (Illinois)
5. Keith Quint (Florida)
6. Todd Dunham (Colorado)

154-lb class
1. Steve Duvall (Minnesota)
2. Brandon Dennington (California)
3. Tom Henderson (California)
4. Roger Phillipi (Pennsylvania)
5. Ron Frank (New Jersey)
6. Shane Boucher (Washington)

165-lb class
1. Dan Russell (Oregon)
2. Warren MacNaughton (New York)
3. Marty Morogan (Minnesota)
4. Scott Edman (Illinois)
5. Chad Gentzler (Pennsylvania)
6. Ethan Bosch (New York)

178-lb class
1. Scott Brown (Virginia)
2. Rex Homan (Ohio)
3. Anton Kossankowski (Illinois)
4. Chris Shorot (Minnesota)
5. Rich Burgdolt (Pennsylvania)
6. Ramon Diaz (California)

191.5-lb class
1. Fritz Lehrke (Wisconsin)
2. Scott Hamilton (Missouri)
3. Jay Rogers (Washington)
4. Matt Mynster (Ohio)
5. Shawn Halal (Oregon)
6. Dennis Malecek (Iowa)

286-lb class
1. Carl Presley (Illinois)
2. Mike Smith (Washington)
3. Cam Strahm (Oregon)
4. Rich Kane (New York)
5. Mike Halac (Nebraska)
6. Tim Simpson (Illinois)

Outstanding Wrestler: David Dameron (Michigan)

1987
Freestyle (Cedar Falls, IA)

Place winners

98-lb class
1. T.J. Jaworsky (Oklahoma)
2. Jason Buxton (South Dakota)
3. Pat Tocci (Pennsylvania)
4. Geoff Glogas (Indiana)
5. Sam Henson (Missouri)
6. Salvadore Gomez (California)
7. Jeff Mirabella (Illinois)
8. Nick Melfi (New Jersey)

105.5-lb class
1. Dan Vidlak (Oregon)
2. Keith Ketcham (New Hampshire)
3. Burke Tyree (Montana)
4. Nick Purler (Missouri)
5. Jeff Vasquez (Georgia)
6. Alfonso Alcarez (Nevada)
7. Tony Purler (Missouri)
8. Anton Burckett

114.5-lb class
1. Jeffery Prescott (New York)
2. Donnie Heckel (Oklahoma)
3. George Chew (New Jersey)
4. John Buxton (South Dakota)
5. Ben Morris (Illinois)
6. Troy Steiner (Indiana)
7. Eric Akin (Kansas)
8. Tim Asher (Iowa)

123-lb class
1. Alan Fried (Ohio)
2. Adam Disabato (Ohio)
3. Terry Brands (Iowa)
4. Wayne McMinn (Arizona)
5. Thomas Brands (Iowa)
6. Marcus Gowens (Oklahoma)
7. Dennis Hall (Wisconsin)
8. Jeff Bedard (Georgia)

132-lb class
1. Tim Anderson (Iowa)
2. Chris Owens (Idaho)
3. Chuck Barbee (Oklahoma)
4. Jodie Wilson (Oklahoma)
5. Sean Bormet (Illinois)
6. Eric Mendoza (Colorado)
7. Lloyd Wurm (Minnesota)
8. Andy Hill (Colorado)

143-lb class
1. T.J. Campbell (Montana)
2. Steve Hamilton (Iowa)
3. Aaron Schetter (Ohio)
4. Troy Sunderland (Pennsylvania)
5. Peter Horst (Pennsylvania)
6. Ken Ramsey (Ohio)
7. Victor Saucedo (California)
8. Jamie Boyd (Michigan)

154-lb class
1. Mark Reiland (Iowa)
2. Todd Chesbro (Oklahoma)
3. Scott Hovan (Pennsylvania)
4. Todd Layton (Kansas)
5. David Myers (Colorado)
6. William Santiago (Vermont)
7. Greg Yager (Wisconsin)
8. Matt Johnson (Colorado)

165-lb class
1. Solomon Fleckman (Florida)
2. Mike Simons (Oregon)
3. Mark Geradi (California)
4. Roy Hall (Michigan)
5. Chris Kwortnik (Pennsylvania)
6. John Harms (Wisconsin)
7. Bill Stanbro (New York)
8. Rob Patton (Virginia)

178-lb class
1. Bart Chelesvig (Iowa)
2. Greg Butteris (Iowa)
3. Adam Mariano (New York)
4. Sean Brunson (Oregon)
5. Ricky Gullet (Florida)
6. John Tripp (California)
7. Chad Gentzler (Pennsylvania)
8. Rick Evans (Oregon)

191.5-lb class
1. Chris Short (Minnesota)
2. Don Finch (Iowa)
3. Matt Ruppel (Montana)
4. Pat Kelly (Iowa)
5. Philip Tomek (Illinois)
6. Bill Elvin (Kansas)
7. Scott Cubberly (Michigan)
8. Craig Lamont (Utah)

220-lb class
1. Jay Rogers (Washington)
2. Paul Haley (Massachusetts)
3. Patrick Halpin (New York)
4. Paul Thomas (Georgia)
5. Jamie Cutler (Iowa)
6. Kirk Mammen (Illinois)
7. Curt Engler (Iowa)
8. Greg Smith (Ohio)

275-lb class
1. Kurt Angle (Pennsylvania)
2. Carl Presley (Illinois)
3. John Morris (Virginia)
4. Ellery Mortenson (Oregon)
5. Marc Pawde (Arizona)
6. Quinton Gough (Maryland)

7. Gregory Rivera (Florida)
8. Tony Edwards (California)

Outstanding Wrestler: T.J. Campbell (Montana)

1987
Greco-Roman (Cedar Falls, IA)

Place winners

98-lb class
1. Sam Henson (Missouri)
2. Tim McQueen (Pennsylvania)
3. Jeff Mirabella (Illinois)
4. Bobby Janisse (Oregon)
5. Pat Gomez (Colorado)
6. Chris Perez (Colorado)
7. Ross Bruno (Illinois)
8. Scott Rollins (Oregon)

105.5-lb class
1. Nick Purler (Missouri) and Tony Purler (Missouri) co-champions
3. Eric Zertuche (Colorado)
4. Gonz Medina (Kansas)
5. Danny Lewis (Colorado)
6. Nick Salatino (Illinois)
7. John Calderon (New Jersey)
8. Tom Pardo (California)

114.5-lb class
1. Sam Geracic (Illinois)
2. Eric Akin (Kansas)
3. James Gruenwald (Wisconsin)
4. Tod Clinefelter (Idaho)
5. Corey Jones (Kansas)
6. Matt Bartlett (Illinois)
7. David Martinez (California)
8. Chris Ward (Oklahoma)

123-lb class
1. Denis Hall (Wisconsin)
2. Broderick Lee (Oregon)
3. Keith Stanford (Pennsylvania)
4. Mike Pankratz (South Dakota)
5. Marco Sanchez (California)
6. Brett Dinovi (New Jersey)
7. Mike Warnick (Pennsylvania)
8. Mark Oldhouse (Pennsylvania)

132-lb class
1. Jack Vatress (Oregon)
2. Tom Best (Pennsylvania)
3. Lloyd Wurn (Minnesota)
4. Weston Hardin (Kansas)
5. Chris Sabo (New York)
6. Jason Jones (Oregon)
7. Matt Lindland (Oregon)
8. Suk Kim (Virginia)

143-lb class
1. Ken Thompson (Illinois)
2. Ken Ramsey (Ohio)
3. Aaron Schetter (Ohio)
4. Mike Tegge (Illinois)
5. Jeff Sconce (Oklahoma)
6. John Sehnert (Illinois)
7. Jim Kennedy (Massachusetts)
8. Darren MacNaughton (New York)

154-lb class
1. Mark Reiland (Iowa)
2. Bert Gustafson (Florida)
3. Gary Witherspoon (Colorado)
4. Greg Yager (Wisconsin)
5. Jon Watson (Idaho)
6. Mike Swift (Pennsylvania)
7. Eric Lemaster (Indiana)
8. Dana Wilkes (Florida)

165-lb class
1. Solomon Fleckman (Florida)
2. Phil Hughes (New Jersey)
3. Tom Henderson (California)
4. Matt McDermott (Illinois)
5. Jess Macias (California)
6. John Trip (California)
7. Dave Malecek (Iowa)
8. Steven Williams (Florida)

178-lb class
1. Brad Knouse (Texas)
2. Rich Powers (Illinois)
3. Ethan Bosch (New York)

4. T.J. Wright (New York)
5. Rich Burgdolt (Pennsylvania)
6. Charlie Krantz (Nebraska)
7. Tom Socker (Pennsylvania)
8. Ric Spires (Indiana)

191.5-lb class
1. Rex Holman (Ohio)
2. Steve Utter (Oregon)
3. Pat Nelson (Minnesota)
4. Bill Cronmiller (New York)
5. Hamilton Munnell (Massachusetts)
6. Bill Elvin (Kansas)
7. Mark Kuehl (Illinois)
8. David Simmons (Iowa)

220-lb class
1. Jay Rogers (Washington)
2. Dave Marti (Iowa)
3. Todd Nelson (Illinois)
4. Greg Theobald (Wisconsin)
5. Ellery Mortenson (Oregon)
6. Ed Evans (Illinois)
7. Tom Mashek (Iowa)
8. Greg Smith (Ohio)

275-lb class
1. Carl Presley (Illinois)
2. Gregory Rivera (Florida)
3. Harry Thanos (Illinois)
4. Joe Cornelius (Florida)
5. Tim Edwards (Ohio)
6. Richard Kane (New York)
7. Bobby Henderson (Wyoming)
8. Robert Stine (Wisconsin)

Outstanding Wrestler: Jack Vantress (Oregon)

1988
Freestyle (Cedar Falls, IA)

Place winners

98-lb class
1. Scott Schlucter (Oklahoma)
2. Wade Gall (Oklahoma)
3. Frank Ingalls (Indiana)
4. Grant Patton (Minnesota)
5. Brian Kupusta (Pennsylvania)
6. Jeff Miller (Pennsylvania)
7. Larry Duran (New Mexico)
8. Chris Thatcher (Pennsylvania)

105.5-lb class
1. Alfonson Alcaraz (Nevada)
2. Bobby Janisse (Oregon)
3. Jason Buxton (South Dakota)
4. Eric Zertuche (Colorado)
5. Rico Jourdan (Oklahoma)
6. Bob Young (Missouri)
7. David Long (Virginia)
8. Jeff Stepanic (Pennsylvania)

114.5-lb class
1. Eric Akin (Kansas)
2. Tony Purler (Missouri)
3. Cale Sponsler (Iowa)
4. Burke Tyree (Missouri)
5. John Bove (Pennsylvania)
6. Shawn Nelson (Ohio)
7. Scott Dooley (Colorado)
8. John Crain (West Virginia)

123-lb class
1. Troy Steiner (North Dakota)
2. Marcus Gowens (Oklahoma)
3. Chad Zaputil (Iowa)
4. Sam Dollyhigh (Virginia)
5. Adam Di Sabato (Ohio)
6. Tim Gallagher (New Jersey)
7. Jody Staylor (Virginia)
8. Bob Simpson (Pennsylvania)

132-lb class
1. Alan Fried (Ohio)
2. Tim Anderson (Iowa)
3. Marco Sanchez (California)
4. Damon Johnson (Oklahoma)
5. Jeff Theiler (Iowa)
6. Wayne McMinn (Arizona)
7. Terry Steiner (North Dakota)
8. Darryl Holiday (Oregon)

143-lb class
1. Troy Sunderland (Pennsylvania)
2. Willy Short (Minnesota)
3. Steve Hartle (Iowa)
4. Sean Bormet (Illinois)
5. Anthony Camacho (Nevada)
6. Tony Piva (Idaho)

7. Randy Street (Missouri)
8. Matt Puckett (Indiana)

154-lb class
1. Pat Smith (Oklahoma)
2. Matt Johnson (Colorado)
3. Lenny Klinglesmith (Colorado)
4. Tom Onorato (Pennsylvania)
5. Torrae Jackson (Michigan)
6. Jamie Byrne (Iowa)
7. Brendan Matthew (South Dakota)
8. J.J. Stanbro (New York)

165-lb class
1. Dan Henderson (California)
2. Roy Hall (Michigan)
3. Pete Welch (New Jersey)
4. Pat Lynch (New Jersey)
5. Chris Kwortnik (Pennsylvania)
6. Ricky Gullett (Florida)
7. George Parker (Oklahoma)
8. Randy Hale (Virginia)

178-lb class
1. Adam Mariano (New York)
2. Brad Knouse (Texas)
3. Robert Zapata (California)
4. J.J. McGrew (Oklahoma)
5. Steven Medina (New Mexico)
6. Jason Loukides (Michigan)
7. Joel Sharratt (Minnesota)
8. Tony Freeman (New Mexico)

191.5-lb class
1. Rex Holman (Ohio)
2. Steve King (Minnesota)
3. Mark Trice (California)
4. Clay Woodward (Oregon)
5. Dan Troupe (Missouri)
6. Kyle Scrimgeour (Colorado)
7. Brett Sharp (Iowa)
8. Bill Elvin (Kansas)

220-lb class
1. Curt Engler (Iowa)
2. Jason Nelson (Colorado)
3. Lorenzo Neal (California)
4. Joe Cornelius (Florida)
5. Don Whipp (Michigan)
6. Kevin Brown (Maryland)
7. Kevin Schiltz (Minnesota)
8. David Boor (Oregon)

275-lb class
1. Mel Crosby (Pennsylvania)
2. Greg Rivera (Florida)
3. Quinton Gough (Maryland)
4. Todd Kinney (Iowa)
5. Brian Rose (Illinois)
6. Dale Simpson (Oklahoma)
7. Tony Barajas (California)
8. Jimmy Jefferson (Georgia)

Outstanding Wrestler: Eric Akin (Kansas)

1988
Greco-Roman (Cedar Falls, IA)

Place winners

98-lb class
1. Len Leonardi (New Jersey)
2. Chris Thatcher (Pennsylvania)
3. Wade Gall (Oklahoma)
4. Randy Miller (Pennsylvania)
5. Bob Chihoski (Illinois)
6. Scott Mendenhall (Indiana)
7. Chris Jordan (New Jersey)
8. Ted Bray (Ohio)

105.5 lb-class
1. Sam Henson (Missouri)
2. Scott Rollins (Oregon)
3. Pat Gomez (Colorado)
4. Tim Queen (Pennsylvania)
5. Corey Ricco (Wisconsin)
6. Duke DiJoseph (New Jersey)
7. Leo Pietrantuono (New Jersey)
8. Neal Shelby (Virginia)

114.5-lb class
1. Nick Purler (Missouri)
2. Tony Purler (Missouri)
3. Rob Prebish (Pennsylvania)
4. Duane Wilson (North Carolina)
5. Mark Eckenrode (Pennsylvania)
6. Tim Turner (Colorado)
7. Tim Gallagher (New Jersey)
8. Kasey Thomas (Wyoming)

123-lb class
1. Dennis Hall (Wisconsin)
2. James Gruenwald (Wisconsin)
3. Sam Dollyhigh (Virginia)

4. Javier Gonzales (California)
5. Jeff Vasquez (Georgia)
6. Ted Kacandes (New Jersey)
7. Ricky Williams (Missouri)
8. Bill Johnson (Washington)

132-lb class
1. Marco Sanchez (California)
2. Joe Block (Minnesota)
3. Gilbert Valerio (New Mexico)
4. Brett Fry (California)
5. Scott Eastman (Utah)
6. Matt Helm (Michigan)
7. Jason Jones (Oklahoma)
8. Pete Schulte (Illinois)

143-lb class
1. Tom Best (California)
2. Heath Sims (Pennsylvania)
3. Chris Saba (New York)
4. Jeff Sconce (Oklahoma)
5. Darren McNaughton (New York)
6. John Meyers (Connecticut)
7. Pat Morrissey (Colorado)
8. Scott Toothman (Iowa)

154-lb class
1. Aaron Schetter (Ohio)
2. Mike Schyck (Florida)
3. Brian Paramski (Illinois)
4. Corey Schroeder (New York)
5. Matt Doyle (Iowa)
6. Ray Brinzer (Pennsylvania)
7. Bobby Green (Minnesota)
8. Travis Smith (Florida)

165-lb class
1. Dan Henderson (California)
2. Gary Witherspoon (Washington)
3. Pete Welch (New Jersey)
4. Pat Lynch (New Jersey)
5. Trucker Waller (Illinois)
6. Ray Phillips (Illinois)
7. Ricky Gullet (Florida)
8. David Rogers (Texas)

178-lb class
1. Dan Ritchie (Illinois)
2. Rick Spires (Indiana)
3. Michael Mosley (New York)
4. Mark Menapace (Wyoming)
5. Robert Lockwood (Illinois)
6. Tony Cipollone (Pennsylvania)
7. Tom Socker (Pennsylvania)
8. Ethan Bosch (New York)

191.5-lb class
1. Rex Holman (Ohio)
2. Steve King (Minnesota)
3. Scott Wessley (Wisconsin)
4. Rusty Castetter (Indiana)
5. Dan Troup (Montana)
6. Mark Trice (California)
7. Clay Woodward (Oregon)
8. Eric Wisch (Illinois)

220-lb class
1. T.J. Wright (New York)
2. Tom Mashek (Iowa)
3. Lorenzo Neal (California)
4. Thomas Breeze (Arizona)
5. Edward Evans (Illinois)
6. Joe Cornelius (Florida)
7. Kevin Schiltz (Minnesota)
8. Shane Ooten (Washington)

275-lb class
1. Greg Rivera (Florida)
2. Bobby Henderson (Wyoming)
3. Jimmy Jefferson (Georgia)
4. Terry Smith (Wisconsin)
5. Rob Stine (Wisconsin)
6. Frank Wellman (Oregon)
7. Brian Rose (Illinois)
8. Mark Smith (California)

Outstanding Wrestler: Sam Henson (Missouri)

Chapter 11

The Junior World Tournaments

World tournaments are held at several levels other than those of the Olympics and Senior World Championships. A young wrestler can compete for a world title in the Espoir World Championships, the Junior World Wrestling Championships, or the University World Games.

The word *espoir* is derived from the French word for "aspirant" or "hopeful." In a wrestling sense, it pertains to the athletes in the 17-20 age group. From its inception in 1969, the international espoir program was known as "Junior World." However, following the 1980 Olympics in Moscow, FILA created a new division for wrestlers ages 17 and 18 and gave the name "Junior World" to that group. Subsequently, it needed to come up with a new name for the 17-20 age group, and the name "espoir" was selected.

Lock Haven, Pennsylvania, was the site of the first national espoir tournament in 1985. John Smith, who won the 136.5-pound title, was named Outstanding Wrestler. The first Greco-Roman nationals were held in Ann Arbor, Michigan, and Bubba Strauss, also at 136.5, was named Outstanding Wrestler.

The Espoir World Championships are held every 2 years on even-numbered years (see Table 11.1 on p. 431 and Table 11.2 on p. 438). The Junior World Tournament is held every 2 years on odd-numbered years.

The first Junior World Wrestling Championships were held July 18-19, 1969, at the University of Colorado in Boulder. The United States team was a smashing success, winning five gold medals in the freestyle competition. "The well-trained, top conditioned U.S. junior freestyle team not only beat the USSR juniors for the championship team trophy, but also edged them in individual competition 5-4-1," reported *Amateur Wrestling News* in its August 1969 edition.

Winning gold medals for the United States were Billy Martin (114.5) of Virginia Beach, Virginia; Larry Morgan (123) of Bakersfield, California; Rich Binek (165) of Waterloo, Iowa; Bill Bragg (178) of Fort Morgan, Colorado; and Mike Brundage (191.5) of Boulder. Silver medals went to Jim Bissell

(105.5) of Haslett, Michigan, and Larry Little (123) of Bakersfield, California, and bronze medals were won by Roger Duty (154) of Royal Oak, Michigan, and Jeff Jackson (heavyweight) of Rolling Hills, California.

The Soviets swept through the Greco-Roman competition with seven champions, and the other three went to Bulgaria. Heavyweight Alan Thompson of Orange, California, led the United States to a third-place team finish by taking a silver medal. Third-place finishers were all from Michigan: Billy Davids (105.5) of Hazel Park, Doug Willer (132) of Berkley, and Bill Eisenheimer (143) of Madison Heights.

The second Junior World meet was held in 1971 in Tokyo, and Berney Gonzales made history. The high school student from Madison, Michigan, pinned all five of his foes at 132 pounds to become the first American to win a gold medal at any international level of Greco-Roman wrestling (see Table 11.3 on p. 440).

The concept of a world university tournament became a reality in the 1960s, and the first World University Championships were held in 1968 in Istanbul, Turkey. Students between the ages of 17 and 28 who were enrolled in undergraduate or graduate programs were eligible to compete, but the United States did not participate.

Operating under very short notice, the United States sent just three wrestlers to the championships in 1968. They arrived on the scene just an hour before competition began and still managed to place third behind Bulgaria and Turkey. Richard Sofman (138.5) of Pennsylvania and Jason Smith (171.5) of Iowa State won gold medals, and Jess Lewis (heavyweight) of Oregon State earned a silver medal. Smith made such an impression by pinning his Bulgarian foe in the finals that he was carried around the stadium on the shoulders of admirers to a standing ovation.

The World University Games were first held in 1973 in Moscow, and wrestling was included among the sports. Wrestling was also included in 1977 and 1981. However, problems arose because American college rules are different from the international rules that the World University Games advocates. Due largely to the rules dilemma, the committee governing the World University Games has elected not to hold wrestling ever since the 1981 Games in Bucharest, Hungary (see Table 11.4 on p. 448).

Table 11.1
Espoir Nationals

1985
Freestyle (Lock Haven, PA)

Team	Points
1. Sunkist Kids	60
2. Hawkeye WC	30
3. Panther WC	27

Place winners

105.5-lb class
1. Eric Milsap (California Jets)
2. Danny McIntire (Talon WC)
3. Jeff Norton (Ohio)
4. Eric Miller (Pennsylvania)
5. Joe Herr (Wisconsin WC)
6. Michael Fingman (Golden Bears)

114.5-lb class
1. Jim Martin (Penn State WC)
2. Dan Buzza (Pennsylvania Grapplers)
3. Cory Baze (Sunkist Kids)
4. Dan Knight (Iowa)
5. Steve Harivel (Rock WC)
6. John Walizer (Pennsylvania)

125.5-lb class
1. John Regan (Hawkeye WC)
2. Laurence Jackson (California Jets)
3. Steve Knight (Hawkeye WC)
4. Bobby Malatesta (Panther WC)
5. Jeff Husick (Lock Haven)
6. Billy Broom (Orange Crush)

136.5-lb class
1. John Smith (Sunkist Kids)
2. Chip Park (Sunkist Kids)
3. Mike Hampton (Orange Crush)
4. Dave Kennedy (Athens)
5. Glenn Jarrett (Sunkist Kids)
6. Jeff Gibbons (Cyclone WC)

149.5-lb class
1. Kurt Shedenhelm (Panther WC)
2. Joe Russell (Oregon)
3. Tim Krieger (Cyclone WC)
4. Jeff Jordan (Wisconsin)
5. George Johnston (Ohio)
6. Mike Bevilacqua (New York)

163-lb class
1. Royce Alger (Iowa)
2. Jody Karam (Lock Haven)
3. David Lee (Sunkist Kids)
4. Jim Gressley (Sunkist Kids)
5. Doug Downs (Seagull)
6. Chris Rossman (Wildcat WC)

180.5-lb class
1. Mike VanArsdale (Cyclone WC)
2. Don Lullo (Wildcat WC)
3. David Held (Edinboro)
5. Mike Seckler (Penn State)
6. Eric Groenedaal (Edinboro)

198-lb class
1. Charlie Sheretz (Hawkeye WC)
2. Todd Seiler (Wisconsin)
3. Dale Freeman (Lock Haven)
4. Jerry Curby (Wolverine WC)
5. Andy Katz (Franklin and Marshall)
6. Bruce Wallace (Bloomsburg)

220-lb class
1. Rod Severn (Sunkist Kids)
2. Harold Pennycoff (Army)
3. Alex Koehler (Peninsula)
4. Bob Fisher (Lock Haven)
5. Bob Carpenito (Edinboro)

286-lb class
1. Tony Koontz (Panther WC)
2. Dean Hall (Sunkist Kids)
3. Ken Young (Washington)
4. Tim Moxley (Ohio)
5. Carleton Haselrig (Johnstown WC)
6. Mark Finley (Franklin and Marshall)

Outstanding Wrestler: John Smith. Most falls: Tim Krieger (5 in 3:44)

1985

Greco-Roman (Ann Arbor, MI)

Team	Points
1. Adirondack Three-Style WC	55
2. California Jets	38
3. Sunkist Kids	20

Place winners

105.5-lb class
1. Bam Pustelnik (Illinois)
2. Eric Millsap (California Jets)
3. Isaac Ramaswamy (ATWA)
4. David Zehnder (UA)

114.5-lb class
1. Dan Knight (Iowa)
2. Jim Sanchez (Wyoming)
3. Kevin Harvey (California Jets)
4. Ben Morris (unat)
5. Franklin Beck (Michigan)
6. Patrick Gianneto (ATWA)

125.5-lb class
1. Laurence Jackson (California Jets)
2. Tim Ige (California Jets)
3. Andre Harnitz (unat)
4. David Deluke (ATWA)
5. Anthony Crater (Black Cats)

136.5-lb class
1. Bubba Strauss (Ohio)
2. Arnold Brown (Michigan)
3. Ron Karns (Lock Haven)
4. Steve Fischbein (ATWA)
5. Greg Buehler (Tiger WC)
6. Tony Massaro (ATWA)

149.5-lb class
1. Joe Russell (Sunkist Kids)
2. John Fisher (Michigan)
3. Tim Obrochta (Wildcat WC)
4. Dave Zarichzny (unat)
5. Jim Sinadinos (Michigan)
6. Kannon Kares (Catfishtown WC)

163-lb class
1. Keith Massey (Panther WC)
2. Jace McKeighan (ATWA)
3. Jim Gioiosa (unat)
4. Tom Martinic (unat)
5. Joe Swanson (Navy)
6. Frank Maczewski (Central Michigan)

180.5-lb class
1. Tony Cook (Oklahoma)
2. Steve Hart (ATWA)
3. Jeff Seaney (Tillamook WC)
4. Todd Coutler (unat)
5. Steve Cantrell (USMC)
6. Roy Eisenhut (ATWA)

198-lb class
1. Jerry Curby (Wolverine WC)
2. Pat Whitcomb (Michigan)
3. Todd Seiler (Wisconsin)
4. Gene Faughman (ATWA)
5. Bill Blair (UA)

220-lb class
1. Chris Tironi (ATWA)
2. Rod Severn (Sunkist Kids)

286-lb class
1. Carleton Haselrig (Johnston WC)
2. Harold Pennycoff (Army)

Outstanding Wrestler: Bubba Strauss. Most Falls: Strauss (4 in 8:42)

1986

Freestyle (Las Vegas, NV)

Team	Points
1. Sunkist Kids	75
2. Penn State WC	38
3. California State (Fullerton)	36

Place winners

105.5-lb class
1. Tim Trimble (South Dakota)
2. Roger Bernstein (Brown)
3. Rob Eiter (Sunkist Kids)
4. Eric Falkins (Cougar WC)
5. Sam Tourville (Nevada WC)
6. Steve Sammons (MTWC)

114.5-lb class
1. Zeke Jones (Sunkist Kids)
2. Bo Steinbach (Sunkist Kids)
3. Cory Baze (Sunkist Kids)
4. Steve Martin (Hawkeye WC)
5. Alfonzo Barajas (Sunkist Kids)
6. Norman Spence (BMWC)

125.5-lb class
1. Ken Chertow (Penn State)
2. Jim Martin (Penn State)
3. Dan Evenson (Wisconsin)
4. Steve Morris (Sunkist Kids)
5. Kevin Harvey (California State, Fullerton)
6. Lyndon Campbell (California State, Fullerton)

136.5-lb class
1. Laurence Jackson (Sunkist Kids)
2. Tom Fitzpatrick (Wisconsin)
3. Marty Calder (MTWC)
4. Bubba Strauss (Hawkeye WC)
5. Tim Ige (California State, Fullerton)
6. Scott Glenn (Oregon)

149.5-lb class
1. Scott Shumm (Utah)
2. Chris Lenbeck (Panther WC)
3. Mike Bevilacqua (Penn State)
4. Tom Henderson (California State, Fullerton)
5. Brian Dolph (Hoosier WC)
6. Jerry Durso (Irish WC)

163-lb class
1. John Heffernan (Hawkeye WC)
2. Joe Pantaleo (Cliff Keen)
3. Dan Russell (Sunkist Kids)
4. E.C. Muellhaupt (Bruin WC)
5. Dan Niebuhr (Wisconsin)
6. Jim Pearson (Hoosier WC)

180.5-lb class
1. Dave Lee (Sunkist Kids)
2. Brad Lloyd (Lock Haven)
3. John Ginther (Sunkist Kids)
4. Chris Barnes (Sunkist Kids)
5. Erik Duus (Hawkeye WC)
6. Chris Genser (Irish WC)

198-lb class
1. Andy Voit (Penn State)
2. Mike Farrell (Sunkist Kids)
3. Darrell Long (Panther WC)
4. Brian Jackson (Sunkist Kids)
5. Mark Whitehead (Wildcat WC)
6. Borislaw Kochey (Little WC)

220-lb class
1. Andy Haman (Hawkeye WC)
2. Steve Lawson (California State, Fullerton)
3. David Beneteau (MTWC)
4. Jim Poe (Kalisfell WC)
5. Brian Krasowski (Wisconsin WC)

286-lb class
1. Carleton Haselrig (Pennsylvania)
2. Tom Crawford (California State, Fullerton)
3. LeeRoy Ligons (Utah)
4. Andrew Borodow (Canada)
5. Paul Miamingos (Palomar)
6. John Miller (Corning)

Outstanding Wrestler: Zeke Jones. Most falls: Scott Shumm (5 in 7:02)

1986
Greco-Roman (La Crosse, WI)

Team	Points
1. Minnesota WC	93
2. Adirondack Three-Style WC	32

Place winners

105.5-lb class
1. Ernie McNeal (Minnesota)
2. Roni Yarkin (NYAC)
3. Isaac Ramaswamy (ATWA)

114.5-lb class
1. Bam Pustelnik (Demons)
2. Jim Sanchez (Wyoming)
3. Todd Enger (Minnesota)

4. Jeff Serriler (Minnesota)
5. Jeff LaMountain (ATWA)

125.5-lb class
1. Lyndon Campbell (California State, Fullerton)
2. Andy Swanson (USA Oregon)
3. Rich Douglas (Minnesota)
4. Dan Honsey (Minnesota)

136.5-lb class
1. Laurence Jackson (California State, Fullerton)
2. Shawn Critelli (USA Oregon)
3. Bubba Strauss (Hawkeye WC)
4. Paul Walker (NYAC)
5. Jeff Marcks (Panther WC)
6. Geoff Johnson (Wisconsin)

149.5-lb class
1. George Johnston (Sunkist Kids)
2. Gordy Morgan (Minnesota)
3. T.J. Saunders (Sunkist Kids)
4. Brad Schafer (Minnesota)
5. Steve Kimpel (Wisconsin)

163-lb class
1. Marty Morgan (Minnesota)
2. James Gioiosa (Michigan)
3. Warren McNaughton (ATWA)
4. Scott Kluever (Wisconsin)
5. Mark Mereles (Pennsylvania)
6. Curt Fossum (Wisconsin)

180.5-lb class
1. Chris Short (Minnesota)
2. Brian Flygare (Minnesota)
3. Fritz Lehrke (Wisconsin)
4. Dan Niebuhr (Wisconsin)
5. James Nelson (Wisconsin)
6. Kurt Olson (Wisconsin)

198-lb class
1. Todd Seiler (Wisconsin)
2. Darrel Long (Panther WC)
3. Mike McDowell (ATWA)

220-lb class
1. Richard Kane (ATWA)
2. Jason Chiles (Minnesota)

286-lb class
1. Jim Richardson (Minnesota), unopposed

Outstanding Wrestler: Laurence Jackson.
Most falls: Marty Morgan (3 in 5:53)

1987
Freestyle (Las Vegas, NV)

Team	*Points*
1. Sunkist	57
2. Wildcat WC	24

Place winners

105.5-lb class
1. Erin Millsap (California Jets)
2. Rob Eiter (Sunkist Kids)
3. Keith Ketcham (NYAC)
4. Roger Burnstein (Bruin WC)
5. Eric Folkins (Gopher WC)
6. Sam Atourville (Nevada WC)

114.5-lb class
1. George Chew (NYAC)
2. Bob LaFranco (Bloomsburg State)
3. Charles Iick (California Jets)
4. David Range (Buckeye WC)
5. Pat Higa (Utah State)
6. Flint J. Yale (Navy)

125.5-lb class
1. Ichiro Saski (Japan)
2. Dan Evensen (Wisconsin)
3. Kendall Cross (Sunkist Kids)
4. Duane Martin (Panther WC)
5. Kevin Harvey (Southern California WC)
6. Gary McCall (Iowa)

136.5-lb class
1. Hiag Brown (Sunkist Kids)
2. Shon Lewis (Sunkist Kids)
3. David Zuniga (Sunkist Kids)
4. Kevin Ramsey (Ohio)
5. Scott Glenn (Lehigh)
6. John Epperly (Hawkeye WC)

149.5-lb class
1. Brian Dolph (Hoosier WC)
2. Dan St. John (Arizona)
3. Mike Carpenter (Hawkeye WC)
4. Larry Gotcher (Cliff Keen)

5. Richard Baily (California State, Bakersfield)
6. Chris Wilson (BMWC)

163-lb class
1. Joe Pantaleo (Cliff Keen)
2. Craig Holiday (Wisconsin)
3. Wes White (Sunkist Kids)
4. Wade Zimmerman (Sunkist Kids)
5. Derek Brophy (Lehigh)
6. Brad Traviola (Wildcat WC)

180.5-lb class
1. Steve Lawson (Army)
2. Mike Funk (Wildcat WC)
3. Chris Short (Minnesota)
4. Neal Chriss (Wildcat WC)
5. Scott Chenoweth (Husker WC)
6. Fritz Lehrke (Cliff Keen)

198-lb class
1. Mark Whitehead (Wildcat WC)
2. Manabu Nakanishi (unat)
3. Brian Jackson (unat)
4. Brooks Simpson (Hawkeye WC)
5. Scott Holman (unat)
6. Matt Ruppel (unat)

220-lb class
1. Dave Beneteau (Vancouver)
2. Gregory Haladay (Penn State)
3. Brian Krasowski (Wyoming)
4. Eric Schultz (Buckeye WC)
5. Jim Poe (Wyoming)
6. Ralph Staley (Bruin WC)

286-lb class
1. Jeff Balcom (Gopher WC)
2. David Jones (Southern California)
3. Jeff Thue (Canada)
4. Jeff Russell (Mesa)
5. Scott Wightman (Mesa, AZ)
6. Randy Gonzales (Cypress)

1987
Greco-Roman (Schenectady, NY)

Team	Points
1. Adirondack Three-Style WC	72
2. Cliff Keen	48

Place winners

105.5-lb class
1. Issac Ramaswamy (ATWA)
2. Frank Fronhofer (ATWA)
3. Dan Vidlak (Sunkist Kids)
4. Pat Leamy (ATWA)
5. Jeff Brewer (Lasers)
6. Sam Cruz (Casita Maria)

114.5-lb class
1. Flin Yale (Navy)
2. Van Fronhofer (ATWA)
3. Mike Leamy (ATWA)
4. Steve Mitola (ATWA)
5. Eric Brown (ATWA)

125.5-lb class
1. Salem Yaffai (Cliff Keen)
2. Vinny Innes (Mohawk)
3. Keith Sanford (FCFC)
4. Marco Sanchez (Sunkist Kids)
5. Angelo DiJoseph (Sea Gull)
6. Davie McCollom (ATWA)

136.5-lb class
1. David Dameron (Cliff Keen)
2. Paul Walker (Wisconsin)
3. Shawn Critelli (USA Oregon)
4. James Goswick (Navy)
5. Darren MacNaughton (ATWA)
6. Chris Saba (unat)

149.5-lb class
1. Travis West (Portland)
2. Davie Mendelsohn (Montreal)
3. Frank Dugo (Navy)
4. Chip Cowles (ATWA)
5. Harry Wigler (Long Island)

163-lb class
1. Justin Stewosk (Cliff Keen)
2. Mike Cronmiller (Rochester, NY)
3. Chris Zogby (ATWA)
4. Warren MacNaughton (ATWA)
5. Chris Graham (Michigan)
6. Mike Mosley (ATWA)

180.5-lb class
1. Steve Lawson (Army)
2. Marty Morgan (Minnesota)
3. Gavin Green (unat)

4. T.J. Wright (ATWA)
5. Jim Marker (Sea Gull)
6. Mike Casanovas (Casida Maria)

198-lb class
1. Fritz Lehrke (Cliff Keen)
2. Bill Cronmiller (unat)
3. Daniel Jaffrie (Montreal)

220-lb class
1. Cam Strahm (Sunkist Kids)
2. Alan Gordon (ATWA)
3. Dave Waring (ATWA)

286-lb class
1. Andy Borrow (Montreal)
2. Harold Bucher (unat)
3. Kenyatta Townsend (Casida Maria)
4. Richard Kane (ATWA)

Outstanding Wrestler: Travis West. Most falls: Justin Stewosk (4 in 4:49)

1988
Freestyle (Reno, NV)

Team	Points
1. Sunkist Kids	54
2. California Jets	40

Place winners

105.5-lb class
1. Jeff Brewer (Nevada)
2. Sam Tourville (Nevada)
3. Andy Fabins (Canada)
4. Gary LaBreck (unat)
5. Imran Akhtar (Canada)

114.5-lb class
1. Erin Millsap (California Jets)
2. Keith Ketcham (NYAC)
3. Jayson Johnstone (California Jets)
4. Tom Prado (unat)
5. Anthony Tamez (Sunkist Kids)
6. Eric Folkins (Gopher WC)

125.5-lb class
1. Kendall Cross (Sunkist Kids)
2. Terry Brands (Hawkeye WC)
3. Dan Knight (Cyclone)
4. Bobby Demeritt (unat)
5. Dan Flood (Foxcatcher)
6. Doug Kittleson (Foxcatcher)

136.5-lb class
1. Chuck Barbee (Sunkist Kids)
2. Mike Donovan (Wyoming)
3. Tom Brands (Hawkeye WC)
4. Ronnie Pino (USMC)
5. Craig Roberts (Canada)
6. Robert Stone (Oregon)

149.5-lb class
1. Todd Chesbro (Sunkist Kids)
2. Jeff Lyons (Hoosier WC)
3. Adam Caldwell (Hoosier WC)
4. Luke Collison (Canada)
5. Layne Billings (Lincoln C)
6. Doug Striecker (Hawkeye WC)

163-lb class
1. Matt Demeray (Foxcatcher)
2. Mark Reiland (Hawkeye WC)
3. John Harms (Foxcatcher)
4. David Myers (Wyoming)
5. Mike Kelly (Cyclone WC)
6. Bob Thompson (Cyclone WC)

180.5-lb class
1. Solomon Fleckman (NYAC)
2. Mike McHenry (Indiana)
3. Darrin Farrell (NYAC)
4. Justin Abdou (Canada)
5. Joe Wypiszzenski (unat)
6. Marty Morgan (unat)

198-lb class
1. Chris Short (Gopher WC)
2. Curt Strahm (Oregon)
3. Matt Ruppel (NYAC)
4. Kirk Mammen (Sunkist Kids)
5. Rick Ravalin (California Jets)
6. Rich Powers (Panther WC)

220-lb class
1. Kurt Angle (Clarion State)
2. Jamie Cutler (Cyclone WC)
3. Fred Miller (Buckeye WC)
4. Cam Strahm (Sunkist Kids)
5. Dean Kelly (Canada)
6. Dave Shaver (Canada)

286-lb class
1. David Jones (California Jets)
2. Jeff Thue (Oklahoma Underdogs)
3. Mark Padwe (Penn State)
4. John Morris (NYAC)
5. Jeff Balcom (Gopher WC)
6. Tom Osendorf (California Jets)

Outstanding Wrestler: Solomon Fleckman. Most falls: Kendall Cross (4 in 7:15)

1988
Greco-Roman (Cedar Rapids, IA)

Team	*Points*
1. California Jets	57
2. Minnesota WC	52

Place winners

105.5-lb class
1. Pat Tocci (Gold Medal)
2. Ross Bruno (unat)
3. Jeff Brewer (Nevada)

114.5-lb class
1. Erin Millsap (California Jets)
2. LeLand Payne (USMC)
3. Damon Olson (Army)
4. Tourdj Derangi (California Jets)

125.5-lb class
1. Dan Knight (Cyclone WC)
2. Ray Leonard (California Jets)
3. Richard Douglas (Minnesota)
4. Rob Dills (unat)
5. David Kelly (USMC)
6. Jim Forgush (unat)

136.5-lb class
1. Bam Pustelnik (Panther WC)
2. Ronnie Pino (USMC)
3. Heath Sims (California Jets)
4. Bret Fry (California Jets)
5. Brian Doyle (USMC)
6. Rod Price (Michigan)

149.5-lb class
1. Todd Enger (Minnesota)
2. Andy Lentz (Minnesota)
3. Anthony Geyer (USMC)
4. Lloyd Wurm (Minnesota)
5. Jay Petrulis (unat)

163-lb class
1. Mark Reiland (Hawkeye WC)
2. Dan Henderson (NYAC)
3. Mark Miley (Minnesota)
4. Peter Varmette (Cyclone WC)

180.5-lb class
1. Marty Morgan (Minnesota)
2. Tom Kirpach (Minnesota)
3. Jason Christenson (unat)
4. Chris Pamsdill (ATWA)
5. Ed Preston (USMC)
6. Pat Jones (California Jets)

198-lb class
1. David Simmons (unat)
2. Michael Snyder (USMC)

220-lb class
1. Cam Strahm (Sunkist Kids)
2. Sean Morrison (California Jets)

286-lb class
1. Michael Anderson (Sunkist Kids)
2. Vince Plymire (California Jets)
3. Andy Samann (Greenville)
4. Robert Bucher (unat)

Outstanding Wrestler: Erin Millsap. Most falls: Ray Leonard (3 in 6:06)

Table 11.2
World Espoir Championships: United States Results

Name	Class	Place
1983 Freestyle (Anaheim, CA)		
Billy Ramos	105.5	
Steve Brown	114.5	5
Ed Giese	125.5	6
Greg Randall	136.5	4
Jim Heffernan	149.5	2
Chris Bevilacqua	163	
Rico Chiapparelli	180.5	
Paul Diekel	198	2
Scott Sabo	220	3
Gary Albright	Heavyweight	2
Russ Hellickson, coach (Team placed 3rd)		
1983 Greco-Roman (Kirstiansund, Norway)		
Shawn Sheldon	105.5	5
Jeff Clark	114.5	
Tony Massaro	125.5	
John Placek	136.5	
Jon Cardi	149.5	
Alan Marwill	163	
Jake Sabo	180.5	
Chris Tironi	198	
Scott Sabo	220	
Gary Albright	Heavyweight	3
Joe DeMeo, coach (Team placed 12th)		
1985 Freestyle (Colorado Springs, CO)		
Eric Milsap	105.5	
Mark Schwab	114.5	5
Ken Chertow	125.5	6
John Smith	136.5	3
Peter Yozzo	149.5	7
David Lee	163	
Craig Costello	180.5	5

Name	Class	Place
Charlie Sheretz	198	5
Mark Finley	220	7
Dean Hall	286	4
Gary Keck and Tim Cysewski, coaches (Team placed 5th)		

1985 Greco-Roman (Colorado Springs, CO)

Name	Class	Place
Bam Pustelnik	105.5	7
No entry	114.5	
No entry	125.5	
Bubba Strauss	136.5	7
No entry	149.5	
No entry	163	
No entry	180.5	
Todd Seiler	198	6
Chris Tirone	220	4
Carleton Haselrig	286	4
Dan Jacobson and Rodger Jehlicka, coaches (Team placed 9th)		

1987 Freestyle (Burnaby, British Columbia

Name	Class	Place
Erin Milsap	105.5	2
Pat Higa	114.5	4
Jack Griffin	125.5	
Joe Bales	136.5	4
Brian Dolph	149.5	5
Joe Pantaleo	163	1
Mike Funk	180.5	9
Mark Whitehead	198	3
Brooks Simpson	220	5
Jeff Balcolm	286	7
Mark Johnson and John Azevedo, coaches (Team placed 3rd)		

Name	Class	Place
1987 Greco-Roman (Burnaby, British Columbia)		
Isaac Ramaswamy	105.5	7
Ernie McNeal	114.5	8
Bam Pustelnik	125.5	10
Shawn Critelli	136.5	9
Travis West	149.5	
Eric Messner	163	10
Marty Morgana	180.5	7
Fritz Lherke	198	
Roger Neff	220	7
Harold Bucher	286	8
Dan Jacobson and Rob Hermann, coaches (Team placed 10th)		

Table 11.3

Junior World Tournament: United States Results

Name	Class	Place
1969 Freestyle (Colorado Springs, CO)		
Jim Bissell	105.5	2
Billy Martin	114.5	1
Larry Morgan	123	1
Larry Little	132	2
Bob Tscholl	143	4
Roger Duty	154	3
Rich Binek	165	1
Bill Bragg	178	1
Mike Brundage	191.5	1
Jeff Jackson	Heavyweight	3
Bill Weick, coach (Team placed 1st)		

Name	Class	Place
1969 Greco-Roman (Colorado Springs, CO)		
Billy Davids	105.5	3
Chris Sones	114.5	5
Bernard Gonzales	123	5
Doug Willer	132	3
Bill Eisenheimer	143	3
Vern Brecke	154	5
Mike Jones	165	5
Mal Poemoceah	178	5
Steve Clark	191.5	3
Alan Thompson	Heavyweight	2
Ron Finley, coach (Team placed 3rd)		
1971 Freestyle (Tokyo, Japan)		
Paul Bartlett	105.5	3
Jim Brown	114.5	
Ron Glass	123	3
Andre Allen	132	5
Dennis Graham	143	3
Robert Hoffman	154	6
Alan Albright	165	3
Ed Vatch	178	3
Tony Sidoti	191.5	3
Mark Bittick	Heavyweight	1
Jack Stanbo and Richard Leffler, coaches (Team placed 3rd)		
1971 Greco-Roman (Tokyo, Japan)		
Kerry Bolen	105.5	3
Dan Mello	114.5	2
Jim Sweeney	123	
Berney Gonzales	132	1
Randy Powers	143	6
Rick Benz	154	5
Robin Richards	165	2
Wes Hines	178	4
Dave Severson	191.5	5

Name	Class	Place
Ray King	Heavyweight	4
Joe Seay and David Abraham, coaches (Team placed 4th)		
1973 Freestyle (Miami Beach, FL)		
Dennis Brighton	105.5	3
Jim Brown	114.5	2
Jimmy Carr	125.5	1
Brad Smith	136.5	4
Chuck Yagla	149.5	2
Joe Carr	163	2
Tom Jackson	180.5	3
David Curby	198	4
John Bowlsby	220	5
Chuck Coryea	Heavyweight	3
Gene Davis, coach (Team placed 3rd)		
1973 Greco-Roman (Miami Beach, FL)		
Bill Rosado	105.5	5
Steve Pivac	114.5	
Dan Mello	125.5	6
Ron Boucher	136.5	
Kenneth Williams	149.5	5
Dennis Graham	163	5
Steve Jentzen	180.5	5
Mike Bull	198	(Injured)
Robert Walker	220	4
Bruce Conger	Heavyweight	4
Gil Sanchez and Gary Bandelean, coaches (Team placed 7th)		
1975 Freestyle (Haskovo, Bularia)		
Bill Rosado	105.5	5
Mike McArthur	114.4	
Jimmy Carr	125.5	5

Name	Class	Place
Benji Williams	136.5	
George Espinosa	149.5	(Injured)
Lee Kemp	163	(Injured)
Mark Lieberman	180.5	
Harold Smith	198	
Larry Bilenberg	220	3
John Bowlsby	Heavyweight	5
Don Murray, coach (Team placed 12th)		
1975 Greco-Roman (Haskovo, Bulgaria)		
Kirby Frank	105.5	
Gary Ellpley	114.4	
Bob Trapino	125.5	
Randy Robinson	136.5	
Steve Egesdal	149.5	
Kevin Kramer	163	
Randy Besaw	180.5	
Scott Ecklund	198	
Keith Nelson	220	6
Ray Slizewski	Heavyweight	4
Ron Johnson, coach (Team placed 13th)		
1977 Freestyle (Las Vegas, NV)		
Bobby Weaver	105.5	2
Bill DePaoli	114.5	2
Randy Lewis	125.5	1
Andre Metzger	136.5	3
Scott Bliss	149.5	6
Mark Churella	163	1
Colin Kilrain	180.5	5
Dan Severn	198	1
Jeff Blatnick	220	3
Steve Duerst	Heavyweight	6
Bill Weick, coach (Team placed 2nd)		

Name	Class	Place
1977 Greco-Roman (Las Vegas, NV)		
Greg Williams	105.5	
Mike Farina	114.5	
Chris Roos	125.5	
John Parisella	136.5	
Mike Salizar	149.5	
Dan Zilverberg	163	
Steve Fraser	180.5	5
Mitch Hull	198	4
David Jack	220	5
George Moskowite	Heavyweight	4
Joe DeMeo, coach (Team placed 7th)		
1979 Freestyle (Ulan Bator, Mongolia)		
Bill Kelly	105.5	6
Randy Willingham	114.5	3
Jeff Kerber	125.5	4
Randy Lewis	136.5	
Roger Frizzell	149.5	4
Mark Schultz	163	
Dave Schultz	180.5	6
Craig Blackman	198	6
Mike Evans	220	4
Ken Chamberlain	Heavyweight	4
Bill Weick, coach (No team scoring)		
1979 Greco-Roman (Haparanda, Sweden)		
Scott Reavis	105.5	
Wilfredo Leiva	114.5	
Frank Famiano	125.5	
John Monolakis	136.5	
Michael Johnson	149.5	
Loren Jenkins	163	
Jim Hall	180.5	
Mike Houck	198	
Ernie Velton	220	

Name	Class	Place
Rick Chandler	Heavyweight	
Ed Yarovinski, coach (Team did not place)		

1981 Freestyle (Vancouver, British Columbia)

Name	Class	Place
Tim Vanni	105.5	
Joe Mallet	114.5	5
Barry Davis	125.5	2
Mark Trizzino	136.5	3
Mark Manning	149.5	
Jim Zalesky	163	
Bill Scherr	180.5	2
Pete Bush	198	2
Khalan O'Hara	220	3
Larry Hamilton	Heavyweight	2
Jim Humphrey and Russ Hellickson, coaches (Team placed 3rd)		

1981 Greco-Roman (Vancouver, British Columbia)

Name	Class	Place
Bill Fuller	105.5	1
No entry	114.5	
Frank Famiano	125.5	5
Cliff Gosse	136.5	5
Andrew Seras	149.5	
Murray Crews	163	4
Bill Maresh	180.5	5
Phil Lanzatella	198	
Morris Johnson	220	3
Curt Olson	Heavyweight	4
Lee Allen and Bill Martell, coaches (Team placed 4th)		

1983 Freestyle (Oak Lawn, IL)

Name	Class	Place
Chris Bollin	105.5	3
Cory Baze	114.5	2

Name	Class	Place
Joe Melchiore	123	1
John Smith	132	2
Eddie Borror	143	
Royce Alger	154	2
Mike VanArsdale	165	2
Jimmy Gressley	178	3
Jeff Curby	191.5	3
Jeff Glenn	Heavyweight	2
Al Bevilacqua and Joe Wells, coaches (Team placed 2nd)		
1983 Greco-Roman (Oak Lawn, IL)		
Bobby Malatesta	105.5	3
Doug Stanford	114.5	
Pat Fitzgerald	123	6
David Olmsted	132	1
Sean Finkbeiner	143	
Jody Karam	154	6
Daemon Knight	165	4
Seann Henry	178	5
Greg Zwilling	191.5	3
Tony Koontz	Heavyweight	3
Dan Jacobson, coach (Team placed 3rd)		
1984 Freestyle (Washington, DC)		
Chris Bollin	105.5	1
Cory Baze	114.4	2
Ken Chertow	123	1
John Fisher	132	1
Lenny Bernstein	143	1
Stan Proctor	154	5
Chris Geneser	165	1
John Ginther	178	1
Dave Williams	191.5	2
Jeff Ellis	Heavyweight	1
Steve Szabo, coach (Team placed 1st)		

Name	Class	Place
1984 Greco-Roman (Washington, DC)		
Kurt Howell	105.5	
Dan Knight	114.5	6
Bobby Malatesta	123	2
Mike Leaman	132	3
Tim Obrachta	143	4
Chris Pencarski	154	2
Fritz Lehrke	165	3
Larry Thompson	178	4
Dave Barbour	191.5	2
William Krantz	Heavyweight	4
Greg Zavala, coach (Team placed 3rd)		
1986 Freestyle (Schifferstadt, West Germany)		
Keith Ketchum	105.5	
Sam Ceraci	114.5	
Kendall Cross	125.5	3
Reagan Hicks	136.5	
David Zuniga	149.5	5
Tobin Roitsch	163	
Bart Chelsvig	180.5	
Brad Knouse	198	5
Matthew Rupple	220	2
Todd Nelson	286	
Robin Ersland and Tom Hutchinson, coaches (Team did not place)		
1986 Greco-Roman (Schifferstadt, West Germany)		
Tommy Gabaldo	105.5	
Sam Ceraci	114.5	
Kelly Acosta Miller	125.5	
Shannon Ward	136.5	
Ken Thompson	149.5	
Mark Reiland	163	
Steve Lander	180.5	

Name	Class	Place
Joe Reasbeck	198	
Joe Luecke	220	
Todd Nelson	286	
Tom Hutchinson and Robin Ersland, coaches (Team did not place)		

Table 11.4
World University Tournament: United States Results

Name	Class	Place
1968 Freestyle (Istanbul, Turkey)		
Richard Sofman	138.5	1
Jason Smith	171.5	1
Jess Lewis	Heavyweight	2
Steve Evanoff, coach (Team placed 3rd)		
1973 Freestyle (Moscow, USSR)		
Joe Cliffe	105.5	6
Stan Opp	114.5	6
Don Behm	125.5	5
Jim Humphrey	136.5	
Rich Lawinger	149.5	3
Jeff Callard	163	4
Bill Reinboldt	180.5	
Floyd Hitchcock	198	2
Buck Deadrich	220	2
Gary Ernst	Heavyweight	6
LeRoy Alitz, coach (Team placed 4th)		

Name	Class	Place
1973 Greco-Roman (Moscow, USSR)		
Larry Horton	105.5	6
Chris Sones	114.5	3
Billy Davids	125.5	3
Mark Davids	136.5	5
Doug Wiler	149.5	
Gary Neist	163	
Mike Bradley	180.5	6
Wes Hines	198	5
Ken Levels	220	3
John Major	Heavyweight	4
Ron Finley, coach (Team placed 4th)		
1977 Freestyle (Sofia, Bulgaria)		
Bobby Weaver	105.5	4
Mark Mysnyk	114.5	7
Ron Castles	125.5	(Injured)
Dan Mello	136.5	
Benje Williams	149.5	7
Wade Schalles	163	1
Mark Lieberman	180.5	4
Ron Jeidy	198	5
Steve Day	220	4
John Bowlsby	Heavyweight	5
Willie Myers, coach (Team placed 5th)		
1977 Greco-Roman (Sofia, Bulgaria)		
Gregg Williams	105.5	(Injured)
Keith Whelan	114.5	
David Clardy	125.5	
John Hughes	136.5	5
Tihamer Toth-Fejel	149.5	
James Andre	163	
Mark Johnson	180.5	4
Keith Nelson	198	

Name	Class	Place
John Major	220	
Ralph Zigner	Heavyweight	3
Ron Bessner, coach (Team placed 8th)		
1981 Freestyle (Bucharest, Romania)		
Richard Salamone	105.5	6
Wade Genova	114.5	6
David Cook	125.5	4
Mike Land	136.5	2
Bill Nugent	149.5	5
Dave Schultz	163	2
Jim Scherr	180.5	4
Mitch Hull	198	3
Steve Wilbur	220	6
Bruce Baumgartner	Heavyweight	1
Bill Weick, coach (Team placed 2nd)		
1981 Greco-Roman (Bucharest, Romania)		
Mark Fuller	105.5	4
Eric Seward	114.5	
Brian Canali	125.5	
Frank Famiano	136.5	4
Scott Bliss	149.5	4
Mike Johnson	163	5
Tom Press	180.5	4
Phil Lanzatella	198	4
Morris Johnson	220	
Scott Dunley	Heavyweight	
Lee Allen, coach (Team placed 5th)		

Chapter 12

Special Honors and Awards

Through the decades various wrestling organizations have honored individuals in the sport for memorable achievements. In 1958, *Amateur Wrestling News* began selecting its Coach of the Year (see Table 12.1). In 1969, *Amateur Wrestling News* turned the process over to the National Wrestling Coaches Association.

The group also began selecting different categories of Coach of the Year as the NCAA changed its structure, branching off into size divisions. In 1983, it began picking an Assistant Coach of the Year. The NAIA and the junior colleges began picking a Coach of the Year in 1963 and 1965, respectively (see Table 12.2).

In 1960, *Amateur Wrestling News* began recognizing writers across the nation who had given special attention to the sport. Bob Dellinger, then the sports editor of the *Oklahoman and Times* newspaper, was selected Wrestling Writer of the Year the first 3 years the award was offered. In 1963, *Amateur Wrestling News* renamed the award in his honor.

The Man of the Year award began in 1962. *Amateur Wrestling News* conceived it as a means of honoring the person who did the most in the course of a year to advance the cause of the sport.

USA Wrestling began honoring its top coach, athlete, official, and man of the year in 1971, when the organization was still known as the USWF.

The AAU has also recognized various achievers through the years but has been inconsistent in the effort, and a complete list of award winners is no longer available.

In 1975, USA Wrestling began its Championship Ring Series. The ring is awarded after each year's competition to the Grand Champion, the athlete who has scored the most points throughout the season.

World champion Lee Kemp was the first winner of the Sun Company Cup, initiated in 1978 to honor the nation's top international-style wrestler. The Sun Company of Radnor, Pennsylvania, offered the award in cooperation with the national AAU coaching staff. Other winners were Bobby Weaver and Andre Metzger (1979), Ben Peterson (1980), and Greg Gibson (1981). The award was discontinued in 1982.

The James E. Sullivan award has come to represent the highest honor an amateur athlete can attain outside the arena of competition. Conceived in 1930, the award is named after one of the founders of the AAU. The roll call of legendary athletes who have won the award includes such champions as Bob Mathias, Mark Spitz, and Bruce Jenner.

As of 1988, no wrestler had ever won the award. Although final placings are not officially released, wrestlers Dan Gable, Chris Campbell, and Bruce Baumgartner reportedly finished second in the balloting in 1972, 1981, and 1986, respectively. On three occasions—in 1946 (Douglas Lee and Henry Wittenberg), in 1972 (Dan Gable and Wayne Wells), and in 1988 (Mark Schultz and John Smith)—two wrestlers made the final 10 listing (see Table 12.3).

Table 12.1
NCAA Coach of the Year Awards

National Wrestling Coaches

Year	*Name*	*School*
1958	Harold Nichols	Iowa State
1959	Myron Roderick	Oklahoma State
1960	Everett Lantz	Wyoming
1961	Dale Thomas	Oregon State
1962	Myron Roderick	Oklahoma State
1963	Tommy Evans	Oklahoma
1964	Jay Wilkinson	Southern Illinois
1965	Harold Nichols	Iowa State
1966	Myron Roderick	Oklahoma State
1967	Grady Peninger	Michigan State
1968	Ed Peery	Navy
1969	Dave McCuskey	Iowa
1970	Dale Thomas	Oregon State
1971	Tommy Chesbro	Oklahoma State
1972	Harold Nichols	Iowa State
1973	Fred Davis	Brigham Young
1974	Rick Bay	Michigan
1975	Gary Kurdelmeier	Iowa
1976	Wally Johnson	Minnesota
1977	Duane Kleven	Wisconsin
1978	Dan Gable	Iowa
1979	Thad Turner	Lehigh
1980	Joe Seay	California State, Bakersfield

National Wrestling Coaches

Year	*Name*	*School*
1981	Rich Lorenzo	Penn State
1982	Bill Lam	North Carolina
1983	Dan Gable	Iowa
1984	Tommy Chesbro	Oklahoma State
1985	Stan Abel	Oklahoma
1986	Bob Bubb	Clarion State
1987	Jim Gibbons	Iowa State
1988	Bobby Douglas	Arizona State

Assistant Coach of the Year

Year	*Name*	*School*
1983	Jay Robinson	Iowa
1984	John Fritz	Penn State
1985	Les Anderson	Iowa State
1986	Mark Johnson	Iowa
1987	Ed Banach	Iowa State
1988	Joe Wells	Michigan

College Division Coach of the Year

Year	*Name*	*College*
1968	Vaughan Hitchcock	California Poly
1969	Chuck Patten	Northern Iowa
1970	Larry Schiacchetano	Maritime Academy
1971	Fred Powell	Slippery Rock
1972	Vaughan Hitchcock	California Poly
1973	Chuck Patten	Northern Iowa

Division II Coach of the Year[a]

Year	*Name*	*College*
1974	Larry Kristoff	Southern Illinois at Edwardsville
1975	Jim Morgan	Tennessee
1976	Joe Seay	California State, Bakersfield
1977	Paul Kendle	Augustana, SD
1978	Chuck Patten	Northern Iowa
1979	Ron Clinton	Eastern Illinois
1980	Joe Seay	California State, Bakersfield
1981	Mike Denny	Nebraska at Omaha
1982	Bucky Maughan	North Dakota State
1983	Joe Seay	California State, Bakersfield
1984	Larry Kristoff	Southern Illinois at Edwardsville
1985	Mark Osgood	Ashland

National Wrestling Coaches

Year	Name	School
1986	Larry Kristoff	Southern Illinois at Edwardsville
1987	T.J. Kerr	California State, Bakersfield
1988	Bucky Maughan	North Dakota State

Division III Coach of the Year

Year	Name	College
1974	Tony Decarlo	John Carroll
1975	Larry Schiacchetano	Montclair State
1976	Chris Ford	Ashland
1977	Frank Cheek	Humboldt State
1978	Jerry Swope	Millersburg State
1979	David Icenhower	Trenton State
1980	Don Murray	Brockport State
1981	Doug Sufty	Minnesota
1982	James Howard	Oswego State
1983	Don Murray	Brockport State
1984	Ron Johnson	Iowa Central
1985	Ron Johnson	Iowa Central
1986	Steve Strellner	Montclair State
1987	Dave Icenhower	Trenton State
1988	John Clark	St. Lawrence

Table 12.2
NAIA and Junior College Coaches of the Year

NAIA Coach of the Year

Year	Name	College
1963	Russell Houk	Bloomsburg State
1964	Bill Garland	Moorhead Sate
1965	Russell Houk	Bloomsburg State
1966	Gray Simons	Lock Haven
1967	Gray Simons	Lock Haven
1968	Frank Powell	Adams State
1969	Don Benning	Nebraska at Omaha
1970	Fran McCann	Winona State
1971	Eric Beardsley	Central Washington
1972	Gene Moses	Adams State
1973	Vern Tate	Huron State

NAIA Coach of the Year

Year	*Name*	*College*
1974	Eric Beardsley	Central Washington
1975	John Grygelko	Augsburg, MN
1976	Curt Byrnes	Eastern Washington
1977	Jim Scott	Grand Valley State
1978	Bob Riehm	Southern Oregon State
1979	Eddie Griffin	Central State, OK
1980	Richard Ulrich	Adams State
1981	Eddie Griffin	Central State, OK
1982	Eddie Griffin	Central State, OK
1983	Bob Riehm	Southern Oregon State
1984	David James	Central State, OK
1985	Fran Hummel	Northern State
1986	David James	Central State, OK
1987	Les Hogan	Alaska Pacific
1988	Mike Jones	Simon Fraser

Junior College Coach of the Year

Year	*Name*	*School*
1965	John Philo	Rochester, MN
1966	William Lanham	Northeastern of Colorado
1967	Ronald Eastin	Phoenix
1968	Stan Holtzler	Worthington
1969	Robert Hartman	SUNY A&T at Farmingdale
1970	Sidney Huitema	Muskegon
1971	Larry Wright	Clackamas
1972	Robert Hartman	SUNY A&T at Farmingdale
1973	Kaye Young	North Iowa
1974	Edroy Kringstad	Bismarck
1975	Les Hogan	North Idaho
1976	John Borszcz	Cuyahoga West
1977	Art Kraft	Triton
1978	John Owen	North Idaho
1979	Robert Carlson	Lakeland, OH
1980	Ron Gaffner	Muskegon
1981	Denny Friederichs	Iowa Central
1982	John Owen	North Idaho
1983	Art Kraft	Triton
1984	Art Kraft	Triton
1985	John Owen	North Idaho

NAIA Coach of the Year

Year	*Name*	*College*
1986	Edroy Kringstad	Bismarck
1987	Norm Berney	Clackamas
1988	Bob Christianson	Ricks

Table 12.3
Athletic, Coaching, and Officiating Honors

Championship Ring Series

Year	*Name*	*College*
1975	Chuck Yagla	
1976	Russ Hellickson	Wisconsin WC
1977	Mark Churella	Michigan
1978	Mark Lieberman	NYAC
1979	Bruce Kinseth	Iowa
1980	LeeRoy Smith	Cowboy WC
1981	Bruce Baumgartner	NYAC
1982	Bill Scherr	Nebraska
1983	Jim Scherr	Nebraska
1984	Charlie Gadsen	Cyclone WC
1985	Jim Scherr	Wildcat WC
1986	Andre Metzger	NYAC
1987	Tom Erickson	Sunkist Kids

Wrestling Writer of the Year[a]
(*Amateur Wrestling News*)

Year	*Name*	*Paper*
1960	Bob Dellinger	*Oklahoman and Times*
1961	Bob Dellinger	*Oklahoman and Times*
1962	Bob Dellinger	*Oklahoman and Times*
1963	Russ Smith	*Waterloo Courier*, IA
1964	Doug McDonald	*Centre Daily Times*, PA
1965	Phil Parrish	*Tulsa World*
1966	Bob Moore	*The Takedown*, OR
1967	Ross Nevel	*Lock Haven Express*, PA
1968	Hal Brown	*Lincoln Star*, NE
1969	Irv Moss	*Denver Post*
1970	Jerry Pogue	*Tulsa Daily World*
1971	Tom Tomashek	*Chicago Tribune*

Championship Ring Series

Year	*Name*	*College*
1972	John Doak	*The Predicament*, IA
1973	Wayne Bishop	*Tulsa Daily World*
1974	Russ & Nancy Hellickson	*The Crossface*, WI
1975	J. Carl Guymon	*Daily Oklahoman*
1976	Mike Chapman	*Fort Collins Coloradoan*
1977	Doris Dellinger	book author, OK
1978	Donald A. Sayenga	historian, PA
1979	Wayne Bishop	*Oklahoma Journal*
1980	Ron Seaman	*The Predicament*, IA
1981	Steve Matthies	*Sioux Falls Argus-Leader*
1982	Rob Sherrill	*The Grappler*, IL
1983	Norm Palovcsik	*Pennsylvania Roundup*
1984	Jim Butler	*Pennsylvania Roundup*
1985	Paul Schultz	*Chattanooga News-Free Press*
1986	Scott Davis	*The Guillotine*, MN
1987	Doug McDonald	*Centre Daily Times*, PA
1988	Mike Chapman	book author, IL

Man of the Year
(*Amateur Wrestling News*)

Year	*Name*	*Paper*
1962	Jess Hoke	*Amateur Wrestling News*
1963	Dr. Albert de Ferrari	contributor
1964	Manuel Gorriaran	contributor
1965	Harold Nichols	Iowa State coach
1966	Joe Henson	contributor
1967	Grady Peninger	Michigan State coach
1968	Tommy Evans	Oklahoma coach
1969	Dan Gable	NCAA champion
1970	Wayne Wells	world champion
1971	Myron Roderick	executive director, USWF
1972	Bill Farrell	1972 Olympic coach
1973	Lloyd Keaser	1973 world champion
1974	Stan Abel	Oklahoma coach
1975	Gary Kurdelmeier	Iowa coach

Championship Ring Series

Year	Name	College
1976	John Peterson	1976 Olympic champion
1977	Steve Combs	executive director, USA Wrestling
1978	Lee Kemp	1978 world champion
1979	Stan Dziedzic	AAU national coach
1980	Russ Hellickson	captain, 1980 Olympic team
1981	Chris Campbell	1981 world champion
1982	Bill Lam	North Carolina coach
1983	Dave Schultz	world champion
1984	Jeff Blatnick	Olympic champion
1985	Mike Houck	1985 Greco-Roman world Dchampion
1986	Bruce Baumgartner	1986 world champion
1987	John Smith	1987 world and NCAA champion
1988	Ken Monday	1988 Olympic champion

Man of the Year
(USA Wrestling)

Year	Name
1971	Bud Lindholm
1972	Mel Jones
1973	Jack Stanbro
1975	Russ Hellickson[b]
1976	Ken Kraft
1977	Vince Zuaro
1978	Werner Holzer
1979	Ben Bennett
1980	Rick Bay
1981	John Roberts
1982	Frank Rader
1983	Don Sondgeroth
1984	Gary Thompson
1985	Dr. Dan Gould
1986	Jeff Blatnick
1987	Dave Rudrud

Athlete of the Year
(USA Wrestling)

Year	Name
1971	Dan Gable
1972	Ben Peterson

Championship Ring Series

Year	*Name*
1973	Lloyd Keaser
1975	Dwayne Keller[c]
1976	Russ Hellickson
1977	Wade Schalles
1978	Mark Lieberman
1979	Lee Kemp
1980	LeeRoy Smith
1981	Greg Gibson
1982	Bill Scherr
1983	Dave Schultz
1984	Steve Fraser
1985	Mike Houck
1986	Bruce Baumgartner
1987	Mark Schultz

Coach of the Year
(USA Wrestling)

Year	*Name*
1971	Doug Blubaugh
1972	Harold Nichols
1973	Dave Abraham
1975	Gary Kurdelmeier[d]
1976	Duane Klevin
1977	Wally Johnson
1978	Chuck Patten
1979	J Robinson
1980	Steve Sanchez
1981	Tim Hutchinson
1982	Floyd Young
1983	Al Bevilacqua
1984	Ron Finley
1985	Pavel Katsen
1986	Art Williams
1987	Jim Humphrey

Official of the Year
(USA Wrestling)

Year	*Name*
1971	Vince Zuaro
1972	Wes Hogland
1973	Dennis Fankhouser
1975	Pat Lovell[e]
1976	Sam Williams
1977	Mick Pickford

Championship Ring Series

Year	*Name*
1978	Charlie White
1979	Jon Schauss
1980	Don Sondgeroth
1981	Steve Bernhardt
1982	Gordon Weeks
1983	Bernadette Norris
1984	Leroy Evans
1985	Carolyn White
1986	Tony Melosi
1987	Sandy Cageao

Sun Company Cup
(Top U.S. international wrestler)

Year	*Name*
1978	Lee Kemp
1979	Bobby Weaver
	Andre Metzger
1980	Ben Peterson
1981	Greg Gibson

Sullivan Award
(Wrestlers who made Top 10 list in final selections)

Year	*Name*
1945	M. Allen Northrup
1946	Douglas Lee
	Henry Wittenberg
1948	Henry Wittenberg
1957	Douglas Blubaugh
1959	Terry McCann
1966	Larry Kristoff
1967	Larry Kristoff
1970	Wayne Wells
1971	Dan Gable
1972	Dan Gable
1973	Lloyd Keaser
1975	Lloyd Keaser
1976	John Peterson
1977	Stan Dziedzic
1978	Lee Kemp
1979	Lee Kemp
1980	Ben Peterson
1981	Chris Campbell
1982	Greg Gibson
1984	Steve Fraser

Championship Ring Series

Year	*Name*
1985	Mike Houck
1986	Bruce Baumgartner
1987	Mark Schultz
	John Smith
1988	John Smith

Sustained Superior Performance Award
(For 50 years of service to wrestling)
(Amateur Athletic Association)

Year	*Name*
Year	Name
1967	Bill Schriver
1968	Maurice "Pat" McGill
1969	John Earecksen
1970	Steere Noda
1971	George Myerson
1972	Fendley Collins
1973	Ivan Olsen
1974	Billy Martin
1975	Sy Mitchell
1976	Roy Moore
1977	Andrew Kovacz
1978	Billy Vandiver
1979	John Shindle
1980	Captain Stephen Archer
1981	Elias George
1982	Frank Crosby
1983	No award
1984	Wes Brown
1985	Dean Rockwell
1986	No award
1987	Murl E. Thrush

[a]Renamed The Bob Dellinger Award in 1963.

[b]Award combined for 1974 and 1975.

[c]Award combined for 1974 and 1975.

[d]Award combined for 1974 and 1975.

Chapter 13

Halls of Fame

Many sporting organizations have a hall of fame where their champions of the past are paid tribute to and where memorable deeds and achievements can be recorded. Amateur wrestling has one such hall and also occupies select spots in several other halls of fame across the country.

National Wrestling Hall of Fame

The National Wrestling Hall of Fame in Stillwater, Oklahoma, was dedicated on September 11, 1976, and is the only museum in the nation dedicated solely to the sport. It was funded entirely by popular subscription at a cost of over $500,000. The opening ceremonies included the induction of 14 charter members and a formal banquet with Frank Gifford, noted television personality, serving as master of ceremonies.

The 14 charter members were elected by a secret committee of wrestling authorities, headed by nonvoting member Cliff Keen of Michigan. The charter members were divided into three categories: founding fathers, wrestlers, and coaches.

The founding-fathers group was composed of Dr. Raymond G. Clapp, University of Nebraska; Edward Clark Gallagher, Oklahoma State University; George N. Mehnert, Newark, New Jersey; Hugo M. Otopalik, Iowa State University; and William Sheridan, Lehigh University.

Representing the wrestlers were Jay T. "Tommy" Evans and Dan Allen Hodge, University of Oklahoma, and Jack Van Bebber and Myron Roderick, Oklahoma State University.

The coaches elected into the hall were Fendley A. Collins, Michigan State; Art Griffith, Oklahoma State; Clifford P. Keen, University of Michigan; David H. McCuskey, University of Northern Iowa and University of Iowa; and Rex A. Peery, University of Pittsburgh.

For many years the hall was operated by USA Wrestling, which made its offices in the museum until its move in June 1988 to the United States Olympic Center complex in Colorado Springs, Colorado. The hall's curator is Bob

Dellinger, a former sports editor of the *Oklahoman and Times* newspaper of Oklahoma City and one of the sport's leading authorities and historians.

The National Wrestling Hall of Fame is overseen by a board of governors. The hall is situated on a corner lot of the Oklahoma State University campus near the athletic field house and the football stadium. Items on display trace the development of wrestling in the United States and around the world.

The main attractions are the Wall of Champions, which features the names of over 3,500 national champions; a central display area that features numerous exhibits and trophy cases; a library of books and videotapes; and the Honors Court, where the sport's legendary figures are enshrined with plaques of native granite and telephone recordings describe their achievements.

Following the 1988 induction ceremonies, there were 78 members in the National Wrestling Hall of Fame. The members are selected through balloting of national wrestling experts and are enshrined each November.

Other Halls of Fame

Wrestling personalities are also honored in several other halls of fame around the nation. The oldest such organization is the First Interstate Athletic Foundation, formerly known as the Citizens Savings Athletic Foundation Hall of Fame and before that as the Helms Athletic Hall of Fame (see Table 13.1). Located in Los Angeles, the hall represents a total of 36 sports. It began a wrestling program in 1956, and by 1987 there were a total of 86 men in the wrestling hall.

The U.S. Olympic Hall of Fame and Museum was created in 1979 by the USOC and Coca-Cola USA. The charter class of 19 athletes was inducted in 1983, with such legendary athletes as Jim Thorpe, Muhammad Ali, and Johnny Weissmuller among those voted into the hall. Dan Gable, the 1972 Olympic champion who also served as Olympic freestyle coach in 1980 and 1984, was voted into the hall in 1985, one of the first 36 athletes so honored. By 1987 Gable was the only wrestler among the 46 athletes voted into the hall.

Although no official building serves as the hall, the USOC announced plans in 1987 to build a first-class museum. It received 150 acres of undeveloped land near Colorado Springs in 1987 and has targeted the land as the future home of the U.S. Olympic Museum and Hall of Fame.

The National High School Sports Hall of Fame was started in 1982. Plaques commemorating inductees are on display in a special room at the National Federation of State High School Associations in Kansas City, Missouri. The 1988 inductions brought the total number of honorees to 90. The four wrestling personalities include two men from the same high school in Iowa and coaches from Illinois and Virginia.

Dan Gable, who was an undefeated three-time state champion at West High School in Waterloo, Iowa, is the sole wrestler in the hall. His coach at West

Waterloo, Bob Siddens, was inducted in 1988 after posting a record of 327-26-3 and winning 11 team state championships.

The other two coaches are Charles Farina of Franklin Park, Illinois, and Billy Martin of Virginia Beach, Virginia. Farina won 524 dual meets for Leyden High School by the time of his induction in 1987. Martin, who retired in 1971, compiled a record of 259-9-4 and won 21 state team titles at Granby High School.

The NAIA Hall of Fame recognizes superior athletic achievement in the NAIA organization. Founded in 1952, the hall actually is a "paper shrine" with no building. A total of 694 athletes, coaches, and contributors had been inducted by 1988. Included in that number are 40 wrestlers, 18 coaches and 6 contributors (see Table 13.2).

The National Junior College Athletic Association, located in Colorado Springs, began wrestling inductions in 1979. By 1988 there were 20 wrestlers and 33 coaches who had been elected to the hall (see Table 13.3). There is no official NCAA hall of fame.

Table 13.1
Helms Athletic Hall of Fame

Stan Abel (athlete/coach)
Charles Ackerly (athlete)
Les Anderson (athlete/coach)
David "Buddy" Arndt (athlete)
Dave Auble (athlete)
Wayne Baughman (athlete)
Richard Beattie (athlete)
Pete Blair (athlete)
Ned Blass (athlete)
Doug Blubaugh (athlete)
Glen Brand (athlete)
Conrad Caldwell (athlete)
Michael Caruso (athlete)
Newt Copple (contributor)
Dick Delgatto (athlete)
Richard DiBatista (athlete)
George S. Dole (athlete)
Ed Eichlberg (athlete)
Finn Ericksen (contributor)
Ross Flood (athlete)
Dan Gable (athlete)
Verne Gagne (athlete)
Anthony Gizzoni (athlete)
Ron Gray (athlete)
Larry Hayes (athlete)
Stanley Henson (athlete)
Robert Hess (athlete)
Dan Hodge (athlete)
John G. Hoke (contributor)
Russell Houk (athlete)
Dick Hutton (athlete)
Burl Jennings (athlete)
Merle Jennings (athlete)
Alan Kelley (athlete)
Bill Kerslake (athlete)
William Koll (athlete)
Lowell Lange (athlete)

George Layman (athlete)	Alan Rice (coach)
Frank Lewis (athlete)	Jack Riley (athlete)
Hardie Lewis (athlete)	Rich Sanders (athlete)
Vernon Logan (athlete)	Joseph Sapora (athlete)
Rometo Macias (coach)	Don Sayenga (contributor)
Lawrence Mantooth (athlete)	Joe Scarpello (athlete)
Wayne Martin (athlete)	John Schultz (coach)
Terry McCann (athlete)	Elliott Simons (athlete)
Earl McCready (athlete)	Virgil Smith (coach)
Charles McDaniel (athlete)	William Smith (athlete)
Joe McDaniel (athlete)	John Spellman (athlete)
George Mehnert (athlete)	Harry Steele (athlete)
Peter Mehringer (athlete)	Ralph Teague (athlete)
Allie Morrison (athlete)	Murl Thrush (coach)
Norvard Nalan (athlete)	Warren Tischler (contributor)
William Nelson (athlete)	Yorijo Uetake (wrestler)
Gene Nicks (athlete)	Jack Van Bebber (athlete)
Robert Norman (athlete)	Russell Vis (athlete)
M.A. ''Doc'' Northrup (athlete)	William Weick (athlete)
Edwin Peery (athlete)	Wayne Wells (athlete)
Hugh Peery (athlete)	Alfred Whitehurst (athlete)
Ben Peterson (athlete)	Shelby Wilson (athlete)
John Peterson (athlete)	Henry Wittenberg (athlete)
Arnold Plaza (athlete)	Keith Young (athlete)
Robin Reed (athlete)	Vince Zuaro (contributor)

Note. Last class inducted in 1980.

Table 13.2
NAIA Hall of Fame

Athletes

Year	*Name*
1972	Jerry Wedemeier (Winona State)
1975	James Hazewinkel (St. Cloud State) Gray Simons (Lock Haven) Jerry Swope (Lock Haven)

Athletes

Year	Name
1976	Dominic Carolla (Adams State)
	Arthur Maughan (Moorhead State)
	Lamoin Merkley (Central Washington)
1977	Bill Blacksmith (Lock Haven)
	Mike Stanley (Adams State)
1978	Dave Hazewinkel (St. Cloud State)
	Ken Monroe (Wayne State, NE)
	John Peterson (Wisconsin—Stout)
1979	Steve Exline (Upper Iowa)
1980	Mel Washington (Nebraska at Omaha)
	William Garson (Bloomsburg State)
	Jim Fallis (Lake Superior State)
	William West (Wisconsin— Parkside)
	Kenneth Melchoir (Lock Haven)
	Roy Washington (Nebraska at Omaha)
1981	Ken Martin (Wisconsin—Parkside)
	Bill Mitchell (Central State, OK)
	Gary Smith (St. Cloud State)
	Dennis Warren (Central Washington)
1982	Lanny Davidson (Eastern Washington)
1983	Wade Winters (Westmar)
	Rick Stuyvesant (Moorhead State)
1984	Bob Billburg (Moorhead State)
	Glen Guerin (Taylor)
	Frank Mosier (Moorhead State)
1985	Robert Dettmer (Bemidji State)
	Bobby Douglas (West Liberty State)
	Floyd Marshall (Findlay)
1986	Mike Allison (Adams State)
	Bob Gruner (Wisconsin— Parkside)
	Rollin Schimmel (Eastern Oregon)
1987	Barry Bennett (Concordia, MN)
1988	Craig Kelso (Adams State)
	Herb Stanley (Adams State)
	Marc Mongeon (Simon Fraser)
	David James (Central State, OK)

Athletes

Coaches

Year	*Name*
Year	Name
1963	Hubert Jack (Lock Haven)
1970	Raymond ''Bucky'' Murdock (Waynesburg)
1975	Chester Anderson (Bemidji State) Erling Odegaard (Eastern Oregon State)
1977	Russ Houk (Bloomsburg State)
1979	Byron James (Wisconsin—River Falls)
1980	Rometo ''Rummy'' Macias (Mankato State)
1981	Eric Beardsley (Central Washington)
1983	Clayton Ketterling (Jamestown)
1984	Bill Garland (Moorhead State)
1985	Fred J. Caro (Edinboro) Michael Olson (Dickinson State)
1986	Milton Martin (Westmar) Willie Myers (Wisconsin—Whitewater)
1987	Vince Monseau (West Liberty State) Jack Ramey (Kearney State)
1988	Mike Clock (Pacific University) Bob Riehm (Southern Oregon State)

Contributors

Year	*Name*
1977	Tony Schavone (Black Hills State)
1978	Manuel Gorriarian (Hook-Fast Specialties)
1980	Bob Jones (Winona State)
1985	Neil ''Doc'' Ersland (Westmar)
1987	Jay Roelen (Saddleback College)
1988	Ed Aliverti (Edmonds Community College)

Table 13.3
National Junior College Hall of Fame

Wrestlers

Year	Name
1980	Ron E. Jacobsen (Lamar)
	Gilbert Sanchez (Lamar)
1981	Donald D. Hunry (Lamar)
	Robert Christensen (Ricks)
	Roger Williams (Northern Oklahoma)
	Richard Keefe (Keystone)
	Harry Geris (Joliet)
	Chris Taylor (Muskegon)
1982	Luis Baiz (Phoenix)
	Glen Karsten (Worthington)
	John Lightner (Garden City)
1983	George Beene (Triton)
	Ronald Ray (Wright)
1984	Les Armes (Black Hawk)
	Willie Gadson (Nassau)
1985	Joel Kislin (Luzerne County)
	Tim Williams (Clackamas)
1986	James McCloe (SUNY A&T at Delhi)
	James Young (Middlesex County)
1987	Robert Geoger (St. Louis at Meramec)

Coaches

Year	Name
1979	Emile Caprara (Grand Rapids Junior)
	Ronald D. Eastin (Phoenix)
	Bob Hartman (SUNY A&T at Farmingdale)
	Edroy Kringstad (Bismarck)
	Bill Lanham (Northeastern of Colorado)
	John R. Philo (Rochester, MN)
1980	James Cranfield (Cayuga County)
	Larry Fornicola (Keystone)
	Art Kraft (Triton)
	Roy Minter (Willmar)
	Joe Nix (Mesa, AZ)
	William S. Haven (SUNY A&T at Alfred)
	John Sacchi (Middlesex County)
1981	Wesley Christensen (Ricks)
	John Howard (Columbia Basin)

Wrestlers

Year	*Name*
	Robert L. Mason (Big Bend)
	Ronald Gaffner (Muskegon)
	John Broszcz (Cuyahoga)
1982	C.A. Patterson (College of the Desert)
	Kaye Young (North Area Iowa CC)
	John J. DeVencenzo (SUNY A&T at Morrisville)
1983	Stanley Hotzier (Worthington)
	Frank Millard (SUNY A&T at Delhi)
1984	Stan Nevins (SUNY A&T at Cobleskill)
	Bob Sweiacher (Northern Oklahoma)
1985	Henry Pillard (Joliet)
	Dennie Friederichs (Iowa Central)
1986	Steve Babcock (SUNY A&T at Alfred)
	Neil Boyd (Waldorf)
	Alvin J. Kaltofen (Dupage)
1987	Chuck Henke (Nassau County)
	Ron Mirikitanc (St. Louis at Meramec)
	Eric Knuutilia (Niagara)

Chapter 14

The Play-for-Pay Ranks

The sport of professional wrestling flowered in the 1890s when barnstorming wrestlers moved into a town and challenged the local grapplers. The winner would receive a share of the gate receipts and perhaps score with a few side bets. These touring professionals were very popular at the turn of the century, but, ironically, they gave rise to the split between amateur and professional wrestling.

The very best wrestlers became so good that only other seasoned professionals could compete with them, and the amateurs were relegated to the sidelines. By 1905 professional matches were attracting sizeable crowds. A bout in 1911 between the great Frank Gotch and the famed Russian Lion, George Hackenschmidt, drew nearly 30,000 fans to recently built Comiskey Park in Chicago.

Gotch is considered the greatest professional star in history. He learned his no-holds-barred wrestling as a youngster in the small Iowa farm community of Humboldt. At the age of 19, he sailed to the gold-mining towns of Alaska and tangled with the rough-and-tumble miners in big-money bouts of winner take all. Gotch never lost a match, and he returned to Iowa after only 6 months with nearly $30,000 in winnings, a veritable fortune in 1901. He then began touring the nation looking for worthy foes.

According to Mac Davis in his book *100 Greatest Sports Heroes* (1954), Gotch's popularity was immense: ''As the idol of millions, Gotch made wrestling a big-time sport in his day. As a matter of fact, he drew larger audiences than did the heavyweight champion of boxing when defending his title. Babies had been named in his honor, as had buildings, toys, farm implements and a hundred other things. The word 'Gotch' was a synonym for quality and strength'' (p. 45).

Gotch was invited to the White House by President Theodore Roosevelt on several occasions and toured the United States as the star of a hit play. When he and Jack Johnson, the heavyweight boxing champion of the world, met each other on a Chicago street corner and began chatting, a huge crowd developed. It took mounted policemen to break up the thousands of fans who were anxious to catch a glimpse of the world's two best-known sports heroes.

Frank Gotch, greatest professional wrestler of all time. (From the Chapman collection)

Graeme Kent, in his book *A Pictorial History of Wrestling* (1969), wrote, "In these years [1900-1914] professional wrestling became the major sport with the greatest audience pull in the English-speaking world, dwarfing boxing and all other activities. The wrestling period was brief, but the interest and attention that it aroused was quite phenomenal" (p. 146).

It was this kind of popularity that gave amateur wrestling a huge boost in the early 1900s. Amateurs, eager to compete against other wrestlers on the same level, banded together to form clubs and organize tournaments. Amateur and professional wrestling differed in that amateur bouts were much shorter, had weight classes, and did not allow choke and submission holds.

Frank Gotch almost never worked for a pin, as he always preferred to make his foe give up. This was a philosophy he learned from his tutor, Farmer Burns, a legendary athlete who took part in over 6,000 matches during his career. Burns was so well respected in the sporting ranks of his day that James J. Jeffries, a former heavyweight boxing champion of the world, hired him to help train for his comeback bout against Jack Johnson.

It was at the Jeffries training camp in Reno, Nevada, that one of the most intriguing yet little known matchups in sports history took place. The protagonists were Burns, almost 50 years old, and Billy Papke, just 24 years old and in his prime, a former middleweight boxing champion of the world.

Burns and Papke engaged in a heated dispute over the training methods of Jeffries, and Papke challenged Burns to a free-for-all contest. Burns quickly accepted. The two squared off, both deadly intent on dispatching the other. Papke launched a series of punches, which Burns either took on his shoulder or evaded, and then Burns shot in for a takedown. He flung Papke to his stomach, secured a submission hold, and made the great fighter capitulate. The entire battle had taken less than 2 minutes!

Burns loved amateur wrestling. In 1921, he worked with a high school team in Cedar Rapids, Iowa, preparing it for the first state high school meet ever held. The team won the title, and Burns was given considerable credit in the newspaper accounts of the day. Many Iowa wrestling coaches point to Burns and Gotch as primary reasons why the state has enjoyed such success and established a great wrestling tradition.

Most authorities tie the demise of professional wrestling to the retirement of Gotch and to the subsequent introduction of theatrical devices to stimulate fan interest. Gotch and his contemporaries held themselves above the sort of antics that would mark the sport in the decades to come. "No breath of scandal ever attached itself to Frank Gotch," wrote Kent (1969). But "by 1913 Gotch had run out of opponents, and retired. When he left the ring the golden age of wrestling came to an end" (p. 116).

Although amateur and professional wrestling share common roots and were once closely aligned, they have since moved poles apart. Hardly any amateur wrestling fan of the 1980s would allow himself or herself to be seen at a professional match. Despite the huge gap between the two sports in the 1980s, the fact of the matter is that some of the biggest names in amateur history have crossed over the line into the play-for-pay ranks, almost from the very beginning.

Earl Caddock came out of tiny Walnut, Iowa, to win AAU national titles in 1914 and 1915 at 175 pounds and in 1915 at heavyweight. Long and lanky, Caddock was considered a tremendous wrestler by all who saw him in action. Four-time AAU national champion Fred Meyer, a bronze medal winner in the 1920 Olympics, said Caddock was the real thing, the master of a thousand holds. Gotch himself said shortly after retiring that Caddock was as fine a wrestler as he had ever seen.

In 1917, just 2 years after winning two AAU national championships, Caddock defeated Joe Stetcher, who had succeeded Gotch, and became the world professional title holder. Some chroniclers of the professional game consider the Caddock-Stetcher bout the last legitimate professional title match ever held.

Caddock was a clean-liver who was highly regarded by high school coaches around the Midwest. He was frequently asked to speak at high school wrestling banquets, and he did so.

After witnessing Caddock's success, other amateur stars of the 1920s and 1930s decided to try the professional sport, hoping to earn a good living. Nearly all left the game after short trial runs, disgusted at the theatrics that were already creeping into the sport. Caddock and Stetcher, true wrestling giants who could attract a crowd merely by their reputations and immense wrestling skills, were among the last of the old breed.

Unfortunately, wrestling matches between two evenly matched athletes were often boring to the nonfanatic. The great Gotch-Hackenschmidt match of 1911 lasted over 2 hours, with much of the time spent on the mat as Gotch rode the Russian Lion and searched for an opportunity to apply a submission hold. By the early 1920s, the nation's sports fans simply were not interested in seeing one man control another for long periods of time, working for a pin or a submission.

It was the Roaring Twenties, the age of Jack Dempsey, Babe Ruth, Red Grange, Bill Tilden, Bobby Jones. The United States was a society that demanded nonstop action and a certain degree of showmanship from its professional sports heroes. Amateur wrestlers who would not showboat were out of favor with professional promoters who were looking to make a buck.

Among the more prominent amateur stars who tried to make the transition into the professional ranks in the 1920s and 1930s were Robin Reed, Russell Vis, Bobby Pearce, Jack Van Bebber, and Pete Mehringer, all Olympic champions.

Vis won four AAU national titles and the 1924 Olympic gold medal (145 pounds) in Paris. He turned professional and wrestled several years, but only half-heartedly. "I'd get out there and make a move and get into position where my opponent couldn't move, and then I'd have to let him go, and (the fans) would wonder how he got out of that," Vis told Carlson and Fogarty, authors of the 1988 book *Tales of Gold*. "To put on a show you've got to make faces, jump up and down, pretend you're hurt, then come from underneath. I was a lousy showman" (p. 44).

Nonetheless, Vis often praised many of the old professional stars. Although Vis was a teammate of the great Robin Reed on the 1924 Olympic team, he ranked professional star Johnny Pesek of Nebraska as the greatest wrestler he ever saw in action, professional or amateur.

Reed never lost a match at any time as an amateur wrestler, and he is generally regarded as one of the four or five greatest amateur wrestlers of all time. And he, like Vis, harbored a very healthy respect for the top professionals. "My greatest discussions were with John Pesek and Farmer Burns," Reed once wrote. "Ah! Those were the masters!"

Pearce, Van Bebber, and Mehringer won Olympic titles in 1932 in Los Angeles, and each wrestled professionally, but only briefly. At 132 pounds, Pearce was very small for the professional game but stayed with it for nearly 5 years. Van Bebber, who won three NCAA titles at 155 and 165, stayed in the professional game less than a year.

Mehringer, big and powerful at 200 pounds, played 5 years of professional football. He also dabbled with professional wrestling at the same time. ''After graduation I did a bit of pro wrestling, but I never did think of it as a career,'' Mehringer reported in *Tales of Gold*. ''I didn't enjoy it. It was just show biz, about like it is today [1986]. I was supposed to wrestle Jim Londos once, but his handlers backed out of the match. I did wrestle Strangler Lewis, and I think I could have beaten him in a real match'' (p. 118).

Londos and Lewis were two of the greatest professional stars of all time, ranked only behind Gotch and Hackenschmidt. Ironically, Mehringer's interest in wrestling first sprouted as a youngster on a Kansas farm when he bought a mail-order wrestling course authored by Burns and Gotch.

In 1930, heavyweight Earl McCready finished his career at Oklahoma A&M unbeaten, becoming the first three-time NCAA champion along the way. The powerful Canadian was the first collegiate star to enter the professional ranks, where he remained for nearly 3 decades. Another great A&M star, LeRoy McGuirk, began a long and lucrative professional career after winning the NCAA 155-pound title in 1931.

Ralph Silverstein captured the NCAA title at 175 pounds for the University of Illinois in 1935 and was a star in Midwest rings for years as ''Ruffy Silverstein.'' Wayne Martin, the Oklahoma Sooners' first three-time NCAA champion (his final year was 1936 at 134 pounds), toured professionally for many years.

The parade into the professional ranks sped up in the late 1940s, with Verne Gagne leading the way. Gagne was a great all-around athlete at the University of Minnesota, excelling in both wrestling and football. He became the first man to win four Big Ten mat titles, and he captured two NCAA titles and was third once. He also was the man who stopped Oklahoma State's Dick Hutton from becoming the sport's only four-time NCAA champion, winning a referee's decision from Hutton in 1949 at the NCAA finals in Fort Collins, Colorado.

The advent of television in the early 1950s made professional wrestling shows very popular, and Gagne became one of the biggest stars of all time. His favorite hold was the ''sleeper,'' which made the opponent pass out. Although it might have looked hokey, it was a legitimate judo technique that worked by shutting off the oxygen flow to the brain.

''That's what people really don't understand about pro wrestling,'' Gagne told the author in 1976. ''The old pros, guys like Burns and Gotch, knew so many techniques that came from judo and ju-jitsu. Submission and choke holds. And they were masters at working them. They were really very, very tough men.''

Gagne was successful as an athlete, promoter, and entrepreneur, but he never forgot his amateur background. For years he pumped energy and money into amateur programs all across Minnesota and continued to attend the NCAA Tournament whenever his schedule allowed.

Verne Gagne, former college and professional star. (Courtesy of Verne Gagne)

His old adversary, Dick Hutton, also turned professional and became a world heavyweight champion. Another top heavyweight of the period was Purdue's Ray Gunkel. In 1947, Hutton, Gunkel, and Gagne finished one-two-three in the NCAA tournament. Gunkel captured AAU national titles in 1947 and 1948 and then turned professional. Jack Dempsey, the legendary boxing champ, was his manager for many years.

Bob Geigel of Iowa lost to Gagne in the semifinals of the NCAA Tournament at 191 pounds in 1948 and became ''Texas'' Bob Geigel in the professional ranks. He had a long and successful career in the ring and then, like Gagne, turned to promoting and matchmaking. His Iowa teammate, Joe Scarpello, was a four-time Big Ten and two-time NCAA champion (175) and wrestled professionally out of Omaha, Nebraska, for nearly 3 decades. Scarpello's bouts with Iowa State Glen Brand for a spot on the 1948 Olympic team are considered classics. Brand made the team and won the gold medal in London without a close match. Geigel and Scarpello were both coached at Iowa by Mike Howard, who wrestled professionally after first coming to the United States from Denmark.

The brightest star of the 1950s college mat scene was Dan Hodge, a man who earned the nickname "Dynamite Dan" for his awesome strength and pinning prowess. Hodge was never beaten in 3 years at the University of Oklahoma and was never even taken down! In 1959 he became only the second man in sports history to win national titles in boxing and wrestling. Hodge, fighting in the finals of the National Golden Gloves Tournament in New York, knocked out the defending champion, Fred Hood, before a roaring crowd of 11,000.

Hodge fought 10 times as a professional boxer, winning 8 of the 10 bouts. He then joined up with LeRoy McGuirk and wrestled professionally for 2 decades, mostly in the South and the Southwest. To this day, Hodge holds the honor of being the only amateur wrestler to appear on the cover of *Sports Illustrated* (April 1, 1957).

"Gorilla Monsoon" gained fame as a professional star in the 1960s and 1970s in the East and became even more popular in the 1980s as cohost of a popular television talk show. In 1958 he was runner-up in the NCAA Tournament in Iowa City but was known simply as Bob Marella of Ithaca College.

Fewer amateurs went the professional route in the 1960s, but two who did became tremendous attractions. Jim Raschke starred at the University of Nebraska in the early 1960s at heavyweight and won a bronze medal in the 1963 World Championships in Greco-Roman. He became known professionally as "Baron Von Raschke," a shaved-headed villain reputedly from Nazi Germany.

After winning the NCAA 191-pound title in 1965 for Oklahoma State, Jack Brisco went to Florida and was very successful. He was billed as heavyweight champion of the world for many years.

The career of North Dakota State's Bob Backlund was meteoric in the 1970s. After capturing the NCAA Division II title at 190 pounds in 1971, he went east and signed up with the group that was eventually to strike it rich with "Hulk Hogan." Backlund, moving up the ranks quickly, developed a huge following with his clean-cut demeanor and penchant for hard training. He ruled the roost for several years as world champion but disappeared virtually overnight, giving up the game to become a junior high school coach.

He was followed several years later by another North Dakota State product, powerful Brad Rheingans. After winning two NCAA Division II titles at 190 pounds, Rheingans switched to Greco-Roman wrestling and won six national titles at 220. He was fourth in the 1976 Olympics and was a good bet to win the first Greco-Roman Olympic medal ever for the United States in 1980 had not President Carter decided to boycott the Moscow Games.

Not all amateur stars who tried the professional version found it to their liking. Evan Johnson was NCAA champion at 190 pounds for Minnesota in 1976 but wrestled about 1 year as a professional. Chris Taylor signed a professional contract amid great fanfare after winning his second NCAA title for

Iowa State in 1973 but was not comfortable in the professional ranks. "The Gentle Giant" never developed into the type of attraction promoters envisioned, despite his immense amateur appeal, and he drifted away from professional wrestling after several years. In the summer of 1979, Taylor died in his sleep at his home in Story City, Iowa, at the age of 29.

Other top amateurs who tried professional wrestling were Olympian Bob Roop and collegiate stars Dale Lewis, Dick Beattie, Jim Shields, Jimmy Jackson, and Steve Williams. As "Dr. Death," Williams became popular in the middle 1980s after placing in the NCAA Tournament for 4 straight years for the Sooners of Oklahoma.

The 1980s saw professional wrestling depart even more radically from the amateur sport, as most of the big stars had very sparse amateur wrestling backgrounds to draw on. With the promoters placing an ever-increasing emphasis on outlandish gimmicks and the performer's size, amateur wrestlers turned their backs on the game in greater numbers than ever before. Their places were taken by iron pumpers and steroid poppers, and the gap between the amateur and professional versions of wrestling widened even further. The two endeavors may have had similarities up through the 1950s, but by the late 1980s there was hardly any resemblance at all between the two.

Although professional wrestling has been regarded more as show business than a true athletic contest since the late 1920s, there is no denying that many professional wrestlers are rough-and-ready individuals blessed with great athletic skills. Men like Caddock, Gagne, Hutton, and Hodge could compete on any level, with anybody, in anything that required strength, courage, and athletic ability. Their amateur records are proof enough.

Appendix

Members of the National Wrestling Hall of Fame

Following are biographical sketches of the 78 men who were members of the National Wrestling Hall of Fame honors court up through 1988. They appear as they did at the time of induction, without updating, and are listed alphabetically:

LLOYD APPLETON (1983)

He was national freestyle runner-up at both 158 and 175 pounds in 1927. The next year, Lloyd Appleton concentrated on one weight class, and won a silver medal in the Olympic Games.

In high school, his sports were baseball and basketball, but when he entered Cornell College of Iowa and encountered the renowned coach, Dick Barker, his wrestling skills soon became evident. He was undefeated as a collegian, competing against Missouri Valley, Big Ten and Midwest Conference opponents from 158 pounds to heavyweight.

After the double runner-up finish in his first national tournament, he returned in 1928 to win the national freestyle championship at 158 pounds. He followed this by winning the Olympic trials and capturing a silver medal in the Olympic Games at Amsterdam.

For the next six years, he was a teacher of sciences and mathematics at prep schools in Maine and Massachusetts, and at each of those three schools he organized a wrestling program. As a 175-pound wrestler, he won New England championships and the national YMCA title in 1931-32, and was runner-up in the Olympic trials—thus making the U.S. team for the second time, although this time as an alternate.

Starting in 1936, he served 19 years as wrestling coach at the United States Military Academy, and remained at West Point 16 more years as a professor of physical education, the first civilian to attain that rank. Not only did he develop consistent winners among his varsity teams, but in his course of Wrestling for Military Leadership he taught the sport to some 15,000 cadets.

During the late 1950s, he established wrestling programs for U.S. troops in Europe, organizing and conducting clinics for coaches and officials, to prepare them along with the wrestlers for the all-Army championships and the international military games.

Throughout his coaching and teaching career, he played an active role in such organizations as the Boy Scouts, the YMCA, the American Heart Association and state and health organizations.

BUDDY ARNDT (1981)

Is it possible for a champion to walk away from the mat for three full years and return to compete at the same high level? Buddy Arndt did just that and became the only wrestler to win National Collegiate championships on both sides of World War II.

His only coach in wrestling, Hall of Famer Art Griffith, was a man who hated to lose. With that leadership in both high school and college, and his own exceptional ability, Arndt never met defeat.

He won every match in three years at Tulsa Central High School and two state championships, missing one state meet because of illness. As a sophomore at Oklahoma State, he captured his first NCAA title at 145 pounds and won all six bouts in the national freestyle tournament, only to settle for second place under the international scoring rules.

But as a junior, in 1942, Buddy was clearly the nation's best wrestler, sweeping National Collegiate and freestyle honors and earning the outstanding wrestler trophy in both tournaments. Both seasons he competed a full class above his normal weight to make room in the Aggie lineup for another national champion.

But athletics then were overshadowed by the war and Arndt spent the next three years as a P-38 fighter pilot, flying more than 100 combat missions over Italy with the 15th Air Corps. He was awarded the Distinguished Flying Cross with four clusters and also collected six Bronze Battle Stars for action in major battles.

He returned to college after the war, this time competing at his natural weight of 136 pounds, won his third NCAA championship and, for the third time, led the Aggies to the team trophy.

WAYNE BAUGHMAN (1982)

As a high school wrestler, his best finish was third in the state. But Wayne Baughman went on to compete in 25 national tournaments and placed as low as third only twice!

He won 16 national championships and was runner-up seven times, and became the first athlete to win a national title in each of the four recognized styles of wrestling—folkstyle (high school and collegiate style), freestyle, Greco-Roman and sombo.

At the University Oklahoma, he sandwiched the 1962 NCAA crown between a pair of runner-up efforts. But it was during his career as an Air Force officer that his wrestling success soared to unparalleled heights.

He won five national championships in freestyle, nine in Greco-Roman and one in sombo. He won eight world-wide Air Force trophies and 15 interservice titles.

He captured the freestyle gold medal in the Pan American Games of 1967 and was a member of three Olympic teams and eight world teams. He was a placewinner in Olympic or world competition in all three of the international styles.

Through a combination of ability, determination and self discipline, Wayne Baughman reaped a rich harvest in the fields of wrestling. And throughout his career he worked with equal diligence to plow those same values back into the sport. He was largely responsible for keeping the U.S. Air Force active in wrestling, and he coached service teams in eight years of international competition before becoming head coach at the Air Force Academy in 1975.

As a wrestler and as a coach, he has been an ambassador for the sport, visiting many junior and senior high schools to stress the importance of academics as a part of athletic success.

Wayne Baughman, winner of 16 national titles and coach of many international teams including the 1976 Olympic team. (Courtesy of Wayne Baughman)

DOUG BLUBAUGH (1979)

In the shadowed ruins of Rome's ancient Basilica, Doug Blubaugh battled the world champion from Iran for the Olympic gold medal. Emamali Habibi never had known defeat.

Three times the Persian attacked, each time throwing the young American into danger. Then a swift counterattack from Blubaugh hurled his opponent to his back—suddenly the struggle was ended.

Thus did an Oklahoma farm boy reach the apex of a brilliant athletic career, earning the 1960 Olympic gold medal at 160.5 pounds, and with it recognition as the outstanding wrestler in the world.

Doug Blubaugh was no stranger to the role of champion. He won national collegiate honors for Oklahoma State University in 1957 and national freestyle titles in 1957, when he was named outstanding wrestler, and 1959.

A year before his Olympic conquest, he won the gold medal in the 1959 Pan American Games at Chicago, matching the 1955 achievement of his older brother, Jack. They are the only brothers to capture Pan American titles.

Blubaugh is remembered, too, for his epic struggles with a former college teammate, Phil Kinyon. Over four years of freestyle competition, they met 13 times. The first 12 bouts ended in draws. 11 of them scoreless. Five of these took place in the 1960 Olympic trials, before Blubaugh crashed through for the takedown and the victory that sent him on to Olympic glory.

After a competitive career totaling more than 400 victories against just 17 defeats, Blubaugh turned to coaching and won added respect for his teaching skills and his honesty and dedication.

After seven years as an assistant at Michigan State, during which he was freestyle coach of the U.S. teams in the 1971 Pan American Games and World Championship, he assumed his present position as head coach at Indiana University in 1972.

GLEN BRAND (1978)

From the day he started wrestling as a sixth grader in Clarion, Iowa, his goal was to be a champion. Glen Brand not only became a national champion, but he attained his ultimate goal in 1948 when he won the gold medal at 174 pounds in the Olympic Games at London.

Along the way, and since, he achieved many other honors.

He was coached in high school by a cousin, Dale Brand, who was a member of the 1936 Olympic team. Glen went directly into the U.S. Marine Corps., serving four years before enrolling at Iowa State University.

Under the guidance of Hall of Fame coach Hugo Otopalik, he became a three-time All-American, winning 54 of 57 matches, with 30 falls, and defeating his last 35 opponents.

Although outweighed substantially, he placed third in the NCAA tournament at heavyweight his freshman year. As a sophomore, he was runner-up at 175 pounds, and then as a junior in 1948 won the National Collegiate championship. He continued undefeated through the U.S. Olympic trials and the London Games.

Returning to school in 1950, he won seven more matches before undergoing surgery which ended his competitive efforts.

In his professional career as a hydraulics engineer, during which he built a one-man firm into one of the nation's finest, he served 14 years as a YMCA wrestling coach and organized youth wrestling activities in Omaha, Nebraska.

An excerpt from the program for his final match at Iowa State sums up his stature as a competitor: "There's more to Glen Brand than his wrestling. He's a true amateur, a gentleman who respects his opponent, but who brooks no interference with his right to rule on the mat."

CONRAD CALDWELL (1981)

He won the National Collegiate championship in only the fifth bout he ever wrestled. But that title was just the beginning of Conrad Caldwell's spectacular career.

He did not compete in wrestling at Commerce, Oklahoma, High School and indeed had never seen the sport until he enrolled at Oklahoma State, where Hall of Fame coach Edward C. Gallagher recruited him from a gym class and promised to turn him into a national champion.

His pre-tournament experience consisted of two matches as a substitute heavyweight. Then in three bouts as a 165-pounder in the 1929 NCAA meet, he fulfilled Coach Gallagher's prophecy. He repeated, at 175 pounds, in 1930 and 1931 to become only the third wrestler to win three collegiate crowns.

Caldwell was a standout amid an awesome array of Aggie talent that included such teammates as Earl McCready, Jack Van Bebber, Bobby Pearce and LeRoy McGuirk. One night in 1931, Caldwell applied the finishing touches to a dual meet victory over Kansas State that required only 19 minutes, 33 seconds of wrestling by the entire team.

In 1932, he moved to California and competed five years for the Los Angeles Athletic Club. The only defeat of his career came in the first round of the 1932 Olympic trials. He came back to win those trials at 191 pounds, only to see another wrestler chosen in his place to take part in the Los Angeles Games.

Through 1936, Caldwell was unbeaten from 174 pounds through heavyweight—and on one occasion, all three weights at one time. In a 1933 dual meet with UCLA, he weighed in at 174 but found his teammates at 191 and heavyweight were absent. He pinned the UCLA 174-pounder, won a decision at 191 and after a 10-minute struggle pinned the heavyweight, an all-Coast football tackle.

DR. RAYMOND CLAPP (1976)

Raymond Gustavus Clapp, Doctor of Medicine, was an outstanding athlete and coach but his principal contribution to the sport of wrestling took place as he led development of early-day collegiate rules and collegiate tournaments.

Dr. Clapp became chairman of the NCAA wrestling rules committee in 1927 and served for 18 years. In many respects, it could be said that he WAS the rules committee during its formative years. Through his leadership, a distinct and progressive code of rules for college and high school competition was developed and adopted.

He organized and conducted the first National Collegiate tournament in 1928. Four years earlier, Dr. Clapp inaugurated the Missouri Valley tournament, forerunner of the present Big Eight Conference championships.

While a student at Yale in 1896, he became the first athlete to clear 10 feet in the pole vault, soaring to the unheard of height of 10 feet, 7 inches. Two years later, he raised the world record to 11 feet, 10 inches. Also excelling in gymnastics, he was the Eastern Collegiate allaround champion in 1899. After earning his medical degree at Keokuk College in Iowa, Dr. Clapp became professor of physical education and gymnastics coach at the University of Nebraska. In 1915, he organized a wrestling team at Nebraska which won the Western Conference championship. Six years later, his team administered one of the five defeats suffered by Oklahoma A&M during the coaching tenure of Edward C. Gallagher.

FENDLEY COLLINS (1976)

Fendley Alexander Collins, one of the quiet gentlemen of a fiercely-competitive sport, enjoyed an outstanding 33-year career as coach at Michigan State University, but his contributions to wrestling spanned more than half a century.

As an undefeated 175-pound wrestler under Edward C. Gallagher at Oklahoma State, he won the Canadian amateur championship in 1926 and the U.S. National amateur title in 1927.

After two brief years of high school coaching, he assumed the reins at Michigan State in 1930 and guided the Spartans to 158 victories, against 84 losses and 11 ties. Three times his teams were runners-up in the NCAA tournament, and his wrestlers won 28 national titles in collegiate and amateur meets.

Collins was active in all phases of wrestling. He served on national rules and officials' committees and on the United States Olympic Committee. He was coach of the U.S. team in the 1955 Pan American Games and manager of the 1964 Olympic team.

Some of his most noteworthy activities concerned international competition, and education of America to the differences in style and procedures. He founded the Pan American Wrestling Confederation, served as its first president, and later was named honorary president for life.

He was the first true interpreter and instructor to the United States on the complicated international bracketing system and was the author of the basic guide to pairings still in use throughout the country.

After his retirement from active coaching in 1962, he served another 10 years at Michigan State as coordinator of special events and as instructor in physical education. He retired in 1972, four years before his death.

STEVE COMBS (1985)

When Steve Combs took the helm of the United States Wrestling Federation in 1974, the six-year-old organization was ready to embark on broad educational, developmental and competitive programs for its 9,000 members.

Under the leadership, USWF enjoyed its decade of destiny. Membership grew tenfold to more than 90,000 athletes, and the federation achieved recognition under its new name of USA Wrestling as the sport's national governing body and international representative.

The structure of one of the largest amateur sport organizations in the country was built on the solid grassroots, educational philosophy of Steve Combs. His tenacity survived and overcame the many arbitrations, court cases and political struggles necessary to return control of the sport to the entire wrestling community.

When Steve became executive director, his foremost goal was to establish strong and active state federations. The states continue to play a vital role in determining national policy and operations.

His creativity, and his ability to envision how ideas would fit together, led to many outstanding programs. He established one of the finest sport science projects in the country, by bringing together experts on sport psychology, physiology, nutrition and training techniques.

He recognized the need for a uniform approach in teaching freestyle and Greco-Roman wrestling. This led him to develop the concept of "Seven Basic Skills" and combine it with sport medicine in the National Coach Certification Program. He also led the way in creating developmental camps, officials' clinics, instructional books, films and video tapes, and other publications.

As a wrestler, Steve was a Big Ten champion and a national finalist for the University of Iowa. He went on to win the national freestyle championship and earn a place on the 1968 Olympic team. As a prelude to his role as executive director, he served 11 years as a successful high school coach in Deerfield, Ill., and established the Illinois Wrestling Federation as the type of strong, vibrant state organization that would serve as a national pattern in the years to come.

GENE DAVIS (1985)

National champion, Olympic medalist, international coach—he has written his name into the most exalted records of wrestling. But perhaps no other in our sport has touched as many lives as Gene Davis has with his personal ministry.

In 17 years as wrestler and coach for the Athletes in Action, a division of the Campus Crusade for Christ, Gene and his colleagues have used the forum of athletics to carry their message to groups of sports fans across the nation. That the AIA wrestlers, always "on the road," won 188 of 224 dual meets and two national team championships is noteworthy, but incidental to their primary goal.

Davis was a four-time state high school champion at Missoula, Montana, undefeated in 66 matches. At Oklahoma State University, he was a National Collegiate champion and three-time All-American at 66-3-1, also outstanding wrestler in the Big Eight Conference.

Upon graduation, he joined the Athletes in Action as wrestler and coach. He continued his spectacular athletic career for 11 years, winning four national freestyle titles and placing fourth and sixth in the World Championships. A member of the 1972 Olympic team, he returned four years later as Olympic captain and earned a bronze medal at Montreal.

Gene's lifelong attitude of placing his team and his teammates before personal goals caused him to make a difficult and painful drop to 136.5 pounds for the 1976 Olympics. He had dominated the 149.5-pound class throughout the year, but felt he could strengthen the team by making way for another U.S. candidate. Despite victories over the reigning world champion and the world silver medalist, the strain of severe weight-cutting thwarted his bid for a gold medal.

A recent world champion talks of Gene Davis: "More important than the wrestling knowledge Gene passed on to me is that he gave me perspective. He taught me that there are things in life more important than wrestling."

In 1979, Davis coached the United States to a sweep of 10 gold medals in the Pan American Games. Two years later he was world team coach.

ALBERT DE FERRARI (1979)

His interest in wrestling surfaced in 1922 from deep under the waters of San Francisco Bay. After more than half a century of service to the sport, Dr. Albert de Ferrari's impact on wrestling had spanned the globe.

His first exposure to the sport followed a shipwreck near the Golden Gate. The ship's cargo of cotton was declared free to any takers. Already a champion swimmer and diver, de Ferrari retrieved a truckload. The mothers of his neighborhood then remade the wrestling mats of the area, stuffing in the free cotton and sewing the canvas covers with heavy thread.

Such interest attracted the attention of the young San Francisco dentist. Soon he would become involved in promoting wrestling in the storied Olympic Club, and would nurture the sport until the club became of national renown on the mats.

Doctor Albert never lost his innovative approach. While serving more than two decades on the U.S. Olympic Committee and the International Wrestling Federation, he brought about this country's first exchange series with Japan and the Soviet Union and inaugurated the Junior World Championships.

When the United States Wrestling Federation was founded in 1968, he was an inspirational leader and a close liaison with the international leaders of the sport until his death in 1976.

His greatest contribution came during the late 1950s when he rescued the vague and indecisive international rules from their pointless pattern. Because of his efforts, the international federation accepted the scoring of points for takedowns, stopping of the clock for out-of-bounds, and requirements that even the touch-fall must be controlled by the offensive wrestler.

Even a shipload of waterlogged cotton would have been easier to salvage from the depths.

BOB DELLINGER (1983)

Without setting foot on the mat, except as an official, Bob Dellinger has made a lasting imprint on the sport of wrestling for more than 30 years.

As a reporter and sports editor of Oklahoma City's daily newspapers, he covered wrestling as a major sport. His articles were marked by enthusiasm, and with a thorough knowledge of the subject. He covered high school wrestling statewide and college wrestling nationwide, and showed other newspapers around the country how the sport should be treated.

In 1960, when Jess Hoke and *Amateur Wrestling News* presented the first national "writer of the year" award, Bob was selected. After he won the trophy again in 1961 and 1962, he withdrew his name from consideration. The award promptly was renamed in his honor.

Another major contribution to wrestling has been in the field of tournament operations. Bob Dellinger literally created the science, or art, of conducting tournaments in a smooth, efficient manner, with total fairness for the athletes, consideration for the officials and appeal for the spectators. He became the leading authority on seeding and bracketing, and all other aspects of tournament planning. He authored two revolutionary rules, the present-day team scoring system in 1959, and the current consolation bracketing in 1971.

Under the tutelage of Fendley Collins, he became one of the first to thoroughly understand the international pairings system, and to teach others across the country. When he left the newspapers in 1972 to join the U.S. Wrestling Federation, Bob established the national series of pairings and tournament operations clinics that have educated most of the capable pairings masters in the nation.

He has participated in operations of more than 100 national and international events, in most of them in a position of primary responsibility.

And as director of the Hall of Fame, he has preserved for our education and enjoyment the great moments of wrestling's heritage in our sport's only national museum.

BOBBY DOUGLAS (1987)

The Making of a Champion is the title of his book, and it also is the pattern of Bobby Douglas' life.

From a small town in eastern Ohio, and a small college in neighboring West Virginia, he rose to become a dominant athlete of the 1960s, and earned national and international acclaim in the years that followed.

At Bridgeport High School, he won two state championships and also captured All-State honors in football and baseball. Bobby emerged on the national scene as a 1962 NAIA champion for West Liberty State. A year later, he reached the NCAA finals, and his 13-8 battle with the defending champion from a much larger school was a classic.

To broaden his horizons and to sharpen his skills, Bobby transferred to Oklahoma State, where he won the Big Eight title but was knocked out of the 1965 nationals by an injury, closing his collegiate career at 72-2.

It was in the international styles where Bobby Douglas earned worldwide renown, for his knowledge of the sport and his technical skills—knowledge and skills he later would share with another generation as coach, clinician and author.

He won three national freestyle titles and represented the United States on two Olympic teams and six world teams. He placed second in the world in 1966, third in 1970 and fourth in 1969, and fourth in the 1964 Olympic Games. He was captain of the 1968 Olympic team and compiled a career record of 303 victories with only 17 defeats.

After serving as an assistant coach at Oklahoma State, Iowa State and Cornell, he took the reins at the University of California at Santa Barbara in 1973. A year later, he moved to Arizona State, where he not only built a collegiate powerhouse, but also launched the Sunkist Kids club toward a series of national championships. He has been assistant coach for seven world and three Olympic teams and is World Cup coach for 1987.

Bobby Douglas was the first black athlete to wrestle for the USA in the Olympic Games, the first to captain our Olympic team, and the first to coach wrestling at a major university. He showed, by example, that others could reach such goals.

FINN ERIKSEN (1982)

As a wrestler, as a high school coach, as an administrator, as an official, Finn Eriksen lived by the rules. Some might say, in truth, that he also lived for the rules.

In the early years, when wrestling had no orderly structure, he helped create one. It stands today as the foundation of wrestling's growth and progress.

In high school in his native Denmark, Finn had no wrestling opportunity, but was an outstanding gymnast. When he entered Northern Iowa in 1927, this skilled athlete soon became a star wrestler.

He emerged onto the coaching scene in 1932 and found the sport in low esteem. There were no elementary or junior high programs, few high schools had practice rooms or mats, there were no summer camps, few qualified coaches and virtually no literature for the novice coach. American wrestling rules were vague and poorly coordinated.

To Finn Eriksen this shambles was intolerable. While building a dynasty at West Waterloo, he worked to lift other programs up to his standards of excellence. When he retired after 12 years as coach and entered three decades as a public schools administrator, his efforts to coordinate the sport increased tenfold.

His brilliant coaching produced many stars. In 1947, six of his proteges competed for various schools in the NCAA tournament. Two became champions, one placed second, another fourth. All of his wrestlers showed the discipline and character so typical of their mentor.

He was an outstanding referee and officiated in the 1952 Olympics, the first Iowan to earn an international license. But most of all he was an educator. He conducted countless clinics for wrestlers, coaches and officials and was the author of many articles in national publications.

As a long-time member of the national rules committee, and as an interpreter of the rules to the schools, he had a profound influence on the sport.

TOMMY EVANS (1976)

Jay Thomas Evans left an indelible imprint on the sport of wrestling as a champion athlete and a champion coach.

Evans wrestled for the University of Oklahoma in 1951, 1952 and 1954, missing the 1953 season because of injury. He won 42 of 43 matches and scored 20 falls, an aggressive style which he carried forward into his coaching career. He was National Collegiate champion in 1952 and 1954 and both times was voted outstanding wrestler of the NCAA tournament, at that time only the second athlete to win such honors twice.

His wrestling career carried Evans around the world, to Helsinki, Finland, in 1952, and to Melbourne, Australia, in 1956, as a member of United States Olympic teams. At Melbourne, he wrestled in both freestyle and Greco-Roman competition.

In the 1952 Olympic finals at Helsinki, Evans took his Swedish opponent to the mat seven times, but under the archaic scoring system then in use was not awarded a point and was forced to settle for the silver medal at 147 pounds.

Evans also won three national amateur titles and a gold medal in the 1955 Pan-American Games.

He succeeded Port Robertson as coach at Oklahoma in 1960 and led his first team to the NCAA title. Only Art Griffith at Oklahoma State ever had achieved that feat. Skipping the 1962 season for active duty as a pilot—his present occupation—Evans returned in 1963 and coached 10 more years, compiling a record of 140 victories, 39 defeats, two ties and two more NCAA team championships. He also coached U.S. teams in the 1967 World Championships and the 1968 Olympic Games.

BILL FARRELL (1987)

Without the benefit of a high school or collegiate wrestling background, Bill Farrell enjoyed a substantial career as a wrestler and coach for the New York Athletic Club. But it was as world team and Olympic coach that he led his country to its best performance in nearly half a century.

Farrell took over the national freestyle team in the late 1960s, at a time when international programs needed his leadership in organization and management, as well as his coaching. He was known for his ability to blend individuals with diverse personalities and different techniques into a successful unit, obtaining maximum effort from each without conflict.

He organized training champs to expose more wrestlers to international techniques and strategy. And his knowledge of the international scoring system short-circuited Iron Curtain "deals" at least twice to protect USA gold medals.

Farrell's 1969 team placed second in the World Championships, this country's highest finish, and produced our first two gold medalists in Rick Sanders and Fred Fozzard. All 10 USA wrestlers placed in the top six. In 1970, the USA placed second, with Wayne Wells as champion among five medalists.

In the 1972 Olympic Games, Farrell guided the Americans to an unexpected six medals: gold for Wells, Dan Gable and Ben Peterson, silver for Sanders and John Peterson, and bronze for the mammoth Chris Taylor.

As a wrestler for the New York AC, Bill chalked up more than 300 victories, gaining All-American stature, winning the Canadian Nationals and placing sixth in the 1962 Worlds. But it was as NYAC coach from 1960 through 1972 that he earned national, then international, acclaim.

When Farrell began selling wrestling shoes out of the trunk of his car in the late 1950s, it was the start of one of the nation's largest wrestling equipment firms, one that since has branched into other areas of physical fitness. His company has supplied equipment and financial support to U.S. teams for three decades.

He has served as secretary of the Olympic Wrestling Committee and as president of the New York Athletic Club. And he was the first "Marlboro Man" when an advertising agency built its campaign around rugged-looking individuals.

ROSS FLOOD (1978)

One of his ancestors, Daniel Boone, was a fair-to-middlin' sharpshooter, and when Ross Flood went hunting for wrestling championships his aim was just as good.

At Blackwell, Ross and his brother John became the first twins to win Oklahoma high school championships. Then Ross pursued his wrestling career at Oklahoma State University under Hall of Fame coach Edward C. Gallagher.

Undefeated in 30 matches at 126 pounds, he won three National Collegiate championships in 1933, '34 and '35, each time leading the Cowboys to NCAA team honors. As a senior he was voted outstanding wrestler of the national tournament.

His achievements continued to mount when he won national freestyle championships in 1935 and 1936 and another Outstanding Wrestler trophy. He then earned a place on the U.S. Olympic team and captured the silver medal at 123 pounds in the Games at Berlin.

In the 1937 Pan American Exposition at Dallas, he won the gold medal at the expense of three other national champions, despite severe rib injuries which brought an end to his competitive career.

For six years he was a successful high school coach in Stillwater, then entered the Navy to spend five years as a physical instructor, including wartime service in the Pacific theater. He returned to coaching in 1946 to revive the wrestling program at Southwestern Oklahoma State, then purchased a livestock auction in Stillwater, which he operated for three decades.

Billy Sheridan, the famed Lehigh coach, often declared that Ross Flood provided the best example he had ever seen of wrestling skills and techniques.

DAN GABLE (1980)

A textbook on dedication, determination and desire should use Dan Gable as its model. His relentless pursuit of excellence carried him to the highest pinnacles of achievement.

Dan Gable won every major championship available to an American wrestler, climaxed by the gold medal in the 1972 Olympic Games.

He was an undefeated, three-time state high school champion at West Waterloo in Iowa. He won six consecutive Midlands Champions. At Iowa State University, he captured three Big Eight Conference titles and national collegiate honors in 1968 and again in 1969. He won 100 college matches in a row.

Such was the stature of this magnificent athlete that he is best remembered for a match he lost, the 101st of his collegiate career, the 1970 NCAA finals to Larry Owings of Washington. Yet defeat only spurred him to new heights.

Starting in 1969, he won three national freestyle championships. In 1971, he was outstanding wrestler of a major international tournament in Russia, and won gold medals at the Pan American Games in Colombia and the world championships in Bulgaria.

Thousands of miles of roadwork, thousands of hours of training had brought Dan Gable within sight of his goal. He was ready for the Olympic challenge. He overwhelmed all opponents in the Games at Munich and was widely acclaimed as outstanding wrestler of the 1972 Olympics.

What now, what new challenge for the world's finest wrestler?

Turning to coaching, Gable joined the University of Iowa staff in 1973 and became head coach in 1977. His Hawkeyes won three NCAA team titles in his first four years at the helm. He also has served as world freestyle coach with notable success, and was the 1980 Olympic coach.

But Dan Gable, the coach, may never discover an athlete with the intense determination of Dan Gable, the wrestler.

EDWARD C. GALLAGHER (1976)

Edward Clark Gallagher was a pioneer, not only of wrestling techniques but also of wrestling tradition. From Oklahoma State University, where his coaching achievements were unparalleled, Ed Gallagher's influence on the sport spread across the nation. Long after his death in 1940, his torch was carried onward by Gallagher's pupils, who became great coaches in their own right at major universities across the land.

As a collegian, Gallagher excelled in football and track. He was clocked once in 9.8 seconds while winning the 100-yard dash in the Southwest Conference meet, and his 99-yard run in the Kansas State football game that same year, 1908, still stands as the OSU school record.

He received his degree in electrical engineering, but chose a career coaching football and track, and teaching physical education. He remained at his alma mater for several years, then went to Baker University in Kansas.

In 1916, he returned to Oklahoma State as director of athletics. Gallagher introduced scientific wrestling to gym classes and put his first varsity team on the mat that year. He applied his engineering knowledge of leverage and stress to the development of more than 300 wrestling holds. He was the first to organize systematic practice situations, and devoted close attention to diet and training methods.

In 23 years of coaching he produced 19 undefeated team. His wrestlers won 138 dual meets, tied four and lost only five. During the 10 years prior to 1932 his teams scored 68 consecutive victories.

When the National Collegiate tournament was inaugurated in 1928, halfway through his coaching career, Gallagher's wrestlers won four of the seven individual titles, earning recognition as the first NCAA championship team. Competing in 13 NCAA tournaments, the Gallagher teams reigned supreme 10 times and shared an 11th title. Along the way, they collected 37 individual NCAA titles, 32 national amateur crowns, and three Olympic Gold Medals.

Ed Gallagher coaching Eldon Jackson at a 1939 meet.

SPRIG GARDNER (1986)

He didn't set out to create a legend, nor to become one. Sprig Gardner simply wanted to start a high school wrestling program, and to teach skills and sportsmanship to young athletes. His success story is without parallel.

In two decades at Mepham High School on Long Island, Sprig Gardner sent his teams to the mats 304 times for dual meet or tournament competition. Ten times only, they failed to finish first (and two of those were ties).

A graduate of Franklin & Marshall, without wrestling experience, he organized his first team at Mepham in 1937 in an abandoned elementary school converted to a high school. Except for three years in World War II as a lieutenant commander on an aircraft carrier, he remained at the helm until 1958. He spent two later years restoring a wrestling program at Gettysburg College.

After a year at the junior varsity level, Mepham burst onto the scholastic scene. Not for eight years would Gardner's teams know defeat. In January 1946, Baldwin High School ended a streak of 100 consecutive victories, yet that loss was merely an interlude to greater success. Mepham would not fall again until January 1955, when a one-point loss to Amityville ended a string of 130 triumphs. In 18 years, Gardner's charges also won 37 consecutive South Shore and Sectional tournaments.

The battle lines spread from Long Island. Mepham overpowered the best teams and even all-star squads from five states. Over-all, Sprig's wrestlers won 254 dual meets, lost five and drew one. His tournament teams won 40 titles, shared another and placed second three times.

Sprig and his Mepham wrestlers were featured in a five-page article in *Life* magazine. Two of his proteges, George Creason and Sid Nodland, won National AAU championships while still in high school. Eighteen went on to win Eastern Intercollegiate titles. Many attained success in both athletics and business.

Innovation was a key to Sprig Gardner's success. His drill system revolutionized the sport. He shared his concepts through books and articles and by turning his wrestling room into an "open house" where anyone might come and learn.

MANNY GORRIARAN (1985)

Seldom if ever has anyone contributed to the sport of wresting in so many ways, in so many places, for so many years, as Manny Gorriaran.

Born in Havana, Cuba, at the turn of the century, he emigrated to the United States in 1936 and founded a firm—now one of the world's largest—specializing in the design and manufacture of jewelry and emblems. Because of his love of the sport, wrestling designs soon made their mark among his wares. He has donated more than 100,000 emblems and trading pins to wrestling teams and organizations around the world.

Before leaving Cuba, he helped add wrestling to the Central American and Caribbean Games, forerunners of the Pan American Games. A year later, he formed the first Cuban wrestling team, bringing opponents from Miami for its first competition.

He is recognized as the father of the sport in Rhode Island, but his activities know no boundaries. He has served as manager of United States teams in Pan American, World and Olympic competition. While acting as announcer and interpreter for the Pan Am Games of 1959, he helped rewrite and translate the organization's bylaws to provide strong and fair rules for wrestling.

He is best known for his insistence on the fall as the ultimate goal of amateur wrestling, and for inaugurating an award given at tournaments everywhere, the Gorriaran Trophy for the wrestler scoring the most falls in the least total time.

In the early 1960s, he decided that wrestling needed its own "Heisman Trophy," and conceived an annual award to wrestling's Man of the Year. The first award, in 1963, was voted to his good friend, Jess Hoke. Two years later, Manny was elected.

For more than 20 years, he has made and donated awards to all tournaments held for blind wrestlers, along with many special awards for conference, regional and national collegiate events.

He is a lifetime member of the U.S. Olympic Committee, the Pan American Wrestling Confederation, the Swedish Amateur Wrestling Federation and the International Wrestling Federation.

ART GRIFFITH (1976)

Art Griffith always felt a coach should lead his wrestlers to championships, and he lived up to that ideal. In 30 years of coaching, he took his teams to 77 tournaments and never left the scene without at least one gold medal.

Griffith's coaching career spanned two great dynasties, first for 15 years at Central High School in Tulsa, Oklahoma, and then for 13 seasons at Oklahoma State University. His records were fabulous.

His high school teams won 94 of 100 matches, 50 of them in a row, and 10 Oklahoma scholastic championships. A dozen times, his Braves were undefeated, and they won the only two national high school tournaments conducted.

Succeeding Edward C. Gallagher, he took the reins at Oklahoma State in 1941 and amassed eight NCAA championships in 13 attempts. His teams produced 78 victories against seven losses and four ties, and 10 times were undefeated. His wrestlers won 27 individual NCAA titles.

When he became the Cowboy coach, they already had won 27 consecutive dual meets. Under his leadership that streak was extended to a record 76 before a loss in 1951. He was U.S. Olympic coach in 1948.

Art Griffith developed his own style of wrestling, with constant motion as the hallmark. "Every technique has its weakness," he said, "but you can't exploit that weakness by standing still. You must move, and you must force your opponent to move with you."

Another lasting contribution was Griffith's development of the point scoring system for wrestling bouts, which in early days were determined only by falls or time advantage.

Griffith served in many roles throughout his career, but the effect of his coaching greatness was most in evidence in 1941. Of the 16 National Collegiate finalists that year, all but two had been coached by Griffith in either high school or college.

RUSSELL HELLICKSON (1988)

One of wrestling's dominant figures of the past two decades, Russ Hellickson ruled the nation's light heavyweights through the 1970s and continued to shine through the 1980s as a coach and contributor to the sport.

Although he was a three-sport high school star at Stoughton, Wisconsin, and a consistent winner at the University of Wisconsin–Madison, Hellickson's career burst into national and international prominence after his graduation in 1970. He won 12 national championships in freestyle and one in Greco-Roman, captured silver and bronze medals and a fourth place in the World Championships, and won the Tbilisi International and the World Cup. Hellickson is the only wrestler ever to win three gold medals in the Pan American Games, in 1971, 1975, and 1979.

Thwarted by injury in 1972, he won the silver medal in the 1976 Olympic Games, battling defending champion Ivan Yarygin of the Soviet Union in a 19-13 spellbinder. Hellickson was captain of the 1980 Olympic freestyle team that was kept at home by the boycott.

During the same period, he served 12 years as assistant coach at the University of Wisconsin, where he became head coach in 1982. After four successful seasons, he moved to Ohio State. As head coach he has produced more than 100 victories, three NCAA champions and a dozen All-Americans.

Russ and his wife, Nancy, founded The Crossface, Wisconsin's state wrestling newspaper, and they were honored together nationally as writers of the year in 1974 and as state editors of the year in 1976.

Hellickson spent five years as Wisconsin state chairman for USA Wrestling, helping develop the state program into the second largest membership in the country. He also has served as a member of USA Wrestling's board of directors, as president of the independent clubs, as freestyle sport chairman and as a member of the national coaching staff. He was Junior World coach in 1981 and in 1983.

His televised coach's talk show and production of instructional and motivational video tapes led to a new phase of his career—television commentator. He was the voice of wrestling for ABC at the 1984 Olympic Games, for TBS at the '86 Goodwill Games and for NBC at the 1988 Olympics.

STANLEY HENSON (1978)

In the never-ending debate over who has been America's greatest wrestler, Stanley Henson always received plenty of support. His record as a competitor speaks for itself.

Henson's career was blessed by the leadership of two Hall of Fame coaches. At Tulsa Central High School, under Art Griffith, he wrestled two years, won two state championships and won the outstanding wrestler award as a senior.

Then he joined the Oklahoma State University team of Edward C. Gallagher. Defeated only once in three seasons, Henson won three NCAA championships and each time led the Cowboys to the team title.

In 1937 he became the first sophomore ever to be voted Outstanding Wrestler of the NCAA tournament. He continued to excel the next two years, but the nation's coaches were not yet ready to present their cherished award to any man a second time.

He also won the Pan-American Exposition in 1937 and scored a 1938 double with the national freestyle title. As his junior year drew to a close with two championships, Henson already was thinking more of medical school than of wrestling.

During a European tour in the fall of 1938, he suffered a severe shoulder injury which hampered him during his senior year but couldn't prevent a third NCAA title, this one at 155 pounds after two at 145.

After five years as a physical instructor and wrestling assistant at the U.S. Naval Academy, Henson was able to concentrate fully on the study of medicine, completing his degree in 1950 at the University of Maryland.

Now a highly-respected surgeon, he was one of the first to combine his athletic and medical interests in the rapidly growing field of sports medicine, where he became a nationally-known lecturer and consultant.

DANNY HODGE (1976)

Dan Allen Hodge was a wrestler of awesome strength, physical prowess so great that often, for his fans at least, it overshadowed his tremendous skills. His grip could shatter a pair of pliers, could crush an apple into applesauce. Had he not studied and carefully utilized proper wrestling techniques, he might well have maimed his opponents instead of dominating them.

In the collegiate style of wrestling, he had no peer, indeed no challenger. He won every one of his 46 bouts for the University of Oklahoma, 36 of them by fall, for an astonishing 78 percent. During his junior and senior years, he pinned 22 consecutive opponents. And no collegiate foe ever took him to the mat from the standing position.

Three times an NCAA champion at 177 pounds, he twice was voted the Outstanding Wrestler of the NCAA tournament.

In one 10-day span in 1956, his junior year, Hodge won the NCAA title, and AAU national championships in both Greco-Roman and freestyle, winning every bout in those three tournaments by fall.

Twice he was an Olympic wrestler, placing fifth in 1952 at Helsinki before his college career started, and winning the silver medal in the 1956 Games at Melbourne. There, in the championship bout, he led his Bulgarian opponent by a wide margin when a controversial fall was called against him. In five years, starting in 1952, his only three defeats in any style of wrestling were administered by three Olympic champions: a Russian, an American and a Bulgarian.

After his collegiate wrestling career, Dan Hodge won national amateur and national Golden Gloves championships in boxing, becoming the first athlete in more than 50 years to win national championships in both sports.

JESS HOKE (1977)

He was neither a wrestler not a coach, but Jess Hoke stands among the giants of the sport as its first true communicator. As founder and editor of *Amateur Wrestling News*, now in its third decade of publication, he has had monumental impact on wrestling's tremendous growth, coast to coast.

His interest in wrestling was stimulated during his days as a student sportswriter in the early stages of Edward C. Gallagher's coaching career at Oklahoma A&M. He had a personal interest, too, in Coach Gallagher, who had been his Scoutmaster and track coach. The account of the first major Cowboy victory, over Nebraska in 1920, carried Jess Hoke's byline.

In the 1950s, as five of his seven sons journeyed north to Michigan State to wrestle for coach Fendley Collins, he discovered that college students then, as now, were inconsistent about writing letters home.

From his interest in Michigan State results came the fullscale idea of a publication to carry wrestling results across the nation. At that time, wrestling was a regional sport. Nobody knew what was happening a few miles away.

Thus was born "Wrestling News and Reports," soon to become "Amateur Wrestling News," annually publishing thousands of dual meet summaries and complete reports on activities from high school tournaments to the Olympic Games.

With "Amateur Wrestling News" as his forum, Jess has inaugurated many projects to stimulate interest throughout the sport: national rankings of college teams, tournament forecasts, and achievement awards to coaches, wrestlers, writers, photographers and other contributors.

In 1962, he was the first recipient of amateur wrestling's Man of the Year trophy. His role in establishing wrestling as a nationally-known sport is without parallel.

WALLY JOHNSON (1985)

For 40 years, and more than 600 dual meets, Wally Johnson has instilled the American "work ethic" into his wrestlers, and both he and his teams have realized the fruits of success.

Throughout his career he has been a man of foresight, a builder. More than three decades ago, he founded wrestling programs at Luther College in Iowa and across the state of South Dakota. He launched Kids wrestling in Minnesota, and was one of the founding fathers of the United States Wrestling Federation, serving as its first president and guiding it over the rocky path of its formative years.

Entering his 35th year of coaching at the University of Minnesota, Johnson has amassed 380 victories with the Golden Gophers. Adding five years at Luther and South Dakota, his career total swells to 419 victories and an astonishing 67 per cent. He also coached football and track at South Dakota and football at Minnesota.

He was a multi-sport athlete for the Gophers, captain of the wrestling team, member of an NCAA champion football team and twice the school's middleweight boxing champion.

He had no opportunity to wrestle in high school, because the state did not adopt the sport until the year after his graduation in 1937. But once a state program was developed, he helped refine it and established its team format. For years, he has offered free clinics to Minnesota youngsters, bringing in top instructors from around the country.

And he has contributed immensely to the growth of Greco-Roman wrestling by opening the doors of his wrestling room to the Minnesota Wrestling Club, helping it develop into the nation's strongest Greco power.

His coaching produced two Big Ten champion teams, 35 individual titlists, four NCAA champs and more than 40 AllAmericans. An even more impressive statistic is the 99 per cent graduation rate of his lettermen, the result of his adamant stand that academics always outrank athletics.

He always has offered his facilities and financial support to senior athletes. His career has encompassed the roles of promoter, coach, team leader and administrator, no matter the age or skill level of the contestants.

CLIFF KEEN (1976)

Clifford Patrick Keen started his coaching career in football. His 1925 high school team at Frederick, Oklahoma, scored 355 points and yielded but three. Then he decided to see what he could do with wrestlers.

After 45 years at the University of Michigan, the longest coaching career in wrestling history, the answer was clear. He could develop champions.

Cliff Keen was an undefeated wrestler under Edward C. Gallagher at Oklahoma State University and won the Missouri Valley national invitational championship. In 1924, he won the Olympic trials but was sidelined by a broken rib. His substitute ultimately lost in the Olympic finals at Paris.

He also was a football and track star.

His Michigan teams twice were NCAA runners-up and they won 13 Big Ten Conference championships, placing in the top three in the conference 40 times. They won 276 dual meets against 88 losses and 11 ties. His wrestlers captured 11 National Collegiate titles and 81 conference crowns.

But Cliff Keen's impact on the world of wrestling has no state or national boundaries. He served on the U.S. Olympic Committee from 1928 to 1952 and was manager of the 1948 Olympic team in London.

He was an original member and later president of the National Wrestling Coaches Association and also presided over the national rules committee. For many years he has pioneered the development of safe, effective wrestling equipment, such as the headgear which bears his name. There is no role of service to wrestling which has not borne the stamp of Cliff Keen.

He obtained a law degree from Michigan in 1933 and served three years as a naval commander during World War II.

Cliff Keen listens to his achievements while standing near his plaque at the National Wrestling Hall of Fame. (Courtesy of National Wrestling Hall of Fame)

PAUL KEEN (1977)

An outstanding collegiate athlete in almost every sport except wrestling, Paul Keen, Cliff's brother, was handed a staggering assignment when he joined the coaching staff at the University of Oklahoma. All he had to do was build the fledgling Sooner mat program to a competitive level with the awesome power of his old school, Oklahoma A&M.

As an Aggie student, he had starred in football, basketball and track. He learned the fundamentals of wrestling by working out with the teams of coach Edward C. Gallagher. When he was a senior, he could have wrestled on the varsity, but he had been elected basketball captain and chose to fulfill that obligation.

His 12-year coaching career at Oklahoma is marked by two historic milestones. In 1932, after four years at the Sooner helm, he led his team to an outstanding upset of Gallagher's Aggies in Stillwater, shattering a winning streak that had spanned 70 dual meets and 10 undefeated seasons.

Four years later, in 1936, he guided Oklahoma to the national collegiate championship, OU's first national title in any sport. Keen's Sooners also finished second twice and third twice in NCAA tournaments and captured 12 individual championships. His wrestlers won six titles in the Big Six Conference and never placed below third.

Another milestone of his coaching career collapsed in the fires of World War II. He was destined to become the 1940 Olympic wrestling coach, but the Olympic torch was snuffed out by the worldwide holocaust.

Throughout his coaching tenure, he recruited and taught without the aid of a single scholarship grant. To further the development of young wrestlers, he joined with Coach Gallagher to establish a strong high school wrestling program in Oklahoma.

BILL KERSLAKE (1982)

He was one of the first giant heavyweights of modern American wrestling, but Bill Kerslake's achievements on the mat far surpassed even his physical stature.

He had no high school wrestling opportunity and little collegiate experience, although he starred in football and track at both levels. But in postgraduate wrestling, he became the dominant figure of the 1950s, winning 15 national championships in freestyle and Greco-Roman.

Over an eight-year span starting in 1953, he won 76 consecutive bouts in national tournament competition, and the national championship in both styles, until his streak was broken in the Greco-Roman finals of 1960. One of his tournament bouts in 1956 ended in just four seconds, still a record for the fastest fall in national competition.

He won a gold medal in the Pan-American Games of 1955 and three times represented the United States in the Olympic Games, placing fifth, eighth and seventh from 1952 through 1960. After his retirement from competition, he remained active in the sport as a referee for more than a decade.

While his collegiate days at Case Tech may not have been the ultimate preparation for competitive wrestling, he took advantage of the exceptional academic opportunities in engineering. Throughout his wrestling career, and to the present, he has been an aerospace research engineer for the National Aeronautics and Space Administration.

He is co-inventor of the first ion thruster for space propulsion at NASA, and has served as chairman of the national technical committee of the American Institute of Aeronautics and Astronautics.

BILL KOLL (1977)

How good was Bill Koll as a collegiate wrestler? Take a look at the record—he wrestled 3 and 1/2 years and won every match in devastating style. Along the way, he earned three consecutive national collegiate championship and three national freestyle titles.

In the midst of his first season, he left college to serve three years with the combat engineers in World War II, earning the Bronze Star. He returned to become a ringleader of the great Iowa Teachers teams developed by coach Dave McCuskey in the late 1940s.

In 1946, at the first post-war NCAA tournament, he won the award for the most falls. A year later, he was voted Outstanding Wrestler of the collegiate championships.

When he was elected Outstanding Wrestler again in 1948, he became the first contestant ever to win the NCAA's most coveted individual trophy a second time. Only four others since have earned that award twice.

Also in 1948, he won the U.S. Olympic trials at 147.5 pounds and placed fifth in the unfamiliar international style at the London Games.

After graduation, Bill Koll turned his masterful skills to coaching, where he has established another outstanding career. Starting at the University of Chicago, then moving to Cornell College, he returned to the Iowa Teachers (now the University of Northern Iowa) to succeed Coach McCuskey.

During his 11 years at UNI, his Panthers won 71 dual meets. He was instrumental in inaugurating the NCAA's College Division national tournament and served as host and tournament director of the first two events in 1963 and 1964.

He then succeeded Charlie Speidel at Penn State University, where his teams always rank high in the eastern and national standings, with more than 100 dual meet wins.

LOWELL LANGE (1981)

He won his first national freestyle championship while still in high school at West Waterloo, Iowa. For three of the next four years, Lowell Lange ruled without serious challenge over the nation's lightweight wrestlers.

Had not severe injuries in an automobile accident knocked him out of competition as a sophomore, in the Olympic year of 1948, he likely would have become collegiate wrestling's only four-time champion, as well as an international medalist.

But he won three NCAA titles and three more national freestyle crowns for Cornell College of Iowa while amassing 160 victories against a single loss. In 1947 he helped the Rams of Coach Paul Scott capture the NCAA team trophy, the only one ever won by a private school.

Returning from injury as a junior, he swept through the 1949 collegiate tournament without surrendering a single point, perhaps the only wrestler to do so since scoring rules were adopted.

Lange spent the 1951 season as Cornell coach, and still regards the selection of his 130-pounder, Walt Romanowski, as the NCAA's Outstanding Wrestler one of his greatest thrills.

In 1964, business interests took Lange to Atlanta, where he immediately set out to revive the long-dormant wrestling program at Georgia Tech, taking over the coaching position he has held to this day. Only two years later, his team defeated Auburn in the Southeastern tournament, handing Swede Umbach his first conference setback in 20 years.

Despite the handicaps of a low-budget program, Lange has maintained wrestling interest at Tech, while contributing to the success of the sport at the national level. He has served as a member of the rules committee and the coaches' executive committee and helped launch U.S. Wrestling Federation programs in Georgia.

GERALD LEEMAN (1977)

Bursting onto the scene as a precocious youngster, Gerry Leeman won his first national freestyle championship at 112 pounds in 1940, while he was still in high school at Osage, Iowa. In fact, Leeman and a high school teammate scored more points in that AAU tournament than the official national team champion.

That event was the forerunner of an outstanding career. Wrestling three years for coach Dave McCuskey at Iowa Teachers College, he lost only one bout and reigned as national collegiate champion and outstanding NCAA wrestler in 1946. His career was interrupted by wartime service as a Navy pilot.

In 1948, he scaled even further heights, winning another national freestyle crown and earning the 125.5 position on the U.S. Olympic team. He brought home a silver medal from the London Games.

During the Olympic trials of 1948, he caught the eye of the great Billy Sheridan of Lehigh. Sheridan knew he had found his eventual successor as coach of the Engineers. And, after two years as a title-winning high school pilot in Iowa, Leeman joined the Lehigh staff in 1950, succeeding Sheridan as head coach in 1953.

During his 18-year tenure, he never suffered a losing season, winning 161 dual meets against only 38 losses and producing six Eastern team champions and 36 individual winners. Six of his wrestlers captured 10 NCAA titles, including Lehigh's only three-time winner, Mike Caruso.

He worked closely with Sheridan to carry on the nation's first summer wrestling camp, which had been established by Sheridan in 1935.

At Lehigh, Leeman also coached varsity tennis, soccer and cross-country, and freshman track. Even after his official retirement as head wrestling coach in 1970, he remained active in wrestling and other athletic programs at Lehigh.

FRANK LEWIS (1979)

As a tall, skinny college freshman, Frank Lewis was "a little tired" after six years of wrestling and planned to give full attention to his studies at Oklahoma State University.

But he needed a physical education credit and figured that wrestling class would provide an easy grade. Members of the class were required to compete in the all-college intramurals and when he failed to win the championship his pride was stung. He decided to concentrate on wrestling again.

Frank Lewis concentrated so well that he became a national champion and the gold medalist in the 1936 Olympic Games at Berlin.

A state high school champion and four-time medalist from 100 to 155 pounds, he possessed the raw talent from which coach Edward C. Gallagher could mold a winner. But because of his rapid growth, the youngster didn't have the stamina to wrestle the longer college matches. And because of a minor heart condition, his coach had to devise a special training routine to build stamina without putting a strain on his health.

Despite these difficulties, he established a collegiate record of 45 victories against just five defeats, winning the NCAA championship in 1935 after placing second the year before. Both years he contributed vital points to the Cowboys' team trophies.

In 1935, he won the national freestyle title and became the first contestant to be officially recognized as the Outstanding Wrestler of the national AAU tournament, receiving a gold watch for this honor.

A year later, he swept undefeated through the series of Olympic trials, then defended his position against his alternate on the boat to Europe.

In the Games, he scored a fall the first day, another the second day. He wrestled three times the third day, but stamina no longer was a problem and two more falls offset a narrow loss to Tur Andersson of Sweden as Frank Lewis became the only American to win a gold medal.

GUY LOOKABAUGH (1983)

As the first superstar of Oklahoma State athletics, Guy Lookabaugh helped establish a wrestling dynasty that spanned half a century. He earned headlines in football, but in wrestling was recognized as one of the greatest athletes of his time.

Guy Lookabaugh enrolled at Oklahoma State, then Oklahoma A&M, in 1917 and immediately became a football hero. He then enlisted in the army, but returned after the war to become known as the first "Super Aggie."

In 1920, Coach Ed Gallagher's wrestlers made a bid for national recognition, facing a mighty Nebraska team that was undefeated for five years. With his team trailing, Lookabaugh took the mat at 158 pounds and battled through a 27-minute overtime match for a difficult decision. In the final bout, the Aggies had victory within reach, but had no one to send against Nebraska's unbeaten 175-pound star. Coach Gallagher again called upon Lookabaugh, and he responded with a "regular" 21-minute decision to give the Oklahomans their first major wrestling triumph.

Lookabaugh, nicknamed "Ducky," never lost a college match. His career preceded the national collegiate tournaments, but in 1921 he won championships of three conferences–the Missouri Valley (now the Big Eight), the Western (Big Ten) and the Southwest.

He was known for his flamboyant style, as shown in his first national freestyle tournament. Facing Eino Leino, the great Finn who would win four Olympic medals, Lookabaugh threw him out of the ring and pinned him on the floor. The referee ruled it an illegal fall.

Lookabaugh turned to coaching in 1922 and 1923, but returned to school to train for the 1924 Olympics. He reached the finals of the Games at Paris, only to lose an unpopular split decision.

After graduation in 1925, he coached three years at Kansas and served with Dr. Raymond G. Clapp on the national rules committee as it formulated plans for the first NCAA tournament. His coaching career continued at Northeastern Oklahoma and Grinnell of Iowa until 1940.

BILLY MARTIN (1980)

Were it not for the high school wrestling coaches of this land, there would be few—if any—collegiate and post-graduate stars to earn national and international acclaim. Among these vital contributors to the sport, Billy Martin stands at the highest level.

His record at Granby High School in Norfolk, Va., is a story of phenomenal success: 259 duals meet victories and but nine defeats, 22 state team titles in 23 years, 106 individual state champions.

Six of his wrestlers went on to capture 10 national collegiate championships. Two of them competed in the Olympic Games. Many others earned All-American honors. One year, 10 of his proteges appeared in the same NCAA tournament, representing a variety of schools.

Yet the measure of a high school coach rests not only on the written records. His true impact on the sport is achieved through his influence on the lives of young men. Here, the diminutive figure of Billy Martin stands among the giants.

He began his education in wrestling as a 1940 graduate of Michigan State. But he has never faltered in extending that education, nor in sharing it with others. Always seeking a new and better method, he has become known as an innovator of wresting maneuvers, such as the Granby Roll series.

His educational efforts for wrestling are not measured by scholastic seasons. Through clinics and summer camps, he has carried his knowledge of wrestling and its values to thousands of youngsters and their coaches.

Billy Martin was the founder of organized wrestling in Virginia, developing programs at all levels across the state—high school, collegiate, intramural, recreational and community activities.

GEORGE MARTIN (1982)

He extended the boundaries of his campus to the state borders. In more than three decades as coach at the University of Wisconsin, George Martin accepted no limits on his efforts to develop the sport he loved.

He was a gifted athlete and a successful coach, but most of all he was a builder. A master craftsman in woodworking, he had the skills to construct the framework of national prominence in wrestling for his university and for his state.

As a wrestler, he was a national collegiate champion for Iowa State in 1933, and as captain led the derby-hatted Cyclones to a share of the team title. The Iowans adopted their dapper headgear in answer to the cowboy attire of their rivals in Oklahoma.

Martin won the national freestyle championship in 1934, but passed up a chance at the Olympics and became coach at Wisconsin. In 1935 there were no high school teams in the state, although some schools had intramural wrestling. He convinced a few to add the sport to their varsity programs, and in 1940 the first state tournament was held.

After a three-year wartime interruption, during which he earned a bronze star for heroism as a naval officer, he returned to coaching and served with honor until his death in 1970.

During those early years in Wisconsin, George traveled some 40,000 miles within the state—equal to nearly two trips around the world—giving demonstrations, presenting clinics and talking with school board, administrators and parents to sell the values of the sport. Today there are more than 400 wrestling schools in Wisconsin.

He patterned his life, and the lives of his students, on those values. He taught that winning is not as important as striving to win, and that the purpose of athletics is to develop the individual to his full potential.

His stature as the father of wrestling in Wisconsin is attested by the fact that the state's wrestling hall of fame is named for him.

CHARLES W. MAYSER (1977)

They called him "Uncle Charlie," but Charles W. Mayser was the father of four outstanding wrestling programs in the first quarter of the 20th century, reaching from the ivy covered halls of Yale to the plains of Iowa.

He entered Yale in 1900, intending to put himself through medical school. But he decided teaching physical education to freshmen was more rewarding, and instead graduated from the New Haven School of Gymnastics. In 1901, he coached Yale gymnasts at the Pan-American Exposition.

He was responsible for introducing wrestling as a varsity sport at Yale, creating the nation's first dual meet team in 1903. Ten years later he became football coach at Franklin & Marshall College. It was a brief stop, but soon he would return for a lifetime.

He became director of athletics at Iowa State in 1915, coaching football and introducing a wrestling program which has ranked consistently among the nation's finest. Five of his eight teams were undefeated.

He also launched Iowa's high school program, perhaps the first in the country and certainly one of the best.

Mayser returned to Franklin & Marshall in 1924 as athletic director and football coach and again introduced the sport of wrestling. His teams won 145 meets against only 20 losses and were undefeated for five consecutive seasons.

He was one of the first coaches to insist that his wrestlers go for the fall at all times, regardless of the score, adding greatly to the sport's appeal.

He became such a legend at Franklin & Marshall that the school named its new athletic complex in his honor in 1962, five years before his death at the age of 91.

Charlie Mayser was the first chairman of the collegiate rules committee in 1918, ten years before the start of the NCAA tournament. He served through 1922.

TERRY MCCANN (1977)

The fires of competition burn brightly within all champion athletes, but never more intensely than in the heart of Terry McCann. And his fierce love of the challenge of sport carried him to supreme heights in wrestling.

Starting in the Chicago playground programs at the age of 12, he advanced through high school championships to the University of Iowa. There, under coach Dave McCuskey, he lost only three matches in three years, winning two NCAA titles.

Business interests took him to Tulsa, Oklahoma, where he joined the YMCA team and won three national freestyle championships, earning Outstanding Wrestler honors in the national tournament of 1959. That same year, he was undefeated in eight dual meets with a Russian national team.

Because of injury, he started the 1960 Olympic trials at the bottom of the 125.5-pound ladder, but earned a trip to the Rome Games on the freestyle team coached by Port Robertson and scaled the ultimate heights to a gold medal.

He coached junior high wrestlers three years in Tulsa, winning conference and state titles. Then, returning to Chicago, he took the helm of the Mayor Daley Youth Foundation Club and coached that team to six national freestyle and five national Greco-Roman championships in seven years.

In 1965, McCann teamed with Myron Roderick and others to spur creation of the United States Wrestling Federation and served as a charter member of the Governing Council.

Upon dedication of the National Wrestling Hall of Fame, Terry's first reaction was to nominate another wrestler, Russell Vis. He wrote: "Since I was a small boy, my heroes were not those of others my age. Instead of idolizing Babe Ruth, Bronko Nagurski or George Mikan, I admired the deeds of America's greatest wrestlers. My heroes were people like George Mehnert, Russell Vis, Robin Reed, Bobby Pearce, Frank Lewis and later, the great Bill Koll. These were my heroes, the men whom I hoped some day I could emulate." Emulate them he did.

EARL MCCREADY (1977)

His nickname was "Moose"—maybe because of his home town in Saskatchewan, Canada, but more likely because of Earl McCready's stature as the first great heavyweight wrestler of the collegiate tournaments.

International recruiting was unheard of in the mid-1920s, but in 1926 Fendley Collins and two teammates from Oklahoma A&M drove to Vancouver and captured the Canadian national freestyle tournament. They liked the looks of the strapping 220-pound youngster named McCready and talked him into following them back to their campus.

Under the guidance of coach Edward C. Gallagher, he won every match for three years, all but three of them by falls. He was the anchor man, the cleanup hitter, for three undefeated championship teams. "We never worried if the match was close," one of his teammates recalls. "We knew Moose would get them, and he always did."

McCready wrestled in the first three NCAA tournaments, in 1928, 1929 and 1930, and won the championship each year, thus becoming the first three-time champion in collegiate history. It was 20 years before another heavyweight could match that feat. In the 1928 finals, he won by a fall in 19 seconds, still a record for an NCAA tournament conducted under collegiate rules.

He also won four national freestyle championships, one in the United States and three in Canada, and represented Canada in the 1928 Olympic Games, carrying his country's banner in the opening ceremonies. He won a gold medal in the 1930 British Empire Games.

As a collegiate athlete, McCready was a three-year football letterman at guard, winning all-star honors in 1929. He wrestled professionally for 28 years, including a match in the famed Royal Albert Hall in London. He was the first wrestler to demonstrate the sport on British television.

DAVID MCCUSKEY (1976)

David Homer McCuskey established two great collegiate wresting programs, both within the state of Iowa, in a career spanning 41 years.

At Iowa State Teachers College (later the University of Northern Iowa), he was an outstanding football halfback, baseball pitcher and track star. Upon graduation, he immediately joined the coaching staff of the college and built it into a national power in the sport of wrestling.

In 21 years there, he produced 102 victories, 31 losses and seven ties. His efforts bore fruit in the form of a National Collegiate team championship in 1950 and national amateur AAU titles in 1949, 1950 and 1951. His Panthers were NCAA runners-up four times.

In 1953, McCuskey moved to the University of Iowa and again embarked on a construction program of great wrestling teams. His Hawkeyes won 160 matches against 69 losses and seven ties and laid the groundwork for NCAA championships in the mid-1970s.

McCuskey's wrestlers at the two schools won 25 individual NCAA titles. Among his 11 Olympians were two gold medal winners. He was coach of the 1956 Olympic team and at one time or another headed such major wrestling associations as the Olympic Committee, coaches association, officials' committee and rules committee.

Many of his wrestlers rank among the nation's leading collegiate coaches and others remain active across the country in the promotion and development of the sport for all age groups.

JOE MCDANIEL (1979)

He was destined to be an Olympic champion, but the Games of the XII Olympiad were engulfed in the holocaust of World War II. So Joe McDaniel had to settle merely for recognition as the outstanding wrestler in the world.

Three times he was a national collegiate champion for Oklahoma State University, each year leading the Cowboys of coach Edward C. Gallagher to the team trophy. As a 118-pound junior, he was voted Outstanding Wrestler of the 1938 NCAA tournament, an honor won a year earlier by his roommate, Stanley Henson.

Three times he reigned as national freestyle champion, twice as a collegian when the Cowboys also won team honors, and again in 1941, two years after graduation.

McDaniel's only serious exposure to international competition came at the close of his junior year, in a 1938 European tour climaxed by a tournament at Stockholm, Sweden, among the leading wrestling nations of the world. He was undefeated in 12 bouts and scored an overwhelming victory over Odon Zombori of Hungary, winner of the Olympic gold two years earlier.

Despite a three-year hitch in the Air Corps and seven years as field representative for a major steel firm, McDaniel never has been far from the sport of wrestling.

After a year of high school coaching and another at Maryland, he returned from the war to coach 11 years at Syracuse University, leading the Orange to a fourth place national finish. In 1963, he moved to Wyoming, coaching two years in high school and eight at the University.

His career turned full circle in 1973, when he returned to his hometown of Sulphur, Oklahoma, where he continues to serve as the high school coach. In 30 years of coaching at all levels, his record stands at 257 victories against 105 defeats.

PETE MEHRINGER (1982)

He learned about wrestling from a mail-order correspondence course. And Pete Mehringer learned his lessons so well that 6 years later he won an Olympic championship.

As a youngster growing up with six older brothers on a western Kansas farm, Pete subscribed to the "Frank Gotch and Farmer Burns School of Wrestling and Physical Culture" course. Two years later, as a high school sophomore, he was appointed the school's wrestling coach, because the football coach wanted nothing to do with it.

Kinsley High School attended the state tournament in 1928, where its student-coach won his first state title and the team finished fourth. The Depression barred further trips, but as a senior Pete hitch-hiked across the state to win another championship.

At the University of Kansas, where he starred in both wrestling and football, he came under the coaching of Leon Bauman, who started him toward three consecutive conference championships. But when Bauman resigned to enter medical school, Mehringer again found himself in the role of his own coach.

In 1932, he suffered his only collegiate defeat, at the hands of Northwestern University heavyweight Jack Riley in the NCAA finals. As they continued to struggle in the Olympic trials, the Olympic coach suggested that Pete drop to 191.5 pounds so both could be in the lineup at Los Angeles. He responded by shedding 17 pounds in 12 days. After that, the stars of Sweden, Canada and Australia looked easy, as he swept to the gold medal.

An All-American in football, he played in the first College All-Star game in 1934 and then earned a professional lineman's top salary of $100 per game with the Chicago Cardinals and the Los Angeles Bulldogs. During his eight-year pro football career, he also was a movie extra and stunt man, appearing as one of Ronald Reagan's teammates in the movie, "Knute Rockne, All-American," and once doubling for Bob Hope in "The Road to Zanzibar."

GEORGE MEHNERT (1976)

George Nicholas Mehnert was the first "superstar" of amateur wrestling and the only United States wrestler ever to win two gold medals in the Olympic Games, in 1904 at 115 pounds and in 1908 at 119 pounds.

Representing the National Turnverein, a sporting club in Newark, New Jersey, Mehnert first attracted attention in 1900 for his skills in wrestling and basketball. He won the metropolitan amateur wrestling title in 1901 and his first of six national amateur championships in 1902.

Virtually unbeatable over a seven-year span through 1908, he wrestled 59 bouts in national amateur tournaments and lost only one—to fellow Olympic champion George Dole of Yale in the 1907 finals. One of Mehnert's victories during this period was by fall in seven seconds, for many years the fastest on record.

Together with his Newark wrestling partner, Gus Bauers, who was silver medalist in the 1904 Games at St. Louis, Mehnert so dominated competition in the lighter weights that he often couldn't find opponents willing to challenge his skills.

The official report of the British Olympic Association for the 1908 Games in London states: "Mehnert showed form quite above any other man in the whole contest, and undoubtedly was the most scientific, both in attack and defense, of any wrestler taking part in the Games."

Mehnert later was active in the development of amateur wrestling in New Jersey and he served on the Olympic wrestling committee during the 1930s.

MIKE MILKOVICH (1983)

When wrestlers talk about winners, they talk about Mike Milkovich. But there's far more to his phenomenal coaching career. Call him winner, yes, but also call him teacher, developer, promoter and builder of the sport.

After success as a high school and college wrestler, he entered high school coaching in 1950 at Maple Heights, Ohio, where there was no organized wrestling program.

Over 27 years, his teams produced 265 dual meet victories against a mere 25 defeats. They enjoyed 16 undefeated seasons, won 10 state championships, eight runner-up trophies and 21 conference titles. Included was a winning streak of 102 dual meets, and another of 59.

Complementing his record on the mat was his flair for promotion of the sport. He attracted attention to his program with the use of mat maids, cheerleaders, pep clubs, booster clubs, junior high and junior varsity matches and the "radical" innovation of holding the meets at night.

Among his greatest wrestlers were two of his own sons—Tom, who won four Big Ten championships and a National Collegiate title, and Pat, a four-time national finalist and twice an NCAA champion. Both followed him into coaching.

Mike Milkovich never limited his horizons to the city limits of Maple Heights. As an educator of coaches and wrestlers, he has conducted clinics across the United States. He developed and published a practice plan for both high school and college coaches. His book on how to teach wrestling has sold thousands of copies. And his video tape series on wrestling techniques has received nationwide acclaim.

His achievements and his efforts for the development of wrestling have earned widespread recognition. In 1969, he served as coach and manager of the first U.S. gold medal junior world team. In 1976, he was chosen National High School Coach of the Year.

And in a rare tribute to any athletic figure, the Mike Milkovich Middle School was dedicated in Maple Heights in September of 1983.

BILL NELSON (1980)

In the golden era of wrestling at the University of Northern Iowa, Bill Nelson played a major role as the Panthers (then known as Iowa State Teachers College) scaled the heights of national prominence.

Three times he won the national collegiate championship, and in 1947 became one of the very few ever to win it as a freshman. An untimely injury during the 1948 tournament thwarted his bid to become the NCAA's only four-time champion. At the close of that sophomore season, he earned a place on the U.S. Olympic team, but an injury in his final qualifying bout in London knocked him out of the Games.

Bill Nelson returned to the NCAA's king row in 1949 and 1950, leading Iowa Teachers to the team championship as a senior. He won national freestyle titles the same two years, and his Panthers captured team honors at both tournaments. In 1950, he was selected by a national magazine as the country's outstanding amateur wrestler.

He was a state high school champion at Eagle Grove, Iowa, and when he launched his coaching career, he returned to the high school ranks, first in Colorado, then Iowa, then Michigan. In 1963, he became coach at the University of Arizona, where he has emerged as one of the most widely respected figures in collegiate wrestling.

He is a member of state halls of fame in Iowa, Michigan, and Arizona.

He has served as president of the National Wrestling Coaches Association and was host director of the 1976 NCAA Championships at Tucson, the only time the tournament has been held in the Southwest.

HAROLD NICHOLS (1978)

He was a national champion wrestler as a collegian, but Harold Nichols has left his indelible stamp on the sport as one of its most successful coaches.

Wrestling at Michigan for another Hall of Fame coach, Cliff Keen, he won the NCAA championship at 145 pounds in 1939. When Don Nichols followed him to the victory stand a year later, they formed one of the first championship brother combinations in collegiate wrestling.

After wartime service as an Air Force pilot, Harold spent six years as a successful coach of wrestling and track at Arkansas State University.

But it was at Iowa State University, starting in 1953, that he truly launched the fabulous coaching career that has produced six national team champions, seven runners-up, 31 individual titlists and a staggering total of nearly 400 dual meet victories. His teams won four national trophies during a five-year span staring in 1969.

Seven of his Cyclones have represented the United States in the Olympic Games, winning two gold medals, a silver and a bronze.

Four times Dr. Nichols has been honored with a national Coach of the Year award, three of them from his colleagues in the National Wrestling Coaches Association. In 1966 he was elected Wrestling Man of the Year.

Alongside his achievements as a coach, he has had a monumental impact on the progress of the sport of wrestling in the United States through long and dynamic service on the NCAA national rules committee, AAU and Olympic committees, and by initiating a host of noteworthy improvements.

Harold Nichols' effect on young wrestlers spreads far beyond the boundaries of his own wrestling room. For two decades he has been one of the nation's leading clinicians, operating his own summer camps and making many appearances as a guest speaker.

HUGO OTOPALIK (1976)

Hugo M. Otopalik was perhaps the first great collegiate wrestler to become a great wrestling coach. He was the 175-pound Western Conference champion for Nebraska, under Dr. Raymond G. Clapp, in 1916 and 1917, and also starred in the backfield of the Cornhuskers' first football powers.

He held the rank of first sergeant during World War I and served with the Red Cross in the European theater during World War II.

Otopalik became director of athletics at Kearney State in Nebraska in 1918 and joined the staff at Iowa State in 1920. He had not planned to become a coach, but when Charles Mayser resigned in 1923, Otopalik agreed to "handle" the wrestling team until a replacement could be found. He continued to "handle" the team for 29 years, developing many individual national champions.

His 1933 Cyclones were recognized as co-champions of the NCAA tournament with Oklahoma A&M. Over the years, his teams compiled a dual meet record of 160 victories, 66 losses and five ties and won seven team championships in the Big Eight Conference.

In 1932, Otopalik coached the United States Olympic team, which won three gold medals and was acclaimed as the championship team. Four years earlier, he had served as host to the first National Collegiate tournament, organized by his former coach, Dr. Clapp.

Otopalik was the first secretary of the National Wrestling Coaches Association, from 1932 to 1936, and played an active role in national amateur wrestling throughout the years. He was vice president of the International Wrestling Federation in 1952.

BOBBY PEARCE (1981)

He took up wrestling as a youngster to strengthen himself physically in a constant struggle with allergies. But despite his frail physique, Bobby Pearce won championships at all levels.

Matt Berg, the high school coach at Cushing, Oklahoma, allowed him to join the squad despite some misgivings. Pearce rewarded him with three undefeated seasons and three state championships. As a high school senior, he reached the semifinals of the 1928 Olympic trials.

Then he joined the awesome array of talent at Oklahoma State, helping extend the winning streak of Coach Edward C. Gallagher's Aggies to 70 consecutive matches. Overall, during his collegiate days, he won 60 bouts, lost four and tied one.

A fast and aggressive wrestler, Pearce liked to go for the quick fall, and once flattened his opponent in just 11 seconds.

Pearce was national freestyle champion in 1930 and 1931, won the NCAA title in 1931 and was runner-up in 1932. Although he was upset in the collegiate finals as a senior, he responded with the ultimate triumph, winning the gold medal in the 1932 Olympic Games at Los Angeles, the first ever for an Oklahoma wrestler.

Although only a 126-pounder, he competed professionally for five years and at the same time turned his hand to coaching. He guided Cushing to the state high school title in 1933 and coached a YMCA team for two years before embarking on a professional career in refinery engineering.

He returned to coaching briefly 20 years later at Mesa College in Colorado, leading that team to two undefeated seasons and a conference championship.

ED PEERY (1980)

His goals as a collegiate wrestler were clear-cut and offered no alternatives. All Ed Peery had to do to keep pace with his father and brother was to win three national championships.

Although he won 51 of 52 matches at the University of Pittsburgh, under the coaching of his father, Rex, the championships did not come easily. In all three of his NCAA finals, Ed came from behind to win.

The most difficult was his third—and the family's ninth—in his senior year of 1957. He trailed Harmon Leslie of Oklahoma State 7-4, in the last minute of the finals, only to rally with a takedown and time advantage to send the match into overtime.

When the extensions ended in a 2-2 draw, Ed Peery was voted national champion by the judges and wrestling owned a family legend without precedent in the world of sport.

Ed Peery was born a few hours before Rex won his third NCAA title for Oklahoma State. He was named for his father's great coach, Ed Gallagher.

After a 48-1 career and two state championships at Shaler High School in Glenshaw, Pa., he followed brother Hugh into the Pittsburgh lineup. For six straight years, coach Rex could find an NCAA champion at his own dinner table, Hugh in 1952-53-54, Ed in 1955-56-57. Adding a few open tournaments, Ed's over-all career numbered more than 100 victories.

For two decades, Ed has been coach at the U.S. Naval Academy, guiding five Eastern team champions, a host of individual winners and nearly 200 dual meet victories. He was National Coach of the Year in 1969. He is a member of the U.S. Wrestling Federation's national teaching staff.

HUGH PEERY (1980)

His story is Chapter Two of wrestling's family legend, but Hugh Peery's record stands by itself among the greatest.

He won three national collegiate championships for the University of Pittsburgh in 1952-53-54. He won all but one of his 57 collegiate matches, the last 48 of them in a row.

But even before he launched that career, he had earned international honors, capturing a gold medal at the 1951 Pan American Games in Argentina. He earned sixth place in the 1952 Olympic Games at Helsinki, winning two of three bouts.

As a wrestler, Hugh was noted for his speed and clever style. He was an exceptional takedown artist with a wide variety of moves, and his usual pattern was to establish an early lead and maintain pressure with a vast repertoire of rides, escapes and pinning holds.

Hugh Peery followed the lead of his father and coach, Rex Peery, to help create wrestling's fabulous family story. Rex was a three-time NCAA champion at Oklahoma State in the 1930s. They were to be joined at that level by younger son Ed, completing a 9-for-9 sweep of national titles.

Under his father's coaching, Hugh was a state high school champion at Tulsa Central in 1949. Rex left for Pittsburgh the next year, but Hugh remained in Oklahoma to win a second state crown.

Hugh launched his Pittsburgh career under Rex' guidance in 1952, recovering from a mid-season defeat to post an 18-1 record and win his first national championship at 115 pounds.

His total competitive record—high school, college and open—numbered more than 100 victories against a mere half a dozen defeats.

REX PEERY (1976)

Rex Anderson Peery fathered the greatest family legend in the history of wrestling. So monumental were his personal achievements, and those of his family, that they tend to overshadow his outstanding coaching career and his many contributions to the development of the sport.

Rex Peery was a three-time NCAA champion at Oklahoma State University under coach Edward C. Gallagher. For the next 29 years, he established a great coaching career, 13 years in Oklahoma high schools and 16 years at the University of Pittsburgh.

Two unforgettable milestones mark his Pittsburgh coaching tenure. In 1952, 1953 and 1954 he coached his elder son, Hugh, to NCAA championships. In 1955, 1956 and 1957, he coached his younger son, Ed, to those same honors.

Can any family, in any sport, equal those achievements of nine national championships in nine attempts?

As a wrestler, Rex Peery was undefeated in dual meets. He added the 1935 national amateur championship to his collegiate laurels.

As a coach, he produced 233 victories, 58 losses and six ties. His Pittsburgh teams twice were NCAA runners-up and he developed 13 individual collegiate champions and 23 Eastern champions.

He was coach of the United States freestyle team in the 1964 Olympic Games in Tokyo. He was a member of the U.S. Olympic Committee for 12 years, and has held many other positions of service in the sport of wrestling.

Rex Peery was one of the founders of United States Wrestling Federation programs in Pennsylvania and serves on both the governing council of the USWF and the board of governors of the National Wrestling Hall of Fame.

He continues to serve in the athletic department of the University of Pittsburgh as an assistant professor.

GRADY PENINGER (1987)

Only once in more than 30 years has the national collegiate team championship escaped from the states of Oklahoma and Iowa. And it took a native Oklahoman, Grady Peninger, to carry the trophy away to Michigan State.

Peninger's 1967 Spartans, featuring individual champions Dale Anderson and George Radman, provided just one of the highlights of his 40-year career as a wrestler and coach. There were many others, and those he treasures most involve the athletes he developed.

He reached national prominence while still in high school in Tulsa, winning the state championship and the first of two national freestyle crowns during his senior year of 1945. After a two-year hitch in the Navy, he enrolled at Oklahoma State, placing as an Olympic alternate in 1948 and as an NCAA finalist a year later.

He entered high school coaching at Ponca City and in eight years guided three state champion teams. His stars included Shelby Wilson and Doug Blubaugh, who went on to capture Olympic gold medals.

In 1960, he was called by Michigan State to assist, and soon to succeed, Fendley Collins at the helm of the Spartans. Peninger's teams dominated the Big Ten Conference, winning seven consecutive titles starting in 1966. He was voted National Coach of the Year after the 1967 triumph.

He was the first Big Ten coach to develop a three-time NCAA champion, Greg Johnson, and a four-time NCAA finalist, Pat Milkovich. One of his wrestlers, Don Behm, was an Olympic silver medalist, and another, Tom Milkovich, won four conference titles.

In all, he produced 43 conference and 11 national champions, 90 Big Ten medalists and 46 All-Americans. His Spartans won 213 of 330 dual meets and enjoyed 23 consecutive winning seasons. He was the first coach to bring a team to Oklahoma, wrestle both the Cowboys and the Sooners, and go home undefeated.

Peninger was president of the National Wrestling Coaches Association, which elected him a lifetime member. While serving on the NCAA Rules

Committee, he pushed through the expanded consolation bracket adopted in 1986, creating more opportunity for the wrestlers.

That's always been his goal—to provide greater opportunity for wrestlers to succeed.

BEN PETERSON (1986)

A high school youngster from Wisconsin, competing in the 1968 Olympic trials, caught the eye of veteran coach Harold Nichols. Soon Ben Peterson would become one of Iowa State's greatest wrestlers and then one of America's brightest stars.

He won nearly 100 collegiate matches, was a three-time Big Eight king and a three-time All-American. He captured NCAA championships in 1971 and 1972.

Encouraged (you might say pushed) by his friend and teammate, Dan Gable, Ben blended athletic skills with determination and strong faith to develop a powerful career. Over the next decade, Ben won seven national freestyle titles, placed twice in the World Championships (winning a bronze in '73), and captured the gold medal in the 1975 Pan-American Games.

Through much of this era, he was joined by his brother John, as they forged one of wrestling's great family legends.

In the '72 Olympics, Ben struggled to a draw with Gennady Strakhov of the USSR. When they emerged as the only survivors at 198 pounds, Ben earned the gold with more falls. John's silver at 180.5 was almost as sweet.

The brothers returned to the Olympic scene in 1976 at Montreal, to spin an equally rewarding but oddly reversed success story. Levan Tediashvili, the superb Soviet who had blocked John's bid at Munich, limited Ben to a silver medal. But John captured the gold, and the Peterson brothers became only the third and fourth two-time Olympic medalists in U.S. wrestling history.

Ben made a third Olympic team in 1980, and only five Americans have done that, but was thwarted by the boycott.

Faith has been a hallmark of Ben Peterson's life. Since 1976 he has coached and taught at Maranatha Baptist Bible College in Wisconsin, and has directed a summer camp to teach his skills and his way of life to young wrestlers. John, too, serves on the camp staff.

Maranatha earns none of today's wrestling headlines, but the golden touch remains. One of Ben's students, Mike Houck, is another super-achiever and in 1985 Houck became the first American ever to win a World Championship in the Greco-Roman style.

JOHN PETERSON (1986)

It can be said that John Peterson followed in the footsteps of his younger brother, Ben. Yet when all is said and done, the brothers stand together at the apex of wrestling success.

Hailing from the tiny farm community of Comstock in northwestern Wisconsin, John earned three conference titles and NAIA All-American honors for the University of Wisconsin at Stout. But only then did his wrestling career blossom.

During his senior year of 1971, John dropped by Iowa State to join Ben and his teammates in preparing for the Pan-American trials. John began to think of a long-shot bid for the 1971 World Championships, although the 177-pounder had met only grief in cutting to the international 163-pound class. An off-the-cuff discussion with Dan Gable proved the turning point.

"Don't cut all that weight," the Cyclone star told John. "You can wrestle and win at 180.5 pounds." With his always strong faith now bolstered by wrestling confidence, John began to practice with intensity, and to succeed. He made the World team that summer of 1971, and again in '73, '78 and '79, winning bronze and silver medals the latter two years.

In the Olympics of 1972, the spotlight was on Gable and Wayne Wells, who won gold medals as expected, and on the mammoth Chris Taylor. But the Petersons stole the show. Ben took the gold at 198 pounds and John won six matches in a row. He bowed to the magnificent Soviet star, Levan Tediashvili, but captured the silver.

John continued to compete in the mid-70s, winning three national AAU titles and three World Cups. And he found a way to blend his wrestling interests with his deep and abiding faith, as a coach and competitor with Athletes in Action. He spent three of seven AIA years in Europe and now lives in Vienna, Austria, as a staff member of the Campus Crusade for Christ.

The 1976 Games in Montreal provided the ultimate wrestling achievement for John Peterson. A closing victory over Mahmet Uzun of Turkey captured the gold medal. Ben collected the silver at 198, and the Petersons became only the third and fourth two-time Olympic medalists in U. S. wrestling history.

ROBIN REED (1978)

He took up wrestling in high school at Portland, Oregon, to escape from mandatory gym classes. Robin Reed quickly learned the fundamentals of the sport, and learned them so well that he never lost a wrestling match to anyone of any size.

"I needed gymnasium credits to graduate from high school, but I didn't want any gym because I was already getting all the exercise I needed operating an air hammer at the shipyards," he said. "I was only 125 pounds and could barely hold onto that air hammer, so I was getting all the gym I needed."

That air hammer may have been the toughest opponent Robin Reed ever wrestled.

While at Oregon State University, he won national freestyle championships in 1921, '22 and '24. He established his stature as world champion by winning the gold medal at 134 pounds in the 1924 Olympic Games at Paris, pinning every opponent he faced.

Had the rules permitted, he might well have won a handful of gold medals. In the Pacific Northwest tryouts for the Olympic team he entered four weight classes, from 145 pounds to 191, and won all four. It is well established that he could pin almost every member of the U.S. Olympic team, including the gold medalists at 191 pounds and heavyweight.

Reed coached a championship team at Corvallis High School while still a student himself at Oregon State. When he returned from the '24 Games, he voluntarily ended his amateur career and was named varsity coach even though he was still attending college. His 1926 team won the national freestyle title.

He appeared as a professional wrestler for a decade, then entered the real estate field. In 1936, he built a house on the rugged Oregon coast where he has lived ever since.

PORT ROBERTSON (1977)

Theodore Roosevelt is quoted, "Speak softly and carry a big stick." Port Robertson took that advice to heart. The "big stick" with which he armed every one of his wrestlers was self-discipline.

As coach at the University of Oklahoma for 15 years, he produced three NCAA championship teams and three national runners-up, and firmly established the Sooners as a national power. His wrestlers captured 15 individual NCAA titles and five outstanding wrestler awards.

Port firmly believes the goal of a wrestler is to win by a fall. Over a span of eight national tournaments, his Sooners pinned 39 opponents, 11 of them in their 1957 championship parade.

In 1960, he coached the U.S. Olympic team to three gold medals, the only such championship harvest between the Olympiads of 1932 and 1972. "Port Robertson raised you up to a level higher than you would set for yourself," one of his wrestlers declares. "He never compromised his standards."

A stickler for physical conditioning and mental preparation, Port told his wrestlers, "A lean dog is lots hungrier than a fat one," and sent them up another 72 steps of the football stadium.

He spelled out his philosophy bluntly: "First of all, a boy has to want to come here to get an education. If he thinks wrestling is more important than that, he's not going to do well in either. Then he has to realize what it takes to be a good wrestler. It depends on how much of himself he wants to spend. He has to learn to know himself. Once he gets self-discipline in wrestling, he'll have it all his life."

An Oklahoma high school champion and star in football and track, he wrestled at OU under coach Paul Keen, winning 20 of 24 bouts and two conference titles. He was a captain of field artillery in World War II, earning a Bronze Star and a Purple Heart in the Normandy invasion.

MYRON RODERICK (1976)

Myron Willis Roderick was a fierce competitor as a wrestler and equally as fierce a competitor when a coach—a winner of championships in both roles.

In his three years as a wrestler at Oklahoma State University, he won 42 of 44 matches and three National Collegiate championships, one at 137 pounds, then two more at 130 pounds. He placed fourth in the 1956 Olympic Games at Melbourne, losing a split decision to the eventual champion.

But it was as coach of the Cowboys that he attained his greatest stature. And there was no interlude between his two careers. From national champion in 1956 to the new torch-bearer of the great Oklahoma State coaching tradition in 1957 was an abrupt but highly-successful transition.

In 1958, when he led the Cowboys to the NCAA team title he was, at 23, the youngest coach ever to guide a national champion team in any sport. In his 13 years of coaching, he produced seven NCAA team champions. His Cowboys won 140 dual meets, lost only 10 and tied seven, once producing 84 consecutive duals without a loss.

His wrestlers won 20 individual NCAA championships and four gold medals in the Olympic Games. He also coached his teams to two national amateur championships, was the United States coach in the 1963 World Games, and was assistant coach in the 1964 Olympics.

Roderick departed from tradition in one respect. He carried his personal intensity into a search for quality wrestlers and, more than any other man, introduced recruiting on a major scale into the sport of wrestling.

As the first executive director of the United States Wrestling Federation, he continued his work toward development of the sport among the youth of America.

Terrific trio: Myron Roderick, Doug Blubaugh, and Shelby Wilson. (Courtesy of National Wrestling Hall of Fame)

RICK SANDERS (1987)

His career was like a meteor—a streak of brilliance then, tragically, he was gone. But for a dozen years, Rick Sanders was the golden boy of wrestling, our first world champion, one who would leave an indelible impact on our sport.

He won three Oregon high school championships, collegiate titles at three levels, five national freestyle crowns and six medals in international competition. He once beat Dan Gable 6-0, the only shutout loss of the Iowan's storied career.

His high school record showed 80 victories, one loss. Across town at Portland State University, he won the NAIA title in 1965, the Division II NCAA in 1967 and 1968, and the Division I collegiates in 1966 and 1967, reaching the finals again as a senior. He was voted Outstanding Wrestler of four of those events.

As early as his freshman year in college, in 1965, Sanders won his first national freestyle championship and made the U.S. world team. He took a world bronze medal in '66, won the Pan-American Games in '67 and was a silver medalist in the 1967 worlds and in the 1968 Olympics.

A year later, at 114.5 pounds, he became the first American ever to win a world championship. He returned to the Olympics in 1972 and captured another silver medal. Of the 11 bouts he won in two Olympics, nine came by fall. But suddenly, Rick was gone, killed in an automobile accident in Yugoslavia while touring Europe after the 1972 Games in Munich.

Rick Sanders was a complex personality, a freethinker. He had his own style of training, his own style of living. He wore long hair and a beard before they were fashionable, to the distress of conservative coaches and administrators. But above all, Rick was a champion. His technique, his expertise were ahead of his time. A self-made man, with little family background, he concentrated on helping youth, giving free clinics anywhere, anytime.

He often left cutting weight to the last minute. One of wrestling's favorite vignettes is that of Rick jogging up and down the aisle of a mammoth jet airliner on his way to a match with the Soviet Union.

In 1970, he won the world team trials at 125.5 pounds, after an epic series with fellow world and Olympic medalist Don Behm. Then, to strengthen the team, he gave up that position to try—unsuccessfully—to cut to 114.5 so both could wrestle.

He is one we shall never forget.

JOE SCALZO (1987)

His career in wrestling spanned the whole gamut of the sport. Joe Scalzo was wrestler, coach, referee, administrator and international delegate. There were other roles as well, such as pioneer, innovator and crusader.

He started as a high school champion in New Jersey and was a national collegiate finalist for Penn State in 1939. During his early years of employment as a chemical engineer, he coached wrestling as a volunteer at the Toledo YMCA, where his teams were unbeaten for a decade and won three national titles.

He became the first wrestling coach at the University of Toledo in 1950. Scalzo promoted all styles of wrestling, but was particularly fond of Greco-Roman. For years his push for Greco met resistance or indifference from the sport's leaders, but he lived to see the USA stand tall among the nations, with two gold medalists in the 1984 Olympics and our first world champion a year later.

He was Olympic coach in 1956 and one of his collegiate stars, Richard Wilson, became a three-time Olympian.

In Toledo, he organized the first two World Championships held in this country, in 1962 and again in 1966. Scalzo conceived the idea of a World Cup among champions of the various continents, convinced the international federation of its value and served as host for 13 of its first 14 years. He was one of the first to see wrestling as an ''event'' to be planned and conducted with the spectators and media in mind.

As an international referee, he held the highest rating of exceptionnelle for 23 years, and he was an active participant—as coach, official or administrator—in nine Olympics and more than 100 continental and world tournaments for all age groups.

He served as vice president of the International Wrestling Federation (FILA) and was elected a lifetime member of the FILA Bureau. He died in the midst of wrestling friends and colleagues, stricken by a heart attack while attending the awards banquet of the 1986 World Championships in Budapest.

His life in wresting, both at home and abroad, was that of a volunteer, a sidelight to his professional careers of engineer, labor negotiator, business executive, attorney at law, management consultant and civic leader, each role earning him accolades from his community, his state and his country.

BILLY SHERIDAN (1976)

William ''Billy'' Sheridan was a wrestler of legendary stature in his native Scotland in the early years of the 20th Century, but it was as coach at Lehigh University that he earned lasting renown.

At the age of 19, in 1905, he won the Scottish wrestling crown at nine stone, or 126 pounds. Wrestling eight or nine times a week without ever losing a bout, he reigned as featherweight and lightweight champion of the British Isles until 1908.

In 1908 he emigrated to Ontario, Canada, but two years later moved to Philadelphia. To earn some extra money, he agreed to pose for the famous sculptor, Tait McKenzie, at the University of Pennsylvania and chanced to observe the wrestling team in action. Unable to resist involvement, he offered suggestions and was invited to serve as coach and trainer. In 1911, he was recommended to Lehigh in a similar role.

Thus began his famed coaching career. It lasted 40 years, until his retirement in 1952, and produced 223 dual meet victories, only 83 losses and seven ties. In this 40-year period, he developed 59 Eastern Intercollegiate champions, five National Collegiate champions, five national amateur titlists and three Olympians. He also coached winning teams in soccer and lacrosse.

In 1936, he was an alternate coach on the United States Olympic team, and in 1951 was both coach and manager for the United States entry in the first Pan-American Games. He refereed every bout in the first NCAA tournament in 1928.

Sheridan was the founder of the first summer wrestling camp in the United States in 1935. His coaching philosophy is summed up: ''Whatever you do, do quickly.''

BOB SIDDENS (1980)

He will always be remembered as ''Dan Gable's coach,'' which isn't a bad way to be remembered. But there's much, much more to the outstanding career of Bob Siddens.

As a high school coach of exceptional stature, as a nationally recognized referee, as a respected clinician both on technique and on officiating, as an author, teacher and counselor, he has made notable contributions to the sport for three decades.

He was a successful wrestler at Eagle Grove High School in Iowa, then at the University of Northern Iowa where he helped launch the Panthers to national prominence. Upon graduation, he coached 1 year at Eagle Grove, then embarked on a 27-year term at West High School in Waterloo.

His teams there won 327 dual meets, 88 in a row, and lost only 26. The Wahawks won 11 state team championships and placed second or third 10 other times. They enjoyed 14 undefeated seasons. During that span, high school wrestling in Iowa grew from 28 schools to more than 300.

Siddens' wrestlers went on to capture 19 Big Eight titles, nine NCAA championships and an Olympic gold medal. In the 1968 collegiate national, two of his proteges—Dale Anderson of Michigan State and Dan Gable of Iowa State—won consecutive titles.

Long respected as one of the nation's finest collegiate referees, he has officiated at two dozen NCAA championships, more than any other official. He has traveled thousands of miles to conduct clinics for wrestlers and for officials, and has published many articles on the sport.

GRAY SIMONS (1978)

During his four years of collegiate competition at Lock Haven State, Gray Simons entered seven national tournaments. He won all seven, and six times and was voted Outstanding Wrestler of the event.

Four years he reigned supreme at 115 pounds in the National Association of Intercollegiate Athletics, and all four years was chosen the NAIA's finest, an unparalleled achievement. Three times he won the University Division title in the NCAA and as a junior and senior was voted the outstanding competitor.

The only two defeats of his 93 collegiate matches came early in his freshman season. He then proceeded to win 84 in a row.

In the two years after his graduation, while stationed at the U.S. Military Academy, he continued to annex national championships in military, YMCA and AAU competition. He won the gold medal in the 1963 World Military Games.

Gray Simons twice represented his country in the Olympic Games, in 1960 and 1964.

On the mat, he was known as a superb technician, with quickness, skill and perfect execution of an infinite variety of moves. His abilities helped spread nationwide the ''Granby Series'' of moves developed by his high school coach in Norfolk, Virginia, Billy Martin.

Since the close of his competitive career, he has served with distinction as a collegiate coach at Lock Haven State, Indiana State and the University of Tennessee, and never has suffered a losing season. Among his proteges are two NCAA champions and several All-Americans.

In both roles, as a wrestler and coach, this quiet man has set an outstanding example for young athletes everywhere.

BILL SMITH (1978)

Championships came early and often for Bill Smith at Iowa State Teachers College (now the University of Northern Iowa), but he scaled the ultimate heights in 1952 when he won the gold medal at 160.5 pounds in the Olympic Games at Helsinki.

He was NCAA champion twice during a college career which saw 52 victories, two draws and no defeats. His second title, in 1950, led the great Iowa Teachers team of Hall of Fame coach Dave McCuskey to the national crown.

Three times, starting in 1949, he was the national freestyle champion at 165 pounds and all three years the collegians from ISTC marched away with the team trophy.

Four years after his gold medal triumph, Bill Smith won the 1956 Olympic trials at 174 pounds, but later was declared ineligible for the Games because he already had launched a coaching career that was to span three levels of competition.

In four seasons at Rock Island, Illinois, he produced a state high school team champion and a 57-5 record. He spent four more years with a winning record at the University of Nebraska, then moved to California for nearly a decade as coach of the Olympic Club of San Francisco, a powerhouse of open competition which won three national team titles in freestyle and four in Greco-Roman wrestling.

He served as Canadian Olympic coach in 1968, then returned to California to the high school ranks. In 1976, his Clayton Valley team from Concord won the California high school championship, marking Bill Smith as one of the few coaches to lead prep winners in more than one state.

CHARLES M. SPEIDEL (1979)

He devoted a lifetime to the sport of wrestling. But in more than 60 years as an athlete, coach and teacher, Charles M. Speidel contributed far more to the lives of others than ever can be recorded in the statistics of achievement.

He was a pioneer for wrestling and helped it gain stature as a major sport in the high schools and colleges of Pennsylvania and all across the eastern states. He traveled extensively, often with arch rival Billy Sheridan, to present clinics and introduce the sport.

The record shows that ''Doc'' Speidel coached 38 years at the Pennsylvania State University. His teams won 191 dual meets and lost 53. Seven of them were undefeated. They won eight Eastern Intercollegiate team championships.

And in 1953, his Nittany Lions became the only eastern squad ever to win the NCAA team championship.

He was an author of wrestling books, and articles for such publications as the *Encyclopedia Brittanica*. During World War II he served four years as fleet recreation officer in the South Pacific.

In 1930, he brought the nation's wrestling coaches together and founded the National Wrestling Coaches Association, later serving two terms as its president. All this is a matter of record.

But Charlie Speidel's contributions cannot be measured by victories and defeats. First of all, he was a teacher, who gave of himself to enrich the lives of young men.

He taught ''total wrestling''—not only the mechanics, but enthusiasm, self-reliance and the importance of deep dedication, hard work and the strength of the will to win. He stressed the importance of education and insisted that his athletes complete their degrees.

DALE THOMAS (1980)

Perhaps no man has left his mark on the sport of wrestling in as many ways as Dale Thomas—as a wrestler, coach, official, teacher and innovator.

He was team captain at Cornell of Iowa in 1947, when it became the only private school to win NCAA and AAU team titles. He went on to amass nine national championships in freestyle and Greco-Roman competition.

He earned a place on the 1952 Olympic team by handing Henry Wittenberg his first defeat in more than 300 matches, but yielded the position to Wittenberg in the final trials in Helsinki. He returned to the Olympics in 1956, placing sixth in Greco-Roman at Melbourne.

In 24 years at Oregon State University, he has recorded more victories than any other coach in history, 432 against 76 defeats. He has coached 10 NCAA champions, 54 all-Americans and 21 national titlists in freestyle and Greco-Roman.

His Beavers were NCAA runners-up in 1973 and have placed third or fourth five times. He was national coach of the year twice. But the only special award he offers to his collegiate wrestlers is compiled by blending their dual meet scores with their academic grade point averages.

He coached U.S. international teams in 1961, 1966 and 1970, and has taught and studied wrestling around the world, from Yugoslavia to Canada to New Zealand, from South Africa to Mexico to southeast Asia.

As a top-ranked international referee, he served as an official in the 1960 and 1964 Olympics, and in several World Championships.

He inaugurated Kids wrestling for children in Oregon 20 years ago, emphasizing fun and fundamentals, a concept that is the cornerstone of today's national Kids programs. He founded state freestyle and international cultural exchange programs for Oregon high school wrestlers.

YOJIRO UETAKE (1980)

After winning the national high school championship of Japan, he came to the United States to complete his education. By the time Yojiro Uetake returned to his native land, he had given a whole generation of American wrestlers an education in winning technique.

He won all 58 of his collegiate matches for Oklahoma State University and three Big Eight Conference titles. Three times a national collegiate champion, he was voted Outstanding Wrestler of the national tournament as a junior and again as a senior.

After his sophomore year of competition in 1964, "Yo-Jo" returned to Japan to win the Olympic gold medal in his home city of Tokyo. Four years later, in Mexico City, he repeated this achievement and became the first Japanese wrestler ever to win two championships in the Olympic Games.

He was the complete wrestler, blending speed, strength and unparalleled skills to dominate all areas of the sport—takedowns, control, escapes and falls. Seldom did any opponent score offensive points against him.

Such was the range of his ability that every match became a small "clinic" in itself, attracting coaches and rival contestants from all parts of the arena to learn from his masterful techniques.

While preparing for his second Olympic crown, he spent two years as an assistant coach at Oklahoma State, then returned home to become Japan's national freestyle coach. He guided his country's wrestlers into the 1972 Olympics at Munich and the 1976 Games at Montreal.

SWEDE UMBACH (1981)

He introduced the sport of wrestling to the Deep South. Swede Umbach then spent the next 27 years as coach at Auburn University showing his opponents what it takes to win wrestling championships.

His Tigers captured 25 team trophies in the conference he founded, the Southeastern Intercollegiate Wrestling Association. They won 249 dual meets, lost just 28 and tied five. Only one of those defeats was at the hands of a conference opponent.

He coached 127 conference champions and four national winners.

Swede Umbach was born in Oklahoma Territory in 1903 and attended Oklahoma A&M Prep in 1919-20, where he learned wrestling from Hall of Fame coach Edward C. Gallagher. After concluding high school in Weatherford, he entered Southwestern Oklahoma State in 1924 and was a four-time conference champion wrestler as well as a football star of note.

He then spent 14 years coaching in Oklahoma high schools, producing state champions in both sports. His college coach, Carl Voyles, called Umbach to accompany him, first to William & Mary in 1941, then to Auburn in 1944. He launched Auburn's first wrestling program in 1946.

Umbach earned reknown not only as an athlete and coach, but also as one of the sport's pioneer officials. He refereed 18 of the storied "Bedlam Series" battles between Oklahoma State and Oklahoma, along with several national and international tournaments.

He has served the sport in many ways, giving hundreds of free clinics, acting as president of the national coaches' association and a member of various rules committees. He is the author of three books and hosted the first NCAA tournament held in the South.

JACK VAN BEBBER (1976)

Jack Francis Van Bebber vanquished the nation's finest wrestlers seven times, but when he set out to conquer the world, he had to hitch-hike.

At the 1932 Olympic Games in Los Angeles, as he awaited his final bout for the gold medal, Van Bebber suddenly learned that the time schedule had been altered and he was due on the mat within the hour, six miles away. No transportation was provided, or available, so he set out afoot. After two miles, a passing motorist gave him a ride to the arena.

Once at the scene, however, his opponent proved no more effective than his earlier victims. And "Blackjack" Van Bebber became champion of the world with a decision over Eino Leino of Finland, a four-time Olympian who already owned gold, silver and bronze medals.

Van Bebber was undefeated as a collegiate wrestler for Oklahoma State University in 1929, 1930 and 1931, winning three NCAA championships at 155 and 165 pounds. He captured national amateur titles the same three years, then moved to Los Angeles in 1932 and won another.

The only defeat of his wrestling career came in an early round of the Olympic trials, but he rallied to win the trials and successfully tackled his 158.5-pound assignment during final challenge bouts in Los Angeles.

Van Bebber served four years in the infantry during World War II, three of them in the Pacific theater. He then joined the Phillips Petroleum Company for 39 years until his retirement, and taught wrestling to sons of company employees and to Boy Scouts.

In 1950, a national poll of U. S. coaches, officials and sports editors selected him as one of the country's top 10 amateur athletes in the first half of the 20th century.

RUSSELL VIS (1977)

He came out of the West as an "unknown" without collegiate experience or publicity, but when Russ Vis exploded onto the national wrestling scene there was no one who could stand in his way.

After winning high school championships in Oregon, he joined the Olympic Club of San Francisco in 1916 and competed in club, city, Pacific Coast and regional tournaments, winning every one he entered.

His family moved to Los Angeles in 1919, leading Russ to the Los Angeles Athletic Club, where he has been a life member nearly 60 years. After dominating all competition in his own area, he traveled at his own expense to national freestyle tournaments in distant parts of the country, and won four consecutive national championships, 1921 through 1924, without ever losing a bout.

He reached the pinnacle of success in 1924 when he captured the gold medal at 145 pounds in the Olympic Games in Paris.

His own career was largely self-developed and self-sponsored, but he has devoted the past half-century to the development and sponsorship of young wrestlers and other young athletes, and continues to encourage others to meet his own high standards.

He is a strong booster of wrestling at all levels from high school to the Olympic Games. Men like Russ Vis provide the foundation for the tremendous growth of the sport.

DICK VOLIVA (1984)

Every university welcomes home-grown talent. So when Indiana University was building a wrestling power in the early 1930s, it was happy to find a young state champion, Dick Voliva, right at home in Bloomington.

As a sophomore he was a member of the Hoosier team that claimed the unofficial 1932 national collegiate championship, first ever for a Big Ten Conference school.

He amassed individual honors the next two years, reaching the national finals in 1933 and winning both Big Ten and NCAA titles as a senior, to close this collegiate career with a 48-4 record. He also starred in football, and as a senior was presented a special award for bringing honor and distinction to his university.

As a high school and college wrestler, Voliva had competed in freestyle, winning several regional tournaments and reaching the national finals in 1932. During a two-year term as graduate assistant at Ohio State, he placed third in 1935 and captured the AAU national championship in 1936. Then, in the Olympic Games at Berlin, he earned the silver medal at 174 pounds.

On returning from the Olympic Games, he joined the faculty at Montclair State in New Jersey and soon launched a wrestling program there, serving as coach until World War II brought a four-year interruption. He had been commissioned a second lieutenant in the U.S. Army upon graduation in 1934, and during active duty he rose in rank to lieutenant colonel.

Voliva returned to New Jersey in 1946, but at the state university, Rutgers. He coached there for 25 years, guiding his teams to 148 victories against 85 losses and eight draws. He was a leader among his colleagues, serving five years on the NCAA rules committee, two of them as chairman. He was president of both the Eastern Intercollegiate Wrestling Association and the National Wrestling Coaches Association.

WAYNE WELLS (1982)

He stood atop the Olympic awards stand, gold medal draped across his chest, and sang the Star Spangled Banner. In the proudest moment of his wrestling career, Wayne Wells thanked his country for the opportunity to excel.

Once given that opportunity, he spent a dozen years of hard work, building upon the cornerstones of skill, desire and conditioning. Those years brought brought many rewards, and just a few disappointments, but each setback proved the spur to higher achievement.

At the University of Oklahoma, Wayne was a three-time Big Eight Conference champion and a three-time All-American. NCAA runner-up as a junior, he won the championship the following year and went on to earn fourth place in the Olympic Games of 1968.

While turning his attention to law school and the foundation of a professional career, Wayne intensified his wrestling efforts. He captured the silver medal in the 1969 world championships, then returned a year later to win the gold.

He won two national freestyle titles and placed second in the Pan-American Games. In the months leading up to the 1972 Olympics he completed his final year of law school, passed the state bar exam, assisted the OU coaching staff and trained five hours a day.

As evidence of his preparation for the Olympic effort, his scores in the strength-endurance tests exceeded those of all other members of the United States wrestling team. And in a final victory over adversity, he dominated his opposition despite a separated and displaced rib, an enlarged spleen and a badly damaged knee.

Throughout his athletic career, and now as a respected member of the legal profession, Wayne Wells has been a positive force for every organization or team with which he was involved, with the knack of contributing his personal maximum and making it count for the success of the organization.

SHELBY WILSON (1982)

To become a champion, an athlete must set a goal. Shelby Wilson not only set a goal, but he pursued it through disappointments and distractions until he scaled the ultimate championship heights.

As a high school wrestler in Ponca City, Oklahoma, he won three conference championships and suffered only three defeats—all in the state meet, two of them in the finals. At Okla. State, after an injury cut short one season, he captured two Big Eight Conference titles and twice charged to the finals of the national tournament, only to suffer disheartening defeats both times.

Even his journey to the Olympic Games of 1960 was beset with obstacles. He competed in the trials, finishing second.

Then, he threw the Greco-Roman champion to assure a trip to Rome. He replaced that assignment with a freestyle ticket by fighting his way up from fourth place among the challengers.

And in the shadowed ruins of Rome's ancient Basilica, Shelby Wilson earned the Olympic gold medal. The road was long, with many detours, but he had attained his goal.

"Without a goal, an athlete isn't really going to struggle to achieve," he says. "Whether or not he wins a victory, the struggle, the discipline, the battle with adversity give him the championship qualities he needs for success in life."

Shelby Wilson's hobby is "repairing anything that's broken." Growing up on a farm, he learned the value of keeping the land and the equipment in condition. During 13 years of high school and college coaching, and now as the founder and director of the Stronghold Youth Foundation, he transferred those values to human needs. An ordained minister who loves people, he works on their behalf with the same dedication that he once devoted to the pursuit of a wrestling goal.

HENRY WITTENBERG (1977)

He never wrestled in high school and he needed a couple of years of college to reach national prominence. But once Henry Wittenberg learned the sport, his was a story of unparalleled success.

Coached at the City College of New York by early-day NCAA champion Joe Sapora, he placed third in the collegiate tournament as a junior as was runner-up as a senior in 1939. But Henry was a "natural" for wrestling and his career was about to reach full bloom.

Over the next 10 years, Henry Wittenberg wrestled more than 300 matches without a loss. He entered eight national freestyle tournaments and won eight championships, representing the West Side YMCA of New York and later the Police Sports Association.

In 1948, he won the gold medal at 191.5 pounds in the Olympic Games at London, then retired from competition. But in 1952, he returned to the mat to lead the U.S. team to the Olympics at Helsinki, where he captured the silver medal and became the first American wrestler since 1908 to win two Olympic medals.

He also won gold medals in the Maccabiah Games in 1949 and 1953.

Wittenberg has coached collegiate wrestlers at Yeshiva University and

CCNY for two decades. He was the United States national team coach in 1959 on the first trip to the Soviet Union and returned to the Maccabiah Games twice as coach of the U.S. team.

He also guided the American Greco-Roman team in the 1968 Olympic Games at Mexico City.

KEITH YOUNG (1979)

He packed more wrestling success into five years than most athletes manage in a lifetime of competition. Keith Young has spent the three decades since returning those rewards to the sport with full interest.

His Algona High School team didn't offer wrestling until his senior year, and when he joined the Iowa State Teachers College squad, you'd hardly expect a youngster of such limited experience to fill the shoes of one of wrestling's all-time greats, Bill Koll.

But fill them he did, winning six national championships in three seasons. Undefeated in collegiate competition, he was NCAA champion at 145 pounds in 1949, 1950 and 1951, leading the Panthers of coach Dave McCuskey to the team title during his junior year.

Young's three collegiate crowns matched Koll's total as ISTC (now Northern Iowa) reigned supreme in the welterweight division for six consecutive seasons. The same three years, Young was national freestyle champion—Outstanding Wrestler in 1950—and each year the Panthers captured the team trophy.

Rather than pursue post-graduate competition, Young turned immediately to high school coaching. In three years at Blue Earth, Minnesota, he produced a state team champion. Then he returned to Iowa, coaching a year at Osage before taking the reigns in 1955 at Cedar Falls.

There he has produced more than 200 dual meet victories, two state champion teams, two runners-up and a host of individual winners. Far more important, however, has been his influence on the lives of young men, as a teaching example of integrity and dedication.

He also served the sport of wrestling for many years as one of its most widely-respected referees, officiating at the high school and collegiate levels all the way to the NCAA and NAIA championships.

VINCE ZUARO (1984)

Because of Vince Zuaro, America knows the rules.

Through half a century of Olympic endeavor, USA wrestlers were handicapped by unfamiliarity with the international styles—the techniques, the rules and their often confusing interpretations. That so many excelled is a tribute to their talent and dedication. But for every achievement, there also was a shadow of what might have been.

Today, America's officials, and thus America's coaches and athletes, know the international rules better than some of the people who wrote them largely because of the U.S. Wrestling Officials Association founded by Vince Zuaro in 1970. That officials association has grown to more than 1,500 members, volunteers at work year around to educate and supervise American athletes of all ages as they compete in the international styles.

Zuaro himself is a referee-judge of exceptional ability, a model of integrity and fair play. Over the past two decades, he has officiated in three Olympic Games, more than a dozen World Championships, four Pan-American Games and a host of national tournaments. Twice he was presented the FILA Cross of Honor, highest award of international wrestling, for his Olympic officiating.

A 1948 graduate of Holy Cross and a member of its 1946 Orange Bowl football team, Zuaro was a highly-successful wrestling coach for 11 years at Freeport High School on Long Island, and for two years at Columbia University, with an overall record of 132 victories against 63 defeats.

But it was as an official and as an educator of officials that he gained national and international acclaim. He is the nation's foremost clinician on freestyle and Greco-Roman rules and officiating techniques, and has trained more than 5,000 referee-judges all across the nation and among the armed forces in Europe.

Never again will American athletes enter international competition without knowing what to expect from their opponents, the referees, and the rules.

References

1. *Amateur Wrestling News* P.O. Box 60387, Oklahoma City, OK 73146.
2. Associated Press & Grolier Enterprises, Inc. *Pursuit of excellence: The Olympic story.* Danbury, CT: Grolier Enterprises.
3. Carlson L., & Fogarty, J. (1987). *Tales of gold.* Chicago: Contemporary Books.
4. Chapman, M. (1981). *Gotch to Gable: A history of wrestling in Iowa.* Iowa City, IA: University of Iowa.
5. Davis, M. (1954). *100 greatest sports heroes.* New York: Grosset and Dunlap.
6. Kelch, D. (1988, March). *Scarlet and Gray*, p. 19. (Available from 635 Park Meadow Road, Suite 208, Westerville, OH 43081)
7. Kent, G. (1969). *A pictorial history of wrestling.* New York: Spring Books.
8. National Wrestling Hall of Fame (official programs for induction). Stillwater, OK 74074.
9. Ragan, D. (1976). *Who's Who in Hollywood: 1900-1976.* New Rochelle, NY: Arlington House.
10. Staff (1987, November). Athletes are heroes to Americans. *The Olym pian Magazine*, p. 37.
11. Willson, C.M. (1959). *The magnificent scufflers.* Brattleboro, VT: Stephen Greene Press.